EQUAL JUSTICE AND THE DEATH PENALTY

DAVID C. BALDUS
GEORGE WOODWORTH
CHARLES A. PULASKI, JR.

EQUAL JUSTICE AND THE DEATH PENALTY

A Legal and Empirical Analysis

NORTHEASTERN UNIVERSITY PRESS   BOSTON

Northeastern University Press

Library of Congress Cataloging in Publication Data
Baldus, David C.
  Equal justice and the death penalty.
  Includes index.
    1. Capital punishment—Georgia. 2. Equality before
the law—Georgia. 3. Capital punishment—United
States—States. 4. Equality before the law—United
States—States. 5. Criminal statistics—United States—
States. I. Woodworth, George. II. Pulaski, Charles A.
III. Title.
KFG565.C2B35   1989   345.758'0773   88–33088
ISBN 1–55553–056–7   347.5805773

Designed by David Ford

Composed in Aldus by BookMasters, Inc., Ashland, Ohio.
Printed and bound by Edwards Brothers, Inc., Ann Arbor,
Michigan. The paper is Glatfelter Offset, and acid-free
sheet.

MANUFACTURED IN THE UNITED STATES OF AMERICA

95 94 93 92 91 90   5 4 3 2 1

To Joyce—D. B.

To Carrol, Zoë, and Griffin—G. W.

To my parents—C. P.

CONTENTS

TABLES

NOTE TABLES

FIGURES

ACKNOWLEDGMENTS

We want to express our great appreciation to the individuals who provided us with data on death sentencing in Georgia and elsewhere. Patsy Morris generously shared with us her ever-growing records on Georgia's death-row inmates. Carol Palmer, formerly of the NAACP Legal Defense and Educational Fund, Inc., provided us with nationwide information on death-row inmates. Jim Henderson and Jack Taylor graciously shared with us their nationwide data set. David Eisner, former Chief Trial Deputy, Office of the Colorado Public Defender, provided our Colorado data, for which we are most grateful. We particularly appreciate the assistance of the officials of the State of Georgia, without whose help this project could not have been undertaken.

We received valuable advice on Georgia criminal practice from Millard Farmer, George Kendall, Patsy Morris, Bud Siemon, and Robert Stroup.

Many law students at The University of Iowa College of Law and Syracuse University College of Law worked on this project. In particular, we want to acknowledge the invaluable assistance of Ronald Chapman, Frederick Kyle, Karen Romano, Kurt Schroeder, and Mary Thee.

Anthony Amsterdam, Jack Boger, and William Bowers provided assistance, guidance, and inspiration throughout the entire study. Barry Nakell and Marvin Wolfgang generously shared with us their data collection instruments, and Jack Boger and Edward Gates made important contributions to the construction of our data collection instruments and protocols.

Richard Berk, Leon Burmeister, and Timothy Wyant gave us helpful advice on statistics. And our statistical computing was greatly facilitated through the expert assistance of Barbara Broffitt, Bruce Riddle, and Kurt Schroeder.

We want to acknowledge the valuable contribution of Edward Gates and Kathy Christian, who were our principal data collectors in the Procedural Reform Study in Georgia. In the Charging and Sentencing Study, Edward Gates skillfully supervised the data collection and was diligently assisted in that effort by Lee Ann de Grazia, Matthew Estes, John Greeno, Orry Korb, and Martha Macgill.

This manuscript has gone through numerous drafts, which were typed and retyped with precision and care by, among others, Sally Laster, Phyllis Monaghan, and Melanie Stutzman.

The quality of the analysis and writing throughout has been greatly enhanced by the comments on earlier drafts of colleagues Hugo Bedau, Leigh Bienen, Jack Boger, William Bowers, William Buss, James Cole, Dennis Dorin, Robert Forsyth, Samuel Gross, Joseph Hoffman, Patrick Hubbard, Gary King, John Monahan, Barry Nakell, Michael Radelet, Robert Stroup, and Gregory Williams. Also, Deborah Kops and Ann Twombly of Northeastern University Press provided extremely valuable editorial advice.

Early work on the Procedural Reform Study was supported by the National Institute of Justice, U.S. Department of Justice, grant No. 80-IJ-CX-0035. Collection and initial analysis of the Charging and Sentencing Study data were supported by a grant from the Edna McConnell Clark Foundation to the NAACP Legal Defense and Educational Fund, Inc. The Law and Social Sciences Program of the National Science Foundation, grant No. SES 8209449, supported analysis of the Charging and Sentencing Study data subsequent to the *McCleskey* hearing in 1983. And during the 1980s we received support from The University of Iowa Law School Foundation, The University of Iowa's University House Interdisciplinary Research Grants Program, Arizona State University College of Law, and the Center for Interdisciplinary Legal Studies, College of Law, Syracuse University.

Earlier versions of portions of this book appeared in Baldus, Woodworth, and Pulaski, "Monitoring and Evaluating Temporary Death-Sentencing Systems: Lessons From Georgia," 18 *U.C. Davis L. Rev.* 1375 (1985). We thank the law review publisher for its permission to republish those items here.

CHAPTER ONE
Introduction

This book is a study of equal justice in death sentencing during the fifteen-year period between two United States Supreme Court decisions from Georgia, *Furman v. Georgia* (1972) and *McCleskey v. Kemp* (1987).[1] In 1972, by a 5–4 vote, *Furman* invalidated every death-sentencing statute then in place in the United States. *Furman* held that all the statutes were arbitrary and potentially discriminatory and, as a consequence, violated the cruel and unusual punishments clause of the Eighth Amendment. In 1987 the *McCleskey* decision, which was also decided by a 5–4 vote, rejected a claim of arbitrariness and discrimination in the administration of Georgia's post-*Furman* death-sentencing system and, in the process, terminated at least for the near future any expectation that the United States Constitution will be read to require comparative or equal justice in the administration of the death-sentencing systems in this country.

Between *Furman* and *McCleskey*, state legislatures and state and federal courts made three promises in an effort to end arbitrariness and discrimination in capital sentencing. The first promise appeared in trial-court sentencing reforms adopted by many state legislatures after *Furman*, with the goal of eliminating arbitrariness and discrimination from capital sentencing at the trial-court level. These statutory reforms sought to channel the exercise of discretion by limiting the range of cases in which prosecutors could seek death sentences and by focusing the attention of sentencing juries on the most relevant aggravating and mitigating circumstances of each case.

The second promise came from expanded appellate oversight, which many state legislatures required of their state supreme courts after *Furman*. The announced objective of this reform was the elimination of effects of any arbitrary or discriminatory death sentencing that persisted in the post-*Furman* period. This expanded oversight, most importantly through a process known as "comparative proportionality review," would enable the state supreme courts to weed out excessive and arbitrary death sentences.

The third promise came from *Furman* and a series of United States Supreme Court decisions in the late 1970s and early 1980s.[2] These decisions developed a constitutional doctrine that, since death sentences are "qualitatively different" from other criminal sentences, courts should provide strict oversight of the state death-sentencing systems to ensure that the states conduct their death-sentencing systems in an evenhanded, nondiscriminatory fashion.[3]

The main theme of this book is that, although the levels of arbitrariness and racial discrimination in capital sentencing have declined in the post-*Furman* period, none of these promises has been fulfilled; moreover, given the Supreme Court's decision in *McCleskey v. Kemp*, little improvement in this regard appears likely.

In our analysis of the effectiveness of both the trial-level and appellate-review reforms of the post-*Furman* period, we consider what may be called two "impossibility" hypotheses. The first, which was formulated by Justice Harlan in 1971 and echoed by numerous commentators, questions whether trial-level reforms, particularly the use of standards and guidelines to channel the exercise of jury discretion, can distinguish rationally between those who should live and those who should die. Justice Harlan believed that such a task was "beyond present human ability," a fact that in the eyes of some observers makes arbitrariness and discrimination in capital sentencing "inevitable."[4]

The second impossibility hypothesis, advanced by Chief Justice Rehnquist and various commentators, questions the ability of state supreme courts to provide the oversight of their death-sentencing systems required to ensure that they operate in a consistent, nondiscriminatory fashion.[5] Speaking in 1976, then-Justice Rehnquist expressed grave doubts about the effectiveness of comparative proportionality review: "All that such review of death sentences can provide is a comparison of fact situations which must in their nature be highly particularized if not unique, and the only relief which it can afford is to single out the occasional death sentence which in the view of the reviewing court does not conform to the standards established by the legislature."[6]

In this book we present the results of two overlapping empirical studies, both of which were designed to test the two impossibility hypotheses. The first study, known as the Procedural Reform Study (PRS), examines 156 pre-*Furman* cases and 594 post-*Furman* cases that resulted in a Georgia jury murder-trial conviction between 1973 and 1978. In the PRS, we compared the pre- and post-*Furman* samples of cases as a basis for estimating the extent to which Georgia's capital-sentencing system became more evenhanded in the post-*Furman* period. We also used data from the Procedural Reform Study to test the second impossibility hypothesis—the ability of state supreme courts to ensure through proportionality review that their death-sentencing systems operate in a consistent nondiscriminatory fashion. The results of the PRS are presented in chapters 5 through 7.

The second study, known as the Charging and Sentencing Study (CSS), was developed to test the first impossibility hypothesis, with special reference to the issue of racial discrimination. It included data on a sample of 1,066 defendants indicted for murder or voluntary manslaughter between 1973 and 1979 whose cases resulted in a murder or voluntary manslaughter conviction. This study was designed both for scholarly purposes and for use in litigation challenging the constitutionality of Georgia's post-*Furman* capital-sentencing system and provided the principal basis for the petitioner's claims of arbitrariness and racial discrimination in *McCleskey v. Kemp*. The results of the Charging and Sentencing Study are presented in chapter 10, which considers the *McCleskey* case.

There are three principal reasons for our heavy (though not exclusive) focus on the state of Georgia in this book. First, Georgia is a leading death-sentencing state; since 1930, more people have been executed there than in any other American jurisdiction.[7] Second, both the Court's 1972 *Furman* decision, which struck down all capital sentencing statutes, and its 1976 decision in *Gregg v. Georgia*, which affirmed the constitutionality of death as a punishment for murder, focused on Georgia's capital-sentencing system. Both decisions rested on several factual assumptions about the operation of Georgia's system, which are empirically verifiable and which we have tested in our studies. Third, as noted, McCleskey's claims of arbitrariness and discrimination were based largely on the results of our Georgia research.

In spite of our belief that the three main promises to bring fairness to death sentencing in the United States remain unfulfilled, we are not yet convinced that arbitrariness and discrimination in death sentencing are inevitable. As we demonstrate, the system has improved since *Furman* and it is clear that even though many of the death sentences imposed since 1973 are arbitrary or racially discriminatory, all the death sentences imposed since then cannot be so characterized. Indeed, many death sentences are imposed each year in highly aggravated cases in which racial features play no role whatever. The problem is that a very large proportion of each year's death sentences are imposed against defendants whose cases are not among the most aggravated and therefore the most blameworthy cases.

The challenge to the system, then, is whether it can be modified to limit death sentencing to the worst offenders. This goal might be achieved by drastically narrowing the categories of cases for which death sentences are authorized, for example, by limiting death sentences to cases involving extreme and systematic torture or mass killings. Under existing state laws, however, the issue is whether the system can mobilize itself to weed out the excessive and discriminatory sentences that are imposed and leave intact only the death sentences imposed against the worst offenders. The administration of such a system would not be easy or inexpensive, as it would require systematic oversight by officials with a commitment to the task and a willingness to vacate death sentences that appear to be arbitrary, excessive, or the likely product of racial discrimination. However, with such a system in place, a reasonably fair death-sentencing system may be possible. (At the moment, we consider state supreme courts to be the institution in the best position to provide this sort of monitoring and oversight.) However, our research convinces us that in the absence of some such system of oversight, a substantial level of arbitrary and discriminatory death sentencing under the laws as currently drawn is inevitable.

This book consists of twelve chapters, which may be divided into five parts. The first part (chapters 2 and 3) addresses the Supreme Court's decision in *Furman* and the response of the states to it. Chapter 2 describes the principal features of the capital-sentencing procedures employed by Georgia and other states at the time of *Furman* and the reasons that a majority of the Supreme Court decided they were constitutionally deficient. Chapter 3 continues this inquiry by describing how the legislatures of Georgia and other death-penalty states responded to *Furman* with new statutory procedures. It also reviews 1976 Supreme Court decisions that determined the constitutionality of these revised sentencing procedures, with particular reference to the factual assumptions that underlay the Court's conclusions. Although this discussion emphasizes the Georgia procedure, we also examine cases arising from other jurisdictions in the interest of completeness.

Part two (chapter 4) describes the methodology both of the Procedural Reform Study and of the Charging and Sentencing Study. (Appendix A presents further detail and analysis on the methodological issues raised by our studies.)

Part three (chapters 5 through 7) reports the findings of the Procedural Reform Study that we conducted on the impact of Georgia's post-*Furman* procedural death-sentencing reforms on the consistency and rationality of the post-guilt-trial stages of Georgia's death-sentencing process before and after *Furman*. The focus of chapters 5 and 6 is on (a) the extent to which the results of Georgia's pre-*Furman* death-sentencing system conform to the assumptions of the Supreme Court justices in *Furman*; (b) differences between the levels of arbitrariness and discrimination in Georgia under its pre- and post-*Furman* death-sentencing systems; (c) the extent to which one can reasonably attribute those differences to Georgia's 1973 capital-sentencing reforms; and (d) the extent to which prosecutors and juries—the major official participants at the post-guilt-trial stages of Georgia's post-*Furman* death sentencing system—actually function as the United States Supreme Court presumed they would in *Gregg v. Georgia*. Chapter 7 examines the extent to which Georgia's post-*Furman* system of comparative proportionality review conducted by the

Georgia Supreme Court functions in the manner contemplated by the United States Supreme Court in *Gregg*.

Part four (chapters 8 and 9) summarizes the empirical literature generally concerning the pre- and post-*Furman* death-sentencing experience in other states. Chapter 8 examines the nationwide evidence of infrequency, arbitrariness, and discrimination in capital sentencing, while chapter 9 examines the experience and effectiveness of the other state supreme courts in their conduct of comparative proportionality review since *Furman*.

Part five (chapters 10 and 11) describes and evaluates *McCleskey v. Kemp* (1987). Chapter 10 presents the legal background against which the case was planned and the circumstances of our involvement in the case. It also describes the *McCleskey* record and adjudications in the Federal District Court, the Eleventh Circuit Court of Appeals, and the United States Supreme Court. Chapter 11 assesses the central issues of interpretation and methodology presented by the decisions of the Eleventh Circuit and the Supreme Court. (In Appendix B we present a technical assessment of the methodological issues raised by the decision of the district court.)

Finally, chapter 12 presents a summary of our methodology and findings, and our conclusions.

NOTES

1. Furman v. Georgia, 408 U.S. 238 (1972); McCleskey v. Kemp, 107 S.Ct. 1756 (1987).

2. Gregg v. Georgia, 428 U.S. 153 (1976); Jurek v. Texas, 428 U.S. 262 (1976); Proffitt v. Florida, 428 U.S. 242 (1976); Woodson v. North Carolina, 428 U.S. 280 (1976); Roberts v. Louisiana, 428 U.S. 325 (1976); Gardner v. Florida, 430 U.S. 349 (1977); Lockett v. Ohio, 438 U.S. 586 (1978); Beck v. Alabama, 447 U.S. 625 (1980); Adams v. Texas, 448 U.S. 38 (1980); Eddings v. Oklahoma, 455 U.S. 104 (1982); Hopper v. Evans, 456 U.S. 605 (1982); Zant v. Stephens, 462 U.S. 862 (1983).

3. United States Supreme Court decisions have also clarified which procedural safeguards a death-sentencing system must include to survive a facial challenge under the Eighth Amendment. Such a statute must include legislatively mandated criteria to identify those defendants convicted of capital crimes who may be considered for the death penalty. Zant v. Stephens, 462 U.S. at 873–80; Gregg v. Georgia, 428 U.S. at 192-95 (plurality opinion). It must provide for a bifurcated sentencing procedure, *id.* at 163–64, Roberts v. Louisiana, 428 U.S. at 356, and for an individualized decision that takes into account any mitigating circumstances that the defendant might wish to proffer. Lockett v. Ohio, 438 U.S. at 604–5; Eddings v. Oklahoma, 455 U.S. at 110; Skipper v. South Carolina, 476 U.S. 1, 2–9 (1986). Such a statute must also provide for an explicit determination of the particular statutorily designated aggravating circumstance that qualified the defendant for the death penalty if that sentence is imposed, Gregg v. Georgia, 428 U.S. at 193–95 (plurality opinion), Zant v. Stephens, 462 U.S. at

865, and for sufficient safeguards to ensure reliable and accurate fact determinations in connection with the sentencing decision, Gardner v. Florida, 430 U.S. at 357–62, Beck v. Alabama, 447 U.S. at 637–38. If, in any respect, the statute entrusts the sentencing decision to the jury (which the Constitution does not require, Spaziano v. Florida, 468 U.S. 447, 465 (1984)), the presiding judge cannot exclude individuals from the jury for cause because of their antipathy toward capital punishment unless it would prevent or substantially impair the performance of their duties as jurors in accordance with their oath as jurors and the trial court's instructions, Adams v. Texas, 448 U.S. at 43–47, Wainwright v. Witt, 469 U.S. 412, 418–26 (1985).

4. McGautha v. California, 402 U.S. 183, 204 (1971). *See also* Black, CAPITAL PUNISHMENT: THE INEVITABILITY OF CAPRICE AND MISTAKE (2d ed. 1981); The Roscoe Pound–American Trial Lawyers Foundation, *The Penalty of Death: Final Report*, 21–39 (1980). Others argue that contemporary capital-sentencing systems are producing evenhanded justice by limiting the death penalty to only the most extreme and heinous cases or that issues of comparative justice are irrelevant. *See* van den Haag, *In Defense of the Death Penalty: A Legal-Practical-Moral Analysis*, 14 CRIM. L. BULL. 15 (1978); van den Haag, *The Collapse of the Case Against Capital Punishment*, 30 NATIONAL REV. 395 (March 1978); Berns, *Defending the Death Penalty*, 26 CRIME & DELINQUENCY 503 (1980), H. Bedau, THE DEATH PENALTY IN AMERICA 305–41 (3d ed. 1982) (excerpts from five authors favoring capital punishment).

5. *Infra*, chap. 7, notes 3 and 4 and accompanying text.

6. Woodson v. North Carolina, 428 U.S. 280, 316 (1976).

7. Bureau of Justice Statistics, Dept. of Justice, SOURCEBOOK OF CRIMINAL JUSTICE STATISTICS: 1982 at 580 (1982). From 1930 to 1980 Georgia, with a 1980 population of 5,463,000, executed 366 people. Close behind are New York, population 17,558,000, with 329, Texas, population 14,229,000, with 297, and California, population 23,688,000, with 292. As of July 1989, Georgia, with 102 inmates on death row, was surpassed by Florida, with 294, Texas, with 283, California, with 247, Illinois, with 120, and Pennsylvania, with 115. As for executions, Georgia had carried out 13. The comparable numbers were 20 in Florida and 30 in Texas. NAACP, Legal Defense Fund, DEATH ROW U.S.A. (July 1989).

CHAPTER TWO

Capital Sentencing and the Impact of *Furman v. Georgia*

CAPITAL SENTENCING BEFORE *FURMAN*

Throughout this century, capital punishment has served as a component of criminal justice in a majority of states of the United States. From a national perspective, therefore, one can view the capital-sentencing process as a large, decentralized, decision-making system.[1] Its purpose is to select, from the thousands of murderers deemed eligible for a death sentence under state law, those defendants considered by prosecutors, juries, and judges to be the most deserving of execution.

Prior to *Furman v. Georgia* (1972) the death-sentencing systems of most states exhibited six general characteristics that acquired potential constitutional significance during the late 1960s and early 1970s. First was the very large number of defendants who, because of the crimes for which they were convicted, were technically eligible for the death penalty ("death eligible") under the applicable state law.[2] In the majority of death-sentencing jurisdictions, any person convicted of first-degree murder ("willful, deliberate, and premeditated killing") was eligible to receive a death sentence.[3] A minority of states, including Georgia, used the broader common-law definition of murder to set the parameters of death eligibility.[4] In those jurisdictions a defendant who killed a spouse during a heated argument was as eligible for a death sentence as one who murdered a stranger in a brutal, premeditated fashion while committing a contemporaneous offense such as rape or armed robbery. In addition, a number of Southern states, including Georgia, authorized the death penalty for rape or armed robbery even if no life was taken and without regard to the degree of aggravation.[5]

The second relevant characteristic of pre-*Furman* death-sentencing systems was the presence in most jurisdictions of approximately four separate steps or decision points commencing with indictment.[6] At each of these decision points, some responsible authority—a prosecutor, judge, or jury— would make a discretionary decision regarding the case that would either retain the defendant in the group of death eligibles or would, in effect, remove him from that group. The first step in a typical pre-*Furman* system usually involved a decision by the prosecutor or a grand jury whether to charge a potentially death-eligible defendant with capital murder or a lesser offense, such as second-degree murder, for which no death sentence was authorized. At the second step in the process, either unilaterally or in exchange for a guilty plea, the prosecutor could reduce the charge of capital murder to some lesser offense. Alternatively, in most states, the prosecutor could waive the death penalty in exchange for a guilty plea to capital murder.

The third step involved a trial, usually by jury, of those defendants charged with capital murder who pleaded not guilty. Typically, in these cases, the jury would decide both the question of the defendant's guilt or innocence and, if it found the defendant guilty of capital murder, the appropriate sentence.[7] Relatively few defendants avoided all punishment at this stage by outright acquittal, but juries convicted many defendants tried for capital murder of only noncapital crimes. Furthermore, of those defendants convicted of capital murder, only a small minority received sentences of death.[8]

An important feature of the capital-murder trials in most states was the use of a single, or "unitary," evidentiary proceeding, at the conclusion of which the jury would decide both the defendant's guilt, and, if appropriate, the ultimate sentence.* Under this unitary-trial procedure the parties presented all their evidence and argument with respect to both the alleged crime and the appropriate punishment at one time. Many observers believed this process put the defendant at a distinct disadvantage.[9] It permitted the state to offer damaging evidence—subject to limiting instructions, of course—that was irrelevant to the question of guilt but did relate to the question of punishment. Furthermore, defendants who might wish to testify about mitigating factors in an effort to avoid the prospect of a death sentence confronted the practical necessity of disclosing their participation, if any, in the alleged crime.†

A third constitutionally relevant feature of most pre-*Furman* systems was the delegation of discretion to sentencing juries without providing any sort of

---

*In many jurisdictions, however, a prosecutor who believed that a death sentence would be inappropriate in a given case could limit the jury's sentencing discretion either by requesting a jury instruction that omitted the option of imposing a death sentence or by telling the jury that a death sentence was inappropriate. Moreover, in some jurisdictions a trial judge who believed a death penalty was not warranted could decline to instruct the jury regarding that option.

†The alternative to the unitary trial involved a two-step, or "bifurcated," procedure. Under this alternative the parties would present evidence solely with respect to the defendant's innocence and guilt. The jury would then decide the guilt question. If the jury convicted the defendant of capital murder and the State wished to seek the death penalty, a second evidentiary proceeding—the "sentencing" or "penalty" trial—would occur, after which the jury would decide the question of punishment. Georgia was one of a handful of states that adopted a bifurcated system before 1972. In 1970 it established a penalty trial in which the prosecutor was authorized to present information on the defendant's prior record. 1970 Ga. Laws 949. Georgia's penalty-trial process became much more extensive after 1973.

authoritative guidelines or standards to regularize their decisions. Basically, these procedures left juries free to impose sentence based on whatever criteria they liked, without regard to their legitimacy or their relevance to the sentencing decision. Furthermore, they provided absolutely no assurance that capital defendants would be judged according to the criteria employed by different juries in other cases.

A fourth relevant characteristic of the pre-*Furman* systems was the limited jurisdiction of state appellate courts reviewing death-sentence cases. Basically, appeals by condemned inmates could seek the correction only of specific legal errors that might have infected the trial-court proceedings. The propriety and reasonableness of a death sentence in a given case was not a subject for review.*

The fifth characteristic of the pre-*Furman* systems was the remarkably small number of defendants who actually received death sentences each year, and the even smaller number of condemned defendants who actually suffered execution. From a high of probably 300 to 400 death sentences imposed and 199 executions carried out in 1935, there was a steady decline to about 100 death sentences a year imposed and fewer than 50 actually carried out in the early 1960s. The number of executions per 100 homicides during this period fell from 1.6 in the 1930s to .45 in the early 1960s.[10] In 1967, all executions were stopped pending the outcome of litigation challenging the constitutionality of capital punishment, while sentences imposed remained at about 100 per year.[11]

The sixth characteristic of the pre-*Furman* systems was the very high proportion of nonwhite defendants sentenced to death. From the 1930s until the 1967 moratorium, nearly 50 percent of the offenders executed for murder nationwide were black. In the South the figure exceeded 60 percent. Moreover, black defendants consistently represented from 80 to 90 percent of the men executed for rape nationwide.[12]

Except for a limited penalty-trial system, which distinguished it from the majority of states, Georgia's pre-*Furman* system of capital sentencing reflected each of the constitutionally relevant characteristics just described. Indeed, it was because of certain of these characteristics that in *Furman* five justices of the United States Supreme Court concluded that Georgia's death-sentencing procedures—and, by implication, those of every other state—violated the Eighth Amendment. Before analyzing *Furman*, however, it is necessary to consider several other constitutional challenges to the death-sentencing procedures asserted during the 1960s.

---

*The appropriateness of imposing death sentences in individual cases clearly did, however, influence appellate-court determinations of whether legal error had occurred and whether such error justified a new trial.

CONSTITUTIONAL CHALLENGES TO
THE PRE-*FURMAN* SYSTEM

During the late 1960s and early 1970s, counsel for death-row defendants and other opponents of capital punishment mounted several major constitutional challenges to then-current death-sentencing practices.[13] The first of these efforts addressed alleged discrimination against black offenders in nonhomicide rape cases. The basis of these claims was an empirical study conducted in the 1960s of death-sentencing results in nonhomicide rape cases in various Southern states.[14] The data suggested that black defendants convicted of raping whites were substantially more likely to receive a death sentence than either white defendants or black defendants whose victims were black. This challenge did not succeed in the lower federal courts, and, since the United States Supreme Court's grant of certiorari in the case did not embrace the discrimination claims, it never squarely ruled upon the question.[15]

The next series of challenges to existing capital-sentencing procedures invoked the due process clause of the Fourteenth Amendment. One fundamental objection raised was that permitting juries to impose death sentences without providing any meaningful guidelines or governing standards violated the principles of procedural due process. A second due process objection was that the unitary-trial procedure compelled defendants either to surrender their privilege against self-incrimination or to forgo the opportunity to testify regarding the appropriate punishment. A third due process objection attacked the liberality with which trial judges granted challenges by prosecutors to exclude from juries persons who expressed doubts or concerns about capital punishment.

This last due process objection prevailed. In 1968 in *Witherspoon v. Illinois*, the United States Supreme Court held that trial judges should not exclude venirepersons from juries in capital cases unless they would automatically vote against imposing a death sentence regardless of the circumstances or unless their attitude toward the death penalty would prevent them from rendering an impartial verdict.[16]

By contrast, in the 1971 decision of *McGautha v. California*, the Court rejected the other two due process objections.[17] Justice Harlan's majority opinion acknowledged that the challenged procedures lacked any meaningful sentencing standards.[18] Nevertheless, he concluded that these procedures were constitutionally unobjectionable. First, he believed legislative drafters were incapable of identifying in language that juries could understand and fairly apply "those characteristics of criminal homicides and their perpetrators which call for the death penalty."[19] Second, he believed juries would exercise their sentencing power conscientiously "with due regard for the consequences of their decision" and would impose the death penalty only in appropriate cases. [20] Consequently, Justice Harlan concluded that a system permitting juries to decide in their "untrammeled discretion" whether defendants convicted of capital crimes should live or die violated no principle of due process. [21]

The Court was equally unsympathetic to the unitary-trial challenge. [22] It ruled that the dilemma faced by defendants when deciding whether to give testimony in mitigation of punishment—either waiving the privilege against self-incrimination or remaining silent— was no greater than other constitutionally permissible dilemmas that criminal defendants and their attorneys confronted in many other contexts. [23] More particularly, the majority concluded that no policy underlying the privilege against compelled self-incrimination was offended when a capital defendant yielded to the pressure to testify on the issue of punishment despite the risk of damaging his case on guilt. [24]

Underlying both of the majority's rulings in *McGautha* was a strong deference to the independent sovereignty of the states and the principles of federalism. [25] The majority recognized that, quite likely, "bifurcated trials and criteria for jury sentencing discretion are superior means of dealing with capital cases if the death penalty is to be retained at all." [26] Nevertheless, it concluded, the Constitution "does not guarantee trial procedures that are the best of all worlds, or that accord with the most enlightened ideas of students of the infant science of criminology, or even those that measure up to the individual predilections of members of this Court." [27]

FURMAN V. GEORGIA

The last basic constitutional challenge to the death-sentencing practices of the late 1960s and early 1970s invoked the prohibitions of the Eighth Amendment. [28] Basically, the argument was that death sentences that juries imposed in only a small minority of all death-eligible cases without any guidelines or standards constituted "cruel and unusual punishments" within the meaning of the Eighth Amendment. [29] This argument closely resembled the procedural due process objections to standardless jury sentencing that the Court had rejected in *McGautha v. California*. Remarkably, however, in the case of *Furman v. Georgia*, which the Court decided less than fourteen months after its *McGautha* decision, this argument persuaded five justices that the death-sentencing procedures of virtually every state that employed capital punishment violated the Eighth Amendment. [30]

Because each of the five justices wrote a separate concurring opinion stating a different rationale for the decision, the exact meaning of *Furman* is difficult to decipher. Consequently, it becomes necessary to extrapolate that meaning from the separate opinion of each concurring justice. Only two of the justices, Brennan and Marshall, concluded, for somewhat different reasons, that imposing the death penalty would violate the Constitution under any circumstances.[31] However, this absolute prohibition of capital punishment did not command the support of the remaining members of the Court.

Rather, the other three members of the *Furman* majority—Justices Douglas, Stewart, and White—chose to decide the case on more narrow grounds. They each concluded that standardless, discretionary jury sentencing was unconstitutional because the death sentences that resulted reflected qualities or characteristics offensive to the Eighth Amendment. Each of them described that impermissible quality or characteristic in a substantially different way. For example, Justice Douglas concluded that standardless, discretionary sentencing violated the Eighth Amendment because it permitted juries to discriminate between defendants for reasons that offended equal protection. In particular, he believed black or impoverished defendants suffered the death penalty to a disproportionate degree.[32]

By contrast, Justice Stewart concluded that standardless, discretionary jury sentencing violated the Eighth Amendment because no logical basis existed to distinguish between most capital offenders, who did not receive the death penalty, and the "capriciously selected random handful" who suffered the ultimate sanction.[33] Indeed, Justice Stewart likened the imposition of the death penalty in those few cases to being struck by lightning.[34] He concluded that the Eighth and Fourteenth Amendments did not permit the death penalty to be "so wantonly and so freakishly imposed."[35]

Justice White took the view that the death penalty would be constitutional if its imposition substantially advanced some legitimate penal purpose, such as incapacitation, general deterrence, or satisfaction of society's demands for retribution. He concluded, however, that the extreme infrequency with which states actually imposed the death penalty, coupled with the usually satisfactory alternative of lengthy incarceration, undercut any justification based on retribution or incapacitation.[36] For the same reasons, Justice White also rejected the argument that discretionary death-sentencing systems were permissible as a general deterrent. He noted that, in practice, the death penalty lacked any real deterrent effect because it was impossible to determine why relatively few individuals convicted of atrocious crimes received the death penalty while many others, convicted of the same crimes, did not. In Justice White's view, the death penalty could serve as a general deterrent only if regularly imposed in identifiable classes of cases.[37]

While these three justices condemned discretionary jury sentencing for different reasons, their opinions shared a common concern. They each suggested that the death-sentencing systems under scrutiny in *Furman* were unconstitutional because of two factors: the infrequency with which juries actually imposed the death penalty, and the lack of any legitimate explanation of why some persons among those convicted of atrocious crimes received life sentences, while others convicted of factually similar crimes were sentenced to death.[38] For this reason, subsequent cases have interpreted *Furman* to prohibit death-sentencing systems that permit the imposition of the death penalty on the basis of constitutionally impermissible factors or that fail to provide any meaningful basis for distinguishing between those relatively few defendants who receive the death penalty and the many other defendants guilty of capital murder who do not.[39]

Another important feature of all five concurring opinions in *Furman* was their willingness to accept the defendants' contentions on the basis of *a priori* assumptions about jury sentencing results. Instead, on the basis of intuition or remarkably fragmentary and incomplete evidence, each of the concurring justices concluded that contemporary death-sentencing systems operated in an essentially arbitrary or discriminatory fashion. On the basis of quite general studies, Justices Douglas, Brennan, and Marshall each expressed concern that racial or other impermissible factors either had influenced actual sentencing outcomes or, at the very least, had created an intolerable risk of such discrimination against minorities and social outcasts.[40] Justice Stewart, by contrast, felt the evidence suggesting discrimination on the basis of race was too fragmentary.[41] Yet, on the question of arbitrariness apart from racial discrimination, he invoked his own intuition and general experience to conclude that death-sentence cases were generally indistinguishable from those of most other capital defendants who received only lesser sentences.[42] Justice White acknowledged that he could not "prove these factual conclusions in the strict sense of the word."[43] Rather, he based his judgment "on 10 years of almost daily exposure to the facts and circumstances of hundreds and hundreds of federal and state criminal cases involving crimes for which death is the authorized penalty."[44]

The *Furman* dissenters did not share the willingness of the majority in *Furman* to elevate their personal impressions to the level of constitutional findings. Although Justice Blackmun expressed some personal doubts that death sentences served any legitimate penal purposes, he strongly criticized the majority for rendering judgment on such a basis.[45] Chief Justice Burger also criticized the majority for an unseemly willingness to void discretionary sentencing on the basis of "sweeping factual assertions, unsupported by empirical data, concerning the manner of imposition and effectiveness of capital punishment in this country."[46] The chief justice was quite satisfied to rely on the "general premise" as indicated in *McGautha* "that juries impose the death penalty in the most extreme cases."[47] The willingness of the five concurring

justices to decide the constitutionality of the nation's death-sentencing procedures on the basis of actual results sharply distinguishes them from the dissenters. It also distinguishes them from the position of the majority in *Mc-
Gautha* and, more significantly, from many of the Court's post-*Furman*
decisions.

DEFINITIONS AND MEASURES OF ARBITRARINESS, EXCESSIVENESS, DISCRIMINATION, AND EQUAL JUSTICE

The opinions of the concurring justices in *Furman* and the Supreme Court's
subsequent Eighth Amendment decisions inform the concept of "equal justice" and provide the basis for the definitions of "arbitrariness," "excessiveness," "discrimination," and, ultimately, "fairness" that we use in this book.
In this section we describe the various senses in which these terms are used by
courts and commentators.

Depending on the context in which it is applied, the concept of arbitrariness
may have quite different although related meanings. When used to characterize the death sentence imposed in an individual case, arbitrariness means that
the case in which that sentence was imposed cannot be distinguished in a
"meaningful" or "principled" way from other cases that generally result in
life sentences or less.[48] Individual death sentences that are arbitrary in this
sense have been described as "random," "freakish," "capricious," "rare,"
"wanton," "excessive," "comparatively excessive," or "excessive in a comparative sense."[49] We regard the last three descriptive terms as particularly
appropriate because they capture the central defect of arbitrary death sentences. The problem is not that the defendant's crime and past record necessarily make a death sentence unthinkable and thereby excessive in the traditional sense that the concept has been employed by the Supreme Court.[50]
Rather, the problem is that imposing a death sentence in such a case is disproportionately severe in comparison to the high frequency with which life sentences are imposed in "similar" cases. In other words, a death sentence is
comparatively excessive if it is so infrequently imposed among a group of
similarly situated capital defendants that it offends basic notions of evenhandedness and comparative justice.[51] Accordingly, our measure of comparative
excessiveness in an individual death-sentenced case is the relative infrequency
with which death sentences are imposed in cases that are comparable to the case
under review in their overall level of moral culpability or blameworthiness.

When used to characterize a death-sentencing system, rather than individual death sentences, arbitrariness has two possible meanings. The first is that
either the system as a whole operates in a capricious or random fashion or that

there is a substantial risk that sentences will be imposed in such a fashion. When the Supreme Court invalidates a death sentence on this ground, it is most often on the basis of the Court's intuitive determination that certain procedures applied in the case fail to minimize the risk that the death sentence may have been the product of whim or caprice.[52]

The second meaning of arbitrariness when used to describe a death-sentencing system refers to the extent to which (a) the death sentences imposed in the system are the product of legally irrelevant or impermissible factors, such as the race or socioeconomic status of the defendant or victim, or (b) there is a substantial risk that impermissible factors are influencing the system. Of course, death sentences imposed for such reasons are obviously discriminatory.[53] But they are arbitrary as well because they cannot be explained in a "principled" way and, therefore, also offend basic notions of even-handed justice. In determining whether a death sentence was imposed under an unacceptable risk that it was the product of discrimination, the Supreme Court has also relied thus far exclusively on its intuition. There are, however, empirical measures that address this issue which we apply in this study.[54]

The concept of discrimination employed in this book refers to conduct prohibited by the equal protection clause of the Fourteenth Amendment. Since 1976, the Supreme Court has required evidence of "intentional" or "purposeful" discrimination as a basis for liability under the Fourteenth Amendment.[55] It is clear that proof of a Fourteenth Amendment violation does not require proof of racial animus or hostility. What is less clear, however, is whether the only purposeful discrimination prohibited by the Fourteenth Amendment is conscious, deliberate discrimination, or whether it also outlaws more intuitive, nonconscious forms of discrimination. Statistical procedures of the type used in this study can support an inference that racial considerations are an influence in a decision-making process. They can also support an inference that race was a "but for" cause in one or more decisions that would have been different had the racial characteristics of the cases been different. However, statistical evidence sheds no light on the degree to which the decisions adversely affecting the minority group were the product of a conscious purpose as opposed to a nonconscious bias or intent to discriminate.

Finally, we conceive of a death-sentencing system as operating fairly and delivering "equal justice" when it shows no significant signs of arbitrariness, excessiveness, or discrimination.

NOTES

1. *See* Gillers, *Deciding Who Dies*, 129 U. Pa. L. Rev. 1 (1980); Greenberg, *Capital Punishment as a System*, 91 Yale L.J. 908 (1982); Gross & Mauro, *Patterns of Death:*

An Analysis of Racial Disparities in Capital Sentencing and Homicide Victimization, 37 STAN L. REV. 27 (1984) (hereinafter Gross & Mauro); Special Project, *Capital Punishment in 1984: Abandoning the Pursuit of Fairness and Consistency,* 69 CORNELL L. REV. 1129 (1984).

2. Furman v. Georgia, 408 U.S. 238, 293 (1972) (Brennan, J., concurring). *See also* H. Bedau, THE DEATH PENALTY IN AMERICA (3d ed. 1982) (hereinafter Bedau); W. Bowers, LEGAL HOMICIDE (1984) (hereinafter Bowers).

3. Bedau, *supra* note 2, at 4, 35.

4. *See* GA. CODE ANN. §26-1101 (1983) (murder is the commission of an unlawful act with malice aforethought that causes the death of a human being, or causing the death of another while committing a felony, regardless of actual malice). Murder in Georgia is not graded into 1st- and 2nd-degree murder.

5. *See* Shapiro, *First-Degree Murder Statutes and Capital Sentencing Procedures: An Analysis and Comparison of Statutory Systems for the Imposition of the Death Penalty in Georgia, Florida, Texas, and Louisiana,* 24 LOY. L. REV. 709, 716n.45 (1978).

6. For another description of the pre-*Furman* procedures, *see* Haller, *Capital Punishment Statutes After Furman,* 35 OHIO ST. L.J. 651 (1974).

7. *See* McGautha v. California, 402 U.S. 183, 199–203 (1971).

8. Furman v. Georgia, 408 U.S. at 292–94, 386n.11.

9. *See* Note, *The Two-Trial System in Capital Cases,* 39 N.Y.U.L. REV. 50 (1964); Knowlton, *Problems of Jury Discretion in Capital Cases,* 101 U. PA. L. REV. 1099, 1108–18 (1953).

10. Bowers, *supra* note 2, at 25–26.

11. *See infra* chap. 8, table 48.

12. Bowers, *supra* note 2, at 59–60. Historically, black defendants have accounted for about 50% of the nation's homicides but far fewer than 80% of the nation's rapes.

13. *See generally* M. Meltsner, CRUEL AND UNUSUAL: THE SUPREME COURT AND CAPITAL PUNISHMENT (1973).

14. Wolfgang & Riedel, *Race, Judicial Discretion and the Death Penalty,* 407 ANNALS 119 (1973).

15. Maxwell v. Bishop, 398 F. 2d 138 (8th Cir. 1968) (statistical evidence proffered by petitioner was insufficient to justify relief), *vacated* on other grounds, 398 U.S. 262 (1970). *See* Dorin, *Two Different Worlds: Racial Discrimination in the Imposition of Capital Punishment in Rape Cases* 72 J. CRIM. L. & CRIMINOLOGY 1667 (1981).

16. 391 U.S. 510 (1968). In subsequent cases, the Court reformulated the circumstances under which a trial court could exclude a juror for cause consistent with *Witherspoon.* The issue is whether the prospective juror's views regarding capital punishment would "prevent or substantially impair the performance of his duties as a juror in accordance with his instructions and his oath." Wainwright v. Witt, 469 U.S. 412, 420 (1985), (quoting Adams v. Texas, 448 U.S. 38, 45 (1980)). The Court has also ruled that the exclusion of prospective jurors pursuant to this test does not deny a defendant's Sixth Amendment right to an impartial jury selected from a fair cross-section of the community. Lockhart v. McCree, 476 U.S. 162 (1986).

17. 402 U.S. 183 (1971). *McGautha* and its companion case, Crampton v. Ohio, both raised the standardless-sentencing issue. *Crampton* also involved a challenge to the use of the unitary trial in capital cases.

18. *Id.* at 197–202.

19. *Id.* at 204.

20. *Id.* at 208.

21. *Id.* at 207.

22. In an earlier case the Court had sustained the unitary-trial procedure despite claims that it permitted the jury to learn adverse information about a defendant relevant to the possible sentence before the jury had decided whether the defendant was, in fact, guilty. Spencer v. Texas, 385 U.S. 554 (1967).

23. McGautha v. California, 402 U.S. at 214–17.

24. *Id.* at 213–14, 217. The court also found no violation of whatever constitutional right of allocution—the right to speak personally prior to sentencing—the defendant might enjoy. *Id.* at 217–20.

25. *Id.* at 195–96, 220–22.

26. *Id.* at 221.

27. *Id.*

28. In the same year that the Court decided *Witherspoon,* it also condemned a federal statute that permitted capital punishment only upon the jury's recommendation. United States v. Jackson, 390 U.S. 570 (1968). The Court ruled that this statute impermissibly penalized defendants who chose to exercise their Sixth Amendment right to a jury trial. Although a victory for death-penalty opponents, *Jackson* was of limited applicability because of the peculiar nature of the statute involved. *See also* Brady v. United States, 397 U.S. 742 (1970) (*Jackson* precedent inapplicable to guilty pleas in capital cases).

29. Reportedly, the impetus for this challenge was Justice Goldberg's dissent to denials of certiorari in Rudolph v. Alabama and Snider v. Cunningham, 375 U.S. 889 (1963). *See* Goldberg, *The Death Penalty and the Supreme Court,* 15 ARIZ. L. REV. 355 (1974).

30. 408 U.S. 238 (1972).

31. Justice Brennan concluded that capital punishment did not comport with the notion of human dignity, which he regarded as the core concern of the Eighth Amendment. Furman v. Georgia, 408 U.S. at 270 (Brennan, J., concurring). He reached this conclusion by applying four principles: punishment by its severity must not degrade human dignity, it must not be inflicted arbitrarily, it must not be in a form rejected throughout society, and it must serve some penal purpose. *Id.* at 281. In concluding, under the last three principles, that capital punishment was constitutionally impermissible, Justice Brennan stressed that the occasions on which convicted defendants suffer the death penalty have grown increasingly rare despite the growing number of capital crimes committed annually. *Id.* at 291–300.

Justice Marshall also stressed the infrequency of actual executions and condemned capital punishment under all circumstances because of its failure to advance legitimate penal purposes and its rejection by contemporary society. *See id.* at 359–60 (Marshall, J., concurring). Unlike Justice Brennan, however, Justice Marshall was not content to argue that the infrequency of capital punishment made it ineffective even as an instrument of a penal policy of retribution. Rather, he contended that retribution was itself unconstitutional. *Id.* at 342–45. Justice Marshall also differed in his evaluation of the death penalty's acceptability to contemporary society. Justice Brennan had argued that the infrequency of capital punishment demonstrated its repugnancy. *Id.* at 299–300 (Brennan, J., concurring). In contrast, Justice Marshall took note of public opinion polls suggesting that a substantial number of those polled favored capital punishment. *Id.* at 361n.144 (Marshall, J., concurring). However, he suggested that the constitutionally relevant question was not whether Americans regarded capital punishment as barbarously cruel, but whether they would do so if fully informed of the haphazard and discriminatory fashion in which the few who actually suffered the death penalty were chosen. *Id.* at 362–69; *see* Sarat & Vidmar, *Public Opinion, the Death Penalty, and the Eighth Amendment: Testing the Marshall Hypothesis*, 1976 WIS L. REV. 171.

32. 408 U.S. at 249–50, 255–58 (Douglas, J., concurring).

33. *Id.* at 309–10 (Stewart, J., concurring). Unlike Justice Douglas, Justice Stewart felt that the evidence concerning the impact of race on sentencing was not sufficient to prove discrimination. *Id.* at 310; *accord, id.* at 389n.12 (Burger, C.J., dissenting); *id.* at 447 (Powell, J., dissenting).

Justice Stewart also suggested that the death penalty is cruel and unusual because it is more severe than the minimum punishment deemed appropriate for any given capital offense subject to discretionary sentencing, and because it is only infrequently imposed. *Id.* at 309 (Stewart, J., concurring).

34. *Id.* at 309.

35. *Id.* at 310.

36. *Id.* at 311–12 (White, J., concurring).

37. *Id.* at 312. Justice White did not reject the notion that capital punishment could serve as an effective general deterrent. In fact, he seemed to concede the constitutional authority of legislatures to resolve that debatable question as they deemed appropriate. *See id.* at 311; *accord*, Gregg v. Georgia, 428 U.S. at 184–87 (plurality opinion). However, he refused to sustain the constitutionality of death-sentencing statutes on that ground because he regarded the legislative practice of delegating the death-sentencing function to individual juries without the benefit of legislative guidance as more a legislative abdication than an exercise of legislative judgment. Furman v. Georgia, 408 U.S. at 314 (White, J., concurring).

38. These factors also influenced the views of Justices Brennan and Marshall that, under any circumstances, imposition of the death penalty would be unconstitutional. *See supra* note 31.

39. *See* Lockett v. Ohio, 438 U.S. 586, 601 (1978); Gregg v. Georgia, 428 U.S. 153, 188 & n.36 (1976); *id.* at 220–21 (White, J., concurring). This interpretation of the *Furman* decision cannot be derived in any strict sense from *Furman* itself. Each of the five concurring justices wrote his own concurring opinion and none of them chose to join in any other justice's concurring opinion. Nevertheless, in subsequent cases, various members of the Court have attempted to extrapolate from the most narrow of the concurring opinions a core principle with which all the concurring justices would presumably agree. *See, e.g.*, Gregg v. Georgia, 428 U.S. at 169 & n.15 (plurality opinion). That this core principle, however described, focuses upon the infrequency of execution under pre-*Furman* sentencing systems and the probability that those cases that resulted in death sentences could not be distinguished on any legitimate basis from other cases that did not also receive the death penalty seems likely in view of the *Furman* dissents. Those opinions characterized the opinions of Justices Stewart and White as reflecting a concern with inconsistent sentencing in capital cases. *See, e.g.*, Furman v. Georgia, 408 U.S. at 396–401 (Burger, C.J., dissenting).

40. 408 U.S. at 249–57 (Douglas, J., concurring); 293–95 (Brennan, J., concurring); 364–66, 368 (Marshall, J., concurring).

41. *Id.* at 310 (Stewart, J., concurring).

42. *Id.* at 309–10 (Stewart, J., concurring).

43. *Id.* at 313 (White, J., concurring).

44. *Id.*

45. *Id.* at 405–6, 410–12 (Blackmun, J., dissenting).

46. *Id.* at 405 (Burger, C.J., dissenting).

47. *Id.* at 389n.12. The unwillingness of the *Furman* dissenters to accept the factual determinations about discretionary jury sentencing upon which the five concurring justices relied was not solely because of inadequate factual support. The dissenting opinions, particularly that of the chief justice, reflect obvious concerns with the doctrinal implications of such conclusions. For one thing, they were obviously inconsistent with the basic rationale of *McGautha*. More fundamentally, however, to reject the notion that juries impose the death penalty in only the most extreme cases is "inconsistent in principle with everything this Court has ever said about the functioning of juries in capital cases." *Id.* at 387 (Burger, C.J., dissenting). As Chief Justice Burger also observed, "to assume from the mere fact of relative infrequency that only a random assortment of pariahs are sentenced to death, is to cast grave doubt on the basic integrity of our jury system." *Id.* at 388–89.

48. Godfrey v. Georgia, 446 U.S. 420, 433 (1980) (plurality opinion) ("no principled way to distinguish" the case before the Court from the many who received lesser sentences); Gregg v. Georgia, 428 U.S. at 206 (plurality opinion) ("If a time comes when juries generally do not impose the death sentence in a certain kind of murder case, the appellate review procedures assure that no defendant convicted under such circumstances will suffer a sentence of death"); Furman v. Georgia, 408 U.S. at 309–10 (Stewart, J., concurring) ("For, of all the people convicted of rapes and murders in 1967 and 1968, many just as reprehensible as these, the petitioners are among a capriciously selected random handful upon whom the sentence of death has in fact been imposed") (footnotes omitted). *Id.* at 313 (White, J., concurring) ("[T]here is no meaningful basis for distinguishing the few cases in which [the death penalty] is imposed from the many cases in which it is not"). *See also* Gross & Mauro, *supra* note 1, at 36.

49. Pulley v. Harris, 465 U.S. 37, 45 (1984) ("capricious," "freakish," "comparative proportionality"); Gregg v. Georgia, 428 U.S. at 173 ("excessive," "wanton," "capricious," "freakishly"); Furman v. Georgia, 408 U.S. at 293, 295, 309, 310, 312, 358 ("freakishly," "rare," "capricious," "random," "excessive"); Note, *Distinguishing Among Murders When Assessing the Proportionality of the Death Penalty*, 85 COLUM. L. REV., 1786, 1793 (1985) ("comparative proportionality").

50. The concept of disproportionality traditionally employed in Eighth Amendment jurisprudence contemplates a judicial judgment, informed by the values of the Court and by such indicia of contemporary community standards as legislative enactments and jury decisions, that a given sanction is a disproportionate and excessive punishment for a particular offense. Enmund v. Florida, 458 U.S. 782, 797 (1982). Because the Eighth Amendment's underlying concern is preventing the "purposeless and needless imposition of pain and suffering," it condemns penal sanctions whose severity or length serve no legitimate social purpose either as a deterrent or as a form of justifiable retribution. Coker v. Georgia, 433 U.S. 584, 592 (1977) (plurality opinion). The United States Supreme Court has invoked the Eighth Amendment's prohibition of disproportionate punishments to invalidate death sentences in four cases. In *Coker*, the Court ruled that death was a "grossly disproportionate and excessive punishment" for the rape of an adult. In *Enmund*, the Court held that death was a disproportionate sanction when imposed upon an accessory to a robbery who was convicted of capital murder solely by means of the felony-murder doctrine. More recently, the Eighth Amendment has been interpreted to bar death sentencing for insane persons, Ford v. Wainwright, 477 U.S. 399 (1986), and for minors below 16 years of age at the time of their homicides, Thompson v. Oklahoma, 108 S.Ct. 2687 (1988). However, in Gregg v.

Georgia, 428 U.S. at 176–87, the Court held that death was a permissible sanction in cases involving intentional, aggravated murder. In each of these cases the Court decided the disproportionality question by considering two basic factors: first, whether the punishment of death, society's harshest and irrevocable sanction, comported with the heinousness of the offense; and, second, whether recent legislative authorization and judicial imposition of the death penalty in such cases occurred with sufficient frequency to be consistent with contemporary community standards.

The concept of comparative excessiveness, with which we are particularly concerned, is analytically distinct from this traditional notion of constitutional disproportionality. Issues of comparative excessiveness arise in cases in which the defendant's death sentence is not disproportionate in the traditional Eighth Amendment sense, given the nature of his crime and the circumstances of his case. Under these circumstances, a death sentence may be comparatively excessive, however, because it is disproportionate to the lesser penalties generally imposed on other defendants whose cases cannot be meaningfully distinguished.

The concept of comparative excessiveness differs from the more traditional notion of disproportionality in at least two important respects. First, disproportionality in the traditional sense directly addresses whether a given sanction is constitutionally excessive because it serves no useful social purpose, while comparative excessiveness approaches the same ultimate question from the perspective of evenhandedness. A prohibition of comparatively excessive death sentences thus contributes to the rational and consistent administration of justice in capital cases.

The second way in which the traditional notion of disproportionality and the concept of comparative excessiveness differ is the manner in which courts conduct each type of inquiry. The Supreme Court has repeatedly emphasized that determinations of disproportionality in the traditional sense are ultimately judicial judgments. Legislative enactments, prior sentencing patterns, and even public opinion surveys are important considerations, but ultimately the justices themselves must assess the severity of the sanction in comparison to the gravity of the offense. By contrast, prior sentencing patterns assume much greater importance when one decides whether a particular death sentence is comparatively excessive. Indeed, the sentences imposed in factually similar cases provide the benchmark by which courts decide whether a particular death sentence is excessive or evenhanded when they engage in the process of true comparative-sentence review.

Thus, although both traditional disproportionality analysis and the comparative excessiveness inquiry reflect a concern with sentencing patterns in similar cases, the degree of importance that each attributes to such patterns differs substantially. Additionally, when engaging in traditional disproportionality analysis, the Court has freely considered sentencing patterns in similar cases on a nationwide basis. Determinations of comparative excessiveness, by contrast, characteristically limit themselves to statewide sentencing patterns.

The concepts of traditional and comparative excessiveness that we employ in this book are analogous to the concepts of "cardinal" and "ordinal" proportionality used in the criminal law literature. Cardinal-proportionality issues arise in "fixing the absolute severity levels" for given crimes, while the issue of ordinal proportionality "concerns how a crime should be punished compared to similar criminal acts." *See* A. von Hirsh, Past or Future Crimes 40–43 (1985).

51. *Furman*, 408 U.S. at 398–99 (Burger, C.J., dissenting) ("The decisive grievance of the [concurring opinions of Justice Stewart and Justice White] . . . is that the

present system of discretionary sentencing in capital cases has failed to produce even-handed justice"). Because the Supreme Court's opinions do not quantify the notion of "evenhandedness," it is unavoidably elastic in terms of the infrequency with which death sentences must be imposed in comparable cases to make any particular death sentence excessive. Also, a frequency approach to excessiveness normally requires a sufficient number of sentencing decisions among a group of similar cases to determine whether the death sentences imposed in the group are sufficiently infrequent to be considered excessive. For example, if only one life and one death sentence have been imposed in a category of similar cases, it may not be possible to determine whether life or death sentences will be the norm for such cases over the long run. For the purposes of analyzing our Georgia data, we classified a death sentence as presumptively arbitrary or excessive if the death-sentencing rate among a reasonably sized sample of cases deemed to be similar was less than .35; we classified as presumptively evenhanded those death-sentence cases for which the comparable death-sentencing rate was .80 or greater. For a discussion of the legal basis for this method of classification, *see infra* chap. 4, note 50, and Baldus, Pulaski, & Woodworth, *Comparative Review of Death Sentences: An Empirical Study of the Georgia Experience*, 74 J. CRIM. L. & CRIMINOL-OGY 661, 695–98 (1983).

52. *See infra* chap. 4, note 49 and accompanying text, for a description of the empirical measures used in this book to evaluate the level of arbitrariness in a death-sentencing system.

53. Furman v. Georgia, 408 U.S. at 257 (Douglas, J., concurring) ("[The death sentencing systems before the Court] are pregnant with discrimination and discrimination is an ingredient not compatible with the idea of equal protection of the laws that is implicit in the ban on 'cruel and unusual' punishments"). Within the decade the Court had determined that proof of intentional discrimination is required to establish a successful claim of racial discrimination under the Fourteenth Amendment. *See* Village of Arlington Heights v. Metropolitan Housing Development Corp., 429 U.S. 252, 265 (1977); Washington v. Davis, 426 U.S. 229, 242 (1976). The Court has yet to determine whether unlawful discrimination under the Eighth Amendment must be purposeful, although in McCleskey v. Kemp, 107 S.Ct. 1756 (1987), the Court clearly implied that proof of widespread purposeful discrimination in a system, as distinct from merely the risk of discrimination, would support an Eighth Amendment claim. *See infra* chap. 10, note 111 and accompanying text.

54. See *infra* chap. 4, note 54 and accompanying text, for a description of these measures.

55. *Washington*, 426 U.S. at 238–39.

CHAPTER THREE

Post-*Furman* Developments

Furman invalidated death sentences imposed on over six hundred defendants.[1] It did not, however, abolish the death penalty altogether, since only Justices Brennan and Marshall flatly condemned capital punishment under all circumstances. As a consequence, many states that wished to retain the death penalty adopted a variety of new procedures in an effort to overcome the deficiencies that made standardless, discretionary sentencing statutes unconstitutional.[2] Some states tried to prevent abuses of sentencing discretion by making the death penalty mandatory in specified classes of cases, an approach the Supreme Court subsequently rejected.[3] Other states, including Georgia, attempted to satisfy *Furman* while preserving some degree of sentencing discretion by enacting explicit sentencing standards to guide the exercise of that discretion and by adopting sometimes elaborate procedures to ensure that those standards were enforced.

THE LEGISLATIVE RESPONSE TO *FURMAN* IN GENERAL

The statutory changes that the Supreme Court approved in the years following *Furman v. Georgia* dramatically changed the procedures that had regulated capital punishment in over thirty jurisdictions.[4] First, the category of murders in which death sentences could be imposed was specifically limited by statute. Most state laws now identify six to twelve aggravating circumstances, at least one of which must be present before a convicted murderer is eligible for a death sentence.* Statutorily designated aggravating circumstances commonly include killing a police officer, killing to avoid arrest or confinement, or endangering the lives of others in the course of the murder.[5] The two most important aggravating circumstances, however, are the "contemporaneous offense" and the "vile murder" circumstances. These two statutorily designated aggravating circumstances lead all others by far, both in the numbers of defendants they

---

*We estimate that only 10% to 25% (or 2,000 to 4,000) of the approximately 18,000 murders and nonnegligent manslaughters annually reported to the FBI qualify as death-eligible homicides under state law. See Baldus, Pulaski, & Woodworth, *Arbitrariness and Discrimination in the Administration of the Death Penalty: A Challenge to State Supreme Courts*, 15 STETSON LAW REVIEW 133, 152 (1986); see *infra* table 48.

make death-eligible and in the number of cases in which they appear that actually result in death sentences.[6] The contemporaneous-offense circumstance makes an offender death-eligible if he commits murder while engaged in the commission of a rape, armed robbery, kidnapping, burglary, or arson. The vile-murder circumstance makes an offender death-eligible if he commits murder in an exceptionally wanton, vile, or horrible manner.

A second major statutory change was the bifurcation of the guilt and jury sentencing phases of capital trials into separate proceedings. The unitary trials that the Supreme Court sustained in *McGautha v. California* are a thing of the past. Under the new procedures, the jury first hears evidence and argument solely with respect to the defendant's guilt. If the jury finds the defendant guilty of capital murder, the case then typically advances to a second proceeding, known as the penalty trial, during which the parties present further evidence and argument with respect to the appropriate sentence.[7] The purpose of this procedural change is to prevent otherwise inadmissible information from affecting the decision on guilt, while ensuring that the jury makes the sentencing decision on the basis of all the relevant evidence. As a result of this reform, the capital-charging-and-sentencing process now includes an additional step. *

A third change, which resulted both from changes in state law and from United States Supreme Court decisions, concerns the aggravating and mitigating circumstances to be considered in capital cases. Once a sentencing jury finds one or more statutory aggravating circumstances present in a case, the Eighth Amendment permits that jury to consider any aggravating circumstances relating to the defendant, the crime, or the victim, whether or not specified as a statutory aggravating circumstance by state law.[8] Some states, however, have restricted the aggravating circumstances that can be considered in determining the appropriate sentence to those designated by the legislature.[9] On the other hand, the Eighth Amendment prohibits the imposition of any limits or restrictions on the mitigating circumstances that may be considered.[10] State laws or instructions from the bench that prohibit the jury from taking any particular mitigating factor into account are unconstitutional.[11] The Eighth Amendment may also impose a further requirement that trial judges ensure that sentencing juries understand the

---

*We note that in Florida and in two other states the jury sentencing decision is only a recommendation that may be reversed by the trial judge. *See* Mellow & Robson, *Judge over Jury: Florida's Practice of Imposing Death over Life in Capital Cases*, 13 FLA. STATE U. L. REV. 31 (1985); Ehrhardt & Levinson, *Florida's Response to Furman: An Exercise in Futility*, 64 J. CRIM. L. & CRIMINOLOGY 10 (1973). Moreover, in five other states the judge makes the sentencing decision with no input from the jury. Because most states use jury sentencing, we discuss that system in the text.

proper function of aggravating and mitigating circumstances.[12] The purpose of these rules is to ensure that each defendant will receive an individualized sentencing decision, based upon a careful balancing of all the relevant factors relating to the appropriate sentence, especially mitigating factors.

Of course, allowing the sentencing judge or jury sufficient discretion to ensure that each defendant receives individualized consideration creates a risk that basically similar defendants will receive different sentences or that some defendants will be treated more or less harshly for unconstitutional or inappropriate reasons.[13] Presumably on these grounds, many states adopted new rules requiring an unusual degree of appellate court scrutiny in cases in which death sentences occurred.[14] At present, state supreme courts perform this enhanced oversight role in more than twenty death-sentencing jurisdictions, mostly by reason of statutory changes, but, in a few cases, by reason of court decisions.[15]

GEORGIA'S LEGISLATIVE RESPONSE TO *FURMAN*

Less than a year after the United States Supreme Court decided *Furman* in 1972, the Georgia legislature enacted new death-sentencing procedures, based in part upon the Model Penal Code, in an effort to retain capital punishment as a penal sanction.[16] Georgia's revised statute made a defendant death-eligible if he was convicted of common-law murder—an unlawful killing with "malice aforethought"—and if the sentencing jury determined that at least one of ten statutorily designated aggravating circumstances was present.[17] These statutory aggravating circumstances included both the contemporaneous-felony and the vile-circumstances criteria.[18] However, in contrast to several other states, of which Florida is a leading example, the Georgia statute did not specify any mitigating circumstances that the sentencing jury should consider; nor did it prescribe the manner in which juries should weigh aggravating and mitigating circumstances. Indeed, it does not even require that sentencing juries should base their decisions upon a weighing of aggravating and mitigating circumstances. The statute merely requires the court to instruct the jury to consider "any mitigating circumstances or aggravating circumstances otherwise authorized by law" and any "statutory aggravating circumstances which may be supported by the evidence."[19] Moreover, the Georgia Supreme Court has interpreted this provision to authorize an instruction (a) that the jury may recommend life imprisonment, no matter how aggravated the case may be, and (b) that once the jury finds a statutory aggravating factor present in the case, the question of whether a death sentence should be imposed is totally discretionary for the jury.[20] However, if a jury does decide to impose a death sentence, it is required to make a written finding of the statutorily designated aggravating circumstances found to be present in the case.[21]

When the Georgia legislature revised its death-sentencing procedure in 1973, it was unnecessary to adopt a new bifurcated-trial procedure since, as previously noted, the legislature, in response to a suggestion of the Georgia Supreme Court, had taken that step in 1970.[22] However, prior to *Furman*, the sentencing phase of Georgia's bifurcated procedure was a perfunctory affair. Normally, the only additional evidence offered during the sentencing hearing was the defendant's prior criminal record, if any. After *Furman* and, perhaps more importantly, after *Lockett v. Ohio*, which sensitized attorneys to the significance of mitigating circumstances,[23] the evidence offered during the sentencing phase of capital cases in Georgia became much more extensive.

The revised Georgia statute also increased the responsibilities of the Georgia Supreme Court in death-sentence cases. It created a new automatic appeal, in the course of which the Georgia Supreme Court is required to review the record and determine whether the evidence supports the jury's finding of a statutorily designated aggravating circumstance.[24] The court also reviews any other claims of legal error affecting the guilt or sentencing phases of the trial and, most importantly, decides whether the death sentence is excessive and disproportionate when compared with other similar cases "considering both the crime and the defendant" and whether its imposition was the product of passion or prejudice.[25]

THE UNITED STATES SUPREME COURT'S DECISIONS APPROVING GUIDED-DISCRETION DEATH-SENTENCING SYSTEMS

In its 1976 decisions in *Gregg v. Georgia, Proffitt v. Florida*, and *Jurek v. Texas*, the Supreme Court approved new death-sentencing systems in Georgia, Florida, and Texas.[26] In these rulings the Court clarified in several respects the constitutional requirements of the Eighth Amendment in the death-sentencing context. First, the Court rejected the argument that the death penalty was an inherently excessive sentence for aggravated murder.[27] Second, it ruled that the Georgia procedures that gave sentencing juries the discretion to impose a life sentence, no matter how aggravated the circumstances, did not violate the Constitution. The Court acknowledged that such a broad grant of discretion would permit juries to impose inconsistent sentences in similar cases, but concluded that "the isolated decision of a jury to afford mercy" in a particular case did not make death sentences imposed on other defendants unconstitutional.[28] In reaching this conclusion, both the plurality and concurring justices stressed the Georgia Supreme Court's statutory obligation to subject every death-sentence case to a proportionality review.[29]

In sustaining the Georgia and Florida statutes, the Court also rejected the argument that the discretion of prosecutors to charge death-eligible defendants with lesser offenses than capital murder for a given homicide created an impermissible risk of arbitrariness. The manner in which the different justices disposed of this argument is interesting, especially in light of some of our empirical findings. We will give this question further attention on pages 28–30 of this chapter.

At the same time that the Court sustained the constitutionality of the Georgia, Florida, and Texas statutes, it invalidated, on Eighth Amendment grounds, the mandatory death-sentencing procedures enacted after *Furman* by the legislatures of Louisiana and North Carolina. The Court found these mandatory statutes unconstitutional either because they denied the sentencing juries sufficient discretion to individualize the sentencing decision or because they lacked sufficient guidelines or safeguards to ensure that the discretion that the Court believed juries would inevitably exercise at the guilt trial would produce rational, evenhanded sentencing results.[30]

Other Supreme Court decisions since 1976 have further developed the constitutional requirements applicable to death-sentencing procedures. By and large, the 1976 decisions sought to vindicate the core concerns of *Furman v. Georgia* while avoiding undue rigidity. Rather than interpreting the Eighth Amendment to mandate specific procedures, the Court accepted as constitutionally sufficient different statutory schemes containing a variety of safeguards, so long as each appeared capable of producing rational, evenhanded sentences while ensuring that each defendant receives a factually reliable, individualized sentencing determination.[31] Furthermore, when reviewing particular death sentences, the Court has carefully distinguished between errors or omissions that violate state law and those that are so severe as to offend constitutional requirements.[32]

For the purposes of this study, certain features of the Court's post-*Furman* decisions stand out. First, in the course of articulating the precise requirements of the Eighth Amendment, the Court effectively transposed the result-oriented character of the *Furman* holding into an essentially procedurally oriented inquiry. Instead of asking whether sentences imposed under the new capital-sentencing procedures were, in fact, rational and evenhanded, the Court asked itself whether the new procedures seemed capable of minimizing the risk of arbitrary or capricious sentences.[33]

Certainly, the Court has always recognized that the five concurring opinions in *Furman*, particularly those of Justices Stewart and White, depended upon the factual characteristics of the death sentences under consideration. In order to apply *Furman* prospectively and to develop workable rules for future cases, however, the Court necessarily shifted its focus to a procedural mode. Thus, in *Gregg,* the Court decided that Georgia's revised capital-sentencing procedures were constitutional because of its assessment that, if properly applied, those procedures were capable of preventing death sentences that would offend *Furman.*[34] Similarly, in each of *Gregg's* companion cases, the Court presumed that the statutory procedures under scrutiny would operate as they were capable of operating, and the Court decided their acceptability under *Furman* on that basis.[35]

Implicit in this approach, of course, lurked at least two factual presumptions capable of empirical verification. The first was that those who were actually to administer death-sentencing procedures would, in fact, observe the statutory requirements and conduct themselves in conformity to the legislature's intent. The second presumption was that if those who administer death-sentencing procedures did conduct themselves in conformity with the new statutes, the sentences imposed would be free of the arbitrariness and excessiveness that *Furman* condemned.

Of these two factual presumptions, the first seemed unsurprising. Courts normally presume that officials will conduct themselves in accordance with their statutory obligations. We discuss this presumption further in the following section. The second presumption, however, seems more remarkable. It certainly required the Court to make a greater leap of faith than did the first and, in contrast to *Furman,* represented a return to the more deferential approach that characterized Justice Harlan's opinion in *McGautha.* More importantly, the Court's use of the second presumption in *Gregg* to uphold the Georgia statute—presuming that, because the Georgia sentencing procedure seemed capable of producing constitutional sentences, it would, in fact, produce such sentences—again demonstrated the Court's willingness to decide important constitutional questions on the basis of essentially factual presumptions untested by the adversary process.

As previously indicated, one major objective of our study of Georgia was to test the Court's second presumption. If, in fact, the study concluded that the Georgia statute had failed to produce rational, consistent sentencing results, such a finding would threaten the central premise of the Court's conclusion in *Gregg* that the Georgia statute was constitutional.[36] On the other hand, a finding that Georgia sentences imposed under the state's post-*Furman* legislation did reflect principled distinctions between those capital defendants who received death sentences and those who did not would strongly confirm the Court's presumptive approach.[37]

FACTUAL ASSUMPTIONS UNDERLYING *GREGG* CONCERNING PROSECUTORS, JURIES, AND THE GEORGIA SUPREME COURT

We also designed our study so we could scrutinize the conduct of the three major decision makers in Georgia's capital-sentencing process. The purpose of this phase of our study was to compare our empirical findings with a series of factual assumptions that the Court employed to decide *Gregg v. Georgia*. In various respects, both Justice Stewart's plurality opinion in *Gregg* and Justice White's concurring opinion, in which the chief justice and Justice Rehnquist also joined, assumed that Georgia's prosecutors and juries, and the state supreme court, would discharge their respective duties under the statute in ways that obviated the constitutional challenge.

Factual Assumptions about Prosecutorial Discretion

In *Gregg* the defendant argued that, under the new Georgia legislation, prosecutors could still affect the sentencing process by the charges they chose to file in potentially capital cases. This power, ran the argument, created a sufficient risk of inconsistent or arbitrary sentencing to make the entire statute unconstitutional. Both Justice Stewart and Justice White rejected this argument, though on different grounds. Justice Stewart's opinion for the plurality asserted that *Furman* should not be read to diminish the prosecutor's traditional discretion in capital cases; its holding applied exclusively to the sentencing authority.[38] Consequently, complaints about the impact of the prosecutor's charging discretion were simply off the mark.

Because *Furman* condemned the cumulative results of the entire death-sentencing process, Justice Stewart's interpretation appears to be rather narrow. However, he clearly believed that eliminating all prosecutorial discretion in capital cases would be "totally unrealistic" and possibly unconstitutional.[39] The tone of his opinion even suggests that he considered the contrary argument to be somewhat frivolous. Perhaps for this reason, he never directly addressed the core of the defendant's argument: that the prosecutor's unrestricted ability to exercise discretion in capital cases, favoring some defendants but not others, created a risk that less-favored defendants might ultimately receive arbitrary or excessive death sentences.

By contrast, Justice White regarded the potential impact of prosecutorial discretion on the ultimate sentencing results as a legitimate issue. He was concerned, in part, because of a deficiency in the Georgia Supreme Court's form of comparative-proportionality review.[40] When deciding if a death sentence on appeal was comparatively excessive, the Georgia court did not scrutinize the cases of potentially death-eligible defendants who escaped the risk of death sentences through prosecutorial charging decisions. Consequently, if prosecutors arbitrarily exercised their discretion by charging some death-eligible cases with manslaughter or other lesser offenses, they could theoretically taint the operation of the entire system without detection.

Having recognized this potential constitutional defect, however, Justice White rejected it as factually unsupported.

> Absent acts to the contrary, it cannot be assumed that prosecutors will be motivated in their charging decision by factors other than the strength of their case and the likelihood that a jury would impose the death penalty if it convicts. Unless prosecutors are incompetent in their judgments, the standards by which they decide whether to charge a capital felony will be the same as those by which the jury will decide the questions of guilt and sentence.[41]

In other words, without contrary evidence, Justice White assumed that Georgia prosecutors would voluntarily observe the same statutory criteria that governed the sentencing decisions by Georgia juries. He was willing to indulge this assumption, presumably, because no death sentence would result anyway, unless those standards were satisfied.

This analysis seems plausible, as far as it goes. Certainly, a prosecutor who wants to obtain a death sentence will undoubtedly consider the applicable statutory standards. But this does not mean that prosecutors will always seek death sentences in every case in which, given the statutory standards, such a penalty is warranted.

This distinction is important. It underscores the critical factual assumption implicit in Justice White's conclusion that the existence of unrestricted prosecutorial discretion created no risk of arbitrary or capricious sentencing results. If one assumes that prosecutors will always exercise their discretion consistently with the statutory standards and their estimate of the strength of the evidence, it follows they will nearly always seek a death sentence if that penalty is the likely result. Justice White was clearly willing to make this assumption. He suggested that a prosecutor might fail to seek a capital conviction or a death sentence despite adequate evidence only through incompetence. His opinion contemplated no other reason why a prosecutor might decline to seek the maximum authorized penalty in such a case.* Presumably, however, he would be willing to reevaluate his position if persuaded that, in fact, prosecu-

---

*Implicit in Justice White's analysis of prosecutorial discretion may be a second factual assumption. The Georgia statute provided that every defendant convicted of capital murder "shall" undergo a penalty trial. Ga Laws, Act. No. 74, p. 162, quoted in Gregg v. Georgia, 428 U.S. at 208n.2. Justice White may have assumed that prosecutorial discretion played no role in the sentencing process once a defendant pleaded guilty to, or a jury convicted a defendant of, capital murder. *See infra* chap. 7, note 70.

tors did sometimes exercise their discretion in an arbitrary, discriminatory, or excessive manner. Indeed, his reference in the foregoing quotation, "[a]bsent acts to the contrary," suggested that such a showing might raise a question of constitutional significance.

Factual Assumptions about Sentencing Juries and the Georgia Supreme Court

In *Gregg*, the defendant also challenged the sentencing jury's unrestricted discretion to be lenient, that is, to impose a life sentence in any case no matter how aggravated the offense or how culpable the offender.[42] This discretion, contended the defendant, created a risk that basically indistinguishable convicted capital offenders might receive different sentences simply because their respective juries disagreed about the appropriateness of the death sentence in such cases.

Justice Stewart's plurality opinion disposed of this argument by invoking two factual presumptions, both of which are susceptible to empirical verification. The first presumption was that in most cases in which the presence of a statutorily designated aggravating circumstance made capital punishment an authorized sanction, the jury would choose to impose a death sentence. This presumption is implicit in Justice Stewart's reference in *Gregg* to "the isolated decision of a jury to afford mercy"[43] and his invocation of Justice White's reference in *Furman* to "the few cases in which [the death penalty] is imposed" and "the many cases in which it is not."[44]

The second factual presumption was that the Georgia Supreme Court would effectively discharge its responsibility to vacate on appeal any death sentence found to be "excessive or disproportionate" in comparison to other similar cases.[45] This presumption buttressed Justice Stewart's conclusion that decisions of sentencing juries to be lenient would create no constitutional defect in the Georgia statute. He clearly believed that, in the exercise of its comparative-sentence review function, the Georgia Supreme Court would screen out any death sentences found to be excessive because, in most similar cases, juries only imposed life sentences.

Justice White's concurring opinion in *Gregg* also rejected the defendant's objection to the sentencing jury's discretion by invoking these two factual presumptions. Under the Georgia system, wrote Justice White, "it becomes reasonable to expect that juries—even given discretion not to impose the death penalty—will impose the death penalty in a substantial portion of the cases" involving statutorily designated aggravating circumstances.[46]

With respect to the Georgia Supreme Court's comparative-sentence review function, Justice White was even more explicit. He noted that in order to ensure that Georgia juries imposed death sentences with reasonable consistency in cases involving serious murders, the Georgia legislature directed the state supreme court to perform the very function that the Supreme Court had performed in *Furman*: deciding whether the death penalty was being administered for any class of crime in a discriminatory, standardless, or rare fashion.[47] "Indeed, if the Georgia Supreme Court properly performs the task assigned to it," wrote Justice White, "death sentences imposed for discriminatory reasons or wantonly or freakishly for any given category of crime will be set aside."[48]

Two Models of Georgia's Sentencing Process

Implicit in the *Gregg* plurality and concurring opinions are two alternate preconceptions or models of how Georgia's revised sentencing procedures would ensure the consistency and rationality that *Furman* requires. The first model presupposes that prosecutors will regularly seek and juries will regularly impose death sentences in most cases in which the presence of a statutory aggravating circumstance makes the defendant death-eligible. Under these circumstances, the case characteristics specified by those statutory aggravating circumstances (e.g., killing a police officer) would themselves distinguish in a meaningful and principled fashion those defendants who received death sentences from other murder defendants who did not. Thus, the fatal weakness of pre-*Furman* sentencing practices—arbitrariness and excessiveness—would be cured without the intervention of the state supreme court.

On the other hand, the Georgia statute does give prosecutors and juries substantial discretion. As Justice White recognized, there was no way to guarantee that prosecutors and juries would always exercise that discretion as this first model presupposes.[49] Thus, even after the post-*Furman* reforms, capital sentencing in Georgia might still reflect the inconsistency and arbitrariness that *Furman* condemned.

It is in this context that the second model comes into play. This second model contemplates that, if Georgia's prosecutors and juries do not seek or impose similar sentences in all factually similar cases, the Georgia Supreme Court's review process can still achieve consistent results.[50] Specifically, this second model presumes that the Georgia Supreme Court will review every death-sentence case in light of all the other death-sentencing decisions in the state. This process would permit the Court to identify those categories of defendants who are regularly sentenced to death and to determine whether the death-sentence case under review conforms to that pattern. If so, the sentence would be affirmed. Otherwise, the Georgia Supreme Court would vacate the sentence. Thus, this model would ensure that every death sentence that survived this systematic appellate review would be distinguishable on some meaningful and principled basis from the larger group of murder cases in which death sentences were imposed only irregularly, if at all.

The critical difference between these two models is that, unlike the first, the second model would produce rational, consistent results even if prosecutors and sentencing juries exercised their discretion selectively. Consequently, this second model would permit a more refined system of community standards of moral culpability to govern the actual operation of the capital-sentencing process than one based solely on the statutory aggravating circumstances. However, this second model presupposes an effective form of appellate review that would eliminate any death sentences that are arbitrary or comparatively excessive.[51]

RACIAL DISCRIMINATION AND THE POST-*FURMAN* CASES

Although the five concurring justices in *Furman* did not explicitly agree whether racially discriminatory sentencing had actually occurred in the past, *Furman* certainly suggested that death-sentencing procedures could create an intolerable risk of discriminatory sentences.[52] In this respect, however, the United States Supreme Court's post-*Furman* opinions are less explicit. Until its 1986 decision in *Turner v. Murray*,[53] the Court had given no special consideration to sentencing decisions that might have been tainted by race or other impermissible factors; nor had the Court specifically addressed the means by which state courts might prevent discriminatory sentences or identify them when they had occurred. To be sure, if impermissible discrimination resulted in a comparatively excessive death sentence, proportionality review would presumably ensure relief. What the Court did not consider, however, was that discriminatory sentences can occur without being excessive.[54] Presumably, state supreme courts would nevertheless monitor their capital-sentencing processes for evidence of racial or other impermissible discrimination and would grant the same sort of classwide or individual relief employed in other contexts when discriminatory practices occurred.

SUMMARY

After *Furman*, many states, including Georgia, revised their capital-sentencing procedures. Those that survived subsequent United States Supreme Court review share several common features. They all restrict the death penalty to those murder cases in which a legislatively designated aggravating circumstance is present. They further permit the sentencing authority to consider any mitigating factors or circumstances in connection with the sentencing process. They all replace the unitary-trial procedure that the Supreme Court had sustained in *McGautha* with the more reliable bifurcated procedure. Finally, in jurisdictions like Georgia, which permit sentencing juries to refrain from imposing the death penalty regardless of the circumstances, they frequently include some form of comparative-sentence review to ensure that no defendant receives a death sentence under circumstances that usually result in a lesser penalty.

In *Gregg v. Georgia* the United States Supreme Court sustained the constitutionality of Georgia's revised procedure against a variety of constitutional objections.[55] The Court reached this decision because it believed that the new Georgia statute included sufficient safeguards to prevent the risk of arbitrary or excessive death sentences that *Furman* had condemned. In reaching this conclusion, both Justice Stewart, who wrote the plurality opinion, and Justice White, who concurred, appeared to rely on several empirically verifiable factual assumptions about the likely conduct of prosecutors, juries, and the Georgia Supreme Court under the new procedures. One such assumption was that prosecutors and juries would regularly seek and impose the death penalty in most death-eligible cases. A second assumption was that the Georgia Supreme Court would conduct the process of comparative-sentence review in an effective manner, correcting any arbitrary or excessive death sentences imposed at the trial court level. The later decision of *Zant v. Stephens* also appeared to assume that the Georgia Supreme Court would perform its comparative-sentence review function in an effective manner.[56]

NOTES

1. Greenberg, *Capital Punishment as a System*, 91 YALE L. J. 908, 915 (1982).

2. *See* Lockett v. Ohio, 438 U.S. 586, 599–600 (1978); *see also* Note, *Discretion and the Constitutionality of the New Death-Sentencing Statutes,* 87 HARV. L. REV. 1690, 1699–1712 (1974); Note, *Furman to Gregg: The Judicial and Legislative History*, 22 How. L.J. 53, 84–95 (1979). F. Zimring and G. Hawkins, CAPITAL PUNISHMENT AND THE AMERICAN AGENDA 38–45 (1986), describe the "backlash" of the states to *Furman* in which over thirty states reenacted death-penalty legislation. In doing so, they perceptively characterize the death penalty as "precisely the type of politically charged, symbolic policy issue," like school prayer, pornography, and abortion, "to which judicial invalidation [by the Supreme Court] has always provoked anger and resentment." *Id.* at 45.

3. *See* Roberts v. Louisiana, 428 U.S. 325, 334–36 (1976); Woodson v. North Carolina, 428 U.S. 280, 302–3 (1976). The Court in *Woodson* left open the possibility of mandatory death sentences for life-term prisoners committing certain violent crimes. *Id.* at 292n.25.

4. For a general description of the post-*Furman* legislation, *see* Gillers, *Deciding Who Dies*, 129 U. PA. L. REV. 1 (1980).

5. *See id.* at 101–19, app. I; Ledewitz, *The New Role of Statutory Aggravating Circumstances in American Death Penalty Law,* 22 DUQ. L. REV. 317, 360–69 (1984); *see also* H. Bedau, THE DEATH PENALTY IN AMERICA 36–37 (3d ed. 1982).

6. Baldus, Pulaski, & Woodworth, *Arbitrariness and Discrimination in the Administration of the Death Penalty: A Challenge to State Supreme Courts,* 15 STETSON L. REV. 133, 138 (1986) (hereinafter Baldus, Pulaski, & Woodworth (86)).

7. For a critical analysis of the penalty trial and its proper function in light of the Supreme Court's decisions, *see generally* Weisberg, *Deregulating Death,* 1983 SUP. CT. REV. 305 (hereinafter Weisberg).

8. *See* Zant v. Stephens, 462 U.S. 862, 878–80 (1983) (if a sentencer imposes a death sentence on the basis of constitutionally relevant aggravating circumstances other than those authorized by state law, no federal constitutional violation occurs); Barclay v. Florida, 463 U.S. 939, 950–51, 962 (1983).

9. *See* Zant v. Stephens, 462 U.S. at 878n.17.

10. *See* Eddings v. Oklahoma, 455 U.S. 104, 110 (1982).

11. *See* Skipper v. South Carolina, 476 U.S. 1, 4 (1986); Lockett v. Ohio, 438 U.S. at 604–5; Mills v. Maryland, 108 S.Ct. 1860 (1988) (jury unanimity on the presence of a mitigating circumstance is not required before an individual juror may weigh it against aggravating factors).

12. *See* Gregg v. Georgia, 428 U.S. 153, 192–93 (1976); *see also* Peek v. Kemp, 784 F.2d 1479, 1494 (11th Cir. 1986) (en banc), *cert. denied,* 479 U.S. 939 (1986) (Constitution requires no specific instructions regarding mitigating circumstances so long as there is no reasonable possibility that jurors will misunderstand the meaning and function of mitigating evidence); Briley v. Bass, 750 F.2d 1238, 1244 (4th Cir. 1984), *cert. denied,* 470 U.S. 1088 (1985).

13. *See* Turner v. Murray, 476 U.S. 28, 37 (1986). The doctrinal tension between the goals of individualized sentencing and consistent sentencing has attracted substantial attention. *See, e.g.,* Lockett v. Ohio, 438 U.S. at 622–24 (White, J., dissenting); *id.* at 628–33 (Rehnquist, J., dissenting); Weisberg, *supra* note 7, at 308.

14. *See* Baldus, Pulaski, & Woodworth (86), *supra* note 6, at 8–9; Baldus, Pulaski, Woodworth, & Kyle, *Identifying Comparatively Excessive Sentences of Death: A Quantitative Approach,* 33 STAN. L. REV. 1, 12–18 (1980) (hereinafter Baldus, Pulaski, Woodworth, & Kyle); Dix, *Appellate Review of the Decision to Impose Death,* 68 GEO. L.J. 97, 109–58 (1979) (hereinafter Dix).

15. *See* Baldus, Pulaski, & Woodworth, *Comparative Review of Death Sentences: An Empirical Study of the Georgia Experience,* 74 J. CRIM. L. & CRIMINOLOGY 661, 663–64 (1983) (hereinafter Baldus, Woodworth, & Pulaski (83)); chap. 9 *infra.*

16. *See* Hancock, *The Perils of Calibrating the Death Penalty Through Special Definitions of Murder,* 53 TUL. L. REV. 828, 832–33 (1979).

17. *See* GA. CODE ANN. §§26-1101(a), (c), 27-2534.1 (Harrison 1978); Gregg v. Georgia, 428 U.S. at 196–97 (plurality opinion).

18. GA. CODE ANN. at §27-2534.1 provides:

(a) The death penalty may be imposed for the offenses of aircraft hijacking or treason in any case.

(b) In all cases of other offenses for which the death penalty may be authorized, the judge shall consider, or he shall include in his instructions to the jury for it to consider, any mitigating circumstances or aggravating circumstances otherwise authorized by law and any of the following statutory aggravating circumstances which may be supported by the evidence:

    (1) The offense of murder, rape, armed robbery, or kidnapping was committed by a person with a prior record of conviction for a capital felony;

    (2) The offense of murder, rape, armed robbery, or kidnapping was committed while the offender was engaged in the commission of another capital felony or aggravated battery, or the offense of murder was committed while the offender was engaged in the commission of burglary or arson in the first degree;

    (3) The offender by his act of murder, armed robbery, or kidnapping, knowingly created a great risk of death to more than one person in a public place by means of a weapon or device which would normally be hazardous to the lives of more than one person;

    (4) The offender committed the offense of murder for himself or another, for the purpose of receiving money or any other thing of monetary value;

    (5) The murder of a judicial officer, former judicial officer, district attorney or solicitor, or former district attorney or solicitor was committed during or because of the exercise of his official duty;

    (6) The offender caused or directed another to commit murder or committed murder as an agent or employee of another person;

    (7) The offense of murder, rape, armed robbery, or kidnapping was outrageously or wantonly vile, horrible, or inhuman in that it involved torture, depravity of mind, or an aggravated battery to the victim;

    (8) The offense of murder was committed against any peace officer, corrections employee, or fireman while engaged in the performance of his official duties;

    (9) The offense of murder was committed by a person in, or who has escaped from, the lawful custody of a peace officer or place of lawful confinement;

    (10) The murder was committed for the purpose of avoiding, interfering with, or preventing a lawful arrest or custody in a place of lawful confinement, of himself or another.

(c) The statutory instructions as determined by the trial judge to be warranted by the evidence shall be given in charge and in writing to the jury for its deliberation. The jury, if its verdict be a recommendation of death, shall designate in writing, signed by the foreman of the jury, the aggravating circumstance or circumstances which it found beyond a reasonable doubt. In non-jury cases the judge shall make such designation. Except in cases of treason or aircraft hijacking, unless at least one of the statutory aggravating circumstances enumerated in Section 27-2534.1(b) is so found, the death penalty shall not be imposed.

In Arnold v. State, 236 Ga. 534, 540, 224 S.E.2d 386, 391 (1976), the Georgia Supreme Court held unconstitutional the portion of the first circumstance, later deleted by the legislature, encompassing persons who have a "substantial history of serious assaultive criminal convictions" because it did not set "sufficiently 'clear and objective standards.' "

19. GA. CODE ANN. at §27-2534.1(b). In Gates v. State, 244 Ga. 587, 597, 261 S.E.2d 349, 357 (1979), cert. denied, 445 U.S. 938 (1980), the Georgia Supreme Court held that the statute:

does not impose the additional requirement that the jury be instructed that mitigating circumstances are to be weighed against aggravating circumstances, but instead allows the jury to consider both, and to impose a life sentence even where there are aggravating circumstances.

As for the fact that the trial court failed to give examples of mitigating circumstances, it is not required that specific mitigating circumstances be singled out by the court in giving its instructions to the jury. To influence the jury by use of examples might limit its discretion to consider other matters in addition to the examples given.

20. *See, e.g.,* Duhart v. State, 237 Ga. 426, 432–33, 228 S.E.2d 822, 826 (1976) (approving the following jury instruction):

> If you find beyond a reasonable doubt that the State has proved the existence in this case of the aggravating circumstance, . . . then you would be authorized to recommend the imposition of the sentence of death, but you would not be required to do so. . . . [Y]ou would also be authorized to recommend the defendant to the mercy of the Court, which is a recommendation you may make either with or without a reason. You may make it for any reason that is satisfactory to you, or without a reason. You may make it arbitrarily, as a matter of course, or as a matter of discretion.

Romine v. State, 251 Ga. 208, 215, 305 S.E.2d 93, 100 (1983), *cert. denied,* 107 S.Ct. 1912 (1987) (approving the following jury instruction):

> Mitigating circumstances are those which do not constitute a justification or excuse for the offense in question but which in all fairness and mercy may be considered as extinuating [*sic*] or reducing the degree of moral culpability or blame.
> ". . . [I]f you see fit . . . to recommend mercy for the Defendant then this recommendation is solely in your discretion and is not controlled by any rule of law. You may make such recommendation with or without reason. . . . In other words . . . if you find beyond a reasonable doubt that the State of Georgia has proved the existence of one or more of the aggravating circumstances given to you in this charge as to either or both counts, you nonetheless are not required to recommend that the Defendant Romine be put to death.
> "You may, if you see fit, and this is a matter entirely in your discretion, provide for a life sentence for the accused Romine based upon any mitigating circumstances or reasons satisfactory to you [with] or without reason if you see fit to do so.

Ross v. State, 254 Ga. 22, 32, 326 S.E.2d 194, 204 (1985), *cert. denied,* 472 U.S. 1022 (1985) (approving the following jury instruction):

> "Now, Ladies and Gentlemen, even if you find beyond a reasonable doubt the State has proved the existence of aggravating circumstances in this case which would justify the imposition of a death sentence, . . . [y]ou may provide for a life sentence for the accused for any reason that is satisfactory to you, [with] or without any reason, if you care to do so."

The Georgia policy on jury instructions was approved by the United States Supreme Court in Zant v. Stephens (1983), *see infra* note 53 and accompanying text. The jury charging practices appear to be the same before and after *Zant.*

21. GA. CODE ANN. §27-2534.1(c) (1983). The sentencing jury may impose the death sentence only upon a unanimous verdict, and if the jury is unable to so agree, the court imposes a life sentence. Additionally, in death-sentence cases, the trial judge must complete a six-page questionnaire to be submitted to the Georgia Supreme Court in connection with its appellate review process. GA. CODE ANN. §27-2537(g) (1983).

22. 1970 GA. LAWS 949. This statute was amended into its present form by 1974 GA. LAWS 352, §7.

23. *Lockett,* 438 U.S. 586 (1978), invalidated death-sentencing procedures that restricted the sentencer's ability to consider mitigating circumstances.

24. GA. CODE ANN. §27-2537(C)(2) (1983).

25. GA. CODE ANN. §27-2537(C)(1), (C)(3) (1983). For descriptions of how the Georgia Supreme Court conducts this process of comparative proportionality review, *see* Liebman, *Appellate Review of Death Sentences: A Critique of Proportionality Review,* 18 U.C. DAVIS L. REV. 1433 (1985); *see also* Baldus, Pulaski, & Woodworth

(83), *supra* note 15, at 672–78; Baldus, Pulaski, Woodworth, & Kyle, *supra* note 14, at 12–22; Dix, *supra* note 14, at 111–17; Bowers, *The Pervasiveness of Arbitrariness and Discrimination under Post-Furman Capital Statutes*, 74 J. CRIM. L. & CRIMINOLOGY 1067, 1090–94 (1983); Bentele, *The Death Penalty in Georgia: Still Arbitrary*, 62 WASH. U.L.Q. 573, 591–97 (1985).

26. Gregg v. Georgia, 428 U.S. 153 (1976); Proffitt v. Florida, 428 U.S. 242 (1976); Jurek v. Texas, 428 U.S. 262 (1976).

27. Gregg v. Georgia, 428 U.S. at 187. In Coker v. Georgia, 433 U.S. 584 (1977), the Court ruled that the death penalty was a constitutionally disproportionate sanction for the crime of rape. *See* White, *Disproportionality and the Death Penalty: Death as a Punishment for Rape*, 38 U. PITT. L. REV. 145 (1977). Zimring and Hawkins, *supra* note 2, at 68, persuasively argue that in rejecting the argument that capital punishment violated the Eighth Amendment the Court was heavily influenced by the rapid and widespread reenactment of capital punishment after *Furman* but that in so responding the Court mistakenly perceived this "legislative backlash" as a reflection of public support for executions.

28. Gregg v. Georgia, 428 U.S. at 203 (plurality opinion).

29. *Id.* at 203 (plurality opinion); 222–24 (White, J., concurring).

30. Woodson v. North Carolina, 428 U.S. at 303–4; Roberts v. Louisiana, 428 U.S. at 333–36.

31. *See* Spaziano v. Florida, 468 U.S. 447, 459 (1984); Pulley v. Harris, 465 U.S. 37, 44–45, 53 (1984); Zant v. Stephens, 462 U.S. at 873–75 (quoting Gregg v. Georgia, 428 U.S. at 195).

32. Barclay v. Florida, 463 U.S. 939 (1983).

33. *See*, e.g., Spaziano v. Florida, 468 U.S. at 466; Pulley v. Harris, 465 U.S. at 45.

34. Gregg v. Georgia, 428 U.S. at 197–98, 206–7 (plurality opinion); 220–24 (White, J., concurring). *See also* Zant v. Stephens, 462 U.S. 862 (1983).

35. Jurek v. Texas, 428 U.S. at 268–77 (plurality opinion); Proffitt v. Florida, 428 U.S. at 247–52, 257–60 (plurality opinion).

36. It was on this basis that the Court rejected the North Carolina and Louisiana statutes. *See supra* note 30 and accompanying text. Furthermore, in some of its most recent decisions, the Court has vacated death sentences because of procedural deficiencies that created an intolerable risk of arbitrariness or discrimination. *See* Caldwell v. Mississippi, 472 U.S. 320, 328–33 (1985) (suggestion to sentencing jury that appellate court would correct an inappropriate death sentence creates an intolerable risk of unreliable sentencing); Turner v. Murray, 476 U.S. at 33 (failure to *voir dire* jury about racial bias in an interracial murder case creates an intolerable risk of discrimination); *see also* Vasquez v. Hillery, 474 U.S. 254, 260-64 (1986) (indictment by an all-white grand jury from which black individuals were systematically excluded creates an intolerable risk that defendant's indictment was a result of discrimination, thereby violating the equal protection clause; that defendant was subsequently lawfully convicted does not cure the taint attributed to a grand jury selected on the basis of race).

37. *Cf.* Godfrey v. Georgia, 446 U.S. 420, 433 (1980) (where appellate review procedure employed did not distinguish death-sentence cases in any "principled way" from life-sentence cases, death sentence is invalid).

38. Gregg v. Georgia, 428 U.S. at 199 (plurality opinion).

39. *Id.* at 199n.50 (plurality opinion).

40. *Id.* at 224–25 (White, J., concurring).

41. *Id.* at 225 (White, J., concurring).

42. *Id.* at 203 (plurality opinion). The defendant also challenged the jury's freedom to convict a defendant charged with capital murder of a lesser included offense. Justice Stewart rejected this argument for the same reason he refused to consider challenges to the prosecutor's charging direction—that *Furman* had no bearing on the presentencing stages of the process. *Id.* at 199 (plurality opinion). *Lockett*, 438 U.S. 586 (1978), invalidated death-sentencing procedures that restricted a sentencer's ability to consider mitigating circumstances.

43. Gregg v. Georgia, 428 U.S. at 203 (plurality opinion).

44. *Id.* at 198 (plurality opinion) (quoting *Furman v. Georgia*, 408 U.S. at 313) (White, J., concurring).

45. Gregg v. Georgia, 428 U.S. at 204–7 (plurality opinion).

46. *Id.* at 222 (White, J., concurring).

47. *Id.* at 222–23.

48. *Id.* at 224.

49. In Georgia and in many other states, the standards employed to identify the statutory aggravating circumstances—which are themselves based on the Model Penal Code and which many other states adopted—are quite general. Indeed, in McGautha v. California, 402 U.S. 183, 208 (1971), a majority of the Court expressed doubt that such standards could ever guide the exercise of discretion in any meaningful way. Furthermore, different prosecutors and juries might very well respond differently to the circumstances of basically similar cases. This is particularly true in Georgia because its law permits sentencing juries to impose life sentences no matter how aggravated the crime and no matter how many statutory aggravating circumstances or how few mitigating circumstances are present in the case.

50. The *Gregg* plurality, 428 U.S. at 222–23, noted that the Georgia legislature had:

> reason to expect that Georgia's current system would escape the infirmities which invalidated its previous system under *Furman*. However, the Georgia legislature was not satisfied with a system which might, but also might not, turn out in practice to result in death sentences being imposed with reasonable consistency for certain serious murders. Instead, it gave the Georgia Supreme Court the power and the obligation to perform precisely the task which three Justices of this Court, whose opinions were necessary to the result, performed in *Furman*: namely, the task of deciding whether *in fact* the death penalty was being administered for any given class of crime in a discriminatory, standardless, or rare fashion.

51. In principle, a process that permits such selectivity by prosecutors and juries seems desirable. It would facilitate a meaningful link between the values of the community and the criminal justice system. Also, by eliminating "excessive" death sentences—those imposed in cases that are essentially indistinguishable from other cases in which lesser sentences usually occur—the second model ensures that death sentences that survive the review process accord with the consensus of the community. *See* Schwartz, *The Supreme Court and Capital Punishment: A Quest for a Balance Between Legal and Societal Morality*, 1 LAW & POL'Y Q. 285 (1979).

52. *See* Turner v. Murray, 476 U.S. at 33–36 (Part II of the opinion); *see also* Gross & Mauro, *Patterns of Death: An Analysis of Racial Disparities in Capital Sentencing and Homicide Victimization*, 37 STAN. L. REV. 27, 31–37 (1984).

53. 476 U.S. 28 (1986). Zant v. Stephens, 462 U.S. at 885, implies that race-of-defendant or race-of-victim discrimination would be impermissible ("[n]or has Georgia attached the 'aggravating' label to factors that are constitutionally impermissible or

totally irrelevant to the sentencing process, such as for example the race, religion, or political affiliation of the defendant").

54. This situation would occur when there is a fairly high death-sentencing rate, say, .90, among a subgroup of similarly situated cases, but racial factors are influencing those decisions. Evidence in such a case may reveal a death-sentencing rate of .80 for white defendants and .95 for black defendants. *See infra* chap. 6 for further discussion of the relationship between excessiveness and discrimination, p. 148 (pre-*Furman*) and pp. 154 & 157 (post-*Furman*).

55. 428 U.S. 153 (1976).

56. 462 U.S. 862 (1983).

CHAPTER FOUR
The Methodology for Two
Death-Sentencing Studies

This chapter describes the research methodology underlying our two empirical studies of death sentencing in Georgia—the Procedural Reform Study (PRS) and the Charging and Sentencing Study (CSS). The results of the Procedural Reform Study are reported in the next three chapters and the results of the Charging and Sentencing Study appear in chapter 10.

In the discussion that follows, we first present a diagram of Georgia's capital-charging-and-sentencing systems. We then describe the PRS, which we commenced in the late 1970s, and then the CSS, which we undertook in 1980. Finally, we consider the key methodological issue presented by this project—the validity and interpretation of empirical measures of arbitrariness and discrimination.

We have prepared this chapter basically for the general reader without a special background in or a passion for empirical methodology or statistics. More technical explanations addressed to statisticians and methodologists appear in the Notes. In addition, in Appendix A we discuss certain aspects of our methodology that affect the validity of our empirical findings.

GEORGIA'S CAPITAL-CHARGING-AND-SENTENCING SYSTEM

Figure 1 presents a diagram of the Georgia capital-charging-and-sentencing system, which was the subject of the Procedural Reform Study and the Charging and Sentencing Study. It identifies the five key decision points in the process for capital-murder cases that reach the indictment stage:

1. indictment for murder, voluntary manslaughter, or a lesser crime;
2. plea bargaining and guilt plea (although some defendants plead guilty to murder without the benefit of a plea bargain);
3. guilt-trial decision for defendants pleading not guilty;
4. prosecutorial decision to advance to a penalty trial cases that result in a capital-murder conviction; and
5. jury death-sentencing decision for cases that advance to a penalty trial.

Our two empirical studies are limited to cases that resulted in a conviction for either murder or voluntary manslaughter. As a result, we have no data on

Figure 1. Georgia's Capital-Charging-and-Sentencing System[1]

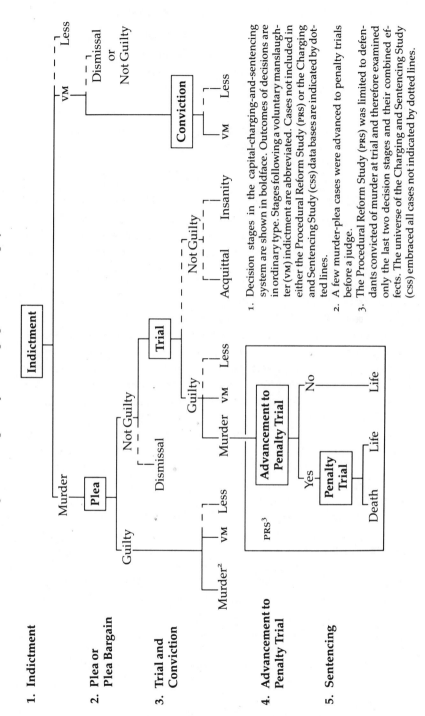

1. Indictment

2. Plea or
   Plea Bargain

3. Trial and
   Conviction

4. Advancement to
   Penalty Trial

5. Sentencing

1. Decision stages in the capital-charging-and-sentencing system are in ordinary type. Outcomes of decisions are in boldface. Stages following a voluntary manslaughter (VM) indictment are abbreviated. Cases not included in either the Procedural Reform Study (PRS) or the Charging and Sentencing Study (CSS) data bases are indicated by dotted lines.

2. A few murder-plea cases were advanced to penalty trials before a judge.

3. The Procedural Reform Study (PRS) was limited to defendants convicted of murder at trial and therefore examined only the last two decision stages and their combined effects. The universe of the Charging and Sentencing Study (CSS) embraced all cases not indicated by dotted lines.

the cases that were dismissed or not prosecuted (before or after indictment) or that resulted in a not-guilty verdict or a conviction for a crime less serious than murder or voluntary manslaughter. The flow of cases on which we have no data is indicated in Figure 1 with dotted lines.

RESEARCH DESIGN, SAMPLE, AND DATA

The Procedural Reform Study (PRS)

The primary purpose of the PRS was to compare how Georgia sentenced defendants convicted of murder at trial, before and after the statutory reforms prompted by *Furman v. Georgia,* and to assess the extent to which those reforms affected the levels of arbitrariness and discrimination observed in its sentencing decisions.[1] Accordingly, the study focuses on the final two stages of Georgia's charging-and-sentencing process, that is, the prosecutor's decision whether to seek a death sentence after obtaining a capital-murder conviction at trial and the jury's decision to impose a life or death sentence after a penalty trial.

We undertook the PRS in 1979 solely for academic research purposes, with no expectation that the results would be used in death-penalty litigation. Financial support for the project was provided by the National Institute of Justice of the U.S. Department of Justice, the University of Iowa Law School Foundation, and the College of Law's Center for Interdisciplinary Legal Studies at Syracuse University.

For several reasons, we limited our data set in the PRS to defendants convicted of murder after trial. The first, and most obvious, involved resources. We felt it was preferable to gather extensive quantities of information about relatively fewer cases than to obtain less information about a greater number. Furthermore, restricting our data set to cases in which there was a murder conviction after trial satisfied several important considerations. First, by including in our data set only cases in which a jury convicted the defendant of murder beyond a reasonable doubt, we obtained a rudimentary control for the strength of the evidence. Furthermore, because there are very few appeals in cases that end in guilty pleas, cases involving murder convictions after trial resemble most closely the sorts of death-sentence cases most commonly appealed to both the Georgia Supreme Court and the United States Supreme Court. This consideration was important, since one purpose of our study was to test empirically the validity of the United States Supreme Court's perceptions, especially in *Furman,* of how state courts actually processed capital cases. The restriction of our universe of cases to murder-trial convictions was

Syracuse University Law School's Center for Interdisciplinary Legal Studies also supported the data analysis. Finally, the National Science Foundation's Law and Social Sciences program provided funds for additional analysis of the data subsequent to the *McCleskey* hearing in 1983.

Second, the primary emphasis of the css was on the extent to which racial and other illegitimate or suspect case characteristics influenced the flow of cases from the point of indictment up to and including the penalty-trial death-sentencing decision. The results of these analyses provided the principal basis of Warren McCleskey's ultimate claim that Georgia's death-sentencing system was applied in a racially discriminatory fashion. The css results presented in *McCleskey v. Kemp* are reported in chapter 10 of this book.[9]

Third, the css covered the period from 1973 through 1979, one year more than the prs, and embraced a much larger universe of cases—2,484 defendants arrested and charged with homicide who were subsequently convicted of murder or voluntary manslaughter. The actual data set is also larger, consisting of a stratified random sample of 1,066 cases from the 2,484-case universe.[10] The sample included 127 death-sentenced defendants. Overall, more than 300 jury-trial murder cases are common to both studies.

Fourth, in comparison to the prs, which examined only the two post-guilt-trial decisions in the Georgia charging-and-sentencing system, the css examined five decision points. This feature of the css permitted us to conduct a more "longitudinal" study that could track the movement of cases through the system, which includes grand-jury indictment decisions, prosecutorial plea-bargaining decisions, jury guilt-trial decisions, prosecutorial decisions to seek a death penalty after the guilt trial, and jury penalty-trial sentencing decisions. The longitudinal design of the css follows a recommendation of a 1983 National Research Council Panel on sentencing that longitudinal studies should be preferred over studies that focus on only one or two of the final stages in a multistage decision-making system.[11] A longitudinal research design avoids the risk of overlooking discrmination and arbitrariness occurring at early stages in a charging-and-sentencing system, particularly if it is offset at later stages in the process. The design of the css also allowed us to examine the combined effects of all decisions from the point of indictment through the penalty-trial sentencing decision. In fact, the principal focus of results from the css reported in chapter 10 is on the combined effects of all prosecutorial and jury decisions from the murder indictment to the sentencing decision.

The fifth difference between the two studies is the number of items included in the data-collection questionnaire. Based on our experience with the prs, the experience of other researchers,[12] and the recommendations of practitioners whom we consulted, we included in the css questionnaire additional variables relating to the defendant's prior record, the circumstances of the offense, any contemporaneous offenses, aggravating and mitigating factors, and the involvement of any codefendants. This data-collection instrument appears in Appendix E. The principal expansion in coverage, however, concerned the strength of the evidence of the defendant's guilt and overall culpability. Thirty-five percent of the items in the css questionnaire related to the strength of the evidence. The data for the css were collected in the summer of 1981 from the files of the Georgia Board of Pardons and Paroles. From this data set we created for each case a file of over 230 variables that were suitable for multivariate statistical analysis;[13] 10 percent of these variables related to strength of evidence.

A sixth difference was that we coded the two studies from overlapping but somewhat different data sources. As noted earlier, we coded one-half of the cases in the PRS from the Georgia Supreme Court's records; we coded the other half from the files of the Georgia Board of Pardons and Parole.[14] By contrast, we coded all cases in the css from the parole board files and used the records of the Georgia Supreme Court only for supplemental data.[15]

The last difference between the two studies was the coding protocol employed for each. A coding protocol is a set of rules and procedures that instructs each coder how to perform his or her task under specified conditions. The protocol that we developed for use in the css was far more detailed and elaborate than that used in the PRS.

MEASURING ARBITRARINESS, EXCESSIVENESS, AND DISCRIMINATION

The "Similar" Case Problem

Furman v. Georgia condemned "arbitrary and capricious" death sentences, that is, those imposed in cases that could not be meaningfully distinguished from many similar cases that resulted in lesser sentences. The Court's concern was prompted primarily by the disparities it perceived to exist in the sentences imposed on similarly situated defendants. The concept of "comparative excessiveness," which underlies the proportionality-review statutes of over twenty death-sentencing jurisdictions, captures this core concern with inexplicable or unprincipled sentencing disparities. For example, in Georgia the state supreme court determines whether a death sentence is "excessive and disproportionate" by examining the sentences imposed in "similar cases, considering both the defendant and the crime." This test embodies an attempt on Georgia's part to ensure evenhanded treatment of equally culpable offenders.

Furman v. Georgia also expressed a concern that standardless jury-sentencing procedures permitted "discrimination" against minorities and the poor. Although not all of the concurring justices specified the sorts of discrimination they had in mind, certainly race and socioeconomic status were matters of concern. It is still an open question whether a showing of intentional discrimination on some impermissible basis is necessary to establish an Eighth Amendment violation. From a methodological standpoint, however, whether the ultimate issue is one of intent or effect, the methods of proof are the same. One must identify groups of cases with legitimate sentencing considerations that are similar with respect to the defendant, the victim, and the crime.

Of course, the ideal measure of similarity would be strict factual comparability with respect to the case characteristics deemed most relevant or most "salient" for sentencing purposes. For example, all twenty-five-year-old defendants with three prior felony convictions who killed police officers in the course of armed robberies might be deemed to be equally culpable or blameworthy. If a sufficient number of such factually similar cases exists, the pattern of sentencing results would provide a statistical basis for assessing the evenhandedness of the sentences imposed in subsequent cases with the same factual characteristics. The problem, however, is that one rarely finds a sufficient number of other cases that match on all relevant case characteristics to conduct a meaningful analysis. Even in large jurisdictions, there will rarely be statistically adequate numbers of cases that match each other with respect to more than three or four salient features.

For this reason, we have used alternative systems for classifying cases as "similar" by using criteria of more general application than strict factual identity. The goal of such systems is to identify cases that are "similar" in relative culpability or blameworthiness, despite factual differences.[16] We believe this approach is appropriate because the decisions of the United States Supreme Court have suggested that a constitutionally satisfactory death-sentencing process will produce consistent sentences in cases of equal culpability or blameworthiness.[17]

Ranking each case in the jurisdiction by its relative culpability or blameworthiness permitted us to construct a culpability map from which we could select different subgroups of cases with similar culpability levels. Thus, after selecting a subgroup of perhaps thirty to fifty cases of relatively equivalent culpability, we could easily determine the frequency with which death sentences occurred within that subgroup and whether that frequency varied within the group depending upon the presence or absence of racial or other impermissible factors.

There are two basic approaches to classifying cases as similar or dissimilar—the *a priori* and the empirical. The *a priori* approach endeavors to classify cases as similar on the basis of criteria that, from a legal or moral perspective, one believes should govern the appropriate sentence. In the capital-sentencing context, for example, one might classify as "similar" all cases involving the same statutorily designated aggravating circumstances. Thus, if the applicable statute authorized a death sentence for any defendant convicted of intentional murder committed in the course of an armed robbery, one might consider all armed-robbery murder cases to be of similar culpability. In this fashion, one could identify other subgroups of comparable cases on the basis of other statutory aggravating circumstances that define death eligibility, such as killing multiple victims, committing a murder for hire, and so forth. Experience proves, however, that capital cases classified under any single statutory aggravating circumstance often result in a wide range of sentences.

This variation in sentencing results among groups of capital cases that share a common single statutory aggravating circumstance appears to be the product of an unequal distribution among such cases of other statutory aggravating circumstances and of nonstatutory aggravating and mitigating factors, all of which quite properly may influence the judgments of prosecutors and juries. As a consequence, the presence of a particular statutory aggravating circumstance in a group of cases is not a sufficient basis for classifying them all as "similar" for comparative purposes. It becomes necessary to refine the classification mechanism by taking into account additional factors that seem relevant from one's *a priori* perspective.

The empirical approach also begins by presupposing that certain factual characteristics of the case being reviewed can serve to identify other cases of "similar" culpability. In contrast to the *a priori* approach—which primarily selects those factual characteristics on a normative basis—the empirical approach tries to employ those legitimate case characteristics that, statistically, best explain the observed sentencing results. Obviously, there may be some overlap between the criteria selected by *a priori* and empirical methods, and, indeed, the degree of overlap may be substantial. The difference between the two methods is that the *a priorist* selects the factors he or she believes *should* influence the sentencing decision, while the empiricist selects the factors that actually appear to do so.[18] The problem is that there is no one uniformly accepted *a priori* or empirical measure of defendant culpability. Rather, we see in the cases and in the literature a variety of possible approaches. Given this lack of consensus, we adopted a "triangulation" approach: when possible, we employed several different methods for measuring defendant culpability and thereby selecting "similar" cases, while still recognizing the potential bias or unreliability of each.[19] This use of different methods serves as a cross-check on the results of each. Our confidence in our ultimate conclusions largely depends on the consistency or inconsistency of the results produced by each of these several methods.

Two *A Priori* Measures

A Legislative-Criteria Measure

One useful *a priori* measure assesses relative culpability based on the number of case characteristics that make the defendant death-eligible under Georgia's post-*Furman* legislation. The Georgia death-sentencing statute incorporates the legislature's *a priori* judgment that the presence of any one of ten case characteristics would justify the imposition of a death sentence. This suggests that the blameworthiness of a given offender may be a function of the number of statutorily designated aggravating circumstances present in his case. We used this measure several times in the PRS.[20]

Qualitative A Priori *Measures*

We also developed qualitative *a priori* measures. The first, which we used in the PRS, assesses culpability by qualitatively weighing the aggravating factors (statutory and nonstatutory) against the mitigating factors present in each case.[21] This measure ranks the cases among various culpability levels based on the number and importance of the aggravating and mitigating factors present.[22] It thereby classifies as "similar" all cases with a common culpability level, even though they may be factually quite distinct.

We applied this measure separately to the pre- and post-*Furman* armed-robbery murder cases in the PRS.[23] First, two law-trained evaluators each read a one hundred- to three hundred-word narrative summary of every case. This summary did not disclose the race of the defendant or the victim or the sentence imposed. On this basis, the evaluators identified the aggravating and mitigating factors present in each case. They then intuitively weighed the aggravating and mitigating factors in each case against each other and distributed them among five culpability levels using the following classification protocol:

- *Category I* (least culpable):
  Defendant was not the triggerman and was an underling; he had no intent to kill and did not participate in any violence or threatening conduct.
- *Category II:*
  Mitigating factor(s) substantially outweigh aggravating factor(s).
- *Category III:*
  No mitigating factors or statutory aggravating factors except the armed-robbery aggravating factor.
- *Category IV:*
  Armed-robbery aggravating factor plus one or more aggravating factors other than those noted in category V, and no (or substantially outweighed) mitigating factor(s).

- *Category V* (most culpable):
  Armed-robbery aggravating factor plus contract killing, mutilation, arson, or execution-style killing, and no (or substantially outweighed) mitigating factor(s).

Finally, within each of these five subgroups, the evaluators ranked the cases according to the degree to which the aggravating circumstances appeared to outweigh the mitigating circumstances. The rankings derived by each evaluator were then compared, and when they disagreed the evaluators worked out by consensus the most appropriate ranking.

Table 1 presents summaries of a sample of two post-*Furman* cases from each of the five levels derived with this measure. Appendix G includes summaries of the entire sample of post-*Furman* Georgia armed-robbery murder cases ranked with this measure.

We also developed three *a priori* measures for use in the CSS. In the first, we subdivided the cases into four subgroups determined by the presence or absence of either of two variables, whether the case involved felony circumstances and whether the defendant had a serious prior record.[24] In our second analysis, we identified all the murder cases in the sample that, because of the presence of a contemporaneous felony (e.g., armed robbery, rape, kidnapping, etc.) were death-eligible under the statute. We then added to this group all of the similarly defined cases from the PRS. This gave us a sample of 438 cases, which we sorted according to the nature of the contemporaneous felony (e.g., armed robbery, rape, etc.). This analysis revealed that only the armed-robbery cases had a sufficient sample size (275 cases) to allow further categorization.[25] We then divided the armed-robbery murder cases into seven subcategories according to the nature of other contemporaneous offenses that may have been present and, for the cases involving no additional offense, the level of aggravation of the armed robbery.[26]

Our third *a priori* measure of case culpability was based on the expert opinion of the presiding district court judge in the *McCleskey* case, J. Owen Forrester. Judge Forrester, who had also been a federal prosecutor, carefully studied our data collection instrument and developed a detailed coding protocol that he believed would identify the most blameworthy offenders.[27] On the basis of this analysis, we were able to define groups of cases of comparable culpability and to estimate race effects within them using cross-tabular and multiple-regression methods.[28]

Two Empirical Measures

A Qualitative Three-Dimensional Classification System

Empirical approaches to classifying cases as similar or dissimilar seek to employ those legitimate characteristics of the cases that best explain the sentences

Table 1. A Sample of Post-*Furman* Armed-Robbery–Murder Cases, Ranked with an *a Priori* Weighting Measure[1]

Case #	Category I (least-aggravated category)
957	rob (B2), defendant driver, co-perp. hit V with gun and kicked him, elderly V, acquaintances, no priors
635	rob (B2), co-perp. beat V and her invalid mother to death (B7), defendant 16 years old, defendant did not beat V, V 55-year-old female neighbor, 7 priors (6 nonviolent)
	Category II
C88	rob (B2), V killed, defendant not triggerman, drinking, defendant 17-year-old, no priors
559	rob (B2), V shot at defendant first, then defendant killed victim, confession, defendant cooperated with authorities, alcohol, defendant in military, no priors
	Category III
648	rob (B2), V shot after rejecting defendant's demand for money and walking toward defendant, 1 nonviolent prior
494	rob (B2), defendant goes to V's home to discuss loan problems with V (bank employee), shoots V 4 × after argument, no priors
	Category IV
755	rob (B2), V shot while calling police (B10), V shot in chest, defendant not trigger, strangers, defendant 19-year-old, 2 nonviolent priors
384	rob bus station (B2), defendant shot V twice in head (B7), killed V so V could not identify him, no priors
	Category V (most-aggravated category)
D21	rob $1,000 (B2), defendant tied V to tree, beat with butt of gun, stab 3 × in neck (B7), defendant 19-year-old hitchhiker, V 58-year-old, unknown priors
265	rob (B2), escapee (B9), female V raped and sodomized (B2), 5 V's (B7), kidnap (B2), female V breast mutilated (B7), 2 priors

1. The statutory aggravating factors in each case are in parentheses.

actually imposed. However, the techniques used to identify these characteristics can vary substantially. One approach, used by some state supreme courts when engaging in proportionality reviews, tries to identify the key factors that distinguish death-sentence cases from life-sentence cases on the basis of intuition and common sense. In a recent study, Professor Arnold Barnett, a consultant to the National Center for State Courts Proportionality Review Project, developed a three-dimensional classification system based on this approach, which he employed to classify the relative culpability of all the post-*Furman* cases in the PRS.[29]

Using factual summaries of the cases (each normally being from one hundred to three hundred words in length), he carefully evaluated their facts and circumstances in light of the sentences imposed and, using intuitive judgment, constructed an internally consistent, systematic protocol for case classification. The result of this effort was a three-dimensional classification scheme that permitted him to categorize cases as similar or dissimilar in the following three dimensions:

1. Certainty the defendant is a deliberate killer—
   (o) Clearly no; (1) Neither o nor 2; (2) Clearly yes
2. Close or prior relationship between defendant and victim—
   (o) Yes; (1) No
3. Vileness or heinousness of the killing—
   (o) Elements of self-defense; (1) Neither o nor 2; (2) A vile killing

Professor Barnett classified the cases in these three dimensions based on the presence or absence of thirty-five specific variables. For example, if a case involved "mutilation" or any one of thirteen other aggravating case characteristics, it received a score of 2 on the vileness dimension. The objective criteria he used for classifying the cases with respect to these three dimensions appear in Appendix H of this book. This three-dimensional classification scheme produced a total of eighteen potential categories of "similar" cases, which one could then examine for evidence of excessiveness or discrimination.

Table 2 lists a sample of cases from seven of these categories. Appendix I includes summaries of additional cases from the different subgroups produced by the system.

Statistically Based Culpability Indexes and Scales

Social scientists and statisticians have also developed quantitative measures that serve to rank cases according to a single dimension that incorporates a variety of case characteristics.[30] For example, employment-discrimination cases frequently require an estimation of the individual productivity of a large number of workers based on such characteristics as age, education, job type, experience, and supervisory ratings.[31] By using statistical techniques to analyze and to weigh the data for each of these variables, one can develop a measure for ranking the productivity of each employee. One then scrutinizes the treatment of employees of similar productivity for evidence of discrimination.

Medical science offers another example of the usefulness of such quantitative measures. One important study examined whether a particular anesthetic, halothane, was more dangerous than other widely used anesthetics.[32] Because the risk of death associated with an operation depends on many factors besides the type of anesthetic used, the investigators developed a composite measure of this risk, using such variables as the patient's age, prior health, weight, and type of surgery. This measure permitted them to estimate the risk

Table 2. A Sample of Post-*Furman* Georgia Murder Cases as Classified with Arnold Barnett's Classification System

---

Sum of Scores
on the Three
Classification
Variables

---

0 (0,0,0)[1]   The two coperpetrators drove to a shopping center with the male victim's girlfriend. During the drive, coperpetrator #1 gave the girlfriend his gun. At the shopping center, the victim and the girlfriend argued, and the girl took the gun out of her purse. At this point, the victim, the girlfriend, and her brother went to the victim's house. The two coperpetrators then met the defendant, and coperpetrator #1 told the defendant that the victim had his gun. The defendant, who had a pistol, and the two coperpetrators then went to the victim's house. The victim came to the door, unarmed, and said, "Niggers, get out of my house." The defendant then shot the victim once in the thigh, at close range. The victim died two days later after going into shock and suffering cardiac arrest. (365)

0 (0,0,0)   The 32-year-old male defendant had been seeing the adult male victim's wife since she and the victim had separated nine months earlier. The victim went to the defendant's home and demanded that his wife follow him to her mother's home. While the wife and the defendant were searching for her car keys, the victim approached the house yelling. The defendant told the victim to stay away from the house and the victim pulled a gun. There was a struggle for the gun, during which it discharged twice. The defendant took the gun and fired it one more time. The defendant claimed he fired the final shot into the ground. None of the three witnesses was sure which of the three shots hit the victim. (748)

1 (0,0,1)   The male defendant and the two male coperpetrators were high school seniors. The male victim had previously assaulted the fiancée of one of the coperpetrators. The perpetrators arranged to lure the victim to the high school tennis courts. When he arrived at the tennis courts, the two coperpetrators opened fire on the victim from the back of the defendant's station wagon. Both coperpetrators emptied their guns into the victim's car. Two shots hit the victim in the head and another in the shoulder. The defendant was driving the station wagon. The parties were arrested two months later on the basis of an anonymous tip. (519)

1 (0,0,1)   The 21-year-old male defendant and the adult male victim had an argument and, according to witnesses, the defendant tried to provoke the victim to fight. The victim walked away. Later, the defendant and the victim argued again. The defendant pulled a knife and stabbed the victim. The victim died sixteen days later. The defendant claimed he was intoxicated and remembered nothing. (808)

2 (0,1,1)   The 26-year-old male defendant, the male coperpetrator, and a female companion (primary witness) went to a bar and were drinking when they saw the male victim and a male companion walk in. The defendant, coper-

Table 2. *(Continued)*

Sum of Scores
on the Three
Classification
Variables

---

petrator, and female friend exchanged "funny looks," indicating they had a plan to rob the victim. The defendant, coperpetrator, and female friend went outside the bar to wait for the victim to come out. The coperpetrator struck the victim in the head and face with a large cement block, causing multiple lacerations and exposing the inside skull. The defendant may have beaten the victim several times. The defendant also attacked the victim's friend with a knife, cutting him in the face and throat. The victim's friend was seriously injured, but did not die. The coperpetrator went through the pockets of the victim and his friend, taking some change and a wallet. The defendant dragged the bodies into some bushes, and the three went to another bar to drink. (324)

2 (1,0,1) The 17-year-old male defendant and his girlfriend were having problems, and the girlfriend was dating the male victim. The defendant threatened to kill the victim if he ever dated the girlfriend again. The victim and the girlfriend went to a movie together. The defendant waited at his girlfriend's house for them to come home. When the victim left the girlfriend's home, the defendant followed him. The defendant caused the victim to stop his car and shot him twice in the chest. The defendant then called his girlfriend and stated, "you thought you could get away with it, didn't you." The defendant left his .22 automatic rifle with a friend and went home, where he was arrested. (656)

3 (1,1,1) The 20-year-old male defendant approached the male victim and a male friend from behind as they walked down the street. The defendant held a gun to the victim and demanded his money. The friend stated that the victim had no money. Then the friend and the defendant struggled for the gun. The defendant broke away, ran ten feet, turned, and shot the friend in the leg. The victim then walked toward the defendant saying, "I'm not afraid of your gun," and the defendant then shot the victim several times. The friend identified the defendant as the killer. (357)

3 (1,1,1) The male victim was driving his wife and his small child in a car. The male defendant, his brother, and two females were driving behind the victim's vehicle. The victim apparently was not going fast enough for the defendant and his passengers, so they began hanging out the windows and yelling at the victim. Thinking that something was wrong, the victim stopped his car. As the victim stepped out of his car, the defendant shot him several times and drove off. The victim's wife provided the police with a description of the defendant and the defendant's car. (D02)

4 (2,0,2) The male defendant and a coperpetrator went to the male victim's house and took him for a ride. The perpetrators and the victim were casual acquaintances. The perpetrators took the victim to a side road and shot him

Table 2. *(Continued)*

Sum of Scores on the Three Classification Variables	

	three times with a shotgun. The murder was very bloody. Immediately afterward, the defendant boasted that all they had to do now was to collect the money, implying that the killing was a murder for hire. (408)
4 (2,0,2)	The male defendant and the male coperpetrator were involved in a check-fraud scheme. They retained the male victim, who was the manager of a local club, to act as a front. The defendant owed the victim money and had previously discussed getting rid of the victim. On the night of the offense, the three men left the bar to deliver some bootleg liquor. While the victim was driving, the defendant shot him several times in the head. The defendant claimed someone else committed the murder. (552)
5 (2,1,2)	The 31-year-old male defendant was hired by a criminal organization, consisting of coperpetrators #1, #2, and #3, to kill a deputy who was investigating cases against them concerning drugs and illegal-liquor operations. The coperpetrators agreed to pay the defendant $3,000 for victim #1 (the male deputy) and an additional $500 if it was necessary to kill victim #2 (victim #1's wife). The defendant went to the home of the victims and shot them with a shotgun. (692)
5 (2,1,2)	The 18-year-old female victim #1 and the male victim #2 were shot-gunned to death in some woods. The male defendant flagged down a police car and reported finding the bodies while he was hunting. The police arrested the defendant more than a month later, after testing his shotgun. (573)

1. The scores for the three variables are included in parentheses. The first score is for the premeditation variable, the second is for the defendant/victim relationship variable, and the third score is for the vileness variable.

of death for each operation without regard to the anesthetic used. The investigators then identified groups of cases with similar risk levels and compared, within these groups, the mortality rate for the patients who received halothane as opposed to the other anesthetics.

We employed comparable statistical methods to determine the relative culpability of different defendants based on the case characteristics that, on a statistical basis, best explained which defendants actually received death sentences. If, for example, the presence of aggravating factors A1, A2, and A3 statistically increased the risk of a death sentence, the presence of those characteristics in an offender's case would suggest that he was relatively more culpable than otherwise. Conversely, if mitigating factors M1, M2, and M3 statistically reduced the risk of a death sentence, the presence of one or more of those factors in a given case would tend to reduce the culpability ranking of that defendant. The principal difference between this approach and the procedure used by Professor Barnett is that one selects the factors used to determine relative culpability by means of a statistical procedure rather than by means of intuition, experience, and common sense.

Procedural Reform Study (PRS)   We developed a regression-based culpability index for the PRS with a logistic multiple-regression analysis designed to identify statistically the factors that best explain which defendants received death sentences. For the post-*Furman* analysis we used the same Georgia cases that Professor Barnett employed for his analysis. This procedure required us, first, to collect information for every case concerning a large number of legitimate case characteristics, such as prior record or a contemporaneous felony, that might have influenced the sentencing decision.[33] We then computed for each such case characteristic a regression coefficient (or "weight") that reflected its individual contribution to the overall culpability index.[34] Next, we calculated the relative culpability or blameworthiness of each case by summing the "weights" of all the legitimate explanatory variables present in that case.[35] We then ranked all the cases according to their relative culpability scores, thereby constructing an overall culpability index along which the cases were distributed. Finally, we defined as "similar" six groups of cases with comparable overall culpability scores.[36]

Because of the aggregate nature of the culpability scores computed for each case, the impact of an aggravating factor (such as "taking the victim hostage"), which on average enhances the risk of a death sentence, may be partly cancelled by the presence of an offsetting, mitigating factor (for example, "defendant was an underling").[37] As a result, the culpability score of a case with both aggravating and mitigating factors may be virtually the same as that of another case with no special aggravating or mitigating features. In other words, the cumulative and compensatory nature of the scoring process frequently produced similar scores for cases that were factually distinct. Nevertheless, in terms of their relative culpability or blameworthiness in the eyes of the prosecutors and juries who processed the universe of cases from which we derived the culpability index, such factually different cases do appear to constitute "near neighbors."

Using the procedures just described, we conducted a logistic-regression analysis for each of the following outcomes: (a) pre-*Furman* death-sentencing decisions among defendants convicted of murder at trial; (b) post-*Furman* death-sentencing decisions among defendants convicted of murder at trial; (c) post-*Furman* decisions by prosecutors to seek a death sentence for defendants convicted of murder at trial; and (d) post-*Furman* jury decisions to impose a death sentence in a penalty trial.[38]

We created two indexes for each of these outcomes—one to be used to measure excessiveness ("type C") and one to be used to measure discrimination ("type B"). For each outcome we started with a basic model, referred to as "type A," which included legitimate, suspect, and illegitimate variables.[39] We constructed the type C excessiveness index strictly on the basis of the legitimate coefficients estimated in the type A model. The type A model had included illegitimate and suspect variables to insure that the coefficients estimated for the legitimate case characteristics did not reflect the influence of inappropriate variables, such as race of the defendant or of the victim, that might be correlated with the legitimate variables.[40] However, to create the excessiveness type C index, we dropped the illegitimate and suspect variables from the index to ensure that their presence did not affect the culpability score of any given case. Finally, using this excessiveness index, we ranked the cases to which it applied and further divided them into six distinct culpability levels.[41] Table 3 lists summaries from a sample of post-*Furman* cases from each of the six levels of the scale derived from the index; this index reflects the combined effects of the prosecutorial decision to seek and the jury decision to impose a death sentence. Appendix K lists more detailed summaries of a larger sample of cases. We used excessiveness indexes of this type in such figures as 4 and 5 and the scale in table 10.

For the purpose of measuring the effects of illegitimate and suspect variables, however, we dropped the illegitimate and suspect variables from the type A model and estimated new partial-regression coefficients for the remaining legitimate factors for each decision point. This was the type B discrimination index. We used these indexes and scales to produce plots of the type shown in figures 20 and 21 and the cross-tabular analysis shown in tables 27, 28, and 36.[42]

Charging and Sentencing Study (CSS) Our principal culpability index for the CSS was a 39-variable overall "input-output" statistical model to explain which of all of the defendants in the study, or those indicted for murder, were ultimately selected to receive a death sentence by Georgia's prosecutors and juries. We developed this model on the basis of the literature, of our knowledge of the Georgia capital-sentencing system, and of our prior experience with the Procedural Reform Study and other capital-sentencing studies.

We also conducted a variety of analyses to test the "robustness" of the racial disparities estimated in logistic multiple-regression analyses with this 39-variable model.[43] Among these were alternate model specifications incorporating quadratic terms and interactions, as well as "influence" diagnostics to

Table 3. A Sample of Post-*Furman* Georgia Murder Cases Ranked with a Multiple-Regression-Based Culpability Measure, from Least to Most Culpable

---

Culpability Level,
from Least to
Most Aggravated

---

1   The 24-year-old male defendant lived with the male victim and two women. One evening the defendant and the victim got into a particularly violent argument, which ended with the defendant stabbing the victim three times, causing his death. The defendant claimed he acted in self-defense. (722)

2   The 29-year-old male defendant and the female victim, his fiancée, got into an argument over an alleged sexual relationship between the victim and another man. The defendant and the victim were in the trailer they shared when the defendant grabbed a butcher knife and stabbed the victim three times. The defendant stated the killing was accidental and also claimed self-defense. (C95)

3   The male defendant, armed with a sawed-off shotgun, entered a store with two coperpetrators. The victim, the storekeeper, told the defendant of his heart condition and begged the defendant not to hurt him or a female patron. The defendant took the victim's wallet, forced him into the back room, forced him down, and struck him in the head with the gun butt. The defendant also threatened to kill the female patron if she interfered. At this point, a milkman entered and the defendant shot at him (unclear whether he was hit) and then fatally shot the victim in the stomach. The defendant then struck the female patron in the back of the head with the gun butt, causing a skull fracture and concussion. (459)

4   The 18-year-old male defendant robbed the store at which the victim was apparently employed. The defendant shot the 50-year-old male victim between the eyes. The victim had pleaded for his life. The defendant had no priors. (407)

5   The defendant, a 22-year-old male with five prior convictions, two of which were for nonviolent crimes, stabbed the victim, a female clerk, several times in the back, chest, and face and beat her in the course of a robbery. He had robbed and beaten another clerk the day before. The defendant gave conflicting statements to the police, first confessing to the crime and then pleading insanity and denying his confession. (512)

6   The defendant, a 35-year-old male with a prior conviction for burglary and two convictions for nonviolent crimes, and three coperpetrators planned to burglarize a home. While the three coperpetrators were in the house, three male victims came home, and the perpetrators shot them. Three more victims then arrived, two of whom were shot. The perpetrators took the remaining victim, the only female, to the woods, where she was raped and sodomized. They then shot her twice, and mutilated her breasts. The defendant claimed to be in another state at the time of the killings, but a coperpetrator testified that the defendant killed one of the victims. (267)

---

determine if results were idiosyncratic to a few cases. In addition, we conducted several multiple-regression analyses to determine if additional variables might account for the racial effects. First, we used linear and logistic
procedures to screen the entire file of variables to identify those (a) that
showed a statistically significant relationship with the outcome variable, and
(b) for which the sign of the coefficient was in the direction one would expect in
a rational death-sentencing system.[44] We then used these two sets of variables
in linear and logistic multiple-regression analyses with racial variables. Also,
using the index based on linear-regression analysis, we created scales comparable to those used in the PRS, first for all cases in the study and then for the 472
most aggravated cases.[45]

We then produced an index with a stepwise linear-regression procedure that
included all variables which showed a statistically significant ($p \le .10$) relationship with the death-sentencing outcome (regardless of the sign of the
coefficient) among all defendants indicted for murder.[46] We then conducted a
factor analysis of the death-sentencing decision among those indicted for murder, which reduced the list of 230 + variables in the file to 126 factors. We
entered those factors into a linear multiple-regression analysis along with the
racial variables.

Finally, we conducted a linear-regression analysis that simultaneously included all 230 + background variables in a single computation.[47]

In addition to the overall models just described, which reflected the combined effects of all decisions from the indictment decision to the penalty-trial
decision, we also developed separately linear and logistic multiple-regression
models of the following outcomes: indictment decisions, plea-bargaining decisions (voluntary manslaughter plea and murder plea with a penalty-trial
waiver), guilt-trial decisions, prosecutorial decisions to seek a death sentence
after obtaining a murder-trial conviction, and the jury penalty-trial decision.
These latter two decision points parallel the prosecutorial and jury decision
points in the PRS.[48]

Measuring Arbitrariness, Excessiveness, and Discrimination

Arbitrariness/Excessiveness

We applied several measures of arbitrariness and excessiveness in the Procedural Reform Study. The first proceeds on the assumption that, in a random or
highly capricious death-sentencing system, there would be little or no relationship between the perceived culpability of those sentenced and the sentences they received. For example, Justice Stewart condemned the standardless jury-sentencing systems in *Furman* as a "lottery" because he could
discern no rational basis to explain why various defendants received different

sentences. More specifically, in a random system one would expect to find little or no difference between the median culpability scores of the life-sentence and the death-sentence cases. In a highly selective system, by contrast, there should be a large difference between those two numbers. Our first measure of excessiveness, therefore, is the approximate difference between the median culpability scores of defendants receiving life sentences and those receiving death sentences. Precise comparisons of systems are not possible with this measure, however, when they are based on indexes estimated with different sets of cases.

Second, one would also expect a random death-sentencing system to produce a nearly complete overlap in the distributions of culpability scores for life- and death-sentence cases. A highly selective system, by contrast, should produce little or no overlap between the culpability scores for the two sets of cases. Our second measure of excessiveness, therefore, focuses on the overlap of the distributions of death- and life-sentence cases on our culpability indexes. Specifically, the measure quantifies the proportion of defendants sentenced to death whose culpability scores are lower than the 95th percentile of the culpability scores for life-sentence cases.[49]

Third, a random system should also produce subgroups of "similar" cases with death-sentencing rates that approximate the overall average rate. A highly selective system, which imposed death sentences in only the most extreme cases, would produce a very different pattern. There would be a small group of highly aggravated cases for which the death-sentencing rates would be quite high. This subgroup would account for most of the death sentences imposed in the entire system. There would also be less aggravated groupings of the remaining cases with very low or zero death-sentencing rates. Our fourth measure, therefore, examines the frequency of death sentencing among cases deemed similar with our estimated indexes and scales. Specifically, it focuses on the magnitude of the death-sentencing rates among groups of similarly situated defendants, and on the proportion of all death sentences that are imposed in categories of cases where the death-sentencing rates are very high or very low.

In this connection, we classify death sentences as presumptively excessive if the frequency with which death sentences occur in other cases classified as "similar" by our various measures is less than .35. If the death-sentencing rate among "similar" cases exceeds .80, we classify a death-sentence case as presumptively evenhanded.[50] Using these criteria, we compare the proportion of death sentences imposed that are presumptively evenhanded and the proportion of the death sentences imposed that are presumptively excessive.

Finally, because a random system would allocate death sentences without regard to case culpability, there should be little, if any, statistical association between the culpability scores and case outcomes in a random system.[51] Statistical measures of the goodness of fit or concordance between predicted and actual sentencing outcomes, therefore, provide some insight into the degree of randomness in a system.[52] Caution in interpretation is required, however, since changes in the overall death-sentencing rate can also affect such measures.[53]

Discrimination

The Measures   There are a number of accepted measures used to estimate discrimination by discretionary decision-making systems. The first approach, which we employ in the PRS and the CSS, estimates differences in the rates at which death sentences are actually imposed among racially distinct subgroups of cases of similar culpability. Thus, we might find that, within a group of cases at a given level of culpability as defined by a particular culpability scale, the death-sentencing rate for black defendants was 20 percentage points higher than it was for white defendants (e.g., .40−.20 or .30−.10). If all the cases involved were comparable in all relevant respects and the sample sizes of the black and white defendant subgroups are adequate, a disparity of this magnitude would constitute compelling evidence of purposeful race-of-defendant discrimination. But if the death-sentencing rates for the two racially differentiated subgroups were essentially the same, the results would suggest the system was evenhanded. Tables 27, 28, and 36 illustrate the use of this type of disparity measure which, for technical reasons, we consider the best measure of discrimination.[54]

A second type of measure, which we use in the PRS and the CSS, is the partial-regression coefficient. It expresses quantitatively the magnitude of the difference between the average predicted death-sentencing rate for the two racial groups being compared, after simultaneous adjustment for the legitimate variables included in the multiple-regression analysis. The difference between the two predicted chances of receiving a death sentence is expressed by either a ratio (for logistic regression) or an arithmetic difference (for linear regression). The partial-regression coefficient for a racial variable or any other type of variable in a logistic multiple-regression analysis can be converted to a ratio measure known as an odds multiplier (the antilog of the partial logistic-regression coefficient). The odds multiplier for a variable such as the defendant's race tells us the ratio of the predicted odds of a death sentence for a black defendant to the predicted odds for a comparable white defendant, after adjustment for all of the legitimate variables in the analysis. For example, the logistic partial-regression coefficient for the race-of-defendant variable may indicate that, on average, a defendant's odds of receiving a death sentence are 1.5 times higher if he is black than if he is white.

In logistic-regression models, the effect of racial variables on the defendant's probability of receiving an adverse outcome can be appreciated by examining graphs like figure 20, in which we plot separately the estimated death-sentencing rates for two or more racial subgroups of cases at each level of case culpability as indicated by their legitimate case characteristics. If the model indicates that the system involved is free of discrimination, the plots for the different racial subgroups would overlap within statistical error. When applied to a discriminatory system, however, this analysis would reveal a substantial gap between the predicted death-sentence probabilities estimated for cases of equivalent culpability in the various subgroups.

The partial-regression coefficient derived from an ordinary-least-squares (O.L.S.) analysis, in contrast, indicates the average arithmetic difference between, for example, a black defendant's predicted probability and the probability predicted for a similarly situated white defendant.[55]

Although not our preferred measure of racial discrimination, we estimated a broad range of linear- and logistic-regression coefficients for racial variables in the PRS and the CSS.[56]

To summarize, Table 4 lists all of the alternative statistical analyses of racial discrimination that we conducted for each study, with an indication of the background variables controlled for in each and a reference to the location of the results reported in this book. Also, a summary of the principal statewide race-of-victim findings, pre- and post-*Furman*, for both studies appears in chapter 12, Table 64.

A Note on the Interpretation of Statistical Disparities If there is no difference in the treatment of the two groups of interest, for example black and white defendants, the racial disparity estimated for the race-of-defendant variable will generally be at or near zero.[57] However, as the race-of-defendant disparity becomes larger and more significant statistically, the inference that purposeful discrimination is an influence in the system becomes more plausible. This assumes, of course, that the analysis includes variables for all legitimate background variables that are statistically and practically related to both the race variable and the death-sentencing results.

It is important to emphasize the inferences such statistical disparities can and cannot legitimately support. "Unadjusted disparities" that control for no background variables are easily understood and interesting, but only suggestive at best. Because they do not take into account the impact of any other case characteristics, unadjusted disparities almost invariably diminish in magnitude and statistical significance upon adjustment for legitimate background variables. If a statistical disparity persists, however, after adjustment for background variables, the extent to which one can legitimately infer the presence of

Table 4. Type and Location of Racial-Discrimination Analyses in This Book[1]

	I. Procedural Reform Study			
A. Analytic Method and Background Variables Adjusted/Controlled For	B. Death Sentences Imposed among Defendants Convicted of Murder at Trial		C. Prosecutorial Decisions to Seek a Death Sentence after Trial: Post-*Furman*	D. Jury Penalty-Trial Sentencing Decisions: Post-*Furman*
	Pre-*Furman*	Post-*Furman*		
1. Unadjusted disparities	T. 26	T. 30	T. 34	T. 34
2. Plot of predicted death-sentencing rates by defendant/victim racial combination, controlling for main culpability index	F. 20	F. 21	F. 23	F. 24
3. Cross-tab controlling for qualitative *a priori* measure	T. 29	T. 31	T. 35	T. 34
4. Cross-tab controlling for main culpability scale	T. 27 T. 28	T. 32	T. 36 T. 38 T. 39 T. 40 T. 41	T. 36 T. 38 T. 39 T. 40 T. 41
5. Cross-tab controlling for Barnett culpability measure		F. 22	F. 25	F. 26

Table 4. *(Continued)*

	App. J, Pt. 4 (model PREFURMA)	App. J, Pt. 1; Ch. 4, n. 39 (N.T.1) (model OVERALLA)	App. J, Pt. 2 (model PROSCUTA)	App. J, Pt. 3 (model JURYA)
6. Multiple-regression coefficients after adjustment for the following legitimate case characteristics:				
a. Main culpability index		Ch. 10, n. 17 (N.T.4) Ch. 6, text at n. 20	Ch. 10, n. 18 (N.T.5); Ch. 10, n. 20 (N.T.6) Ch. 6, text at n. 39	Ch. 10, n. 18 (N.T.5); Ch. 10, n. 21 (N.T.7) Ch. 6, text at n. 39
b. From 5 to 51 background factors (multiple analyses)				
c. 150-plus background factors				
7. Urban/rural analyses		T. 42	T. 42	T. 42

II. Charging and Sentencing Study Statewide

A. Analytic Method and Background Variables Adjusted/Controlled For	B. Death Sentences Imposed among All Cases or Murder-Indicted Cases		C. Prosecutorial Decisions to Seek a Death Sentence after a Murder Trial	D. Jury Penalty-Trial Sentencing Decisions
	Statewide	Fulton Co.		
1. Unadjusted disparities	T. 50	T. 59–61	T. 56	T. 56
2. Adjustment for felony circumstances and prior record	F. 31			
3. Plot of predicted death-sentencing rates for white- and black-victim cases involving black defendants, controlling for 39-variable core model	F. 32			

4. Cross-tab controlling for a qualitative *a priori* measure	T. 54 T. 58	T. 59		
5. Cross-tab controlling for a culpability scale	T. 53 T. 57			
6. An alternative culpability index (most aggravated 472 cases)	T. 53			
7. Multiple-regression coefficients after adjustment for the following legitimate case characteristics:				
a. Main 39-variable culpability index	Ch. 4, n. 43 (N.T. 2.); T. 52			
b. 13 to 136 variables (multiple analyses)	T. 51	T. 63	Ch. 10, n. 18 (N.T. 5); Ch. 10, n. 20 (N.T. 6)	Ch. 10, n. 18 (N.T. 5); Ch. 10, n. 21 (N.T. 7)
c. 230+ variables				
d. Main 39-variable culpability index—limited to 647 highly aggravated cases as determined by Judge J. Owen Forrester	T. 51 Ch. 10, n. 38 and accompanying text			
8. Urban/rural analysis	Ch. 10, n. 54 (N.T. 10); Ch. 10, n. 54 (N.T. 11)			

1. "T." refers to table, "F" refers to figure, "N.T." refers to note table, "Ch." refers to chapter, and "n." refers to note. Summaries of the results of the race-of-victim analysis are shown in chap. 6, table 43 (pre- & post-*Furman* overall effects, PRS); chap. 6, table 44 (post-*Furman* prosecutor and jury results, PRS); chap. 10, table 55 (principal CSS evidence in McCleskey v. Kemp); and chap. 12, table 64 (brief summary, CSS and PRS). Also, Appendix L contains a series of multiple-regression models from the CSS and PRS.

purposeful discrimination depends upon two factors. The first is the magnitude and statistical significance of the disparity—the larger and more statistically significant it is, the more confident one can become that it is not an artifact of chance. The second important factor is the likelihood that the addition to the analysis of omitted variables that have not been controlled for would reduce the magnitude and statistical significance of the estimated racial disparity. If that likelihood appears to be small, based on one's knowledge of the system and other available information, the inference of purposeful discrimination is enhanced. By contrast, the inference is weakened if it appears likely that omitted variables are correlated with both the racial and the outcome variables. When they are so correlated, their inclusion in the analysis could normally alter the size and statistical significance of the estimated racial disparity.[58]

In the context of this study, therefore, our ultimate judgments about the likely influence of race or other suspect factors on Georgia's capital-sentencing system are not simply a matter of statistics. They also reflect our understanding of how that system functions in Georgia and how similar systems function elsewhere. In addition, they reflect our confidence that the many background variables included in the analyses satisfactorily control for plausible alternative hypotheses that could produce the disparities we observe.

Finally, as we noted above, at their best statistical analyses of the type presented in this book can identify by inference those case characteristics, such as the number of victims or the race of the victim, that apparently influenced prosecutors and juries. They do not tell us the reason for their influence. Specifically, they do not indicate whether the response to such case characteristics was conscious or nonconscious.[59]

NOTES

1. In order to obtain full coverage of death sentences, however, we also included in our data set two cases in which the defendant received a death sentence after pleading guilty to capital murder. See supra chap. 2, note 4, for a definition of the crime of murder in Georgia.

2. The dates of the 25 supplemental death sentences were 1965 (3), 1966 (3), 1967 (5), 1968 (8), and 1969 (6). To adjust for the differential sampling rates among life- and death-sentence cases in the second, supplemental part of the pre-*Furman* sample (i.e., 0% life- and 100% death-sentence cases), we weighted the life-sentence cases in the original sample by a factor of 2.23 to achieve an overall ratio of life- to death-sentence cases in the entire pre-*Furman* data set equal to that in the original sample. As a result, the unweighted sample of 112 life-sentence cases and 44 death-sentence cases generalizes to a universe of 250 life-sentence cases and 44 death-sentence pre-*Furman* cases. However, since the life-sentence cases are weighted, round-off errors sometimes produce variations in the total number of cases in a given tabulation of the pre-*Furman* data, particularly when they are broken into small subgroups.

3. In the twenty-three cases in which we did not know whether a penalty trial was held, we used a multiple-regression estimation procedure to impute the variable's value. *See infra* app. B, note 44 and accompanying text.

4. Also, in a number of cases, we obtained information on the status of defense counsel and whether there was a penalty trial from questionnaires sent to prosecutors and defense attorneys.

5. The main data-collection effort proceeded in two stages. All of the post-*Furman* death-sentence cases and one hundred of the post-*Furman* life-sentence cases were coded, by law students in Iowa City, from a detailed abstract of each case that had been prepared, in the summer of 1979, from the records of the Georgia Supreme Court by a law school graduate and a law student. Also, these first two hundred cases were initially coded into a larger questionnaire that was the forerunner of the questionnaire at app. C. The data in those original questionnaires were later transformed, by way of a computer program, into the format of the app. C questionnaire, which we used to collect data on the three hundred remaining post-*Furman* cases and all of the pre-*Furman* cases. The data coded in the format of the questionnaire at app. C were then transformed into a variety of substantive variables embodying specific characteristics of the cases that were amenable to machine analysis (for example, the variable MITCIR indicates the presence of any of a list of mitigating circumstances). A listing of the variable names and labels that were used in the substantive analysis are in app. D, which also includes the frequency distribution for those variables for both the pre- and post-*Furman* data sets.

6. A summary of the race-of-victim findings from the PRS is presented *infra* in chap. 6, tables 43 & 44.

7. *Infra* chap. 10, note 16 and accompanying text.

8. However, we did not learn that the results would be presented on behalf of Warren McCleskey until nine months before the hearing was actually held. The background of our involvement in the *McCleskey* case is described *infra* chap. 10, page 310.

9. *Supra* chap. 10, note 27 and accompanying text.

10. The universe of cases for the Charging and Sentencing Study consists of 2,456 offenders who were listed in the records of Georgia's Department of Offender Rehabilitation as having a "date sentence began" (which usually means the date of arrest, since most murder defendants do not make bail) after March 27, 1973, and before January 1, 1980. This population included 100 offenders with death sentences, 876 offenders with a murder conviction and a life sentence, and 1,480 offenders with voluntary-manslaughter convictions.

The first step in the sampling procedure was the separate selection from each judicial district of a 25% random sample stratified according to the three major conviction and sentencing outcomes (voluntary manslaughter, murder–life imprisonment, and murder–death sentence). In the second stage of the sampling procedure, we supplemented the sample to include at least 18 cases in circuits in which the random sample had not produced that number of cases. In the two circuits with fewer than 18 cases in the universe, all cases were included in the sample. The cases selected for this supplementation were picked randomly and the selections were stratified to insure that the final sample from each circuit approximated the distribution of voluntary-manslaughter and murder-life cases in the universe of each circuit. This sampling procedure resulted in a stratified random sample of 1,038 cases. Our third supplementation involved the addition of 28 death-sentence cases, not listed in the Department of Offender Rehabilitation list of murder cases but falling within the time frame of the study. These cases brought the total sample to 1,066 cases.

Because of the different sampling rates between circuits and between murder and voluntary-manslaughter cases within individual circuits, it was necessary to weight the cases for the purpose of obtaining estimates of the characteristics of the entire universe of cases.

11. 1 RESEARCH ON SENTENCING: THE SEARCH FOR REFORM 27 (A. Blumstein, J. Cohen, S. Martin, & M. Tonry eds. 1983) (hereinafter Blumstein et al.). B. Nakell & K. Hardy, THE ARBITRARINESS OF THE DEATH PENALTY (1987), is a good, early example of a longitudinal study that includes all homicide cases processed through North Carolina's death-sentencing system in a single year, including those cases that did not result in a homicide conviction. Bienen, Weiner, Denno, Allison, & Mills, *The Reimposition of Capital Punishment in New Jersey: The Role of Prosecutorial Discretion*, 41 RUTGERS L. REV. 27 (1988), is a more recent example covering all New Jersey homicides that occurred during a period of about three years. See *infra* chap. 8 for a description of these and other studies.

12. We are grateful to Professors Nakell and Hardy for the use of their questionnaire in the planning stages of the CSS. We also drew heavily on questionnaires developed by Marvin Wolfgang for his southern rape studies and by the Stanford Law Review for its California death-sentencing study. *Infra* chap. 8, notes 97 & 50.

13. A frequency distribution for each of these variables appears in app. F. In addition, we also secured for each case, as we had in the PRS, a 100- to 300-word narrative summary that permitted qualitative analyses of defendant culpability.

14. *Supra* note 5 and accompanying text.

15. The coders in the Charging and Sentencing Study had available the opinion of the Georgia Supreme Court in all cases appealed to the Georgia court. In addition, the files of the Georgia Supreme Court were consulted in every known penalty-trial case to learn which aggravating circumstances were charged and found by the jury.

The data sets for the PRS and the CSS, with documentation, are available at the University of Michigan's Inter-University Consortium for Political and Social Research: Criminal Justice Archive.

16. Throughout this book we use the terms case "culpability," "seriousness," "aggravation level," and "blameworthiness" interchangeably in characterizing and rank-ordering cases. In this context, defendant "culpability" refers to "moral culpability," a broader concept than the traditional criminal-law reference of culpability to the mental state, or *mens rea*, of a defendant that must be established for each "material element" of the offense. Model Penal Code §2.02 (1962).

17. Various United States Supreme Court opinions before *McCleskey* had suggested that defendant moral culpability and blameworthiness is the principal concern in determinations of whether death-sentenced defendants can be meaningfully distinguished from defendants receiving lesser sentences. See Furman v. Georgia, 408 U.S. 238, 311–13 (1972) (White, J., concurring), 309–10 (Stewart., J., concurring), 387–89 (Burger, C. J., dissenting); Godfrey v. Georgia, 446 U.S. 420, 433 (1980). Similarly, some state supreme courts have recognized the relevance of overall case culpability in the conduct of comparative-proportionality review. Baldus, Pulaski, & Woodworth (86), *supra* chap. 3, note 6, at 175–78 & notes 90–91.

18. In practice, the distinction between the *a priori* and empirical approaches is often less sharp than suggested. One's determination of the case characteristics that should influence decisions is likely to be affected by an intuitive understanding of the case characteristics that are in fact important to prosecutors and juries. Similarly, the use of empirical methods may be influenced by normative considerations that limit the

case characteristics whose influence an investigation will seek to determine statistically. Such obviously irrelevant factors as hair color, or such illegitimate and suspect factors as race and socioeconomic status, would not be included in a culpability measure, regardless of their explanatory power. See Fisher & Kadane, *Empirically Based Sentencing Guidelines and Ethical Considerations*, in 2 RESEARCH SENTENCING: THE SEARCH FOR REFORM 184 (A. Blumstein, J. Cohen, S. Martin, & M. Tonry eds. 1983).

19. "Frequently, there may be more than one approach to estimating the same quantity. When this happens we have the opportunity to make comparisons based on the several methods. This approach is sometimes called triangulation, since it gives more than one fix on a quantity. Triangulation has many merits: it may show us what our method is especially sensitive to; it may tell something about the uncertainty overall; and it may call our attention to some unreasonable numbers we have been using in one or another of the analyses." Mosteller, *Assessing Unknown Numbers: Order of Magnitude Estimation*, in STATISTICS AND PUBLIC POLICY 163, 175 (W. Fairley & F. Mosteller ed. 1977).

20. *See infra* tables 9 & 16, and fig. 10.

21. In this respect our measure conforms to practices that the Supreme Court has either condoned, Zant v. Stephens, 462 U.S. 862, 878–79 (1983) (Constitution permits sentencing authority to weigh nonstatutorily designated aggravating factors), or required, Lockett v. Ohio, 438 U.S. 586, 601–5 (1978) (state law cannot preclude consideration of nonstatutory mitigating factors.)

22. The weight attributed to each aggravating or mitigating factor present in a case reflects a normative judgment about its respective bearing on the appropriate sentence. Development of a measure of this type involves some trial and error. One selects the criteria used to define the different culpability levels on a normative basis and then ranks the cases accordingly. If some cases seem misclassified, one may revise the factors used to define the culpability levels, or reclassify some of the cases.

23. *See infra* tables 7 & 12.

24. *See infra* fig. 31.

25. *See infra* tables 54 & 58.

26. We divided the 275 armed-robbery cases into the following subcategories:

1. with kidnapping, burglary, or arson (30);
2. with more than one victim (8);
3. with another contemporaneous offense other than kidnapping, burglary, or arson (26); and
4. with no other contemporaneous offense (150).

The armed-robbery cases with no other contemporaneous offense were then divided into three levels of culpability. The criteria used to define those levels are as follows:

5. More aggravated (43)
   1. More than one victim
   2. Prior history of armed robbery or homicide
   3. Clear premeditation to murder before the robbery
   4. Defendant inflicts excessive pain or mutilation
   5. Helpless victim
   6. Defendant is an escapee or on parole
6. Less aggravated (45)
   1. Defendant had no intent to kill, e.g., random shot
   2. Evidence that defendant acted in self-defense
   3. No prior felony conviction

    4. Defendant is clearly under the influence of alcohol or drugs

    5. Defendant is mentally deficient

  7. Less aggravated because defendant was not the actual killer (61).

The remaining sixty-two armed-robbery cases were classified as typical because there was only one victim, the defendant was the triggerman, and none of the aggravating or mitigating factors that would make them "more" or "less" aggravated was present.

    27. Judge Forrester's coding protocol included over 170 of the foils (items) in the CSS data collection instrument at app. E.

    28. *See infra* chap. 10, note 38 and accompanying text.

    29. Barnett, *Some Distribution Patterns for the Georgia Death Sentence*, 18 U.C. Davis L. Rev. 1327 (1985); Baldus, Woodworth, & Pulaski, *Monitoring and Evaluating Contemporary Death Sentencing Systems: Lessons from Georgia*, 18 U.C. Davis L. Rev. 1375, 1381–82 (1985).

    30. Among these techniques are multiple-regression analysis (linear and logistic), factor analysis, and discriminant analysis.

    31. See Finkelstein, *The Judicial Reception of Multiple Regression Studies in Race and Sex Discrimination Cases*, 80 Colum. L. Rev. 737 (1980); Fisher, *Multiple Regression in Legal Proceedings*, 80 Colum. L. Rev. 702 (1980); D. Baldus & J. Cole, Statistical Proof of Discrimination chap. 8 (1980); D. Barnes & J. Conley, Statistical Evidence in Litigation chap. 8 (1986).

    32. J. Bunker, W. Forrest, Jr., F. Mosteller, & L. Vandam, The National Halothane Study (1969).

    33. The codebook used to collect the data is at app. C, and the variables created from the original data in app. C are listed in app. D.

    34. We identified the variables included in each model with a screening procedure that enabled us to reduce to a manageable size the number of variables used in the culpability index while retaining the essential information reflected by the omitted variables. In stage 1 of the procedure, we estimated a logistic model that included from twenty to thirty legitimate variables previously identified as significant by an OLS (ordinary-least-squares) analysis. This produced index 1.

Illegitimate and suspect factors were included in stages 2–4. In stage 2 we determined which of the omitted variables had a statistically significant partial correlation (at the .10 level) with the outcome variable after controlling statistically for index 1. We then included these variables with the variables comprising index 1 in a backward-elimination logistic-regression procedure that excluded variables that did not achieve a level of significance beyond the .10 level. The results of this analysis produced index 2. In this analysis, we used the logistic-regression procedures in the Statistical Analysis System (SAS) and the BMDP statistical software packages. BMDP Statistical Software 1981 (W. J. Dixon, chief ed., 1981); SUGI Supplemental Library User's Guide (1983 ed.).

In stage 3 we created interaction terms between all of the variables comprising index 2. Depending on the decision point involved, this produced between 78 and 496 two-way interaction terms between pairs of legitimate variables, and between 26 and 64 two-way interaction terms between legitimate variables and variables for the race of the victim and the race of the defendant. We then screened these interactions to identify those that had significant partial correlations with the outcome variable at the .10 level of statistical significance, after controlling for index 2.

In stage 4, we computed multicollinearity diagnostics on the variables in index 3 and the interaction terms that survived the screen conducted in stage 3 and eliminated variables that had perverse signs due to collinearity.

In stage 5, we placed all the variables that survived the multicollinearity checks in a backward-elimination logistic-regression analysis that selected for the final index (a) all legitimate variables that achieved a .10 level of statistical significance and (b) variables for the race, sex, and socioeconomic status of the defendant, which we retained in the analysis regardless of their statistical significance.

The results of the regression analyses are presented in app. J. The key measures of the impact of a given variable are the logistic-regression coefficient, which is difficult to interpret in its own right, and the odds multiplier, which is the antilog of the logistic-regression coefficient. The latter indicates the degree to which the odds of selection are, on average, increased or decreased by the presence of the relevant case characteristic after adjustment for the other variables in the analysis. An odds multiplier of 4 for a given case characteristic means the presence of that characteristic, on average, would quadruple the odds of receiving a death-penalty sentence (for example, 2:1 odds would increase to 8:1). A negative logistic coefficient, in contrast, produces an odds multiplier of less than 1, which indicates that the case characteristic to which it relates will, when present, reduce the average odds of receiving a death sentence. For example, an odds multiplier of .07 estimated from a negative 2.63 logistic-regression coefficient indicates that the factor's presence will on average reduce level odds (1 to 1) to .07 to 1 (7 to 100). *See* S. Gross and R. Mauro, DEATH & DISCRIMINATION 248–52 (1989) for further discussion of logistic-regression coeficients.

The formula $P = \frac{O}{1 + O}$ converts odds (O) to probabilities (P). Thus, if the odds are 1 to 2, $P = \frac{1/2}{1 + 1/2} = \frac{.5}{1.5} = .33$ The formula $O = \frac{P}{1 - P}$ converts probabilities to odds. Thus, $P = .33$ corresponds to: $O = \frac{.33}{1 - .33} = \frac{.33}{.66} = 1/2 = .5$.

The odds multiplier shows the average impact of a case characteristic if present in an individual case. The statistic R measures the aggregate influence of a characteristic over all cases. For example, a characteristic like "insurance proceeds motive" may have a great impact on the disposition of those few cases where it is present, but its systemwide impact, as measured by R, is comparatively small since this characteristic is so rare. SUGI SUPPLEMENTAL LIBRARY USER'S GUIDE 183 (1983 ed.).

35. The procedure is somewhat more complicated than the text suggests, since the numbers summed for each variable to produce the overall culpability score are a product of its regression coefficients and the coding for the variable involved; e.g., a coefficient at 1.7 for the "multiple stabs" variable (coded 1 when multiple stabs are present and 0 when they are not) produces a weight of 1.7 when multiple stabs are present (1.7×1) and a weight of 0 when no multiple stabs are present (1.7×0).

36. The range of culpability scores for the six levels of each scale are presented in app. J.

37. To the extent that the procedure weights aggravating and mitigating case characteristics, it parallels the *a priori* measure discussed earlier, *supra* note 21 and accompanying text.

38. The regression model for each of these decision points is presented in app. J. Two of the post-*Furman* decision points presented a question about the degree to which the analyses should be limited to death-eligible cases, i.e., defendants who were candidates for the death penalty because of the presence of a statutory aggravating factor in their cases, whether or not the prosecutor sought a death sentence or the jury found the

factor present in the case. Indeed, our data indicate that prosecutors sought a death sentence in only 41% (194/471) of the cases we deemed to be death-eligible, while juries found a statutory aggravating factor present and imposed a death sentence in 54% (112/206) of the cases that advanced to a penalty trial. If the measures for all of the statutory aggravating circumstances were perfect, we would have limited our post-*Furman* analyses to death-eligible cases, since cases without a statutory aggravating factor present have no risk of resulting in a death sentence. In fact, however, because of the vagueness of a number of the statutory aggravating circumstances, and the wide discretion enjoyed by Georgia's prosecutors in determining whether an aggravating circumstance was present, we did not believe that our measures of death eligibility correlated perfectly with the perception of Georgia's prosecutors. Indeed, there were seven cases that we deemed to be *not* death-eligible that were advanced to a penalty trial because the prosecutor perceived an aggravating circumstance to be present in the case (each of these cases resulted in a life sentence). It is clear, therefore, that to some degree our measures of death eligibility are not coextensive with prosecutorial perceptions of death eligibility. Indeed, it may be appropriate to perceive all of the cases in the file as being death-eligible to a certain degree. For this reason, in the analyses of both the post-*Furman* prosecutorial decisions to seek a death sentence after trial and the combined effects of post-*Furman* prosecutorial and jury decisions, we included all cases in the sample whether or not our measures classified them as death-eligible. (This issue did not exist for the pre-*Furman* cases, since all of them were death-eligible; similarly, all the post-*Furman* cases that reached a penalty trial were death-eligible in the eyes of the prosecutors.) The results of the regression analysis differed, however, only slightly when they were limited to the cases we deemed death-eligible. Moreover, the results of the substantive excessiveness and race-discrimination analyses differed only slightly using the two different files of cases.

The excessiveness analysis presents, however, the system in a slightly better light when it is limited to death-eligible cases. For this reason, we limited those analyses to the penalty-trial cases and to those cases defined as death-eligible by our measures. In contrast, in our discrimination analyses, the race-of-victim effects estimated in the system were slightly less strong when all cases were included. For this reason, all of our substantive analyses of the impact of race and other illegitimate or suspect variables were conducted using all cases in the sample.

39. The variables, coefficients, standard errors, and *P* values for the principal Type A model (OVERALLA) appear in note table 1, *infra*.

40. See Blumstein et al., *supra* note 11, at 23.

41. The coding for the four culpability scales is presented in app. J.

42. In preparation for the hearing in McCleskey v. Kemp, we developed a series of alternative-regression indexes for the PRS. These captured the combined effects of both the prosecutorial decision to seek and the jury decision to impose a death sentence. One was based on a linear analysis of all statutory aggravating circumstances and 44 variables for mitigating circumstances (schedule 14, app. L). Another was based on a linear analysis of the full file of 150-plus nonracial aggravating and mitigating factors and 4 suspect factors (schedule 15, app. L). The third was based on a linear analysis of the 32 variables that showed a statistically significant relationship ($p \leq .10$) with the death-sentencing results (schedule 16, app. L). We also developed two indexes of nonperverse variables that showed a statistically significant relationship to the separate outcomes of the prosecutorial decisions to seek a death sentence after the guilt trial (schedule 12, app. L—from a linear analysis) and the jury penalty-trial decision (schedule 13, app.

Note Table 1. Logistic-Regression Coefficients for Main Post-*Furman* Model (OVERALLA), PRS: Outcomes—Death Sentence (1) or Life Sentence (0)[1]

Variable Label and Name	Logistic-Regression Coefficient (Standard Error)	p Value	Variable Label and Name	Logistic-Regression Coefficient (Standard Error)	p Value
1. Black defendant (BLACKD)	−.57 (.50)	.25	15. Victim police- or fireperson (VICPFIR)	2.00 (.89)	.02
2. White victim (WHVICRC)	2.66 (.65)	.0001	16. Victim twelve years or younger (YNGVIC)	2.3 (.97)	.02
3. One or more mitigating circumstances and a white victim (MCIRAWHV)	−1.65 (.54)	.002	17. Defendant lay in wait (AMBUSH)	2.16 (.63)	.001
			18. Defendant in military (MILDEFN)	2.43 (.86)	.005
4. Low-status defendant (LSTATDEF)	.85 (.48)	.08	19. Race-hatred motive (RACE)	4.68 (1.97)	.02
5. High-status defendant (HISTD)	1.88 (.95)	.05	20. Victim low status (VICLSTAT)	−2.63 (.80)	.001
6. Female defendant (DFEM)	−.59 (1.03)	.56	21. Bloody murder (BLOODY)	1.43 (.49)	.004
7. Number of statutory aggravating circumstances, plus number of B7 (vile murder) circumstances in the case (DELB7EX)	1.22 (.20)	.00001	22. Kidnap and multiple shots (KDNPAMSH)	−2.60 (1.03)	.012
			23. Neither kidnap nor multiple shots (NKNPOMSH)	−2.46 (.52)	.00001
			24. Aggravated motive and one or more prior felony convictions (AGMOTAPF)	1.69 (.58)	.004
8. Female victim (FEMVIC)	2.26 (.52)	.00001	25. Number of convictions for violent personal crimes (other than murder, rape, armed robbery, kidnap) and number of statutory aggravating circumstances interaction (DLXXW15D)	0.36 (.19)	.07
9. Defendant an underling in the murder (DUNDERLG)	−6.88 (1.51)	.00001			
10. Victim a stranger (VICSTRAN)	1.00 (.51)	.051			
11. Multiple stabs (MULSTAB)	1.71 (.71)	.01			
12. Defendant killed two or more people (TWOVIC)	1.66 (.65)	.01			
13. Victim a hostage (HOST)	3.69 (2.03)	.07	26. Defendant resisted arrest and one or more prior felony convictions (DEFRAAPF)	1.38 (.70)	.06
14. Defendant cooperated with authorities (STMIT9)	2.64 (.81)	.001			

[1] The model is also reported with odds multipliers for each variable, *infra* app. J, part 1.

L—from a logistic analysis). All of these indexes were forerunners of those reported in app. J, which we developed after the *McCleskey* hearing.

43. Because 94% of the cases in the study were indicted for murder, the results were nearly identical for analysis involving all cases and those limited to defendants indicted for murder. The names, labels, regression coefficients, and supporting statistics for the thirty-nine legitimate variables in this model, as well as the two racial variables, are listed in app. L, schedule 4. The names, labels, logistic-regression coefficients, and level of statistical significance for the coefficients in this model also appear in note table 2, *infra*.

A robustness test indicates the extent to which the magnitude and statistical significance of the partial-regression coefficients produced by a model may be affected by or be the product of (a) the basic characteristics of the statistical analysis that produced it (e.g., logistic regression assumes a certain relationship between the dependent and independent variables—*see infra* app. A, figure 33 and accompanying text) or (b) the failure of certain assumptions about characteristics of the data on which the model rests (e.g., a normal distribution of the values for the outcome data).

44. The variables identified in these analyses are listed in schedules 5 and 6 of app. L. An example of a "perverse" variable would be one that showed a negative (mitigating) sign for the presence of torture in the case. Also, in contrast to the screening analyses described above for the PRS, which included suspect and illegitimate variables, these CSS analyses excluded such variables from the outset.

45. The variables comprising this index are listed in schedule 5 of app. L. See *infra* chap. 10, table 53, for an analysis of the 472 most aggravated cases.

46. The 43 variables that survived this screen are listed in schedule 7 of app. L. As suggested in the text, the difference between this analysis and the analyses described in note 44 is that it did not exclude variables that showed a perverse sign, i.e., signs that were different than what was expected in a rational death-sentencing system on the basis of prior knowledge and existing law.

47. The variables in the 230+ analysis are listed in schedule 3 of app. L.

48. The variables included in the indexes estimated with logistic methods for these decision points are listed in schedules 8 (prosecutor) and 9 (jury) of app. L. After the *McCleskey* hearing, we produced an additional index for each of the five stages of Georgia's charging-and-sentencing system, plus the combined effects of those decisions leading to the death sentence. We developed each index with logistic multiple-regression analysis.

49. We used the 95th-percentile life-sentence case as the basis of the measure so it would reflect the general tendency of the sentencing system and would minimize the influence of occasional and possibly abberational acts of mercy by prosecutors and jurors in not seeking or imposing death sentences in highly aggravated cases. The measure based on the 95th-percentile life-sentence case indicates less comparative excessiveness in the system than would a measure based on the percentage of life-sentenced cases that were less aggravated than the most aggravated life-sentenced cases.

50. Although McCleskey v. Kemp suggests that comparatively excessive death sentences may no longer be a matter of constitutional concern, we previously defined a death sentence to be comparatively excessive if other defendants of similar culpability receive the death penalty only infrequently (*supra* chap. 2, notes 48 through 51 and accompanying text). We base this definition upon the United States Supreme Court's opinion in Gregg v. Georgia, which approved of Georgia's comparative-sentence review procedure. There is, however, no Georgia court opinion that provides a quantified

Note Table 2. Logistic-Regression Model for 39-Variable Aggravation Index, css: Outcomes—Death Sentence (1), Life Sentence, or Term of Years (0)

Variable	Logistic-Regression Coefficient	Level of Stat. Sig. (p)[1]	Variable Label
CONSTANT	−6.1497	0.000	
BLACKD	−0.0638	0.852	Def. was black
WHVICRC	1.4473	0.000	One or more white victims (recode)
BLVICMOD	−0.6128	0.147	Family, lover, liquor, barroom quarrel
DEFADMIT	−1.2747	0.061	Def. admit guilt, no defense asserted
VWEAK	1.1261	0.124	Victim weak or frail
HATE	−0.3426	0.631	Hate motive
DROWN	0.9625	0.219	Victim was drowned
LDFB3	0.1400	0.748	Def. caused deathrisk in pub. place to >2
INSMOT	3.0106	0.001	Def. motive to collect insurance
LDFB10	0.4118	0.245	Kill to avoid, stop arrest of self, other
VICCHILD	1.5558	0.021	Victim was 12 or younger
LDFB4	−0.2249	0.669	Pecuniary gain for self/other
LDFB1	1.3985	0.005	Prior rec. of mur, armrob, rap, kid w/bod inj
NONPROPC	0.3505	0.570	Nonproperty-related contemp. crime
TWOVIC	2.0693	0.000	Def. killed two or more people
LDFB6	1.7724	0.029	Murder for hire
MITDEFN	−0.6119	0.576	Def. retired, student, juvenile, housewife
LDFB7D	0.5981	0.136	Rape/armrob/kid/sil. wit/exec/vic pleaded
TORTURE	3.3126	0.000	Victim tortured physically
NOKILL	−2.7504	0.000	Defendant not triggerman
DRGHIS	−1.0111	0.003	History of drug or alcohol abuse
SMYOUTH	−0.8758	0.183	Def. under 17 years of age
STRANGER	1.0345	0.002	Victim a stranger
LDFB8	0.5163	0.502	Victim police/corrections/fireman on duty
FEMDEF	0.2812	0.668	Defendant a female
AVENGE	3.3650	0.055	Motiv to aveng role by jud. off, D.A., lawyr
VBED	1.0369	0.277	Victim bedridden/handicapped
MULSH	0.7885	0.018	Multiple gunshots
KIDNAP	1.0601	0.093	Kidnapping involved
LDFB9	2.0401	0.001	Def. prisoner or escapee
DLEADER	0.5503	0.236	Def. prim. mover plan homicid, contemp. off.
MENTORT	2.2735	0.001	Mental torture
MULSTAB	1.5408	0.000	Multiple stabbing
MURPRIOR	1.6628	0.173	Num. of prior mur. convict def.
ARMROB	1.4355	0.007	Armed robbery involved
COPERP	0.2424	0.533	One or more coperpetrators involved
JEALOUS	−0.7452	0.491	Jealousy motive
VPCARBR	0.3022	0.424	One or more convictions: vpc/burg/arson
CPLESSEN	0.7851	0.052	Coperp received a lesser sentence
RAPE	2.5475	0.000	Rape involved
PRISONX	0.0814	0.593	No. of def. felony prison terms

1. This column reports the nominal estimated level. *See infra* app. L, sched. 4, for the "safe" estimated level.

measure of comparative excessiveness. In Eberheart v. State, 232 Ga. 247, 206 S.E.2d 12 (1974), *vacated*, 433 U.S. 917 (1977), the Georgia Supreme Court approved imposition of the death penalty in a case involving a nonfatal kidnap-rape, although only seven of the fourteen "similar" cases cited in its opinion resulted in death sentences for similar offenses. On the other hand, in the earlier decision of Coley v. State, 231 Ga. 829, 204 S.E. 2d 612 (1974), which also involved a nonfatal rape, the Georgia Supreme Court vacated the death penalty as excessive based upon the results of twelve other cases involving fourteen defendants, of whom only 36% (5/14) received death sentences. Although these two decisions are by no means conclusive, they suggest that the Georgia Supreme Court may classify a death sentence as excessive if the death-sentencing frequency in "similar" cases is somewhat less than .35. Complicating this attempt at quantification is Moore v. State, 233 Ga. 861, 213 S.E. 2d 829 (1975), *cert. denied*, 428 U.S. 910 (1976). In *Moore*, the Georgia Supreme Court stated that "we view it to be our duty under the similarity standard to assure that no death sentence is affirmed unless in similar cases throughout the state the death penalty has been imposed generally." *Id.* at 864, 213 S.E. 2d at 832. Indeed, the United States Supreme Court invoked this language to describe the Georgia procedure in Gregg v. Georgia, 428 U.S. 153, 205 (1976). In fact, however, juries imposed death sentences in only 39% of the cases identified by the Georgia Supreme Court in *Moore* as similar. Nevertheless, the Georgia court affirmed Moore's death sentence because "juries faced with similar factual situations have imposed death sentences." 233 Ga. at 866, 213 S.E. 2d at 833.

We have found only two decisions outside Georgia in which the reviewing court addressed the meaning to be given to the concept "generally" in the context of proportionality review. In a dissenting opinion in State v. Jeffries, 105 Wash. 2d 398, 437, 717 P. 2d 722, 744 (1986), *cert. denied*, 479 U.S. 922 (1986), Justice Utter argued that it clearly implied a rate significantly greater than .50. In contrast, the North Carolina Supreme Court vacated a death sentence in which the death-sentencing rate among cases it deemed comparable was .18 (5/23). State v. Young, 312 N.C. 669, 688, 325 S.E. 2d 181, 192–93 (1985). The court emphasized, however, that the magnitude of the death sentencing was not the critical consideration in its eyes:

> While we wish to make it *abundantly clear* that we do not consider this numerical disparity dispositive of our proportionality review, our careful examination of these cases has led us to the conclusion that although the crime here committed was a tragic killing, "it does not rise to the level of those murders in which we have approved the death sentence upon proportionality review." State v. Jackson, 309 N.C. at 46, 305 S.E. 2d at 717. The facts presented by this appeal more closely resemble those cases in which the jury recommended life imprisonment than those in which the defendant was sentenced to death.

The approach to a quantified measure of comparative excessiveness that we are suggesting is also consistent with Justice Stewart's plurality opinion in Gregg v. Georgia. When describing the Georgia Supreme Court's appellate-review process in death-penalty cases as an important statutory safeguard, Justice Stewart commented:

> The provision for appellate review in the Georgia capital-sentencing system serves as a check against the random or arbitrary imposition of the death penalty. In particular, the proportionality review substantially eliminates the possibility that a person will be sentenced to die by the action of an aberrant jury. *If a time comes when juries generally do not impose the death sentence in a certain kind of murder case*, the appellate review procedures assure that no defendant convicted under such circumstances will suffer a sentence of death. Gregg v. Georgia, 428 U.S. at 206 (plurality opinion) (emphasis added).

In other words, like the Georgia Supreme Court, Justice Stewart seemed to regard comparative-sentence review as a safeguard only against the type of aberrant, lightning-strike death sentences he condemned in *Furman*. By contrast, Justice White, in his concurring opinions in *Furman* and *Gregg*, suggested a different approach to the quantification of comparative excessiveness.

Justice White's *Furman* opinion expressed concern with the impact of erratic and infrequent death sentences upon the viability of capital punishment as a general deterrent. In Justice White's view, the death penalty could not serve as an effective (and, therefore, constitutional) deterrent unless imposed "with sufficient frequency." Furman v. Georgia, 408 U.S. at 312 (White, J., concurring). Similarly, when concurring in *Gregg*, Justice White asserted that if Georgia juries imposed the death penalty in "a substantial portion" of capital cases involving statutory aggravating circumstances, the sanction would demonstrate its usefulness and, therefore, its constitutionality, 428 U.S. at 222. Implicit in this deterrence-oriented approach, however, is the notion that, if the frequency of death sentences within an identifiable class of murder cases is less than substantial, the constitutional concerns that Justice White expressed in *Furman* would remain unsatisfied. In other words, unless the death penalty is regularly imposed in identifiable classes of cases, its usefulness as a deterrent remains suspect.

This concern with regularity of imposition, which characterizes Justice White's concurring opinions, takes on added force when one also considers the Court's repeated reference to "evenhanded" sentencing in capital cases as a constitutional goal. In a variety of opinions, a number of different justices have identified the absence of evenhandedness as the central defect condemned in Furman v. Georgia. In this respect, Justice White's concern with regularity in the imposition of the death penalty was more consistent with the "evenhandedness" mode of analysis than Justice Stewart's apparent concern with preventing only aberrant death sentences.

The potential tension between Justice Stewart's notion of what constitutes impermissible excessiveness and that implicit in both Justice White's opinions and the "evenhandedness" approach emerges when one considers a case like Eberheart v. State, 232 Ga. 247, 206 S.E.2d 12 (1974), *vacated*, 433 U.S. 917 (1977). In *Eberheart*, the frequency of death sentences among cases deemed "similar" by the Georgia Supreme Court was .50. Certainly, from Justice Stewart's perspective, under these circumstances Eberheart's own death sentence would not be aberrant. But, conceivably, Justice White might not regard a .50 death-sentencing rate as sufficiently regular to make the death penalty in that class of case a viable deterrent. And, certainly, imposing the death penalty in only one out of every two factually similar cases does not satisfy the conventional notion of evenhandedness.

As a result, one can plausibly argue that comparatively excessive death sentences can occur even if the frequency of death sentences among similar cases is substantially greater than .35. So long as that frequency is too low to comply with notions of evenhandedness or regularity—something less than .80, for example—one can contend that imposition of the death penalty in any such case is comparatively excessive.

51. As an experiment, we conducted analyses of artificially constructed pre-*Furman* and post-*Furman* data in which we randomly assigned to cases the same number of death sentences that were actually imposed during each period. To determine the ability of the variables in our file to appear to explain randomly assigned death sentences, we conducted stepwise regressions using more than 150 potentially explanatory variables. In the analysis of the pre-*Furman* data, only 4 of the more than 150 variables showed a statistically significant relationship ($\leq.10$) with the death-sentencing outcome; in the post-*Furman* analysis, 7 variables showed such a relationship. Also, in these analyses the R^2 statistic, a measure of how well the independent

variables explain the sentencing outcomes, was .15 for the pre-*Furman* analysis and .05 for the post-*Furman* analysis. In a logistic multiple-regression analysis involving the variables that best explain the actual death-sentencing results, i.e., the "A" models referred to in app. J in which the outcome variable was randomly distributed, no variables showed a statistically significant relationship with the death-sentencing outcome variables in either the pre- or post-*Furman* periods. Also, in linear-regression analyses of these models using the random dependent variables, the R^2 statistics were .03 and .02, respectively.

52. Although the coefficient of determination, or R^2, will be familiar to many readers, it must be interpreted with great caution in models with dichotomous dependent variables (such as "life or death" sentence, "penalty trial or not") since under such conditions, unlike the continuous case, R^2 has no information-theoretic interpretation. It is more appropriate to use the information-theory based measure of predictability discussed *infra* chap. 5, note 7.

53. R^2 is the ratio of explained variance to total variance. The total variance of a dichotomous variable, such as a life or death sentence, is a function of the rate of occurrence of the adverse outcome. Consequently, R^2 will be influenced by the rate of death sentencing.

54. *See infra* app. A, pp. 441–42.

55. Logistic regression models the logarithm of the odds of a death sentence as an exponential function of regression coefficients; consequently the regression coefficient for a given case characteristic measures the difference in the logarithm of the odds of death for cases with and without the characteristic. For a fuller discussion of the interpretation of logistic-regression coefficients, *see* Gross & Mauro, *Patterns of Death: An Analysis of Racial Disparities in Capital Sentencing and Homicide Victimization*, 37 STAN L. REV. 27, 147–49 (Appendix 3) (1984); Baldus, Pulaski, Woodworth, & Kyle, *Identifying Comparatively Excessive Sentences of Death: A Quantitative Approach*, 33 STAN L. REV. 1, nn. 80 & 71 (Appendix) (1980).

Coefficients in a linear-probability model (linear regression or O.L.S.) estimate average incremental increases in the rate of occurrence of the event being modeled (death sentence or prosecutor seeking a death sentence) for a unit change in the independent variable. For example, suppose that in a linear-regression model for jury decisions a coefficient of .07 is associated with having a female victim. Since "female victim" is coded 0 (no) or 1 (yes), the presence of a female victim corresponds to a unit (one-point) increase in this variable. Consequently, the presence of a female victim, on average, raises the predicted jury death-sentencing rate by .07 (7 percentage points). The situation is slightly different for such multivalued variables as "number of prior convictions for violent personal crimes." If this variable had a regression coefficient of .005, say, then on average the predicted death-sentencing rate increases by .005 for each additional prior conviction.

56. When the results produced interaction terms between race variables and legitimate case characteristics, further calculations were required to estimate the overall race effects. *See, e.g., infra* chap. 6, notes 9, 15, & 16 and accompanying text. In our discrimination analysis in chap. 5, we place less weight on estimates of racial discrimination calculated with the coefficients for the racial variables than on the race effects estimated from the case rankings. The reason is that the validity of an individual regression coefficient for such a variable as the race of the victim depends not only upon the validity of the case ranking produced by the regression, but also on the validity of a variety of other technical assumptions that are discussed in app. A. We do, however,

report the coefficients for illegitimate and suspect variables. And we have the greatest confidence in our findings when both the regression coefficients, for the race of the defendant and the victim, and the disparities estimated with our ranking procedures are comparable.

57. Even if there is no difference in the treatment of two groups, chance factors associated with random effects that are not controlled for in the analysis and that influence the system may produce a disparity in the treatment of two groups, even though in fact they are treated the same. It is a major purpose of statistical tests of significance to indicate the likelihood that disparities observed at given magnitudes could be the product of chance forces such as these, even though there is no difference in the treatment of the two groups involved. This estimated likelihood is quantified with a probability value, e.g., .03. The lower the value, the higher is the "level of statistical significance" of the disparity of interest. Also, the higher the level of statistical significance estimated for a disparity (i.e., the lower the value), the lower the probability that the observed disparity is in fact the product of chance.

58. A principal exception to this rule occurs when the omitted variable that is correlated with both the race and outcome variables is itself highly correlated with a variable that is already controlled for in the analysis. The omission of such a variable has no effect on the magnitude or statistical significance of the estimated racial disparity. *See infra* app. A, text accompanying note 7, and app. B, note 67 and accompanying text, for further discussion of the omitted-variable problem.

59. For example, prosecutors and jurors whose assessments of the relative culpability of an offender are influenced by the race of the victim are in most cases probably quite unaware of the connection between their culpability perceptions and the race of the victim. *See* Nisbett & Bellows, *Verbal Reports About Causal Inferences on Social Judgments: Private Access Versus Public Theories*, 35 J. PERSONALITY & SOCIAL PSYCHOLOGY 613 (1977) (subjects were given a "job application portfolio," which varied five characteristics of the applicant; their reports about the effects of the factors on their judgment were in general highly inaccurate); Nisbett & Wilson, *Telling More Than We Can Know: Verbal Reports on Mental Processes*, 84 PSYCHOLOGICAL REV. 231 (1977) ("Subjects are sometimes (a) unaware of the existence of a stimulus that importantly influenced a response, (b) unaware of the existence of the response, and (c) unaware that the stimulus has affected the response").

CHAPTER FIVE

Arbitrariness and Excessiveness in Georgia's Capital-Sentencing System before and after *Furman*

In this chapter we consider the extent to which the data from the final stages of Georgia's capital-sentencing system provide evidence of randomness, caprice, and excessiveness. We first present the evidence of randomness and excessiveness at the trial-court level of Georgia's capital-sentencing system observed in our Procedural Reform Study data before and after *Furman*. We then consider whether the procedural reforms that Georgia adopted in 1973 explain the differences we observed between the pre- and post-*Furman* periods. Next we explore the likely sources of randomness, caprice, and excessiveness in Georgia's capital-sentencing system.

THE EVIDENCE OF EXCESSIVENESS

Pre-*Furman*

In *Furman v. Georgia*, the infrequency with which juries actually imposed death sentences in death-eligible cases concerned each of the concurring justices.[1] The *Furman* opinions suggest that the justices estimated that the national death-sentencing rate among convicted murderers was less than .20.[2] Our pre-*Furman* data from Georgia indicated an unadjusted death-sentencing rate of .15 (44/294) in cases that resulted in murder convictions after trial, all of whose defendants were death-eligible under Georgia law. This figure is quite consistent with the Court's estimate of the national rate.

Of course, a low death-sentencing rate does not necessarily mean the system is capricious or random. As the minority justices contended in *Furman*, a low death-sentencing rate might result under a highly selective system that only imposes death sentences in the most extreme cases.

For that reason, we used a variety of measures of case culpability and a variety of analytic procedures to assess the degree to which Georgia's pre-*Furman* death-sentencing system was arbitrary or excessive in a comparative sense. The purpose of each analysis was to determine whether those defendants who received sentences of death can be meaningfully distinguished from the many other defendants who received only life sentences.

To illustrate the utility of our measures, we begin by describing the results we might see in systems ranging from a purely random system of the type condemned by the concurring justices in *Furman* to a highly selective system that reserves death sentences for only the most extreme cases. Figure 2 illustrates what we would expect to see in a purely random system when analyzed with our first measure of arbitrariness, which compares the distributions of life- and death-sentence cases in terms of overall culpability as determined by our post-*Furman* regression-based index. Figure 2 shows the results produced with such an analysis of our post-*Furman* sample of 483 death-eligible cases after the 112 death sentences were assigned by lot.[3] The vertical axis indicates the culpability level of the cases; the life-sentence cases are distributed on the left and the randomly assigned death-sentence cases are distributed on

Figure 2. Distribution of Life- and Death-Sentence Cases on Culpability Index in a Hypothetical Random Death-Sentencing System[1]

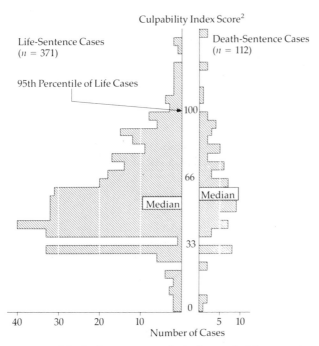

1. Ninety-six percent of the death-sentence cases have a lower culpability score than the culpability score of the 95th-percentile life-sentence case.
2. The underlying index is OVERALLC, *infra* app. J, part 1, which is described *supra* chap. 4, note 38 and accompanying text.

the right. The resulting distributions of the life- and death-sentence cases on the culpability index are quite similar, with only a small gap separating the median life- and the median death-sentence cases. A measure of the lack of selectivity of a sentencing system is the proportion of death cases that are less aggravated than "normal" life cases. We define "normal" life cases as those between the 5th and 95th percentiles; consequently, our measure of lack of selectivity is the proportion of death cases with culpability scores below the 95th percentile of the life-sentence cases. As expected, in this purely random system 96 percent of the death-sentence cases (108/112) have culpability scores lower than the 95th percentile of the culpability scores of the life-sentence cases.

By contrast, Figure 3 depicts the results to be expected of a rational, nearly perfectly selective system. There is no death-sentence case with a culpability

Figure 3. Distribution of Life- and Death-Sentence Cases on Culpability Index in a Hypothetical Selective Death-Sentencing System[1]

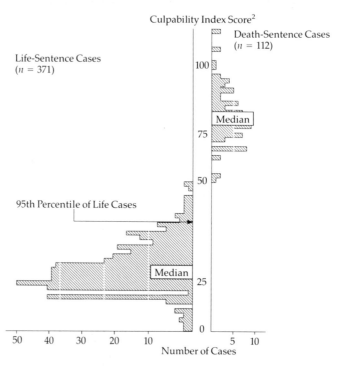

1. No death-sentence cases have a culpability score lower than the culpability score of the 95th-percentile life-sentence case.
2. The underlying index is OVERALLC, *infra* app. J, part 1, which is described *supra* chap. 4, note 38 and accompanying text.

score less than the 95th percentile of life-sentence cases. Indeed, only a single life-sentence case overlaps the cohort of death-sentence cases. As a result, a very large gap exists between the median culpability scores of the life- and death-sentence cases.

Figure 4 presents the actual distribution of life- and death-sentence cases from our pre-*Furman* data. The substantial overlap between the life- and death-sentence cases on the culpability index indicates a less than perfectly selective system. Indeed, the culpability scores of 61 percent of the death-sentence cases are at or below the equivalent score of the life-sentence case at the 95th percentile of the life-sentence cases. Although this measure suggests that Georgia's pre-*Furman* system was far from random, the sentencing results approximate the random model displayed in Figure 2 much more closely than they do the rational, highly selective model.

Our second measure of excessiveness scrutinizes the numbers and propor-

Figure 4. Distribution of Life- and Death-Sentence Cases on Culpability Index (Pre-*Furman*)[1]

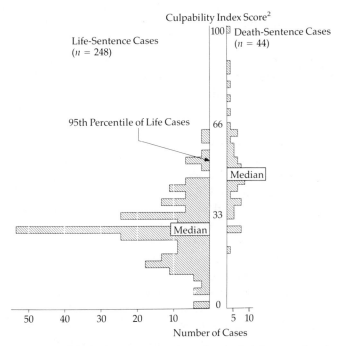

1. Sixty-one percent of the death-sentence cases have a lower culpability score than the culpability score of the 95th-percentile life-sentence case.
2. The index is PREFURMC, *infra* app. J, part 4, which is described *supra* chap. 4, note 38 and accompanying text.

tions of death sentences imposed among cases of comparable culpability that appear to be either excessive or evenhanded in a comparative sense. We first divided the cases into subgroups with similar culpability levels and calculated the death-sentencing rate for each subgroup; we then computed the proportion of all the death sentences imposed that appeared in subgroups of cases for which the death-sentencing rate was either quite high or quite low. For this purpose we considered death sentences to be presumptively evenhanded if they occurred in subgroups of cases with death-sentencing rates of .80 or higher. Conversely, death sentences in subgroups with a death-sentencing rate below .35 were characterized as presumptively excessive in a comparative sense.[4]

As noted earlier, in a highly selective system death sentences would occur only in subgroups of comparably culpable cases with very high death-sentencing rates. As a result, no death sentence would be excessive in a comparative sense, and the legitimate characteristics of the subgroups of cases with high death-sentencing rates would meaningfully distinguish them from the other subgroups of cases for which life sentences were the norm. By contrast, a purely random sentencing system would produce subgroups of "similar" cases, and the death-sentencing rates for each would approximate the average rate for all cases. Consequently, the factual differences between the various subgroups would not meaningfully distinguish those defendants who received death sentences from the others who did not. Moreover, with an overall death-sentencing rate among these factually indistinguishable cases of under .35, every death sentence imposed would be presumptively excessive, as we define that concept.

Table 5 presents this sort of comparative-excessiveness analysis of Georgia's pre-*Furman* system. The six rows in the first part of the table sort the cases into six subgroups according to their culpability scores, using the index employed for Figure 3. Column B indicates the death-sentencing rate for each subgroup. A comparison of these rates again indicates that Georgia's pre-*Furman* sentencing system was not purely random; the death-sentencing rates are generally higher for the more culpable subgroups of cases. On the other hand, one cannot say Georgia's pre-*Furman* system was particularly selective, since only a handful of death sentences (those in culpability level 6) occurred in subgroups of cases with very high death-sentencing rates. In fact, as shown in the second part of the table, over 43 percent (19/44) of the pre-*Furman* death sentences appear to be comparatively excessive. Only the ten death-sentence cases in row six, which constitute 23 percent (10/44) of all the pre-*Furman* cases, appear to be presumptively evenhanded.

Table 6 presents thumbnail sketches of a sample of the death-sentence cases that appear to be either excessive or evenhanded under this analysis. Consider,

Table 5. Death-Sentencing Rates, Controlling for Case Culpability Level Measured with a Regression-Based Index (Pre-*Furman*)

A. Case Culpability Level from 1 (low) to 6 (high)[1]	B. Death-Sentence Rate
1	.01 (1/110)
2	.08 (8/95)
3	.23 (10/43)
4	.53 (8/15)
5	.35 (7/20)
6	1.00 (10/10)

Proportion and Number of Death-Sentence Cases for Which the Death-Sentence Frequency in Similar Cases Was:

A. Less than .35	.43 (19/44)
B. .80 or more	.23 (10/44)

1. The index is PREFURMC, *infra* app. J, part 4, which is described *supra* chap. 4, note 38 and accompanying text.

for example, defendant Q72 (at level 5), who, in fact, was the defendant in *Furman v. Georgia*. Our data suggest that in pre-*Furman* Georgia, convicted murderers whose overall culpability approximated that of *Furman* received death sentences only one-third of the time. This finding supports Justice White's intuitive judgment that *Furman*'s crime seemed no more serious than hundreds of other cases he had reviewed that had resulted only in prison sentences.[5] Moreover, Justice White's characterization of Furman's death sentence as excessive contributed to our decision to classify death-sentence cases for which the death-sentencing rate among similarly situated defendants was less than .35 as presumptively excessive.

Our final estimate of the degree of comparative excessiveness in the pre-*Furman* system employs an analysis of death-sentencing rates among sixty pre-*Furman* armed-robbery–murder cases, which we subdivided using a qualitative measure of case culpability. As noted earlier, this qualitative measure is based upon an intuitive, commonsense assessment of the aggravating and mitigating circumstances of the armed-robbery–murder cases in our sample. For our pre-*Furman* data, this procedure produced the three subgroups of cases depicted in Table 7. These results indicate a difference of 45 percentage points between the death-sentencing rates in the most and least aggravated cases, which again demonstrates that the system was not completely random. Nevertheless, even among the most aggravated cases, the death-sentencing rate was only .45. The results in the second part of Table 7 show that no death sentence imposed in this sample of pre-*Furman* armed-

Table 6. Summaries of Selected Pre-*Furman* Cases in Which Death Sentences Imposed Appear Presumptively Excessive When Compared with the Sentences Imposed in Cases with Similarly Situated Defendants

Level 1 (from Table 5)	20-year-old male defendant and coperpetrator in liquor store. Coperpetrator pointed gun at store manager, the male victim, who then pulled out a gun and pointed it at coperpetrator. Five or six shots were exchanged and victim fell. Defendant ran from the scene, victim fired two more shots. Victim died en route to hospital. No criminal record. Defendant not trigger. One eyewitness. (B07)
Level 2	The 23-year-old male defendant shot the victim, his wife, two times with a rifle after an argument. Several prior convictions. (B32) The 19-year-old male defendant and a coperpetrator, dressed as females, attempted to rob a cabdriver, the victim. The victim was shot three times in the neck. Some dispute as to who was trigger. (C17)
Level 3	Defendant, 23-year-old male, and two coperpetrators shot victim, 22-year-old male with polio, during an armed robbery. Victim shot once, then another time as he was lying on floor. Defendant was trigger. Two witnesses, one struck on head with gun by a coperpetrator. (I44) The 33-year-old male defendant burglarized the victim's home. Victim, a female who had previously employed the defendant as a handyman, returned home as burglary was in progress. Defendant choked victim until she "went limp," then placed victim in bathtub in attempt to make it appear that she had drowned. Coroner's report stated victim died of drowning. (Q84)
Level 4	The 20-year-old male defendant and a coperpetrator attempted to rob the victim, a 61-year-old gas-station attendant. Victim was shot five times. The defendant was AWOL at the time. Defendant attempted robbery and shot at (but did not kill) another person two weeks later. (71) 21-year-old male defendant robbed victim, semi-invalid, 72-year-old male operator of grocery store/service station. Defendant then stabbed victim several times in the stomach and chest and beat victim with his pistol. Victim died in hospital after giving information about defendant (and identifying defendant as brother-in-law of someone known to victim) to police. (Q87)
Level 5	18-year-old defendant discovered by male victim while burglarizing victim's home. Victim shot in chest. Defendant was drunk. Ten prior convictions for burglary. Prior prison term. (Q72) 23-year-old defendant, on escape, stole car and burglarized lumber company of $4,000. Victim, a police officer investigating the burglary, was shot several times. Five prior convictions, other violent crimes. (Q85)

Table 7. Death-Sentencing Rates Among Pre-*Furman* Armed-Robbery Cases, Controlling for Culpability Measures with an *a Priori* Measure that Weighs Aggravating and Mitigating Circumstances

A. Case Culpability Level from 1 (low) to 3 (high)[1]	B. Death-Sentence Rate
1 (Category I)	.00 (0/16)
2 (Category II)	.08 (2/24)
3 (Category III)	.45 (9/20)
All cases	.18 (11/60)

Proportion and Number of Death-Sentence Cases for Which the Death-Sentencing Frequency in Similar Cases Was:

A. Less than .35	.18 (2/11)
B. .80 or more	.00 (0/11)

1. *See supra* chap. 4, note 21 and accompanying text, for a description of the measure underlying this table.

robbery–murder cases appears to be comparatively evenhanded. One possible interpretation is that the *a priori* measure used to classify the cases in Table 7 does not adequately distinguish between cases of high and low culpability.

Our next measure of arbitrariness examines the extent to which the legitimate variables in our data set explained statistically why particular defendants received life or death sentences. Specifically, we determined the proportion of the life- and death-sentence cases that our best-fitting logistic multiple-regression model correctly predicted, using only legitimate case characteristics. In a random system legitimate case characteristics would explain only a small proportion of the sentences actually imposed; that is exactly what we observed when, as noted earlier, we modeled an artificially generated system in which life and death sentences were randomly distributed without regard to case culpability. In a rational, highly selective system, by contrast, legitimate case characteristics would explain virtually all of the sentences imposed. What we actually found when we subjected our pre-*Furman* data to this analysis was that, prior to 1973, Georgia's death-sentencing system exhibited a high level of unpredictability. Our best-fitting model, using only legitimate case characteristics, could correctly predict 97 percent of the life-sentence cases but only 43 percent of the death-sentence cases.[6]

Another common measure of predictability in a decision-making system is the R^2 statistic generated by a multiple-regression analysis. Although the measure is not entirely appropriate for our study (because the "outcome" or "dependent" variable allows only a "yes" or "no" answer), it has the virtue of familiarity to many readers. The R^2 statistic indicates the proportion of variation in sentencing outcomes explained by the legitimate case characteristics. The adjusted R^2 for our best-fitting model was .25, which is consistent with the results commonly obtained in other sentencing studies. Because our data account for a very large number of legitimate case characteristics, however, the resulting R^2 statistic should be quite high if Georgia's pre-*Furman* death-sentencing system had functioned rationally and consistently. We, therefore, consider the relatively low R^2 that we actually obtained to further reflect the high degree of arbitrariness in the pre-*Furman* system.[7]

Summary

Our statistical analysis of Georgia's pre-*Furman* sentencing patterns confirms the largely intuitive judgments of the five concurring justices in *Furman v. Georgia*: the appellant Furman's death sentence was most probably excessive. Our data suggest no meaningful way to distinguish Furman from the many other defendants who received only life sentences.

However, our data also suggest that, at least as to Georgia, none of the justices was completely correct in characterizing or making assumptions about the death-sentencing systems operating in the United States prior to *Furman*. Justices correctly observed that death sentences occurred in only a small proportion of the cases that resulted in a murder conviction, all of which became death-eligible under Georgia law. That system was clearly not random, however, since legitimate case characteristics do explain the distribution of life and death sentences to a much greater degree than one would find in a truly random system. In short, Justice Stewart's metaphor of lightning striking, although memorable, was off the mark, both with respect to the frequency with which death sentences were imposed and the random quality of their distribution.

On the other hand, the contention of the *Furman* dissenters that the low death-sentencing rate reflected the operation of a rational and highly selective system was also clearly wrong. Even our most conservative measure classifies nearly one-half of the death sentences imposed as presumptively excessive.[8] Similarly, even in the most favorable light, fewer than one-quarter of the death sentences imposed appear to be evenhanded. Clearly, then, the random qualities of Georgia's pre-*Furman* sentencing system outweighed its selective capacity.

Post-*Furman*

Among all the post-*Furman* cases in our study that resulted in jury-trial convictions for murder, the unadjusted death-sentencing rate was .19 (112/606). This is up from .15 among pre-*Furman* cases. This statistic is somewhat misleading, however. Under Georgia's revised procedures, evidence of at least one statutorily designated aggravating circumstance was also necessary in order to make a defendant convicted of murder a statutory candidate for the death penalty. This additional requirement insulated more than one hundred murder defendants from death eligibility. Among those post-*Furman* defendants who were death-eligible, the overall death-sentencing rate was .23 (112/483), an 8-percentage-point increase over the pre-*Furman* rate of .15 among the murder cases in our sample, all of whom were death-eligible.

This 8-percentage-point increase represents an increase of 53 percent over the comparable pre-*Furman* death-sentencing rate, which appears quite substantial. However, in terms of the increased likelihood that the average defendant would receive a death sentence, the eight-point increase was really quite modest. Moreover, a death-sentencing rate of only .23 for all death-eligible defendants suggests that the presence of a statutory aggravating factor in a case did not, in and of itself, meaningfully distinguish those defendants who received death sentences from the larger groups of defendants who did not. Table 8 illustrates this point. It depicts the death-sentencing rates among defendants who were death-eligible under each of Georgia's statutorily designated aggravating factors. In only one narrow category of cases (B9) does the death-sentencing rate exceed .50. For the two statutory categories that accounted for most of the death sentences imposed (B2 and B7), the death-sentencing rate is well below .50.

By contrast, the presence of multiple statutory aggravating circumstances in a case is strongly associated with the prospect of receiving a death sentence. Indeed, of the more than 150 variables in our PRS data set, the number of

Table 8. Death-Sentencing Rates for Death-Eligible Defendants Under Each of Georgia's Statutory Aggravating Factors (Post-*Furman*)[1]

A. Georgia Statutory Aggravating Factors	B. Death-Sentencing Rate
1. Prior capital record (B1)	.34 (14/41)
2. Enumerated contemporaneous offense (B2)	.37 (99/271)
3. Risk of death to two or more in public (B3)	.22 (21/96)
4. Money/value motive (B4)	.37 (78/212)
5. Victim judicial officer, D.A. (B5)	NC[a]
6. Murder for hire (B6)	.20 (4/20)
7. Murder vile, horrible, or inhuman (B7)	.30 (93/308)
8. Victim police- or fireperson (B8)	.35 (6/17)
9. Defendant prisoner or escapee (B9)	.56 (10/18)
10. Killing to avoid/stop arrest (B10)	.33 (41/125)

1. This measure refers to the presence of a statutory aggravating factor in a case regardless of whether it was found by the jury or whether there was a penalty trial in the case.
a. NC means no cases.

statutory aggravating circumstances present played by far the major role in distinguishing between those defendants who received a death sentence and those who did not.[9] The data in Table 9 illustrate the strong association between the number of aggravating circumstances and the probability of receiving a death sentence. Specifically, the risk of a death sentence increases steadily and substantially as the number of statutory factors in the case increases. Yet, even among the most aggravated cases, the death-sentencing rate was only .63. Thus, if cases were matched only by statutory aggravating factors, the post-*Furman* system would appear to be at least as random as the pre-*Furman* system viewed most favorably (compare Tables 5 and 9). More than half (.57) of the death sentences imposed under the revised procedures were presumptively excessive, compared to .43 for the pre-*Furman* period. Perhaps even more significantly, there would be no subcategory of cases, defined by a specific statutory aggravating circumstance, for which the death-sentencing rate equalled our benchmark for presumptive evenhandedness, a rate of .80. These data clearly suggest that statutory aggravating circumstances increased the consistency of the post-*Furman* system but that they alone fell far short of producing the consistency contemplated by the Supreme Court in *Gregg*.

However, this analysis concerns only the impact of statutorily designated aggravating circumstances on Georgia's post-*Furman* sentencing results. Our regression-based culpability indexes demonstrate that a variety of nonstatutory aggravating and mitigating factors did play an important role in the post-*Furman* system. Specifically, our "overall culpability" index ranks the

Table 9. Death-Sentencing Rates, Controlling for the Number of Georgia Statutory Aggravating Factors Present (Post-*Furman*)[1]

A. Number of Statutory Aggravating Factors Present	B. Death-Sentence Rate
1	.04 (6/152)
2	.13 (17/130)
3	.34 (41/119)
4	.58 (38/66)
5 and 6	.63 (10/16)
All cases	.23 (112/483)

Number and Proportion of Death-Sentence Cases for Which the Death-Sentencing Frequency in Similar Cases Was:

A. Less than .35	.57 (64/112)
B. .80 or more	.00 (0/112)

1. This measure refers to the number of statutory aggravating factors in the case regardless of whether they were found by the jury or whether there was a penalty trial in the case.

cases according to the presence or absence of seventeen legitimate case characteristics and combinations thereof that share a statistically significant relationship with the sentences imposed.[10]

Using this index, we compared the culpability distributions of the post-*Furman* life- and death-sentence cases that had at least one aggravating circumstance present. Figure 5 reveals a considerable overlap of the distribution of life- and death-sentence cases, indicating that the system is not highly selective. Nevertheless, in comparison to Figure 4, the comparable figure for the pre-*Furman* period, there is more selectivity in the post-*Furman* system. For example, only 29 percent of the post-*Furman* death-sentence cases possessed culpability scores equal to or less than the culpability score of the 95th percentile life-sentence case, a decline from the comparable pre-*Furman* figure of 61 percent.

Figure 5. Distribution of Life- and Death-Sentence Cases on Culpability Index (Post-*Furman*)[1]

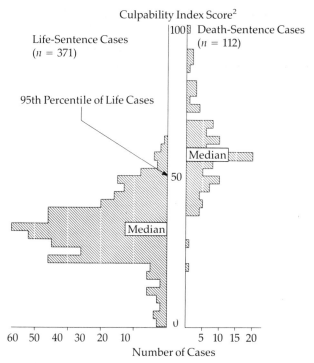

1. Twenty-nine percent of the death-sentence cases have a lower culpability score than the culpability score of the 95th-percentile life-sentence case. The death-sentence cases include twelve cases in which two death sentences were imposed.
2. The index is described *infra* app. J, part 1, and *supra* chap. 4, note 38 and accompanying text.

Table 10 presents further evidence of increased selectivity under Georgia's post-*Furman* death-sentencing system. Column B indicates the death-sentencing rate for six groups of cases with similar scores on the regression-based culpability index used for Figure 5. Only 13 percent of the post-*Furman* death sentences appear in categories of cases with death-sentencing rates of less than .35, and more than half (.51) of the post-*Furman* death sentences occurred in cases for which the death-sentencing rate among similar cases exceeds .80.

The resulting proportion of presumptively excessive sentences has dropped from .43 (19/44) pre-*Furman* to .13 (15/112) post-*Furman*, and the proportion of evenhanded sentences has grown from .23 (10/44) pre-*Furman* to .51 (57/112) post-*Furman*. This is evidence of increased selectivity. Nevertheless, when one considers all the post-*Furman* death sentences, one observes that nearly one-half (55/112) fall within groups of similar cases in which death sentences did not regularly occur.

Table 11 presents thumbnail sketches of a sample of the death-sentence defendants included in levels 1 through 3 of Table 10. We consider the fifteen death sentences at levels 1 and 2 to be presumptively excessive, while those at levels 3 and 4 fall in a midrange between the presumptively excessive and the presumptively evenhanded cases. Included in the level 3 cases, with a death-sentencing rate of .38, is defendant Z15, whose death sentence the United

Table 10. Death-Sentencing Rates, Controlling for Case Culpability Level (Post-*Furman* Georgia)

A. Case Culpability Level from 1 (low) to 6 (high)[1]	B. Death-Sentence Rate
1	.02 (6/276)
2	.14 (9/65)
3	.38 (18/47)
4	.65 (22/34)
5	.85 (23/27)
6	1.00 (34/34)
All cases	.23 (112/483)

Number and Proportion of Death-Sentence Cases for Which the Death-Sentencing Frequency in Similar Cases Was:

A. Less than .35	.13 (15/112)
B. .80 or more	.51 (57/112)

1. This index and scale are described *supra* chap. 4, note 38 and accompanying text, and *infra* app. J (OVERALLC AND CSCALC).

Table 11. Summaries of Selected Post-*Furman* Cases in Which the Death Sentences Imposed Appear Presumptively Excessive When Compared with the Sentences Imposed in Cases with Similarly Situated Defendants

Level 1 (from Table 10)	Defendant, 22-year-old male, and coperpetrator lived with male victim, defendant's cousin. Defendant and coperpetrator took out insurance policy (changed beneficiary from victim's father to defendant) on victim two weeks before shooting victim three times in head. Primary witness heard defendant and coperpetrator discuss killing victim for insurance money. Unclear if defendant was trigger. Defendant led police to murder weapon. (515)
	20-year-old female defendant and coperpetrator (husband of victim) planned to murder victim. Coperpetrator established alibi while defendant went to victim's home and shot victim three times, twice in face. Coperpetrator admitted crime, defendant led police to murder weapon. (052)
	Defendant, 15-year-old male, and coperpetrator robbed store. Victim, 19-year-old male cashier, shot in chest. Defendant identified by witness as one of the two leaving store with gun in hand. No proof defendant was trigger. (953)
Level 2	Defendant had been fired from job (and had sworn to get revenge) one week before two victims (male office manager and female secretary) were killed with large sword or machete. Female victim nearly decapitated. (250)
	28-year-old defendant and coperpetrator (primary witness) planned to rob victim's liquor store. Coperpetrator remained in car while defendant, in stocking mask and hat, entered store. Victim shot once, in the eye. Victim's wife and sister made to lie on floor while defendant took $3,100 and fled. Defendant confessed after arrest. (893)
	22-year-old male defendant, after drinking and taking drugs, broke into victim's apartment. Victim was a 78-year-old female who had, on occasion, hired defendant to do repair work. Defendant knocked victim unconscious, then carried victim to bedroom, where victim was raped, assaulted, and sodomized. Defendant also raped victim with a plastic bottle. Cause of victim's death ruled as suffocation or heart attack. Defendant claimed victim fell from chair in fright and was knocked unconscious, that he carried her into bedroom but could not perform rape and left, and that someone else later came in and assaulted, raped, and sodomized victim. (D27)
Level 3	Male defendant, with long history of marital problems (possibly alcohol related), drove to his mother-in-law's home and shot his wife (victim #1) and his mother-in-law (victim #2) as they sat playing cards. Defendant's wife had told defendant she was leaving him. Defendant's (and victim #1's) 11-year-old daughter was witness to the crime. Defendant called police, confessed, and waited for police to arrive. Defendant admitted that he had been considering committing that crime for eight years and "would do it again." (Z15)

(continued)

Table 11. *(Continued)*

Male defendant, with prior history of assault, attacked 62-year-old female victim, a stranger, while she was shopping. Victim was stabbed four times in the chest. Some indication that defendant may have been insane. (426)

The male defendant and three coperpetrators robbed small store where male victim worked. Defendant struck victim in head with gun, then shot victim in temple. No prior criminal record. (497)

States Supreme Court vacated in *Godfrey v. Georgia* because it was indistinguishable from many other cases that did not result in death sentences. By contrast, the case of the defendant in *Gregg v. Georgia* appears at level 4 of table 10, for which the death-sentencing rate among similar cases is .65. Given the nature of Troy Gregg's crime—the deliberate murder of two victims—no member of the Supreme Court even suggested that his death sentence might be comparatively excessive. On the contrary, both the plurality and the concurring justices appear to have assumed that death would be the regular sentence in such cases.[11] That the observed death-sentencing rate for the cases classified as similar to Gregg's by our regression-based index is only .65 suggests the existence of some variance between the Supreme Court's expectations in 1976 and the actual operation of Georgia's death-sentencing system.

A similar impression of Georgia's post-*Furman* system emerges from a comparative-excessiveness analysis conducted using the three-dimensional classification system developed by Arnold Barnett.[12] Figure 6 presents the distribution of the post-*Furman* cases among the eighteen categories generated by this classification system. Each cell indicates the number of cases and the number and proportion of death-sentence cases, as well as the characteristics of the cases in terms of the three relevant dimensions. For example, the cell to the extreme right includes the seven cases with the most aggravated set of characteristics (2,1,2), that is, the deliberate, vile killing of a stranger; 86 percent (6/7) of these cases resulted in death sentences.

The distribution of death-sentence rates in Figure 6 resembles that shown in Table 10 (founded on our regression-based culpability index) in at least two respects. First, the overall pattern of rates is comparable. For a small proportion of the cases the death-sentencing rates are quite high; for a very large proportion of the cases the death-sentencing rate is under .05. There is also a group of cases in the mid-aggravation range, with death-sentencing rates between .09 and .80. Second, and more striking, the proportion of presumptively evenhanded death sentences suggested by the two measures is almost identical—.58 (65/112) in the Barnett analysis and .51 (57/112) in our anal-

Figure 6. Death-Sentencing Rates among Subgroups of Death-Eligible Cases Defined by Three Barnett Dimensions (Post-*Furman* Georgia)[1]

0	1	2	3	4	5
	.0 (0/1) (0,1,0)	.05 (1/22) (0,0,2)	.09 (1/11) (2,0,1)		
.0 (0/3) (0,0,0)	.03 (1/31) (1,0,0)	.0 (0/9) (1,1,0)	.25 (15/59) (1,1,1)	.81 (59/73) (1,1,2)	.86 (6/7) (2,1,2)
	.0 (0/42) (0,0,1)	.02 (1/41) (0,1,1)	.30 (6/20) (0,1,2)	.56 (10/18) (2,0,2)	
		.01 (1/106) (1,0,1)	.28 (11/39) (1,0,2)		
		.0 (0/1) (2,0,0)			

Sum of Scores for the Three Barnett Dimensions

0	1	2	3	4	5

Least Aggravated ──────────────────────────────────────→ Most Aggravated

1. The three numbers in parentheses at the foot of each cell indicate the coding for Barnett's three dimensions: (a) certainty that killing was deliberate (0 = low, 1 = medium, 2 = high); (b) relationship between defendant and victim (0 = family/friend, 1 = stranger); and (c) vileness of the killing (0 = element of self-defense, 1 = neither self-defense nor vile, 2 = vile killing). The death-sentencing rate and the number of cases (death cases/all cases) are in the center of each cell. There were no cases in cells (2,1,0) and (2,1,1). The figure includes twelve cases in which two death sentences were imposed. *See supra* chap. 4, note 29 and accompanying text, for a further explanation of the classification system used for this figure.

ysis. By contrast, the Barnett analysis identifies a higher proportion of presumptively excessive sentences, .33 (37/113), than the .13 (15/113) for cases matched by our regression-based case culpability index.

The Barnett analysis also supports the Court's conclusion in *Godfrey v. Georgia* that the death sentence in that case was comparatively excessive. Barnett's analysis placed Godfrey in the cell coded (1,0,2), for which the death-sentencing rate among forty-two similar cases was .26. Interestingly, Barnett also places the defendant in *Gregg v. Georgia* in the same cell. According to the Barnett analysis, what distinguishes cases like *Gregg* and *Godfrey* from those for which death is the regular sentence is the existence of a prior relationship between the defendant and the victim. If the victims in *Godfrey* or *Gregg* had been total strangers, Barnett's analysis suggests that the applicable death-sentencing probability would have been approximately .81 (59/73).[13]

Table 12 presents the results of an excessiveness analysis of post-*Furman* armed-robbery—murder cases, employing our qualitative measure of case culpability that weighs aggravating and mitigating circumstances. Thumbnail sketches indicating the sentencing outcome for each of the cases in Table 12 appear in Appendix G. Table 12 presents a much less favorable picture of the post-*Furman* sentencing system than those just discussed, which used empirical measures of relative case culpability. Except among the most and the least extreme cases, for which the death-sentencing rates are .07 and .85 respectively, increasing death-sentencing rates rise far less steeply with culpability levels. As a consequence, the proportion of presumptively evenhanded death sentences calculated from column C is low, .15 (11/71), and the proportion of presumptively excessive death sentences suggested by this analysis is also not particularly large, .24 (17/71). Thus, Table 12 provides no assurance that death sentences are imposed evenhandedly among this most important subgroup of homicide cases, which accounts for 63 percent (71/112) of all the death sentences imposed in post-*Furman* Georgia (although this may be because of the inability of this intuitive culpability index to identify highly aggravated cases). Finally, we note that this analysis also puts Troy Gregg in the midrange of cases, for which death sentences are neither clearly excessive nor clearly

Table 12. Death-Sentencing Rates among Subgroups of Georgia Armed-Robbery—Murder Cases Defined with an *a Priori* Weighting Measure of Case Culpability[1]

A. Case Culpability Level, from I (low) to V (high)	B. Case Subgroups	C. Death-Sentencing Rate
I	1	.07 (1/14)
II	2	.33 (3/9)
III	3	.11 (2/19)
	4	.20 (4/20)
IV	5	.09 (3/33)
	6	.59 (20/34)
	7	.68 (23/34)
V	8	.33 (4/12)
	9	.85 (11/13)
All cases		.38 (71/188)

Proportion and Number of Death-Sentence Cases for Which the Death-Sentence Frequency in Similar Cases Was:

A. Less than .35	.14 (10/71)	.24 (17/71)
B. .80 or more	.00 (0/71)	.15 (11/71)

1. *See supra* chap. 4, note 21 and accompanying text, for a description of this index.

evenhanded. Specifically, his case falls in case subgroup 7, which has a death-sentencing rate of .68 (23/34).

Our final measure of consistency in the post-*Furman* period is the R^2 statistic generated by the least-squares multiple-regression analysis. The adjusted R^2 for our best-fitting model of the post-*Furman* data was .50, which is twice the comparable statistic for the pre-*Furman* period.[14]

Summary

Our comparison of the sentencing patterns in the trial stages of Georgia's pre- and post-*Furman* death-sentencing systems permits four observations. First, in both the pre- and post-*Furman* periods, the number of death sentences imposed was substantially lower than that authorized by law. The behavior of both prosecutors and juries reflects much less enthusiasm for capital punishment in practice than the theoretical support for it expressed in public opinion polls and in broad death-sentencing statutes of the type found in Georgia law.[15]

Second, in contrast to the sentences imposed during the pre-*Furman* era, the post-*Furman* system was more consistent with respect to the cases that resulted in murder trials.[16] The degree of improvement depends, however, upon which measure of case culpability one uses to select groups of similar cases. From the perspective of the largely intuitive measure that we used to rank pre- and post-*Furman* armed-robbery–murder cases, there is a sharp decline in the percentage of clearly excessive sentences, from 100 percent to 24 percent. By this measure, however, there was only a slight increase in the proportion of presumptively evenhanded death sentences (from 0 percent to 15 percent). By contrast, when we evaluated the pre- and post-*Furman* systems using empirical measures of case culpability, we found a sharp decline in the proportion of presumptively excessive sentences (from 43 percent to 13 percent) and a substantial increase in the proportion of presumptively evenhanded sentences (from 23 percent to 51 percent).

The third observation is that the statutorily designated aggravating circumstances in Georgia's post-*Furman* law do not serve in practice to distinguish murder cases in which death sentences are routinely imposed from those that normally result in a life sentence. This outcome is not surprising if one accepts the somewhat primitive model of how the Georgia system should function espoused by the Georgia Supreme Court and, perhaps, by the United States Supreme Court in *Zant v. Stephens*.[17] It is, however, contrary to the expectations that the United States Supreme Court expressed in the earlier case of *Gregg v. Georgia*.

The fourth observation is that, under Georgia's post-*Furman* procedures, prosecutors and juries do not reserve the death penalty for only the most extreme cases. From 15 percent to 30 percent of the death sentences imposed appear to be presumptively excessive as we define that term, and nearly one-half of all of Georgia's post-*Furman* death sentences show some evidence of excessiveness.

We want to emphasize, however, that our findings provide no basis for assessing the consistency of Georgia's entire capital-charging-and-sentencing system, either before or after *Furman*. The PRS is limited to an analysis of defendants convicted of murder at trial. As a result, our findings do not reflect the impact of pretrial prosecutorial charging and plea-bargaining decisions that may have enabled highly culpable offenders to avoid the risk of a death sentence.[18] For this reason, the levels of excessiveness we report for both the pre- and post-*Furman* periods probably understate the level of excessiveness one would observe in the system as a whole.[19]

POSSIBLE EXPLANATIONS FOR THE DECLINE OF COMPARATIVE EXCESSIVENESS IN THE POST-*FURMAN* PERIOD IN GEORGIA

Our observation that the proportion of presumptively excessive death sentences imposed in Georgia declined after *Furman v. Georgia* raises an obvious question: to what extent can one properly attribute that decline to the procedural reforms that Georgia adopted in response to the *Furman* decision? Those reforms limited death sentencing to ten statutorily defined categories of cases, facilitated the introduction of additional information at the penalty trial, expanded the instructions given to sentencing juries, and required the jury to make specific factual findings whenever it imposed a death sentence.[20]

Because the purpose of these procedural changes was to reduce the risk of excessive or arbitrary death sentences, the decline in the observed level of excessiveness suggests that they worked. However, other factors may have been responsible for that decline. The first rival hypothesis is that the increased level of consistency that we observe in the post-*Furman* period is an artifact of altered record-keeping practices in the post-*Furman* period. *Furman* suggested that a minimal level of consistency would thereafter be required and that capital-sentencing systems may be subject to increasing scrutiny by the federal courts. Moreover, Georgia's 1973 proportionality-review statute mandated state-court oversight of Georgia's death-sentence system to promote evenhandedness. These developments could reasonably have led to heightened post-*Furman* scrutiny and documentation of the circumstances of the cases that were related to the statutory aggravating circumstances enumerated in Georgia's post-*Furman* death-sentencing statute. Because the parole board and state-court records from which we obtained both our pre- and post-*Furman* data would reflect the effects of any changes in post-*Furman* record-keeping practices, a comparison of the results of our pre- and post-*Furman* analyses could suggest a greater post-*Furman* improvement in both consistency and the number of comparatively excessive death sentences than actually occurred. As we note below, for example, the presence or absence of the post-*Furman* statutory aggravating factors, which we specified in both the pre- and post-*Furman* cases, have more than twice the statistical explanatory power (for predicting who will receive a death sentence) in the post-*Furman* cases than they do in the pre-*Furman* cases. The question is whether this increased predictive power reflects a greater influence of the statutory aggravating factors post-*Furman* or simply greater information on those factors.

We tested the record-keeping hypothesis in two ways. First, we compared the degree to which variables for important legitimate case characteristics were coded "unknown" in the pre-*Furman* and post-*Furman* periods. The results of this analysis were inconclusive because, for some variables, the proportion of missing information was slightly larger pre-*Furman* while, for others, the post-*Furman* results showed slightly more missing information. In our second test, we focused on the post-*Furman* statutory aggravating circumstances and compared their distribution in the pre- and post-*Furman* cases. Here we found some weak support for the record-keeping hypothesis. Specifically, in the post-*Furman* period, a slightly higher but not statistically significant proportion of the cases that resulted in a murder-trial conviction had one or more post-*Furman* statutory aggravating factors present than was the case pre-*Furman* (.72 pre- versus .78 post-*Furman*); among the cases deemed death-eligible in both periods, the average number of statutory aggravating circumstances was virtually identical.[21]

Because the increase in the number of statutory aggravating factors, including those relating to the wanton/vile statutory aggravating circumstances before and after *Furman*, is small, it is distinctly possible that the increased level of aggravation among the post-*Furman* cases correctly mirrors an upward trend in the aggravation level of homicides generally. For example, we would expect to see what we did see if the aggravation level of homicides generally were higher in the post-*Furman* period. Since this possibility is plausible and we have no basis for dismissing it, we are not inclined to attribute a significant proportion of the post-*Furman* increases in consistency that we observe to changes in record-keeping practices. Our only caution about the validity of this interpretation is that the increase in the aggravation level of the cases was not uniform across the cases. (The largest increase in the number of statutory aggravating circumstances occurred in the black-defendant/white-victim cases, a point we discuss further in chapter 6.) To the extent that disparate post-*Furman* record-keeping practices may have enhanced the presence of statutory aggravating circumstances in this subgroup of cases, many of which are highly aggravated, we could expect some bias toward a finding of increased overall consistency. On balance, we consider it likely that the post-*Furman* improvements reported in this chapter may not have been quite as dramatic as the numbers may initially suggest.

Moreover, to the extent there was an actual improvement in the system, we sought to estimate the degree to which it was the product of Georgia's 1973 procedural reforms. We first examined how the selectivity of Georgia's death-sentencing system changed each year between 1970 and 1978. For this purpose we constructed a regression-based culpability index using a pooled data set of both pre- and post-*Furman* cases.[22] This permitted us to measure the selectivity of the two periods on the same index.

Figure 7 presents for the years 1970–78 the distributions of life-sentence and death-sentence cases on the culpability index. For each year, there are two columns of numbers. The left column represents the distribution of life sentences on the culpability index, while the right column represents a similar distribution of the death-sentence cases for that year. The numbers in each column indicate the number of cases located at each point on the culpability index. The figure also includes two trend lines that indicate the median culpability scores for life- and death-sentence cases for each year.

The information presented in Figure 7 suggests that Georgia's 1973 statutory reforms caused the observed differences in Georgia's pre- and post-*Furman* capital-sentencing patterns. The data for 1974, the first post-*Furman* year with a large number of death sentences, indicate a considerably greater degree of selectivity compared to the pre-*Furman* period. The trend lines in Figure 7, which indicate the yearly median-culpability scores for life- and death-sentence cases, also suggest that the impact of the post-*Furman* procedural changes was, except in 1976, a sustained one.[23] The data in Figure 8, which presents the average rather than the median culpability scores for the life- and death-sentence cases from 1970 to 1978, suggest an even greater increase in selectivity post-*Furman*.

The second measure of impact is the change, after the 1973 reforms, in the degree of overlap of culpability index distributions for life-sentence and death-sentence cases. A visual examination of Figure 7 shows an increased degree of overlap after the early 1970s. A further reflection of this phenomenon appears in Table 13, which indicates the proportion of death-sentence cases with culpability scores at or below the score for the 95th percentile life-sentence case for the years 1970–78.

Figure 8 sheds further light on the possible impact of the post-*Furman* reforms with a comparison of the average culpability scores (as contrasted with median scores in Figure 7) of the life and death sentences imposed each

Figure 7. Distribution of Life- and Death-Sentence Cases at Each Level of Aggravation/Mitigation for Each Year 1970–78 with Trend Line of Median Aggravation/Mitigation Scores for Life-Sentence and Death-Sentence Cases (For each year the left column is the distribution of life-sentence cases and the right column is the distribution of death-sentence cases [each number indicates the number of cases at each point on the index])

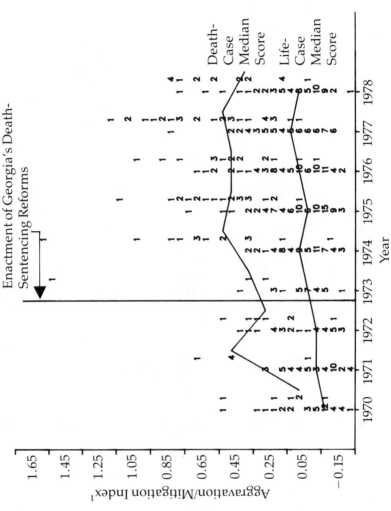

1. See chap. 5, note 22, for a description of the index underlying this figure.

Table 13. Proportion of Death-Sentence Cases with a Culpability Score Below the
Score for the 95th-Percentile Life-Sentence Case

Year	Proportion
1970	.83 (5/6)
1971	.17 (1/6)
1972	.86 (6/7)
1973	.33 (1/3) ⎫ .09 (2/22)
1974	.05 (1/19) ⎭
1975	.45 (10/22)
1976	.67 (10/15)
1977	.37 (11/30)
1978	.50 (9/18)

year. It suggests a larger initial improvement in the early post-*Furman* years
and a gradual weakening of the system's capacity to limit death sentences to
the most extreme cases.

Figures 7 and 8 also suggest an improvement in the system's selectivity
during the pre-*Furman* period between 1970 and 1971. Possibly Georgia's
adoption of a bifurcated death-sentencing system on March 27, 1970, contributed to this development. Assuming that implementation of the change took
some time, one would not expect whatever effects it produced to appear until
1971. The data are consistent with this hypothesis. The distribution of life and
death sentences in 1970 closely approximates the random model illustrated in
Figure 2, with a nearly complete overlap of each category of cases on the
culpability scale. For each of the next three years, however, there is an increasingly greater degree of selectivity than in 1970. Although the annual samples
of death cases in the pre-*Furman* period are too small to reach statistical significance and include no pre-1970 data, the results are consistent with the
hypothesis that bifurcated trials increased the selectivity of Georgia's capital-
sentencing process after 1970.

To what extent, therefore, is it plausible to attribute the post-*Furman* improvements in selectivity to Georgia's 1973 procedural reforms? One thing is
certain. The statutory aggravating circumstances have eliminated death sentencing among the least aggravated cases—those in which the defendant is no
longer death-eligible under the post-*Furman* statute. However, more than 90
percent of the pre-*Furman* death sentences were imposed in cases whose facts
would have made them death-eligible under Georgia's post-*Furman* statute.

Conceivably, the institution of statutorily designated aggravating circumstances might also have invited juries to impose death sentences more fre-

Figure 8. Average Level of Aggravation/Mitigation for Cases Receiving Life or Death Sentences for Each Year, 1970–78

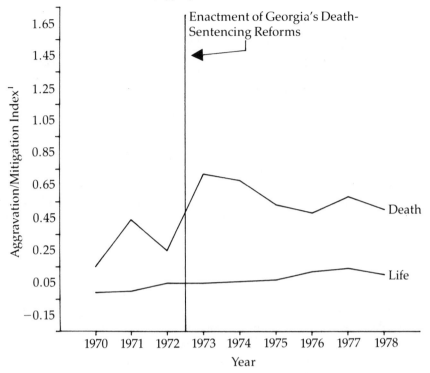

1. *See* chap. 5, note 22, for a description of the index underlying this figure.

quently in those cases in which they learned that, on the basis of legislatively enacted criteria, the defendants were death-eligible.[24] The higher death-sentencing rates in the post-*Furman* period tend to support this hypothesis. Among the twenty-one circuits with five or more murder cases, both pre- and post-*Furman*, the death-sentencing rate increased in thirteen of the circuits, or 62 percent (13/21). The average increase among these thirteen circuits was 17 percentage points. In the other one-third (7/21) of these circuits in which death-sentencing rates declined, the average drop was 7 percentage points.[25] As we noted earlier, however, the magnitude of the overall death-sentencing rate increased by only 8 percentage points.[26]

Further evidence of the influence of the statutory aggravating factors are the pre- and post-*Furman* death-sentencing rates among cases in which evidence supporting the presence of a statutory aggravating factor existed. Table 14 presents this comparison. It indicates generally higher death-sentencing

Table 14. Pre- and Post-*Furman* Death-Sentencing Rates, Controlling Separately for the Presence of Post-*Furman* Statutory Aggravating Factors in the Case

A. Georgia Statutory Aggravating Circumstances	B. Pre-*Furman*[1]	C. Post-*Furman*[2]
1. Prior capital record (B1)	.18 (4/22)	.34 (14/41)
2. Enumerated contemporaneous offense (B2)	.24 (24/100)	.37 (99/271)
3. Risk of death to two or more in public (B3)	.23 (6/26)	.22 (21/96)
4. Money/value motive (B4)	.19 (18/96)	.37 (78/212)
5. Victim judicial officer, D.A. (B5)	.75 (6/8)	NC[a]
6. Murder for hire (B6)	.33 (1/3)	.20 (4/20)
7. Murder wantonly vile, horrible, etc. (B7)	.20 (22/109)	.30 (93/308)
8. Victim police- or fireperson (B8)	.42 (8/19)	.35 (6/17)
9. Defendant prisoner or escapee (B9)	.67 (4/6)	.56 (10/18)
10. Killing to avoid/stop arrest (B10)	.25 (19/77)	.33 (41/125)

1. The denominators include weighted life-sentence cases. *See supra* chap. 4, note 2 and accompanying text, for a description of the weighting procedure used.
2. The counts include all sentencing decisions, including twelve cases in which two penalty trials were held.
a. NC means no cases.

rates for the post-*Furman* era. Of particular interest are the increases in the rate of death sentencing, after the 1973 revisions took effect, in cases involving the two most numerically important aggravating circumstances in the post-*Furman* system—a serious contemporaneous felony (B2) and a wantonly vile, horrible, or inhuman killing (B7). For the contemporaneous-felony factor, the increase was from .24 to .37, or 13 points; for the wantonly vile factor, there was a 10-point increase, from .20 to .30. The increased death-sentencing rates in these two categories of cases markedly affected the composition of death row in the post-*Furman* period. As a proportion of all murder cases, the proportion of cases with the contemporaneous-felony and wantonly vile factors present increased only slightly in the post-*Furman* period (from .57 to .68). By contrast, the proportion of all death-sentenced defendants in whose cases the contemporaneous-felony factor was present increased from .54 pre-*Furman* to .88 post-*Furman*. For the wantonly vile circumstance, the comparable increase among death-row defendants was from .50 to .83.[27]

Although our data shed no light on the impact of the other trial-level reforms that Georgia adopted after *Furman*—the increased information available to juries or the expanded jury instructions—we would expect these reforms to have contributed as well to the greater selectivity and consistency observed in the post-*Furman* period.

There are also, however, three rival hypotheses that might plausibly explain the post-*Furman* improvements in selectivity in death sentencing that we have observed. The first is a general trend toward consistency and reasonableness on the part of Georgia's prosecutors and juries during the 1970s, perhaps resulting from increased education and improved living standards. Collateral evidence does show some improvement in these areas.[28] But, even if this trend were present, it would not account for the abrupt change that occurred after 1973. Moreover, the declining level of selectivity in the system between 1974 and 1978 undercuts the hypothesis, since education and living standards did not decline during this period.

The second rival hypothesis is that the 1973–74 improvements resulted from some initial uncertainty, on the part of prosecutors and judges, concerning the degree of oversight to which the Georgia and United States Supreme Courts might subject their actions. Such uncertainty might prompt both prosecutors and judges to be more cautious and discriminating when deciding whether to advance particular defendants to a penalty trial. By 1976, any such uncertainty about judicial supervision would undoubtedly have declined, thus producing the reduced degree of selectivity that we observed.[29] Although admittedly speculative, this hypothesis may partly explain the backsliding of the system after its initial sharp improvement.

The third rival hypothesis is that the increased selectivity and resulting consistency observed in the system are attributable to a general decline in racial discrimination. The data support this hypothesis, since it appears that the greatest decline in racial prejudice probably occurred prior to 1973.[30] However, we consider it unlikely that the change in public attitude could by itself explain the abrupt improvement in performance in 1973 and 1974.

In summary, these three rival hypotheses may, in fact, explain some of the increased selectivity that we observed in our post-*Furman* sample. They do not, however, either separately or in combination, provide a satisfactory alternative explanation for all of that increase or the variations we observe from year to year. We remain persuaded, therefore, that Georgia's 1973 statutory reforms contributed significantly to the decline of excessiveness that we observe in our post-*Furman* data.

SOURCES OF ARBITRARINESS AND EXCESSIVENESS IN GEORGIA'S CAPITAL-SENTENCING SYSTEM

The preceding section discussed the consistency with which Georgia's capital-sentencing system imposed sentences on death-eligible defendants convicted of murder after jury trials. The death sentences imposed in these cases resulted from two discrete decisions made after the defendant's conviction of capital murder. First, the prosecutor must decide to advance the case to a penalty trial.

Second, the jury must decide to impose a death sentence, if a penalty trial occurs. In this section, we examine separately the consistency of prosecutorial and jury decision making in the post-*Furman* period. We also test the oft-stated hypothesis that geographic differences in attitudes toward punishment explain most of the sentencing disparities observed in capital-sentencing systems.

The Consistency of Post-*Furman* Prosecutorial and Jury Decision Making

One might legitimately wonder why prosecutorial discretion or consistency in its exercise after a defendant has been found guilty of capital murder is even an issue. The Georgia Code clearly states that all defendants found guilty of capital murder by plea or at trial "shall" be presented to a judge or jury for sentencing in a penalty trial.[31] In *Gregg v. Georgia*, the Supreme Court clearly assumed that this provision was mandatory.[32] To be sure, the Supreme Court did acknowledge that prosecutors could exercise substantial discretion with respect to death-eligible defendants prior to trial. After a capital-murder conviction, however, the Court assumed the sentence imposed was strictly a matter for the sentencing judge or jury. In this respect the Court's preconception in *Gregg* of how the Georgia system functioned in practice was mistaken. In Georgia, even after the defendant's conviction for capital murder, a prosecutor who considers a death sentence to be inappropriate or unwarranted may waive the penalty trial. The trial judge will then automatically impose a life sentence. In such cases, the jury plays no role whatsoever in the sentencing decision.[33] The questions of interest, therefore, are (a) the number and proportion of life sentences that were set as a consequence of prosecutorial decisions waiving the death penalty; (b) the relative appetite of prosecutors and sentencing juries for capital punishment, as reflected in their decisions to seek and to impose the death penalty; (c) how consistently prosecutors exercise their discretion in this context, in comparison to sentencing juries; (d) to what extent prosecutors and sentencing juries probably contribute to the excessiveness we observed in the sentences imposed upon defendants convicted of murder; and (e) to what extent the observed levels of excessiveness and evenhandedness would change if the case of every defendant convicted of capital murder were advanced to a penalty trial, as state law appears to require.

Among all death-eligible cases, prosecutors advanced 41 percent (194/471) to a penalty trial. Therefore, in 59 percent of the death-eligible cases, a life sentence was imposed by default when the prosecutor unilaterally waived the penalty trial.

Figure 9 depicts the respective roles of prosecutors and juries in the disposi-

Figure 9. Distribution of Outcomes in Death-Eligible Cases (Death Sentence, Life Sentence in a Penalty Trial, Life Sentence without a Penalty Trial), Controlling for the Presence of Separate Statutory Aggravating Circumstances (Post-*Furman*)

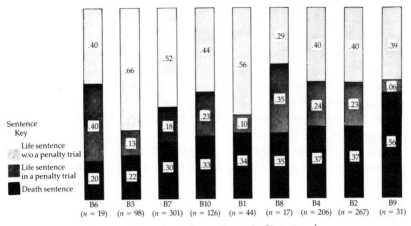

Georgia Statutory Aggravating Circumstances[1]

1. The aggravating circumstances are ordered by ascending frequency of death sentence: B6 (murder for hire), B3 (risk of death to two or more in public), B7 (murder vile, horrible, or inhuman), B10 (killing to avoid/stop arrest), B1 (prior capital record), B8 (victim police- or fireperson), B4 (money/value motive), B2 (enumerated contemporaneous offense, including armed robbery), and B9 (defendant prisoner or escapee). The study included no cases that were death-eligible under the B5 factor (murder of a judge or prosecutor).

tion of cases that are death-eligible under each statutory aggravating circumstance. The different shading in Figure 9 indicates whether the defendant received: (a) a life sentence because the prosecutor waived a penalty trial (lighter shading); (b) a jury-imposed life sentence after the prosecutor advanced the case to a penalty trial (medium shading); or (c) a jury-imposed death sentence after the prosecutor advanced the case to a penalty trial (dark shading). In all but two small categories of cases (B8, B9), prosecutors ensured a life sentence by unilaterally waiving penalty trials in a larger proportion of the cases in the subgroup than the proportion of defendants who actually received death sentences.

Figure 10 presents a similar distribution, controlling for the number of statutory aggravating circumstances in the case. It indicates that prosecutors seek death sentences in more than 50 percent of the cases only if three or more statutory aggravating factors are present. And in no group of these cases does the rate exceed .80.

Only when we classify the cases by a variety of nonstatutory aggravating and mitigating factors do we observe categories of cases in which prosecutors regularly seek death sentences. Figure 11 presents such an analysis. Among most of the less aggravated cases, fewer than 50 percent ever reach a penalty trial. However, among the most highly aggravated three categories of cases, prosecutors seek a death sentence more than 85 percent of the time.

Together, these three figures clearly suggest that prosecutors play a dominant role in the sentencing of death-eligible offenders, especially among the less aggravated cases.

Figures 9, 10, and 11 also indicate the relative appetite of prosecutors and juries for capital punishment. The data in each of the figures provide a basis for calculating the rates at which prosecutors seek and juries impose death sentences among classes of cases deemed comparable with three different measures of culpability.

First, from the data in Figure 9, we compared the rates at which prosecutors sought and juries imposed death sentences in death-eligible cases classified by

Figure 10. Distribution of Outcomes in Death-Eligible Cases (Death Sentence, Life Sentence in a Penalty Trial, Life Sentence without a Penalty Trial), Controlling for the Number of Statutory Aggravating Circumstances (Post-*Furman*)

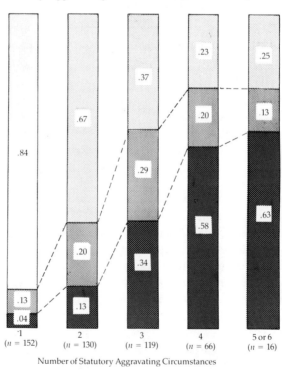

Figure 11. Distribution of Outcomes in Death-Eligible Cases (Death Sentence, Life Sentence in a Penalty Trial, Life Sentence without a Penalty Trial), Controlling for Case Culpability (Post-*Furman*)

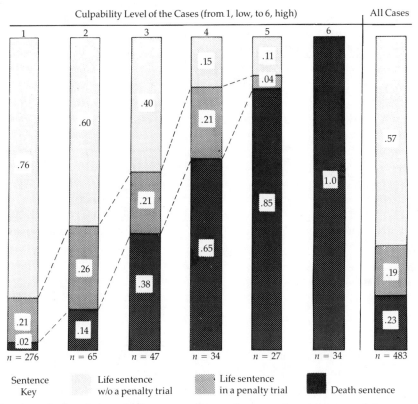

Culpability Level of the Cases (from 1, low, to 6, high) | All Cases

Sentence Key | Life sentence w/o a penalty trial | Life sentence in a penalty trial | Death sentence

1. The index and scale underlying this figure are OVERALLC and CSCALC, *infra* app. J, part 1, and chap. 4, note 38 and accompanying text.

each of the statutory aggravating circumstances. The results presented in Table 15 indicate a generally higher selection rate for juries, suggesting a more punitive reaction on their part. The differences, however, are not entirely consistent nor all that great. More important, since prosecutors routinely waive the penalty trial in the less aggravated death-eligible cases, we would expect the cases that do reach a penalty trial to be more aggravated in their nonstatutory aggravating factors than the population of death-eligible defendants initially screened by the prosecutors.

We also conducted a similar analysis of the data in Figures 10 and 11, which more effectively control for case culpability. For example, part I of Table 16 shows the rates at which prosecutors sought and juries imposed death sentences in cases that had one or more statutory aggravating circumstances

Table 15. Rates at Which Prosecutors Seek and Juries Impose Death Sentences, Controlling for Individual Statutory Aggravating Factors (Post-*Furman*)

A. Georgia Statutory Aggravating Circumstances	B. *Prosecutor* Proportion of Cases Advanced to Penalty Trial[1]	C. *Jury* Penalty Trial Death-Sentencing Rate[2]
1. Prior capital record (B1)	.43 (17/40)	.78 (14/18)
2. Enumerated contemporaneous offense (B2)	.58 (149/259)	.61 (99/161)
3. Risk of death to two or more in public (B3)	.33 (31/94)	.64 (21/33)
4. Money/value motive (B4)	.59 (120/204)	.61 (78/128)
5. Victim judicial officer, D.A. (B5)	NC[a]	NC
6. Murder for hire (B6)	.60 (12/20)	.33 (4/12)
7. Murder wantonly vile, horrible, etc. (B7)	.47 (139/298)	.62 (93/149)
8. Victim police- or fireperson (B8)	.69 (11/16)	.50 (6/12)
9. Defendant prisoner or escapee (B9)	.59 (10/17)	.91 (10/11)
10. Killing to avoid/stop arrest (B10)	.55 (66/121)	.59 (41/70)
Average rate	.41 (194/471)	.54 (112/206)

1. The counts do not include repeat penalty trials for death sentences vacated on appeal to the Georgia Supreme Court.
2. The counts include all sentencing decisions, including twelve cases in which more than one penalty trial was held.
a. NC means no cases.

present. The data in part II of the table present a similar comparison of selection rates for prosecutors and juries in cases of similar culpability, as measured by our overall culpability index. Even though the measures of case culpability in Table 16 are more refined than those used for the analysis in Table 15, we still expected that the screening function of the prosecutors would have passed to the juries, in each culpability level, a sample of cases that had more aggravated case characteristics not captured by our culpability indexes than those initially confronted by the prosecutors. As a result, we anticipated considerably higher selection rates for juries than for prosecutors, particularly in the analysis based on the count of statutory aggravating circumstances, a measure that we know omits many factors which influence prosecutorial and jury decisions. The data in Table 16, however, show quite comparable selection rates on the part of juries and prosecutors, a result susceptible to three possible explanations. The first is that the prosecutors are in fact advancing to penalty trials cases that have more aggravated case characteristics not reflected in the measures underlying Table 16, and the sentencing juries are applying a higher standard of proof than are the prosecutors before they are willing to vote for a death sentence. This theory does not explain, however, the comparability of the selection rates at each culpability level. A second possible explanation is that the pools of death-eligible offenders that prosecutors and juries confront are of

Table 16. Rates at Which Prosecutors Seek and Juries Impose Death Sentences, Controlling for the Number of Statutory Aggravating Circumstances (I) and a Culpability Index (II) (Post-*Furman*)

I. Statutory Aggravating Circumstances		
A. Number of Statutory Aggravating Circumstances	B. Rates at Which Prosecutors Sought Death Sentences[1]	C. Rates at Which Juries Imposed Death Sentences[2]
1	.17 (25/151)	.24 (6/25)
2	.32 (41/128)	.40 (17/43)
3	.62 (72/116)	.55 (41/75)
4	.75 (46/61)	.75 (38/51)
5 or 6	.73 (11/15)	.83 (10/12)
II. Regression-Based Culpability Index[3]		
A. Culpability Level, from least (1) to most (6) culpable	B. Rates at Which Prosecutors Sought Death Sentences[1]	C. Rates at Which Juries Imposed Death Sentences[2]
1	.24 (65/276)	.09 (6/65)
2	.39 (25/64)	.35 (9/26)
3	.59 (27/46)	.64 (18/28)
4	.84 (26/31)	.76 (22/29)
5	.88 (22/25)	.96 (23/24)
6	1.00 (29/29)	1.00 (34/34)

1. The prosecutorial analysis does not include multiple penalty trials.
2. Jury decisions include both decisions in twelve cases that had two penalty trials.
3. *See supra* chap. 4, note 38 and accompanying text, and *infra* app. J (OVERALLC and CSCALC) for a description of this culpability index, which reflects the impact of both prosecutorial decisions to seek and jury decisions to impose death sentences.

comparable culpability, and that both prosecutors and juries consider about the same proportion to be death-worthy. This unexpected result would be consistent with the theory that the system imposes a de facto quota on the number and proportion of death sentences occurring at all levels of culpability.[34] A third possible explanation, which we consider extremely unlikely, is that the similarity of the selection rates for prosecutors and juries is a pure coincidence or a statistical fluke.

Whatever the explanation for the apparent agreement of prosecutors and juries on the proportion of defendants at different culpability levels who should be executed, the frequent jury reluctance to follow the prosecutor's recommendations substantially reduces the overall death-sentencing rate among death-eligible offenders. The relative infrequency of prosecutorial death-sentence recommendations among the less aggravated cases also suggests that prosecutors may be a source of inconsistency and excessiveness in the post-*Furman* period. This hypothesis seems plausible for several reasons. Most prosecutors confront capital cases relatively infrequently, and death-sentence cases impose high economic, emotional, and sometimes political costs. Furthermore, prosecutors are often sensitive to public opinion and political pressures, which may also influence their decisions regarding specific murder cases. All these factors would encourage not necessarily consistent choices of which cases to pursue to a death sentence. Furthermore, although one might expect that the prosecutor's greater training and experience would produce more consistent results than a series of ad hoc jury decisions, the literature suggests that group decision-making processes, like those of a jury, are generally more consistent and rational.[35]

We next evaluated this hypothesis with two measures of arbitrariness and excessiveness. The first measure examined the comparative culpability distributions of the cases in which prosecutors either waived or demanded a penalty trial (Figure 12) and the comparative distributions for the cases in which juries imposed a life or a death sentence (Figure 13). A comparison of these two distributions provides only weak support for the hypothesis that prosecutors are a major cause of excessiveness. The overlap of culpability scores for cases advanced or not advanced to penalty trial in Figure 12 is not substantially different from that of life- and death-sentence cases in Figure 13. Furthermore, 43 percent of the jury death-sentence cases had culpability scores lower than the 95th percentile life-sentence case, while the comparable statistic for the prosecutorial decision to seek a death sentence was 46 percent.

When we apply our second measure of consistency, which compares selection rates at various culpability levels using the same indexes employed for Figures 12 and 13, the differences between prosecutors and juries become more evident. Tables 17 and 18, respectively, indicate the rates at which prosecutors sought and juries imposed death sentences in six subgroups of cases, with culpability in each tabulation separately defined by defendant culpability. The regression-based index in Table 17 was derived from prosecutorial decisions to seek a death sentence; the regression-based index in Table 18 was derived from jury decisions to impose death sentences. The data in Table 18 indicate that, in spite of the extensive screening of cases by Georgia's prosecutors, there is still a significant proportion of penalty-trial cases in which juries extend mercy. Indeed, in the 28 percent (59/206) of the jury cases that represent the least-aggravated category in Table 18, the death-sentencing rate is less than .10.

When we examine the consistency of prosecutorial and jury decision making using Professor Barnett's three-dimensional measure of case culpability, the results, shown in Figures 14 and 15, are comparable to Tables 17 and 18. Among the most aggravated cases, we see very high selection rates for both prosecutors and juries and very low rates among the least aggravated death-

Figure 12.   Distribution on Culpability Index of Prosecutorial Decisions either to Seek or to Waive the Death Penalty (Post-*Furman*)[1]

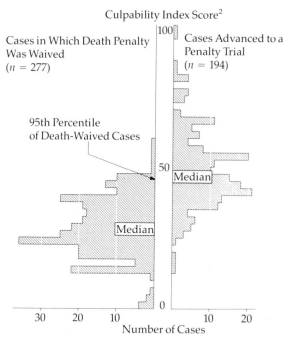

Culpability Index Score[2]

Cases in Which Death Penalty Was Waived
($n = 277$)

Cases Advanced to a Penalty Trial
($n = 194$)

95th Percentile of Death-Waived Cases

Median

Median

30   20   10   10   20
Number of Cases

1. Forty-six percent of the cases in which the prosecutors sought a death sentence have a lower culpability score than the culpability score of the 95th percentile case in which prosecutors waived a penalty trial.
2. This index (PROSCUTC) is described *supra* chap. 4, note 38 and accompanying text, and *infra* app. J, part 2.

eligible cases. Figure 15 also indicates that among nearly .24 (49/206) of the penalty-trial cases, the death-sentencing rate among similarly situated cases is under .15.

These findings also suggest the obvious question of whether Georgia's prosecutors could enhance evenhandedness in the system by advancing all murder-conviction cases to penalty trials.[36] To answer this question, we analyzed the cases of all convicted murder defendants, whether or not they actually underwent a penalty trial, using a logistic multiple-regression index consisting of the eleven legitimate case characteristics that best explain which defendants juries considered most deserving of a death sentence.[37] This allowed us to estimate the number of cases (in which the prosecutor waived a penalty trial) that the jury probably would have imposed a death sentence if a penalty trial had occurred. Table 19 presents the results. The first part of the

Figure 13. Distribution of Jury life- and Death-Sentencing Decisions on Culpability Index (Post-*Furman*)[1]

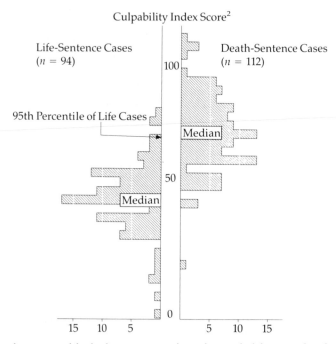

1. Forty-five percent of the death-sentence cases have a lower culpability score than the culpability score of the 95th-percentile life-sentence case.
2. This index (JURYC) is described *supra* chap. 4, note 38 and accompanying text, and *infra* app. J, part 3.

table compares, for six different culpability levels (col. A), the actual post-*Furman* death-sentencing rates among all death-eligible cases (col. B) (even though juries imposed the sentence in only 40 percent of the cases), with the probable results that would have been obtained if prosecutors had advanced every death-eligible case that resulted in a murder-trial conviction to a penalty trial (col. C). Table 19 indicates that a mandatory penalty-trial policy may have increased the number of death sentences from 112 to 182, an increase of 63 percent. As a consequence, the overall death-sentencing rate for all death-eligible defendants could have increased 58 percent, or 14 percentage points, from .24 (112/476) under the actual system to .38 (182/476). We emphasize, however, that this analysis assumes that the cases in which the prosecutor waived a penalty trial are indistinguishable from others at the same

Table 17. Rates at Which Prosecutors Seek Death Sentences, Controlling for Case Culpability Scores (Post-*Furman*)

Case Culpability Level, from 1 (low) to 6 (high)[1]	Rates at Which Prosecutors Seek Death Sentences among Death-Eligible Defendants Convicted of Murder at Trial[2]
1	.06 (10/162)
2	.27 (20/73)
3	.50 (51/103)
4	.70 (40/57)
5	.91 (32/35)
6	1.00 (41/41)
Average rate	.41 (194/471)

1. *See supra* chap. 4, note 38 and accompanying text, and *infra* app. J, part 2, for a description of this index and scale (PROSCUTC and PSCALC).
2. These tabulations do not include the second prosecutorial decision in twelve cases that had two penalty trials.

Table 18. Rates at Which Juries Impose Death Sentences in Penalty Trials, Controlling for Case Culpability (Post-*Furman*)

Case Culpability Level, from 1 (low) to 6 (high)[1]	Jury Death-Sentencing Rate[2]
1	.07 (4/59)
2	.35 (14/40)
3	.69 (18/26)
4	.92 (24/26)
5	.82 (14/17)
6	1.00 (38/38)
Average rate	.54 (112/206)

1. *See supra* chap. 4, note 38 and accompanying text, and *infra* app. J, part 3, for a description of this index and scale (JURYC and JSCALC).
2. Jury decisions include both decisions in twelve cases that had two penalty trials.

level of defendant culpability. If the cases screened out of a penalty trial by the prosecutors were less aggravated than those presented to a sentencing jury, even though classified as having similar culpability by our methodology, the increase in the number of death sentences would have been smaller than our

Figure 14. Rates at Which Prosecutors Seek Death Sentences among Subgroups of Death-Eligible Cases Defined by Three Barnett Case Dimensions (Post-*Furman* Georgia)[1]

0	1	2	3	4	5
	1.0 (1/1) (0,1,0)	.23 (5/22) (0,0,2)	.64 (7/11) (2,0,1)		
.00 (0/3) (0,0,0)	.13 (4/31) (1,0,0)	.44 (4/9) (1,1,0)	.63 (37/59) (1,1,1)	.88 (59/67) (1,1,2)	.83 (5/6) (2,1,2)
	.17 (7/42) (0,0,1)	.32 (13/41) (0,1,1)	.65 (11/17) (0,1,2)	.83 (15/18) (2,0,2)	
		.11 (12/106) (1,0,1)	.35 (13/37) (1,0,2)		
		1.0 (1/1) (2,0,0)			

Sum of Scores for the Three Barnett Dimensions

0	1	2	3	4	5

Least Aggravated ——————————————————————————→ Most Aggravated

1. The three numbers in parentheses at the foot of each cell indicate the coding for Barnett's three dimensions: (a) certainty that killing was deliberate (0 = low, 1 = medium, 2 = high); (b) relationship between defendant and victim (0 = family/friend, 1 = stranger); and (c) vileness of the killing (0 = element of self-defense, 1 = neither self-defense nor vile, 2 = vile killing). The rate at which cases advance to a penalty trial and the number of cases (penalty-trial cases/all cases) are in the center of each cell. *See supra* chap. 4, note 29 and accompanying text, for a further explanation of the classification system used for this figure. There were no cases in cells (2,1,0) and (2,1,1). The figure does not include twelve cases that had two penalty trials.

estimate suggests. For example, the culpability index on which the analysis was based included no measure for defendant demeanor.

The second part of Table 19 indicates how a mandatory penalty-trial policy may have changed the number and proportion of presumptively excessive and presumptively evenhanded death sentences. First, we estimate that there would have been a decrease in both the number and the proportion of presumptively excessive death sentences. The data also suggest that we would see a substantial increase in the actual number of evenhanded sentences (from 38 to 99) and a 20-percentage-point increase in the proportion of such sentences.

On balance, therefore, it appears that a mandatory penalty-trial policy and the resulting jury-dominated system would likely produce a dramatic increase in the absolute number of death sentences imposed and a significant increase in the number and proportion of both evenhanded and excessive death sentences. From the standpoint of overall arbitrariness, however, the ultimate effects of

Figure 15. Jury Death-Sentencing Rates among Subgroups of Cases Defined by Three Barnett Case Dimensions (Post-*Furman* Georgia)[1]

1	2	3	4	5
.00 (0/1) (0,1,0)	.20 (1/5) (0,0,2)	.14 (1/7) (2,0,1)		
.25 (1/4) (1,0,0)	.00 (0/4) (1,1,0)	.41 (15/37) (1,1,1)	.91 (59/65) (1,1,2)	1.0 (6/6) (2,1,2)
.00 (0/7) (0,0,1)	.08 (1/13) (0,1,1)	.43 (6/14) (0,1,2)	.67 (10/15) (2,0,2)	
	.08 (1/12) (1,0,1)	.73 (11/15) (1,0,2)		
	.00 (0/1) (2,0,0)			

Sum of Scores for the Three Barnett Dimensions

Least Aggravated ————————————————————————→ Most Aggravated

1. The three numbers in parentheses at the foot of each cell indicate the coding for Barnett's three dimensions: (a) certainty that killing was deliberate (0 = low, 1 = medium, 2 = high); (b) relationship between defendant and victim (0 = family/friend, 1 = stranger); and (c) vileness of the killing (0 = element of self-defense, 1 = neither self-defense nor vile, 2 = vile killing). The death-sentencing rate and the number of cases (death cases/all cases) are in the center of each cell. There were no cases in cells (2,1,0) and (2,1,1). *See supra* chap. 4, note 29 and accompanying text, for further explanation of the classification system used for this figure. The figure includes the second penalty-trial decision in twelve cases that had two penalty trials.

such a policy change would depend on how well the Georgia Supreme Court's system of proportionality review served to identify and to vacate the increased number of excessive death sentences we would likely see in such a system.

Geographic Death-Sentencing Disparities

There are two aspects of our analysis of geographic disparities in death sentencing. The first concerns the extent to which defendants convicted of murder at trial face differing risks of receiving a death sentence in different parts of the state. Since attitudes toward both crime and punishment frequently vary from place to place, some geographic disparity would not be surprising.

Our second concern is with the geographic distribution of death sentences that we characterize as "presumptively" excessive or evenhanded. The preceding analysis suggests that from 15 percent to 30 percent of Georgia's post-

Table 19. Actual and Hypothetical Death-Sentencing Rates in Georgia's Capital-Sentencing System, Controlling for the Culpability Level of the Cases

A. Case Culpability Level, from 1 (low) to 6 (high)[1]	B. Actual System[2]	C. Hypothetical System without Prosecutorial Discretion[3]	D. Change in Number of Death Sentences (Col.C − Col.B)
1	.02 (4/226)	.07 (16/233)	+12
2	.15 (14/96)	.35 (34/96)	+20
3	.38 (18/48)	.69 (33/48)	+15
4	.56 (24/43)	.93 (40/43)	+16
5	.67 (14/21)	.81 (17/21)	+3
6	.90 (38/42)	1.00 (42/42)	+4
Total death sentences	112	182	+70

Proportion and Number of Death-Sentence Cases for Which the Death-Sentence Frequency in Similar Cases Was:

A. Less than .35	.16 (18/112)	.09 (16/182)
B. .80 or more	.34 (38/112)	.54 (99/182)

1. *See supra* chap. 4, note 38 and accompanying text, and *infra* app. J, part 3, for a description of the culpability index (JURYC) and scale (JSCALC) underlying this table.
2. Death-sentencing rates among all death-eligible cases, including more than two hundred that prosecutors did not advance to a penalty trial, classified on jury case culpability index JURYC. This analysis includes repeat penalty trials.
3. Estimated death-sentencing rates among all death-eligible cases are based on the assumption that all death-eligible cases advance to a penalty trial and are sentenced at the same rate as cases of similar culpability that resulted in a penalty-trial death sentence. The analysis includes twelve cases with more than one penalty trial.

Furman death sentences are probably excessive in a comparative sense. The second phase of our analysis seeks principally to explain the distribution of the excessive death sentences.

The Distribution of Death-Sentencing Rates

Table 20 presents the pre- and post-*Furman* distribution of unadjusted death-sentencing rates by judicial circuits. Column A shows the range of possible death-sentencing rates. Columns B and E indicate the proportion and number of judicial circuits with death-sentencing rates at the different levels indicated in column A. Columns B through G present the distribution of circuits, all cases, and death-sentence cases, by the frequency with which death sentences are imposed in their respective circuits. For example, row 3 of columns B, C, and D indicate that 79 percent of the circuits had a pre-*Furman* death sentencing rate of between .00 and .19 and that 82 percent of all murder-trial cases and 55 percent of the death-sentence cases were found in those circuits.

Table 20. Distribution of Judicial Circuits by the Rates at Which Death Sentences Are Imposed, with a Listing of the Proportion of Cases and Death Sentences in Each Category (Pre- and Post-Furman)

A	B	C	D	E	F	G
	Pre-Furman[2]			Post-Furman		
	Proportion and Number of			Proportion and Number of		
Death-Sentencing Rate[1]	Circuits (n = 40)	Cases (n = 291)[a]	Death Sentences (n = 44)	Circuits (n = 42)	Cases (n = 483)	Death Sentences (n = 112)
.0	.43(17)	.22(64)	.00(0)	.26(11)	.13(63)	.00(0)
.0+	.08(3)	.11(32)	.07(3)	.02(1)	.02(11)	.01(1)
.10+	.28(11)[b]	.49(142)	.48(21)	.19(8)	.31(151)	.19(21)
.20+	.05(2)	.07(21)	.11(5)	.17(2)	.28(134)	.29(33)
.30+	.08(3)	.03(9)	.07(3)	.10(4)	.06(31)	.10(11)
.40+	.03(1)	.06(19)	.18(8)	.17(7)	.16(75)	.30(34)
.50+				.05(2)	.02(12)	.06(7)
.60+						
.70+	.08(3)	.01(4)	.09(4)	.02(1)	.01(4)	.03(3)
1.00				.02(1)	.004(2)	.02(2)

1. Circuits in each category include cases with rates above the rate indicated; e.g., the .10+ category includes all circuits with rates above .10 up to and including .20.

2. Two circuits had no cases.

a. Count is 291 instead of 294 because of rounding of weighted life-sentence cases.

b. Cases at the median are underlined.

A comparison of the data presented in Table 20 for the pre- and post-*Furman* periods suggests there was considerably more geographic disparity in the post-*Furman* period. There were almost as many post-*Furman* circuits with death sentencing rates of .40 or more ($n = 11$) as with a rate of zero ($n = 10$). By contrast, the narrow variation in the rates for the pre-*Furman* period does not support the hypothesis that geographic disparities explain much of the excessiveness observed prior to 1973.

Table 21 examines separately the rates at which prosecutors sought and juries imposed death sentences for the post-*Furman* period. The figures in columns B and C reveal substantial disparities in selection rates for both decisions. In the median circuit, prosecutors sought death sentences at rates between .40 and .50; juries imposed death sentences at rates between .50 and .60.

Table 21. Proportion of Circuits with Different Rates at Which Prosecutors Seek and Juries Impose Death Sentences

A. Circuit Selection Rate[1]	B. Prosecutorial Decision to Seek a Death Sentence: Proportion and number of circuits with rate indicated in Column A ($n = 42$)	C. Jury Decision to Impose a Death Sentence: Proportion and number of circuits with rate indicated in Column A[2] ($n = 38$)
.0	.10 (4)	.18 (7)[a]
.0+	.02 (1)	
.10+	.10 (4)	.05 (2)
.20+	.02 (1)	
.30+	.21 (9)	.08 (3)
.40+	.19 (8)[b]	.18 (7)
.50+	.14 (6)	.08 (3)
.60+	.10 (4)	.13 (5)
.70+	.10 (4)	.08 (3)
.80+		
.90		
1.00	.02 (1)	.21 (8)[c]

1. Seeking a death penalty for the prosecutors; imposing a death penalty for the juries. Circuits in each category include cases with rates above the rate indicated; e.g., the .10+ category includes all circuits with rates above .10 up to and including .20.
2. Four circuits had no penalty trials.
a. Four circuits in this category had only one penalty trial, one had two, and one, Western, had five.
b. Median circuits are underlined.
c. Five circuits in the category had one or two penalty trials, two had three, and one, Coweta, had eight.

We sought next to determine the extent to which the unadjusted disparities we observed are correlated with urban/rural regional distinctions.[38] Table 22 shows the unadjusted rates for the urban and rural areas of the state and for its five regions. There are two noteworthy features of the pre- and post-*Furman* results. The first is their consistency for the urban areas. The second is a sharp increase in rural areas. Another comparison tells the same story. Both before and after *Furman*, just over half the state's capital murders occurred in rural areas, .53 (157/294) before *Furman* and .56 (267/476) after. However, the proportion of death sentences attributable to crimes in rural Georgia increased after *Furman* by two-thirds, from .39 to .65.

The pre- and post-*Furman* data for the five regions of the state reveal similar changes. There was a very slight change in the death-sentencing rate for Fulton County, but a very sharp increase in the North Central and Southwest regions, which together account for more than one-half of the death-eligible cases.

Table 23 indicates, however, that there was still extensive variability in death sentencing rates within the regions in the post-*Furman* period, suggesting that a variety of factors beyond broad regional characteristics play an important role in the death-sentencing process.[39]

The degree of this variability in death-sentencing rates within regions, both

Table 22. Death-Sentencing Rates, Controlling Separately for Urban versus Rural Location and Region (Pre- and Post-*Furman*)

Area	Pre-*Furman*	Post-*Furman*
I. Urban/Rural Location[1]		
A. Urban places	.20 (27/137)	.19 (40/212)
B. Rural places	.11 (17/157)	.27 (72/271)
II. Region[2]		
A. North	.07 (2/29)	.09 (4/47)
B. North Central	.14 (13/93)	.33 (53/162)
C. Fulton County	.16 (7/43)	.13 (9/72)
D. Southwest	.12 (7/58)	.23 (23/98)
E. Southeast	.21 (15/71)	.22 (23/104)

1. *See* chap. 5, note 38, for a listing of the urban judicial circuits.
2. Regional groupings of circuits are as follows: North (Lookout Mountain, Conasauga, Blue Ridge, Mountain, Northeastern, Rome, Cherokee); North Central (Tallapoosa, Cobb, Coweta, Griffin, Clayton, Stone Mountain, Gwinnett, Alcovy, Piedmont, Western, Ocmulgee, Northern, Toombs, Flint); Fulton County (Atlanta); Southwest (Chattahoochee, Macon, Houston, Southwestern, Pataula, Cordege, Tifton, Dougherty, South Georgia, Southern, Alapaha); Southeast (Augusta, Middle, Dublin, Ogeechee, Oconee, Atlantic, Eastern, Waycross, Brunswick). W. Bowers, LEGAL HOMICIDE 234 (1984).

Table 23. Distribution of Death Sentences by Judicial Circuits, Controlling for Region

Death-Sentencing Rate[1]	All Circuits (n = 42)	Region				
		North (n = 7)	North Central (n = 14)	Fulton County (n = 1)	Southwest (n = 11)	Southeast (n = 9)
.0	.26 (11)	.57 (4)	.07 (1)		.27 (3)	.33 (3)
.0+	.02 (1)	.14 (1)				
.10+	.19 (8)	.14 (1)	.21 (3)	1.0 (1)	.18 (2)	.11 (1)
.20+	.17 (7)[a]		.21 (3)		.09 (1)	.33 (3)
.30+	.10 (4)	.14 (1)	.07 (1)		.18 (2)	
.40+	.17 (7)		.29 (4)		.09 (1)	.22 (2)
.50+	.05 (2)		.14 (2)			
.60+						
.70+	.02 (1)				.09 (1)	
.80+						
.90+						
1.00	.02 (1)				.09 (1)	

1. Circuits in each category include cases with rates above the rate indicated; e.g., the .10+ category includes all circuits with rates above .10 up to and including .20.
a. Circuits at the median are underlined.

before and after *Furman*, is also depicted in the maps shown in Figures 16 and 17. Figure 16, especially, shows the strong concentration of circuits with high death-sentencing rates in the North Central region and, to a lesser extent, in the Southwest.

Figures 18 and 19 present, separately for each judicial circuit, the rates at which prosecutors sought and juries imposed death sentences in the post-*Furman* period. The data in Figure 18 indicate that prosecutors in the North Central region are generally more prone to seek a death sentence than are prosecutors in other sections of the state. Figure 19 also indicates that juries in the North Central region are more prone to impose death sentences than their counterparts in most other sections of the state. These data suggest, therefore, that the high post-*Furman* death-sentencing rates in the North Central region surrounding Fulton County, shown in Figure 17, are the product of both prosecutorial and jury decisions.

Of course, none of these comparisons adjusts for the seriousness of the cases in the various regions. Some have suggested that higher death-sentencing rates occurred in rural Georgia because a higher proportion of seriously aggravated homicides took place in rural areas, while others have suggested that

Figure 16. Distribution of Pre-*Furman* Death-Sentencing Rates by State Judicial Circuit

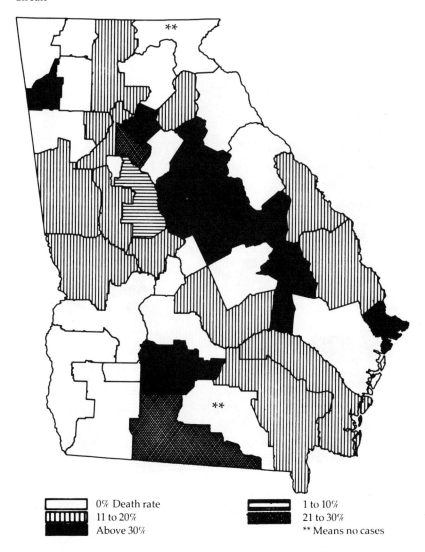

	0% Death rate		1 to 10%
	11 to 20%		21 to 30%
	Above 30%		** Means no cases

the most aggravated homicides are committed in urban areas. To test these competing hypotheses, we conducted multivariate analyses that, after adjusting for legitimate case characteristics affecting each defendant's culpability, estimated the likelihood that death sentences would be imposed in rural or in

Figure 17.   Distribution of Death-Sentencing Rates among Post-*Furman* Death-Eligible Cases by State Judicial Circuit

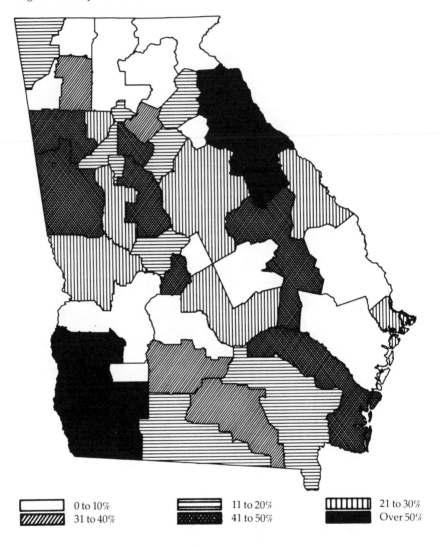

	0 to 10%		11 to 20%		21 to 30%
	31 to 40%		41 to 50%		Over 50%

urban areas, in particular regions of the state, and in particular circuits.[40] The analysis for the pre-*Furman* period identified no geographic area with a death-sentencing rate significantly different from the statewide rate.

The post-*Furman* overall analysis also revealed no statistically significant geographic effects after adjusting for legitimate case characteristics.

Figure 18. Distribution of Rates at Which Prosecutors Seek Death Sentences in Death-Eligible Cases, by State Judicial Circuit (Post-*Furman*)

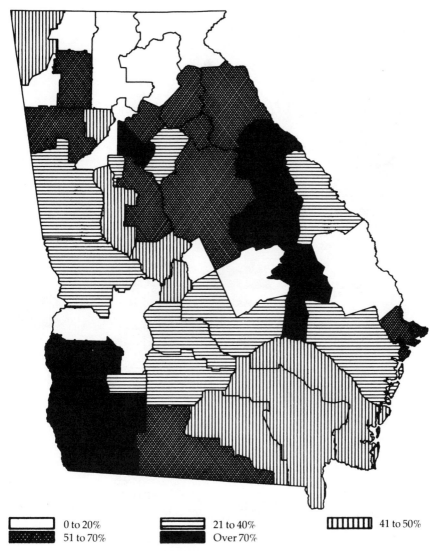

| | 0 to 20% | | 21 to 40% | | 41 to 50% |
| | 51 to 70% | | Over 70% | | |

Separate analyses of jury and prosecutorial post-*Furman* decisions showed no geographic effects on the former. The analysis of prosecutorial decisions showed a statistically significant above-average penalty-trial rate in only one circuit—Ocmulgee in the North Central region.[41] These data suggest a fairly

Figure 19. Distribution of Rates at Which Juries Impose Death Sentences in Penalty Trials, by State Judicial Circuit (Post-*Furman*)

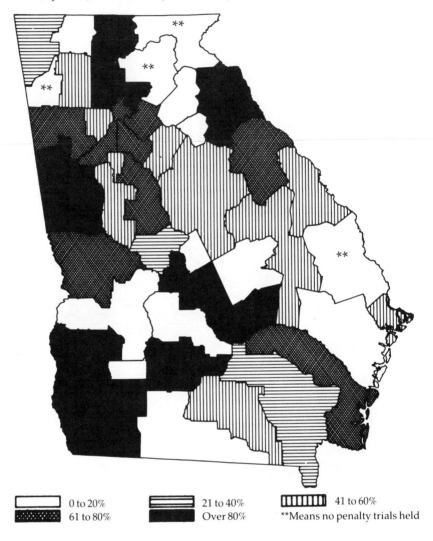

☐ 0 to 20%	▤ 21 to 40%	▥ 41 to 60%
▦ 61 to 80%	■ Over 80%	**Means no penalty trials held

uniform consensus among the prosecutors and juries of the state concerning which defendants were most deserving of a death sentence.[42]

The results of our statistical analysis of geographic disparities provide an interesting point of comparison with the findings of Ursula Bentele, who interviewed a number of Georgia prosecutors in 1982.[43] She reports that "[p]rosecutors in the different Georgia judicial circuits articulated vastly different charging standards . . . concerning when it is appropriate to charge a capital crime." Some prosecutors charge a defendant with a capital murder whenever they can make out a prima facie case for an aggravating circumstance. Others suggested a need for evidence of premeditation, clear intent, or a total disregard for human life. Reasons given for not seeking a death sentence when the facts would support such a request include:

- the high cost of capital trials in time and in resources;
- the difficulty of obtaining executions after death sentences are imposed;
- a low level of public reaction to the crime;
- a low standing of the victim in the community;
- the presence of mitigating circumstances related to the defendant's mental condition; and
- a sentence less than death has been imposed for a more culpable codefendant.

These interviews are consistent with the results of our regression analyses, which identify several of the factors mentioned in the interviews (premeditation, defendant mitigating circumstances, the status of the victim, and the brutality of the killing) as important in explaining statewide patterns in the exercise of prosecutorial discretion. Professor Bentele's interviews are also consistent with the unadjusted data on prosecutorial decisions reported in Table 21, which show substantial intercircuit variation. However, the results of our multivariate analysis, which adjusts for the aggravation level of the cases, suggest considerably less disparity among prosecutors. One explanation for this apparent inconsistency may be that the self-reported policies of the prosecutors do not accurately reflect their policies as applied. Another explanation may be that the levels of intercircuit variation observed in our multiple-regression analyses did not attain statistical significance more often because of the small numbers of cases found in most circuits.

The Distribution of Excessive and Evenhanded Death Sentences

We first examined the distribution of both excessive and evenhanded death sentences by region. The results shown in Table 24 reveal, in each region of the state, both excessive death sentences (those in levels 1 through 3) and evenhanded death sentences (those in levels 5 and 6).[44] If the death sentences that appeared excessive when viewed statewide were in fact the product of very high sentencing rates among less aggravated cases in one or more circuits, Table 24 would show this effect. In fact, among the least aggravated cases statewide, there is relatively little variation in death-sentencing rates across regions.

Table 25 explores the characteristics of the fifteen of thirty-one death-sentencing judicial circuits that produced one or more death sentences that we would classify as comparatively excessive. Column D of the table indicates that

Table 24. Distribution of Death-Sentencing Rates and Death Sentences among Death-Eligible Cases Statewide and by Region, Controlling for Culpability Level

Case Culpability Level, 1 (low) to 6 (high)[1]	Statewide	Region				
		North	North Central	Fulton County	Southwest	Southeast
1	.02 (6/276)	.0 (0/33)	.05 (4/78)	.0 (0/47)	.02 (1/64)	.02 (1/54)
2	.14 (9/65)	.0 (0/6)	.21 (5/24)	.09 (1/11)	.10 (1/10)	.14 (2/14)
3	.38 (18/47)	.40 (2/5)	.45 (9/20)	.50 (3/6)	.33 (1/3)	.23 (3/13)
4	.65 (22/34)	.50 (1/2)	.85 (11/13)	.25 (1/4)	.83 (5/6)	.44 (4/9)
5	.85 (23/27)	1.00 (1/1)	.79 (11/14)	1.00 (1/1)	1.00 (5/5)	.83 (5/6)
6	1.0 (34/34)	NC[a]	1.00 (13/13)	1.00 (3/3)	1.00 (10/10)	1.00 (8/8)
Percent of all death sentences in region		.04	.48	.08	.20	.20
Percent of all excessive death sentences in region		.06	.55	.12	.09	.18

1. The culpability index (OVERALLC) and scale (SCALC) underlying this table are described *supra* chap. 4, note 38, and *infra* app. J, part 1.
a. NC means no cases.

in eight circuits more than 40 percent of the death sentences imposed are presumptively excessive. Moreover, column C indicates that one-half of those circuits are located in the North Central region. A similar analysis of the sixteen death-sentencing circuits that produced no excessive death sentences revealed, however, a quite similar proportion of circuits from the North Central region. What makes the North Central region stand out is the high proportion of its districts that have high death-sentencing rates.

The comparison of the circuits with and without excessive death sentences also revealed that the excessive death sentences are disproportionately located in urban circuits. Of the eight urban circuits in which death sentences were imposed, only the two that imposed no death sentences were without excessive death sentences. Moreover, the Cobb and Stone Mountain circuits, both quite urban, were among the circuits with the largest proportion of excessive sentences imposed. Although entirely speculative, it is possible that the lower visibility of homicides in urban criminal-justice systems may give prosecutors in those areas a scope of discretion that leads to inconsistency.

A. Proportion of Death Sentences Imposed that Are Comparatively Excessive	B. Circuit Name[2]	C. Region of the State[3]	D. Proportion of Death Sentences that Are Comparatively Excessive	E. Circuit Death-Sentencing Rate[4]
.00	Alcovy, Augusta,* Blue Ridge, Clayton, Flint, Griffin, Gwinnett, Houston, Oconee, Pataula, Piedmont, S. Georgia, Southern,* Tifton, Toombs, Waycross		.00	.27 (37/136)
.01–.19	Chattahoochee*	4	.13 (1/8)	.24 (8/34)
.20–.39	Brunswick	5	.20 (1/5)	.42 (5/12) +
	Coweta	2	.25 (2/8)	.44 (8/18) +
	Middle	5	.25 (1/4)	.44 (4/9) +
	Macon*	4	.33 (1/3)	.16 (3/19)
	Northern	2	.33 (1/3)	.60 (3/5) +
	Alapaha	4	.33 (1/3)	.33 (3/9) +
.40–.59	Atlanta*	3	.44 (4/9)	.13 (9/72) −
	Lookout Mountain	1	.50 (1/2)	.18 (2/11)
	Tallapoosa	2	.50 (2/4)	.44 (4/9) +
	Eastern*	5	.57 (4/7)	.23 (7/30)
.60–.79	Ocmulgee	2	.63 (5/8)	.29 (8/28)
	Cobb*	2	.67 (2/3)	.27 (3/11)
.80+	Stone Mountain*	2	.86 (6/7)	.50 (7/14) +
	Cherokee	1	1.00 (1/1)	.33 (1/3) +

1. "Comparatively excessive" death sentences are those found in levels 1–3 on Table 24.
2. Circuits not listed in Column B imposed no death sentences.
3. The regions of the state are (1) North, (2) North Central, (3) Fulton County, (4) Southwest, and (5) Southeast. See supra table 22, note 2.
4. The statewide average death-sentencing rate, based on both excessive and other death sentences, was .23 (112/483) among all circuits, including 11 in which no death sentences were imposed. Among circuits imposing death sentences, the rate was .27 (112/420). Circuits with substantially above-average death-sentencing rates (10 or more percentage points above the statewide average) are identified with a "+"; circuits with rates 10 or more percentage points below the statewide average are identified with a "−".
*The asterisk identifies the urban judicial circuits.

We also tested the hypothesis that excessive death sentences were more likely to be found in circuits with above-average death-sentencing rates. The data provided only weak support for this theory. The circuits with excessive death sentences were only slightly more likely to have above average death-sentencing rates. We did note, however, that none of the circuits with excessive sentences showed death-sentencing rates significantly below the statewide average, while 25 percent of the circuits with no excessive sentences had rates substantially below average.[45] These findings suggest that while it is possible to conduct a punitive capital-sentencing program without also producing excessive death sentences, punitive sentencing practices do, on the average, increase somewhat the risk of excessive death sentences.

The upshot of our analysis of the distribution of excessive death sentences is that none of the variables for legitimate case characteristics that we examined is capable of explaining much of the variations between regions and circuits. This suggests that excessive sentences are either the product of suspect or illegitimate case characteristics (such as the race of defendant or victim), or of unmeasured idiosyncratic factors (such as the vagaries of plea bargaining among coperpetrators, the luck of the draw in juror selection, the competence, level of preparedness, and diligence of the prosecutor, the court, and the defendant's attorney, and the type of impression the defendant made on the jury).[46]

CONCLUSION

The data presented in this chapter support a number of observations concerning capriciousness at the trial stage of Georgia's capital-sentencing system. As we noted earlier, our study analyzed only prosecutorial and jury-trial decisions. As a result, our findings do not reflect the impact of pretrial prosecutorial charging and plea-bargaining decisions, which may have enabled highly culpable offenders to avoid the risk of a death sentence. For this reason, the levels of excessiveness we report for both the pre- and post-*Furman* periods may very well understate the level of excessiveness one would observe in the system as a whole.[47]

Our first observation is that, both before and after *Furman*, the number of death sentences imposed was substantially less than Georgia law authorized. The actual decisions made both by prosecutors and by juries reflect much less enthusiasm for capital punishment in practice than the theoretical support for it expressed in public opinion polls and in the broad death-sentencing statutes enacted by the Georgia legislature.[48] This finding provides strong support for Franklin Zimring and Gordon Hawkins's hypothesis that the *Gregg* court misread the legislative backlash after *Furman* as reflecting strong public support for both the imposition and execution of death sentences.[49]

Our second conclusion is that, as they pertain to Georgia, the empirical assertions and assumptions of neither the concurring nor the dissenting justices in *Furman v. Georgia* were completely correct. Georgia's pre-*Furman* system for sentencing defendants convicted of murder at trial was clearly not a lottery, as several concurring justices suggested, although it was much closer to being a lottery than the highly selective system envisioned by Chief Justice Burger.[50]

Third, in its consistency Georgia's post-*Furman* system represents an improvement over the pre-*Furman* period, although the degree of improvement depends on the measure of case culpability used to identify similar cases.[51] Also, there is a possibility that altered record-keeping practices in the post-*Furman* period, which may have emphasized the collection of case data on statutory aggravating circumstances, could have exaggerated somewhat the degree of consistency that we observe. The most important improvement is a substantial reduction in the proportion of excessive death sentences (those found among the least aggravated cases, for which death sentences are quite infrequent). Also, a considerably higher proportion of the death-sentence cases appear to be evenhanded, that is, imposed in categories of highly aggravated cases that regularly result in death sentences.

Fourth, the post-*Furman* improvements in Georgia's death-sentencing system appear to be attributable in significant part to Georgia's 1973 reforms of its death-sentencing procedure. To a substantial degree, those reforms served to restrict the kinds of murder cases in which the death sentence was a permissible sanction and to guide the exercise of sentencing discretion by juries. The reforms were also expected to have an indirect effect on the decision of prosecutors acting in anticipation of jury sentencing patterns.[52]

Fifth, in spite of these improvements, the post-*Furman* system in Georgia is far from the chief justice's vision of a selective system that limits death sentences to the most extreme cases. Even when viewed in the most favorable light, only 50 percent to 60 percent of Georgia's death-sentence cases appear to be presumptively evenhanded, and nearly a third of them are presumptively excessive.[53]

Sixth, the post-*Furman* death-sentencing rate among the cases defined as death-eligible under each of Georgia's statutory aggravating factors is quite low. As a result, those statutory aggravating circumstances do not provide a meaningful basis for distinguishing between the relatively few defendants who are sentenced to death and the vast majority who receive life sentences or less. However, by taking other, nonstatutory factors into account, it is possible, in a meaningful and principled way, to distinguish about half of the post-*Furman* death-sentence cases from the larger group of life-sentence cases.[54]

Seventh, Georgia's prosecutors play a much more prominent role in the post-*Furman* capital-sentencing system than the Supreme Court contemplated in *Gregg v. Georgia*.[55] The Court presumed in *Gregg* that defendants guilty of capital crimes would routinely undergo penalty trials. In fact, penalty trials occurred in only a small proportion of capital cases because prosecutors generally chose to waive the death sentence. Moreover, the data indicate that those cases in which Georgia prosecutors chose to waive the penalty trial were not limited to the relatively unaggravated cases in which juries were unlikely to impose a death sentence. Many quite serious cases that would have probably resulted in death sentences never reached a penalty trial.

Eighth, the data are plain that, contrary to the assumption of the Court in *Gregg*, prosecutors do not regularly seek nor do juries regularly impose death sentences in death-eligible cases. The data are somewhat unclear, however, about the relative appetite of prosecutors and juries for capital punishment. Among cases of similar levels of blameworthiness, as determined by our measures of culpability, prosecutors and juries tend to seek and impose the death sentence at essentially the same rate. If, however, our measures are overlooking intangibles that influence levels of case culpability as perceived by the juries, and the cases they encounter are in fact more aggravated than those confronted by the prosecutors, juries would appear to be applying a higher threshold of culpability before imposing a death sentence than prosecutors do in seeking a death sentence. In any event, the relative lack of enthusiasm for capital punishment among the less aggravated cases on the part of both prosecutors and juries holds the overall death-sentencing rate to the quite low levels that we observe among the death-eligible cases as a whole.

Ninth, our data from Georgia suggest that if prosecutors advanced all capital-murder-conviction cases to a penalty trial, thereby enhancing the jury's role in the death-sentencing process, there would be a dramatic increase—well over 50 percent—in the number of death sentences imposed.[56] This change would also result in a significant increase in the number and proportion of both evenhanded and excessive death sentences. At the same time, the number and proportion of death-sentence cases falling between these two extremes would decline. We conclude, therefore, that the heavy influence of Georgia's prosecutors in the posttrial sentencing process substantially reduces both the total number of death sentences imposed and the number of death sentences imposed that are excessive in a comparative sense.

Tenth, unadjusted data show substantial variations in death-sentencing rates in different parts of the state. However, adjustment for case culpability reduced these apparent disparities significantly.

Finally, we examined the distribution of death sentences that our measures suggested were excessive and evenhanded in a comparative sense. We found both types of death sentences in each of the state's five regions, but the excessive death sentences were somewhat overrepresented in the North Central region. Also, excessive death sentences are disproportionately found in urban areas and somewhat more likely to occur in circuits with above-average death-sentencing rates. Nevertheless, much of the variation in the distribution of excessive sentences could not be explained with the data available on legitimate case characteristics, suggesting that excessive sentences most likely result from suspect and illegitimate factors, such as the race and socioeconomic status of the defendant or the victim, or, perhaps, other idiosyncratic factors that are not well understood.[57]

NOTES

1. See 408 U.S. 238, 249–50 (1972) (Douglas, J., concurring); id. at 291–95 (Brennan, J., concurring); id. at 309–10 (Stewart, J., concurring); id. at 311–13 (White, J., concurring); id. at 314–74 (Marshall, J., concurring).

2. Id. at 386n.11 (Burger, C.J., dissenting).

3. For the purposes of this illustration, we allocated the post-*Furman* death sentences randomly across all 594 cases in our post-*Furman* sample.

4. See supra chap. 4, note 50, for discussion of the rationale for defining excessive and evenhanded death sentences.

5. Furman v. Georgia, 408 U.S. at 311–12 (White, J., concurring). See also id. at 309–10 (Stewart, J., concurring); id. at 398, 402–3 (Burger, C.J., dissenting).

6. See supra chap. 4, note 39 and accompanying text, and app. J for a description of the pre-*Furman* regression model (PREFURMC) used for this test. A case was deemed to be correctly predicted if the model predicted more than a .50 probability the sentence that was actually imposed.

7. Because, as noted in the text, the analysis involves a dichotomous outcome variable (death or life sentence), a more appropriate measure of the predictability of the pre-*Furman* system is an "analysis of information"; see Baldus, Pulaski, Woodworth, & Kyle, *Identifying Comparatively Excessive Sentences of Death: A Quantitative Approach*, 33 STAN L. REV. 1n.86 (1980). The total information required to predict the 44 pre-*Furman* death sentences in our sample is 172 bits; however, the statistically significant variables in our best logistic regression provided only 60 bits of information. In this sense, the system is only 35% predictable.

8. See supra table 8 and accompanying text.

9. The frequency distribution of these variables is shown in app. D. The most predictive version of the "number of statutory aggravating circumstances" variable treated each of five circumstances satisfying the requirement for the heinous, vile, and outrageous statutory aggravating circumstance (B7) as a separate statutory aggravating factor. This modification raised the simple correlation between the death-sentencing results and a count of statutory aggravating circumstances present from .49 to .58. For some time after *Gregg*, it was unclear to what extent it was permissible for juries to consider nonstatutory aggravating circumstances in their death-sentencing deliberations. Zant v. Stephens, 462 U.S. 862 (1983), held that they could be so long as a single statutory aggravating circumstance was found by the sentencing authority.

10. The seventeen variables are (1) number of statutory aggravating circumstances plus the number of B7 (vile murder) circumstances in the case, (2) female victim, (3)

defendant underling in the murder, (4) victim stranger, (5) multiple stabs, (6) defendant killed two or more people, (7) victim hostage, (8) victim police- or fireperson, (9) victim twelve years or younger, (10) defendant lay in wait, (11) defendant in military, (12) race-hatred motive, (13) a bloody murder, (14) neither kidnap nor multiple shots, (15) aggravated motive and one or more prior felony convictions, (16) number of convictions for violent personal crimes (other than murder, rape, armed robbery, kidnap) and number of statutory aggravating circumstances interaction, and (17) defendant resisted arrest and one or more prior felony convictions. The coefficients for the variables are listed in app. J *infra*, Model OVERALLC; *see supra* chap. 4, note 34 and accompanying text, for a description of the process used for selecting the variables.

11. Justice White was most explicit about the assumption in his concurrence. *Gregg v. Georgia*, 428 U.S. 153, 207 (1976) (White, J., concurring).

12. *See supra* chap. 4, note 29 and accompanying text, for a description of the Barnett classification system.

13. Although some readers may not consider the defendant/victim relationship an appropriate basis to assess the blameworthiness of a capital defendant, it is clearly an important factor for prosecutors and juries. We also believe the legitimacy of the factor is problematic, but believe it probably serves as a proxy for an assumption of the risk by the victim. Barnett's rationale is as follows: "This status dimension has little explicit basis in law. It is hard to avoid speculating that, in killings in which jurors can imagine themselves or their loved ones as victims, death penalties are more likely to be imposed. To say this is not to impute cynicism to the juries; when a case evokes genuine fear, considerations of deterrence may more greatly affect the sentencing decision than otherwise." Barnett, *Some Distribution Patterns for the Georgia Death Sentence*, 18 U.C. DAVIS L. REV. 1327, 1341 (1985). *See infra* chap. 6, note 25 and accompanying text, for a discussion of "legitimate, suspect, and illegitimate" case characteristics, including the defendant/victim relationship.

14. Using an analysis-of-information approach, *supra* note 7, Georgia's post-*Furman* system is 61% predictable (418 bits of information are required to predict the death-sentence cases, but the variables in the logistic model provided only 255 bits of information).

15. Although we doubt it, it is possible that opinion-poll respondents who state that they favor capital punishment for murder are expressing support for the practice of the last fifteen years of regularly imposing death sentences but rarely executing them. Unfortunately, the questions put to citizens in death-penalty opinion polls do not permit a definitive answer to the question.

16. We have no basis for comparing the consistency of Georgia's system before and after *Furman* with respect to its consistency in the treatment of all death-eligible offenders, including those whose cases, because of plea bargains, did not result in a jury murder-trial conviction.

17. The Zant v. Stephens, 462 U.S. 862 (1983), model (which is discussed *infra*, chap. 10, note 4) holds that once a jury finds one or more statutory aggravating circumstances present, it may consider any legitimate factors it deems important.

18. Figure 1 in chap. 4 illustrates the relatively small scope of the PRS's examination of Georgia's entire charging-and-sentencing system. The only defendants included in our study are those whom juries convicted of murder (or who received death sentences after entry of a guilty plea). The PRS sheds no light at all upon the manner in which prosecutors decided whether to seek a capital-murder indictment in a homicide case or whether to permit a defendant indicted for capital murder to plead guilty in exchange

for a life sentence or to plead to a lesser crime. For example, of fifty defendants arrested for armed robbery–murder, prosecutors might choose not to seek capital-murder indictments in a handful of cases and permit twenty-five of those indicted for capital murder either to plead guilty to murder in exchange for a waiver of the death penalty or to plead to a lesser offense. Conceivably, some or all of the defendants who thereby avoided the risk of a capital-murder conviction at trial through pretrial prosecutorial intercession might have been convicted of capital murder at trial and have found their way into our study. If these cases had resulted in life sentences, either through a post-trial waiver of the death penalty by the prosecutor or a jury life-sentence decision, their presence in the study would have increased the pool of life-sentence cases in the study. This in turn would have made the death sentences imposed among the similarly situated defendants appear less frequent and relatively more excessive in a comparative sense than is apparent in our analysis, limited as it is to defendants convicted of murder at trial.

19. Data from the Charging-and-Sentencing Study (CSS), which includes information on earlier stages in the process, support this view. They indicate that, for the period it covers, the PRS includes approximately 40% of the death-eligible cases that resulted in either a murder or a voluntary-manslaughter conviction. Also, among the total population of death-eligible defendants in the CSS convicted of murder or voluntary manslaughter, the death-sentencing rate was only .08 (128/1,576).

20. Another major component of the 1973 procedural reforms was a requirement of comparative-proportionality review, GA. CODE ANN. §§27-2537(c)(3) (1983). This reform would affect the results at the trial level only indirectly through its potential influence on the exercise of prosecutorial discretion in seeking the death penalty.

21. The average number of statutory factors was 2.22 pre-*Furman* and 2.3 post-*Furman*. When we made the comparison with variable DELB7EX, which emphasizes the variables related to the B7 (wanton/vile statutory aggravating) circumstance, we saw a somewhat larger increase in the number of aggravating factors among the death-eligible cases, 1.7 pre-*Furman* versus 2.2 post-*Furman*, a difference significant at the .06 level. We are grateful to Samuel R. Gross for suggesting the record-keeping rival hypothesis in the context of this research.

22. The index score for each case was based on the combined results of three separate regression analyses, which for the post-*Furman* period included all cases whether or not they were classified death-eligible by our measures. Two analyses were designed to include comparable numbers of cases pre- and post-*Furman*. The first used the 1970–72 pre-*Furman* cases and all of the post-*Furman* cases that advanced to a penalty trial. The second analysis used all of the 1970–72 pre-*Furman* data and the post-*Furman* data for 1973–74. The third analysis used the 1970–72 pre-*Furman* data and the 1973–75 post-*Furman* data, which ensured coverage for equal periods pre- and post-*Furman*. See Baldus, Pulaski, & Woodworth, *Comparative Review of Death Sentences: An Empirical Study of the Georgia Experience*, 74 J. CRIM. L. & CRIMINOLOGY 661, 689n.98 (1983) for details of the index.

23. The median culpability score for either the life- or death-sentence cases is a score at the 50th percentile on the culpability index. In contrast, the average or mean score, referred to below, is calculated by summing the culpability scores for all the cases and dividing by the number of cases.

24. Weisberg, *Deregulating Death*, 1983 SUP. CT. REV. 305, 379–82, argues that the bifurcated sentencing procedures in the post-*Furman* period, as well as the "language of legalism" that pervades jury instructions in the post-*Furman* period, may lead

jurors to believe that under certain circumstances they have no discretion to impose anything but a death sentence. In contrast, in the pre-*Furman* period the instructions left the entire question to the conscience of the jury with no guidance from the court on how their discretion should be exercised, a procedure that may well have enhanced the influence of emotional appeals from the prosecutor and defense counsel.

25. The death-sentencing rate in one circuit did not change.

26. *See supra* text following note 8.

27. Another measure of the importance of the statutory aggravating factors is the amount of "variance" (variation in the death-sentencing results) that they explain in an ordinary-least-squares (O.L.S.) multiple-regression statistical analysis. For the pre-*Furman* period, the explained variance, measured with an R^2 statistic, was .09, while for the post-*Furman* period it was .23. In addition, in a logistic multiple-regression analysis that estimated the impact of each of the ten post-*Furman* statutory aggravating circumstances after simultaneous adjustment for all of the others, four of the ten emerged as statistically significant beyond the .05 level in the pre-*Furman* analysis, while seven were significant beyond the .05 level in the post-*Furman* analysis.

28. Educational levels increased in Georgia from 1960 to 1980. The percentage of all persons twenty-five years and older who graduated from high school, but did not attend college, increased from 18.4% in 1960 to 22.4% in 1970 to 28.5% in 1980. The percentage of whites twenty-five years and older with this much education increased from 22.3% in 1960 to 25% in 1970 to 29.4% in 1980; for blacks, the figures were 7% in 1960, 13.3% in 1970, and 25.6% in 1980. The percentage of people twenty-five years and older with a four-year college degree or more increased from 6.2% in 1960 to 9.2% in 1970 to 14.6% in 1980; by race, the increase for whites was from 7.5% in 1960 to 10.7% in 1970 to 16.6% in 1980; the increase for blacks was from 2.5% in 1960 to 4.0% in 1970 to 7.5% in 1980. 1980 CENSUS OF POPULATION, 1 *Characteristics of the Population*, pt. 12: Georgia, ch. C, at 12–65 (Dep't. Commerce 1983) (data for 1970 & 1980); CENSUS OF POPULATION: 1960, 1 *Characteristics of the Population*, pt. 12: Georgia, at 12–192 (Dep't. Commerce 1963). In addition, the median income for families in Georgia increased from $4,208 in 1960 to $8,167 in 1970 to $17,414 in 1980. 1980 CENSUS OF POPULATION, 1 *Characteristics of the Population*, pt. 12: Georgia, ch. C, at 12–76 (Dep't. Commerce 1983); 1970 CENSUS OF POPULATION, 1 *Characteristics of the Population*, pt. 12: Georgia, at 12–238 (Dep't. Commerce 1973) (data for 1960 & 1970).

29. By 1976, it was apparent that the Georgia Supreme Court would not provide rigorous oversight of the system to ensure consistency through its comparative-proportionality review. *See infra* chap. 7.

30. Nationwide responses to the following question give some idea of the change that has taken place: "Do blacks have a right to live wherever they want?"

	1964	1968	1970	1972	1974	1975	1976
Yes: blacks can live where they choose	57.1%	67.8%	70.5%	76.4%	83.4%	83.0%	85.3%
No: whites can keep blacks out	26.5%	22.2%	19.1%	15.7%	9.5%	12.5%	8.2%
Don't know	16.5%	10.1%	10.4%	7.9%	7.1%	4.5%	6.5%

P. Converse, AMERICAN SOCIAL ATTITUDES DATA SOURCEBOOK, 1947–1978, at 65 (1980). The degree of change has probably not been so dramatic in the South, however, as responses from the South to a 1983 Gallup Poll suggest. When asked about the propriety of interracial marriages, there was a 50% disapproval rate nationwide and a 60% disapproval rate in the South. G. Gallup, THE GALLUP POLL: PUBLIC OPINION 1983, at 96–98 (1984).

31. GA. CODE ANN. §§26-1101(c), 26-3102, 27-2528 (1983).

32. Gregg v. Georgia, 428 U.S. 153, 196 (1976).

33. As noted earlier (supra chap. 2, text following note 8), in the pre-*Furman* period, before the bifurcated trial was established, prosecutors could influence or determine the jury's death-sentencing decision by not requesting a jury charge on death as a sentencing option or by stating to the jury that the state did not seek a death sentence.

34. See infra chap. 8, note 3 and accompanying text, for discussion of the theory that the United States death-sentencing system behaves as if it were subject to a 250–300 annual quota of death sentences. The jury death-sentencing rates do indicate, however, that sentencing juries frequently disagree with the prosecution's assessment of which individual defendants are most deserving.

35. See, e.g., H. Kalven Jr. & H. Zeisel, THE AMERICAN JURY 498 (2d ed. 1971) ("the group nature of the jury decision will moderate and brake eccentric views"). However, in large prosecutorial offices, like Fulton County, the decision to seek a death sentence will normally involve consultation, although the decision not to seek a death sentence in a death-eligible case is more likely to be made by the prosecutor handling the case. For a thorough review of the literature, see M. Saks, SMALL GROUP DECISION MAKING AND COMPLEX INFORMATION TASKS 26 (Federal Judicial Center 1981).

36. Making a penalty trial mandatory in every case of a capital-murder conviction would carry a significant price tag; but, before one can address that question, the issue discussed in the text must be answered.

37. The eleven background variables used in the analysis were (1) number of statutory aggravating circumstances plus the number of B7 (vile murder) circumstances in the case, (2) female victim, (3) defendant in military, (4) a bloody murder, (5) kidnap and multiple shots, (6) defendant was accomplice to relatively minor act, (7) multiple shots, (8) insurance motive, (9) victim kidnapped, (10) defendant had history of drug or alcohol abuse, and (11) prior convictions for murder/armed robbery/rape/kidnap and other violent personal crimes. These comprise the JURYC index and underlie the JASCALC scale found in app. L, part 3.

38. Counties were defined as "metropolitan" if they were SMSA counties with a population of 50,000 or more, or suburban counties with three or more judges and having more than 70% urban population in 1970, density of more than 500 per square mile, and less than 10% farmland. Other counties with a city of 25,000–50,000 population in 1970 were deemed "urban." Our urban/rural analysis treats judicial circuits with either a "metropolitan" or an "urban" county as an "urban circuit." See generally, A HISTORY OF GEORGIA (K. Coleman ed. 1977).

The urban circuits, with their "urban" or "metropolitan" county (in parentheses), plus the number of death-eligible cases in the circuit, are as follows: Atlanta (Fulton: 72), Augusta (Richmond: 19), Chattahoochee (Muscogee: 34), Cobb (Cobb: 11), Dougherty (Dougherty: 15), Eastern (Chatham: 30), Macon (Bibb: 19), Rome (Floyd: 7), Southern (Lowndes: 9), Stone Mountain (DeKalb: 14), and Western (Clarke: 8).

39. See Tabak, The Death of Fairness: The Arbitrary and Capricious Imposition of the Death Penalty in the 1980's, 14 N.Y.U. REV. L. & SOC. CHANGE 797 (1986) (hereinafter Tabak), for a perceptive summary of these factors; Amsterdam, The Supreme Court and Capital Punishment, 14 HUMAN RIGHTS 14 (A.B.A. Sec. on Individual Rights & Responsibilities) (Winter 1987).

40. In a data set in which the death sentence was sought in about two hundred cases and was imposed in about one hundred cases scattered among forty-two judicial circuits, it is extremely difficult to evaluate geographic variations in death-seeking and death-sentencing rates for two reasons. First, in most judicial circuits, there will be only a handful of cases in which the death sentence was sought or imposed, so that estimated rates will have large standard errors. Second, logistic regression is extremely sensitive to influential observations, or "leverage points."

In general, a leverage point is a single case that, if deleted, would substantially alter the size of a regression coefficient. In our Georgia data, we find that leverage points most often are instances in which the adverse outcome is consistently associated with the presence of a rare characteristic in cases that otherwise are not highly aggravated. Since most judicial circuits are comparatively "rare," making up less than 2% or 3% of the data, the problem of leverage points is particularly acute when studying geographic variation. We used three strategies to make our analysis more powerful and less sensitive to leverage points. First, we aggregated judicial circuits into larger units: we made a regional aggregation into five broad, comparatively homogeneous areas of the state and an urban/rural aggregation into two categories for urban circuits and rural circuits. See *supra* Table 22 and note 38 and accompanying text for detail on the regional and urban/rural classifications.

For each geographic level, we created a geographic variable(s), and interaction terms between each geographic variable(s) and the race-of-defendant and race-of-victim variables. Thus, we had 3 variables for the urban/rural dimension, 15 (5 × 3) variables for the regional dimension, and 126 (42 × 3) variables for the circuit dimension.

To measure geographic variations, we conducted a separate logistic analysis for each of the three different geographic levels. Each included the appropriate geographic variables and interaction terms plus the culpability-index variable embracing the legitimate aggravating and mitigating circumstances of OVERALLA index (*see* app. J) or its components. To minimize the leverage-point problem referred to above, we randomly split the data into halves and "screened" the geographic variables and geographic-racial interactions in each set of analyses by computing weighted correlations between candidate variables and logistic residuals, in effect adjusting for the OVERALLA culpability index. (A logistic residual is $(y-\hat{p})/\hat{p}\hat{g}$, where y is the dichotomous outcome and $\hat{p}$ the fitted probability; the weight is $\hat{p}\hat{g}$.) A geographic area or a race-geography interaction was accepted as deviating from the statewide model only if it correlated significantly in both halves of the data ($p \leq .15$). We presented candidate variables that passed this screening step to a stepwise logistic regression conducted on the entire data set and that included the component variables of the culpability index (which included variables for the race of the defendant and race of the victim). Geographic variables and interactions that entered these analyses beyond the .15 level of statistical significance we considered to be important evidence of geographic variability.

41. The logistic-regression coefficient for the Ocmulgee circuit was $b = 1.92$ (S.E. = .66), which carries an odds multiplier of 6.8.

42. We expected to find lower jury death-sentencing rates in circuits with more punitive prosecutorial policies, since those juries would likely confront cases that are less aggravated than average with respect to factors not included in our data.

43. Bentele, *The Death Penalty in Georgia: Still Arbitrary*, 62 WASH. U.L.Q. 573, 616 (1985).

44. See *supra* chap. 4, note 50 and accompanying text, for a description of the rationale used to classify death sentences as excessive and evenhanded.

45. We considered a death-sentencing rate to be substantially above or below the statewide average if it were 10 or more percentage points above or below the statewide average.

46. *See* Tabak, *supra* note 39. We consider racial discrimination as a source of excessiveness, *infra* chap. 6, notes 18 & 24 and accompanying text (post-*Furman*), and on p. 148 (pre-*Furman*).

47. *See supra* notes 19 and 20.

48. The Gallup polls report the following proportion of people nationwide in favor of the death penalty for murder: 1953, 68%; 1960, 51%; 1965, 45%; 1971, 49%; 1976, 65%; 1978, 62%; 1980, 56%; 1981, 66%; 1982, 72%; 1985, 75%. G. Gallup, THE GALLUP POLL: PUBLIC OPINION 1978, at 115 (1979); PUBLIC OPINION 1980, at 250 (1981); PUBLIC OPINION 1981, at 43–44 (1982); PUBLIC OPINION 1982, at 251 (1983); and PUBLIC OPINION 1985, at 268–69 (1986). In 1983, 80% of the residents of the South Atlantic states, which include Georgia, favored the death penalty for murder. PUBLIC OPINION, "Opinion Roundup," Feb./Mar. 1983 (Vol. 6, No. 1), at 26. *See infra* chap. 12, note 43 and accompanying text, for a discussion of the implications of this finding. As we have previously remarked, *supra* note 15, the support expressed in these polls may be for frequent death sentencing and rare execution.

49. *See supra* chap. 3, note 2.

50. *See supra* note 8 and accompanying text.

51. *See supra* notes 9 and 10 and accompanying text.

52. *See supra* notes 21 to 28 and accompanying text.

53. *See supra* table 10 and figures 5 and 6 and accompanying text.

54. *See supra* table 10 and figure 6 and accompanying text.

55. *See supra* note 33 and accompanying text.

56. *See supra* note 36 and accompanying text.

57. *See supra* notes 39 to 46 and accompanying text.

CHAPTER SIX

The Influence of Racial and Suspect Factors in the Postconviction Phases of Georgia's Capital-Sentencing System

In this chapter we assess the influence of racial and other suspect factors on postconviction decisions by prosecutors and juries in pre- and post-*Furman* capital-murder cases; the results are from the Procedural Reform Study (PRS). The race-discrimination results from the Charging and Sentencing Study (CSS) that were used in *McCleskey v. Kemp* are presented in chapter 10.[1] From a legal standpoint, our findings bear on both the issue of racial discrimination under the Fourteenth Amendment and the issue of arbitrariness under the Eighth Amendment.[2]

PRE-*FURMAN*

In one manner or another, virtually all of the justices who participated in the *Furman* decision addressed the question of racially discriminatory death sentences. Several of the concurring justices expressed concern that unrestrained sentencing discretion in capital cases left jurors free to consider racially discriminatory or other suspect factors, such as the defendant's sex or socioeconomic status, when imposing sentence.[3] Indeed, Justice Marshall flatly asserted that, based on the available evidence, racially discriminatory death sentences had occurred. By contrast, Justice Stewart and the dissenting justices disagreed. They felt that the available evidence was simply inadequate to justify such a finding. But they did agree that, in principle, racially discriminatory death sentences were unconstitutional.

One major purpose of our study of Georgia was to determine, if possible, what impact racial or other suspect factors actually exerted on the postconviction phases of Georgia's death-sentencing process both before and after the *Furman*-prompted legislative reforms enacted in 1973. Because of the nature of our data, we can only report, for the pre-*Furman* period, the extent to which the combined decisions of Georgia prosecutors and juries responded to racial or other suspect factors.[4] For the post-*Furman* period, however, our data permitted separate analyses of prosecutorial and jury decisions.

Race Effects

Table 26 presents the pre-*Furman* death-sentencing rates for defendants convicted at trial, controlling for the race of defendant and victim, but without adjustment for the culpability level of the cases. These data suggest both race-of-defendant and race-of-victim effects. The overall race-of-defendant effect is an 11-percentage-point difference; among the white-victim cases, where we would anticipate the strongest race-of-defendant effect, the disparity is 23 percentage points (.31 versus .08). The overall race-of-victim effect is 8 percentage points; among the black-defendant cases, where we would expect to see the largest impact of the victim's race, the disparity is 21 points (.31 versus .10).

Simple associations between racial characteristics and death-sentencing rates, such as those shown in Table 26, do not, of course, establish that racial factors actually influenced the system. A variety of other factors could explain the associations. For this reason, we estimated the pre-*Furman* race effects after adjusting for various background factors that juries and prosecutors legitimately consider when evaluating the culpability of capital defendants. Then we further controlled for geographic factors and for other suspect factors, such as the sex and socioeconomic status of the defendant and the victim. If racial and other suspect factors exerted no influence on death-sentencing decisions, we would expect to see no significant statistical association between the variables representing such factors and the outcome variables.[5]

Table 26. Unadjusted Race-of-Defendant and Race-of-Victim Disparities in Death-Sentencing Rates (Pre-*Furman*)

A. Race of Defendant	
Black	.19 (35/182)
White	.08 (9/112)
Difference	11 pts.
Ratio	2.4
B. Race of Victim	
White	.18 (32/179)
Black	.10 (12/115)
Difference	8 pts.
Ratio	1.8
C. Defendant/Victim Racial Combination	
1. Black defendant/white victim	.31 (24/77)
2. White defendant/white victim	.08 (8/102)
3. Black defendant/black victim	.10 (11/105)
4. White defendant/black victim	.10 (1/10)

We used three methods to adjust for the legitimate background factors. The first method involves fitting a logistic-regression model that included the defendant's and victim's race among the explanatory variables. Figure 20 is a plot of the death-sentencing rates predicted for the cases involving each of the four defendant/victim racial combinations after taking account of both the culpability level of the cases and their racial characteristics. The X axis in Figure 20 indicates the culpability scores of the cases, estimated with a logistic multiple-regression analysis of legitimate case characteristics, while the Y axis indicates the predicted likelihood of a death sentence for each. Thus, each case is plotted according to its culpability score and the likelihood of receiving a death sentence predicted for each case given its racial characteristics and level of case culpability. If racial factors exerted no effect on the system, the estimated plots for each subgroup of cases would perfectly overlap.[6] If there are measurable race effects in the system, the predicted plots for the subgroup will separate.

The coefficients for both the race-of-victim and race-of-defendant variables were statistically significant in the logistic-regression analysis that underlies

Figure 20.   Logistic Model of Race Effects in Pre-*Furman* Georgia

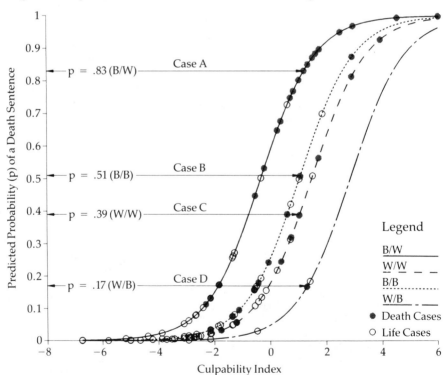

the plots in Figure 20. Morever, the magnitude of the gaps between the plots for the four subgroups of cases further suggests that the impact of the two racial variables was substantial. One gains a sense of the magnitude of this impact by comparing the estimated death sentences for the four cases labelled A, B, C, and D in Figure 20. Each of these four cases is comparable in terms of its location at approximately the midpoint along the culpability index; however, the predicted likelihood of a death sentence for the four cases varies considerably. For case D, the white-defendant/black-victim case, the predicted likelihood of a death sentence is .17, while for case C, the white-defendant/white-victim case, the predicted rate is .39. For the two black-defendant cases the rates are .51 for B, whose victim was black, and .83 for A, whose victim was white.

Figure 20 also suggests that each of these two racial factors—the victim's race and the defendant's race—exerted a significant independent influence on Georgia's post-*Furman* sentencing results. Even after adjustment for legitimate background factors, Figure 20 indicates that the predicted rate for all black defendants is higher than the predicted rate for any white defendant with comparable culpability scores. There is also a strong race-of-victim effect, reflected by the higher predicted rates for white-victim cases, among both white- and black-defendant cases.

Our second method of describing the impact of racial, as opposed to legitimate, factors involved the calculation of partial-regression coefficients for the race-of-defendant and race-of-victim variables.[7] These partial-regression coefficients serve as overall average estimates of the race effects shown in Figure 20. The logistic-regression analysis displayed in Figure 20 estimated that the average black defendant's odds of receiving a death sentence were 12 times higher than a comparable white defendant's. The estimated odds of receiving a death sentence if the defendant killed a white person were 4.3 times those applicable to a comparable defendant with a black victim.

Our third measure of race effects involves a comparison of the actual death-sentencing rates for racially defined subgroups of cases of comparable culpability. The results appear in Table 27. The table first subdivides the cases into six subgroups with comparable levels of culpability (column A); it then separates the white-victim cases (columns C through F) and the black-victim cases (columns G through J). Within each of those subgroups it compares the death-sentencing rates for the black and white defendants. The results of this analysis are particularly telling, in our judgment, because the estimates are much less dependent on the validity of the assumptions of multiple-regression analysis.

The key columns in Table 27 are E and F. They compare the death-sentencing rates for black and white defendants after controlling for legitimate background factors and the race of the victim. Because the number of white-

Table 27. Race-of-Defendant Disparities in Death-Sentencing Rates, Controlling for Race of Victim and Case Culpability Level (Pre-*Furman*)

A	White-Victim Cases					Black-Victim Cases			
	B	C	D	E	F	G	H	I	J
Culpability Level, 1 (low) to 6 (high)[1]	All Cases	Black-Defendant Cases	White-Defendant Cases	Difference (Col. C − Col. D)[2]	Ratio (Col. C/ Col. D)	Black-Defendant Cases	White-Defendant Cases	Difference (Col. G − Col. H)[2]	Ratio (Col. G/ Col. H)
1	.02	.05 (2/42)	.00 (0/60)	5 pts.	Infinite	.04 (2/56)	.00 (0/5)	4 pts.	Infinite
2	.10	.10 (1/10)	.08 (1/12)	2 pts.	1.3	.11 (2/18)	NC[a]	—	—
3	.20	.71 (5/7)	.05 (1/19)	66 pts.	14.2	.18 (4/22)	.00 (0/2)	18 pts.	Infinite
4	.46	.67 (4/6)	.33 (1/3)	34 pts.	2.0	.33 (1/3)	NC	—	—
5	.62	1.00 (8/8)	.60 (3/5)	40 pts.	1.7	.20 (1/5)	.33 (1/3)	−13 pts.	.61
6	1.00	1.00 (4/4)	1.00 (2/2)	0	1.0	1.00 (1/1)	NC	—	—
All cases	.15 (44/294)	.31 (24/77)	.08 (8/101)[b]	23 pts.	3.9	.10 (11/105)	.10 (1/10)	0	1.0

1. The index and scale underlying this table are PREFURMB and PFSCALB, *supra* chap. 4, note 38 and accompanying text, and *infra* app. J, part 4.
2. The weighted-average, race-of-defendant disparity for both white- and black-victim cases is 12 percentage points, significant at the .001 level.
a. NC means no cases.
b. Case total is 101 instead of 102 because of rounding of weighted life-sentence cases. *See supra* chap. 4, note 2.

defendant/black-victim cases in the sample is small, the disparities in columns I and J do not contribute much to the 12-percentage-point overall race-of-defendant disparity noted in footnote 2 of the table.

Table 28 presents the results of a similar analysis of race-of-victim effects in the pre-*Furman* system. The principal difference in the table is that the initial sort of cases in columns C through F and columns G through J is between the black- and white-defendant cases, with a further division of the cases under each of these groups by race of the victim. Again, columns E and F are most important because of the small number of white-defendant/black-victim cases in column H. The overall race-of-victim effect reported in footnote 2 of the table is 12 percentage points, significant at the .005 level.

The patterns of racial disparity observed in column E of Tables 27 and 28 and in our post-*Furman* data (Table 32) are a central finding of this research. They suggest that race-of-victim and race-of-defendant effects are not uniform across the cases, but appear primarily in cases in the midaggravation range, where the average death-sentencing rates for the various subgroups of cases range from .10 to .60. In other words, the magnitude of the impact of the racial factors on the sentencing outcome varies with the culpability level of the cases.

This phenomenon is an example of what methodologists describe as an "interaction" effect. This interaction between racial factors and case culpability is consistent with earlier jury research by Harry Kalven and Hans Zeisel.[8] They suggested that juries were most influenced by legally irrelevant or impermissible considerations when the evidence of guilt was ambiguous and the case was close. In such situations, they observed, the less than compelling evidence "liberated" the jury to take into account other factors when deciding the defendant's innocence or guilt. Similarly, we found that, when the crime involved was either extremely aggravated or comparatively free from aggravating circumstances, the choice between a life and a death sentence was relatively clear; and, regardless of racial factors, Georgia prosecutors and juries responded accordingly. By contrast, our pre-*Furman* data suggest that in the midaggravation range racial factors did play a significant role, probably for the very reasons that Kalven and Zeisel suggested.[9]

As a further check, we also analyzed the impact of racial factors on our pre-*Furman* sample of Georgia armed-robbery–murder cases. The results were consistent with those just described. Table 29 presents the death-sentencing rates for a group of sixty-one pre-*Furman* armed-robbery–murder cases divided into three culpability levels. It reveals persistent race-of-defendant and race-of-victim effects at all three levels. Specifically, the overall race-of-defendant disparity is 9 percentage points, while the race-of-victim disparity is 3 points, although neither disparity is significant beyond the .10 level.

Table 28. Race-of-Victim Disparities in Death-Sentencing Rates, Controlling for Race of Defendant and Case Culpability Level (Pre-*Furman*)

A	B	Black-Defendant Cases					White-Defendant Cases			
Culpability Level, 1 (low) to 6 (high)[1]	All Cases	C White-Victim Cases	D Black-Victim Cases	E Difference (Col. C − Col. D)[2]	F Ratio (Col. C/Col. D)	G White-Victim Cases	H Black-Victim Cases	I Difference (Col. G − Col. H)[2]	J Ratio (Col. G/Col. H)
1	.02	.05 (2/42)	.04 (2/56)	1 pt.	1.3	.00 (0/60)	.00 (0/5)	0	—
2	.10	.10 (1/10)	.11 (2/18)	−1 pt.	.90	.08 (1/12)	NC[a]	—	—
3	.20	.71 (5/7)	.18 (4/22)	53 pts.	3.9	.05 (1/19)	.00 (0/2)	5 pts.	Infinite
4	.46	.67 (4/6)	.33 (1/3)	34 pts.	2.0	.33 (1/3)	NC	—	—
5	.62	1.00 (8/8)	.20 (1/5)	80 pts.	5.0	.60 (3/5)	.33 (1/3)	27 pts.	1.8
6	1.00	1.0 (4/4)	1.00 (1/1)	0	1.0	1.0 (2/2)	NC	—	—
All cases	.15 (44/294)	.31 (24/77)	.10 (11/105)	21 pts.	3.1	.08 (8/101)[b]	.10 (1/10)	−2 pts.	.80

1. The index and scale underlying this table are PFSCALB, *supra* chap. 4. note 38 and accompanying text, and *infra* app. J, part 4.
2. The weighted-average, race-of-victim disparity among both the white- and black-defendant cases is 12 percentage points, significant at the .005 level (Mantel-Haenszel $Z = 2.91$).

a. NC means no cases.
b. Case total is not 102 because of rounding of life-sentence cases; *see supra* chap. 4, note 2.

Table 29. Death-Sentence Rates in Pre-*Furman* Armed-Robbery–Murder Cases, Controlling for the Defendant/Victim Race Combination and the Culpability Level of the Cases[1]

	Defendant/Victim Racial Combination			
Case Culpability, from 1 (low) to 3 (high)[2]	Black Defendant/ White Victim	White Defendant/ White Victim	Black Defendant/ Black Victim	White Defendant/ Black Victim
1	0 (0/4)	0 (0/4)	0 (0/7)	NC[a]
2	.22 (2/9)	0 (0/11)	0 (0/4)	NC
3	.56 (5/9)	.33 (2/6)	1.0 (1/1)	.33 (1/3)

1. The weighted-average, race-of-defendant effect is 9 percentage points, not significant at the .10 level (Mantel-Haenszel $Z = 1.14$). The weighted-average, race-of-victim effect is 3 percentage points, not significant at the .10 level (Mantel-Haenszel $Z = .26$).
2. *See* text accompanying chap. 4, note 21, for a description of this index.
a. NC means no cases.

The practical consequences of racial discrimination in the pre-*Furman* period were substantial. If the black defendants represented in Table 27 had received death sentences at the same rate as white defendants of comparable culpability, there would have been eighteen fewer death sentences. This would have represented a 41 percent (18/44) decline in the number of death sentences imposed. If death sentences had occurred in the white-victim cases represented in Table 28 at the same rate as in the black-victim cases, there would have been seventeen fewer death sentences, a decline of 39 percent (17/44).[10]

Another indicator of the impact of racial factors in the pre-*Furman* cases involves a comparison of their significance with that of other, legitimate factors. Our multiple-regression analysis of the pre-*Furman* data suggests these racial factors exerted a statistical impact on the sentencing results that was considerably stronger than any of the following statistically significant case characteristics: elderly victim; coperpetrator(s) involved; defendant resisted arrest; defendant had a prior conviction for rape or kidnapping; a nonviolent contemporaneous felony was involved in the case; and the case involved a defendant-related mitigating factor, such as the defendant's age.

Indeed, we found that there were only four legitimate case characteristics that exerted a comparable or stronger effect statistically on the death-sentencing results than the race of the defendant or of the victim: the number of major aggravating circumstances in the case; the presence of multiple victims; the defendant's role as a leader; and the defendant's commission of additional crimes after the murder.[11]

Our final measure of the impact of racial factors in the pre-*Furman* system was a comparison of the accuracy with which our logistic multiple-regression analyses could correctly predict who received a death sentence when racial factors were taken into account and when they were not. As we noted earlier, the model, which did not include racial factors, was able to predict only 43 percent (19/44) of the death sentences that were imposed. However, when racial considerations were taken into account, the proportion of correctly predicted death sentences rose to 64 percent (28/44).

Tables 27 and 28 also show a significant relationship between racial factors and excessiveness. The most clearly excessive death sentences were those found in levels 1 through 3 of the two tables. All of those sentences involved either a black defendant or a white victim. In fact, no white-defendant/black-victim case at those levels of culpability resulted in a death sentence. These data certainly support Justice Stewart's observation in *Furman* that race appears to be the principal case characteristic that distinguishes the defendants who were sentenced to death from those who received life sentences.

The pre-*Furman* race-of-victim disparities presented above are summarized in Table 43 in the conclusion of this chapter.

Suspect Case Characteristics

Another concern expressed in *Furman* was that other suspect factors besides race, such as sex or socioeconomic status, might influence jury-sentencing decisions. Our pre-*Furman* data did reveal an unadjusted association between the defendant's sex or socioeconomic status and the sentence imposed. However, when we used multiple-regression analyses to control for legitimate case characteristics, these effects weakened or disappeared. The introduction of controls for case culpability similarly reduced the unadjusted association between the victim's race or socioeconomic status and the sentence imposed.[12]

Conclusion

In *Furman,* the concurring justices all agreed that unrestrained jury sentencing in capital cases entailed unacceptable risks of arbitrary and capricious death sentences. Several of the justices also specifically condemned the risk that racial factors might play a role in certain cases. Our pre-*Furman* data from Georgia underscore the validity of this concern. Defendants who were black or whose victims were white received more punitive sentences than other equally culpable defendants. The combined impact of these two forms of discrimination was particularly harsh in black-defendant/white-victim cases. However, these racial factors exerted relatively little influence except in moderately aggravated cases, the circumstances of which did not clearly dictate either a life or death sentence. Consequently, our results do not support the contention that in all Georgia death-sentencing cases before *Furman* racial factors were determinative. Nor do they support the contention by certain justices in *Furman* that other suspect case characteristics, such as gender or the defendant's socioeconomic status, also influenced jury-sentencing decisions.

POST-*FURMAN*

One purpose of the post-*Furman* sentencing reforms adopted in Georgia and elsewhere in the early 1970s was to reduce the risk that racial considerations or other suspect factors could influence death-sentencing decisions. To accomplish this objective, state legislators reduced the scope of jury discretion and mandated detailed jury instructions to focus the jury's attention on the relevant aggravating and mitigating circumstances of the case. By contrast, no steps were taken to restrain the traditional discretion exercised by prosecutors in capital cases. Presumably, lawmakers felt that professionally trained prosecutors would not respond to such impermissible factors as race and would seek death sentences only when the legitimate circumstances of the case so warranted. Opponents of the death penalty argued, however, that these statutory changes still gave prosecutors and juries too much discretion. Consequently, they did not believe that the post-*Furman* death-sentencing reforms would reduce significantly the influence of racial or other suspect factors. Our data from Georgia shed considerable light on the merits of this contention.

Race Effects

Table 30 presents the unadjusted post-*Furman* death-sentencing rate among defendants convicted of murder at trial for subgroups defined by the race of the defendant and the victim.[13] The data in parts B and C of the table suggest a significant race-of-victim effect; the rates for the white-victim cases exceed the rates for all black-victim cases. Part A suggests a race-of-defendant effect that appears to work to the disadvantage of white defendants. Part C, however, which controls for both the race of the defendant and the race of the victim, also suggests a race-of-defendant effect adverse to black defendants that is considerably less than what we observed in the pre-*Furman* data. Specifically, the gap between the death-sentencing rates for the black-defendant/white-victim cases and white-defendant/white-victim cases dropped from 23 points (.31–.08) pre-*Furman* to 13 points (.35–.22) post-*Furman*; moreover, among the post-*Furman* death-eligible cases, the disparity is only 5 points.

The post-*Furman* picture suggested by the unadjusted data in Table 30 is largely consistent with the results of our multivariate analysis. Figure 21 presents a distribution of the predicted likelihood of a death sentence, after

Table 30. Unadjusted Race-of-Defendant and Race-of-Victim Disparities in Death-Sentencing Rates (Post-*Furman*)

A. Race of Defendant	
Black	.16 (59/362)
White	.22 (53/244)
Difference	−6 pts.
Ratio	.74
B. Race of Victim	
White	.27 (96/360)
Black	.07 (16/246)
Difference	20 pts.
Ratio	3.86
C. Defendant/Victim Racial Combination	
1. Black defendant/white victim	.35 (45/130)
2. White defendant/white victim	.22 (51/230)
3. Black defendant/black victim	.06 (14/232)
4. White defendant/black victim	.14 (2/14)

1. This analysis includes all cases in the study, including those not deemed death-eligible by our measures (see chap. 4, note 38). When limited to cases deemed death-eligible by our measures, the race-of-defendant disparity was −5 points (.21 for black defendants versus .26 for white defendants). The race-of-victim disparity was 22 points (.31 for white-victim cases and .09 for black-victim cases). The rates by defendant/victim combination were B/W .36, W/W .31, B/B .09, W/B .15.

adjustment for legitimate case characteristics based on our post-*Furman* data, for four subgroups defined by the defendant/victim racial combination. What is most striking about these results is the total absence of any race-of-defendant effect. In fact, at each point on the culpability index, the predicted likelihood of a death sentence is lower for the black-defendant/white-victim cases than it is for the white-defendant/white-victim cases. However, as we explain in more detail on page 179, a race-of-defendant effect reemerges when one examines separately the cases from urban and rural areas. The rural cases suggest black defendants were still at a slight disadvantage, although the effect is not statistically significant. In urban Georgia, we find a statistically significant race-of-defendant effect that disadvantaged white defendants.[14]

In contrast to this apparent decline under Georgia's post-*Furman* procedures in the impact of the defendant's race, our post-*Furman* data indicate that the victim's race remained important. Defendants whose victims were white were nearly as disadvantaged after *Furman* as they were before. As Figure 21 indicates, the predicted death-sentencing rates for all of the white-victim cases exceeds the predicted level for all comparable black-victim cases. Our mea-

Figure 21. Logistic Model of Race Effects in Post-*Furman* Georgia, 1973–78[1]

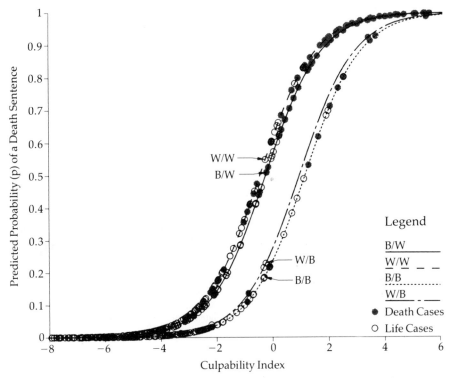

1. Not shown are fifty-one life-sentence cases below −8 and twelve death-sentence cases above 6 on the culpability index.

sures comparing actual death-sentencing rates after adjustment for case culpability quantify this effect.

Table 31 presents a race-of-victim analysis of actual death-sentencing rates among the 188 post-*Furman* armed-robbery–murder cases in our sample, after adjustment for case culpability with a qualitative measure that weighed aggravating and mitigating circumstances without regard to the outcome of the cases. The death-sentencing rates for the white-victim and black-victim cases at each culpability level appear in columns C and D, respectively, while columns E and F present difference and ratio measures of the race-of-victim disparities within each subgroup.

The last row of the figures in Table 31 ("All cases") indicates an unadjusted disparity of 36 percentage points between the death-sentencing rates for the white- and black-victim cases; column F indicates that, without adjustment for

Table 31. Race-of-Victim Disparities in Death-Sentencing Rates among Georgia Armed-Robbery–Murder Cases, Adjusted for Case Culpability with an *a Priori* Measure that Weighs Aggravating and Mitigating Circumstances (Post-*Furman*)

A	B	C	D	E	F
Case Culpability Level from 1 (low) to 6 (high)[1]	Death-Sentencing Rates				
	Overall Rate	White-Victim Rate	Black-Victim Rate	Difference[1] (C−D)	Ratio (C/D)
1	.14 (6/42)	.16 (5/31)	.09 (1/11)	7	1.8
2	.20 (4/20)	.27 (4/15)	.00 (0/5)	27	Infinite
3	.09 (3/33)	.15 (3/20)	.00 (0/13)	15	Infinite
4	.59 (20/34)	.64 (18/28)	.33 (2/6)	31	1.9
5	.59 (27/46)	.67 (26/39)	.14 (1/7)	53	4.8
6	.85 (11/13)	.85 (11/13)	—	—	—
All cases	.38 (71/188)	.46 (67/146)	.10 (4/42)	36	4.6

1. Differences are in percentage points. In order to ensure sufficient sample size among the black-victim cases, this table collapses subgroups 1 and 3 from table 12 into level 1 and subgroups 7 and 8 from table 12 into level 5. *See supra* chap. 4, note 23 and accompanying text, for a description of the culpability index.

The overall disparity after adjustment for culpability level is 25 percentage points, significant at the .01 level (Mantel-Haenszel $Z = 3.07$).

culpability, death sentences are, on average, 4.6 times more likely to occur in white-victim cases than in black-victim cases. Moreover, when we subdivide the cases by relative culpability, the disparities decline only slightly. The adjusted overall disparity in death-sentencing rates for white- and black-victim cases reported in the second part of the note to Table 31 is 25 percentage points, significant at the .01 level.[15] Also, after adjustment, the ratio of the death-sentencing rates within most subgroups is about two to one, or higher.

Our next measure of post-*Furman* race-of-victim effects compared actual death-sentencing rates for white- and black-victim cases of comparable culpability using the three-dimensional classification system developed by Arnold Barnett. Figure 22 presents those results. It shows the death-sentencing rates for white- and black-victim cases in each of the sixteen cells defined by those three dimensions in which cases were found. Figure 22 also indicates, for each cell, the overall death-sentencing rate and the disparity between the death-sentencing rates for black- and white-victim cases. Figure 22 shows a race-of-victim effect in four of the six cells in which the overall death-sentencing rate exceeded .10 and quite substantial effects in the midrange of cases, where the death-sentencing rate for all cases ranged from .10 to .30. The overall

Figure 22. Post-*Furman* Georgia Race-of-Victim Disparities, Controlling for the Three Barnett Dimensions[2]

	0,1,0 (.00)	0,0,2 (.04)	2,0,1 (.09)		
	WV .0 (0/1) BV NC[a]	WV .07 (1/14) BV .00 (0/9) 7 pts.	WV .14 (1/7) BV .00 (0/4) 14 pts.		

0,0,0 (.00)	1,0,0 (.02)	1,1,0 (.00)	1,1,1 (.25)	1,1,2 (.81)	2,1,2 (.88)
WV .0 (0/3) BV .0 (0/5) 0 pts.	WV .00 (0/13) BV .03 (1/30) −3 pts.	WV .0 (0/6) BV .0 (0/4) 0 pts.	WV .34 (14/41) BV .05 (1/19) 29 pts.	WV .83 (53/64) BV .67 (6/9) 16 pts.	WV .86 (6/7) BV 1.00 (1/1) −14 pts.

	0,0,1 (.00)	0,1,1 (.02)	0,1,2 (.29)	2,0,2 (.56)	
	WV .0 (0/30) BV .0 (0/25) 0 pts.	WV .03 (1/32) BV .00 (0/16) 3 pts.	WV .38 (6/16) BV .0 (0/5) 8 pts.	WV .55 (6/11) BV .57 (4/7) −2 pts.	

		1,0,1 (.01)	1,0,2 (.26)		
		WV .01 (1/89) BV .00 (0/95) 1 pt.	WV .31 (8/26) BV .19 (3/16) 12 pts.		

		2,0,0 (.0)			
		WV .0 (0/1) BV NC			

1. The distribution of cases is not the same as in Figure 6, which is limited to death-eligible cases. Each cell indicates the coding on the three Barnett dimensions, the overall death-sentence rate (in parentheses), the death-sentencing rates for white-victim (WV) and black-victim (BV) cases, respectively, and the arithmetic difference between the two rates in percentage points. *See supra* chap. 4, note 29 and accompanying text, for a further explanation of the classification system used for this figure. The figure includes twelve cases that resulted in two penalty trials.

The overall race-of-victim disparity after controlling for the levels of case culpability defined by the three Barnett dimensions is 8 percentage points, significant at the .006 level.

a. NC means no cases.

race-of-victim effect, after controlling for the three Barnett dimensions, is 8 percentage points, significant at the .006 level.[16]

Our third analysis of actual death-sentencing rates estimates the race-of-victim effect, after adjustment for case culpability, with our regression-based index. These data, shown in Table 32, indicate an overall race-of-victim disparity of 7.4 percentage points, significant at the .0005 level. This 7.4-point disparity is, however, an average race-of-victim effect. As in the pre-*Furman* period, the race-of-victim effects are concentrated in the midaggravation

Table 32. Race-of-Victim Effects in Death-Sentencing Rates, Controlling for Case Culpability (Post-*Furman*)

A	B	C	D	E	F
Case Culpability Level, from 1 (low) to 6 (high)[1]	Death-Sentence Rate			Difference[2] (Col. C− Col. D)	Ratio (Col. C/ Col. D.) Case
	All Cases	White-Victim Cases	Black-Victim Cases		
1	.01	.02 (4/207)	.00 (0/193)	2 pts.	Infinite
2	.12	.14 (6/44)	.10 (2/21)	4 pts.	1.4
3	.31	.35 (11/31)	.21 (3/14)	14 pts.	1.7
4	.79	.89 (25/28)	.33 (2/6)	56 pts.	2.7
5	.89	1.00 (19/19)	.67 (6/9)	33 pts.	1.5
6	1.00	1.00 (31/31)	1.00 (3/3)	0 pts.	1.0
All cases	.19	.27 (96/360)	.07 (16/246)	20 pts.	3.9

1. *See supra* chap. 4, note 38 and accompanying text, and *infra* app. J, part 1, for a description of the index (OVERALLB) and scale (CSCALB) underlying this table.
2. The overall average race-of-victim disparity is 7.4 percentage points, significant at the .0005 level (Mantel-Haenszel Z = 3.51).

range of cases, and in that range they are very large. For example in rows 3, 4, and 5 of Table 32, the average race-of-victim disparity is 24.6 points, significant at the .002 level.[17] We also note that, while the race-of-victim effect in row 1 is only 2 percentage points when measured by the arithmetic difference between the death-sentencing rates for the white- and black-victim cases, the race-of-victim effect appears to be largest for row 1 when it is measured by the ratio measure in column F. Although the exact value of the ratio is indeterminate, statistical analysis indicates that if the defendants in the white-victim cases in row 1 had been sentenced to death at the same rate as the defendants with black victims, it is as likely as not that none of the white-victim cases would have resulted in a death sentence; moreover, the odds are 2:1 that no more than one of the defendants with a white victim in row 1 would have received a death sentence.[18]

We next estimated a logistic-regression coefficient for the race-of-victim variable, after adjusting for twenty-three non-racial case characteristics, which included the socioeconomic status of the victim. The average race-of-victim effect estimated in the analysis suggests that, among offenders convicted of murder at trial, the odds of receiving a death sentence for the average defendant whose victim was white were 4.3 times greater than those of a similarly situated defendant whose victim was black, a disparity that was statistically significant at the .001 level.[19] This analysis estimates that statewide, after similar adjustment for the victim and the nonracial background variables, the average black defendant's odds of receiving a death sentence were .57 the odds of a comparable white defendant, although the disparity was significant only at the .25 level.

Finally, we conducted a large-scale linear multiple-regression analysis that estimated coefficients for the race-of-victim and the race-of-defendant variables, after adjusting simultaneously for the 23 variables noted above, plus more than 140 additional legitimate case characteristics. The average race-of-victim disparity estimated in this analysis was 9 percentage points, significant at the .01 level, which is comparable to the 7.4-percentage-point average race-of-victim effect estimated in Table 32.[20]

*Assessing the Magnitude and Impact of Post-Furman
Race-of-Victim Discrimination*

In order to illustrate the magnitude of the post-*Furman* race-of-victim effects, we first compared the power of the race-of-victim variable in explaining the death-sentencing results with the power of the variables we used for the nonracial case characteristics in our culpability index. This analysis revealed that the only aggravating circumstance, statutory or nonstatutory, with more explanatory power than the race-of-victim variable was the number of statutory aggravating circumstances in the case.[21] Legitimate case characteristics with statistical power comparable to the race-of-victim variable were, for example, that the victim was a female and the defendant lay in wait. Moreover, the influence of the victim's race was more pronounced statistically than the following legitimate variables: the victim was a stranger, multiple victims, multiple stab wounds, hostage victim, and victim under twelve years of age.

Another method for assessing the influence of the victim's race on sentencing results is to estimate the number and proportion of cases in which no death sentence would have been imposed "but for" the presence of a white victim. We employed two approaches. First, using a model based on an analysis of all of the cases, we estimated the number of death sentences that would have resulted if death sentences had occurred in white-victim cases at the same rate as in similarly situated black-victim cases. If death sentences had resulted in all the cases in each cell shown in Table 32, at the rate observed for the black-victim cases in each cell, there would have been thirty-two fewer death sentences, a 29 percent reduction of the total number imposed. By contrast, if death sentences had occurred in all the cases in each cell at the white-victim rate, there would have been an increase of 13 death sentences, or 12 percent, in the size of death row.[22]

Our second method for extrapolating overall death-sentencing results, based on black- and white-victim case results, involved multiple-regression analyses. We first analyzed, separately, the white-victim cases by screening in a stepwise linear-regression analysis over 150 legitimate variables to develop the regression model of nonracial variables statistically significant at the .10 level that best explained which defendants with white victims received a death sentence. We then used the variables that survived this linear screening procedure to estimate for the white-victim cases a logistic multiple-regression model of the death-sentencing process applied to those cases. We then applied that logistic model to the black-victim cases to determine how those defendants would have fared if they had been processed in the manner suggested by the white-victim model. The results indicated that, instead of the sixteen death sentences actually imposed in the black-victim cases, there would have been twenty-one death sentences in black-victim cases if they had been treated in the same way as the white-victim cases. This would have represented a 23 percent increase in the number of death sentences in the black-victim cases, and an overall increase in the death-sentencing rate of 6 percent.

We also sought to develop a comparable model with the black-victim cases to apply to the white-victim cases. However, because of the small number of death sentences imposed in the black-victim cases ($n = 16$), the results of the logistic-regression analysis were not sufficiently stable to construct the model.

We also estimated what changes would have occurred in the racial composition of death row had the white- and black-victim cases been treated the same. Since almost all of the defendants in black-victim cases are themselves black, the application of any evenhanded sentencing model, whether it increased or reduced the total number of defendants on death row, could be expected to increase the proportion of those defendants on death row who are black. Specifically, an analysis of the data underlying Table 32 indicates that if the white-victim rate had been applied to all of the cases, the percentage of black defendants on death row would have increased 5 percentage points, from 53 percent to 58 percent; if the black-victim rate had been applied to all cases, the increase would have been the same.[23]

Our final measure of the impact of racial factors in the post-*Furman* system was a comparison of the accuracy with which our logistic multiple-regression analyses could correctly predict who received a death sentence when racial factors were taken into account and when they were not. The model without racial factors was able to correctly predict 72 percent (69/112) of the death sentences, while the model with the racial variables included correctly predicted 80 percent of the death sentences. This 8-percentage-point improvement stands in sharp contrast to the 21-point improvement we observed in a similar analysis of the pre-*Furman* data and reflects the complete reversal of the overall race-of-defendant effects in the post-*Furman* system.

The data in Table 32 illustrate another important point: the extent to which the excessiveness we observed in the post-*Furman* data is attributable to race-of-victim discrimination. The most likely excessive death sentences appear to be the 26 shown in levels 1 through 3 of the table. Of the twenty-one death sentences imposed in that category in white-victim cases, 29 percent (6/21) are a likely product of race-of-victim discrimination.[24]

The post-*Furman* race-of-victim disparities presented above are summarized in Table 43 in the conclusion of this chapter.

The Influence of Other Variables of Interest Besides Race

Table 33 lists the major case characteristics that we found to be related to a statistically significant degree with the sentencing outcome in our post-*Furman* cases. We have divided these factors into three categories based on their relative legitimacy as sentencing considerations. Following each characteristic we have included in parentheses a number that indicates the factor's statistical impact. Not listed in Table 33 are five statistically significant interaction terms that we constructed from combinations of legitimate case characteristics listed in column A.

Table 33. Major Case Characteristics with a Statistically Significant Impact in Determining Who Is Sentenced to Death[1]

A. Clearly Legitimate Case Characteristics[2] ($n = 13$)	B. Neutral Case Characteristics ($n = 3$)	C. Suspect Case Characteristics ($n = 7$)
Number of statutory aggravating factors (25)	Female victim (16)	White victim (16)
Defendant an underling (17)	Military defendant (9)	Low-status victim (12)
Ambush (12)	Victim a stranger (5)	Bloody (11)
Multiple stabs (9)		Race motive (9)
Multiple victims (9)		Low-status defendant (5)
Young victim (9)		Court-appointed attorney (6)
Victim a hostage (6)		Defendant had an out-
Victim a police officer (7)		of-state residence (5)

1. The number in parentheses after each variable name, the R statistic estimated for its coefficient, is a measure of its statistical impact (*supra* app. J, part 1, model OVERALLA). *See* chap. 4, note 34 (last paragraph), for a description of the R statistic. Because of missing data, the variables for "Court-appointed attorney" and "Defendant had an out-of-state residence" were not included in model OVERALLA (*see infra* app. A, notes 37 and 38 and accompanying text).

2. The statistical model OVERALLA also included five interaction terms created with legitimate case characteristics; *see supra* chap. 4, note 38.

To classify a case characteristic as "clearly legitimate," "neutral," or "suspect," we evaluated it in terms of the legitimate goals of capital punishment and the Supreme Court's dictum that death, society's most severe and irrevocable sanction, should be reserved for only the most extreme and aggravated cases.[25] In particular, we asked ourselves whether a death-sentencing statute that specifically described the case characteristic under scrutiny as either an aggravating or mitigating circumstance to be considered by the jury would withstand constitutional attack.

Using this approach, we have classified seven of these statistically significant case characteristics as "suspect." By this we mean that, as a reason for imposing a death sentence, the characteristic is either unconstitutional or highly questionable. Two of the suspect characteristics relate to the defendant's socioeconomic status. After adjustment for all other legitimate case characteristics and the defendant's race, defendants with court-appointed attorneys faced odds of receiving a death sentence that were 2.6 times higher than defendants with retained counsel. And defendants classified more generally as having low socioeconomic status faced odds that were 2.3 times higher than the balance of the sample of cases.[26] The Supreme Court has indicated several times that a statute or jury instructions that invited the jury to treat low economic status as an aggravating factor would not withstand constitutional attack.[27] The evidence also suggests that out-of-state defendants, another questionable case characteristic, are treated more harshly than local residents.[28]

Two of the suspect characteristics relate to the victim. We have already described our reasons for including the first characteristic, that the victim was white, in this category. We also included the victim's low socioeconomic status in this group of "suspect" factors, even though we recognize that the perceived status of the victim frequently influences many kinds of criminal-justice decisions. We reasoned that a statute which described a victim's low socioeconomic status as a mitigating circumstance would be unconstitutional because it bears no relationship to the defendant's culpability or any legitimate goal of capital punishment.[29]

Another important factor that statistically influenced the sentencing decisions included in our study was the sex of the victim. However, despite the questionable nature of gender-based discrimination, we did not classify this variable as "suspect." Although Georgia prosecutors and juries tend to treat defendants more harshly when the victim is a female, we do not believe sex discrimination is reasonably at work. Rather, we are persuaded that this punitive response is more probably a reaction to the greater physical vulnerability of many female victims.

The other two factors that we classified as "suspect"—the bloodiness of the killing and the presence of a racially antagonistic motive—deserve a brief comment. We classified bloodiness as an illegitimate factor because the Supreme Court recently so opined.[30] On the other hand, we also classified the presence of a racial motive as illegitimate despite a Supreme Court suggestion to the contrary.[31] Our data suggest that "race hatred" really serves as a proxy for the defendant/victim racial combination, and it does so in a particularly virulent way. We found that the presence of a racially antagonistic motive increases the likelihood of a death sentence in white-victim cases when, presumably, the defendant is black. By contrast, in black-victim cases, presumably with a white defendant, a "race hatred" motive is a statistically significant *mitigating* circumstance.

We classified two variables as "neutral" because, although they seemed to bear no obvious relationship to the legitimate goals of capital punishment, an indirect relationship probably does exist. For example, that the victim and the defendant had previously known one another is a statistically significant mitigating factor. Whether a statute could constitutionally mandate less protection to previously acquainted or related victims in comparison to strangers is problematic. However, it seems likely that this factor serves as a crude proxy for a sort of assumption of the risk by the victim. Similarly, treating the defendant's prior service in the military as an aggravating factor also seems questionable. However, in doing so prosecutors and jurors may be responding to the expertise in the use of weapons that many military personnel acquire— making them more dangerous—or to the somewhat higher code of conduct with which officers and enlisted men are expected to comply.

Finally, one important legally suspect variable, the defendant's sex, does not appear in Table 33. The defendant's sex showed an unadjusted association with the sentencing result in the expected direction. And after we controlled for case culpability, using a multivariate analysis, it still showed female defendants operating at an advantage (a .56 × odds multiplier), but the coefficient failed to achieve statistical significance beyond the .10 level.[32]

The significance of the data presented in Table 33 should not be overlooked. These were factors that, statistically, were important in explaining which defendants received sentences of life or death in our post-*Furman* cases. Almost one-fourth of the important variables in our post-*Furman* multiple-regression analysis were constitutionally illegal or suspect, and in a number of cases they probably determined the sentence imposed. The conclusion is inescapable that during the post-*Furman* years covered by our study Georgia's death-sentencing procedures did not function in an exclusively rational manner.

Conclusion: Post-*Furman*

The data indicate that, after *Furman*, there was a decline statewide in the level of discrimination against black defendants that was so prominent in pre-*Furman* Georgia. Such discrimination persists at reduced levels in rural areas, but it is masked in statewide statistics by observable discrimination against white defendants in urban areas.

By contrast, the victim's race is nearly as influential in the post-*Furman* period as it was pre-*Furman*, particularly in cases that fall within the mid-range in defendant culpability. Among these cases, the presence of a white victim increases the risk of a death sentence by a factor of two or more and by as much as 20 percentage points. Moreover, we estimate that up to one-third of the death sentences imposed in the white-victim cases may have been the product of race-of-victim discrimination. It also appears that the principal beneficiaries of this race-of-victim discrimination were black defendants, whose proportionate representation on death row would increase slightly if death-sentencing decisions after trial were made without regard to the victim's race.[33]

As for suspect and questionable case characteristics, our post-*Furman* data reflect a decline in the influence of the defendant's sex, but an increase in the impact of the victim's sex and socioeconomic status. On the other hand, certain other ethically questionable case characteristics assumed importance, including the defendant's socioeconomic status, the defendant's out-of-state residence, the victim's socioeconomic status, the presence of a race motive, and bloody circumstances of a murder.

THE SOURCES AND DETERMINANTS OF DISCRIMINATION IN GEORGIA'S CAPITAL-SENTENCING SYSTEM

In this section we report our findings regarding the sources of discrimination in Georgia's post-*Furman* capital-entencing system.[34] We first compare the contributions of post-*Furman* prosecutors and juries and then examine the impact of case type, place, and time.

Prosecutors and Juries

Racial Discrimination

The analysis of discrimination presented in the first two sections of this chapter examined sentencing patterns among defendants convicted of murder at trial. As we have noted, these sentences result from two different decisions—the prosecutor's decision to seek or to waive the death penalty following the defendant's conviction, and the jury's decision at the penalty trial to impose a life or a death sentence. A separate analysis of these two decisions provides a clearer picture of the injury that defendants suffer because of race-of-victim discrimination and helps clarify whether the evidence of such discrimination establishes disparities of sufficient magnitude and statistical significance to indicate "purposeful" discrimination on the part of prosecutors and juries. Table 34 presents the unadjusted rates at which prosecutors seek and juries impose death sentences. The data show no race-of-defendant effect in the jury decisions. In the prosecutorial decisions, we see a race-of-defendant effect among the white-victim cases, but in the absence of adjustment for the victim's race there is an average race-of-defendant effect that favors black defendants. The unadjusted data for the race of the victim, however, show very strong effects in the prosecutorial decisions and substantial effects in the jury decisions.

As in our earlier analysis, we employed a variety of multivariate techniques to estimate race effects in the prosecutorial and jury decisions after adjustment for legitimate case characteristics. Figures 23 and 24 plot the predicted likelihood that prosecutors would seek and juries would impose a death sentence in the four categories of post-*Furman* cases defined by defendant-victim racial combination, after adjustment for the legitimate case characteristics that best explain the outcomes at these two stages. The prosecutorial plot shows a slight race-of-defendant effect (disadvantageous to blacks), but it is not statistically significant, while the plot for the jury decisions shows white defendants operating at a slight and not statistically significant disadvantage. Both plots do, however, indicate a strong race-of-victim effect.[35]

The results of our analyses of actual decisions tell a similar story, that is, no significant race-of-defendant effects but strong evidence of race-of-victim discrimination. First, Table 35 presents a race-of-victim analysis of prosecutorial and jury decisions among the 188 post-*Furman* armed-robbery–murder cases in our sample, after adjustment for case culpability with a qualitative measure that weighed aggravating and mitigating circumstances without regard to the outcome of the cases. In both the prosecutorial and jury analyses there are substantial average race-of-victim effects in the range of 15 to 40 percentage points. However, because of the small number of black-victim cases that reached a penalty trial, the race-of-victim disparity in the jury analysis is statistically significant only at the .10 level.

Figures 25 and 26 depict the estimated race-of-victim effects among cases of comparable culpability as determined using the three case dimensions developed by Arnold Barnett. The disparities between white- and black-victim cases, on average, were 15 percentage points for prosecutors and 14 percentage points for juries, as compared to the 8.5 percentage-point overall disparity

Table 34. Unadjusted Race Effects in Prosecutorial and Jury Decisions
(Post-*Furman*)[1]

I. *Prosecutorial Decisions to Seek a Death Sentence*	
A. Race of Defendant	
Black	.30 (106/356)
White	.37 (88/238)
Difference	−7 pts.
Ratio	.81
B. Race of Victim	
White	.45 (157/349)
Black	.15 (37/245)
Difference	30 pts.
Ratio	3.0
C. Defendant/Victim Racial Combination	
1. Black defendant/white victim	.58 (72/125)
2. White defendant/white victim	.38 (85/224)
3. Black defendant/black victim	.15 (34/231)
4. White defendant/black victim	.21 (3/14)
II. *Jury Penalty-Trial Decisions*	
A. Race of Defendant	
Black	.53 (59/112)
White	.56 (53/94)
Difference	−3 pts.
Ratio	.95
B. Race of Victim	
White	.57 (96/168)
Black	.42 (16/38)
Difference	15 pts.
Ratio	1.4
C. Defendant/Victim Racial Combination	
1. Black defendant/white victim	.58 (45/77)
2. White defendant/white victim	.56 (51/91)
3. Black defendant/black victim	.40 (14/35)
4. White defendant/black victim	.67 (2/3)

1. The prosecutorial analysis does not include multiple penalty trials in the same case, while the jury analysis does. Also, the prosecutorial analysis includes cases deemed not to be death-eligible with our measures. When the prosecutorial analysis is limited to cases deemed death-eligible with our measures, the unadjusted prosecutorial disparities are −7 points for race of defendant (.38 for black defendants v. .45 for white defendants) and 30 points for race of victim (.52 for white-victim cases v. .22 for black-victim cases). The penalty-trial rates by defendant/victim racial combination among the death-eligible cases are B/W .61, W/W .47, B/B .22, and W/B .23. *See supra* chap. 4, note 38, on the use of all cases versus the cases deemed death-eligible by our measures as a basis for estimating racial disparities.

Figure 23. Logistic Model of Race Effects in Prosecutorial Decisions Advancing
Defendants Convicted of Murder at Trial to a Penalty Trial (Post-*Furman*)[1]

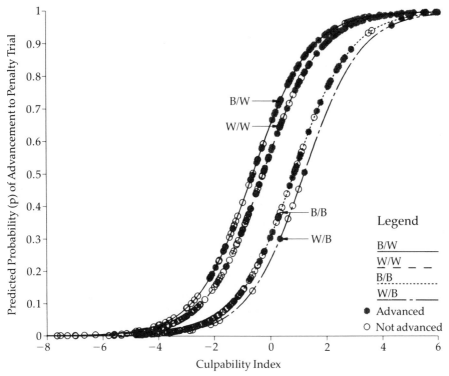

1. Not shown are three penalty-trial cases below −8 and fifteen nonpenalty-trial cases above 6 on
    the culpability index.

reported earlier in Table 32. Moreover, these estimated race-of-victim disparities for prosecutors and juries are only averages for all of the cases in each
sample. As Figures 24 and 25 indicate, the impact in the midrange of cases is
considerably greater. Adding to the significance of this midrange effect is the
high concentration of cases within the midrange, as compared to the low- and
high-aggravation extremes.

  Table 36 depicts the statewide race-of-victim disparities for the prosecutor
and jury decisions, after adjusting for culpability levels using regression-
based indexes generated separately for the two decision points. The race-of-
victim disparities are 11.3 percentage points for prosecutors and 14.5 percentage points for juries, as contrasted to an 8.5-point disparity in the overall
analysis. In the midaggravation range of cases, the disparities are even larger,
in the 20- to 30-percentage-point range.[36]

Figure 24. Logistic Model of Race Effects in Jury Penalty-Trial Sentencing
(Post-*Furman*)[1]

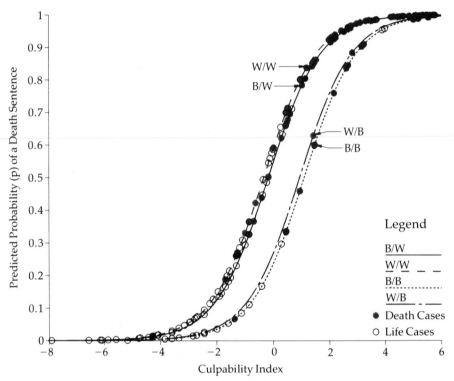

1. Not shown are two life-sentence cases below −8 and thirteen death-penalty cases above 6 on
   the culpability index.

Logistic-regression coefficients in our multiple-regression models of prosecutorial and jury decisions for the race-of-victim variable show a comparable
effect for each category of cases. The presence of a white victim increased the
odds that the prosecutor would seek a death sentence by a factor of 5.5 (significant at the .001 level); the odds that a jury would impose a death sentence
increased by a factor of 7 (significant at the .001 level). The statistical impact of
the victim's race in prosecutorial decisions became particularly strong in cases
involving victims who were strangers, while the analysis of the jury decisions
suggested that the race-of-victim effect tended to rise as the number of statutory aggravating circumstances present in the case increased.[37]

Finally, we conducted large-scale linear multiple-regression analyses to estimate race-of-victim and race-of-defendant effects in prosecutorial and jury
decision making.[38] After adjusting simultaneously for the variables in the

Table 35. Race-of-Victim Effects in the Rates at Which Prosecutors Seek and Juries Impose Death Sentences among Georgia Armed-Robbery–Murder Cases, Adjusted for Case Culpability with an *a Priori* Measure that Weighs Aggravating and Mitigating Circumstances

	I. Prosecutorial Decision to Seek a Death Sentence					II. Jury Decision to Impose a Death Sentence				
A	B	C	D	E	F	G	H	I	J	K
Case Culpability Level, from 1 (low) to 6 (high)[1]	Overall Rate	White-Victim Rate	Black-Victim Rate	Difference[2] (Col. C − Col. D)	Ratio (Col. C/ Col. D)	Overall Rate	White-Victim Rate	Black-Victim Rate	Difference[2] (Col. H − Col. I)	Ratio (Col. H/ Col. I)
1	.48 (20/42)	.61 (19/31)	.09 (1/11)	52 pts.	6.8	.30 (6/20)	.26 (5/19)	1.00 (1/1)	−74 pts.	.26
2	.55 (11/20)	.60 (9/15)	.40 (2/5)	20 pts.	1.5	.36 (4/11)	.44 (4/9)	.00 (0/2)	44 pts.	Infinite
3	.42 (14/33)	.55 (11/20)	.23 (3/13)	32 pts.	2.4	.21 (3/14)	.27 (3/11)	.00 (0/3)	27 pts.	Infinite
4	.79 (26/33)	.81 (22/27)	.67 (4/6)	14 pts.	1.2	.74 (20/27)	.78 (18/23)	.50 (2/4)	28 pts.	1.6
5	.71 (30/42)	.77 (27/35)	.43 (3/7)	34 pts.	1.8	.79 (27/34)	.84 (26/31)	.33 (1/3)	51 pts.	2.5
6	.91 (10/11)	.91 (10/11)	NC[a]	–	–	.92 (11/12)	.92 (11/12)	NC	–	–
All cases	.61 (111/181)	.71 (98/139)	.31 (13/42)	40 pts.	2.3	.60 (71/118)	.64 (67/105)	0.31 (4/13)	33 pts.	2.1

1. *See supra* chap. 4, note 21 and accompanying text, for a description of the index and scale underlying this table. In seven cases that resulted in two penalty trials, both trials are included in the jury analysis (Part II), but only the first decision is included in the prosecutorial analysis (Part I).

2. Differences are in percentage points. The average race-of-victim disparity for the prosecutorial decisions, after adjustment for case culpability level, is 31 percentage points, significant at the .001 level (Mantel-Haenszel Z = 3.7); for the jury decisions, the average disparity is 16 percentage points, significant at the .100 level (Mantel-Haenszel Z = 1.7).

a. NC means no cases.

Figure 25. Race-of-Victim Disparities in Rate at Which Prosecutors Seek Death Sentences, Controlling for the Three Barnett Dimensions[1]

	0,1,0 (1)	0,0,2 (.22)	2,0,1 (.64)			
	WV 1.00 (1/1) BV NC[a]	WV .36 (5/14) BV .00 (0/9) 36 pts.	WV .86 (6/7) BV .25 (1/4) 61 pts.			
0,0,0 (.00)	**1,0,0 (.09)**	**1,1,0 (.40)**	**1,1,1 (.61)**	**1,1,2 (.88)**	**2,1,2 (.83)**
WV .0 (0/3) BV .0 (0/5) 0 pts.	WV .15 (2/13) BV .07 (2/30) 8 pts.	WV .50 (3/6) BV .25 (1/4) 25 pts.	WV .73 (30/41) BV .35 (7/20) 38 pts.	WV .90 (52/58) BV .78 (7/9) 12 pts.	WV .80 (4/5) BV 1.00 (1/1) −20 pts.
	0,0,1 (.13)	0,1,1 (.27)	0,1,2 (.61)	2,0,2 (.83)	
	WV .17 (5/30) BV .08 (2/25) 9 pts.	WV .34 (11/32) BV .13 (2/16) 21 pts.	WV .69 (9/13) BV .40 (2/5) 29 pts.	WV .91 (10/11) BV .71 (5/7) 20 pts.	
	1,0,1 (.07)	1,0,2 (.33)			
	WV .11 (10/89) BV .02 (2/95) 9 pts.	WV .32 (8/25) BV .33 (5/15) −1 pt.			
	2,0,0 (1)				
	WV 1.00 (1/1) BV NC				

1. The distribution of cases is not the same as in Figure 14, which is limited to death-eligible cases. Each cell indicates the coding on the three Barnett dimensions, the overall rate at which death sentences are sought (in parentheses), the rates for white-victim (WV) and black-victim (BV) cases, respectively, and the arithmetic difference between the two rates in percentage points. See supra chap. 4, note 29, for further explanation of the classification system used for this figure.

The overall race-of-victim disparity after controlling for the levels of case culpability defined by the three Barnett dimensions is 15 percentage points, significant at the .001 level.

a. NC means no cases.

models underlying Figures 23 and 24 and Table 36, as well as for more than 125 additional legitimate and suspect case characteristics, the average race-of-victim effect estimated in the prosecutorial analysis was 12 percentage points, significant at the .01 level. The average race-of-victim effect in the jury analysis was 20 percentage points, significant at the .01 level.[39] In contrast, the race-of-defendant coefficients in the prosecutorial and jury analyses were $-.01$ ($p = .97$) and $-.04$ ($p = .50$), respectively.

Figure 26. Race-of-Victim Disparities in the Rates at Which Juries Impose Death Sentences, Controlling for the Three Barnett Dimensions[1]

0,1,0 (.00)	0,0,2 (.20)	2,0,1 (.14)		
WV .00 (0/1) BV NC[a]	WV .20 (1/5) BV N.C. 20 pts.	WV .17 (1/6) BV .00 (0/1) 17 pts.		
1,0,0 (.25)	1,1,0 (.00)	1,1,1 (.41)	1,1,2 (.91)	2,1,2 (1.0)
WV .00 (0/2) BV .50 (1/2) −50 pts.	WV .00 (0/3) BV .00 (0/1) 0 pts.	WV .47 (14/30) BV .14 (1/7) 34 pts.	WV .91 (53/58) BV .86 (6/7) 5 pts.	WV 1.0 (5/5) BV 1.0 (1/1) 0 pts.
0,0,1 (.00)	0,1,1 (.08)	0,1,2 (.43)	2,0,2 (.67)	
WV .00 (0/5) BV .00 (0/2) 0 pts.	WV .09 (1/11) BV .00 (0/2) 9 pts.	WV .50 (6/12) BV .00 (0/2) 50 pts.	WV .60 (6/10) BV .80 (4/5) −20 pts.	
	1,0,1 (.08)	1,0,2 (.73)		
	WV .10 (1/10) BV .00 (0/2) 10 pts.	WV .89 (8/9) BV .50 (3/6) 40 pts.		
	2,0,0 (.00)			
	WV .00 (0/1) BV NC			

1. The distribution of cases is not the same as in Figure 15, which is limited to death-eligible cases. Each cell indicates the coding on the three Barnett dimensions, the overall rate at which death sentences are sought (in parentheses), the rates for white-victim (WV) and black-victim (BV) cases, respectively, and the arithmetic difference between the two rates in percentage points. *See supra* chap. 4, note 29, for further explanation of the classification system used for this figure.

The overall race-of-victim disparity after controlling for the levels of case culpability defined by the three Barnett dimensions is 14 percentage points, significant at the .12 level.

a. NC means no cases.

Although the estimated race-of-victim disparities are slightly larger for the jury decisions, the victim's race appears to be a more systematic and important influence on prosecutorial decisions. First, the statistical significance of the race-of-victim effect at the prosecutorial level is considerably greater in the prosecutorial decisions. Furthermore, at the prosecutorial level, the race-of-victim effect was more powerful statistically than any variable for a legitimate case characteristic.[40] By contrast, the analysis of jury decisions identified ten

Table 36. Race-of-Victim Effects in Prosecutorial and Jury Decisions (Post-*Furman*)

A	B	C	D	E	F	G	H	I	J	K
	Prosecutorial Decision to Request a Death Sentence					Jury Decision to Impose a Death Sentence				
Case Culpability Level, from 1 (low) to 6 (high)[1]	Overall Rate	White-Victim Rate	Black-Victim Rate	Difference (Col. C − Col. D)[2]	Ratio (Col. C/ Col. D)	Overall Rate	White-Victim Rate	Black-Victim Rate	Difference (Col. H − Col. I)[3]	Ratio (Col. H/ Col. I)
1	.03	.05 (6/124)	.01 (2/144)	4 pts.	5.0	.05	.04 (2/49)	.07 (1/14)	−3 pts.	.57
2	.14	.21 (10/48)	.05 (2/39)	16 pts.	4.2	.33	.37 (11/30)	.00 (0/3)	37 pts.	Infinite
3	.49	.56 (40/72)	.34 (11/32)	22 pts.	1.6	.71	.74 (17/23)	.50 (3/6)	24 pts.	1.5
4	.86	.95 (38/40)	.67 (12/18)	28 pts.	1.4	.96	1.00 (19/19)	.83 (5/6)	17 pts.	1.2
5	.91	.93 (31/33)	.80 (8/10)	13 pts.	1.2	.89	1.00 (13/13)	.60 (3/5)	40 pts.	1.0
6	1.00	1.00 (32/32)	1.00 (2/2)	0 pts.	1.00	1.00	1.00 (34/34)	1.00 (4/4)	0 pts.	1.0

1. Two separate indexes, PROSCUTB and JURYB, underlie the two scales, PSCALB and JSCALB, used in this table; *see supra* chap. 4, note 38 and accompanying text, and *infra* app. J, parts 2 and 3. Also, since each model is estimated from a different data set, the cases at each level of culpability are not coterminous; nor does the prosecutorial analysis include second penalty trials, while the jury data do.
2. The overall average disparity ia 11.3 percentage points, significant at the .001 level (Mantel-Haenszel Z = 3.83).
3. The overall average disparity is 14.5 percentage points, significant at the .055 level (Mantel-Haenszel Z = 1.92).

legitimate case characteristics with a higher level of statistical significance than the victim's race, and five of them showed a larger practical impact on sentencing outcomes. Finally, a comparison of the predictive power of the logistic-regression models for the jury and prosecutorial decisions, with and without race variables, showed a 5 percent improvement in the capacity of the prosecutorial model to predict which case would advance to a penalty trial, while the addition of the racial variables to the jury model produced only a 1 percent improvement in predictive power.

To better understand the exercise of jury discretion in penalty trials, we focused on the frequency with which juries found specific aggravating factors (such as the B2 contemporaneous-offense factor) to be present in cases in which they were instructed to determine whether the given factor was present. The narrow focus of this analysis provides a reasonable control for strength of evidence since, presumably, the prosecutor would not have requested a charge on the issue in the absence of good evidence. The analysis is also instructive since the jury was asked for a factual determination, after which it could decide to impose a life sentence even if it found the statutory aggravating factor to be present in the case. The race-of-victim disparities presented in Table 37, although not statistically significant beyond the .10 level, suggest that perceptions about the race of the victim, consciously or unconsciously, influence not only judgments about when mercy is due under a given set of facts but also perceptions of what transpired in a given case.

The race-of-victim disparities presented above for prosecutorial and jury decision making are summarized in Table 44 in the conclusion of this chapter.

The Impact of Suspect and Legitimate Case Characteristics

Our comparison of prosecutorial and jury decision making revealed other differences of emphasis. Prosecutors tended to place more weight on the socioeconomic status and less weight on the role of the defendant (as an underling or nontriggerperson) than did juries. And while prosecutors were more lenient with women, juries treated men more easily than women.[41] Also, in contrast to juries, prosecutors placed more weight on the number of victims, the age of the victims, and the defendant-victim relationship, but placed less weight on the sex and socioeconomic status of the victim. Finally, prosecutors placed more weight on the amount of premeditation than did juries. Otherwise, the statewide responses of prosecutors and juries to the legitimate and suspect variables for which we have data are quite comparable.

Inside the Dual System

The strong race-of-victim effects we observed in the post-*Furman* period indicate that prosecutors and juries evaluate white- and black-victim cases dif-

Table 37. Rates at Which Juries Find Aggravating Circumstances Present After Being Charged on the Factor in a Penalty Trial

A	B	C	D	E	F
Statutory Aggravating Circumstances Charged	All Cases	White-Victim Cases	Black-Victim Cases	Difference[1] (Col. C−Col. D)	Ratio (Col. C/Col. D)
Contemporaneous offense (B2)	.67 (70/105)	.70 (64/92)	.46 (6/13)	24 pts.	1.5
Pecuniary gain motive (B4)	.47 (17/36)	.52 (14/27)	.33 (3/9)	19 pts.	1.6
Heinous, wanton, vile killing (B7)	.64 (65/102)	.68 (55/81)	.48 (10/21)	20 pts.	1.4

1. None of the disparities reached a level of statistical significance beyond the .10 level. The power of this analysis is limited by the number of penalty-trial cases with missing data on the specific aggravating circumstances charged and found: 38% (36/94) in the life-sentence cases and 5% in the death-sentence cases. A logistic multiple-regression analysis of the B2 cases, which controlled for the components of the JURYA model (infra app. J, part 3), produced a race-of-victim logistic-regression coefficient of 1.3 (p = .16) and a 3.7× odds multiplier. A similar analysis of the B7 cases, with controls for the same background variables, produced a race-of-victim logistic-regression coefficient of 1.3 (p = .16) and a 3.7× odds multiplier. There were too few B4 cases to conduct a multiple-regression analysis.

ferently. Although our data shed no direct light on why this is so, they can suggest certain ways in which prosecutors and juries perceive black- and white-victim cases differently.

The first insight into the quite different ways the cases are treated emerged from our effort to predict the sentences in black-victim cases using a multiple-regression model that we developed with the white-victim cases alone. The white-victim-case model correctly predicted 97 percent (218/225) of the life sentences imposed in the black-victim cases, which is the same success rate the model had in predicting life sentences in the white-victim cases. The success of the white-victim-case model in predicting death sentences, however, was quite different. It correctly predicted only 56 percent (9/16) of the death sentences actually imposed in the black-victim cases, while the comparable rate for the white-victim cases was .86 (83/96).[42]

Our second approach to the dual-system question was to estimate, in multiple-regression analyses, the importance and statistical significance of race-of-victim "interaction terms," which indicate the extent to which race-of-victim effects vary with other features of the case. In general, these analyses substantiated our earlier finding that the race-of-victim effects were concentrated in the midrange of cases in terms of case culpability. For example, the overall model, reflecting the combined effects of both prosecutorial and jury decisions, showed much stronger race-of-victim effects in the roughly one-quarter of the cases with no mitigating circumstances present (a 14 × race-of-victim odds multiplier) than in cases with one or more mitigating circumstances present (only a 4.3 × odds multiplier). Similarly, the analyses of prosecutorial decisions showed much stronger race-of-victim effects in cases where the victim was a stranger (a 10 × race-of-victim odds multiplier) than in those cases in which the defendant and victim were acquaintances (a 4 × odds multiplier). Finally, the analyses of jury-sentencing decisions showed a strong positive correlation between the level of race-of-victim discrimination and the number of statutory aggravating factors in the case.[43]

We sought further clues to differences in the treatment of the white- and black-victim cases by analyzing separately the impact of legitimate case characteristics in cases involving white and black victims. The results of this inquiry provide further evidence of differences in the treatment of the two groups of cases.

For each set of cases, we estimated two multiple-regression models that best explained who received a death sentence. In the first analysis, we developed a model for each set of cases, starting from scratch with over 150 possible explanatory legitimate and suspect variables. In the second analysis, we estimated separate models for the two groups of cases using the legitimate variables that emerged as important when all of the cases were evaluated together. The results of these analyses suggest several conclusions. First, the single most important factor in both black- and white-victim cases is the number of statutory aggravating circumstances. Also, the following case characteristics carry approximately equal weight in both white- and black-victim cases: defendant's prior record, multiple victims, victim a stranger, young victim, female victim, defendant cooperated with the authorities,[44] and defendant resisted arrest. Since the relative impact of these case characteristics does not vary substantially depending upon the victim's race, they do not explain the race-of-victim effects we see in the post-*Furman* system.

There was, however, a differential response to other important variables. First, the race of the defendant has no perceivable effect in the white-victim cases, but in the black-victim cases white defendants operate at a relative disadvantage vis-à-vis black defendants, suggesting either that killings that cross caste and class lines in this subcategory of murders are treated more harshly, or that white defendants are held to higher standards than black defendants. A second differential response in the two classes of cases is the importance of the defendant's role in the crime. It matters a great deal in the white-victim cases whether or not the defendant was the triggerman or an underling. Also, the defendant's military status has an aggravating effect only in the black-victim cases.

The level of violence in the case appears to be somewhat more important in the white-victim cases. But there are two characteristics that have a significantly different impact in the two classes of cases. Mitigating factors related to drugs and alcohol are much more important in the black-victim cases, as are the mental and emotional state of the defendant. Also, premeditation is of less importance in the black-victim cases. And in that regard, the response to a murder motivated by race hatred is quite different in black- and white-victim cases. In the latter, a race-hatred motive is treated as a strong aggravating characteristic, while in the black-victim cases a race-hatred motive has a mitigating effect, truly a perverse and troubling finding.

Preferential Treatment of Black Defendants as a Cause of Race-of-Victim Disparities

It has been suggested that the race-of-victim effects observed in the United States capital-sentencing system are not a result of differential treatment of white- and black-victim cases but, rather, are an artifact caused by more lenient treatment of black defendants. Because black defendants are more likely to have killed black victims, the argument goes, the reduced death-sentencing rates for black defendants reduces the death-sentencing rate in black-victim cases.[45]

It is true that in Georgia, at least, after adjustment for case culpability, black defendants, on average, have a lower risk of receiving a death penalty than do similarly situated white defendants. Specifically, the odds that the average black defendant will receive a death sentence are .56 of those faced by a white defendant in a comparable case, although the disparity is not statistically significant at the .05 level. Also, as we have indicated above, if the Georgia capital-sentencing system operated in an evenhanded fashion with respect to the race of the victim, there would be slightly more black defendants sentenced to death, since most black victims die at the hands of a black defendant.[46] The alternative hypothesis, however, is that the below-average death-sentencing rate for black defendants is, to a considerable degree, the product of reduced death sentencing in the black-victim cases.

There are two straightforward ways to test the validity of these two competing hypotheses: first, by comparing the death-sentencing rates of white- and black-victim cases while holding constant the race of the defendant; and second, by comparing the death-sentencing rates for white- and black-defendant cases while holding constant the race of the victim. If the "artifact" hypothesis were correct, death-sentencing rates for both black and white defendants would be essentially the same regardless of the race of the victim. Similarly, the artifact theory would predict that, among both white- and black-victim cases, death-sentencing rates should be appreciably higher for the white defendants than for the black defendants.

The data from Georgia do not support the artifact hypothesis on either of these points. Tables 38 and 39 compare the treatment of white- and black-victim cases by prosecutors and juries after adjustment for case culpability—first in cases involving black defendants and then in cases involving white defendants. In each of these analyses involving a reasonable sample size, the selection rate, on average, is substantially higher in the white-victim cases, a result that undercuts the artifact theory and supports the hypothesis that the race-of-victim effect we observe reflects a differential response to the race of the victim.

The results of the second analysis, presented in Tables 40 and 41, also refute the artifact hypothesis. Within the white-victim cases, white defendants have a lower risk of advancing to penalty trial and only a slightly greater risk of receiving a death sentence in a penalty trial (in neither case is the disparity significant beyond the .10 level). Among the black-victim cases, after adjustment for case culpability, black defendants also have a slightly higher, but not statistically significant, risk of advancing to a penalty trial. Before sentencing juries, however, the white defendants are worse off, but the small sample of only three white-defendant cases makes the result inconclusive.

In conclusion, we believe that the data in these four tables fatally undercut the argument that the race-of-victim effects we observe in the post-*Furman* Georgia data are an artifact of preferential treatment for black offenders.

A Skewed Distribution of White-Victim Cases and Death-Sentencing Rates as a Source of Race-of-Victim Disparities

The death-sentencing disparities we observe repeatedly in our Georgia data, using a wide variety of analyses, strongly suggest that racial factors are influencing the posttrial sentencing decisions in capital cases. It is possible, however, that the observed disparities simply result from a disproportionate concentration of white-victim cases in judicial circuits with high death-sentencing rates. For example, if all white-victim cases arose in circuits or regions with very high death-sentencing rates, the statewide death-sentencing rate estimated for white-victim cases might be higher than the estimate for the black-victim cases, even if racial factors exerted no impact on capital-charging or sentencing decisions anywhere in the state. Such a phenomenon would be an

Table 38. Race-of-Victim Disparities in Prosecutorial and Jury Decision Making in Cases Involving Black Defendants, Controlling for Case Culpability (All Cases with Black Defendants)

A	Prosecutorial Decisions				Jury Decisions			
Case Culpability Level, from 1 (low) to 6 (high)[1]	B White-Victim Cases	C Black-Victim Cases	D Difference[2] (Col. B – Col. C)	E Ratio (Col. B/ Col. C)	F White-Victim Cases	G Black-Victim Cases	H Difference[3] (Col. F – Col. G)	I Ratio (Col. F/ Col. G)
1	.05 (1/22)	.01 (2/140)	4 pts.	5.0	.00 (0/22)	.08 (1/13)	-8 pts.	0.0
2	.24 (6/25)	.06 (2/36)	18 pts.	4.0	.36 (4/11)	.00 (0/3)	36 pts.	Infinite
3	.66 (21/32)	.36 (10/28)	30 pts.	1.8	.77 (10/13)	.40 (2/5)	37 pts.	1.9
4	1.00 (20/20)	.69 (11/16)	31 pts.	1.4	1.00 (12/12)	.83 (5/6)	17 pts.	1.2
5	.85 (11/13)	.78 (7/9)	7 pts.	1.1	1.00 (4/4)	.50 (2/4)	50 pts.	2.0
6	1.00 (13/13)	1.00 (2/2)	0 pt.	1.0	1.00 (15/15)	1.00 (4/4)	0 pt.	1.0
All cases	.58 (72/125)	.15 (34/231)	43 pts.	3.9	.58 (45/77)	.40 (14/35)	18 pts.	1.5

1. The separate indexes underlying the two scales (PSCALB & JSCALB) used in this table are described *supra* chap. 4, note 38 and accompanying text, and *infra* app. J, parts 2 and 3. Also, since each model is estimated from a different data set, the cases at each level of culpability are not coterminous; nor does the prosecutorial analysis include second penalty trials, while the jury data do.

2. The overall average disparity is 13 percentage points, statistically significant at the .0002 level (Mantel-Haenszel Z = 3.7).

3. The overall average disparity is 14 percentage points, statistically significant at the .100 level (Mantel-Haenszel Z = 1.8).

Table 39. Race-of-Victim Disparities in Prosecutorial and Jury Decision Making Involving White Defendants, Controlling for Case Culpability (All White-Defendant Cases)

| | Prosecutorial Decisions | | | | | Jury Decisions | | | |
| A | B | C | D | E | | F | G | H | I |
Case Culpability Level, from 1 (low) to 6 (high)[1]	White-Victim Cases	Black-Victim Cases	Difference[2] (Col. B − Col. C)	Ratio (Col. B / Col. C)		White-Victim Cases	Black-Victim Cases	Difference[3] (Col. F − Col. G)	Ratio (Col. F / Col. G)
1	.05 (5/102)	.00 (0/4)	5 pts.	Infinite		.07 (2/27)	.00 (0/1)	7 pts.	Infinite
2	.17 (4/23)	.00 (0/3)	17 pts.	Infinite		.37 (7/19)	NC[a]	–	–
3	.48 (19/40)	.25 (1/4)	23 pts.	1.9		.70 (7/10)	1.00 (1/1)	−30 pts.	0.7
4	.90 (18/20)	.50 (1/2)	40 pts.	1.8		1.00 (7/7)	NC	–	–
5	1.00 (20/20)	1.00 (1/1)	0 pt.	1.0		1.00 (9/9)	1.00 (1/1)	0 pt.	1.0
6	1.00 (19/19)	NC	–	–		1.00 (19/19)	NC	–	–
All cases	.38 (85/224)	.21 (3/14)	17 pts.	1.8		.56 (51/91)	.67 (2/3)	−11 pts.	.84

1. The separate indexes underlying the two scales (PROSCUTB and JURYB) are described *supra* chap. 4, note 38 and accompanying text, and *infra* app. J, parts 2 and 3. Also, since each model is estimated from a different data set, the cases at each level of culpability are not coterminous; nor does the prosecutorial analysis include second penalty trials, while the jury data do.

2. The overall average disparity is 12 percentage points, not statistically significant at the .100 level (Mantel-Haenszel Z = 1.3).

3. The overall average disparity is −1.3 percentage points, not statistically significant at the .100 level (Mantel-Haenszel Z = .58).

a. NC means no cases.

Table 40. Race-of-Defendant Disparities in Prosecutorial and Jury Decision Making Involving Cases with White Victims, Controlling for Case Culpability (All White-Victim Cases)

A	Prosecutorial Decisions				Jury Decisions			
	B	C	D	E	F	G	H	I
Case Culpability Level, from 1 (low) to 6 (high)[1]	White-Defendant Cases	Black-Defendant Cases	Difference[2] (Col. B − Col. C)	Ratio (Col. B/ Col. C)	White-Defendant Cases	Black-Defendant Cases	Difference[3] (Col. F − Col. G)	Ratio (Col. F/ Col. G)
1	.05 (5/102)	.05 (1/22)	0 pt.	1.00	.07 (2/27)	.00 (0/22)	7 pts.	Infinite
2	.17 (4/23)	.24 (6/25)	−7 pts.	0.71	.37 (7/19)	.36 (4/11)	1 pt.	1.03
3	.48 (19/40)	.66 (21/32)	−18 pts.	0.73	.70 (7/10)	.77 (10/13)	−7 pts.	0.91
4	.90 (18/20)	1.00 (20/20)	−10 pts.	0.90	1.00 (7/7)	1.00 (12/12)	0 pt.	1.00
5	1.00 (20/20)	.85 (11/13)	15 pts.	1.18	1.00 (9/9)	1.00 (4/4)	0 pt.	1.00
6	1.00 (19/19)	1.00 (13/13)	0 pt.	1.00	1.00 (19/19)	1.00 (15/15)	0 pt.	1.00
All cases	.38 (85/224)	.58 (72/125)	−20 pts.	0.66	.56 (51/91)	.58 (45/77)	−2 pts.	0.97

1. The separate indexes underlying the two scales (PROSCUTB and JURYB) are described *supra* chap. 4, note 38 and accompanying text, and *infra* app. J, parts 2 and 3. Also, since each model is estimated from a different data set, the cases at each level of culpability are not coterminous; nor does the prosecutorial analysis include second penalty trials, while the jury data do.

2. The overall average disparity is −4.2 percentage points, not statistically significant at the .100 level (Mantel-Haenszel Z = −1.1).

3. The overall average disparity is 1.3 percentage points, not statistically significant at the .100 level (Mantel-Haenszel Z = .02).

Table 41. Race-of-Defendant Disparities in Prosecutorial and Jury Decision Making with Black-Victim Cases, Controlling for Case Culpability (All Black-Victim Cases)

A	Prosecutorial Decisions				Jury Decisions			
	B	C	D	E	F	G	H	I
Case Culpability Level, from 1 (low) to 6 (high)[1]	White-Defendant Cases	Black-Defendant Cases	Difference[2] (Col. B – Col. C)	Ratio (Col. B/ Col. C)	White-Defendant Cases	Black-Defendant Cases	Difference[3] (Col. F – Col. G)	Ratio (Col. F/ Col. G)
1	.00 (0/4)	.01 (2/140)	–1 pt.	0.0	.00 (0/1)	.08 (1/13)	–8 pts.	0.0
2	.00 (0/3)	.06 (2/36)	–6 pts.	0.0	NC[a]	.00 (0/3)	–	–
3	.25 (1/4)	.36 (10/28)	–11 pts.	0.69	1.00 (1/1)	.40 (2/5)	60 pts.	2.5
4	.50 (1/2)	.69 (11/16)	–19 pts.	0.72	NC	.83 (5/6)	–	–
5	1.00 (1/1)	.78 (7/9)	22 pts.	1.3	1.00 (1/1)	.50 (2/4)	50 pts.	2.0
6	NC	1.00 (2/2)	–	–	NC	1.00 (4/4)	–	–
All cases	.21 (3/14)	.15 34/(231)	6 pts.	1.4	.67 (2/3)	.40 (14/35)	27 pts.	1.7

1. The separate indexes underlying the two scales (PROSCUTB and JURYB) used in this table are described *supra* chap. 4, note 38 and accompanying text, and *infra* app. J, parts 2 and 3. Also, since each model is estimated from a different data set, the cases at each level of culpability are not coterminous; nor does the prosecutorial analysis include second penalty trials, while the jury data do.
2. The overall average disparity is –3.6 percentage points, not statistically significant at the .100 level (Mantel-Haenszel Z = –.17).
3. The overall average disparity is 13 percentage points, not statistically significant at the .100 level (Mantel-Haenszel Z = .44).
a. NC means no cases.

example of Simpson's paradox, which occurs when disproportionate distributions within aggregated output data produce results for the aggregate that conflict with the results one would observe if the data were separately analyzed for each relevant decision-making entity. [47]

One way to test this hypothesis would be to examine separately the cases processed in each state judicial circuit. However, the small number of capital cases found in each circuit made the systematic use of this approach impossible. As an alternative, we created separate variables for region, judicial district, and whether the district was urban or rural. [48] The rationale for these variables was that the population of one of these geographic areas had either a particularly punitive or conservative attitude about the imposition of the death penalty that produced very high or very low death-sentencing rates, and the separate geographic variables would capture this effect. Moreover, if the statewide race-of-victim effect that we observe in our data were in fact the result of a disproportionate concentration of white-victim cases in certain areas with high death-sentencing rates, adjustment for these geographic variables in a multiple-regression analysis, along with a measure of case culpability, would substantially decrease (or reduce to zero) the estimated race-of-victim effect.

Accordingly, each of the multiple-regression analyses we conducted to test this hypothesis controlled simultaneously for case culpability, three suspect variables, the region, the urban or rural character of the judicial circuit, and those judicial circuits that showed a statistically significant relationship with the outcome variable beyond the .10 level. The results of all the runs were the same: the race-of-victim effect never experienced more than a trivial change, usually an enhancement, and always remained statistically significant beyond the .05 level. On the basis of these analyses, we believe there is no basis whatsoever for believing that the racial effects we observe in the data are a statistical artifact caused by Simpson's paradox.

GEOGRAPHIC VARIATIONS IN THE IMPACT OF RACIAL AND OTHER FACTORS OF INTEREST

Georgia's procedures for processing capital cases, both before and after *Furman*, were not only discretionary and complex but also decentralized throughout the state. Thus, it would be no surprise to find substantial variation in the attitudes of prosecutors and juries in different parts of Georgia toward capital punishment and in their responses to racial and other case characteristics. Therefore, we further analyzed our data on racial discrimination and the influence of suspect case characteristics in an effort to discover any geographic variations.

Urban and Rural Distinctions

Table 42 summarizes the data on urban/rural distinctions both before and after *Furman*, after adjustment for case culpability.[49] The entry for each variable indicates the odds multipliers estimated for it in a logistic multiple-regression analysis, with the level of statistical significance in parentheses. If the difference between the coefficients estimated for the urban and rural areas was not statistically significant beyond the .10 level, we report only the odds multiplier estimated for the variable statewide. As noted earlier, our pre-*Furman* data do not permit us to analyze prosecutorial and jury decisions separately. The pre-*Furman* results reported in Table 42 reflect, therefore, the combined effects of both prosecutorial and jury decisions.

For the pre-*Furman* period, row 1 of Table 42 reveals no statistically significant different race-of-defendant effects in urban and rural places. Post-*Furman*, however, the impact of the defendant's race changed dramatically. Black defendants are worse off in rural areas, particularly at the hands of prosecutors, whose more punitive treatment of black offenders is statistically significant at the .05 level (column G). The overall result is that black defendants in rural areas suffered only a slight disadvantage, which is not statistically significant (column E). In urban areas, by contrast, we see a complete reversal of the pre-*Furman* pattern. Our post-*Furman* data definitely suggest that urban prosecutors and juries favor black defendants or discriminate against white defendants, to a degree that overall the relative advantage of black defendants is statistically significant at the .003 level (column D). In other words, after *Furman* it is white rather than black defendants who are more at risk of a death sentence in Georgia's urban areas.

The overall patterns of race-of-victim discrimination reveal no significant differences between the rural and urban areas, either pre- or post-*Furman*. However, the separate analyses of prosecutors and juries show particularly strong effects among rural prosecutors and urban juries (columns G and H). These results therefore weaken slightly our earlier reported finding that prosecutorial decisions contribute more to the overall race-of-victim effects than do jury decisions.[50]

With respect to the defendant's sex, socioeconomic status, and place of residence, we found few clear patterns. We cannot estimate the effects of the defendant's sex prior to *Furman* because of the small number of female defendants in the sample. After *Furman*, women received more lenient treatment from rural prosecutors, probably acting in anticipation of jury reactions.

Table 42. Evidence of the Impact of Racial and Suspect Case Characteristics on Prosecutorial and Jury Decision Making in Urban and Rural Areas, after Adjustment for Case Culpability in a Logistic Multiple-Regression Analysis[1] (Numbers are logistic-regression odds multipliers for the case characteristics in Column A, with the level of statistical significance (p value) of the estimate in parentheses. If there is no statistically significant difference (p≤.10) between the urban and rural coefficients, or if they could not be estimated validly, we present only the odds multiplier estimated from the statewide models in App. J.)

Case Characteristic	Overall Effects				Post-Furman			
	Pre-Furman		Post-Furman		Prosecutorial Decisions		Jury Decisions	
A	B	C	D	E	F	G	H	I
	Urban	Rural	Urban	Rural	Urban	Rural	Urban	Rural
1. Black defendant	12.0 (.002)		.023 (.003)	4.0 (.12)	.41 (.15)	3.0 (0.5)	.18 (.17)	4.9 (.19)
2. White victim	4.3 (.01)		4.3 (.001)		1.7 (.36)	12.9 (.0001)	>6.6 (.005)[a]	2.5 (.48)
3. Female defendant	.01 (.84)		.56 (.56)		1.2 (.85)	.042 (.007)	11.5 (.17)	
4. Socioeconomic status of defendant:								
a. Low	3.2 (.21)	.44 (.49)	1.9 (.45)	22.5 (.003)	1.8 (.08)		2.1 (.22)	
b. High	.35 (.56)		6.6 (.05)		13.5 (.003)	.44 (.41)	1.3 (.84)	

1. The indexes used for the analyses in this table were, respectively, PREFURMA for the pre-Furman analysis reported in columns B and C, OVERALLA for the post-Furman analysis reported in columns D and E, PROSCUTA for the post-Furman prosecutorial analysis reported in columns F and G, and JURYA for the post-Furman jury analysis reported in columns H and I. See supra chap. 4, note 38 and accompanying text, and infra app. J.

a. Because of the comparatively small number of jury cases, we did not obtain a precise estimate of this quantity; we are 95% confident it exceeds the amount shown.

Prior to *Furman*, defendants with low socioeconomic status were worse off in urban areas, but in neither place was the effect statistically significant. Post-*Furman*, such defendants were at a particular disadvantage in rural areas, largely as a consequence of jury sentencing decisions. The data do not suggest, however, that high-status defendants received any preferential treatment. Indeed, high-status defendants were at a disadvantage before urban prosecutors.

Regional and Judicial-Circuit Variations in Race Effects

Because of the considerable regional differences within Georgia—historical, cultural, and demographic—we first considered the extent to which the impact of racial factors might vary among the five major regions of the state.[51] To test for this possibility, we conducted logistic multiple-regression analyses that estimated the extent to which the race-of-defendant and race-of-victim effects in each region and circuit varied from the statewide norm, after adjustment for legitimate and suspect case characteristics and the urban/rural classification of the circuit in which the sentence was imposed.[52]

The analysis of the pre-*Furman* data revealed no statistically significant region or circuit variations. The overall results for the post-*Furman* period also show no significant regional deviations, but Ocmulgee circuit emerged with a substantially higher-than-average death-sentencing rate for black defendants and Eastern circuit emerged with a substantially lower rate for black defendants.[53] Overall, only Stone Mountain circuit showed an above-average death-sentencing rate in white-victim cases.[54]

When we analyzed post-*Furman* prosecutorial decisions separately, we found that the penalty-trial rate in white-victim cases in the Northern region was substantially below the statewide average and approximated the black-victim rate there.[55]

No substantial deviations from the statewide norms emerged in the analysis of jury decisions.

THE EFFECT OF THE 1973 REFORMS ON THE INFLUENCE OF RACIAL AND SUSPECT CHARACTERISTICS

The preceding analysis clearly indicates that the impact of racial factors on Georgia's capital-sentencing process has changed in the post-*Furman* period. Before inferring a causal connection between the 1973 statutory reforms and the observed changes, however, one must evaluate any rival hypothesis that may offer a more plausible explanation.

The most striking post-*Furman* change has been the statewide decline in the race-of-defendant effect. Indeed, on average, black defendants appear to enjoy a slight overall advantage compared to white defendants, although the effect is not statistically significant. The first rival hypothesis is that the observed decline in race-of-defendant discrimination is a likely artifact of changes in record-keeping practices in the aftermath of the *Furman* decision. *Furman* indicated that racial discrimination in capital sentencing was unacceptable and suggested that increased oversight of racial disparities from the courts may be a distinct possibility. A consequence of this perception may have been a tendency on the part of law-enforcement officials to scrutinize more closely black-defendant cases for the presence of aggravating case characteristics, particularly statutory aggravating circumstances. Such a practice could make the post-*Furman* black-defendant cases appear to be, in the records from which we coded our questionnaires, more aggravated than similarly situated pre-*Furman* black-defendant cases. To test this hypothesis, we compared the difference in the average number of statutory aggravating circumstances (as defined by the post-*Furman* statute) in white-defendant and black-defendant cases, before and after *Furman*. Before *Furman*, the average number of statutory aggravating circumstances was lower in black-defendant cases (1.44) than it was in white-defendant cases (1.83). Post-*Furman*, there was a reversal of this relationship, with the average black-defendant cases having slightly more statutory aggravating circumstances (1.86) than the average white-defendant case (1.77), a change from the pre-*Furman* figure that is statistically significant at the .06 level. However, when we restricted the analysis to white-victim cases, where any race-of-defendant effects would primarily be found, we discovered stronger support for the record-keeping hypothesis. Specifically, in the pre-*Furman* period, the number of statutory aggravating circumstances in the black-defendant/white-victim cases and in the white-defendant/white-victim cases was nearly identical (1.92 in the black/white cases versus 1.85 in the white/white cases). In the post-*Furman* period, however, the average number of aggravating circumstances in the black-defendant/white-victim cases increased by .96 (i.e., almost 1 additional aggravating circumstance; $p = .001$), while the white-defendant/white-victim cases revealed an insignificant decrease of .09. Moreover, post-*Furman*, the average number of mitigating factors in the black-defendant/white-victim cases declined sharply relative to the white-defendant/white-victim cases.[56]

In addition, a similar comparison of the average number of minor nonstatutory aggravating factors showed a uniform slight increase across each defendant/victim racial combination. We also compared white-victim and black-victim cases pre- and post-*Furman*, bearing in mind that race-of-victim (as distinct from race-of-defendant) discrimination was not specifically mentioned in *Furman* and was not perceived to be a significant problem in the immediate post-*Furman* years. The results showed, for both white- and black-victim cases, a small, virtually identical, and not statistically significant increase in the number of statutory aggravating factors (an increase of .3 in white-victim cases versus an increase of .2 in black-victim cases).

Of course, the changes just noted in the relative observed seriousness of the black- and white-defendant cases involving white victims could reflect a differential increase post-*Furman* in the actual aggravation level of these two groups of cases that result in murder-trial convictions. It could also reflect post-*Furman* prosecutorial policies requiring a higher level of aggravation before black-defendant/white-victim cases are advanced to a murder trial. However, we consider it implausible that a disparate change in general case composition of the magnitude we observed (in both the statutory aggravating factors and the mitigating factors) could occur naturally in such a short period. And we consider it even more implausible that altered prosecutorial policies could have caused the disparate change. However, we are not willing, on the strength of statistical analyses alone, to attribute all of the decline in the post-*Furman* race-of-defendant disparities to changes in data-collection practices. Our final judgment is that the post-*Furman* decline in race-of-defendant discrimination may not be as dramatic as the numbers suggest at first blush, but that it is quite likely that there was some decline.

To the extent there has been an actual post-*Furman* decline in race-of-defendant discrimination, its source is found primarily in the urban areas, where black defendants receive more lenient treatment from both prosecutors and juries than similarly situated white defendants. This may be a result of the increased numbers of black citizens living in urban areas and of their increased participation in local government and on urban juries. In the rural areas of the state, by contrast, prosecutors continued to discriminate against black defendants to a statistically significant degree. However, our data reveal only very weak evidence of discrimination against black defendants by rural juries. In fact, the rural juries largely neutralized the more punitive attitudes of rural prosecutors toward black defendants.[57] Our data also provide other evidence of changing racial attitudes over the period covered by our study. The pre-*Furman* analysis, which includes the earliest death-sentence cases (ranging from 1964 to 1969), reveals a strong race-of-defendant effect, while the analysis largely limited to 1970-72 cases does not yield a statistically significant race-of-defendant effect, although its coefficient is in the expected direction.

When set against the post-*Furman* race-of-defendant results, these two analyses strongly suggest a gradual trend toward equal treatment of black defendants, which first occurred in urban areas and by the late 1970s was still taking place in the rural areas of the state.[58] Our data suggest, however, that this sharp declining trend in discrimination occurred *only* with respect to the defendant's race. Discrimination on the basis of the race of the victim persists in the post-*Furman* period, although at a somewhat declining rate. Moreover, particularly in rural areas, the socioeconomic status of both the defendant and the victim exerts a statistically significant post-*Furman* effect. If the statutory standards and other procedures adopted in 1973 had actually reduced the influence of illegitimate or suspect factors, these other forms of discrimination, besides race of defendant, should also have declined. In fact, however, they have persisted during the post-*Furman* period. Consequently, it does not appear that the decline in discrimination based on the defendant's race is attributable to Georgia's 1973 statutory changes.[59]

Why did the post-*Furman* trial-level reforms fail to reduce the race-of-victim effects in the system? The most plausible explanation has two parts. First, the new system still leaves prosecutors and juries extremely broad discretion, limited only by the statutory aggravating factors. Second, the political, economic, and personal considerations that appear to produce the race-of-victim effect have not declined in the post-*Furman* period. Indeed, they may have intensified. First, common experience in the United States suggests that white-victim cases generally produce greater publicity and public pressure on prosecutors for a punitive response than do black-victim cases. Similarly, the families and friends of white victims are more likely to have influence with the prosecutor, and those relatives and friends are more likely to demand a death penalty than are the families of black victims.[60] Since the early 1970s, support for capital punishment has risen sharply in the white community but has remained low among blacks.[61] Second, capital cases are much more expensive than life cases, and this cost has increased substantially in the post-*Furman* period. Particularly among the less aggravated death-eligible cases, these costs require a significant reason to justify the expense of a penalty trial. Third, at a personal level, prosecutors (who, to our knowledge, in Georgia are largely white) are more likely to identify with the families of white victims.[62]

Fewer pressures converge on juries to produce a race-of-victim effect; most important, they are not subject to the political, financial, and personal constraints under which prosecutors work. Juries are, however, subject to the influence of community sentiments and the greater identification of predominantly white jurors with white victims and their families. Curiously, however, race-of-victim effects among juries are much stronger in urban than in rural areas.

CONCLUSION

On the issue of racial discrimination, the system pre-*Furman* was as bad as the majority justices in *Furman v. Georgia* feared it to be. There is evidence of discrimination against black defendants in both urban and rural areas, although the data suggest a trend from the 1960s toward a decline in such discrimination. There is also evidence of race-of-victim discrimination. And both forms of discrimination affected a large proportion of the cases. Only among cases where the defendant's culpability was either very high or very low is there no evidence of discrimination pre-*Furman*. Moreover, racial discrimination appears to be a major source of the excessiveness that plagued the pre-*Furman* system. Unexpectedly, the pre-*Furman* data do not reveal evidence that such suspect factors as the socioeconomic status of the defendant and victim were important in trial-level decisions.

The post-*Furman* data present a somewhat different picture. Statewide, we see no evidence of race-of-defendant discrimination, although there is some evidence that altered record-keeping practices post-*Furman* may have suppressed somewhat evidence of discrimination against black defendants in white-victim cases. Also, the picture is different in urban and rural areas.[63] Black defendants are at a disadvantage in rural areas, particularly with prosecutors, although the overall race-of-defendant effect is not statistically significant. In urban areas, we see white defendants operating at a disadvantage with both prosecutors and juries.[64]

The evidence on race-of-victim discrimination, however, is different. Tables 43 and 44 summarize the quantitative evidence on race-of-victim discrimination from the Procedural Reform Study presented in this chapter. Table 43 presents the evidence pre- and post-*Furman* among cases that resulted in a murder-trial conviction. Table 44 compares the results of our separate analyses of prosecutorial and jury decision making in the post-*Furman* period only. The data summarized in Tables 43 and 44 do not show a decline in race-of-victim effect similar to that observed in the pre- and post-*Furman* analyses of race-of-defendant discrimination. Indeed, they suggest that the race-of-victim effects are about the same or stronger in the post-*Furman* period.

The consistency of the post-*Furman* results obtained with a wide variety of methods strongly supports the inference that the race of the victim is a potent influence in the system. Also, the data indicate that, for both the pre- and post-*Furman* periods, the race-of-victim effects were particularly strong in the midrange of cases when prosecutors and juries have the greatest room for the exercise of discretion. In this zone of cases, the race of the victim appears to determine the outcome of more than one-third of the cases. Also, the effects are comparable in both rural and urban areas.

Table 43. Summary of Results of Race-of-Victim Discrimination Analyses, Pre- and Post-*Furman*, among Cases that Resulted in a Murder-Trial Conviction (Procedural Reform Study)[1]

A. Analytic Method and Background Variables Adjusted/Controlled for	B. Statewide Death-Sentencing Disparities among Defendants Convicted of Murder at Trial	
	Pre-*Furman*	Post-*Furman*
1. Unadjusted disparities	8 pts.[a]	20 pts.[b]
2. Cross-tab controlling for qualitative *a priori* measure (armed-robbery cases)	3 pts. n.s.[c]	25 pts.[d]
3. Cross-tab controlling for main culpability scale	12 pts.[e]	7.4 pts.[f]
4. Cross-tab controlling for Barnett culpability measure		8 pts.[g]

5. Multiple-regression estimates after adjustment for the following legitimate case characteristics and the race of defendant:
a. Main culpability index
  (1) Statewide
  (2) Urban
  (3) Rural
b. 150-plus background factors
	4.3 o.m.[h]
	N^{2j}
	N^l
		4.3 o.m.[i]
		N^k
		N^m
		9 pts.[n]

1. Arithmetic disparities are reported as percentage-point differences (e.g., 8 pts. means an 8-point difference in the average death-sentencing rate for white- and black-victim cases). The "odds multiplier" estimates in logistic-regression analyses are designated "o.m." All disparities are statistically significant beyond the .05 level unless indicated "not significant" with "n.s." "T" and "F" in the footnotes stand for tables and figures; "n" stands for a note in this chapter.

2. N means no statistically significant ($p \leq 10$) difference between the race-of-victim effect in rural and urban places.

a. T. 26	g. F. 22	j. T. 42
b. T. 30	h. App. J, pt. 4, model	k. T. 42
c. T. 29	PREFURMA, and text	l. T. 42
d. T. 31	following n.7	m. T. 42
e. T. 28	i. App. J, pt. 1, model	n. Text at n.20
f. T. 32	OVERALLA, and text at n.19	

The statewide results summarized in Table 44 show generally stronger race-of-victim effects in prosecutorial decisions than in jury decisions. The strongest effects, however, are seen in the decisions of urban jurors and rural prosecutors. The pattern of race-of-victim discrimination is common to the five major regions of the state, but strongest in the Southeast.

Table 44. Summary of Results of Race-of-Victim Discrimination Analyses, Post-*Furman*, Prosecutorial and Jury Decision Making (Procedural Reform Study)[1]

A. Analytic Method and Background Variables Adjusted/Controlled for	B. Disparities in Prosecutorial Decision to Seek a Death Sentence After Trial	C. Disparities in Jury Penalty Trial Sentencing Decisions
1. Unadjusted disparities	30 pts.[a]	15 pts.[b]
2. Cross-tab controlling for qualitative *a priori* measure (armed-robbery cases)	31 pts.[c]	16 pts.[d]
3. Cross-tab controlling for main culpability index		
a. All cases	11 pts[e]	14.5 pts. n.s.[f]
b. Black-defendant cases	13 pts.[g]	14 pts. n.s.[h]
c. White-defendant cases	12 pts. n.s.[i]	−1.3 pts. n.s.[j]
4. Cross-tab controlling for Barnett culpability measure	15 pts.[k]	14 pts. n.s.[l]
5. Multiple-regression estimates after adjustment for the following legitimate case characteristics and the race of defendant:		
a. Main culpability index		
(1) Statewide	5.5 o.m.[m]	7 o.m.[n]
(2) Urban	1.7 o.m. (n.s.)[o]	6.6 o.m.[p]
(3) Rural	12.9 o.m.[q]	2.5 o.m. (n.s.)[r]
b. 150-plus background factors	12 pts.[s]	20 pts.[t]

1. Arithmetic disparities are reported as percentage-point differences (e.g., 8 pts. means an 8-point difference in the average death-sentencing rate for white- and black-victim cases). The "odds multiplier" estimates in logistic-regression analyses are designated "o.m." All disparities are statistically significant beyond the .05 level unless indicated "not significant" with "n.s." "T" and "F" in the footnotes stand for tables and figures; "n" stands for a note in this chapter.

a. T. 34
b. T. 34
c. T. 35
d. T. 35
e. T. 36
f. T. 36
g. T. 38
h. T. 38
i. T. 39

j. T. 39
k. F. 25
l. F. 26
m. Text at n. 37 and App. J, Pt. 2, model PROSCUTA
n. Text at n. 37 and App. J, Pt. 3, model JURYA

o. T. 42
p. T. 42
q. T. 42
r. T. 42
s. Text at n. 39
t. Text at n. 39

Race-of-victim discrimination is a major source of comparative excessiveness in the post-*Furman* system. The data also indicate that the socioeconomic status and residence of the defendant, and the socioeconomic status of the victim, influence the decisions of juries. Overall, our findings are squarely at odds with the Supreme Court's assumption in *Gregg v. Georgia* that the only factors that would influence decisions in post-*Furman* Georgia were the culpability of the offender and the strength of the evidence.

We see no plausible basis for attributing the overall decline in race-of-defendant discrimination between the pre- and post-*Furman* periods to the enactment of Georgia's 1973 sentencing reforms. We consider this change more likely the product of demographic trends and increased access of black citizens to the criminal justice system.

In spite of the Supreme Court's expectations, sentencing reforms of the type adopted in Georgia appear likely to have little effect on the role that illegitimate and suspect factors play in the criminal justice system.

NOTES

1. The CSS results presented in *McCleskey* are reported *infra* chap. 10, note 24 and accompanying text. A summary of the race-of-victim results from both studies is found *infra* chap. 12, table 64. Earlier versions of several of the PRS post-*Furman* race-of-victim findings reported in this chapter were presented in the *McCleskey* case, *see infra* chap. 10, note 16 and accompanying text.

2. *See supra* chap. 2, note 52 and accompanying text, and *infra* chap. 10, note 8 and accompanying text, for a discussion of the relevance of racial discrimination under the Fourteenth and Eighth Amendments.

3. *See supra* chap. 2, note 32 and accompanying text.

4. Under the pre-*Furman* system, prosecutors routinely waived the death penalty in death-eligible cases in which they did not consider death to be an appropriate punishment. Before the bifurcated trial system was established in 1970, the prosecutor could request that the jury not be instructed on the death-penalty option or request the jury to impose only a life sentence. After the bifurcated trial system was established in 1970, the prosecutor could effectively fix the sentence at life imprisonment simply by waiving the second stage of the process, the penalty trial. The fragmentary evidence that we do have on the issue suggests that the death penalty was waived pre-*Furman* at about the same rate that we observe post-*Furman*.

5. When we allocated death sentences randomly, *supra* chap. 5, note 3 and accompanying text, the racial and suspect factors in a logistic multiple-regression analysis had no effect at all on the death-sentencing results.

6. If there were no race effects, the distribution of cases would be identical to the one shown in figure 33, *infra* app. A.

7. For an explanation of partial-regression coefficients, see *supra* chap. 4, note 55 and accompanying text; *see infra* app. J, model PREFURMA, for the coefficients estimated in this analysis.

8. H. Kalven & H. Zeisel, THE AMERICAN JURY 164–67 (1966); *see also* Baumeister & Parley, *Reducing the Biasing Effect of Perpetrator Attractiveness in Jury Simulation*,

8 PERSONALITY & SOC. PSYCH. BULL. 286, 288 (1982) ("Sentencing bias in favor of an attractive defendant operates more strongly when the facts of the case are incomplete or equivocal than when evidence is more thorough"); M. Gottfredson & D. Gottfredson, DECISION MAKING IN CRIMINAL JUSTICE: TOWARD THE RATIONAL EXERCISE OF DISCRETION 261 (2d ed. 1988) ("As the reviews of empirical studies . . . have shown, when the offense is less serious, characteristics of the decision maker (for example, attitudes) and of the situation (such as complainant's preference) and extralegal characteristics (including demeanor) have a greater influence on the decision").

9. Another interaction in the pre-*Furman* data emerged in the logistic multiple-regression analysis reported in Appendix J (model PREFURMA). It showed much stronger race-of-victim effects in cases involving coperpetrators than in cases in which the defendant acted alone. The main-effects variable for the race-of-victim variable was $b = 1.74$ ($S.E. = .61$); the coefficient for the (race-of-victim) $\times$ (coperpetrator) interaction term was $b = 2.13$ ($S.E. = 1.23$).

10. If white defendants had been sentenced at the same rate as black defendants, we would have seen a 27% increase in the number of death sentences; similarly, if black-victim cases had been sentenced at the rate of white-victim cases, we would have seen an increase of 20% in the number of death sentences.

11. The coefficients and related statistics on which this analysis is based are reported *infra* app. J, model PREFURMA.

12. *See infra* app. A, note 37 and accompanying text, for a description of the defendant's socioeconomic status. The impact of those variables is probably more sharply felt at earlier stages in the process.

13. The post-*Furman* results presented in this subsection reflect the combined effects of prosecutorial and jury decision making. We examine separately the pattern of prosecutorial decisions and jury decisions in the post-*Furman* period on pages 160–69.

14. *See supra* chap. 5, note 38, for a listing of the urban judicial circuits.

15. *See supra* chap. 4, note 21 and accompanying text, for a description of the scale underlying Table 31. By way of contrast, the linear race-of-victim regression coefficient in an analysis of the armed-robbery–murder cases in Table 31, which adjusts for the components of our overall culpability index (OVERALLA), *infra* app. J, was 17 percentage points ($p = .02$), with a coefficient of $-.02$ ($p = .73$) for the white victim by mitigating-circumstances interaction term .

16. When we added dummy variables for the three basic Barnett case dimensions and his prior-record variable to our basic model of the overall death-sentencing results (OVERALLA), *infra* app. J, plus variables for the location of cases in the eighteen different cells created with the three basic case dimensions, we produced a significantly better-fitting logistic-regression model from a statistical standpoint. However, the estimated race-of-victim effects were virtually identical: (a) the main race-of-victim effects were $b = 2.69$ ($p = .0001$) with only OVERALLA variables, and $b = 2.64$ ($p = .002$) with the Barnett variables also added; and (b) the race-of-victim interaction variable (white victim with mitigating circumstances present) was $b = -1.72$ ($p = .002$) with only OVERALLA variables, and $b = -1.36$ ($p = .04$) with the Barnett variables also added.

Professor John Monahan has raised a question about Professor Barnett's second dimension used to classify cases, i.e., the defendant-victim relationship. Since most social relationships in the United States, and particularly in the South, are intraracial, will it not tend to be true, he asks, that cases with a close defendant-victim relationship will be predominantly intraracial, while the stranger cases are more likely to be interracial? And because the defendants in Georgia's interracial cases are much more likely to be black than white, might not the higher death-sentencing rates in the stranger-victim cases be a product of race-of-defendant discrimination rather than the defendant-victim relationship? For example, when we compare the cell coded 1, 1, 1 (with a death-sentencing rate of .25) with the cell coded 1, 0, 1 (with a rate of .02), the difference may be the product of a higher proportion of black defendants in the white-victim cases coded 1, 1, 1 (the stranger relationship) than in the white-victim cases coded 1, 0, 1 (the close relationship). To test the effects of a possible confound between race of the defendant and the defendant/victim relationship, we estimated an overall race-of-defendant effect, after adjusting for all three Barnett dimensions, and found none. And to test for the possibility that the relationship between the race of the defendant and the defendant/victim relationship may be confounded with the race-of-victim effect apparent in Figure 22, we recomputed the tabulation in that figure separately for white and black defendants. The results indicated that the overall race-of-victim effect, comparable to the adjusted 8-point disparity indicated in the second part of note 1 of Figure 22 for all cases, was 10 points within the white-defendant cases and 7 points within the black-defendant cases. We thus conclude that the correlation between the defendant-victim relationship and the race of the defendant biased neither the apparent influence of the defendant/victim relationship on the death-sentencing rate nor the race-of-victim disparity estimated in Figure 22.

17. (Mantel-Haenszel $Z = 3.27$). When the cases in row 2 are included, the average effect for rows 2 through 5 is 18.1 percentage points, significant at the .003 level (Mantel-Haenszel $Z = 2.98$).

18. This calculation is based on the posterior predictive distribution of the number of death sentences that would occur among white-victim cases if they were sentenced to death at the same rate as the corresponding black-victim cases. The statement is fairly robust since it is valid for prior distributions of the black-victim death-sentencing rate, which are locally uniform near zero.

Another commonly used ratio or multiplier measure used in death-penalty research is the "odds ratio," which compares the odds ("death odds") that individual members of different groups will receive a death sentence. The estimated death odds for a class of defendants is the number of death sentences divided by the number of life sentences in that class. To avoid division by zero, it is customary to add a small number (typically, .5) to the numerator and denominator of the ratio. For example, for white-victim cases in level 1 of table 32, there are 4 death and 203 life sentences, yielding estimated death-odds of 4.5/203.5, or about .022. Because death odds are a measure of a defendant's risk of receiving a death sentence, odds of .022 indicate a rather small risk (for every 1000 life sentences there are only 22 death sentences). The usual measure for comparing the odds on death for the white-victim cases to the odds on death for black-victim cases is the odds ratio—the ratio of the death odds for the white-victim cases to the death odds for the black-victim cases. For example, the odds ratio for level 3 in table 32 is 1.8, indicating that the odds of receiving a death sentence are 80% greater in the white-victim cases than in the black-victim cases at this level of aggravation. The remaining odds ratios are 8.6 for level 1, 1.3 for level 2, 13.1 for level 4, 21 for level 5, and 9 for level 6. Thus, white-victim cases are at a greater risk of death at all levels of aggravation.

Ratio measures are a particularly probative basis for inferring purposeful discrimination in a discretionary selection process, since the absolute-difference measure shown in column E of Table 32 is sensitive to the death-sentencing rate for "All cases" in column B. Ratio measures, in contrast, are insensitive to the overall rate and keep the focus squarely on the relative treatment of the average defendant with white and black victims. D. Baldus & J. Cole, STATISTICAL PROOF OF DISCRIMINATION 157 (1980).

19. See infra app. J, model OVERALLA, for the details of the logistic-regression model. It indicates that there is a substantial interaction effect between the race-of-victim disparity and the seriousness of the case. In the presence of mitigating circumstances, the race-of-victim effects are significantly reduced: $b = .99$ ($S.E. = .63$) with a $2.7 \times$ odds multiplier. In the 23% of the death-eligible cases with no mitigating circumstances present, the race-of-victim logistic coefficient equals 2.66 ($S.E. = .65$) with a $14.5 \times$ odds multiplier. The $4.3 \times$ odds multiplier reported in the text is the average effect for cases with and without mitigating circumstances present.

20. The results of this large-scale model are presented infra app. L, schedule 15. The race-of-victim coefficient estimated in a linear-regression analysis is comparable to the arithmetic-disparity measure reported in col. E of Table 32 (see supra chap. 4, note 55). The race-of-victim effect in cases without mitigating circumstances was 19 percentage points, significant at the .0008 level, while the disparity in cases with one or more mitigating circumstances present was 5 percentage points ($S.E. = .037$), which was not significant at the .10 level. The 9-percentage-point race-of-victim effect reported in the text is a weighted average of these two disparities.

In anticipation of the McCleskey hearing in 1983, we prepared a series of least-squares race-of-victim analyses, which were the forerunner of the results presented above. These results are reported infra chap. 10 (note table 4) in connection with our discussion of the McCleskey case. In a series of six analyses, the least-squares disparities ranged from 8 to 9 points, all significant beyond the .05 level.

21. See infra app. J, model OVERALLA, for the statistics on which this analysis is based. Also, one mitigating factor—"defendant was an underling"—had a slightly larger statistical impact in explaining who received a death sentence than did the race of the victim.

22. The data presented in Table 31 also suggest that a large proportion of the death sentences imposed in the Georgia armed-robbery–murder cases are the product of race-of-victim discrimination. If all defendants in subgroups 1 through 5 had received death sentences at the black-victim rate, there would have been thirty-eight fewer death sentences among the white-victim cases. This would have resulted in a 55% decline in the total number of death sentences imposed in armed-robbery–murder cases.

23. Using this analysis, the application of the white-victim rate would have increased the size of death row by 12%, while the application of the black-victim rate would have reduced the size of death row by 29%; see supra note 22 and accompanying text.

24. If the black-victim death-sentencing rate had been applied to the white-victim cases at levels 1–3, there would have been 6 fewer death sentences in the white-victim cases, a 23% (6/26) decline overall in the number of death-sentence cases in that category.

25. Zant v. Stephens, 462 U.S. 862, 877 (1983) ("an aggravating circumstance must genuinely narrow the class of persons eligible for the death penalty and must reasonably justify the imposition of a more severe sentence on the defendant compared to others found guilty of murder") (footnote omitted). Furman v. Georgia, 408 U.S. 238, 294 (1972) (Brennan, J., concurring) (a constitutionally acceptable capital-sentencing

system should select "only the worst criminals or the criminals who commit the worst crimes" for the death penalty); *id.* at 388 (Burger, C. J., dissenting) ("death is no longer a routine punishment for the crimes for which it is made available").

26. The coefficient was significant at the .05 level. This variable was not included as a suspect variable in the model OVERALLA because there were missing data in 19% (112/594) of the cases. The impact reported in the text was observed in the cases in which there were no missing data. The variable for court-appointed attorney was used, however, to create the LSTATDEF variable, on which data is missing in only a single case. *See infra* app. A, note 37 and accompanying text. LSTATDEF, significant at the .08 level, is included in model OVERALLA. The variable for high-status defendant, HISTD, also had a statistically significant effect, but in an unexpected direction; the odds of a death sentence were 6.6 times higher for high-status defendants. *See* model OVERALLA, *infra* app. J.

27. *Furman v. Georgia*, 408 U.S. at 255–56 (Douglas, J., concurring) ("In a Nation committed to equal protection of the laws there is no permissible 'caste' aspect of law enforcement") (footnote omitted); *see generally Zant v. Stephens*, 462 U.S. at 885 (suggesting that an aggravating circumstance would be invalid if based on such constitutionally protected conduct as political activity, such impermissible or irrelevant factors as race or religion, or "conduct that actually should militate in favor of a lesser penalty," such as a defendant's mental illness).

28. The odds multiplier estimated for this variable, with missing data in 8% (47/594) of the cases, was $2.9 \times$, but the coefficient ($b = 1.06$) was significant only at the .08 level. Because of the considerable proportion of cases with missing data, this variable was also not included in model OVERALLA, *infra* app. J.

29. *See Godfrey v. Georgia*, 446 U.S. 420, 432–33 (1980) (plurality opinion) (suggesting that the finding of an aggravating factor, and subsequent imposition of a death sentence, must be "based on reason," "in light of the facts and circumstances of the murders that [the particular defendant] was convicted of committing").

30. *Godfrey v. Georgia*, 446 U.S. at 433n.16 (plurality opinion) ("An interpretation of [aggravating circumstance] §(b)(7) so as to include all murders resulting in gruesome scenes would be totally irrational").

31. *Barclay v. Florida*, 463 U.S. 939, 949 (1983) (plurality opinion) ("The United States Constitution does not prohibit a trial judge from taking into account the elements of racial hatred in this murder").

32. The simple Pearson correlation coefficient (r) was $-.14$ ($p = .001$). After adjustment for the variables in model OVERALLA, the logistic partial-regression coefficient was $-.59$, significant at the .56 level (*see infra* app. J).

33. *See supra* note 23 and accompanying text.

34. Because our pre-*Furman* data do not allow us to analyze the prosecutorial and jury decisions separately, our comparison of these decisions is limited to the post-*Furman* period.

35. The logistic-regression coefficients for the racial variables, with supporting statistics, underlying these analyses are reported *infra* app. J in the PROSCUTA and JURYA models.

36. One may wonder why the separate race-of-victim effects observed in the prosecutorial and jury decisions are so much larger than the race-of-victim effects for these two decisions combined (*see supra* table 32). The apparent discrepancy is a consequence of using the arithmetic difference in sentencing rates as the measure of the race-of-victim effect. For these data, the overall race-of-victim (ROV) disparity within a

given category of similar cases is the sum of (the prosecutorial arithmetic ROV disparity) × (the jury death-sentencing rate) and (the jury ROV disparity) × (the rate at which prosecutors seek the death sentence). The relationship between the overall disparity and the disparities estimated for prosecutor and jury is analogous to the relationship between the selection rates for the prosecutors and juries and the death-sentencing rate for all defendants convicted of murder at trial, which reflects the combined effects of both prosecutorial and jury decisions. For example, a selection rate of .50 at both the prosecutorial and jury levels results in an overall rate of .25 (.50 × .50), which is substantially lower than either the jury or the prosecutorial rates. However, when the measure in the ROV disparity used is the *ratio* of white-victim and black-victim selection rates (WV rate/BV rate), the disparities observed at each jury and prosecutorial level are essentially the same as those observed in the analysis of the combined overall effects of the two decision points. *See also infra* chap. 11, note 55.

37. These estimates are based on the PROSCUTA and JURYA models reported *infra* app. J. The race-of-victim disparities reported in the text for each model are the average effects after adjustment for interactions between variables for legitimate case characteristics and the race of the victim.

38. Large-scale logistic models of this magnitude are not possible with existing computer software.

39. The prosecutorial model, with more than 150 variables, produced an adjusted R^2 of .56, a main-effects race-of-victim linear-regression coefficient of .15 ($p = .0007$), and a coefficient for the (race-of-victim) × (stranger-victim) interaction term of .16 ($p = .032$). In the jury analysis, because of the small ratio of cases to variables in the model (1.3 [206/159]), we did not consider the estimated coefficients to be valid (the race-of-victim coefficient in the large model was .43 [$p = .01$], with an adjusted R^2 of .57). Instead, we conducted a forward stepwise regression that included all nonracial variables ($n = 18$) that achieved a statistically significant relationship with the sentencing results. The race-of-victim and race-of-defendant coefficients reported in the text are from this stepwise analysis, which reported an unadjusted R^2 of .57.

40. *See supra* chap. 4, note 34, for a description of the R statistic used to measure the statistical power of the variables discussed in the text.

41. The analysis in the text is based on the results of the "A" type models reported *infra* app. J. The overall statewide statistics, which reflect the combined effects of both prosecutorial and jury decisions, show a logistic coefficient for women defendants of $b = -.50$ ($p = .56$) (model OVERALLA, *infra* app. J), which suggests a slight advantage for women that is not statistically significant beyond the .05 level. The prosecutorial and jury models estimated the following logistic coefficients for the female-defendant variable: prosecutor ($b = -1.4; p = .05$); jury ($b = 2.4; p = .17$).

42. The analyses in the text classified a prediction as correct if the actual sentence imposed was predicted at a probability greater than .50, e.g., a predicted death case of .55 was classified correct if the case received a death sentence. Also of relevance is that only 43% (9/21) of the predicted death sentences among the black-victim cases actually resulted in a death sentence, whereas the comparable statistic among the white-victim cases was 91% (83/91).

43. *See infra* app. J for statistical details on the interaction results reported in the text.

44. In both analyses, cooperation with the authorities, which generally meant a confession, had an aggravating effect. This seemingly perverse outcome is likely explained by the strength that a confession adds to the government's case, particularly if

it involves a full description of gruesome details. The propriety of such an effect may be questionable, however. *See* Zant v. Stephens, 462 U.S. 862, 885 (1983) ("Nor has Georgia attached the 'aggravating' label . . . to conduct that actually should militate in favor of a lesser penalty, such as perhaps the defendant's mental illness").

45. Johnson, *The Executioner's Bias*, 37 NAT. REV., Nov. 15, 1985, at 44. ("The history of the death penalty statutes and cases since 1972 encourages the courts to bend over backward to make sure they are not executing a disproportionate number of blacks. So they end up executing a disproportionate number of whites and murderers of whites").

46. *See supra* note 23 and accompanying text.

47. *See infra* app. A, note 21 and accompanying text, for further discussion of this issue.

48. *See supra* chap. 5, note 38, for a listing of the urban circuits.

49. *Id.*

50. *Supra* note 36 and accompanying text.

51. *See supra* chap. 5, table 22, for an enumeration of the judicial circuits in each of the five regions.

52. *See infra* app. A, note 21 and accompanying text, for a description of the methodology we used to estimate the likelihood that race-of-defendant and race-of-victim effects may be an artifact of region and circuit variations in death-sentencing rates.

53. The black-defendant logistic-regression coefficients were $b = 2.9 (S.E. = .9)$ for Ocmulgee circuit and $b = -3.5 (S.E. = 1.5)$ for Eastern circuit. The average statewide race-of-defendant effect is $b = -.5 (S.E. = .5)$.

54. The white-victim logistic-regression coefficient was $b = 1.8 (S.E. = .9)$. The average statewide race-of-victim effect was $b = 1.9 (S.E. = .7)$.

55. The white-victim coefficient for the Northern circuit was $b = -2.29$ $(S.E. = .76)$, compared to an average statewide coefficient of $b = 2.09 (S.E. = .41)$.

The evidence of racial disparities presented thus far is based on an analysis of prosecutorial and jury decisions for the entire 1973–78 period. It is possible that disparities existed during the 1973–75 transition period following the enactment of Georgia's post-*Furman* death-sentencing statute, but disappeared thereafter. To test this hypothesis, we conducted a logistic-regression analysis controlling for case culpability and the year in which sentence was imposed. The results produced an estimate of the extent to which the race-of-defendant and race-of-victim effects for each year deviated from the coefficients estimated for the entire 1973–78 period. For the race-of-defendant variable, the results showed insignificant fluctuations. However, for the race-of-victim variable, the results showed a downward trend in the race-of-victim disparity for each year. Specifically, the years 1973–74 showed a race-of-victim effect that was 1.8 points higher than the five-year average logistic coefficient. However, for the years 1975 through 1978, the race-of-victim effect fell below the five-year average by the following amounts: 1975 (−.14), 1976 (−.22), 1977 (−.79), and 1978 (−.66). Thus, although the race-of-victim effect persisted throughout the period of the study, the results suggest a slight decline from year to year.

56. The average number of mitigating circumstances in the black-defendant/white-victim cases decreased .63 ($p = .001$), as contrasted to an insignificant .07 decrease in the number of mitigating circumstances in the white-defendant/white-victim cases. The results of this analysis are consistent with Radelet & Pierce, *Race and Prosecutorial Discretion in Homicide Cases*, 19 LAW & SOC. REV. 587 (1985), which found evidence that, in Florida cases with black defendants and white victims, prosecutors were most

likely to upgrade and least likely to downgrade the police-report classification of a case as involving a contemporaneous felony, a decision that made the higher-graded cases stronger candidates for a death penalty.

To estimate the possible impact of altered record-keeping practices on our post-*Furman* analysis, we adjusted the variable in our main culpability model (OVERALLA), which reflects the number of statutory aggravating circumstances in the cases (DELB7EXP), so that its post-*Furman* increase in the black-defendant/white-victim cases was the same as that observed in the other post-*Furman* cases. The resulting race-of-defendant logistic-regression coefficient changed from $-.57$ ($p = .25$) to .63 ($p = .16$). In a second, less conservative procedure, we assumed that differential recording practices may have affected the data for other variables used in the aggravation index. For this analysis, we adjusted the post-*Furman* aggravation index used in discrimination analyses (OVERALLB) to make the post-*Furman* increase in the aggravation level of the black-defendant/white-victim cases the same as the average aggravation level increase in the other post-*Furman* cases. After this adjustment, the race-of-defendant disparity (black defendant $= 1$ and white defendant $= 0$) changed from $-.57$ ($p = .25$) to 1.25 ($p = .008$), with an odds multiplier of 3.5. We are grateful to Samuel Gross for suggesting the record-keeping hypothesis in the context of this research.

57. *See supra* table 42 and text accompanying note 49. The proportion of Georgia's "central cities" populations reported as black by the Census Bureau rose from 37% in 1960 to 44% in 1977 to 51% in 1980. Similarly, the proportion of the state's rural population reported as black declined from 27% in 1960 to 22% in 1970 to 19% in 1980. During this same twenty-year period, the percentage of blacks in the population of the entire state declined from 29% to 27%. U.S. Department of Commerce, 1980 CENSUS OF POPULATION, 1 *Characteristics of the Population*, pt. 12: Georgia, chap. C, at 12–7 (Dept. Commerce 1983); 1970 CENSUS OF POPULATION, 1 *Characteristics of the Population*, pt. 12: Georgia, at 12–55, 56 (Dept. Commerce 1973); CENSUS OF POPULATION: 1960, 1 *Characteristics of the Population*, pt. 12, Georgia, at 12–36 (Dept. Commerce 1963).

58. The pre-*Furman* sample is described *supra* chap. 4, note 2 and accompanying text. The race-of-defendant logistic coefficient, estimated from the largely 1970–72 data in our original unaugmented pre-*Furman* sample (with only twenty death cases), was 1.9 ($6.6 \times$ odds multiplier), significant at the .14 level, in contrast to a coefficient of 2.49 ($12 \times$ odds multiplier), significant at the .002 level for the entire pre-*Furman* sample (see app. J). Because of the structure of the pre-*Furman* sample (1969 was the earliest life-sentence case), we could not conduct a separate analysis of the 1960s cases.

59. We believe that more plausible explanations of any decline of race-of-defendant discrimination in Georgia's post-*Furman* sentencing system are the impact of United States Supreme Court decisions prohibiting discrimination against black citizens in the criminal justice system and in local government generally, the large-scale movement of blacks to urban areas, and the general decline of racial prejudice against blacks. On this last point, nearly all of the changes in the attitudes of whites toward blacks occurred in the U.S. generally between 1964 and 1976 (*see supra* chap. 5, note 30).

60. A recent article by Michael Radelet and Michael Mello, *Executing Those Who Kill Blacks: An Unusual Case Study*, 37 MERCER L. REV. 911 (1986), illustrates how both media publicity and the lack of support for capital punishment in the black community can produce race-of-victim effects in death sentencing. Pressure from the media tends to increase the risk of a death sentence in white-victim cases, while pres-

sure from the black community tends to reduce the probability of a death sentence in black-victim cases.

The article describes the case of James Henry, a black defendant who was executed in Florida in 1984 for the murder of his neighbor, Z. Riley, a prominent eighty-one-year-old black civil rights leader. The defendant had broken into the victim's home and cut, bound, and gagged him (in a manner that eventually strangled the victim on the gag). Several days after the killing, a white police officer went to the defendant's home to take him into custody. The defendant attacked the officer, took his gun, and shot him twice, although the wounds were not life threatening. The newspaper coverage of the case suggested that local journalists and editors perceived the defendant's assault on the white police officer to be more important than the murder of the black civil rights leader. Specifically, the authors analyzed thirteen newspaper articles and documented that 51% of the lines devoted to the defendant's case focused on the white police officer's assault, while only 28% discussed the killing:

> Despite the fact that Mr. Riley was one of the most prominent citizens in central Florida, had contributed far more to the community and for a much longer time than Officer Ferguson, and was murdered rather than wounded, the newspaper devoted more coverage to the shooting of the officer than to the slaying of Mr. Riley. *Id.* at 920 (footnote omitted).

On the strength of this analysis, Radelet and Mello conclude that, in fact, the death sentence in Henry's case was more the product of outrage at the injury to the white police officer than it was reaction to the killing of the black victim. *Id.* at 919.

The case also illustrates the importance of black community attitudes toward capital punishment. The victim's son and two nieces appealed to the governor to spare the defendant's life, as did the local branch of the NAACP, in which the victim had been active. Although their appeals had no effect in this case, to the extent that these and similar pleas from families of black victims to spare the lives of capital defendants have an effect, their tendency is normally to reduce the likelihood that death sentences will be imposed in black-victim cases.

61. In 1985, 15% of the nation's white population opposed the death penalty, while 43% of the black population opposed it. G. Gallup, THE GALLUP POLL: PUBLIC OPINION 1985, at 268–69 (1986). In a 1986 Georgia poll, 18% of white respondents, as compared to 53% of blacks, opposed the death penalty. R. H. Thomas and J. D. Hutcheson, Jr., GEORGIA RESIDENTS' ATTITUDES TOWARD THE DEATH PENALTY, THE DISPOSITION OF JUVENILE OFFENDERS AND RELATED ISSUES, at 8 (December 1986). *See supra* chap. 5, note 48, for trends in support of the death penalty since the 1950s.

62. *See* Gross and Mauro, *Patterns of Death: An Analysis of Racial Disparities in Capital Sentencing and Homicide Victimization,* 37 STAN. L. REV. 27, 106–10 (1984); Zeisel, *Race Bias in the Administration of the Death Penalty: The Florida Experience,* 95 HARV. L. REV. 456, 467 (1981). In states like Florida, where sentencing is done by judges, they are likely subject to pressures and influences comparable to those felt by prosecutors.

63. Evidence of the statewide change in race-of-defendant discrimination pre- and post-*Furman* is a comparison of the odds multiplier in our main model developed for each period. The pre-*Furman* model shows a race-of-defendant death odds multiplier of 12 ($p = .002$) for defendants convicted of murder at trial (app. J, part 4, model PRFURMA), while the odds multiplier for the comparable analysis post-*Furman* was $-.57$ ($p = .25$) (*see* app. J, part 1, model OVERALLA). The race-of-defendant coeffi-

cients for the post-*Furman* prosecutorial and jury models were .15 (p = .69) and −.53 (p = .39) (*see* app. J, part 2, model PROSCUTA; part 3, model JURYA). A comparison of cross-tabular analyses based on these indexes shows similar differences. *See supra* Table 27 (pre-*Furman*) and Tables 40 & 41 (post-*Furman*). The degree to which these changes may be an artifact of altered record-keeping practices post-*Furman* is discussed *supra* note 56 and accompanying text.

64. *See supra* Table 42 and accompanying text.

CHAPTER SEVEN

State Appellate Court Review of Arbitrariness
and Discrimination in Capital Sentencing:
The Georgia Experience

INTRODUCTION

The preceding two chapters indicate that, despite Georgia's 1973 procedural reforms, defendants have received arbitrary or excessive death sentences at the trial-court level. In many cases, there is strong evidence of race-of-victim discrimination as well. For these reasons, the manner in which the Georgia Supreme Court has discharged its responsibilities in the review of death-sentence cases is of particular interest. Under the 1973 statute, the Georgia Supreme Court must review every death-sentence case. As part of its appellate review, the court must determine whether the death sentence imposed was excessive or disproportionate or was imposed under the influence of passion, prejudice, or any other arbitrary factor.

In *Gregg v. Georgia*[1] the United States Supreme Court gave Georgia's appellate-review process substantial attention. Justice Stewart's plurality opinion, in particular, invoked the Georgia Supreme Court's extensive oversight role, especially the process of proportionality review, as a basis for deciding if Georgia's 1973 death-sentencing procedures were constitutional. The United States Supreme Court repeated its belief in the importance of proportionality review on several occasions subsequent to *Gregg*. Indeed, some observers during that period expected the Court would eventually require proportionality review, at least for the death-sentencing systems with very broad jury-sentencing discretion. However, in 1984 the Court ruled in *Pulley v. Harris* that no such review was constitutionally required.[2]

Even before *Pulley*, some justices had disclaimed any belief in the efficiency of proportionality review. Indeed, as early as 1976 Justice Rehnquist advanced what we call the second impossibility hypothesis when he expressed strong reservations about the capacity of state courts to identify the "similar" cases required for comparative purposes.[3] Professor George Dix echoed this theme in his 1979 analysis of proportionality review by the Georgia and Florida supreme courts:

> The expectation of effective appellate review assumes that objective and rational decisions can be made concerning which killers should live and which should die.

198

The appellants, however, have all committed atrocious crimes. Given the enormity of their crimes, the task of identifying specific characteristics that society may use to determine whether a particular appellant should be executed may be impossible.[4]

This chapter describes our efforts to evaluate the accuracy of this impossibility hypothesis in Georgia. We began by examining all of the Georgia Supreme Court's opinions regarding the proportionality-review process. We also analyzed empirically sixty-eight of the first sixty-nine cases that the Georgia court reviewed for excessiveness under the new statute prior to the United States Supreme Court's decision in *Pulley v. Harris*, when the constitutional status of proportionality review was still unclear.[5] Further, we attempted to assess statistically the impact of Georgia's appellate-review process generally on the levels of excessiveness and discrimination observed in trial-court decisions.

This chapter also reports the findings of three other investigators who have evaluated the Georgia Supreme Court's system of proportionality review. And in chapter 9 we discuss the effectiveness of proportionality review and the problems associated with its use in other jurisdictions.

GEORGIA'S SYSTEM OF COMPARATIVE-SENTENCE REVIEW

Comparative-sentence review—what the United States Supreme Court has sometimes described as "proportionality review"—is a procedure by which a court determines whether a death sentence is consistent with the usual pattern of sentencing decisions in similar cases or is comparatively excessive.[6] The reviewing court must identify other cases from the same jurisdiction that are "similar" in some pertinent respect to the death-sentence case under review and decide, in light of the sentences imposed in those other "similar" cases, whether the death sentence being scrutinized passes constitutional muster.[7] Legislation in more than twenty states requires their supreme courts to conduct some form of comparative-sentence review in death-sentence cases.[8]

Georgia's statute requires the state supreme court to determine whether each death sentence is "excessive or disproportionate to the penalty imposed in similar cases, considering both the crime and the defendant." The statute further provides that the Georgia court "shall include in its decision a reference to those similar cases which it took into consideration" in its proportionality analysis. To assist the court in selecting similar cases, the Georgia statute requires the trial judge in each death case to complete a standardized questionnaire prepared and supplied by the Georgia Supreme Court. In addition, the statute authorizes the appointment of an "Assistant to the Supreme Court," whose functions include accumulating the records of "all capital felony cases in which sentence was imposed after January 1, 1970, or such earlier date as the Court may deem appropriate." The statute requires this assistant to provide the court with whatever information it desires with respect to each of these prior cases, "including but not limited to a synopsis or brief of the facts in the record concerning the crime and the defendant."[9] During the post-*Furman* period covered by the empirical component of this study, 1973–78, a principal function of this assistant was to receive and to file the questionnaire sent to the court in each death case.[10] In addition, the assistant prepared for the court's use a brief synopsis of every appealed capital-murder case decided after January 1, 1970, whether or not it resulted in a death sentence.[11]

The Universe of Potentially Similar Cases

The Georgia statute does not explicitly define the universe of cases from which the court is to select "similar" cases when conducting a comparative-sentence review. The statute's requirement that the court collect data on "all capital felony cases in which sentence was imposed after January 1, 1970," does imply that this universe of potentially similar cases should include all murder convictions, whether by plea or at trial, in which sentence was imposed. In practice, the court limits its search to post-1969 capital-murder cases in which there was a trial, a murder conviction, and an appeal.[12] Because the Georgia Supreme Court always reviews death-penalty cases, one consequence of this policy is that the universe of potentially similar cases includes all death-sentence cases, but excludes life-sentence cases in which no appeal occurs, as well as death-eligible cases that resulted in a negotiated guilty plea to murder or a noncapital crime such as voluntary manslaughter.[13] The court includes in the universe of potentially similar cases death-sentence cases in which no comparative-sentence review was conducted because the court reversed the conviction or vacated the death sentence on unrelated grounds.[14]

Review of Individual Death Cases

As a matter of Georgia Supreme Court practice, the "author judge" assigned to write the court's opinion in any death-sentence case chooses the other cases selected as "similar" for the purpose of proportionality review.[15] This practice may explain the diversity of approaches one finds in the court's different opinions.[16] In some cases, the author judge has requested the court's assistant for proportionality review to provide summaries of cases with the characteristics specified by the author judge. This requires a manual search of more than seven hundred case summaries.[17] However, it appears that, at least before

1979, such requests for assistance were infrequent. For the most part, author judges relied principally upon their own records and their memory of prior decisions when selecting similar cases.[18]

The Identification of Similar Cases

The opinions of the Georgia Supreme Court do not reveal a uniform method for selecting the characteristics from the death-sentence case under review to be used for determining "similar" cases. In many cases, especially in the 1970s, the methodology is not disclosed; the court simply states that it compared the review case with the evidence and sentence in similar cases, and that those listed in the appendix support the determination that the death sentence under review is not disproportionate or excessive.[19]

However, when one reviews the entire corpus of the Georgia court's proportionality-review opinions, two methods for identifying similar cases seem to predominate. The first and most commonly discussed method is a fact-specific or salient-feature matching method, which employs a variety of quite explicit case classifications. Some are as broad as a given statutory aggravating circumstance such as murder "in the commission of another capital felony."[20] More commonly, however, the court describes the salient factors used for selecting similar cases in a more fact-specific manner. The following are some of the more commonly used classifications:

- [F]or the purpose of receiving money or any other thing of monetary value.[21]
- [E]xecution-style murders or murders following invasion of the victim's home.[22]
- [An] absolutely unprovoked murder while the appellant was in the commission of armed robbery, kidnapping, and rape.[23]
- [A] coldblooded killing perpetrated solely for the purpose of monetary gain.[24]
- [An] execution-style slaying of a police officer engaged in the performance of his official duties.[25]
- [A] brutal killing of an armed-robbery and kidnap victim for the sole purpose of financial gain and in order to eliminate witnesses.[26]
- [V]ictim suffered severe physical abuse prior to death.[27]
- [D]eliberate, unprovoked killing of a victim in conjunction with a sex crime.[28]
- [V]ictim was abducted at gunpoint, taken to a remote area, and coldbloodedly murdered.[29]
- [D]efendant is found to have been the actual perpetrator of, or active participant in, double murders committed upon victims who are unrelated to the defendant.[30]
- [A]n adult defendant commits murder during an unlawful intrusion into a private home.[31]
- [C]ontract murder cases.[32]

When the Georgia Supreme Court does identify the factual circumstances used for selecting similar cases, mitigating factors appear to play only a minor role. Occasionally, the court will include a mitigating circumstance among the criteria used for selecting similar cases.[33] Usually, however, the court discusses mitigating factors only when explaining why the mitigating circumstances invoked by a defendant are insufficient to distinguish his case from other cases in which death sentences were imposed.[34]

The second method that the Georgia Supreme Court appears to use for selecting comparable cases—although no opinion has discussed it explicitly—involves an assessment of the overall culpability of different cases. The use of this approach can be detected in some court opinions that use quite general and subjective terms to classify the case under review. Examples include "cold-blooded and callous nature of the offense,"[35] and the defendant's "brutality and depraved intent . . . is similar" to that found in other cases.[36] Other evidence of the use of an overall culpability method can be derived by analyzing the factual circumstances of cases identified by the court, in its appendices, as "similar." On occasion, the court sometimes selects as "similar" cases that are factually quite different from the death-sentence case under review. Presumably, therefore, the court selected these cases because it regards the death-sentence defendant before it and those in the "similar" cases as comparable in terms of relative culpability.

An example of this overall culpability method at work may be Case 495, one of the cases included in our empirical analysis of Georgia's proportionality-review system. Before committing the murder for which the jury sentenced him to death, defendant 495 shot another person, who survived. Then, without provocation, he shot and killed the victim, a defenseless stranger who had responded to the defendant's request for assistance. Later, in an effort to avoid arrest, the defendant engaged in a shoot-out with the police. In ruling that defendant 495's death sentence was not disproportionate, the Georgia Supreme Court cited fourteen "similar" death-sentence cases.[37]

In seven of these cases the facts were clearly more aggravated because of the number of victims or the level of violence and cruelty.[38] Many of the other cases cited as "similar" were factually quite different. However, after weighing the aggravating factors in these appendix cases, especially the level of pain inflicted, against the mitigating factors, one could reasonably conclude that, despite their factual dissimilarities, they are roughly comparable to Case 495 in overall culpability.[39] Finally, the opinions of the Georgia court have not clearly identified and defended the substantive standards that the justices apply in making their determination of whether a given death sentence is excessive. Although there have been some suggestions in the opinions analyzed in detail below, on the whole we believe the court has been fairly criticized[40] for failing to articulate the standards it applies for deciding the merits of the proportionality issues it routinely confronts.[41]

THE RESULTS OF GEORGIA'S PROPORTIONALITY-REVIEW SYSTEM

Since 1973, the Georgia court has conducted annually approximately ten comparative-sentence reviews in death-penalty cases. In only two of the cases, however, has the Georgia court vacated the death sentence on the grounds that it was "excessive or disproportionate." In neither of these two cases, however, did the court vacate the death sentence on the grounds that it was a rare or infrequent imposition of that penalty in similar cases generally. In one case, the jury had resentenced to death a defendant who had previously received a life sentence;[42] in the other, the defendant's coperpetrator, the actual trigger-man, had received only a life sentence.[43] In every other case, the Georgia Supreme Court affirmed the death sentence as neither excessive nor disproportionate.

The findings reported in chapter 5 of this book suggest that the Georgia court affirmed a number of the death sentences that were probably excessive. For this reason, we conducted an extensive analysis of sixty-eight of the first sixty-nine death-sentence cases that the Georgia Supreme Court reviewed pursuant to the post-*Furman* legislation.[44] In this connection we employed three different measures of case culpability to identify similar cases. The results of this inquiry, published earlier, suggest that from 13 percent (9/68) to 25 percent (17/68) of the death sentences that the court affirmed were probably excessive, in that death-sentencing rates among other defendants of comparative culpability were below .35. We also found that 20 percent to 30 percent of the death sentences in the affirmed cases were probably evenhanded, in that .80 or more of the defendants that our measures classified as similarly situated received death sentences. The measures ranged from 10 percent (7/68) to 50 percent (34/68). In the remaining death-sentence cases, which account for nearly one-half of the total, the death-sentencing rate among similar cases fell between .35 and .80.

By comparison, an examination of the appendixes of the Georgia Supreme Court's opinions, which list the cases that the court considered similar to each death case under review, reveals a completely different picture of the level of consistency in the Georgia death-sentencing system. Figure 27 presents a distribution of the sixty-eight death-sentence cases that we reanalyzed according to the proportion of death-sentence cases that were included in the Georgia court's appendixes. These data indicate that in almost 90 percent of the sixty-eight cases that we analyzed, every case identified in the court's appendix as similar to the death case under review resulted in a death sentence. For only five of the sixty-eight cases was the death-sentencing rate among the appendix cases less than .75, and for only one case was it less than .50.[45]

Figure 27. Distribution of 68 Death-Sentence Cases Reviewed by the Georgia Supreme Court for Excessiveness or Disproportionality According to the Proportion of Death-Sentenced Cases among the Cases Identified as Similar in the Court's Appendix

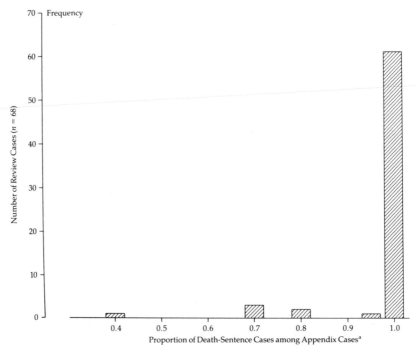

a. Except for 1.0, points on the scale include cases with the proportion indicated plus cases immediately above the next lower point on the scale; e.g., the bar at 0.7 represents cases with death-sentencing frequencies among similar cases ranging from more than 0.6 to and including 0.7.

In other words, our quantitative methods for selecting similar cases with respect to the sixty-eight death-sentence cases that we examined produced very different pools of comparable cases from those selected by the Georgia Supreme Court. If our methods for selecting similar case are reliable, this means that the Georgia Supreme Court has, on occasion, failed to identify death sentences that were, in fact, comparatively excessive and has denied relief in cases in which it was warranted.

We make this statement cautiously, because its accuracy depends on the validity of our measures of comparative excessiveness. A possibility does exist that the observed disparity between the Georgia court's record and our findings has resulted from our use of inaccurate or inappropriate measures. As previously noted, the critical feature of any system of comparative-sentence review is the process of selecting the cases deemed to be "similar" to the death-sentence case under review. None of the computer-assisted methods we have employed for that purpose in our study is foolproof. It is always possible that some special, nonquantifiable features of any case that does not appear in our computerized data files may have determined the appropriate results.

We consider this prospect unlikely, however. Our data files include every factor that the Georgia Supreme Court has identified as salient in any of its opinions. We also doubt that the Georgia Supreme Court has reached different conclusions about the degree of excessiveness involved in any particular case from those indicated by our results on the basis of obscure or unquantifiable factual distinctions. Certainly, the court's opinions have never invoked any idiosyncratic features of the death-sentence cases under review that were not apparent from the face of the record or did not appear in our list of variables.

It is more likely, we believe, that the discrepancies between our findings and the court's sentence-review decisions have resulted from the manner in which the court conducts the sentence-review process. Specifically, when selecting "similar" cases, it appears that the Georgia court systematically overlooks life-sentence cases that are comparable to the case under review. As a consequence, death sentences that our analysis may identify as excessive appear to be evenhanded when compared to the "similar" cases listed in the Georgia court's appendixes.

Two other studies of the Georgia court's proportionality-review process have also concluded that the court's procedure for selecting similar cases biases its proportionality-review process in favor of finding that no death sentence is excessive or disproportionate. William Bowers analyzed the first thirty-six cases in which the Georgia Supreme Court conducted a proportionality review.[46] For this purpose, he also analyzed the pattern of cases the court cited as being similar to the case under review. He concluded:

> In all, the Georgia Supreme Court cited only eighteen life cases . . . , or less than 10 percent, of the more than 200 life sentences appealed to the Court between 1970 and 1977. Moreover, seventeen of these were pre-April 1973 life cases. . . . In only one case (Moore) were more life than death sentences cited as similar. . . .
>
> Thus, from the substantial pool of almost 300 cases available for proportionality review by 1977, the Georgia Supreme Court repeatedly relied upon a small and highly selective subsample. It cited predominantly death cases, then exclusively death cases, and increasingly death cases it had affirmed in previous proportionality reviews: fewer than one in ten of the available life cases and virtually nine out of ten previously affirmed post-*Furman* death cases.
>
> This is not proportionality review as mandated by the Georgia capital statute and approved by the U.S. Supreme Court in *Gregg*, but a process of legally rationalizing trial court decisions to impose death as punishment, regardless of proportionality or excessiveness relative to the sentences in similar cases.[47]

In the second study, Ursula Bentele analyzed the system of proportionality review applied by the Georgia Supreme Court in twenty death-sentence cases in 1981.[48] Using a methodology similar to that of Bowers, Bentele concluded:

> Almost uniformly, appellate proportionality reviews cite only to those cases that also resulted in a death sentence and that were in some sense "similar" to the case on appeal. If the court considers any similar cases in which a life sentence was imposed, it does not list or discuss such cases in its opinions. . . .
>
> At best, Georgia's proportionality review may insure that if a court imposes a death sentence in a case which is in no way similar to other death penalty cases, the supreme court may vacate the sentence. Because, however, the categories of aggravating circumstances are virtually all-inclusive, that situation has never arisen.[49]

In other words, our analysis and the studies by Bowers and Bentele all reach a similar conclusion: the Georgia Supreme Court regularly affirms death sentences as evenhanded and not excessive because, when it selects other "similar" cases for comparative purposes, the court customarily overselects other cases that resulted in death sentences and underselects life-sentence cases. There are several possible reasons that might explain why the Georgia court's proportionality-review analyses rely disproportionately on death-sentence cases. We attempted to evaluate each.

A Precedent-Seeking Approach to Proportionality Review

One possible explanation is that the Georgia Supreme Court frequently uses what one might call a "precedent-seeking" form of sentence review. This means that the court will affirm a death sentence as appropriate and even-handed on the basis of a small number of "similar" cases if they also resulted in death sentences. The precedent-seeking approach is basically result-oriented. It begins with an intuitive judgment about the propriety of the death sentence under review. Then the court cites as authority one or more prior cases that appear to be factually comparable to the case on appeal and that resulted in a similar sentence. Thus, if the court concludes that the death sentence under review is reasonably appropriate, it will cite one or more "similar" cases that also resulted in death sentences. Conversely, if the court considers the death sentence under review to be unreasonable or inappropriate—which the Georgia court did only twice during the period of our study—it will cite a group of "similar" life-sentence cases to support its decision to vacate the death sentence as excessive or disproportionate. A number of state courts explicitly declare that this is the method they employ in their proportionality reviews.[50]

In contrast to the precedent-seeking review-process approach, a comparative-sentence review of the type envisioned by the plurality in *Gregg v. Georgia* contemplates a procedure that will allow the court to determine how frequently death sentences are imposed among similar cases. Such an inquiry will allow the court to determine, for example, if death sentences are "regularly," "infrequently," or "rarely" imposed in cases of comparable culpability. A proportionality-review process that focuses on the frequency of death sentencing requires three determinations. First, the reviewing court must decide which features of the death-sentence case under review will govern the selection of other cases as "similar." Second, using those criteria, the court must identify those other "similar" cases and determine the frequency with which defendants received death sentences in such cases. Finally, the court must decide whether death sentences were imposed so infrequently in this class of similar cases as to make imposition of the death penalty in the case under review comparatively excessive. In making this judgment, the court must consider with what regularity death sentences must be imposed in an identifiable class of cases either to serve as an effective deterrent to others or to constitute a justifiable form of retribution in light of contemporary community standards.

Justice Stewart's opinion in *Gregg* leaves little doubt that the frequency of death sentencing among similar cases should be the principal focus of the court's inquiry in a comparative-proportionality review. When describing the Georgia Supreme Court's appellate-review process in death-penalty cases as an important statutory safeguard, Justice Stewart commented:

> The provision for appellate review in the Georgia capital-sentencing system serves as a check against the random or arbitrary imposition of the death penalty. In particular, the proportionality review substantially eliminates the possibility that a person will be sentenced to die by the action of an aberrant jury. If a time comes when juries generally do not impose the death sentence in a certain kind of murder case, the appellate review procedures assure that no defendant convicted under such circumstances will suffer a sentence of death. [51]

Similarly, Justice White's concurring opinion in *Gregg* reflected the same understanding when he asserted that if Georgia juries imposed a death sentence in "a substantial proportion" of capital cases involving statutory aggravating circumstances, the sanction would demonstrate its usefulness and, therefore, its constitutionality. [52]

As the foregoing discussion indicates, there are certain similarities between the precedent-seeking form of appellate review and the frequency approach characteristic of a true comparative-sentence review. Furthermore, the precedent-seeking approach can, on occasion, identify death sentences that are comparatively excessive. The difference between the two methods, however, deserves emphasis. They both require the reviewing court to scan prior cases and to evaluate the death sentence under review on the basis of the sentences imposed in prior cases regarded as comparable. A precedent-seeking court, however, will be satisfied upon finding one or two prior cases, the circumstances of which make them suitable benchmarks for the death sentence on appeal. By contrast, the frequency approach requires a survey of the sentencing results in all prior cases deemed to be similar to the case on appeal, because it is the relative frequency with which life sentences result in that entire class of cases that determines whether the death sentence on appeal is excessive or evenhanded. For this reason, while a precedent-seeking approach may be a useful tool for deciding whether a given death sentence is disproportionate in the traditional sense, only a comparative-sentence review using the frequency approach can adequately address the question of comparative excessiveness.

One can readily understand why a court might employ a precedent-seeking approach to sentence review. Collecting and systematically analyzing data case-by-case can be a complex, time-consuming process. Also, for some cases that did not result in a death sentence, the process can raise close questions as to whether the evidence in them was sufficiently strong to support a capital murder conviction and a finding that one or more statutory aggravating circumstances were present in the case. Moreover, except when a death sentence is clearly excessive, the process may involve difficult questions of interpretation and line drawing for which there is little guidance. The precedent-seeking approach is easier to apply and may avoid hard legal issues. Furthermore, in comparison to the frequency approach characteristic of true comparative-sentence review, the precedent-seeking approach more closely resembles the methodology of conventional legal research and analysis and seems more comfortable to the law-trained mind. The danger, however, is that the precedent-seeking approach usually fails to identify all the cases in the universe of potentially similar cases that are comparable to the death-sentence case under review.

The question, then, is what approach to proportionality review has the Georgia court adopted? Unfortunately, the court has not described its methodology or documented its holdings with enough specificity for us to be absolutely certain. Moreover, the court's opinions present conflicting evidence on the issue. On balance, however, we believe those opinions support the conclusion that the court has strictly adopted neither of the two models of proportionality review that we have just described. Rather, the evidence suggests the predominate approach is either a modified form of frequency analysis or an expanded and more extensive form of the precedent-seeking approach. Indeed, there is a distinct possibility that both these approaches, as well as others, may be used by various justices.

Three items of evidence support the hypothesis that the court is conducting a modified form of frequency analysis. The first is that the court considers both life- and death-sentence cases. The opinions of the Georgia court make this quite plain.[53] In contrast, some courts using pure precedent-seeking approaches limit their inquiry strictly to death-sentence cases.[54] Second, language implying a frequency analysis appears in a number of opinions, the most common being that death sentences are not appropriate "unless in similar cases throughout the state the death penalty has been imposed generally and not 'wantonly and freakishly imposed.' "[55] Indeed, it was this very language that appears to have led the Supreme Court in *Gregg v. Georgia* to believe that the Georgia court used a frequency approach.[56] Moreover, in one death-sentence case involving four victims that was affirmed by the Georgia court, the opinion stated that "no case" appealed to the court since 1970 involving three or more victims had resulted in a life sentence—by implication a death-sentencing frequency of 1.0.[57] The third item of evidence suggesting a frequency approach is the fairly substantial number of cases included in the appendixes of the court's opinions. Most state courts using a strict precedent-seeking approach cite to only a small handful of death-sentence cases.[58]

There is also, however, considerable evidence in the opinions of the Georgia court indicating that it is not primarily interested in the relative frequency of death sentences in given classes of death-eligible cases and that its primary concern is with the absolute number of death sentences imposed in various case categories. First, the court has never quantified the death-sentencing rate among a group of similar cases, except as indicated above to state occasionally that the evidence suggests that juries "regularly" impose death sentences in cases like the one under review. Second, most opinions appear consciously to avoid language that implies the relevance of the relative frequency of death sentences. The opinions alluding to the issue state that the death sentences referred to in the appendix are evidence of the "willingness of juries" to impose death sentences in similar cases or that juries find death the "appropriate" sentence in similar cases.[59] The implication of these statements is that the key concern is with the identification of some minimum absolute number of death cases in similar cases, no matter how infrequently as a relative matter death sentences may have been imposed among them. Indeed, the court's opinions frequently highlight the absolute number of death sentences that have been imposed in similar cases.[60] The most striking evidence on this point is the court's treatment of domestic slayings. The opinions admit that life sentences are "frequent" in such cases, but the court regularly sustains the death penalty by specifically stating that six or seven other domestic killings, as the case may be, have resulted in a death sentence.[61]

The third item of evidence arguing against a frequency approach is the infrequency with which the court cites life-sentence cases in the appendixes to its opinions. Both our reanalysis of sixty-eight Georgia cases and the research of Bowers and Bentele found an inflated proportion of death-sentence cases in these appendixes.[62] Each of these studies proceeded on the assumption that the cases in the appendixes represented the entire pool of cases found by the court to be similar to the case under review. This assumption was based on the statutory requirement that the court "shall include in its decision a reference to those similar cases which it took into consideration" in its proportionality review.[63] Although the court's opinions were unclear on this point at the outset, it is now plain that the Georgia court does not purport to include in its appendixes all cases that it considers similar to the case under review. Thus, even though the court considers many life-sentence cases, it generally lists in the appendixes only the death-sentence cases and at most a handful of life cases. The strongest evidence of the court's policy of disproportionately reporting death-sentence cases is found in its proportionality reviews of death-sentence cases, which it analyzes in such broad categories as "domestic" or "armed robbery–murder"[64] that clearly include many life-sentence cases. The best example is the "domestic" killings category. As noted above, the court routinely acknowledges that such cases "frequently" result in sentences less than death; but generally no reference is made to any life-sentence domestic cases in the court's appendixes.[65] The only possible explanation is that the court is reporting in its appendixes only a fraction of the similar cases in its data file.

The reported opinions of the Georgia court are consistent with at least two possible approaches to proportionality review. The first is a modified frequency approach in which the court is concerned with the relative frequency of death sentencing but is simply failing to report the data from which one could calculate the death-sentencing frequency in a group of similar cases. The approach might be referred to as an undocumented frequency approach.

The court's reported opinions are also consistent with another and, we believe, more plausible explanation—the court is principally concerned with whether death sentences in a given class of cases are imposed with sufficient frequency in an absolute sense to sustain an appearance of regularity and reasonableness. This hypothesis implies that the court has little or no independent concern about the relative frequency with which death sentences are imposed in the classes of cases it has identified as similar to the death-sentence case under review. This policy would constitute an expanded and somewhat more systematic application of the precedent-seeking approach that we described above. It would explain the court's concern with the absolute numbers of death sentences imposed; the court's concern that death sentences were imposed in a large number of cases (which is reflected in the often lengthy appendix lists); and the court's concern that the death sentences are imposed "throughout" the state. This approach would also explain why the quite broad classifications of cases used for identifying similar cases produce no particular analytic problem for the court. No matter how large the pool of similar cases, the only relevant consideration is that the classification produces a reasonably large group of death-sentence cases. Indeed, for this purpose, the broader the classification used, the more likely the list of death cases identified will include death-sentence cases imposed "throughout" the state.

If either of these explanations correctly depicts how one or more of the Georgia justices approach the task of proportionality review, it would go a long way toward explaining why the court's system of oversight has fallen so far short of the process contemplated by the Supreme Court in *Gregg*.

The Penalty-Trial Hypothesis

Another policy that would contribute to the distinct underrepresentation of life-sentence cases in the Georgia court's proportionality analyses is what we call the penalty-trial hypothesis. The suggestion is that the Georgia Supreme Court may consider as potentially similar only those cases in which a penalty trial occurred.[66] The earlier opinions of the Georgia court suggested that it would consider all life- and death-sentence murder-conviction cases brought to it on appeal. A more recent opinion has flatly stated that in its proportionality reviews the court did consider cases in which "the death penalty could have been sought by the prosecutor but was not."[67] Nevertheless, the tendency of some opinions to distinguish life-sentence cases from the death case under review on the ground that the prosecutor waived the death penalty in the life-sentence case suggests that such cases are not viewed in the same way as life-sentence penalty-trial cases.[68] The same implication flows from the very frequent references in the court's opinions to what juries do or believe to be appropriate.[69] Therefore, the court's policy on the penalty-trial issue is not entirely free of doubt.

The constitutional implications of a penalty-trial requirement deserve emphasis. As previously mentioned, the United States Supreme Court sustained the constitutionality of the Georgia capital-sentencing statute in *Gregg* because a majority of the Court believed that Georgia's post-*Furman* statutory reforms could prevent arbitrary and capricious death sentences. The Court specifically identified Georgia's system of comparative-sentence review as an important safeguard against excessive or discriminatory death sentences. The Court reached this conclusion on the basis of an apparent assumption that, as Georgia law seemed to require, a penalty trial would occur in every case in which the defendant was convicted of capital murder.[70]

In fact, however, not every case in which the jury convicts the defendant of capital murder results in a penalty trial. Penalty trials occur in just over 40 percent of death-eligible cases. In this respect alone, a penalty-trial requirement excludes from the universe of potentially similar cases a substantial number of capital convictions, all of which resulted in life sentences.[71] Moreover, even if the Supreme Court were aware of the frequency with which penalty trials were waived after the guilt trial, the Georgia proportionality-review statute appears to contemplate that the Georgia court will consider "all capital felony cases in which sentence was imposed," regardless of how the conviction was obtained (i.e., by plea or at trial) and regardless of whether the prosecutor sought a death sentence.

There is a further distortion that results from a penalty-trial-only policy. Defendants who receive life sentences following penalty trials are less likely to appeal than defendants who received life sentences without undergoing penalty trials (.62 versus .71).[72] This statistic is important because the Georgia Supreme Court also limits the universe of potentially similar cases to those in which the defendant appealed.[73] Thus, the penalty-trial requirement and the appealed-case requirement operate together to exclude from the universe of potentially similar cases 84 percent of the capital convictions in which the defendant received a life sentence. As a consequence, the efficacy of comparative-sentence review in Georgia—an important factor in the *Gregg* decision—is substantially diminished.

In order to test the effects of the penalty-trial requirement, we compared death-sentencing frequencies among groups of post-*Furman* cases selected as similar by an index method, first including all life-sentence cases in the universe of potentially similar cases and then including only life-sentence cases that involved a penalty trial.[74] Table 45 depicts the results of this analysis. Column D of Table 45 indicates the disparity in death-sentencing rates among the two groups of cases. It suggests that, except in the most aggravated cases, the penalty-trial requirement increases the proportion of death-sentence cases within these groupings of similar cases by an average of more than 20 percentage points. An additional analysis, not reported here, that used the salient-features method for identifying similar cases showed the same degree of disparity in death-sentencing rates.

These results suggest that the Georgia Supreme Court's apparent policy of restricting the universe of potentially similar cases to those in which a penalty trial occurred removes from the court's scrutiny the disposition of a substantial proportion of the death-eligible cases. A further result of this policy is to render all the consequences of prosecutorial discretion totally immune to judicial oversight.

Table 45. Average Death-Sentencing Frequencies among Groups of Appealed Cases when All Life-Sentence Cases Are Included and when Only Penalty-Trial Life-Sentence Cases Are Included in the Analysis, Controlling for the Predicted Likelihood of Receiving a Death Sentence

A	B	C	D	E
Predicted Likelihood of Receiving a Death Sentence, from 3 (low) to 8 (high)[1]	All Appealed Cases	Only Appealed Cases with Penalty Trial	Disparity (Col. C − Col. B)	Ratio (Col. C/Col. B)
3	.07 (7/101)	.32 (7/22)	.25[a]	4.6
4	.21 (11/52)	.37 (11/30)	.16	1.8
5	.39 (16/41)	.84 (16/19)	.45[a]	2.2
6	.81 (26/32)	.93 (26/28)	.12	1.2
7	.67 (10/15)	.91 (10/11)	.24	1.4
8	.96 (26/27)	.96 (26/27)	.0	1.0
Average[2]	.52	.72	.20	1.4

1. *See supra* chap. 5, note 22, for a description of the index underlying this scale. Levels 1 and 2 are omitted from this scale because no death sentences were imposed among cases at those levels.
2. Calculated by dividing the sum of the proportions in each column by 6 (levels 3 through 8).
a. Statistically significant beyond the .05 level.

THE DE FACTO REVIEW HYPOTHESIS

Although the Georgia Supreme Court has never vacated a death sentence in a murder case because of the infrequency of death sentences in similar cases generally, there is a possibility, as George Dix has hypothesized, that the court in effect conducts a de facto comparative-sentence review by reversing, ostensibly on procedural grounds, death sentences it regards as excessive. The Georgia Supreme Court vacates approximately 20 percent of the death sentences it reviews, either by reversing the underlying murder conviction or by vacating the death sentence itself for some procedural error. To the extent that these decisions actually reflect judgments about excessiveness or disproportionality, the court's record of never formally vacating a death sentence on excessiveness grounds is misleading. If this thesis is correct, formal comparative-sentence reviews may occur only in cases the court believes are not excessive or disproportionate.

If this hypothesis is correct, one would expect to see higher rates of reversal on procedural grounds among the less aggravated death-sentence cases.[75] Table 46, which depicts the reversal for death-sentence cases at different levels of

Table 46. Rates at Which Death Sentences Are Vacated on Appeal on Procedural Grounds, Controlling for the Predicted Likelihood of a Death Sentence

A. Predicted Likelihood of a Death Sentence, from 3 (low) to 8 (high)[1]	B. Reversal Rates
3	.43 (3/7)
4	.36(4/11)
5	.25(4/16)
6	.12(3/26)
7	.20(2/10)
8	.23(6/26)

1. *See supra* chap. 5, note 22, for a description of the index underlying this scale. Levels 1 and 2 are omitted from this scale because no death sentences were imposed among cases at those levels.

aggravation, indicates that among the most aggravated cases the reversal rate is approximately one-half that observed among the least aggravated cases.[76] Another possible explanation for this pattern, however, is that procedural errors in the more aggravated cases are less likely to result in a finding of harmless error.[77]

Table 47 depicts the extent to which the procedural reversals of death sentences have reduced the level of excessiveness in the system, as estimated with an index measure. Columns B and C indicate the number and proportion of death-sentence cases before and after appellate review at each aggravation

Table 47. Death-Sentencing Rates among Groups of Similar Cases before and after Appellate Review

A	B	C	D
Predicted Likelihood of Receiving a Death Sentence, from 3 (low) to 8 (high)[1]	Before Review	After Review	Reduction in the Number of Death Cases after Appellate Review (Col. B − Col. C)
3	.07 (9/136)	.03 (4/131)	5
4	.14 (12/87)	.09 (7/82)	5
5	.33 (17/51)	.26 (12/46)	5
6	.74 (26/35)	.72 (23/32)	3
7	.67 (10/15)	.62 (8/13)	2
8	.96 (26/27)	.95 (20/21)	6

1. *See supra* chap. 5, note 22, for a description of the index underlying this scale. Levels 1 and 2 are omitted from this scale because no death sentences were imposed among cases at those levels.

level. Of particular interest are the death-sentence cases included in levels three to five, for which the death-sentencing frequency is less than .35. Column B indicates that there were originally thirty-eight death-sentence cases in this potentially excessive category. Column D indicates, however, that the Georgia Supreme Court reversed fifteen of these cases on procedural grounds, reducing the size of the group by 39 percent.

Thus, our data provide some support for the hypothesis that the Georgia court conducts de facto comparative-sentence reviews by vacating excessive death sentences on procedural grounds. Certainly, these procedural reversals have eliminated a substantial number of the death sentences that our measures suggest may be comparatively excessive. On the other hand, it also seems clear that the Georgia Supreme Court's appellate-review processes result in the affirmation of even a more substantial number of cases that also appear to be excessive. In other words, even if the de facto review hypothesis is correct, the Georgia court is still overlooking many cases in which the death sentence warrants reversal for excessiveness.

Finally, a word about the impact of post-conviction judicial proceedings beyond the defendant's direct appeal to the Georgia Supreme Court. Before their execution, most condemned defendants exhaust their right to challenge their death sentences in state post-conviction proceedings and then in federal habeas corpus proceedings. Moreover, many of these challenges are successful. Indeed, in our sample of one hundred death sentences imposed between 1973 and 1978, by the summer of 1986, 69 percent of the death sentences had been permanently vacated in such proceedings, with no further risk of reimposition, and 31 percent had been sustained (in the first instance or upon reinstitution) against all challenges.[78] In terms of the culpability levels of the death sentences left standing, 65 percent fall into the most aggravated category (death-sentencing rate $\geq .80$), 35 percent fall in the midrange (rates from .10 to .79), and none is among the least aggravated cases (rates $< .10$). Also, by the summer of 1986, six of the death-sentenced defendants in our sample had been executed.[79]

THE IMPACT OF APPELLATE REVIEW ON THE INFLUENCE OF RACE AND SUSPECT FACTORS

Georgia's post-*Furman* procedures require the state supreme court to review every death case and to determine whether it was imposed by reason of "passion" or "prejudice."[80] However, the court has never vacated a death sentence on the grounds of racial discrimination.[81] This is understandable, given the difficulty of inferring whether racial factors determined or influenced a given death sentence. Moreover, so far as we know, the court has made no effort to identify the magnitude or possible sources of race-of-victim or race-of-defendant effects in its capital-sentencing system.[82] As a consequence, because the Georgia court has never vacated death sentences either as racially discriminatory or as comparatively excessive, we find the court affirming many presumptively excessive death sentences in the midaggravation range of culpability, where the race effects are concentrated.

On the other hand, for procedural reasons the Georgia court has reversed more than 20 percent of the death sentences that it has reviewed. These reversals have reduced the magnitude of the race-of-victim effect observed in the system. This was particularly true when we recomputed the statistical impact of racial factors, classifying all cases reversed on appeal as life-sentence cases. This adjustment reduced the estimated overall race-of-victim dispute in a logistic multiple-regression analysis by about 30 percent.[83]

Treating cases reversed on appeal as life-sentence cases, however, might seem questionable. In most of these cases the Georgia Supreme Court remands the defendant for a new trial or resentencing. At least in theory, therefore, these defendants still remain at risk.[84] However, approximately two-thirds of the death sentences reversed by the Georgia court do not, in fact, result in subsequent death sentences.[85] We estimate, therefore, that the actual impact of the Georgia court's appellate review is to reduce the race-of-victim effects by approximately 25 percent.

As noted above, as of the summer of 1986 only 31 percent of the original sample of death-sentenced cases remained in place (or had been successfully reimposed). Of those cases, 65 percent involved black defendants, as compared to 53 percent of the defendants in the original sample of death cases. Also, 85 percent of the remaining death cases involved white victims, as compared with 86 percent in the original sample. Of the seven defendants executed as of the spring of 1987, six were blacks whose victims were white, while one was a white with a white victim.

SUMMARY AND CONCLUSION

In *Gregg v. Georgia,* the United States Supreme Court emphasized the importance of Georgia's post-*Furman* system of comparative-sentence review as a safeguard against excessive death sentences. The Court reemphasized the constitutional importance of the proportionality-review process most recently in *Zant v. Stephens.*[86] Some have argued, however, that an effective comparative-sentence review is extremely difficult, if not impossible, and beyond the capability of state appellate courts. One purpose of our study was to test this hypothesis by examining the Georgia Supreme Court's actual performance of this function, with a special focus on sixty-eight death-sentence cases that the court reviewed and affirmed between 1973 and 1979.

The Georgia Supreme Court has never formally vacated a death sentence as "excessive or disproportionate" because of the infrequency of death sentences among similar cases generally. Moreover, in the lists of "similar" cases appended to its opinions, the court almost exclusively chooses cases that resulted in death sentences.

Based on our measures, about one-fourth of the sixty-eight death-sentence cases that were the subject of our reanalysis and were affirmed by the Georgia court on appeal were presumptively excessive. To be sure, we did find some evidence to support the hypothesis that the Georgia Supreme Court vacates sentences or orders new trials on procedural grounds at a higher rate in cases involving arguably excessive death sentences. Moreover, these decisions eliminated a significant portion of the death sentences that we classified as presumptively excessive. But this form of de facto comparative-sentence review did not serve to correct the majority of the cases in which, according to our analyses, relief was probably warranted.

There are several possible explanations for the court's apparent bias in favor of finding that death sentences are not excessive or disproportionate. The available evidence suggests that the most plausible explanation is that the court is principally concerned with whether death sentences are imposed with sufficient frequency in an absolute sense to sustain an appearance of regularity and reasonableness, and that the court has little or no independent concern about the relative frequency with which death sentences are imposed among the similar cases it has identified as relevant. This policy appears to constitute an expanded and somewhat more systematic application of the strict precedent-seeking approach.

We can understand why an appellate court, frustrated by the apparent complexity of a truly effective comparative-sentence-review process, might opt for some form of a precedent-seeking approach. It is comfortably similar to the methodology of conventional legal research and avoids difficult questions regarding the appropriate criteria for selecting similar cases or the degree of infrequency of death sentences among similar cases that will warrant a finding of excessiveness.

Another possible explanation for the disproportionate use of death-sentence cases in the court's proportionality-review analyses is that it has adopted certain rules or conventions that bias its perceptions of the system. To test this hypothesis, we analyzed the impact of several policies that the court sometimes appeared to employ when prescribing the universe of similar cases it would consider in its reviews. We found that the court's practice of including pre-*Furman* cases in the universe of potentially similar cases tended to overstate the proportion of death-sentence cases in that universe, but that the magnitude of the impact was not great. Similarly, we found that the effects of limiting the universe of potentially similar cases to appealed cases and of classifying death-sentence cases vacated on procedural grounds as death-sentence cases for comparative purposes were much the same—they tended to encourage overreliance on death-sentence cases, but the extent of the impact was not substantial. Certainly, by themselves, these practices do not explain the marked variations between the Georgia Supreme Court's sentencing-review decisions and the results of our analyses.

We also considered the possibility that in its proportionality analyses the Georgia court only considers cases in which a penalty trial occurred. Such a policy would exclude from the universe of potentially similar cases nearly two-thirds of all the life-sentence cases appealed to the court. A further result of this policy would be that all of the consequences of prosecutorial discretion are totally immune to judicial oversight. Our tests indicate, moreover, that such a policy would explain a substantial portion of the disparity between the cases listed as "similar" in the court's appendixes and those identified as "similar" by our alternate methods. The court's opinions suggest that most of the justices probably consider in their reviews life-sentence cases in which the prosecutor waived a penalty trial after obtaining a conviction at trial. However, because the court does not report all of the cases that it considers similar to the death-sentence cases it reviews, it is not possible to determine the exact weight the court places on cases in which the prosecutor waived the death penalty.[87]

We also found that the Georgia court does not systematically monitor its cases for evidence of racial discrimination, and it has never vacated a death sentence for this reason. Nevertheless, since the court does vacate a substantial number of death sentences because of procedural error, it may indirectly reduce by as much as 25 percent the impact of race-of-victim discrimination in the system.

Whatever the actual explanation for the Georgia court's performance, it is apparent that its proportionality-review processes have not functioned in the manner contemplated by the United States Supreme Court in *Gregg v. Georgia*. Indeed, the Georgia court's performance is much more like Justice Rehnquist's description in *Woodson v. North Carolina*, that is, it is capable at best of identifying only the "occasional death sentence which in the view of the reviewing court does not conform to the standards established by the legislature."[88] Whether an effective system of proportionality review is impossible, however, is another question. For reasons that we discuss in chapter 9, we do not believe that the impossibility hypothesis has yet been proven.

NOTES

1. 428 U.S. 153, 206 (1976).

2. *See infra* chap. 10, note 7 and accompanying text, for further discussion of this case.

3. *Supra* chap. 1, note 6 and accompanying text. The first impossibility hypothesis relates to the capacity of statutory aggravating circumstances to guide effectively the exercise of discretion by sentencing juries.

4. Dix, *Appellate Review of the Decision to Impose Death*, 68 GEO. L.J. 97, 160–61 (1979) (hereinafter Dix).

5. We omitted one of the first sixty-nine cases from the analysis through oversight.

6. *See* Bentele, *The Death Penalty in Georgia: Still Arbitrary*, 62 WASH. U.L.Q. 573, 577 (1985) (hereinafter Bentele); W. Bowers, LEGAL HOMICIDE 359–63 (1984) (hereinafter Bowers); Dix, *supra* note 4, at 110–23; and Liebman, *Appellate Review of Death Sentences: A Critique of Proportionality Review*, 18 U.C.DAVIS L. REV. 1433, 1442–58 (1985) (hereinafter Liebman) for descriptions and extensive critiques of the Georgia proportionality-review process.

7. *See* GA. CODE ANN. §27-2537(c)(3) (Harrison 1983).

8. *See infra* chap. 9, note 1.

9. GA. CODE ANN. §27-2537(a). It provides as follows:

(a) Whenever the death penalty is imposed, and upon the judgment becoming final in the trial court, the sentence shall be reviewed on the record by the Supreme Court of Georgia.

(b) The Supreme Court of Georgia shall consider the punishment as well as any errors enumerated by way of appeal.

(c) With regard to the sentence, the court shall determine:
   (1) Whether the sentence of death was imposed under the influence of passion, prejudice, or any other arbitrary factor, and
   (2) Whether, in cases other than treason or aircraft hijacking, the evidence supports the jury's or judge's finding of a statutory aggravating circumstance as enumerated in section 27-2534.1 (b), and
   (3) Whether the sentence of death is excessive or disproportionate to the penalty imposed in similar cases, considering both the crime and the defendant. . . .

(f) There shall be an Assistant to the Supreme Court, who shall be an attorney appointed by the Chief Justice of Georgia and who shall serve at the pleasure of the court. The court shall accumulate the records of all capital felony cases in which sentence was imposed after January 1, 1970, or such earlier date as the court may deem appropriate. The Assistant shall provide the court with whatever extracted information it desires with respect thereto, including but not limited to a synopsis or brief of the facts in the record concerning the crime and the defendant.

(g) The court shall be authorized to employ an appropriate staff and such methods to compile such data as are deemed by the Chief Justice to be appropriate and relevant to the statutory questions concerning the validity of the sentence.

10. *See* GA. CODE ANN. §27-2537(f),(g).

11. *See* Deposition of Dennis York, Esq., former Assistant for Proportionality Review, Nov. 13, 1978, in House v. Balkcom, No. C78-1417A, at 13, 34–35 (N.D. Ga. filed Nov. 15, 1978) (hereinafter York Deposition (1978)).

12. *Id.* at 34–36, 47–49. Because all Georgia defendants found guilty of common-law murder are death-eligible (if an aggravating circumstance is present in the case), this universe eliminates any concern with respect to cases that do not result in a death sentence about whether the *mens rea* (mental state) and conduct requirements for capital murder have been satisfied. *See infra* chap. 2, note 4. The only factual issue in such cases is whether the evidence would have been sufficient to support a finding that an aggravating circumstance was present in the case if the case had been prosecuted as a capital case.

13. This policy excludes negotiated-murder-plea cases and murder convictions from which no appeal was taken. The Georgia Supreme Court has defended the policy of considering only appealed cases on the ground that they "represent a sufficient cross section of similar cases upon which an adequate comparative review can be made." Ross v. State, 233 Ga. 361, 366, 211 S.E.2d 356, 359 (1974), *cert. denied,* 428 U.S. 910 (1976). The United States Supreme Court approved of this policy in Gregg v. Georgia, 428 U.S. at 204n.56 (1976) ("The Georgia court has the authority to consider [unappealed] cases").

14. In our sample of 112 death sentences, four cases involved no appeal in part because the trial court vacated the jury's death sentence.

15. So far as we know, the Georgia Supreme Court has never addressed the propriety of this practice in any reported opinion.

16. *See* York Deposition (1978), *supra* note 11, at 39. Neither the deposition nor the court's opinions indicate the role of court as a body in resolving comparative-sentence-review issues.

17. The principal variation observed is the procedure for selecting the facts of the death-sentence case under review used to identify similar cases.

18. *See* York Deposition (1978), *supra* note 11, at 50–54.

19. *See* Deposition of Dennis York, Esq., former Assistant for Proportionality Review, May 14, 1979, in McCorquodale v. Balkcom, No. C79-95A, at 26–27, 34–35 (N.D. Ga. filed May 17, 1979) (hereinafter York Deposition (1979)).

20. *See, e.g.,* Gates v. State, 244 Ga. 587, 600, 261 S.E.2d 349, 358 (1979), *cert. denied,* 445 U.S. 938 (1980).

21. *See, e.g.,* Douthit v. State, 239 Ga. 81, 90, 235 S.E.2d 493, 499 (1977), *cert. denied,* 445 U.S. 938 (1980).

22. *See, e.g.,* Hill v. State, 237 Ga. 794, 802–3, 229 S.E.2d 737, 743 (1976).

23. *See, e.g.,* Brooks v. State, 244 Ga. 574, 585, 261 S.E.2d 379, 387 (1979), *vacated,* 446 U.S. 961 (1980).

24. *See, e.g.,* Dick v. State, 246 Ga. 697, 708, 273 S.E.2d 124, 135 (1980), *cert. denied,* 451 U.S. 976 (1981).

25. *See, e.g.,* Stevens v. State, 247 Ga. 698, 709, 278 S.E.2d 398, 408 (1981), *cert. denied,* 463 U.S. 1213 (1983).

26. *See, e.g.,* Cervi v. State, 248 Ga. 325, 334, 282 S.E.2d 629, 637 (1981), *cert. denied,* 456 U.S. 938 (1982).

27. *See, e.g.,* Krier v. State, 249 Ga. 80, 90, 287 S.E.2d 531, 538 (1982), *cert. denied,* 457 U.S. 1140 (1982).

28. *See, e.g.,* Buttrum v. State, 249 Ga. 652, 657, 293 S.E.2d 334, 340 (1982), *cert. denied,* 459 U.S. 1156 (1983).

29. *See, e.g.,* Wilson v. Zant, 249 Ga. 373, 388, 290 S.E.2d 442, 454 (1982), *cert. denied,* 459 U.S. 1092 (1982).

30. *See, e.g.,* Putnam v. State, 251 Ga. 605, 614, 308 S.E.2d 145, 153 (1983), *cert.*

denied, 466 U.S. 954 (1984); Wilson v. State 250 Ga. 630, 639, 300 S.E.2d 640, 648 (1983), *cert. denied*, 464 U.S. 865 (1983); Burden v. State, 250 Ga. 313, 316, 297 S.E.2d 242, 245 (1982), *cert. denied*, 460 U.S. 1103 (1983); Rivers v. State, 250 Ga. 288, 302, 298 S.E.2d 10, 21 (1982).

31. *See, e.g.*, Williams v. State, 250 Ga. 553, 565, 300 S.E.2d 301, 310(1983), *cert. denied*, 462 U.S. 1124 (1983).

32. *See, e.g.*, Castell v. State, 250 Ga. 776, 795, 301 S.E.2d 234, 250 (1983).

33. *See* Hawes v. State, 240 Ga. 327, 341, 240 S.E.2d 833, 842 (1977) (Hill, J., concurring). One explanation for the infrequent reference to mitigating circumstances may be the policy of the assistant for proportionality review during the period of this study not to include all mitigating circumstances in his case summaries. *See also* York Deposition (1978), *supra* note 11, at 43.

34. *See, e.g.*, Tucker v. State, 244 Ga. 721, 732–33, 261 S.E.2d 635, 643 (1979), *cert. denied*, 445 U.S. 972 (1980); Bowen v. State, 241 Ga. 492, 495–96, 246 S.E.2d 322, 325 (1978). *Tucker* suggests that a mitigating circumstance in a death sentence will not distinguish it from other "similar" death-sentence cases if juries have given a death sentence in any other cases in which that same mitigating feature was also present. *See* Liebman, *supra* note 6, at 1455–58 for an extended discussion of the Georgia court's treatment of arguments based on mitigating circumstances.

35. Patrick v. State, 245 Ga. 417, 426, 265 S.E.2d 553, 559 (1980), *vacated*, 449 U.S. 988 (1980).

36. Stevens v. State, 245 Ga. 583, 586, 266 S.E.2d 194, 197 (1980), *cert. denied*, 449 U.S. 891 (1980).

37. *Id.* at 586, 266 S.E.2d at 197.

Case 074: The defendant bound and killed two victims in their home while committing robbery. He was later characterized as depraved of mind after laughing about the murders.

Case 576: With premeditation, the defendant bound, strangled, tortured, and robbed two elderly victims, both of whom died.

Case 551: The defendant sexually tortured, mutilated, and killed a woman he forcefully brought home from a bar. Motive: "To teach that 'nigger-lover' a lesson."

Case 571: While on a crime spree, the defendant beat, robbed, and killed three elderly victims in their homes.

Case 553: The defendant sodomized and strangled two 7-year-old boys, killing both.

Case 362: Characterized as having a mental disorder, the defendant forced entry and robbed his victim's home. He terrorized the family and shot the victim, who died the following day. Premeditation may or may not have been involved.

Case 577: The mentally unbalanced defendant killed a stranger who reminded him of his stepmother.

Case 420: The young defendant, characterized as a sexual deviant, raped and murdered his victim without premeditation.

Case 494: The defendant, a disgruntled bank customer, beat, shot, and killed a bank vice-president in his home. Later, the defendant sought to extort money from the bank with a hostage claim.

Case 578: The mentally retarded defendant killed his former wife after beating her and carving initials in her body.

Case 581: Seeking revenge, the sexually frustrated defendant threw his girlfriend's 2-year-old child off a bridge.

Case 627: The defendant and his coperpetrator robbed, bound, gagged, beat, and shot the victim five times before burying him alive to prevent their identification. Defense claimed insanity and the use of drugs; neither claim was substantiated by experts. Prosecution claimed the defendant confessed.

Case 628: Defendant was a 20-year-old equipment operator, with two coperpetrators. Victim was a male insurance salesman. Defendant and coperpetrator 1 killed victim when he came to collect insurance premiums. Victim was robbed, taken to wooded area, tied to a tree, and forced to watch while defendant and coperpetrator 1 dug a shallow grave. Victim was pleading for his life. Victim was put into grave and shot five times (once in head). None of these shots killed victim, so coperpetrator 1 hit victim with a shovel. Victim was buried while still trying to speak.

Case 307: Defendant, 18-year-old male, forced victim (a stranger picked at random at a shopping center) to a wooded area and shot her three times in the head with a .45 caliber revolver.

See Baldus, Pulaski, & Woodworth, *Comparative Review of the Death Sentence: An Empirical Study of the Georgia Experience,* 75 J. CRIM. L. & CRIMINOLOGY 661, 733–52 (1983) (hereinafter Baldus, Pulaski, & Woodworth (83)) (Appendix A), for a similar listing of review and appendix cases from thirteen additional death-sentence cases affirmed by the Georgia Supreme Court.

38. *See* cases 074, 576, 551, 571, 553, 627, and 628, *supra* note 37.

39. *See* cases 362, 577, 420, 494, 578, and 581, *supra* note 37. Another example of a judge's intuitively applying an overall culpability approach is State v. Mercer, 618 S.W.2d 1, 20-22 (Mo. 1981) (Seiler, J., dissenting), *cert. denied,* 454 U.S. 933 (1981).

40. *See* Dix, *supra* note 4, at 111–17; Liebman, *supra* note 6, at 1442–58.

41. The Georgia court's inadequacies in this regard are widely shared with other state supreme courts, *see infra* chap. 9, note 40 and accompanying text.

42. Ward v. State, 239 Ga. 205, 208–9, 236 S.E.2d 365, 368 (1977). The decision drew an interesting dissent in which Justice Bowles argued that all similar cases, not just the defendant's prior case, should have been considered on the issue of disproportionality. The rule of the Georgia Supreme Court in *Ward* was adopted by the United States Supreme Court in Bullington v. Missouri, 451 U.S. 430, 437–41 (1981), on the ground that the double jeopardy clause prevented imposition of a death sentence upon retrial when a jury had imposed life imprisonment at the first trial.

43. Hall v. State, 241 Ga. 252, 258-60, 244 S.E.2d 833, 838–39 (1978). The Georgia court has not, however, established a per se rule to the effect that a death sentence is disproportionate in all cases in which coperpetrators receive life sentences. The question turns upon who the triggerman was, how clear it was who the triggerman was, and whether the coperpetrator who received less than a death sentence did so at a penalty trial, by way of a plea bargain, or upon the basis of other distinguishing characteristics. *See also* Dick v. State, 246 Ga. 697, 707-8, 273 S.E.2d 124, 134 (1980); Baker v. State, 243 Ga. 710, 712-13, 257 S.E.2d 192, 194 (1979), *vacated,* 446 U.S. 961 (1981).

In both *Ward* and *Hall,* the court appears to have been applying a concept of intracase proportionality resting upon a notion of fairness that goes beyond the concept underlying the prohibition against excessive and disproportionate death sentences generally. The sole reason given in each case for deviating from the more common approach is that "equal justice" requires similar treatment of offenders who engage jointly in a single crime. *See* Liebman, *supra* note 6, at 1445–50 for a thoughtful analysis of proportionality among coperpetrators.

44. The results of this investigation are reported in detail in Baldus, Pulaski, & Woodworth (83), *supra* note 37, at 703–6. (The three methods were a "salient factors"

measure that matched cases on fact-specific characteristics, an "index method" that ranked cases according to their predicted likelihood of receiving a death sentence, and a "main determinants method" that matched cases on the basis of variables that were generally influential in explaining in a regression analysis who was sentenced to death.)

45. *Id.* at 703–6.

46. *See* Bowers, *supra* note 6, at 362.

47. *Id.* at 361, 363 (footnotes omitted).

48. Bentele, *supra* note 6, at 590–92.

49. *Id.* at 592–94 (footnotes omitted). Professor Bentele also reanalyzed her sample of death-sentence cases for evidence of excessiveness. She placed these cases in three broad categories and reported the following death-sentencing rates for each: .29 (5/17) for robbery–murder, *id.* at 589; .33 (4/12) for store robbery–murder, *id.* at 590; and .50 (2/4) for peace-officer murder, *id.* She also found a lack of consistency in the disposition of three other narrower categories of murder: .33 (1/3) for murder by poison, *id.* at 585–86; .50 (1/2) for murder by fright, *id.* at 587–88; and .50 (1/2) for murder of a friend for money, *id.* at 588–89. On these comparisons, limited by sample size, she concluded that, within each category, no meaningful basis existed to distinguish between the death-sentence and the life-sentence cases.

50. *See infra* chap. 9, note 10 and accompanying text.

51. Gregg v. Georgia, 428 U.S. 153, 206 (1976) (plurality opinion).

52. *Id.* at 222 (White, J., concurring).

53. *See, e.g.,* Cargill v. State, 255 Ga. 616, 648, 340 S.E.2d 891, 918 (1986), *cert. denied,* 479 U.S. 1101 (1987); Ford v. State, 255 Ga. 81, 96, 335 S.E.2d 567, 581 (1985), *vacated,* 479 U.S. 1075 (1987); Castell v. State, 250 Ga. 776, 795, 301 S.E.2d 234, 250 (1983); Williams v. State, 250 Ga. 553, 565, 300 S.E.2d 301, 310 (1983), *cert. denied,* 462 U.S. 1124 (1983); Burden v. State, 250 Ga. 313, 316, 297 S.E.2d 242, 245 (1982), *cert. denied,* 460 U.S. 1103 (1983); Hill v. State, 250 Ga. 277, 287, 295 S.E.2d 518, 525–26 (1982), *cert. denied,* 460 U.S. 1056 (1983); Horton v. State, 249 Ga. 871, 880–81, 295 S.E.2d 281, 289–90 (1982), *cert. denied,* 459 U.S. 1188 (1983); Krier v. State, 249 Ga. 80, 90, 287 S.E.2d 531, 538 (1982), *cert. denied,* 457 U.S. 1140 (1982); Wilson v. Zant, 249 Ga. 373, 388, 290 S.E.2d 442, 454–55 (1982), *cert. denied,* 459 U.S. 1092 (1982); Gilreath v. State, 247 Ga. 814, 840–41, 279 S.E.2d 650, 673–74 (1981), *cert. denied,* 456 U.S. 984 (1982); Godfrey v. State, 248 Ga. 616, 624-25, 284 S.E.2d 422, 430 (1981), *cert. denied,* 456 U.S. 919 (1982); Tyler v. State, 247 Ga. 119, 126, 274 S.E.2d 549, 555 (1981), *cert. denied,* 454 U.S. 882 (1981); Blake v. State, 239 Ga. 292, 300–301, 236 S.E.2d 637, 644 (1977), *cert. denied,* 434 U.S. 960 (1977); Dix v. State, 238 Ga. 209, 216, 232 S.E.2d 47, 52 (1977), *cert. denied,* 445 U.S. 946 (1980); Ward v. State, 239 Ga. 205, 208–9, 236 S.E.2d 365, 368 (1977); Harris v. State, 237 Ga. 718, 732, 230 S.E.2d 1, 10–11 (1976), *cert. denied,* 431 U.S. 933 (1977); Stephens v. State, 237 Ga. 259, 262, 227 S.E.2d 261, 263–64 (1976), *cert. denied,* 429 U.S. 986 (1976).

54. *See infra* chap. 9, note 16 and accompanying text.

55. Moore v. State, 233 Ga. 861, 864, 213 S.E.2d 829, 832 (1975), *cert. denied,* 428 U.S. 910 (1976).

56. Gregg v. Georgia, 428 U.S. at 205.

57. Burden v. State, 250 Ga. 313, 316, 297 S.E.2d 242, 245 (1982), *cert. denied,* 460 U.S. 1103 (1983).

58. *See infra* chap. 9, note 16 and accompanying text.

59. *See e.g.,* Ingram v. State, 253 Ga. 622, 639, 323 S.E.2d 801, 817 (1984), *cert. denied,* 473 U.S. 911 (1985); Williams v. State, 250 Ga. 553, 565, 300 S.E.2d 301, 310

(1983), *cert. denied,* 462 U.S. 1124 (1983); Wilson v. State, 250 Ga. 630, 639, 300 S.E.2d 640, 648 (1983), *cert. denied,* 464 U.S. 865 (1983); Brown v. State, 250 Ga. 66, 76, 295 S.E.2d 727, 736 (1982); Burden v. State, 250 Ga. 313, 316, 297 S.E.2d 242, 245 (1982), *cert. denied,* 460 U.S. 1103 (1983); Buttrum v. State, 249 Ga. 652, 657, 293 S.E.2d 334, 339-40 (1982), *cert. denied,* 459 U.S. 1156 (1983); Hill v. State, 250 Ga. 277, 287, 295 S.E.2d 518, 526 (1982), *cert. denied,* 460 U.S. 1056 (1983); Rivers v. State, 250 Ga. 288, 302, 298 S.E.2d 10, 21 (1982); Rivers v. State, 250 Ga. 303, 312, 298 S.E.2d 1, 9 (1982); Smith v. State, 249 Ga. 228, 235, 290 S.E.2d 43, 48 (1982), *cert. denied,* 459 U.S. 882 (1982); Cervi v. State, 248 Ga. 325, 334, 282 S.E.2d 629, 637 (1981), *cert. denied,* 456 U.S. 938 (1982); Waters v. State, 248 Ga. 355, 370, 283 S.E.2d 238, 251 (1981), *cert. denied,* 463 U.S. 1213 (1983); Tucker v. State, 245 Ga. 68, 74, 263 S.E.2d 109, 113 (1980), *cert. denied,* 449 U.S. 891 (1980); Wilson v. State, 246 Ga. 62, 69, 268 S.E.2d 895, 901 (1980), *cert. denied,* 449 U.S. 1103 (1981).

60. *See, e.g.,* Berryhill v. State, 249 Ga. 442, 453, 291 S.E.2d 685, 695 (1982), *cert. denied,* 459 U.S. 981 (1982) ("The 19 cases in the appendix in which the death penalty was imposed support the death penalty in the instant case"); Buttrum v. State, 249 Ga. 652, 657, 293 S.E.2d 334, 340 (1982), *cert. denied,* 459 U.S. 1156 (1983) (15 cases); Mathis v. State, 249 Ga. 454, 461, 291 S.E.2d 489, 495 (1982), *cert. denied,* 463 U.S. 1214 (1983) (11 cases).

61. *See, e.g.,* Godfrey v. State, 248 Ga. 616, 624, 284 S.E.2d 422, 430 (1981), *cert. denied,* 456 U.S. 919 (1982); *see* Liebman, *supra* note 6, at 1452–53.

62. Professors Bowers's and Bentele's analyses, *supra* note 6, focused on the infrequency of life-sentence cases in the Georgia court's appendix cases and did not use indexes or measures of defendant culpability to identify alternative pools of comparable cases.

63. GA. CODE ANN. §27-2537(e) states:

> The court shall include in its decision a reference to those similar cases which it took into consideration. In addition to its authority regarding correction of errors, the court, with regard to review of death sentences, shall be authorized to:
> (1) Affirm the sentence of death; or
> (2) Set the sentence aside and remand the case for resentencing by the trial judge based on the record and argument of counsel. The records of those similar cases referred to by the Supreme Court in its decision and the extracts prepared as provided for in subsection (a) of Code Section 17-10-37 shall be provided to the resentencing judge for his consideration.

64. *See, e.g.,* Gilreath v. State, 247 Ga. 814, 841-42, 279 S.E.2d 650, 674 (1981), *cert. denied,* 456 U.S. 984 (1982) (13 cases total in appendix, 13 death cases); Godfrey v. State, 248 Ga. 616, 625, 284 S.E.2d 422, 430-31 (1981), *cert. denied,* 456 U.S. 919 (1982) (9 cases total in appendix, 9 death cases); Tyler v. State, 247 Ga. 119, 126-27, 274 S.E.2d 549, 555 (1981), *cert. denied,* 454 U.S. 882 (1981) (6 cases total, 6 death cases); Dix v. State, 238 Ga. 209, 217, 232 S.E.2d 47, 52 (1977), *cert. denied,* 445 U.S. 946 (1980) (17 cases total, 16 death cases, 1 life case).

65. *See, e.g.,* Cunningham v. State, 248 Ga. 558, 565–66, 284 S.E.2d 390, 397 (1981), *cert. denied,* 455 U.S. 1038 (1982) (22 cases total in appendix, 22 death cases).

66. The possibility that some justices may have applied such a policy is suggested by such decisions as Goodwin v. State, 236 Ga. 339, 345, 223 S.E.2d 703, 707 (1976) ("not unusual for juries in Georgia to impose the death penalty"), *cert. denied,* 431 U.S. 909 (1977); Pryor v. State, 238 Ga. 698, 708, 234 S.E.2d 918, 927 (1977) ("Diverse juries in widely separated counties . . . have imposed the death penalty"), *cert. denied,* 434 U.S.

935 (1977); Tucker v. State, 244 Ga. 721, 732, 261 S.E.2d 635, 643 (1979)("juries have given the death penalty"), *cert. denied,* 445 U.S. 972 (1980); Jarrell v. State, 234 Ga. 410, 425, 216 S.E.2d 258, 270 (1975) ("juries generally throughout the state"), *cert. denied,* 428 U.S. 910 (1976). A formal penalty-trial requirement for inclusion in the universe of potentially similar cases exists in other jurisdictions. *See, e.g.,* State v. Mercer, 618 S.W.2d 1, 20–21 (Mo. 1981) (Seiler, J., dissenting), *cert. denied,* 454 U.S. 933 (1981).

67. *See* Horton v. State, 249 Ga. 871, 880n.9, 295 S.E.2d 281, 289n.9 (1982), *cert. denied,* 459 U.S. 1188 (1983).

68. *See, e.g.,* Horton v. State, 249 Ga. 871, 880n.9, 295 S.E.2d 281, 289n.9 (1982), *cert. denied,* 459 U.S. 1188 (1983); Baker v. State, 243 Ga. 710, 712, 257 S.E.2d 192, 194 (1979), *vacated,* 446 U.S. 961 (1980); Hill v. State, 237 Ga. 794, 804, 229 S.E.2d 737, 743–74 (1976) (Ingram, J., concurring and dissenting).

69. *See, e.g.,* Allen v. State, 253 Ga. 390, 396, 321 S.E.2d 710, 716 (1984), *cert. denied,* 470 U.S. 1059 (1985); Ingram v. State, 253 Ga. 622, 639, 323 S.E.2d 801, 817 (1984), *cert. denied,* 473 U.S. 911 (1985); Roberts v. State, 252 Ga. 227, 241, 314 S.E.2d 83, 97 (1984), *cert. denied,* 469 U.S. 873 (1984); Spivey v. State, 253 Ga. 187, 207, 319 S.E.2d 420, 439 (1984), cert. denied, 469 U.S. 1132 (1985); Castell v. State, 250 Ga. 776, 795, 301 S.E.2d 234, 250 (1983); Mincey v. State, 251 Ga. 255, 274, 304 S.E.2d 882, 897 (1983), *cert. denied,* 464 U.S. 977 (1983); Putnam v. State, 251 Ga. 605, 614, 308 S.E.2d 145, 153 (1983), *cert. denied,* 466 U.S. 954 (1984); Brown v. State, 250 Ga. 66, 76, 295 S.E.2d 727, 736 (1982); Burden v. State, 250 Ga. 313, 316, 297 S.E.2d 242, 245 (1982), *cert. denied,* 460 U.S. 1103 (1983); Hill v. State, 250 Ga. 277, 287, 295 S.E.2d 518, 526 (1982), *cert. denied,* 460 U.S. 1056 (1983); Wilson v. Zant, 249 Ga. 373, 388, 290 S.E.2d 442, 454 (1982), *cert. denied,* 459 U.S. 1092 (1982); Brown v. State, 247 Ga. 298, 304, 275 S.E.2d 52, 59 (1981), *cert. denied,* 454 U.S. 882 (1981); Godfrey v. State, 248 Ga. 616, 624, 284 S.E.2d 422, 430 (1981), *cert. denied,* 456 U.S. 919 (1982); Cape v. State, 246 Ga. 520, 529, 272 S.E.2d 487, 495 (1980), *cert. denied,* 449 U.S. 1134 (1981); Dampier v. State, 245 Ga. 427, 437–38, 265 S.E.2d 565, 574–75 (1980); Tucker v. State, 244 Ga. 721, 732-33, 261 S.E.2d 635, 643 (1979), *cert. denied,* 445 U.S. 972 (1980); Pryor v. State, 238 Ga. 698, 708, 234 S.E.2d 918, 927 (1977), *cert. denied,* 434 U.S. 935 (1977).

70. The court's assumption in this regard was based upon the Georgia statute, which states that "[i]n all cases in which the death penalty may be imposed and which are tried by a jury, upon a return of a verdict of guilty by the jury, the court shall resume the trial and conduct a presentence hearing before the jury." GA. CODE ANN. §27-2503(b). In the event the defendant pleads guilty to murder, the trial court conducts the penalty trial and passes sentence. GA. CODE ANN. §27-2528. If the court's assumption were correct, a penalty-trial requirement would be redundant, since every capital conviction would result in a penalty trial. If this occurred, the universe of potentially similar cases would include all defendants convicted of capital crimes and the comparative-sentence-review process would take into consideration every sentencing decision in every capital case.

71. Since the decisions of prosecutors not to seek a death sentence and of juries not to impose a death sentence when it is sought by the prosecutor are subject to no direct review by the Georgia court, comparative-sentence review provides the sole basis for reviewing, albeit indirectly, the impact of those decisions on the evenhandedness of the state's death-sentencing system.

72. During part of the period considered in this study, defendants convicted of cap-

ital murder and sentenced to life imprisonment exposed themselves to the possibility of a death sentence if a successful appeal resulted in a new trial and reconviction. Bullington v. Missouri, 451 U.S. 430 (1981), has since eliminated this possibility on constitutional grounds. Ward v. State, 239 Ga. 205, 208–9, 236 S.E.2d 365, 368 (1977), eliminated this possibility when the first life sentence was imposed by a jury.

73. *See supra* note 12 and accompanying text.

74. We also tested the hypothesis that the pro-death-case bias that we observed in the Georgia court's system of proportionality review may be partially the result of the rules the court uses to define the population of cases it deems potentially similar in its proportionality review process. The court defines the scope of its inquiry with the following criteria:

(1) The universe consists of capital cases decided under both the pre- and post-*Furman* penalty statutes
(2) The universe is limited only to those cases in which the defendant appeals to the Georgia Supreme Court
(3) Cases in which the jury imposed a death sentence that, on appeal, the Georgia court vacated on procedural grounds are classified as death-sentence cases for comparative purposes.

The results of our investigation indicate that the effect of including pre-*Furman* cases in the analyses biased the results in the direction of finding that death sentences are not excessive or disproportionate but that the magnitude of the bias is trivial.

Our findings with respect to the policy of limiting the inquiry to only appealed cases were similar—it enhances the death-case bias but the effects on average are small. Our findings on this point, however, are conservative, since the alternative analysis used as the point of comparison with the actual results only included unappealed cases that resulted in a jury trial and did not include, as the Georgia statute also appears to suggest, capital cases in which the defendant pled guilty to capital murder and the prosecutor waived the death penalty.

On the third rule, however, we found that the treatment of death cases earlier reversed on appeal as death cases enhances the death-case bias, thus favoring a finding that the death sentences under review are not excessive or disproportionate. When one compares the results obtained under the Georgia court's practice of continuing to treat reversed cases as death cases, with the results obtained by treating such cases as life-sentence cases, the degree of bias is substantial. However, if one excludes the vacated death-sentence cases from the analysis altogether, the impact is not significant.

75. This expectation rests upon the assumption that a death sentence in a less aggravated class of cases is more likely to be comparatively excessive.

76. It should be noted, however, that between categories three, four, and five on the index-based scale there were four death sentences imposed by a jury that were changed to life sentences at the trial level, and the case was not appealed to the Georgia Supreme Court. We can only surmise that concerns about excessiveness influenced those decisions. Since the data in table 45 are limited to cases that were appealed to the Georgia Supreme Court, the impact of those trial-court decisions is not reflected in table 45.

77. In a highly aggravated case, the court would be likely to consider a procedural irregularity, such as a misleading trial-court jury instruction on aggravating and mitigating circumstances, less likely to have been a determining factor in the jury's death-sentence decision than it would if the case were only a "borderline" death case.

78. Note Table 3 indicates the manner of disposition and reimposition, when applicable, for the death sentences vacated in postconviction proceedings.

Note Table 3. Disposition of Death-Sentence Cases in the Procedural Reform Study on Direct Appeal, State Postconviction Proceedings, Federal Habeas Corpus, and on Remand as of June 1986

I. Summary	
A. Death sentence affirmed or reinstated and still standing	31% (31)
B. Death sentence vacated and not reinstated or pending[a]	69% (69)
II. Categories of Disposition ($n = 100$)	
A. Death sentence sustained in all courts	22% (22)
B. Death sentence vacated on direct appeal or in state postconviction proceeding, with the following subsequent disposition	
1. Jury reimposed death sentence 3% (3)	
2. Defendant received life sentence 24% (24)	
3. Case currently pending 8% (8)[b]	
Total	35% (35)
C. Death sentence vacated in federal habeas corpus, with the following subsequent disposition	
1. Jury reimposed death sentence 6% (6)	
2. Defendant received less than death 5% (5)[c]	
3. Case currently pending 29% (29)[d]	
Total	40% (40)
D. Case not finally adjudicated	3% (3)[e]

a. Four death sentences were vacated by the trial court.
b. This count includes four cases currently pending for longer than five years.
c. This count includes one case that resulted in a voluntary-manslaughter conviction.
d. This count includes one case currently pending for longer than five years.
e. This count includes one case in which the defendant died in prison while the case was on appeal and two cases in which the charges were dropped.

79. In overall culpability, three of the cases were among the most aggravated and three were in the midrange.

80. GA. CODE ANN. §27-2537(c)(1).

81. Moreover, the issue has been raised only infrequently; *see, e.g.*, Lewis v. State, 246 Ga. 101, 106, 268 S.E.2d 915, 920 (1980) (claim of passion and prejudice); Davis v. State, 255 Ga. 598, 612, 340 S.E.2d 869, 882 (1986), *cert. denied*, 479 U.S. 871 (1986) (claim of race-of-defendant discrimination rejected on procedural and substantive grounds); Cargill v. State, 255 Ga. 616, 647-48, 340 S.E.2d 891, 918 (1986), *cert. denied*, 479 U.S. 1101 (1987); (claim of race-of-defendant discrimination rejected because defendant was white).

82. From time to time the court refers to the frequency with which it reverses death sentences in black- and white-defendant cases; *see, e.g.*, Drake v. State, 241 Ga. 583, 588n.3, 247 S.E.2d 57, 61n.3 (1978) *cert. denied*, 440 U.S. 928 (1979) (30% [13/43] reversal rate in black-defendant cases versus a 26% [8/31] rate in white-defendant cases).

83. The average race-of-victim disparity dropped from a 4.3 odds multiplier ($b = 1.45$; $p = .01$) to a 2.9 odds multiplier ($b = 1.05$; $p = .07$). The estimated impact of appellate review is the proportionate decline in the odds multiplier.

84. For this reason we also recomputed the impact of the racial factors after removing the reversed cases from the analysis altogether. Using this approach we found that

the decisions of the Georgia Supreme Court have had no effect on the observed level of race-of-victim discrimination in the system.

85. P. Morris, *Sentence Reversals and Subsequent Disposition of Georgia Death Cases: 1973–86*, at 10 (mimeo 1986).

86. 462 U.S. 862 (1983). In McCleskey v. Kemp, 107 S.Ct. 1756, 1774 (1987), Justice Powell referred approvingly to the Georgia court's proportionality review of McCleskey's death sentence and its ruling that it was "not disproportionate to other death sentences imposed in the State." In the next paragraph, however, Justice Powell appeared to suggest that a comparatively excessive death sentence did not create a constitutional concern, a remark that will reduce even further the incentive of state appellate courts to conduct thoroughgoing proportionality reviews.

87. Another possible explanation, which we consider unlikely, might be the court's method of physically selecting similar cases. However, our experience working with the data available to the court indicates that manual systems of the type available to the court are adequate for the task, even when large numbers of cases are involved. *See infra* chap. 9, notes 34 and 63 and accompanying text.

88. Woodson v. North Carolina, 428 U.S. 280, 316 (1976) (Rehnquist, J., dissenting).

CHAPTER EIGHT

Evidence of Infrequency, Arbitrariness, and
Discrimination in Capital Sentencing
in Other States

Our findings about Georgia's pre- and post-*Furman* death-sentencing systems are part of a growing body of empirical evidence on death sentencing nationwide. The capital punishment literature spans a fifty-five-year period commencing in 1930, during which the research has grown in scope and methodological sophistication.

In this chapter we review that evidence and assess the extent to which the patterns we observed in Georgia also appear in other states. Although the available information about nationwide sentencing practices is incomplete, it suggests that the experience of some other states before and after *Furman* has resembled that of Georgia.

THE EVIDENCE OF EXCESSIVENESS

Death-Sentencing Frequencies around the Nation

One of the most striking features of Georgia's capital-sentencing system is that only a small fraction of the defendants for whom a death sentence is authorized under existing law actually receive such a sentence. Specifically, the death-sentencing rate among the death-eligible cases that resulted in a murder-trial conviction increased from .15 pre-*Furman* to .23 post-*Furman*. While our data elsewhere are less refined, they suggest a similar pattern in other death-sentencing jurisdictions. Figure 28 shows for the period 1960 through 1985 the number of defendants received by all state prisons under sentence of death. These statistics understate the actual death-sentence counts slightly because courts occasionally vacate death sentences before the defendant is transferred to a state prison, but they provide a reasonable basis for comparing the pre- and post-*Furman* periods.

The average number of death sentences during five-year periods before and after *Furman*, shown in Figure 28, is also summarized in column B of Table 48. These data reveal a substantial increase in the number of death sentences

Figure 28. Death Sentences Imposed for Murder, before and after *Furman*[1]

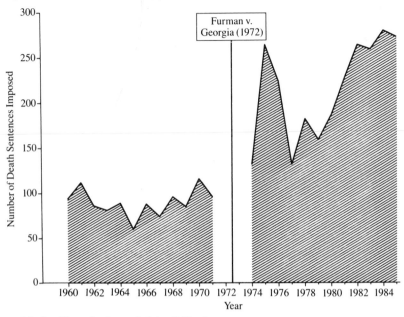

1. Calculated from the data underlying Table 48.

imposed after 1972. Indeed, there was an annual increase of almost 190 percent (269/93) between the 1960–63 and 1982–85 periods. This is not totally surprising, however, because the number of homicides committed each year more than doubled during the same twenty-year period (see column A of Table 48). As a result, the more relevant data are the death-sentencing rates shown in Figure 29 and Table 48. They present the death-sentencing rate per 1,000 reported homicides (murder and nonnegligent manslaughter) in states that authorized the death penalty before and after *Furman*; column C of Table 48, which averages those rates for four-year periods, indicates that adjustment for homicide rates does diminish the apparent increase in the level of death sentencing, but does not eliminate it. The strong surge in death-sentencing rates immediately following *Furman* no doubt reflects the impact of the mandatory-sentencing laws that operated in ten states until they were invalidated in 1976.[1] The next four-year period reported in Table 48 shows an average death-sentencing rate which is about the same as that observed for the 1960–63 period. However, the most recent data show a rate 50 percent higher than the 1960–63 period, and twice as high as the 1964–71 period. Also, because the proportion of reported homicides that involve a death-eligible murder is lower post-*Furman* than it was pre-*Furman*, the statistics in Table 48

Table 48.   Average Number of Homicides (Murder and Nonnegligent Manslaughter), Average Number of Death Sentences Imposed for Homicide, and Death-Sentencing Rates per 1,000 Homicides for Selected Periods in Jurisdictions Authorizing Capital Punishment

Years	A. Average Number of Homicides Annually[1]	B. Average Number of Death Sentences Imposed Annually[2]	C. Annual Death-Sentencing Rates per 1,000 Homicides
Before *Furman*			
1960–63	8,225	93	11.3
1964–67	8,978	78	8.7
1968–71	12,812	98	7.6
After *Furman*			
1974–77	14,792	188	12.7
1978–81	17,672	189	10.7
1982–85	17,521	269	15.4

1. The estimated homicides are reported in FBI, U.S. Dept. of Justice, CRIME IN THE UNITED STATES (1960–85). These figures have been adjusted in column A to reflect only those homicides that occurred in states with statutory authorization for the death penalty. The legal status of state death-penalty statutes is reported by year in Bureau of Justice Statistics, U.S. Dept. of Justice, CAPITAL PUNISHMENT (1980–86); Law Enforcement Assistance Administration, U.S. Dept. of Justice, CAPITAL PUNISHMENT (1972–79); Bureau of Prisons, U.S. Dept. of Justice, CAPITAL PUNISHMENT (1969–71); and Bureau of Prisons, U.S. Dept. of Justice, EXECUTIONS (1961–68). The adjustments were made as follows: (1) if a state did not have a death-penalty statute for any homicide offense or if the death-penalty statute had been formally invalidated by a state court or state legislature during any period of the year, then the homicides in that state have been omitted; (2) if a state had reenacted the death penalty following invalidation or repeal during any period of the year, the number of estimated homicides in that state have been included in the total estimate for that year.
2. The number of death sentences for murder are reported in Bureau of Justice Statistics, U.S. Dept. of Justice, CAPITAL PUNISHMENT (1980–86); Law Enforcement Assistance Administration, U.S. Dept. of Justice, CAPITAL PUNISHMENT (1972–79); Bureau of Prisons, U.S. Dept. of Justice, CAPITAL PUNISHMENT (1969–71); and Bureau of Prisons, U.S. Dept. of Justice, EXECUTIONS (1961–68). The figures given reflect the number of inmates as they are admitted to a state or federal correctional facility, rather than when the court hands down the sentence. Therefore, no prisoners held in local or county jails pending sentence or appeals (with the exception of those at the Cook County Jail in Chicago, Illinois, the parish jails in Louisiana, and the District of Columbia Jail for certain reporting years) are counted.

tend to understate somewhat the post-*Furman* death-sentencing rates.[2] As in Georgia, therefore, nationwide we see increased death-sentencing rates post-*Furman*, but rates that are still relatively low compared to the number of death-eligible cases processed each year and when considered against the Supreme Court's assumption in *Gregg*—that, in death-eligible cases, prosecutors would regularly seek and juries would regularly impose the death penalty.

Figure 29.   Death Sentences per 1,000 Homicides in Death-Penalty States, before and after *Furman*[1]

1. Calculated from data underlying Table 48.

Another striking feature of the death-sentencing patterns of both the pre- and post-*Furman* periods is their stability from year to year. From 1960 to 1971, the number of death sentences imposed annually ranged from about sixty to about one hundred-twenty. And during the twelve years (1974–85) of the post-*Furman* period reported here, the annual number has ranged from approximately one hundred-fifty to somewhat more than three hundred per year. Moreover, considering original or first death sentences imposed, only in 1986, which saw 302 such sentences, did their number exceed 300. The data for both these periods suggest a de facto flow-control mechanism that produces a surprising stability, both in the absolute number of sentences imposed and in the overall death-sentencing rates.[3]

Some have suggested that the elevated post-*Furman* death-sentencing rates were to be expected. One hypothesis is that under the new penalty-trial procedures, judges now instruct sentencing juries in the terms required by sometimes complex legislative formulations; and by casting the sentencing question in a nonemotional "language of legalism," they often lead the jury to believe it has no choice but to impose a death sentence.[4] An alternative hypothesis is that the elevated rates post-*Furman* merely reflect the increased public support for capital punishment.[5]

Some scattered evidence of jury death-sentencing rates pre- and post-*Furman* lends support to both these hypotheses. For example, between 1936 and 1961 the death-sentencing rate in New Jersey among cases ending in a murder-trial conviction was .39 (62/159).[6] In California penalty-trial cases between 1958 and 1966, the rate was .43 (102/239).[7] In Southern rape-trial-conviction cases, the death-sentencing rate was approximately .10.[8] Other studies suggest that the rate of death sentencing in pre-*Furman* murder cases resulting in a trial conviction was between .10 and .20.[9]

The available information about post-*Furman* death-sentencing rates is also incomplete, but it does suggest slightly higher jury death-sentencing rates in some (but clearly not all) jurisdictions: .55 in Georgia, .48 in California,[10] .36 in Colorado,[11] .64 in Cook County, Illinois,[12] 1.0 in Dallas,[13] .25 in Delaware,[14] .74 in Florida, .49 in Louisiana,[15] .42 in Maryland,[16] .50 in North Carolina,[17] .36 in New Jersey,[18] and .60 in Mississippi.[19]

Despite these slightly higher post-*Furman* jury death-sentencing rates, the prosecutors still dominate the nation's capital-sentencing system. And, in general, they appear to be no more willing after *Furman* than they were previously to seek death sentences in capital-murder cases. The data clearly suggest that the frequent reluctance of Georgia's prosecutors to seek death sentences is not unique. Our data from Colorado for the period 1980–84 are instructive on this point.[20] Figure 30 shows an initial pool of 179 death-eligible cases (stage 1), which resulted in four death sentences (stage 5). Stage 1 indicates that in 95 percent of these cases the state initially files a charge of capital murder. However, substantial attrition occurs through plea bargaining, which permits a majority of death-eligible offenders to escape the possibility of a death sentence by pleading guilty, frequently to a lesser included offense.

Of the 67 defendants who pleaded not guilty, 64 percent (43/67) were convicted at trial of capital murder, but penalty trials occurred in only 11 of these cases. This means that fewer than one-third of the defendants who were tried and convicted of capital murder actually underwent a penalty trial and, of these 11 defendants, only 4 received death sentences.

Although the number of death sentences imposed in Colorado is well below the national average, the degree of attrition in the number of cases retained in the system at each step of the death-sentencing process is fairly typical. The proportions of death-eligible cases that end in a guilty plea prior to trial in a sample of other jurisdictions are as follows: Georgia 48%,[21] Maryland 59%,[22] Dallas County, Texas, 86%,[23] Cook County, Illinois 70%,[24] California 49%,[25] North Carolina 67%,[26] Mississippi 35%[27], and New Jersey 77%.[28] In

Figure 30.   Disposition of Colorado's Death-Eligible Cases, 1980–84[1]

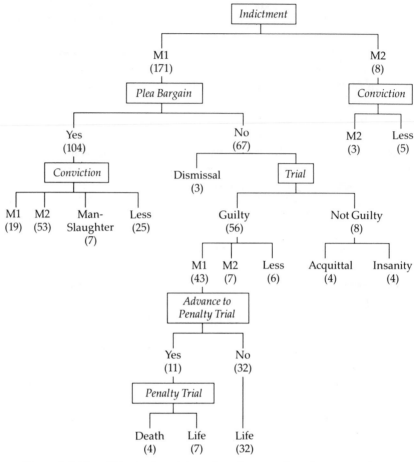

1. The symbols M1 and M2 signify capital murder and noncapital murder, respectively. "Less" indicates conviction on a lesser charge. Decision points (stages) in the process are in italic type in boxes; outcomes of decisions are shown along with the number of cases experiencing the outcomes.

addition, prosecutors in other jurisdictions besides Georgia and Colorado also frequently waive a penalty trial after the jury has convicted the defendant of capital murder. South Carolina prosecutors waive the death penalty in such cases 64% of the time. In California the rate is 50%, and in Cook County, Illinois, it is 75%.[29] Thus, even if post-*Furman* juries are slightly more punitive than their pre-*Furman* counterparts, prosecutors still substantially reduce the number of cases that ever reach sentencing juries.

To obtain a more accurate picture of recent death-sentencing patterns, we estimated the death-sentencing rate for death-eligible cases processed in each state during 1982–84. The results appear in Table 49. The most appropriate estimate of the death-sentencing rate set forth in Table 49 for a given state is a function of two factors: first, whether the scope of the state's statutory aggravating circumstances is broad or narrow;[30] and, second, whether one includes in the category of death-eligible offenders only those actually convicted of capital murder or also includes defendants whom juries could have found to be death-eligible, based on the applicable statute, but who were actually convicted of a lesser offense than capital murder.[31] The "broad" statute estimates (shown in columns D and E of Table 49) are most appropriate for states like Georgia and Colorado whose statutory factors include both the "contemporaneous felony" and "vile" killing aggravating circumstances. For these states the estimate in column D applies to death-eligible defendants convicted of either murder or voluntary manslaughter, while the estimate in column E considers only defendants convicted of capital murder. The "narrow" statute estimates in columns F and G are more relevant for states like Texas whose statutes do not specify "vile" killings as a circumstance authorizing the death penalty.

The data set forth in Table 49 indicate that, in the aggregate, the nation is processing from 2,000 to 4,000 death-eligible cases annually. From this enormous pool, the states actually impose death sentences in 250 to 300 cases, thus producing an annual death-sentencing rate of .06 to .15.

The data permit two additional observations concerning the post-*Furman* death-sentencing rates. First, the annual death-sentencing rates are quite stable within the various jurisdictions.[32] Second, there is less regional variation in death-sentencing rates than one might anticipate. We expected to observe higher rates in the South, but, as the data in Table 49 indicate, the larger numbers of death sentences imposed by Southern states are associated with larger numbers of murder prosecutions. For example, in absolute numbers, Florida, Texas, and California are the nation's leading death-penalty states. Our estimated death-sentencing rates for those states range between 4 percent and 21 percent, which is quite comparable to the rates estimated for such states as Pennsylvania and Indiana. In comparing post-*Furman* death-sentencing rates among the states, it is worth noting that the states whose statutes require death sentencing by the judge rather than by the jury tend to have the highest rates in the region (e.g., Indiana in the East North Central region, Florida in the South Atlantic region, Alabama in the East South Central region, and Arizona and Idaho in the Mountain region). The high death-sentencing rates of the judges are noteworthy, since judicial sentencing was originally conceived as a means of guarding against aberrant jury-sentencing decisions.[33]

Table 49. Estimated United States Death-Sentencing Rates among Death-Eligible Defendants, 1982–84

			Death-Sentencing Rates[1] (number of death-eligibles in parentheses)			
			Broad Death-Eligibility Statutes		Narrow Death-Eligibility Statutes	
Region/State[2]	Average Annual Number of Death Sentences Imposed, 1982–84[a]	Number of Murder and Nonnegligent Manslaughter Offenses Reported to FBI, 1983[b]	Rates among All Death-Eligible Defendants Convicted of Homicide[3]	Rates among Death-Eligible Defendants Convicted of Murder[4]	Rates among All Death-Eligible Defendants Convicted of Homicide[5]	Rates among Death-Eligible Defendants Convicted of Murder[4]
Northeast						
New Jersey (1)	3.33	399	.03 (117)	.06 (58)	.09 (36)	.13 (26)
Pennsylvania (1)	22.33	583	.13 (171)	.26 (85)	.43 (52)	.59 (38)
East North Central						
Illinois (2)	14.67	1,112	.05 (325)	.09 (163)	.15 (100)	.20 (72)
Indiana (2)	6.00	286	.07 (84)	.14 (42)	.23 (26)	.33 (18)
Ohio (2)	11.67	600	.07 (176)	.13 (88)	.22 (54)	.30 (39)
West North Central						
Missouri (1)	7.00	403	.06 (118)	.12 (59)	.19 (36)	.27 (26)
Nebraska (3)	.67	42	.06 (12)	.11 (6)	.17 (4)	.22 (3)
South Atlantic						
Delaware (1)	.67	25	.09 (7)	.17 (4)	.34 (2)	.34 (2)
Florida (1)	37.33	1,199	.11 (351)	.21 (175)	.35 (108)	.48 (77)
Georgia (1)	11.00	483	.08 (141)	.15 (71)	.26 (43)	.35 (31)

Maryland (2)	4.33	367	.04 (107)	.08 (54)	.13 (33)	.18 (24)
North Carolina (1)	11.00	490	.08 (143)	.15 (72)	.25 (44)	.34 (32)
South Carolina (1)	6.67	321	.07 (94)	.14 (47)	.23 (29)	.32 (21)
Virginia (2)	5.33	387	.05 (113)	.09 (57)	.15 (35)	.21 (25)
East South Central						
Alabama (1)	11.67	364	.11 (106)	.22 (53)	.35 (33)	.49 (24)
Kentucky (2)	4.33	364	.04 (106)	.08 (53)	.13 (33)	·18 (24)
Mississippi (1)	8.67	290	.10 (85)	.21 (42)	.33 (26)	.46 (19)
Tennessee (1)	6.67	410	.06 (120)	.11 (60)	.18 (37)	.26 (26)
West South Central						
Arkansas (2)	2.00	178	.04 (52)	.08 (26)	.13 (16)	.17 (12)
Louisiana (1)	7.67	629	.04 (184)	.08 (92)	.13 (57)	.19 (41)
Oklahoma (3)	9.67	249	.13 (73)	.27 (36)	.44 (22)	.60 (16)
Texas (2)	27.00	2,239	.04 (655)	.08 (327)	.13 (202)	.19 (145)
Mountain						
Arizona (3)	12.67	213	.20 (62)	.41 (31)	.66 (19)	.91 (14)
Colorado (1)	1.00	202	.02 (59)	.03 (30)	.06 (18)	.08 (13)
Idaho (3)	3.67	35	.37 (10)	.73 (5)	1.00 (3)	1.00 (2)
Montana (3)	.33	30	.04 (9)	.08 (4)	.11 (3)	.17 (2)
Nevada (1)	5.33	114	.16 (33)	.31 (17)	.53 (10)	.76 (7)
New Mexico (2)	1.00	124	.03 (36)	.06 (18)	.09 (11)	.13 (8)
Utah (1)	.67	56	.04 (16)	.08 (8)	.13 (5)	.17 (4)
Wyoming	.67	30	.07 (9)	.17 (4)	.22 (3)	.34 (2)
Pacific						
California (1)	33.67	2,639	.04 (772)	.09 (386)	.14 (238)	.20 (170)
Washington (2)	1.33	212	.02 (62)	.04 (31)	.07 (19)	.10 (14)
Total Estimated Death-Eligible Cases, per year[5]			4,408	2,204	1,357	977

1. See *supra* note 31 for a description of the methodology underlying these estimates. Because no death sentences were imposed in Connecticut, New Hampshire, Oregon, South Dakota, and Vermont, and only one was imposed in New York (which has very narrow statutory aggravating circumstances), these states were omitted from the tabulation.

2. The notation in parentheses for each state indicates which of the following main statutory aggravating circumstance(s) are in its law:

   (1) statute includes both vile-murder and felony-circumstance factors (broad eligibility estimates are most appropriate);

   (2) statute includes felony-circumstance factor, but not vile-murder factor (narrow eligibility estimates are most appropriate but biased upward to the extent the minor statutory aggravating circumstances such as police-officer victim, enlarge the pool of death-eligibles); and

   (3) statute includes vile-murder or torture factor but not felony-circumstance factor (narrow eligibility estimates are a rough approximation).

3. "Homicide" conviction includes murder (capital and noncapital) and voluntary manslaughter.

4. "Murder" convictions are by plea or by trial conviction.

5. These estimates do not include death-eligible cases from New York, and from Connecticut, New Hampshire, Oregon, South Dakota, and Vermont, which imposed no death sentences.

a. The Legal Defense Fund is the source of the average annual number of death sentences imposed in the years 1982, 1983, and 1984. Approximately 20–30% of the sentences were ultimately vacated on appeal to state supreme courts. Accordingly, all of the estimated death-sentencing rates would be lower if the calculations were based only on cases affirmed by the state supreme courts.

b. The number of murders and nonnegligent manslaughters reported to the FBI for 1983. FBI, DEPT. OF JUSTICE, UNIFORM CRIME REPORTS 52–63 (1984).

Other studies also report relatively low post-*Furman* death-sentencing rates. A nationwide survey for the period 1977-84 reports an average death-sentencing rate of less than 10 percent for all homicides reported to the FBI involving a contemporaneous offense.[34] From 1978 through 1984, the death-sentencing rate in Pennsylvania for murders reported to the FBI involving a contemporaneous felony was .06.[35] A similar study of Louisiana for the period 1977–82 reported a rate of .12.[36] In Dallas, Texas, the death-sentencing rate among defendants indicted for capital murder and convicted of some crime between 1977 and 1984 was .14.[37] In Cook County, Illinois, from 1977 to 1980, the death-sentencing rate for defendants convicted of capital murder was .08.[38] In Colorado the comparable rate was .06 (4/62).[39]

Indications of Excessiveness

As previously noted, a low death-sentencing rate does not by itself establish excessiveness in a death-sentencing system. It does, however, raise questions about the consistency with which the system processes death-eligible cases. To answer those questions one must be able to rank or otherwise classify by overall culpability all death-eligible cases within a given jurisdiction so that one can determine the frequency with which death sentences occur among comparable cases. Six studies have taken this approach, three pre-*Furman* and three post-*Furman*.

Pre-Furman *Studies*

Several of the pre-*Furman* studies found distinct evidence of excessiveness. One of the more fine-grained studies of comparative excessiveness in the pre-*Furman* period is a chapter in *The American Jury*, by Harry Kalven and Hans Zeisel. The sample for the entire study was 3,576 criminal jury trials conducted in 1955–56 and 1958 in all states (except the District of Columbia) and the federal district courts.[40] The research design called for the trial judge in each case to determine, before the jury returned its verdict, how he or she would have decided the case if it had been a bench trial tried before the judge without a jury.[41]

The sample in *The American Jury* included 111 cases in which the defendant was convicted of capital murder and the jury had to decide whether the defendant should be sentenced to death. Here also the authors compared the responses of the judge and jury.[42]

Rather than comparing the cases of the death-sentenced defendants with the cases of the life-sentenced defendants, the authors address the issue of even-handedness in sentencing by comparing the cases in which both jury and judge voted for a death sentence with those in which jury and judge disagreed on the appropriate sentence. The authors first present brief narrative sketches of the cases in which there was agreement on a death sentence and find that they "stand out as especially vicious." Continuing, they state that the "trouble is that some aspects of this viciousness verge so much on the clearly pathological that the criterion loses some of its usefulness."[43] The authors then examined the narrative summaries of the twenty-one cases in which the judge and jury disagreed; in nineteen of those cases they identified a factor that appeared to provide some basis for leniency by either the judge or the jury. The authors conclude, however, that while this analysis has a "plausible ring . . . , the brute fact is that each time one of the factors listed was persuasive to one of the deciders, it was unpersuasive to the other."[44] They also observe that the cases in which the judge and jury disagree on the death penalty "appear no less heinous than those in which they agree."[45] On the basis of this analysis, Kalven and Zeisel conclude:

> But even these techniques for locating a hard core of capital cases do not put to rest the concern about evenhanded justice. In the end the task is one of deciding who, among those convicted of capital crimes, is to die. Whatever the differences on which this decision hinges, they remain demeaningly trivial compared to the stakes. The discretionary use of the death penalty requires a decision which no human should be called upon to make.[46]

To a surprising degree, Kalven and Zeisel's analysis carries the implicit message of equal justice in death sentencing that informed the decision of the United States Supreme Court in *Furman v. Georgia* and inspired many of the procedural reforms of the post-*Furman* period designed to promote rationality and consistency in death sentencing.

In 1976 Franklin Zimring, Joel Eigen, and Sheila O'Malley examined in detail the disposition of 204 homicides reported to the Philadelphia police in 1970.[47] Twenty-four of these cases resulted in first-degree-murder convictions, for which death was an authorized sanction. In three of these cases, two involving armed robberies and one involving a racially motivated killing of a white graduate student by black defendants, the defendants actually received death sentences. The authors searched for distinctions between the three death-sentence cases and the other capital murders, but could "sense no pattern other than the fact that all of the capital cases were tried before a jury and the lack of death sentences for confederates who do not kill." In comparison to the 163 other cases that resulted in convictions for lesser crimes than first-degree murder, "the three selected for death seemed more blameworthy, but it is difficult to justify the enormous difference in punishment outcome by the difference in culpability. The random selection and execution of a white stranger is shocking and senseless, but how much less shocking and senseless than an epidemic of teen-gang killings?"[48]

In 1976 Hugo Adam Bedau evaluated the disposition of 128 defendants in Massachusetts between 1946 and 1970, all of whom were indicted for some form of criminal homicide. Seventeen of these defendants were convicted as well of an associated sex offense; the applicable statutes included both a discretionary death penalty for first-degree murder and a mandatory death penalty for rape-murder. As a result of prosecutorial decisions both before and at trial, none of the seventeen sex-murder defendants was sentenced to death. The study concluded that the sentences imposed frustrated the purpose of the mandatory death statute and that the administration of criminal trials under this statute failed to obtain "evenhanded justice."[49]

In 1980 we published an analysis of data gathered by the *Stanford Law Review* concerning 239 penalty trials conducted in California between 1958 and 1966, 43 percent (102/239) of which had resulted in death sentences. The purpose of the original study was to examine these 239 cases for evidence of racial and socioeconomic discrimination.[50] We reanalyzed the data for evidence of excessiveness.

More specifically, we selected four of the death-sentence cases and identified a group of factually similar cases for each, which we used for comparative purposes. We found that two of the four death sentences were probably excessive, one was plainly evenhanded, and one presented a close case. We also employed a logistic-regression analysis to construct a culpability index on the basis of thirteen variables similar to the culpability index we used for our analysis of excessiveness in Georgia, described in chapter 5. With this index, we ranked all the 239 cases included in the *Stanford Law Review* data set. We found that about half of the death sentences imposed were probably evenhanded in that similarly situated defendants regularly received death sentences. For only about 15 percent of the death-sentence cases was the death-sentencing rate in similar cases less than .50.[51] In other words, our reanalysis of these 239 California penalty-trial cases revealed a lower incidence of excessiveness than we probably would have found in pre-*Furman* Georgia using comparable methods.[52]

Post-Furman *Studies*

The first investigation of excessiveness under post-*Furman* legislation was a 1980 study by Steven Arkin. He examined 350 murder cases in which grand juries in Dade County, Florida, returned indictments for first-degree murder between 1973 and 1976.[53] Arkin's data included the race of the defendant and of the victim, the circumstances of the crime, and the disposition of the case. Twenty-three percent (81/350) of the cases resulted in a first-degree-murder conviction under circumstances that made the defendant death-eligible under Florida law. In ten of those cases (3 percent of the total) the defendant received a death sentence that was not later reduced to life imprisonment.[54] Arkin examined the extent to which the ten death sentences, all of which involved an armed robbery or an execution-type slaying, could be distinguished in a meaningful way from the forty-four of the eighty-one first-degree-murder convictions that also involved felony circumstances. Based on a systematic comparison of narrative summaries of the death- and life-sentence cases, Akrin identified eight legitimate case characteristics that at least arguably distinguished the ten death-sentence cases from most of the life-sentence cases.[55] However, six of the life-sentence cases were essentially indistinguishable from the death-sentence cases. Thus, the death-sentencing rate among this group of indistinguishable cases was .63 (10/16). On the basis of his findings, Arkin concluded that the infrequent imposition of the death penalty in Dade County "reflects *both* selectivity and arbitrariness."[56] The process was selective because the ten death-sentence cases were distinguishable from the great majority of the life-sentence cases; it was also arbitrary because those ten death sentences could not be distinguished from six life-sentenced cases.

Barry Nakell and Kenneth A. Hardy's 1987 study of North Carolina's death-sentencing system focuses on the disposition of homicide cases from June 1, 1977, to May 31, 1978, the first year of death sentencing under that state's discretionary post–*Woodson v. North Carolina* statute.[57] The study embraced all reported homicides and produced a sample of 489 cases, nine of which resulted in a death sentence. For each case, the investigators consulted a variety of official records and conducted interviews with prosecutors and defense attorneys. The result was an extensive data set, with great detail on the strength of evidence organized around the following issues:

1. the defendant's identity as the perpetrator
2. the defendant's mental state or culpability
3. evidence of self-defense
4. statutory aggravating and mitigating circumstances
5. the defendant's prior record
6. the number of victims
7. the district in which the case was processed.[58]

The authors' analysis of excessiveness and irrationality in the North Carolina system had four parts. First, they presented a flow diagram of the cases moving through the system. The picture is similar to what we observed in Colorado and Georgia, with prosecutors screening out the bulk of the cases before trial. Of the 319 cases indicted for first-degree murder, 67 percent (213/319) resulted in pleas to less serious crimes. Moreover, of the sixty cases tried on first-degree murder charges, 30 percent (18/60) resulted in a first-degree-murder conviction and, as noted above, nine of this group received a death sentence. Although the data did not report the precise proportion of defendants who were death-eligible under the state law, it is plain that only a small percentage of their cases resulted in a death sentence. Moreover, only one of the death sentences imposed survived appellate review by the North Carolina Supreme Court, and that defendant was ultimately executed.[59]

The second phase of the excessiveness analysis documented substantial geographic disparities in prosecutorial decisions both to indict for capital murder and to advance cases to a first-degree-murder trial. The authors used both cross-tabular and multiple-regression analyses to demonstrate that these disparities cannot be explained by other legitimate case characteristics, especially the strength of the evidence.[60]

The third phase of the excessiveness analysis focused on the rationality of the case characteristics that best explained which defendants moved through successive stages of the state's charging-and-sentencing system. Surprisingly, their logistic multiple-regression analyses indicate that only two of the legitimate variables in their model had a consistent statistically significant effect on case-processing decisions, the variables for the defendant's mental state or culpability and prior criminal record. In addition, both aggravating and mitigating circumstances had a perverse effect in that the aggravating-circumstances variable had a mitigating effect in explaining who was convicted of first-degree murder and sentenced to death, while the mitigating-circumstances variable had an *aggravating* effect on these decisions, although in neither case was the effect statistically significant.[61]

The fourth stage of the authors' excessiveness analysis compared the cases that resulted in death and life sentences at a penalty trial by the quality of the evidence and the number of aggravating circumstances in each case. The quality of the evidence was only slightly stronger in the death cases, and the number of aggravating circumstances present in the two groups of cases was virtually identical (2.75 for the death cases versus 2.5 for the life cases).[62]

In spite of the highly random appearance of the results produced in the first year of the North Carolina death-sentencing system, the one execution was reserved for a case in which a death sentence would not be unexpected. The defendant was a grandmother convicted of killing her boyfriend by putting ant poison in his food. She also admitted killing three other people, including her mother, in the same manner, and the prosecutor presented evidence that she had also killed her husband with ant poison. Thus, it appears that the North Carolina Supreme Court did limit executions to a very serious case, although the study does not indicate how many cases of equal overall culpability in the sample resulted in lesser sentences.[63]

Another investigation of excessiveness under a post-*Furman* sentencing scheme is a study we conducted in Colorado. It examined the disposition of 179 death-eligible cases processed in Colorado between August 7, 1979, and June

30, 1984.[64] As previously noted, from this group there were sixty-two first-degree-murder (M1) convictions and eleven penalty trials in which the following four defendants actually received death sentences:

1. A 30-year-old male defendant, with two death sentences in another state, kidnapped a female victim in her twenties. He bound, gagged, and raped the victim and then killed her by manual strangulation and suffocation. He moved the victim's nude body to a motel where it was later found. It is unclear if the victim and defendant were acquainted. (1-11)
2. The 30-year-old male defendant, with four prior felony convictions, rode his bicycle to a gas station where the 20-year-old male victim, a stranger, worked as an attendant. Defendant asked the victim to fill up the tires and then killed him by striking him on the head six to seven times with a small sledgehammer. Defendant dragged the body into the station and stole $14 from the cash box. Defendant waited on a customer before leaving on his bicycle. (19-2)
3. The 44-year-old male defendant, with three prior felony convictions, met the 31-year-old male victim and two male coperpetrators at a homosexual party in a motel. The perpetrators kidnapped the victim and held him in a house handcuffed and tied to a pole with a dog chain. They forced the victim to write $9,400 in checks before taking him to a field and killing him. The defendant stabbed the victim three times and passed the knife on to the other coperpetrators. The victim was stabbed twelve times in the back, three times in the chest, and his throat was slit. The victim was handcuffed and gagged and his arms and legs were bound with tape. (19-6)
4. The 26-year-old male defendant, with three prior convictions for bad checks, hired his brother to kill the defendant's 24-year-old wife for insurance proceeds. The defendant remained at work while the murder took place. The brother stabbed the sleeping victim twelve times. She awoke and struggled violently before dying. (21-2)

We used culpability measures similar to those reported in chapter 5 to identify cases similar to each of these death cases. Because of Defendant 1's prior murder conviction, the contemporaneous rape, and the brutal method of killing, his was the most aggravated case in the study. However, there were numerous cases with overall levels of aggravation comparable to those of the other three defendants that did not result in death sentences. For this reason, their death sentences appear to raise issues of excessiveness.[65]

Another major study is Leigh Bienen, Neil Weiner, Deborah Denno, Paul Allison, and Douglas Mills's 1988 report on New Jersey's capital-sentencing system, which focuses on the disposition of 703 cases initiated with a formal homicide charge that resulted in a final disposition at the trial-court level.[66] Their study, which included all cases known to them during 1982–86, embraces 404 death-eligible cases.[67] The data set was developed from court records and interviews with defense attorneys, and includes data on over 200 independent variables concerning the offender, the victim, and the circumstances of the crime.

In the exercise of prosecutorial discretion, New Jersey's capital-sentencing system differs from the Georgia system in two important particulars. First, before a prosecutor can obtain a penalty trial, he or she must have given notice well before trial of an intent to seek a death sentence under specified statutory aggravating circumstances. Second, if a notice of intent to seek a death sentence has not been withdrawn prior to trial, the prosecutor lacks the discretion to waive the penalty trial once a capital-murder conviction is obtained.

Like the other systems we have seen, New Jersey has a low death-sentencing rate largely as a result of the exercise of prosecutorial discretion at the pretrial stages of the process. Specifically, among the 404 death-eligible defendants indicted for murder, only 6 percent (25/404) received a death sentence. Among the cases in which the prosecutor originally filed a statement of intent to seek a death sentence, the death-sentencing rate was 19 percent (25/131); among the cases that resulted in a capital-murder trial, the rate was 27 percent (25/94); and for those that advanced to a penalty trial, the rate was 36 percent (25/69).[68] The impact of prosecutorial discretion is reflected in the fact that prosecutors seek death sentences in only a third (131/404) of the death-eligible cases and that fewer than 25 percent (94/404) of the death-eligible defendants actually advanced to a murder trial.[69]

And as in other similar studies, the New Jersey data show substantial variations between the judicial districts of the state in prosecutorial diligence in seeking and obtaining death sentences.[70]

Two additional post-*Furman* studies have analyzed geographic disparities in capital sentencing. Bowers and Pierce (1980) studied capital sentencing in Florida during the five-year period following the adoption of that state's post-*Furman* statute. They found geographic sentencing disparities in Florida comparable to those we observed in post-*Furman* Georgia.[71] Without adjustment for background factors, Bowers and Pierce found that the overall probability of a death sentence was 2.4 (.048/.020) times greater in the Florida panhandle than it was in the southern region; the comparable probabilities for the northern and central regions fell between these extremes.[72] When the authors controlled for the presence of an accompanying felony in the case, these regional disparities increased. For murder in conjunction with another felony, the probability of a death sentence was four to five times higher in the panhandle than in the southern and northern regions, and more than twice as great as the probability in central Florida.[73] For simple murder cases the disparities between different regions were somewhat different, but the highest regional rate was about three times higher than the rate for next highest region.[74]

Professor Bowers also examined geographic disparities in a 1983 multivariate study of 613 Florida defendants indicted for a capital murder during the period 1973–77.[75] A multiple-regression analysis that controlled for ten legitimate case characteristics and three suspect or illegal factors indicated that, to a statistically significant degree, defendants charged with criminal homicide in the central region were substantially more likely to be indicted for capital murder than comparable defendants in other parts of Florida. Bowers also found that the probability of a capital-murder conviction among defendents indicted for capital murder was substantially higher in the central region of the state. By contrast, for defendants who actually underwent penalty trials, the probability of receiving a death sentence was significantly higher in the northern region of the state.[76]

Bowers's 1983 study also reported the results of interviews with Florida prosecutors, judges, and defense attorneys, conducted by the Florida Justice Institute, which sought to identify "what influences the decision to indict for first degree murder."[77] The results very much paralleled Ursula Bentele's findings based on her interviews with Georgia prosecutors.[78] The most important considerations, according to the Florida prosecutors, were how well the facts of the case conformed to the statutory aggravating circumstances and the extent of the defendant's culpability. Also important were other factors that would inevitably vary from place to place:

- The concerns of prosecutors regarding personal advancement, their philosophy toward punishment, and their attitudes toward certain types of defendants and victims
- Such situational considerations as plea-bargaining strategy, docket pressures, and pressure from the victim's family or the police
- Such social pressures as media coverage, community response, and the political/racial climate.[79]

A 1986 study by Ronald J. Tabak provides a useful overview of the many sources of inconsistency and irrationality in contemporary capital-charging-and-sentencing systems.[80] Most analyses of the subject, including our own, have focused on geographic disparities in death-sentencing rates, race-of-defendant and race-of-victim discrimination in jury and prosecutorial decision making, and the effectiveness of comparative-proportionality reviews conducted by state supreme courts. Tabak's analysis, which is drawn in large part from his pro bono legal representation of nearly a dozen death-row inmates, outlines several additional sources of inconsistency and irrationality operating at the trial level and in the postconviction appeals process.

He discusses four features of the trial process of particular interest:

1. The competence and energy of the defendant's trial lawyer, who is usually appointed by the state
2. The values and predispositions of the jurors and their tendency toward misconduct
3. The willingness of the prosecutor to mislead and inflame the jury in the guilt- and penalty-trial phases

4. Juror misconceptions about the prison time life-sentenced defendants actually serve and about the likelihood a death sentence imposed by a jury will be vacated on appeal.[81]

Tabak's article also dwells on six features of the appeals process in both the state and federal courts that introduce distinctly random features to the process:

1. The availability and competence of the defendant's volunteer counsel, following direct review by the state supreme court
2. Judicial rules that determine the time available to counsel to prepare habeas corpus papers
3. State and federal procedural bars to the consideration of meritorious claims of constitutional error
4. Harmless-error rules that place on defendants the burden of showing that they would not have received a death sentence if constitutional violations had not occurred
5. The infrequent and unpredictable granting of executive clemency
6. The impact of impending state elections on prosecutors and appellate judges involved in capital litigation.[82]

Tabak reviews recent constitutional litigation addressing these issues and concludes that neither the state nor the federal courts have reduced to a reasonable level the risk of error and inconsistency flowing from them. Tabak's analysis raises the question of whether tolerable levels of consistency are attainable at the price society is likely to allocate to the problem. Tabak is skeptical, and closes with the following:

> Our legal system is incapable of providing justice in these highly emotional cases. Too many prosecutors are unable to restrain themselves from seeking the death penalty for tactical or political reasons, from demanding that trials occur in locales reeking with prejudicial publicity, from striving to keep biased people eligible for jury service, or from making highly misleading closing arguments. Too many attorneys for capital defendants, due to a combination of inexperience and lack of time and resources, fail to mount adequate defenses, particularly in sentencing proceedings. Too many jurors vote for the death penalty without really intending that the defendant be executed. Too many state judges seem insensitive to the federal constitutional rights of death-sentenced prisoners. Too many federal judges themselves "abuse the writ" of habeas corpus by imposing procedural bars, by adopting scheduling rules which turn death sentence cases into rollercoasters, and by placing on death row inmates the enormous burden of proving that the deprivations of their constitutional rights probably changed the outcomes of their cases. Too many state governments provide indigent capital defendants with egregiously underfunded or underqualified trial and direct appeal counsel and then deny them funds for counsel in subsequent judicial proceedings. Too many state governors and pardon boards are abdicating their responsibility to consider grants of clemency. And too many members of the public are blindly favoring capital punishment without really understanding how it operates.

In view of these basic problems with the death penalty and the arbitrary and capricious way in which it still operates, it is apparent that this country cannot administer capital punishment fairly. For that reason—if for no other—it should be abolished.[83]

Summary

In summary, the emerging evidence nationwide suggests there is much in common between Georgia and other death-sentencing states. Prosecutors dominate the system and handle most death-eligible cases in much the same fashion as other felonies. Plea bargaining is commonplace, and, for a variety of reasons, prosecutors quite often unilaterally waive the penalty trial after obtaining a capital-murder conviction at trial. When penalty trials do occur, juries impose death sentences in about half of the cases. The result is a low death-sentencing rate, yielding approximately 250 to 300 death sentences each year. The extent to which the relatively few death sentences imposed each year are excessive is not fully known. The limited data available for the pre-*Furman* period suggest that in Georgia and elsewhere a serious problem did exist. What we know about the post-*Furman* era suggests that there has been some improvement in states that process large numbers of capital cases, although many excessive death sentences still occur each year. In states that impose only a very few death sentences, like Colorado, the problems of inconsistency and a lack of evenhandedness are probably much more severe.

THE INFLUENCE OF RACIAL DISCRIMINATION AND SUSPECT FACTORS ON CAPITAL SENTENCING

Most of the empirical research on capital charging and sentencing during the past fifty years has investigated the influence of racial factors and, to a lesser extent, of such other suspect characteristics as the defendant's socioeconomic status. The literature includes studies conducted in a variety of jurisdictions with varying degrees of methodological sophistication. The results have varied considerably depending upon the jurisdiction, the time of the study, and the stage of the process under scrutiny.

Pre-*Furman* Studies

The pre-*Furman* studies of discrimination in the capital-charging-and-sentencing process fall into four categories. The first two categories consist of a series of pioneering studies of defendants convicted in the South of murder and of rape, respectively. The third group of studies involved various samples of murder defendants from non-Southern jurisdictions. The last group of studies examined commutation decisions by governors in death-sentence cases. Also of interest is Gary Kleck's 1981 study of death-sentencing and execution rates, which falls into none of these four categories.

Murder Studies from the South

In 1930, H. C. Brearley in his general study *The Negro and Homicide* noted that for the years 1920–26, the conviction rate for black defendants tried for murder or manslaughter in South Carolina was .64; the comparable rate for white defendants was .32.[84] He attributed the difference to "such factors as race prejudice by white jurors and court officials and the Negro's low economic status, which prevents him from securing 'good' criminal lawyers for his defense." Brearley concluded that for the years 1915–27, South Carolina executed seven whites and fifty-three Negroes, or "one white for every 101 white homicides and one Negro for every 38 Negro homicides."[85]

Other evidence from the early decades of the twentieth century includes studies by Thorsten Sellin and William Bowers. Sellin studied 687 males prosecuted in Arkansas between 1912 and 1924 for all degrees of murder. He found that, in general, blacks were substantially more likely than whites to be convicted (.72 versus .53). However, among a small group of capital-murder cases prosecuted in 1923 and 1924, the conviction rate for black defendants (.31) was actually lower than it was for white defendants (.33).[86] Bowers surveyed those defendants nationwide who received death sentences from 1864 through 1967 and were ultimately executed. He found that black defendants were considerably less likely than whites to have appealed their conviction before being executed.[87]

These studies of the early twentieth century suffer from two important flaws—they lack any control for the defendants' relative culpability, and they include no information about the race of the victim. A somewhat later study by Guy Johnson, published in 1941, included information on the race of both the defendant and the victim. Johnson examined 330 defendants indicted for murder in five North Carolina counties between 1930 and 1940.[88] He found the following distribution of death-sentencing rate among the four possible defendant/victim racial combinations:[89]

Black defendant/white victim	.32 (6/19)
White defendant/white victim	.13 (8/61)
Black defendant/black victim	.04 (11/247)
White defendant/black victim	.00 (0/3)

These results are strikingly comparable to our pre-*Furman* findings in Georgia in two respects. There is a large disparity between death-sentencing rates for black and white defendants with white victims (.32 for black versus .13 for white). There is also a strong race-of-victim effect.

In 1949 Harold Garfinkel published an expansion of Johnson's study that embraced a sample of 821 cases from ten North Carolina counties over the eleven-year period extending from January 1930 through December 1940.[90] His data revealed the following distribution of death sentences among defendants indicted for first-degree murder:

Black defendant/white victim	.37 (15/41)
White defendant/white victim	.11 (11/101)
Black defendant/black victim	.04 (15/372)
White defendant/black victim	.00 (0/11)

Garfinkel's study was also of interest because he examined separately three different steps in North Carolina's capital-charging-and-sentencing process. He found that, by far, the race-of-defendant and the race-of-victim effects most strongly influenced decisions by judges and juries regarding the defendant's innocence or guilt.[91]

Rape Studies from the South

A second group of studies from the South investigated the use of the death penalty in rape cases. Donald Partington's 1965 study reported that in the period 1908–64 every rapist executed in Virginia was black.[92] He also reported that, in the eighteen states that authorized the death penalty for rape, blacks constituted 90 percent (399/444) of the defendants executed between 1930 and 1962 for that crime. In addition to Virginia, he found that in five Southern jurisdictions (the District of Columbia, Louisiana, Mississippi, Oklahoma, and West Virginia) blacks (sixty-six in all) were the only rapists executed during this period.[93]

In the early sixties Marvin Wolfgang conducted a major empirical study of capital punishment in rape cases.[94] He collected extensive data on a sample of over three thousand cases that resulted in a rape conviction between 1945 and 1965 in 230 counties of eleven Southern and border states (Alabama, Arkansas, Florida, Georgia, Louisiana, Mississippi, North Carolina, South Carolina, Tennessee, Texas, and Virginia). Wolfgang's data set included information on a wide variety of legitimate case characteristics. Indeed, in terms of the number of legitimate background variables for which data were available, his was the most sophisticated empirical investigation of sentencing yet conducted at that time. The data allowed Wolfgang to control one at a time for over two dozen variables (such as prior record, contemporaneous robbery, weapon, and victim's age). Before adjustment for these variables, the probability that a black defendant convicted of raping a white victim would receive a death sentence was .36. This was 34 percentage points higher than the equivalent probability for any other defendant/victim racial combination.[95] Wolfgang found that adjusting for none of these legitimate background variables reduced the strong race effects initially observed.[96]

In a subsequent multivariate analysis of the Georgia cases in the Wolfgang sample, Wolfgang and Marc Riedel estimated race effects after simultaneous adjustment for the effects of ten legitimate background factors.[97] They found that the defendant/victim racial combination was by far the most important variable for explaining which defendants would receive death sentences. There was a substantial statistical association between the likelihood of a death sentence and the presence of a black defendant and white victim.[98]

Murder Studies from Non-Southern Jurisdictions

There are five pre-*Furman* sentencing studies from outside the South. In 1964, Edwin Wolf analyzed the sentences imposed on 159 defendants convicted of murders in New Jersey during the period 1937–61.[99] He found that for black defendants the death-sentencing rate was .48 (38/80), while the rate for white defendants was .30 (24/79).[100]

Wolf's data allowed him to control separately for three legitimate case characteristics (felony circumstance, type of weapon, and defendant's age). He found that the race-of-defendant effect was strongest for cases involving a related felony (.60 for black versus .41 for white defendants), but was relatively weak in the nonfelony cases (.27 for black versus .21 for white defendants). The control for weapon type showed a very strong race-of-defendant effect: the rate for beating killings was .64 for blacks (versus .31 for whites), but for murders committed with guns the rate for white defendants (.48) was actually higher than for black defendants (.44). Finally, Wolf found that adjusting for the defendant's age produced a strong race-of-defendant effect among the defendants under the median age (.51 for blacks versus .29 for whites), but only a weak effect among older defendants (.41 for blacks versus .30 for whites).[101]

Wolf did not obtain data on the race of every victim in his study. What information he did acquire suggested that there was a race-of-victim effect. Specifically, for a group of thirty-seven black defendants, the death-sentencing rate was .72 (18/25) in the white-victim cases versus .50 (6/12) in the black-victim cases.[102]

The most thoroughly controlled pre-*Furman* study outside the South was the 1969 investigation by the *Stanford Law Review* described earlier.[103] It analyzed the outcome of 239 penalty trials conducted in California between 1958 and 1966. Employing a multivariate analysis known as "partial correlation analysis," the study estimated race-of-victim and race-of-defendant effects after adjustment for 18 legitimate background factors and certain suspect factors, such as the defendant's occupation. After adjustment for these background variables, the analysis produced no evidence of race-of-victim or race-of-defendant effects. The data did, however, indicate that blue-collar defendants were at a disadvantage with sentencing juries.[104] In 1980, we reanalyzed the *Stanford Law Review* data using a logistic multiple-regression analysis, a procedure designed to analyze dichotomous (yes-no) outcome variables.[105] Our analysis also showed no race-of-victim or race-of-defendant effects. However, after adjusting for 13 statistically significant legitimate background variables screened from over 150 potentially influential variables, we too found a substantial relationship between the death-sentencing outcome and 2 variables relating to the defendant's socioeconomic status.[106]

The results of two other studies of non-Southern jurisdictions are merely suggestive because of the few death sentences involved. In 1976 Hugo Bedau reported a study of defendants indicted for capital murder in two populous Massachusetts counties between 1946 and 1970. This population included seventeen defendants indicted for rape-murder, the statutory penalty for which was a mandatory death sentence.[107] Four of the seventeen cases involved a black defendant and a white victim. Bedau found that none of these or any of the other rape-murder cases resulted in a death sentence.[108]

Franklin Zimring, Joel Eigen, and Sheila O'Malley's 1976 study of the first 204 homicides reported to the Philadelphia police in 1977 documented 171 eventual convictions, 3 of which resulted in death sentences.[109] Each of these cases involved one or more black defendants and a white victim. The defendants were all under twenty years of age; two of the victims were elderly (fifty-six and sixty); and the third victim was the target of a racially motivated killing. In terms of relative culpability the authors could not distinguish these three death-sentence cases from other cases that resulted in lesser sentences, but because the number of death sentences was too small, the authors could make no judgment whether these death sentences reflected race-of-defendant or race-of-victim discrimination.[110]

Gubernatorial Commutation Decisions

The fourth group of pre-*Furman* capital-sentencing studies examined gubernatorial decisions whether to commute the sentences imposed on defendants condemned to death. Two of these studies examined commutation decisions in rape cases from the South. Neither employed any control variables. One study by O. Johnson showed a race-of-defendant effect in Louisiana over the period 1900–1950, while a study by E. Johnson in North Carolina for the period 1909–54 did not.[111] Hugo Bedau's 1964 analysis of New Jersey commutation decisions between 1907 and 1960, which controlled for felony and nonfelony circumstances, showed no race-of-defendant effect.[112] In a similar study of Oregon from 1903 through 1964, Bedau also found no race-of-defendant effect in commutation decisions.[113] However, in a 1962 Pennsylvania study covering the 1914–58 period, Wolfgang, Kelly, and Nolde reported a race-of-defendant effect in cases with felony circumstances but no effect in other cases.[114]

Kleck's 1981 Study

Also of interest is Gary Kleck's 1981 analysis of execution rates since 1930 and death-sentencing rates since 1967 for black and white defendants.[115] Kleck derived his reported annual execution rates by calculating how many defendants from each racial group were executed for each one thousand victims from the same racial group killed during the previous year. Nationwide, he found generally lower execution rates for black defendants. However, when he calculated the execution rates for different regions, he found a higher rate for black defendants in the South, but generally lower rates elsewhere.[116]

Using a comparable method of calculation, Kleck also derived death-sentencing rates for black and white defendants. Between 1967 and 1971, the death-sentencing rate nationwide was generally lower for nonwhite defendants. Kleck did not break down these death-sentencing rates by regions, so that information is unavailable.[117]

Kleck's death-sentencing data did not permit him to control either for the race of the victim or for the relative culpability of the defendant. Quite probably the absence of a race-of-victim control tended to obscure any discrimination against black defendants in white-victim cases; but the lack of any control for culpability level probably exerted an opposite effect. Whatever the limits of Kleck's data, his findings are generally consistent with those of the other pre-*Furman* studies.

Summary

The results of these pre-*Furman* studies of racial discrimination in capital sentencing suggest that the defendant's race did influence the sentence imposed in the South, particularly in rape cases. Moreover, the unadjusted disparities between death-sentencing rates in the South for black and white murder defendants strikingly resemble those that we observed in our pre-*Furman* Georgia sample.

Outside the South, however, the evidence is inconclusive. Two studies of sentencing decisions in Massachusetts and Philadelphia produced different results, but they involved very few death-sentence cases. In the two studies with adequate sample size, the pattern was the same. A study of California with good controls for background variables indicated no race-of-defendant or race-of-victim effects, while a New Jersey study with limited controls did identify race-of-defendant effects.

Post-*Furman* Studies

Post *Furman* empirical research has focused primarily on the South. As in the pre-*Furman* era, it varies considerably in its scope and methodological sophistication. In general, however, regardless of the methodology used, the post-*Furman* results from the South are similar to our Georgia findings: there appears to be no systematic race-of-defendant effect, but a strong and consistent race-of-victim effect is quite evident. The few studies of post-*Furman* sentencing outside the South also disclose no race-of-defendant effects; race-of-victim effects appear to be present, but are less strong than in the South.

National Studies

The first study of post-*Furman* racial discrimination was published by Marc Riedel in 1976.[118] Riedel assumed that a decline in discrimination in the post-*Furman* period would reduce the proportion of black offenders on death row compared to the pre-*Furman* era. Accordingly, he examined the racial composition of death row before and after *Furman* (1971 versus 1974). He found that the proportion of nonwhites on death row actually increased after *Furman* (62 percent after versus 53 percent before).[119] These data are only suggestive, however, because they fail to adjust for the proportion of nonwhite defendants arrested for or convicted of murder. Furthermore, the proportionate increase in black defendants on death row as of 1974 that Riedel reported has not persisted; nonwhites currently constitute approximately 48 percent of the death-row population, a decline since *Furman*.

Gary Kleck's 1981 study also provides some evidence of post-*Furman* race-of-defendant discrimination among persons arrested for homicide from 1974 through 1978. The results continue to show lower death-sentencing rates nationally for black defendants.[120] On the basis of these unadjusted results, Kleck hypothesizes that any discrimination that might occur against blacks "at one or more stages" in the process must be offset by "compensating effects, favoring blacks, at other stages."[121]

Using an approach similar to Kleck's, Lawrence Greenfeld and David Hinners calculated the respective death-sentencing rates for blacks and whites arrested for murder or nonnegligent manslaughter for the years 1980 through 1984.[122] For every one thousand black arrestees, they found there were 11.6 admissions to prison under a death sentence; the comparable rate for white defendants was 15.8.[123] Neither the Kleck nor the Greenfeld and Hinners studies controlled for race of victim or case culpability.

State-Specific Studies

Since 1980 a number of studies have appeared, primarily in the South, that concentrate on a single or a small number of jurisdictions. The first of these studies, reported by William Bowers and Glenn Pierce in 1980, analyzed state-wide death-sentencing patterns in Florida, Georgia, Texas, and Ohio for a five-year period after *Furman*.[124] Their basic procedure was to compare the number of defendant/victim racial combinations represented on each state's death row with the number of murder and nonnegligent homicides involving the same defendant/victim racial combinations. The unadjusted results indicated strong race-of-defendant and race-of-victim effects,[125] but, after adjustment for the presence of felony circumstances, the race-of-defendant effects found to exist in the three Southern states dropped sharply. The race-of-victim effects, however, remained strong.[126]

Bowers and Pierce also analyzed three stages in Florida's charging-and-sentencing system—indictment, conviction, and penalty-trial sentencing by the judge. The data included a sample of more than seven hundred cases from twenty Florida counties processed during the years 1973–77. The unadjusted results for each of the three stages indicated that cases of black defendants who killed white victims were more likely to advance to the next stage of the process than were white-defendant/white-victim cases. The results also showed strong race-of-victim effects at each stage.[127] Again, adjusting for the presence of felony circumstances virtually eliminated the race-of-defendant effects at each of the three stages; but the race-of-victim effects remained strong at each stage.[128] As a result, the overall probability of a death sentence in a felony-circumstances case was twice as high in white-victim cases as it was in black-victim cases. A similar disparity appeared in cases involving no felony circumstances.

Michael Radelet conducted a similar longitudinal study of over six hundred Florida cases that resulted in homicide indictments from twenty of the state's sixty-seven counties.[129] His analysis measured race-of-victim and race-of-defendant effects at each stage in the process while controlling for whether the defendant and victim were acquainted or were strangers. The analysis indicated no race-of-defendant or race-of-victim effects among the former category of cases. However, among the 326 cases in which the victim was a stranger, there was a statistically significant higher probability that defendants who killed white victims would receive a death sentence. The source of this increased probability was the greater likelihood in such cases that grand juries would return indictments for capital murder if the victim was also white. However, even among these cases, Radelet also observed race-of-victim effects in the postindictment stages of the process—.17 (30/182) of the white-victim cases resulted in a death sentence, while only .10 (6/60) of the black-victim cases did so.[130]

In 1981 Hans Zeisel examined the distribution of death sentences in Florida after 1972 and before 1977 in cases involving a concurrent felony.[131] The data indicated a strong race-of-victim effect in death-sentencing rates—the rate was .31 (83/268) among the arrestees in white-victim cases versus .01 (1/110) among the arrestees in black-victim cases.[132] The data also showed that in white-victim cases involving a contemporaneous felony, the likelihood of receiving a death sentence was nearly twice as great for black defendants as for white defendants (.47 versus .24).[133]

In 1982 Linda Foley and Richard Powell reported a longitudinal study of a Florida data set that overlapped with the Radelet file.[134] They examined all 829 defendants indicted for capital murder in twenty-one Florida counties between 1972 and 1978. In contrast to the other earlier studies, this analysis adjusted for ten legitimate background factors and for the race and sex of both the defendant and victim. The study examined three decision points in the process: whether the case pled out or advanced to a guilt trial; if there was a penalty trial, whether the jury recommended a life or death sentence; and whether the trial judge imposed a life or death sentence. After adjusting for the various background factors, Foley and Powell observed no race-of-defendant effects at any stage in the process. Nor did they observe any race-of-victim effects with respect to the prosecutor's decision to advance the case to a guilt trial or the jury's sentencing recommendation. However, the actual sentences imposed by the trial judges did reflect a statistically significant race-of-victim effect.[135]

Steve Arkin's 1980 study of the disposition of 350 homicides processed between 1973 and 1976 in Dade County, Florida, included all cases presented to a grand jury for a first-degree-murder indictment.[136] Of such cases, 142 involved contemporaneous felonies, and ten of them ultimately resulted in death sentences. Nine of the death-sentence cases involved white victims. The resulting death-sentencing rates were .08 for the white-victim cases versus .03 for the black-victim cases. The principal reason for the disparity was that juries returned first-degree murder convictions in white-victim cases at nearly twice the rate observed for black-victim cases—.45 (51/113) versus .21 (6/29).[137]

In 1983 William Bowers reported the results of his reanalysis, with multiple-regression procedures, of the Florida data used by Hans Zeisel and Michael Radelet (508 homicide indictments from 1976-77).[138] After adjusting for fourteen legitimate background factors, Bowers found that killers of white victims were more likely to be indicted for first-degree murder than killers of black victims.[139] His analysis of the guilt-trial stage also revealed a strong race-of-victim effect and a weak race-of-defendant effect.[140] Finally, among 191 cases that advanced to a penalty trial, Bowers's analysis identified a mild race-of-victim effect that approached statistical significance.[141]

Bowers's analysis also included variables for the type of defense attorney (court-appointed, public defender, or privately retained), which served as a proxy for the defendant's socioeconomic status. After adjustment for ten legitimate case characteristics and for racial and regional variables, the analysis indicated that defendants with court-appointed attorneys were more likely to be indicted for first-degree murder.[142] By contrast, the type of defense attorney did not affect the probability of a first-degree-murder conviction. On the other hand, in those cases that advanced to a penalty trial, defendants with court-appointed attorneys and public defenders were significantly more likely than those with privately retained attorneys to receive a death sentence.[143]

Raymond Paternoster has extensively analyzed decisions by prosecutors to seek a death sentence in South Carolina.[144] His sample consisted of three hundred homicides involving statutory aggravating factors that were committed between June 1977 and December 1981. After controlling for eight legitimate background factors and the sex of the defendant, Paternoster observed a statistically significant race-of-victim effect in cases involving a contemporaneous felony. The analysis also revealed an interaction between the seriousness of the offense and the race-of-victim effect—the race-of-victim effect is strongest in single-felony cases and becomes insignificant in homicides involving multiple felonies.[145]

Paternoster found relatively little evidence of prosecutorial discrimination on the basis of the defendant's race. The coefficient for the race-of-defendant variable suggests that black defendants are slightly disadvantaged, but the disparity is not statistically significant.[146] With respect to the race of the defendant, the race of the victim, and their interaction with the seriousness of the case, Paternoster's results parallel our Georgia findings.

In 1983 Elizabeth Murphy reported her analysis of 230 Cook County, Illinois, defendants convicted of capital murder during the period 1977–80.[147] Eighteen of these cases resulted in death sentences. There were 164 white-victim cases in the sample, which resulted in 52 capital-murder convictions. Murphy found that, in these 52 white-victim cases, prosecutors were more than twice as likely to seek a death sentence against black defendants than against white defendants (.40 [12/30] for black-defendant cases versus .18 [4/22] for the white defendants). However, the penalty-trial decisions of the Cook County jurors tended to offset the effect of this prosecutorial discrimination against black defendants. Consequently, among all defendants convicted of the capital murder of a white victim ($n = 52$), black defendants were only slightly more likely than white defendants to receive a death sentence (.16 versus .13).[148]

On the other hand, Murphy also reported a strong unadjusted race-of-victim effect. Prosecutors were substantially more willing to seek a death sentence in cases involving white victims—.32 (19/60) in white-victim cases versus .21 (28/134) in black-victim cases. Nor did the participation of the sentencing juries modify the effects of these prosecutorial decisions. The over-all race-of-victim effect among all defendants convicted of first-degree murder was 13 percentage points (.18 [11/60] for white-victim cases versus .05 [7/134] for black-victim cases).[149]

A 1984 study by Samuel Gross and Robert Mauro focuses principally on the South (Florida, Georgia, Mississippi, and North Carolina), but also includes data from Arkansas, Illinois, Oklahoma, and Virginia.[150] This is an extensive study covering homicides reported by local officials to the FBI from January 1, 1976, through December 31, 1980. The authors controlled for five legitimate case characteristics (felony circumstances, relationship of defendant and victim, number of victims, victim's sex, and weapon used). After adjusting for these variables, they found that Arkansas was the only state in which the analysis revealed a statistically significant race-of-defendant effect, which disadvantaged black defendants.

With respect to the race of the victim, however, the results were quite different. After adjusting for the five background variables and the defendant's race, Gross and Mauro found strong, statistically significant race-of-victim effects in Georgia, Florida, Illinois, Oklahoma, North Carolina, and Mississippi. In two other states, Virginia and Arkansas, death-sentencing rates were higher in white-victim cases, but the coefficients estimated in the multiple-regression analysis were not statistically significant beyond the .05 level.[151]

Of particular relevance to our study are Gross and Mauro's findings with respect to Georgia. Their data overlap our data chronologically, and their results are comparable. For example, they estimated a race-of-victim logistic-regression coefficient from their 1976–80 Georgia data that was similar to the race-of-victim coefficient we estimated with our 1973–78 Georgia data set after adjusting for the same background variables that they employed.[152] The odds multiplier estimated from their race-of-victim logistic-regression coefficient was 7.2, significant beyond the .001 level; our odds multiplier was 4.4 (significant beyond the .001 level).[153] The Gross and Mauro results also show a race-of-victim interaction effect, with the strongest race-of-victim effects observed among cases with a death-sentencing rate above .10, a category of cases roughly comparable to the midrange of cases in our Georgia study.[154]

There are four recent multivariate studies of note. Richard Berk and Joseph Lowery have reported preliminary results from their 1985 study of the operation of Mississippi's capital-charging-and-sentencing system between November 1, 1976, and April 30, 1982.[155] From a universe of approximately 1,100 cases that resulted in a murder or manslaughter conviction, they selected a sample of 404 cases, which included all cases that advanced to a penalty trial. Their data-collection instrument, a modified version of our "Charging and Sentencing Study" questionnaire found at Appendix E of this book, provided for data on hundreds of variables. Their data sources were the files of the Mississippi Department of Corrections and the Mississippi Department of Vital Statistics, the opinions of the Mississippi appellate courts, and in many cases field interviews with prosecutors, sheriffs, and police officers. The data were collected and coded by law students working under the supervision of the law student who supervised the collection of our data set in Georgia.[156] From their questionnaire, Berk and Lowery developed approximately 200 machine-readable variables, from which they selected thirty-nine legitimate and geographic variables on the basis of recommendations of the National Academy of Sciences Sentencing Panel and the work of other capital-punishment researchers.[157]

Berk and Lowery estimated race-of-victim and race-of-defendant effects at four stages in the Mississippi capital-sentencing system with logistic multiple-regression procedures. Specifically, they sought to estimate the cumulative race-of-victim effects produced by the decisions leading up to and including the following four stages in the process: indictment for capital murder, conviction for capital murder, advancement to a penalty trial, and the imposition of a death sentence.[158]

Berk and Lowery presented their findings with respect to the race-of-victim and race-of-defendant effects in the system after adjustment for the thirty-nine legitimate variables in their core-model analysis. Their first analysis, which employed a logistic multiple-regression procedure, showed a strong and statistically significant race-of-defendant and race-of-victim effect in the decisions leading up to and including each of the four decision points. At the penalty-trial death-sentencing stage, black defendants had odds of receiving a death sentence that were four times higher than their white counterparts, while defendants with white victims faced odds of receiving a death sentence that were six times greater than those faced by similarly situated defendants in black-victim cases.[159]

However, in a series of alternative logistic "propensity analyses," the race-of-defendant effects were sharply lower and failed to achieve statistical significance.[160] According to the penalty-trial analysis, black defendants faced odds of receiving a death sentence that were only 1.5 times higher than those faced by white defendants, and the disparity was only significant at the .40 level. Because of the discrepancy in the race-of-defendant results obtained in the two different sets of analyses, the authors minimize the strength of their race-of-defendant findings. However, the race-of-victim effects in these alternative analyses were just slightly smaller, and remained statistically significant. Specifically, defendants in white-victim cases faced odds of receiving a death sentence that were 4.9 times higher than defendants in black-victim cases (significant at the .03 level). This finding is similar to the results of comparable analyses of the Georgia data, which showed that for both defendants indicted for murder and defendants convicted of murder at trial the odds that the average defendant would receive a death sentence were approximately 4.3 times higher in white-victim cases.[161]

Berk and Lowery conclude with the following:

[O]ur substantive conclusions essentially replicate Baldus, Woodworth and Pulaski and Gross and Mauro despite differences in site, data, and methods. Among the legitimate factors affecting sentencing in manslaughter and homicide cases are aggravating circumstances and the defendant's prior record. Mitigating factors are far less visible. Among the influences of questionable legitimacy, geographical region often matters. Homicide cases seem to be taken somewhat more seriously in the Gulf Coast region and somewhat less seriously in the Delta region. And among the illegitimate factors, the victim's race has large and statistically significant effects virtually any way we examined the data. White victim cases are treated far more harshly, holding a large number of potentially confounded variables constant. In addition, these effects are comparable in magnitude to a number of legitimate variables such as aggravating features and prior felony record. . . .

[T]here are also hints here and there that black defendants are treated more punitively than white defendants, holding all else constant. However, a lot depends on the method of analysis and the particular set of predetermined variables in the equation. What can be concluded with great confidence is that white defendants are not treated more punitively, other things equal; however one approaches the data the sign of the effect indicates exactly the reverse. We suspect that with a somewhat larger sample, the more punitive experiences of black defendants would have been both statistically and substantively significant.[162]

The Nakell and Hardy study of the disposition of 489 North Carolina homicide cases in 1977 and 1978 showed race-of-victim and race-of defendant effects quite comparable to those found in other studies. The results emerged in a series of logistic multiple-regression analyses that included variables for six legitimate case characteristics, a series of geographic variables, race variables, and interaction terms between the race variables and variables for the defendant's prior record and the number of aggravating circumstances in the case. The regressions focused on the cumulative effects of the race of defendant and race of victim on decisions prior to and including six successive stages in the process. Early stages in the process show race-of-victim effects in the expected direction, but they do not become statistically significant until the authors reach the analysis of the decisions leading up to and including the jury's first-degree-murder conviction.[163] Here we see a statistically significant ($p = .04$) race-of-victim effect indicating that, all other things being equal, the average defendant's odds of receiving a first-degree-murder conviction are reduced by a factor of .16 when the defendant's victim is black. However, the analysis of decisions leading up to and including the penalty-trial death-sentencing decision does not show a statistically significant effect for the "race and sex of defendant and victim."[164] Unfortunately, the separate effects of each of these variables was not presented. Also, a sample size of only eight death sentences further reduces the significance of these penalty-trial findings.

The race-of-defendant analysis indicates that after adjustment for legitimate case characteristics black defendants face odds both of advancing to a first-degree-murder trial and of being convicted of first-degree murder that are more than three times larger than those faced by white defendants. These disparities are not, however, statistically significant.[165] The only statistically significant race-of-defendant effects are the coefficients for the interaction terms between the race of the defendant, the seriousness of the case, and the defendant's prior record. Since these findings are complex, we rely on Nakell and Hardy's description of them:

> The race of the defendant had a significant effect when the seriousness of the case was controlled for, that is, in interactions of that factor with the degree of culpability factor and also the aggravating circumstances factor. With everything other than the race of the defendant being equal, including the quality of evidence in the cases, in less serious cases a white defendant generally stood a greater chance of being brought to trial on a first degree murder charge than a nonwhite defendant. In more serious cases, however, the nonwhite defendant stood the greater chance of enduring trial on a capital charge.
>
> For the cases that went to trial, the race of the defendant continued to be a significant factor in the determination of whether the first degree murder charge was submitted to the jury, again in interaction with variables regarding the seriousness of the case. At this stage of the trial, if neither the nonwhite nor the white defendant had a prior record, their odds of risking a jury verdict on murder one were fairly close. If both defendants had two aggravating circumstances, their odds were even. But if both had one aggravating circumstance the odds of the nonwhite defendant having the murder one charge considered by the jury were 1.7 times those of the white defendant, and if neither had any aggravating circumstances, the odds of the nonwhite defendant were three times greater. The differential was much more dramatic, however, for defendants with a prior record. If both defendants had a prior record score of 10, the odds of having the jury deliberate the first degree murder charge for the nonwhite defendant were much greater than for the similarly situated white defendant: 19.8 times greater if both defendants' cases had two aggravating circumstances, 31.4 times greater if both cases had only one aggravating circumstance, and a striking 56 times greater if they had no aggravating circumstances.[166]

The results of the Bienen, Weiner, Denno, Allison, and Mills study of capital sentencing in New Jersey between 1982 and 1986 are similar to but weaker than the results from Georgia and elsewhere. Among the death-eligible cases (those cases in which the facts appear to authorize the imposition of a death sentence), the death-sentencing rate among white-victim cases was .09 (14/162), versus .04 (10/238) in cases involving black and Hispanic victims.[167] Particularly striking is the zero death-sentencing rate in the fifty-nine death-eligible cases involving Hispanic victims.

The study by Bienen and her colleagues also reports the results of two logistic multiple-regression analyses that estimated race effects after controlling for more than thirty case characteristics that were screened from a pool of variables for more than two hundred case characteristics. The first analysis sought to identify the case characteristics that best explained prosecutorial decisions, before trial, to seek a penalty trial by serving the defendant with a "notice of factors." The second analysis sought to explain which potentially capital murder cases advanced to a guilt trial rather than ending with a guilt plea, usually arranged through a plea bargain. In the notice-of-factors analysis, after controlling for legitimate case characteristics, black and Hispanic defendants appear to have the highest risk of being served if the victim is white or black. However, when the victim is Hispanic, white defendants are the most likely to be served. The race-of-victim analysis indicated that notice of factors was most likely to be served in white-victim cases when the defendant was black or Hispanic. But when the defendant was white, the risk of a notice of factors was highest when the victim was Hispanic.[168]

In the guilt-trial-versus-plea model, the results were more straightforward. They showed no statistically significant race-of-defendant effect. They also indicated that there is a higher risk (statistically significant at the .10 level) that a case will advance to a capital trial if the victim is white than if the victim is black or Hispanic.[169]

In a study of capital sentencing in Louisiana, Margaret Klemm examined first-degree-murder convictions appealed to the Louisiana Supreme Court from 1979 to 1984. She collected data on 104 variables for case characteristics from the reports of the Louisiana Supreme Court and case files. Unadjusted disparities showed a small race-of-defendant effect (.36 for white defendants versus .39 for black defendants) and only a modest race-of-victim effect (.25 for black-victim cases versus .33 for white-victim cases). After adjustment for the four key variables in a linear multiple-regression analysis, the data showed no race-of-defendant effects, but suggested that defendants with white victims faced a statistically significant 5-percentage-point greater risk of receiving a death sentence than defendants in black-victim cases.[170]

Finally, the race-discrimination analysis in our Colorado study of the disposition of 179 death-eligible cases between 1979 and 1984 produced two findings.[171] First, all four of the death sentences were imposed in white-victim cases, even though 31 percent of the death-eligible cases had nonwhite victims.

Death sentences were concentrated exclusively among the white-victim cases because, among similarly situated cases, defendants with white victims are much more likely to be convicted of capital murder and far more likely to have their cases advanced to a penalty trial than are their counterparts in cases with nonwhite victims.

Second, nonwhite defendants were not disproportionately represented in the four death-sentence cases. There is evidence, however, of race-of-defendant discrimination against minorities in jury guilt-trial decisions. Currently, these effects are offset by the tendency of prosecutors to advance to a penalty trial a higher proportion of white than nonwhite defendants convicted of first-degree murder at trial. If in the future prosecutors were to advance all such convictions to a penalty trial, as appears to be contemplated by Colorado's capital punishment statute, nonwhite defendants would likely face a higher risk of a death sentence than similarly situated white defendants.

One theme of particular interest in the post-*Furman* studies we have reviewed is the absence of strong evidence of race-of-defendant discrimination. In contrast to the pre-*Furman* studies from the South, the more recent data suggest that minority defendants are at a disadvantage only in certain classes of cases and at certain stages of the state systems. It is an interesting question whether these findings can be reconciled with the virtually unanimous opinion of practitioners who represent capital defendants and death-row inmates. Each practitioner known to us believes that, given the same evidence, a minority defendant, particularly a black, is more likely to be sentenced to death than a white defendant. The offered explanations are bias (largely nonconscious) on the part of prosecutors and, in the words of Percy Foreman (a Houston, Texas, lawyer, who by his own estimation has tried more death-penalty cases than anyone else), "racial prejudice on the part of the jurors."[172] It is possible that the perceptions of these practitioners are correct with respect to the cases they have handled and that those cases are responsible for the limited race-of-defendant effects that we see in the data. It is also possible that the discrimination they perceive is offset in the statistics by cases in which black defendants are treated less punitively than their white counterparts. Whatever the reason for the discrepancy between the data and practitioner opinion, a recent Texas study by news reporters Ed Timms and Steve McGonigle sheds light on one likely source of race-of-defendant discrimination, to the extent that it does exist.[173] Timms and McGonigle examined the racial composition of 133 juries that resulted in death sentences in fifteen randomly selected Texas counties, which were the source of 60 percent of the inmates on Texas's death row as of August 1, 1986. They also investigated the manner in which prosecutors exercised peremptory challenges in fifteen Dallas County capital cases, each of which resulted in a death sentence.

The fifteen-county survey of 133 cases produced sixty-one death-sentenced black defendants; in 51 percent (31/61) of their cases, the sentencing jury was all-white.[174] The Dallas County study of the exercise of peremptory challenges examined fifteen capital cases that resulted in a death sentence. Five of those defendants were black and four had all-white juries. The fifth jury had one black juror who "told prosecutors that Texas' form of execution—lethal injection—was too humane. 'It's too quick,' he testified, 'they don't feel the pain.' "[175]

Timms and McGonigle's statistics and the results of their interviews with prosecutors also indicated that black jurors are disproportionately excluded in capital cases involving white defendants because black jurors are perceived to empathize excessively with defendants. The data from the fifteen Dallas County trials indicated that 90 percent (56/62) of the sixty-two black venirepersons were struck by prosecutorial peremptory challenges, while only 2 percent (1/62) of the blacks were struck by a defense peremptory challenge. The result was that only 8 percent (5/62) of the qualified black venirepersons actually served. In contrast, 33 percent of the white venirepersons and 25 percent of the Hispanic venirepersons served as jurors.[176]

The final state-specific study of interest is the analysis of Jim Henderson and Jack Taylor, reporters for the *Dallas Times Herald* who obtained data from each U.S. death-sentencing jurisdiction for the period 1977 through 1984.[177] Their report is the product of a remarkable research effort that involved the collection of data (frequently by telephone) from state corrections officials, state and local ACLU offices, state vital-statistics units, and local medical examiners' and coroners' offices. As a result of this relatively rudimentary data-collection effort, there is a fair degree of imprecision and looseness in their study. Nevertheless, the findings they report and the results of our reanalysis of the raw data in their articles are consistent with the general pattern of research in the other studies that we have reported.

Specifically, our reanalysis of the Henderson and Taylor data indicates that, for cases involving contemporaneous felonies reported to the FBI, black defendants are at a statistically significant disadvantage in only one state, Texas. Moreover, in three states, New Jersey, Florida, and Tennessee, white defendants confront a statistically significant greater risk of receiving a death sentence than do black defendants. Generally, however, there does not appear to be a substantial difference in the rates at which black and white defendants receive a death sentence, even after adjustment for the race of the victim.

Our reanalysis of the Henderson and Taylor data also produced state-by-state estimated race-of-victim disparities in death-sentencing rates for homicides involving contemporaneous felonies that were reported to the FBI from 1977 to 1984. Here we saw considerable state-to-state variation, with no effect apparent in five states (Nevada, North Carolina, Ohio, Pennsylvania, and New Jersey). In seven states (Illinois, Missouri, Florida, Georgia, Alabama, Mississippi, and Tennessee), we found statistically significant higher death-sentencing rates in white-victim cases. Only in Delaware did we find a higher death-sentencing rate in black-victim cases, but the numbers involved are small. In the remaining states, we observed disparities that run in the expected direction, but they are not significant at the .05 level. Because of the imprecision of the Henderson and Taylor data, and the inconsistency between the results produced with their data and the results estimated in more finely tuned studies of New Jersey (Bienen and her colleagues) and North Carolina (Nakell and Hardy), these results can only be treated as tentative. Nevertheless, their general consistency with the results of the literature is revealing.[178]

CONCLUSION

To a surprising degree, the results of our study of Georgia's capital-sentencing system both before and after *Furman* parallel the findings reported for other jurisdictions. This is reassuring, especially in view of the relatively sparse data available and the diversity of research designs and statistical methods employed in the different studies. In fact, this consistency in results, despite the weaknesses and limitations of virtually every study, tends to validate the findings of each. Thus, with some confidence, we can make several observations.

First, while the number of death sentences imposed annually is substantially greater now than it was before *Furman*, death-sentencing rates have not increased appreciably. Although there are some variations, this is generally a nationwide pattern. Moreover, both the number of death sentences imposed annually and the resulting death-sentencing rates have remained quite stable in recent years. Second, the available evidence about pre-*Furman* sentencing patterns in other states is consistent with our findings about Georgia: for the most part, defendants sentenced to death under pre-*Furman* statutes could not be meaningfully distinguished from the large majority of other defendants who did not receive death sentences.

Third, there are relatively few studies of the frequency of excessive death sentences, and the findings are mixed. Our studies of Georgia and Colorado suggest excessive death sentences do occur, and their number may be substantial. Other studies have also identified probably excessive death sentences in other jurisdictions; but because the number of death sentences involved was too small to permit definitive statistical analyses, one must be cautious about such findings. With respect to racial discrimination, more post-*Furman* data are available. They generally indicate a nearly complete reversal of the pre-

Furman pattern of discrimination against black defendants, who appear to receive, on average, slightly more lenient treatment than whites. The advantage is only slight, however, and the suggested statistics mask considerable variation between and within states.

Finally, there is persuasive evidence that, in many jurisdictions, defendants who killed white victims receive more punitive treatment than those whose victims were black. Furthermore, the few studies that have focused on the issue, such as our study of Georgia, find that these race-of-victim effects appear primarily in the midaggravation range of cases rather than at the extremes.

Our survey of the literature is consistent with other surveys of discrimination in capital sentencing and with broader surveys of discrimination in the criminal justice system generally. Several recent surveys suggest that statistical evidence of racial discrimination in capital sentencing against black defendants is largely a product of the pre-*Furman* years and that, although observable in the post-*Furman* period in certain subgroups of cases and in certain phases of selected jurisdictions' capital-sentencing systems, its effect is not strong and consistent. There is also a consensus that there is significant evidence of race-of-victim discrimination in a number of jurisdictions.[179]

Surveys of the empirical literature focused on discrimination throughout the criminal system tell a similar story with respect to race-of-defendant disparities.[180] However, most of the race-of-defendant studies do not control for the race of the victim. Moreover, because until recently criminal-justice-discrimination research did not include information on the race of the victim, the story is not complete on the level of race-of-victim discrimination in the criminal justice system generally.

Another reason for caution in concluding that race-of-defendant discrimination is entirely a thing of the past in capital and noncapital criminal sentencing is the substantial evidence of race-of-defendant discrimination in mock-jury studies.[181] These studies are distinguishable from the observational field studies that constitute the great bulk of the literature on racial discrimination in sentencing. They are true experiments in which all features of the cases remain fixed from one trial to the next except the race of the defendant and the race of the victim, which are manipulated by the investigators. Although the findings from the mock-jury studies are far from uniform, they suggest a race-of-defendant effect that is correlated with the race of the decision maker. Specifically, black defendants are generally treated more punitively by white jurors, and white defendants are treated more punitively by black jurors.[182] While it is true that these studies involve college-student jurors who vote without joint deliberation, their results lend credence to our Georgia findings that black defendants are at a disadvantage in predominantly white rural areas, and white defendants are at a disadvantage in urban communities with heavily minority populations.

NOTES

1. Woodson v. North Carolina, 428 U.S. 280, 313 (1976) (Rehnquist, J., dissenting) ("following *Furman* 10 states enacted laws providing for mandatory capital punishment").

2. In the pre-*Furman* period, most statutes authorized death sentencing for either common-law murder or first-degree murder. In the post-*Furman* period, death eligibility has been restricted to cases including specific statutory aggravating circumstances, the most important one being the presence of such a contemporaneous offense as robbery, rape, burglary, or arson.

3. The nationwide totals in recent years, including both original sentences and reinstated death sentences, are 190 (1974), 288 (1975), 273 (1976), 180 (1977), 242 (1978), 189 (1979), 241 (1980); Greenberg, *Capital Punishment as a System*, 91 YALE L. J. 908, 929–36 (1982); 249 (1981), 295 (1982), 266 (1983), 283 (1984), 330 (1985), 334 (1986), 300 (1987); source, NAACP Legal Defense Fund. Approximately 25% to 40% of these death sentences are vacated by state supreme courts. *See* Dix, *Appellate Review of the Decision to Impose Death*, 68 GEO. L. J. 97 (1979) (Fla., Ga., & Tex.).

4. Weisburg, *Deregulating Death*, 1983 SUP. CT. REV. 305, 379.

5. *Id.*

6. Bedau, *Death Sentences in New Jersey 1907–1960*, 19 RUTGERS L. REV. 1, 60 (1964) (Appendix II: *Abstract of Analysis of Jury Sentencing in Capital Cases: New Jersey: 1937–1961*, by E. Wolf); Baldus, Pulaski, Woodworth, and Kyle, *Identifying Comparatively Excessive Sentences of Death: A Quantitative Approach*, 33 STAN. L. REV. 1, 64 (1980) (hereinafter Baldus, Pulaski, Woodworth, & Kyle).

7. Kopeny, *Capital Punishment—Who Should Choose*, 12 W. ST. U. L. REV. 383, 388n.33 (1985) (hereinafter Kopeny).

8. Wolfgang & Riedel, *Race, Judicial Discretion, and the Death Penalty*, 407 ANNALS 119, 129 (1973) (hereinafter Wolfgang & Riedel).

9. Furman v. Georgia, 408 U.S. 238, 386–87n.11 (1972) (Burger, C.J., dissenting) ("Although accurate figures are difficult to obtain, it is thought that from 15% to 20% of those convicted of murder are sentenced to death in States where it is authorized." Four studies cited).

10. Kopeny, *supra* note 7, at 388n.33.

11. Baldus, Pulaski, & Woodworth, *Arbitrariness and Discrimination in the Administration of the Death Penalty: A Challenge to State Supreme Courts*, 15 STETSON L. REV. 133, 150 & n.41 (1986) (hereinafter Baldus, Pulaski, & Woodworth (86)).

12. *See* Murphy, *Application of the Death Penalty in Cook County*, 73 ILL. B. J. 90, 91 (1984) (hereinafter Murphy).

13. *See* Henderson & Taylor, *Racist Justice: Discrimination Even in Death*, DALLAS TIMES HERALD, Nov. 17, 1985, at A-17, col. 4 (hereinafter Henderson & Taylor).

14. *See* Flamer v. State, 490 A.2d 104, 157–58 (Del. 1983), *cert. denied*, 464 U.S. 865 (1983).

15. *See* Radelet, *Rejecting the Jury: The Imposition of the Death Penalty in Florida*, 18 U.C. DAVIS L. REV. 1409, 1415 (1985) (calculated from data in table 1) (herein-

after Radelet); M. F. Klemm, THE DETERMINANTS OF CAPITAL SENTENCING IN LOUISI-ANA, 1979–84, table 6-10, p. 226, dissertation, University of New Orleans (1986) (hereinafter Klemm) (death-sentencing rate among death-eligible first-degree murder convictions appealed to Louisiana Supreme Court).

16. *See* Tichnell v. State, 297 Md. 432, 468, 468 A. 2d 1, 19–20 (1983), *cert. denied*, 466 U.S. 993 (1984).

17. B. Nakell & K. Hardy, THE ARBITRARINESS OF THE DEATH PENALTY 108–9 (1987) (hereinafter Nakell & Hardy).

18. Bienen, Weiner, Denno, Allison, & Mills, *The Reimposition of Capital Punishment in New Jersey: The Role of Prosecutorial Discretion*, 41 RUTGERS L. REV. 27, 169 (table 1) (1988) (hereinafter Bienen et al.); Fox, *Death Verdict More Frequent in South Jersey*, SUNDAY RECORD (Bergen, N.J.), February 15, 1987, p. A-2.

19. *See* Berk & Lowery, "Factors Affecting Death Penalty Decisions in Mississippi," 14–15 (June 1985; unpublished manuscript) (calculated from data in text) (hereinafter Berk & Lowery).

20. The sample of Colorado cases includes all death-eligible homicides that resulted in a homicide prosecution and were known to the state public defender's office. D. Baldus, G. Woodworth, and C. Pulaski, *Arbitrariness and Discrimination in Colorado's post-Furman Capital Charging and Sentencing Process: A Preliminary Report*, 44 (1986; unpublished manuscript) (hereinafter Colorado Study).

21. These data are from the Charging and Sentencing Study (CSS). *See* chap. 10 for the race-discrimination results from that study.

22. Flamer v. State 490 A. 2d 104, 153–58 (Del. 1983) (attrition among cases charged with capital murder), *cert. denied*, 464 U.S. 865 (1983) .

23. *See* Henderson & Taylor, *supra* note 13, at A-17 (attrition among cases indicted for murder).

24. *See* Murphy, *supra* note 12, at 91 (attrition among capital-murder indictments; however, ninety-nine murder guilty pleas resulted in ten penalty trials and three death sentences).

25. Kopeny, *supra* note 7, at 388n.33.

26. Nakell & Hardy, *supra* note 17, at 109.

27. *See* Berk & Lowery, *supra* note 19, at 18–19 (the figure is the proportion of those indicted for capital murder who were later convicted of a homicidal crime less than capital murder).

28. *See* Bienen et al., *supra* note 18, at 169 (figure 1) (the figure is the percentage of death-eligible cases that do not advance to a capital-murder trial).

29. Paternoster, *Prosecutorial Discretion in Requesting the Death Penalty: A Case of Victim-Based Racial Discrimination*, 18 L. & SOC'Y REV. 437, 451 (1984) (hereinafter Paternoster (84)). Kopeny, *supra* note 7, at 388n.13; Murphy, *supra* note 12, at 91.

30. *See* table 49 n. 2 for definition of "broad" and "narrow" death-eligibility statutes and table 49 notes a & b for table 49 data sources.

31. The population of death-eligible offenders underlying each estimate is based on Georgia arrest and conviction rates during the period 1974–79. Of the murders and nonnegligent manslaughters reported to the FBI during this period, 17% (767/4,472) resulted in murder convictions, by trial or by plea; 86% of these offenders were death-eligible under Georgia's broad death-sentencing statute. However, if one considers all convictions for either murder or voluntary manslaughter during the same period, one finds that 45% (1,999/4,472) of the reported crimes resulted in a conviction and that

65% of those defendants were death-eligible under Georgia law. We applied these conviction and death-eligibility rates to the FBI data for each state to produce the estimated pools of death-eligible offenders that underlie the estimates in columns D and E of table 49.

The estimates in columns F and G assume that only cases with felony circumstances are death-eligible. In Georgia, felony circumstances were present in the cases of 38% of the defendants convicted of murder (by plea or at trial); for those convicted of either murder or voluntary manslaughter the rate was 20%. We applied these death-eligibility rates to produce the estimated pools of death-eligible offenders that underlie the estimates shown in columns F and G. Accordingly, the relevance of these estimates to a given state will, of course, depend on the extent to which its conviction rates differ from Georgia's.

Because various factors, such as the strength of the evidence in a case or a prosecutorial grant of immunity in exchange for testimony, may legitimately remove many cases from the death-eligible category, we made two alternative estimates to take such factors into account. For the first estimate we reduced the final pool of death-eligible cases by 25%. For the second estimate we reduced the final pool by 50%. The 25% reduction caused a 38% increase in the estimated death-sentence rates in Table 49; the 50% reduction in the pool of eligibles increased the estimated death-sentence rates on the order by 100%. For example, the .14 estimated death-sentencing rate for South Carolina (when based only on murder convictions) rises to .19 when 25% of the death-eligible murder convictions are excluded from the pool of death-eligible defendants for strength-of-evidence reasons and to .28 when 50% of the cases are excluded.

32. This judgment is based upon our review of the NAACP Legal Defense Fund's annual state-by-state death-sentence counts. *See supra* note 3 and accompanying text for data on the stability of the rates nationally.

33. We are grateful to Michael Radelet for suggesting the relationship between the practice of judge rather than jury death sentencing and death-sentencing rates. *See generally* Radelet, supra note 15.

34. Henderson & Taylor, *supra* note 13, at A-18, col. 1. This statutory aggravating circumstance accounts for nearly three-quarters of all death sentences imposed.

35. Waseleski, *Grim Equality*, PITTSBURGH POST-GAZETTE, Nov. 28, 1985, at 28.

36. DeParle, *A Matter of Life or Death*, TIMES PICAYUNE (New Orleans), Apr. 7, 1985, at 5 (Special Report).

37. Henderson & Taylor, *supra* note 13, at A-17, col. 1.

38. Murphy, *supra* note 12, at 91.

39. *See supra* figure 30 and accompanying text.

40. H. Kalven and H. Zeisel, THE AMERICAN JURY 33–38 (1966).

41. *Id.* at 45. The results from the full sample showed that the judge and jury agreed in 75% of the cases, 13% of the time to acquit and 62% of the time to convict.

42. *Id.* at 435–36. The jury opted for capital punishment in 19% of the cases, while the judge would have imposed the death sentence in 26% of the cases. Overall, the rate of agreement on sentencing was .81 (90/111)—68% of the time the judge and the jury agreed on a prison sentence and 13% of the time they agreed on a death penalty.

43. *Id.* at 438.

44. *Id.* at 444.

45. *Id.* at 439.

46. *Id.* at 448–49 (footnote omitted).

47. Zimring, Eigen, & O'Malley, *Punishing Homicide in Philadelphia: Perspectives on the Death Penalty*, 43 U. CHI. L. REV. 227 (1976) (hereinafter Zimring, Eigen, & O'Malley).

48. *Id.* at 247.

49. Bedau, *Felony Murder and the Mandatory Death Penalty: A Study in Discretionary Justice*, 10 SUFFOLK U. L. REV. 493, 518 (1976) (hereinafter Bedau).

50. Special Issue, *A Study of the California Penalty Trial in First-Degree-Murder Cases*, 21 STAN. L. REV. 1297 (1969) (the original study) (hereinafter Special Issue); Baldus, Pulaski, Woodworth, & Kyle, *supra* chap. 3, note 14 (our reanalysis).

51. Baldus, Pulaski, Woodworth, & Kyle, *id.* at 66–67. The thirteen variables used to create the culpability index showed a statistically significant relationship with the death-sentencing outcomes and were screened from a pool of over 150 variables for legitimate case characteristics, the balance of which failed to show a significant relationship with the death-sentencing results after adjustment for the thirteen variables used in the model.

52. This comparison is speculative, however, since the pre-*Furman* Georgia data in our analysis, which show substantial excessiveness, were the product of both prosecutorial and jury decisions, while the California data were exclusively the product of jury penalty-trial decisions. If the excessiveness in the pre-*Furman* Georgia data were primarily the product of posttrial prosecutorial decisions, a similar analysis limited to pre-*Furman* Georgia jury decisions might have produced results comparable to those from California.

53. Arkin, *Discrimination and Arbitrariness in Capital Punishment: An Analysis of Post-Furman Murder Cases in Dade County, Florida, 1973–1976*, 33 STAN. L. REV. 75 (1980) (hereinafter Arkin).

54. *Id.* at 86.

55. *Id.* at 94–98. The author found that the following factors did distinguish the life-sentence cases from the death-sentence cases in a meaningful way: (a) the defendants were aged eighteen and twenty years (two cases); (b) the victim was a drug dealer (one case); (c) codefendant sentenced to life (one case); and (d) victim was a participant in a theft (one case). *Id.* at 98–100.

56. *Id.* at 101 (emphasis in original).

57. Nakell & Hardy, *supra* note 17.

58. *Id.* at 104–11.

59. *Id.* at 108–9.

60. *Id.* at 130–44.

61. Further evidence of excessiveness is the fact that the great bulk of the first-degree-murder trials were held in cases in which the multiple-regression model predicted less than a .30 probability that a murder trial would be held in the case. *Id.* at 142.

62. *Id.* at 142.

63. The jury in the case discounted evidence that the defendant was a drug abuser and was under the influence at the time of the killings. The study reports two other female defendants who poisoned their husbands, but overall those cases appear less blameworthy.

64. Colorado Study, *supra* note 20, at figure 30.

65. Because of the low overall death-sentencing rate, the salient-feature method of case matching was the most probative. For Defendant 2, we found one murder-plea case that matched his in terms of the robbery, brutality of the killing, prior record, and the victim having been a stranger. We found two other murder-plea cases that matched his

on all dimensions except prior record, but were comparable in overall culpability because they involved elderly female victims (sixty-three and seventy-nine years of age). We compared Defendant 3 with one coperpetrator, who testified for the state in exchange for a ten-year sentence, and his second coperpetrator, who was given a life sentence at a penalty trial. Two other cases with overall culpability similar to Case 2 resulted in life sentences—one at a penalty trial, the other by a prosecutorial waiver of the death penalty. Case 4's coperpetrator (the actual killer) received a seven-year sentence as an accessory to first-degree murder. Although we found no other case that involved both a contract killing and an insurance motive, as did Case 4, there were seven cases of comparable overall culpability that involved either an insurance motive (one case) or a contract killing (six cases). Five resulted in plea bargains, and the death penalty was unilaterally waived in the other two cases.

66. Bienen et al., *supra* note 18.

67. The authors classify as "death-possible" cases that we have defined as death-eligible through this study.

68. Bienen et al., *supra* note 18, at 169 (table 1).

69. *Id.*

70. *Id.* at 178 (table 7); Fox, *supra* note 18, at A-2, col. 1 (reports penalty-trial death-sentencing rate of .17 [6/35] in northern New Jersey and .40 [25/63] in the state's southern counties).

71. Bowers & Pierce, *Arbitrariness and Discrimination under Post-*Furman *Capital Statutes*, 26 CRIME & DELINQ. 563 (1980) (hereinafter Bowers & Pierce).

72. *Id.* at 602–3.

73. In Georgia, the regional disparities were also substantial for this type of murder, with the highest probability, in the central region (.05), being almost nine times higher than in Fulton County (.006); only the southwest and southeast regions had probabilities about half that of the central region. *Id.* at 603 (table 4).

74. *Id.* at 604.

75. Bowers, *The Pervasiveness of Arbitrariness and Discrimination Under Post-*Furman *Capital Statutes*, 74 J. CRIM. L. & CRIMINOLOGY 1067 (1983) (hereinafter Bowers).

76. *Id.* at 1073, 1079, 1084. As we suggested for Georgia, this result may indicate that closer screening of cases by prosecutors would be expected to produce higher death-sentencing rates among those that reach the penalty-trial stage. Kopeny shows a range of California death-sentencing rates among death-eligible defendants from .06 in Alameda and Los Angeles counties to .46 in San Bernardino County. *Id.* at n.36. Gross & Mauro, *Patterns of Death: An Analysis of Racial Disparities in Capital Sentencing and Homicide Victimization*, 37 STAN. L. REV. 27, 65 (table 18) (1984) (hereinafter Gross & Mauro), report higher death-sentencing rates in rural areas of Georgia, Florida, and Illinois. *See also* S. Gross & R. Mauro, DEATH & DISCRIMINATION: RACIAL DISPARITIES IN CAPITAL SENTENCING (1989). Unadjusted data presented in the Supreme Court Reports of Maryland also suggest substantially higher death-sentencing rates in the rural counties. Tichnell v. State, 468 A.2d at 44 (Md.).

77. Bowers, *supra* note 75, at 1075.

78. Professor Bentele's results are reported *supra* chap. 5, note 43 and accompanying text.

79. Bowers, *supra* note 75, at 1076.

80. Tabak, *The Death of Fairness: The Arbitrary and Capricious Imposition of the Death Penalty in the 1980's*, 14 N.Y.U. REV. L. & SOC. CHANGE 797 (1986).

81. *Id.* at 799–820.

82. *Id.* at 826–47.

83. *Id.* at 848. An interesting comparison to the evidence of infrequency and excessiveness reported in this chapter for the pre- and post-*Furman* periods are the results of M. C. J. Olmesdahl's 1982 study of South African death sentencing in the 1970s. Olmesdahl, *Predicting the Death Sentence*, 6 SACC/SASK 201 (1982) (hereinafter Olmesdahl). Olmesdahl is a senior lecturer in law at the University of Natal, Durban, South Africa. Olmesdahl's analysis proceeds at three levels. First, he presents nationwide death-sentencing rates for all "alleged murders" in South Africa. Second, he describes the disposition of 530 murder indictments processed in Natal in 1979 and in Durban from January 1970 to September 1979. Third, he describes the results of cross-tabular and multiple-regression analyses of death-sentencing decisions in the 542 cases that resulted in a murder-trial conviction in the Durban area from 1971 to 1979. For this part of his study, Olmesdahl read the records or listened to the tapes of each case and prepared a questionnaire with over 120 variables relating to the personal characteristics of the accused and the victim, the nature of the crime, the conduct of the trial, and the personnel of the trial. *Id.* at 206.

The first striking feature of Olmesdahl's data is the high annual homicide rate in South Africa, which appears to be three times greater than the average U.S. rate. Specifically, South Africa's homicide rate appears to be about 25 per 100,000, in contrast to an average rate of about 8 per 100,000 in the U.S. However, the South African rate is comparable to the U.S. 1984 rates in such large urban areas as Washington, D.C. (29 per 100,000), and Detroit (46 per 100,000). *See* FBI UNIFORM CRIME REPORTS: 1984 48, 81 (1985). South Africa's population increased from 16 to 28 million people between 1960 and 1980, with a near doubling of the black population from 11 to 20 million. At the same time, the white population increased by less than 50%, from 3 million to 4.5 million.

Another interesting feature of the South African capital punishment system is the degree to which the numbers of death sentences imposed and executed vary over short periods. During the 1960s, the average number of death sentences imposed was 154, ranging from 107 to 206; the figure declined to an average of 92 from 1970 to 1977. However, in the late 1970s, the number rose again, with an average of 170 for 1977–79. Olmesdahl attributes the decline of the 1970s to rising domestic and international concern about racial discrimination in South Africa generally and in its criminal justice system in particular. He attributes the increased rates of the late 1970s to a "changing political perception" and a perceived need "for a strong hand." The changes cannot be explained by increased homicide rates. *Id.* at 205. There were similar variations in the annual numbers of executions, with an average of 96 in the 1960s, 65 in the early 1970s, and 127 in the late 1970s.

During the two more punitive periods reported in Olmesdahl's article, the number of death sentences imposed appears very high for a country of only 15 to 25 million. Indeed, in the 1960s and late 1970s the rate per 1,000 alleged murders was 29 and 26, respectively. However, during the less punitive period of the early and mid 1970s, the death-sentencing rate per 1,000 murders was only 12, which is comparable to the post-*Furman* rate in this country of 12 death sentences per 1,000 reported murders and nonnegligent manslaughters. *See supra* Table 48. If the South African "alleged murders" category were actually limited to murder, the U.S. rate for murder would probably approach the South African rate during its more punitive periods.

The South African system is also similar to the systems in this country in the high level of pretrial attrition in cases originally indicted for murder. For example, in Natal during 1979 only 33% of the cases indicted for murder resulted in a murder conviction, and only 6% of the murder-indicted cases resulted in a death sentence, a figure almost identical to that observed in Georgia in the period 1973 through 1979. *Id.* at 205 (table E). In Durban during the 1970s the average death-sentencing rate among murder-indicted cases was well under 5%. *Id.* at 204 (diagram A). The rate in Georgia from 1973 to 1979 was 5% among defendants indicted for murder and convicted of murder or voluntary manslaughter.

The results of Olmesdahl's analysis of 542 judicial sentencing decisions in his Durban sample of cases that resulted in a murder-trial conviction are also comparable to our Georgia results. The average death-sentencing rate was .15 (84/542), the same rate observed in our pre-*Furman* Georgia sample, and a rate only somewhat lower than the rate in the post-*Furman* sample. As we note below (*see infra* note 178), 88% of the cases in Olmesdahl's sample involved black victims; these had a death-sentencing rate of .11, while the white-victim cases had a rate of .63.

Olmesdahl also used a multiple-regression analysis of the Durban data to identify the factors that were important in explaining who received death sentences among those convicted of murder. In its level of judicial discretion, the South African system appears quite comparable to the pre-*Furman* systems in this country in that the law prescribes no standards or guidelines for the sentencing authority and also leaves the matter strictly within the discretion of the sentencing judge. Olmesdahl documents variations in death-sentencing rates between magistrates in the same court that rival the geographic disparities in this country, that is, from .o to .28, with good numbers of cases for 16 judges. *Id.* at 205. Of the 100-plus variables for legitimate case characteristics, only 7 showed a statistically significant relationship with the death-sentencing outcomes after adjustment for other factors in a linear multiple-regression analysis: theft motive; the presentation of photographs of the decedent at the sentencing hearing; an alibi defense; use of a gun; the degree of premeditation; the psychiatric history of the defendant; and whether the motive was "exorcism from the evil machinations of a suspected witch or wizard."

The author appears to have used ordinary-least-squares regression procedures, and he reports only total R^2 and R^2 changes associated with the addition of individual variables. The relationship of the defendant and the victim also had an unadjusted strong association with the sentencing outcome, but it was highly correlated with the variables noted above and apparently lost statistical significance in the multiple-regression analysis. *Id.* at 216. The few legitimate variables in Olmesdahl's model explain approximately the same amount of variation in the Durban death-sentencing results as did our models of Georgia's post-*Furman* death-sentencing systems. He reports an R^2 of .46, which contrasts with an R^2 of about .50 for post-*Furman* Georgia models with many more variables. *Id.* The comparison is of interest because the South African "hearing in extenuation," which approximates our postconviction penalty trial, appears to have few of the procedural safeguards that regulate the conduct of penalty trials in this country. Also, South Africa's extenuation hearings are quite perfunctory. Olmesdahl reports that "comparatively little information concerning the offender's personal circumstances is placed before the trial court and whatever is presented has an insignificant effect on whether or not the death sentence is imposed." *Id.* at 217. Nevertheless, it produces an apparent level of consistency that is equivalent to what we observed in Georgia; it is noticeably better than what we see in Colorado and are likely to see in other states with very low death-sentencing rates. *See also* Bruck, *On Death Row in Pretoria Central*, 197 NEW REPUBLIC, July 13 & 20, 1987, at 18 .

84. Brearley, *The Negro and Homicide*, 9 SOC. FORCES 247, 252 (1930).

85. *Id.*

86. T. Sellin, THE PENALTY OF DEATH 57 (1980).

87. W. Bowers, LEGAL HOMICIDE 74 (table 3.1) (1984) (59% for black defendants versus 69% for white defendants).

88. Johnson, *The Negro and Crime*, 217 ANNALS 93 (1941).

89. *Id.* at 99 (calculated from table 1).

90. Garfinkel, *Research Note on Inter- and Intra-racial Homicides*, 27 SOC. FORCES 369 (1949).

91. *Id.* at 374. *See also* W. Bowers's LEGAL HOMICIDE 207–8 (1984) (reanalysis of Johnson's data). The three stages of the process evaluated were indictment for murder versus lesser offense; plea bargain versus trial; and the murder-trial outcome, with a conviction resulting in a mandatory death sentence.

92. Partington, *The Incidence of the Death Penalty for Rape in Virginia*, 22 WASH. & LEE L. REV. 43, 68–70, 72–75 (1965).

93. *Id.* at 52–53.

94. Wolfgang & Riedel, *supra* note 8.

95. *Id.* at 129.

96. *Id.* at 132–33.

97. Wolfgang & Riedel, *Rape, Race, and the Death Penalty in Georgia*, 45 AM. J. ORTHOPSYCHIATRY 658 (1975).

98. *Id.* at 666 (table 1) (F statistic 45.66 with 1,219 degrees of freedom).

99. Wolf, *supra* note 6, at 56.

100. *Id.* at 60 (table III).

101. *Id.* at 61–63 (tables VII, IX, XII).

102. *Id.* at 64n.17.

103. Special Issue, *supra* note 50.

104. *Id.* at 1368–78. After adjustment for "the 18 variables that associate significantly with both penalty and blue-collar defendants," the partial-correlation coefficient for blue-collar defendants increases from -0.0247 to $+0.1241$, "falling just short of significance."

105. Baldus, Pulaski, Woodworth, & Kyle, *supra* chap. 3, note 14.

106. The analysis estimated for the variables "Defendant unemployed at time of crime," a $3\times$ odds multiplier ($p = .05$), and "Defendant had an unstable job history," a $2\times$ odds multiplier ($p = .10$). *Id* at 27–28 (table 1).

107. Bedau, *supra* note 49, at 505.

108. *Id.* at 516. Also, the 111 death-eligible murder cases involving a female victim but no rape resulted in two discretionary death sentences, but the study does not report the race of those two defendants or their victims. *Id.* at 512.

109. Zimring, Eigen, & O'Malley, *supra* note 47, at 227.

110. *Id.* at 247.

111. O. Johnson, *Is the Punishment of Rape Equally Administered to Negroes and Whites in the State of Louisiana?* in CIVIL RIGHTS CONGRESS, WE CHARGE GENOCIDE 216 (W. Patterson ed. 1970); E. Johnson, *Selective Factors in Capital Punishment*, 36 SOC. FORCES 165, 169 (1957).

112. Bedau, *Death Sentences in New Jersey 1907–1960*, 19 RUTGERS L. REV. 1, 19–21 (1964).

113. Bedau, *Capital Punishment in Oregon, 1903–64*, 45 OR. L. REV. 1, 10–12 (1965)("an inference of bias in the use of commutation authority . . . is not supportable in Oregon").

114. Wolfgang, Kelly, & Nolde, *Comparison of the Executed and the Commuted among Admissions to Death Row,* 53 J. Crim. L., Criminology & Police Sci. 301, 306–7 (1962).

115. Kleck, *Racial Discrimination in Criminal Sentencing: A Critical Evaluation of the Evidence with Additional Evidence on the Death Penalty,* 46 Am. Soc. Rev. 783 (1981) (hereinafter Kleck).

116. *Id.* at 794. Kleck's choice of a numerator for the calculation of execution rates serves as an "approximation of the number of persons of that race who committed a homicide." *Id.* at 793.

117. *Id.* at 797–98.

118. Riedel, *Discrimination in the Imposition of the Death Penalty: A Comparison of the Characteristics of Offenders Sentenced Pre-Furman and Post-Furman,* 49 Temp. L. Q. 261 (1976).

119. *Id.* at 276 (table 2).

120. Kleck, *supra* note 115, at 798 (table 6).

121. *Id.* at 797.

122. Greenfeld & Hinners, *Capital Punishment 1984,* in U.S. Dept. of Justice, Bureau of Justice Statistics Bulletin 1, 9 (1985) (table A-2).

123. *Id.* Greenfeld and Hinners also note that while 55% of the victims of murder and nonnegligent homicide were white, it would be reasonable to expect that a larger percentage of those sentenced to death would have white victims, since such contemporaneous felonies as robbery and rape are statutory aggravating circumstances in most death-sentencing jurisdictions and collateral data show that about 77% of rape and robbery victims were white. *Id.* at 10.

124. Bowers & Pierce, *supra* note 71, at 593.

125. *Id.* at 594 (table 2).

126. *Id.* at 599 (table 3).

127. *Id.* at 609 (table 7).

128. *Id.* at 611 (table 8).

129. Radelet, *Racial Characteristics and the Imposition of the Death Penalty,* 46 Am. Soc. Rev. 918 (1981).

130. *Id.* at 925–26. The disparity was not, however, statistically significant beyond the .05 level. *See also,* Radelet & Pierce, *Race and Prosecutorial Discretion in Homicide Cases,* 19 Law & Soc. Rev. 587 (1985) (evidence of prosecutorial bias in the classification of cases as death-eligible because they involve a contemporaneous felony).

131. Zeisel, *Race Bias in the Administration of the Death Penalty: The Florida Experience,* 95 Harv. L. Rev. 456 (1981).

132. *Id.* at 459 (table 1).

133. *Id.* at 461 (figure 2).

134. Foley & Powell, *The Discretion of Prosecutors, Judges, and Juries in Capital Cases,* 7 Crim. Just. Rev. 16 (1982).

135. *Id.* at 18–22.

136. Arkin, *supra* note 53.

137. *Id.* at 89 (table 4). White-victim cases also resulted in either a life or a death sentence, rather than a less severe disposition, at a slightly higher rate than did black-victim cases—.62 (70/113) for the white-victim cases versus .52 (15/29) for the black-victim cases.

138. Bowers, *supra* note 75.

139. *Id.* at 1073 (table 1). (The linear-regression coefficients were black defendant/

white victim, .19, significant at the .05 level; white defendant/white victim, .15, significant at the .01 level; and white defendant/black victim, −.08, not statistically significant beyond the .05 level.)

140. *Id.* at 1079 (table 3). (The linear-regression coefficients were black defendant/white victim, .29, significant at the .01 level; white defendant/white victim, .18, significant at the .01 level; white defendant/black victim, −.07, not statistically significant beyond the .05 level.)

141. *Id.* at 1084–85 (table 4). (The linear-regression coefficient for white-victim cases was .13, significant at the .11 level.)

142. *Id.* at 1073 (table 1). (The linear-regression coefficient for the court-appointed-attorney variable was .17, significant at the .01 level.)

143. *Id.* at 1084 (table 4). (The linear-regression coefficients were .22 for the court-appointed-attorney variable, significant at the .01 level, and .16 for the public-defender variable, significant at the .05 level.)

144. Paternoster (84), *supra* note 29; Paternoster, *Race of Victim and Location of Crime: The Decision to Seek the Death Penalty in South Carolina,* 74 J. CRIM. L. & CRIMINOLOGY 754 (1983).

145. Paternoster (84), *supra* note 29, at 467. (The race-of-victim ordinary-least-squares coefficient in single-felony cases was .519, significant at the .05 level; table 1A.)

146. *Id.* at 466. (The linear-regression coefficient for black defendants was .12, not significant beyond the .10 level.)

147. Murphy, *supra* note 12.

148. *Id.* at 93 (tables 4, 5).

149. *Id.*

150. Gross & Mauro, *supra* note 76.

151. *Id.* at 97n.187, 78 (table 24), 96 (table 32).

152. *Id.* at 78 (table 24). The logistic-regression coefficient in the Gross & Mauro analysis was 1.97, significant beyond the .001 level. The same statistic estimated in an analysis of our PRS data with the same five background variables (weapon was a gun, victim was a stranger, contemporaneous felony, two or more victims, and a female victim) was 1.2, significant beyond the .0001 level.

153. Their analysis reflected the combined effects of decisions from arrest to sentence, while ours reflected the combined impact of only the final two stages in the process—the prosecutorial decision to seek and the jury decision to impose a death sentence.

154. Gross & Mauro, *supra* note 76, at 74 (table 23).

155. Berk and Lowery, *supra* note 19.

156. *Id.* at 10–16.

157. *Id.* at 19–20.

158. In terms of the flow of the cases through the system, the results were generally comparable to what we have seen in similar studies, with one key exception. The decision to indict appears to be much more selective in Mississippi. Of the 404 defendants in the sample, only 26% (*n* = 105) were indicted for murder. Of these cases, 65% resulted in a capital-murder conviction, and 58% of these cases advanced to a penalty trial. Of the penalty trials, 60% resulted in a death penalty, yielding a death-sentencing rate of .22 among those indicted for murder, which is much higher than, for example, Georgia or Colorado. *Id.* at 18–19.

159. *Id.* at 23 (tables 1–4).

160. *Id.* at 44–45 (tables 7–8). A propensity analysis sorts cases with an index comprising the variables that best predict whether a case has a white or a black victim, rather than whether it receives a death sentence. The procedure then determines the extent to which death-sentencing (or other selection) rates are the same for white- and black-victim cases with comparable propensity scores.

161. *Supra* chap. 6, note 19 and accompanying text.

162. Berk & Lowery, *supra* note 19, at 48–49.

163. Nakell & Hardy, *supra* note 17, at 132–46.

164. *Id.* at 147.

165. *Id.* at 146 (table 23 shows a race-of-defendant coefficient of 1.3, significant at the .11 level).

166. *Id.* at 158–59.

167. Bienen et al., *supra* note 18, at 170–71 (table 2).

168. *Id.* at 235–39 (table 33). The article does not provide sufficient information for us to compute the levels of statistical significance of the observed racial disparities, and the small sample sizes of some of the subgroups of cases (e.g., only five white/Hispanic crimes) suggests some of the estimates may be unstable.

169. *Id.* at 226–27 (table 32). The logistic-regression coefficients in the trial (1) versus plea (0) analysis by race of victim were 1.06 (significant at the .10 level) for white-victim cases and −.59 (not significant at the .10 level) for black-victim cases, with the Hispanic-victim cases as the reference population. The study does not present the results of a multivariate analysis of the actual death-sentencing results.

170. Klemm, *supra* note 15, at 124 (for the unadjusted data) and at 236 (for the regression results that did not indicate the statistical significance of the race-of-victim disparity, which we calculated from the data reported).

171. Colorado Study, *supra* note 20, at 44.

172. Timms & McGonigle, *Blacks Rejected From Juries in Capital Cases*, Dallas Morning News, Dec. 21, 1986, at 20A, col. 3.

173. *Id.*

174. *Id.* at 20A, col. 3–4. In the three largest counties, the overall percentages of blacks in the population, in the jury venire, and on the capital juries were approximately as follows: Harris County (Houston), .20, .20, .08; Dallas County (Dallas), .18, .16, .04; and Bexar County (San Antonio), .06, .05, .05. *Id.* at 1, col. 3.

175. *Id.* at 20A, col. 1.

176. The data reported by Timms and McGonigle relate to a period before the Supreme Court decision in Batson v. Kentucky, 106 S.Ct. 1712 (1986), which limits the freedom of prosecutors to use peremptories to exclude minority jurors. *Id.* at 21A, col. 2–3. The discriminatory use of peremptory challenges in Texas is not restricted to capital cases. Timms & McGonigle, *Race Bias Pervades Jury Selection*, Dallas Morning News, March 9, 1986, p. 1, presents the results of a study of 100 Dallas County felony trials in 1983 and 1984 that were randomly selected from a universe of 1,036 felony trials. The data indicated that while blacks constitute 18% of the population of Dallas County and 16% of the people summoned for jury service, they constitute only 4% of those selected for jury service. As a result of the exercise of peremptory challenges, only 2 of the 54 black male defendants in the sample had a black male on their juries. In contrast, all 38 of the Anglo defendants had a majority of Anglos on their juries. *Id.* at 28A, col. 2.

While the jury call for these 100 cases produced 467 eligible black potential jurors, 87% (405/467) were struck by the exercise of prosecutorial peremptory challenges.

Three % (16/467) were struck by defense counsel peremptory challenges, which left only 10% (46/467) of the original call who actually served as jurors. *Id.*

177. Henderson & Taylor, *supra* note 13. *See also* Radelet & Vandiver, *Race and Capital Punishment: An Overview of the Issues,* 25 CRIME & SOC. JUS. 94 (1986).

178. The 1982 Olmesdahl study of death sentencing in Durban, South Africa, from January 1971 to December 1979, *supra* note 83, contrasts with the race-of-defendant and race-of-victim disparities observed in American death-sentencing jurisdictions. The Olmesdahl data show an unadjusted death-sentencing rate that is higher for white defendants than for black defendants (.29 for white defendants versus .15 for black defendants). Olmesdahl, *Predicting the Death Sentence,* 6 SACC/SASK 201, 208, table F (1982). There are two problems with his analysis, however. First, it does not control for the race of the victim; second, there are only 7 white-defendant cases, as opposed to 461 black-defendant/black-victim cases, which would swamp any differential treatment of black and white defendants in the cases that do not involve a black victim. *Id.* at 210 (table I). The article presents no data on the number of white defendants indicted. But the trial-conviction figures suggest either that there are very few white homicide defendants or that whites are permitted to plead to *lesser* offenses and avoid the risk of a death sentence before trial.

The unadjusted race-of-victim data show death-sentencing rates of .11 for black-victim cases (*n* = 470), .63 for white-victim cases (*n* = 24), .46 for Asian-victim cases (*n* = 37), and .0 for "coloured"-victim cases (*n* = 11). *Id.* at 209 (table H). Regrettably, the article does not present death-sentencing rates broken down by the defendant-victim racial combination. The comparable unadjusted Georgia death-sentencing rates for 1973–78 are .07 for the black-victim cases and .27 the white-victim cases. *See supra* chap. 6, table 30.

Olmesdahl further reports the results of a multiple-regression analysis, presumably an ordinary-least-squares procedure, in which the race of the accused is "not associated with" the death-sentencing decision. He also reports that the "race of the victim (though at first examination a highly significant factor) drops out as a variable with high explanatory power when the compounding effects of other variables are removed." *Id.* at 216. It is possible, of course, that the race of the victim has no effect, since 89% of the cases involve black victims. It is possible, however, that the race-of-victim effect in Olmesdahl's regression analysis is obscured by the "pictures of the deceased admitted at trial," the second most important variable in his analysis. Because this variable has a .45 correlation with the race-of-victim variable, its presence in the regression analysis could be masking a race-of-victim effect. Regrettably, the article does not provide enough information to test that possibility. Also, the limitation of the analysis to posttrial sentencing decisions makes it impossible to determine the magnitude of both race-of-victim and race-of-defendant effects that may be felt earlier in the process. Olmesdahl notes in passing an earlier empirical study that suggested there was racial bias in the imposition of the death sentence in South Africa. For his efforts, the author of that study was charged with criminal contempt but acquitted after trial. *Id.* at 204.

179. Kleck, *supra* note 115, at 799; Kleck, *Life Support for Ailing Hypotheses: Modes of Summarizing the Evidence for Racial Discrimination in Sentencing,* 9 LAW & HUM. BEHAV. 271, 272 (1985) (hereinafter Kleck (85)); W. Wilbanks, THE MYTH OF A RACIST CRIMINAL JUSTICE SYSTEM 119–20 (1987) (hereinafter Wilbanks).

180. Kleck, *supra* note 115, at 799; Kleck (85), *supra* note 179, at 272; Wilbanks, *id.* at 120; 1 RESEARCH ON SENTENCING: THE SEARCH FOR REFORM 88–108 (A. Blumstein, J. Cohn, S. Martin, & M. Tonry eds. 1983).

181. Johnson, *Black Innocence and the White Jury*, 83 MICH. L. REV. 1611, 1625–34 (1985).

182. Only a few mock-jury studies focus on race-of-victim discrimination; however, the results of those that do are consistent with the findings in the nonexperimental literature in that they show strong and fairly consistent race-of-victim effects.

CHAPTER NINE

Comparative-Proportionality Review in Other State Courts

In chapter 7, we described the Georgia Supreme Court's system of proportionality review in death-sentence cases. Since 1973, Georgia's post-*Furman* death-sentencing reforms, including its provision for proportionality review, have been adopted in a large number of jurisdictions.[1] Many of these adoptions occurred following United States Supreme Court decisions in the mid and late 1970s invalidating mandatory death sentencing and systems that failed to provide adequately for the admissibility of mitigating evidence in the penalty trial.[2] However, since *Pulley v. Harris*, which ruled that a system of proportionality review is not constitutionally required, a small countertrend may be developing. At least four states that originally adopted the Georgia system have repealed the statutory requirement of comparative proportionality review.[3]

In this chapter we compare the Georgia experience with comparative proportionality review, which we reported in chapter 7, with the experience of the other states that conduct proportionality review. The available evidence indicates that while the basic statutory schemes in these other jurisdictions are quite comparable to Georgia's, the systems that have evolved vary quite a bit. In spite of these differences, however, a common characteristic of most of these state courts is an apparent inability or unwillingness to monitor their capital-sentencing systems in a sufficiently consistent, comprehensive, and principled manner to identify excessive or discriminatory sentences when they occur. To the extent that this conclusion is correct, it tends to support the hypotheses of Justice Rehnquist and Professor Dix that proportionality-review procedures are either inherently ineffective or impossible to apply in an effective way.[4] While we agree that to date the average performance of the state supreme courts has not been encouraging, we do not believe the impossibility hypothesis has been proven. First, the process is new and complicated, and the state courts have been working with it for a relatively short time. Second, during the past twelve years the foundation for a reasonably effective system has been laid in several states, while in others there has been progress in identifying, although not satisfactorily resolving, the problems presented by proportionality review.

280

THE IMPACT OF PROPORTIONALITY REVIEW

In his dissenting opinion in *Pulley v. Harris*, Justice Brennan characterized the impact of the proportionality-review system as slight.[5] Specifically, he could identify only twelve murder cases in which death sentences had been vacated on the ground of excessiveness. Our survey, which was exhaustive through 1986, has identified an additional ten cases that were vacated on the ground of excessiveness before *Pulley v. Harris* and an additional nine cases since that decision. All together, we have identified thirty-one death sentences that have been vacated on the ground of comparative excessiveness.[6] Unlike Georgia, cases involving successful claims of disproportionality elsewhere are more likely to be based on findings of intercase disproportionality (75 percent) than on findings of intracase disproportionality in the sentences of coperpetrators.

THE PATTERN OF FREQUENCY AND PRECEDENT-SEEKING PROPORTIONALITY-REVIEW SYSTEMS

In this section, we describe the various types of proportionality-review systems and policies reflected in the reported decisions of the various state courts. We make this presentation against the background of the findings and recommendations of the National Center for State Courts (NCSC) Project on Comparative Proportionality Review in Death Sentence Cases (1982–84).[7] For this project, the NCSC impaneled a task force of prosecutors, defense attorneys, state supreme court administrative officials, and academics to develop technical support for state supreme courts seeking to implement an effective comparative-sentence-review process. The task force also developed a series of recommendations on the methodology and procedures most likely to enhance the effectiveness of a review process.

As we mentioned in chapter 7, there are two basic approaches to the conduct of proportionality reviews, although, as our study of the Georgia system indicated, there are numerous possible variations. The first of these approaches we refer to as "precedent-seeking," since courts applying it affirm or vacate a death sentence on the basis of even one or two prior death-sentence cases that seem comparable. In other words, so long as death sentences have occurred in one or more prior cases of comparable or less culpability, this expression of community values is sufficient to justify the reasonableness of the death case before the court.[8] Some courts, however, seek out considerably more than two or three life or death cases to justify affirmance of the death sentence under review.

The other general approach is the "frequency approach." A court following this strategy identifies both life- and death-sentence cases comparable to the case being reviewed, determines the proportion of defendants in those similar cases who were sentenced to die, and makes a legal judgment as to whether the relative frequency of death sentences within that group is insufficiently large to warrant affirming the death sentence on appeal. In making this judgment the reviewing court must decide what minimum frequency is necessary to justify the death penalty as an effective deterrent or as a justifiable form of retribution in light of contemporary community standards.

Obviously, the frequency approach to proportionality review is more complicated and demanding than the precedent-seeking approach. Nevertheless, the NCSC task force strongly recommended the frequency approach as the only conceivable way to achieve an effective proportionality-review process.[9] One reason for the NCSC task force's support of the frequency approach to proportionality is that a reviewing court is unable to assess whether the death-sentencing statute in its jurisdiction is being applied in a principled and consistent fashion unless the court is aware of the relative frequency of the imposition of the death sentence among cases of similar culpability. Also, the frequency of death sentencing is a useful measure of both the extent to which death sentences in a given class of cases are likely to have a deterrent effect and the extent to which they reflect a judgment of the community that death is the appropriate punishment in such cases.

Our investigation indicates that not a single state court has explicitly raised the question of whether it should adopt a precedent-seeking rather than a frequency approach to proportionality review. Moreover, we have found only four courts (Louisiana, North Carolina, Pennsylvania, and Virginia) that appear to be applying a frequency approach.[10] None of these courts, however, quantifies the death-sentencing frequencies observed among similar cases. Further, neither the North Carolina nor the Virginia court documents its analysis with sufficient specificity to enable one to calculate the frequencies it observes. The Pennsylvania court, in contrast, reports the number of death and life cases in the pool of similar cases. Its system appears to come closest to the model envisioned by the NCSC task force on proportionality review.[11] In all other jurisdictions with reported cases, the court either has expressly adopted a precedent-seeking approach[12] or has, as we found in Georgia, left the matter of basic approach in a state of some uncertainty.[13]

THE SCOPE OF THE SEARCH FOR SIMILAR CASES

Regardless of the basic approach to proportionality review used by a reviewing court, it is essential for the court to define the boundaries or parameters of the universe or pool of potentially similar cases in which it conducts its search for cases that are similar to the death-sentence case under review. Five populations of cases provide the most commonly mentioned alternatives:

1. Cases indicted for capital murder that result in a homicide conviction
2. Cases resulting in a capital-murder conviction by plea or at trial
3. Cases resulting in a capital-murder conviction at trial
4. Cases that advance to a penalty trial
5. Cases that result in a death sentence

On this issue, the NCSC task force recommended that:

> the pool of cases for a proportionality review system should contain, as a minimum, all cases in which the indictment included a death-eligible charge, and a homicide conviction was obtained. In most jurisdictions, this guideline will mean all cases in which the defendant was charged with first-degree murder and convicted of first- or second-degree murder or manslaughter.

The task force also recommended that the pool should include "convictions resulting from a plea of guilty as well as those following a trial."[14]

The task force's recommendation recognizes that the typical capital-charging-and-sentencing system consists of five or six decision points, ranging from indictment to the penalty-trial decision. Further, the recommendation assumes that concerns about arbitrariness or discrimination relate to the operation of the entire capital-charging-and-sentencing process and are not limited to the final one or two decision points. The task force's recommendations ensure that the decisions of prosecutors and juries at all stages beyond indictment are subject to judicial oversight.[15]

Whether a court considers life-sentence cases in its proportionality-review analysis and how broad a pool of cases it considers are particularly important if the court applies a frequency approach, since the number of life-sentence cases that the court identifies as similar will directly affect the observed death-sentencing frequency among similar cases. For example, if seven death sentences have been imposed in a given class of case, the relative frequency of death sentencing in the class will be quite different if the court finds three similar life cases, .70 (7/10), from its finds thirty similar life cases, .19 (7/37). The issue is also important in a precedent-seeking jurisdiction, since the scope of the court's inquiry will influence the likelihood that it may find significant numbers of life-sentence cases that it considers comparable to the death-sentence case under review.

The policies of the state supreme courts on this issue vary considerably, and none that have conducted proportionality reviews appears to comply with the recommendation of the NCSC task force. Specifically, at least six states narrowly restrict their inquiry by limiting their search to cases that resulted in a death sentence.[16] This practice has been widely criticized by commentators and by a number of dissenting justices.[17] Limiting the inquiry to death-sentence cases significantly enhances the likelihood that any death-sentence case reviewed by the court will not be found excessive or disproportionate.

Such a policy does not, however, totally foreclose the likelihood of finding a death sentence to be excessive and disproportionate. For example, the Mississippi court, which limits its review to death-sentence cases, found one death sentence disproportionate because the case was less aggravated than any of the death-sentence cases in its comparison pool.[18] More important, however, the exclusion of life-sentence cases from the review process distorts the picture of comparative-sentencing practices, a problem that exists even if the court applies a strict precedent-seeking approach.

The most common practice both in the jurisdictions applying a frequency approach and in the precedent-seeking jurisdictions that consider both life and death cases is to limit the inquiry to cases that advance to a penalty trial.[19] This policy has also been criticized because it excludes from judicial oversight such a large part of the state's capital-sentencing system, especially the decisions of prosecutors.[20] Other state courts follow Georgia's declared policy of considering life-sentence capital-murder cases that did not reach a penalty trial.[21] Finally, in a number of states there is a further policy restricting the court's inquiry to appealed cases.[22] This policy excludes not only trial convictions from which no appeal was taken, but also all cases that end in plea bargains, many of which are highly aggravated.[23]

State courts also impose a variety of geographic and temporal limitations on the scope of their proportionality-review inquiries. On the geography issue, most courts consider cases from throughout the state. The principal exception is the Louisiana court, which initially limits its analysis to cases that arose in the parish in which the death sentence under review was imposed.[24] If there are insufficient cases to conduct a review at a parishwide level, however, the court looks for similar cases throughout the state.[25] In addition, some states with small populations and low homicide rates have looked at the sentencing patterns in other states as a source of precedent.[26] Problems with small samples have also induced some states to consider sentencing decisions made in their jurisdiction before either *Furman* or the effective date of the post-*Furman* statute adopted in the late 1970s.[27] Although these practices have been criticized,[28] they appear to have become less common as the pools of post-*Furman* homicides have inevitably grown.

PROCEDURAL IMPEDIMENTS TO EFFECTIVE PROPORTIONALITY REVIEW

Needless to say, the manner in which state supreme courts define the outer limits of the pool of potentially similar cases can handicap even their best efforts to monitor a death-sentencing system effectively. Another potentially distortive practice employed by some state courts is to include in the pool of potentially similar cases death-sentence cases that were reversed on appeal. In this respect the NCSC task force made the following recommendations:

> A second guideline agreed upon by the task force is that cases in which the conviction or sentence is reversed should be dropped from the pool, regardless of the grounds for reversal. Although it can be argued that when the sentencing procedure itself is not directly tainted, the sentence reflects an expression of a community's attitude regarding the crime and the offender and should, therefore, remain in the pool, it is difficult to discern what effect an error during the trial may have had on the sentencing decision. Therefore, the safer and wiser course is to remove a case from the pool of potentially similar cases if either the conviction or the sentence is overturned on appeal or pursuant to a *habeas corpus* petition or other collateral attack, and to enter the sentence imposed if the defendant is reconvicted for homicide.[29]

Our survey of state court practices indicates that this issue has been raised in several jurisdictions. A number of states' policies are consistent with the recommendations of the NCSC task force in that no vacated death sentences are included.[30] Other jurisdictions regularly include vacated death sentences in their proportionality analysis,[31] while still other jurisdictions examine the reason for the reversal to determine if it suggests a reason for excluding it from the analysis.[32]

A third limitation on effective proportionality review characteristic of current practices is the general failure of state courts to develop general measures of case culpability so that they can identify comparable cases regardless of factual differences. Many courts appear to structure the search for comparable cases in terms of factual similarities. This measure of case culpability is highly relevant when it can be applied. But even in jurisdictions with large numbers of capital cases, the number of factually similar cases is nearly always too small to permit a reliable judgment about the kinds of cases that usually result in death sentences.[33] Furthermore, this approach totally deprives the appellate court of the ability to compare the case under review and other factually different cases of comparable culpability. A principal conclusion of our research is that perhaps the major barrier to the emergence of effective systems of proportionality review is the failure of the courts thus far to develop overall measures of case culpability that will allow a reviewing court to compare cases without regard to strict factual identity. Whether such a measure is based on intuition or an objective classification system, an overall culpability measure will allow a court to rank or otherwise categorize all of the cases in its jurisdiction. Such a system will permit the court to identify in an objective and principled manner the types of cases in which it considers death sentencing appropriate and inappropriate. A further conclusion of our research is that the development of effective and valid measures of overall case culpability is feasible without the use of complicated statistical procedures.[34]

Our reading of the state supreme court opinions suggests that some courts do use an overall measure of case culpability that does not demand strict factual comparability.[35] These opinions, however, do not explain the rationale and basis for the approach when it is used.

Finally, state supreme courts have generally impeded the proportionality-review process by failing to make available to the parties to the litigation the case-file information on the cases considered by the court in its proportionality-review process. The National Center for State Courts task force considered this failure an important concern. It recommended that, at a minimum, state supreme courts should inform counsel of the selection criteria and analytic methods that they used in the review process. The task force also stated its belief that

> means should be provided for counsel to use the system in preparing their briefs and arguments on proportionality. . . . [T]he proportionality review process will work most effectively and fairly when counsel for both parties are able to conduct analyses using the same pool of cases, information, and techniques available to the appellate court.[36]

We have seen only a limited willingness on the part of state supreme courts to provide this sort of information to the parties.[37] Indeed, some courts have suggested that securing the necessary information to challenge the proportionality of a death sentence is the responsibility of the defense counsel.[38] Based on our own experience in collecting information of this type—which, in Georgia alone, required several years' work and substantial expense—we believe that to expect defense attorneys to secure such information is patently unreasonable. This attitude is particularly regrettable when the information is, in fact, available in the appellate court's own files.

Further, because state supreme courts have generally failed to adopt methods of proportionality review that would enable them to identify sentencing patterns within their jurisdiction, they are also unable to identify evidence of racial discrimination in the imposition of death sentences. Indeed, we have found no case in which an appellate court vacated a death sentence on the ground that racial considerations actually influenced the sentence imposed.[39]

PRINCIPLE AND OBJECTIVITY IN THE PROPORTIONALITY-REVIEW PROCESS

The enactment of proportionality-review statutes in the middle and late 1970s presented state supreme courts with difficult legal and methodological issues in a highly charged and very visible area of public policy. It was to be expected that there would be a substantial amount of experimentation on the part of the state courts as the issues became better understood and the experiences of the courts became more widely known. Indeed, the last few years have seen a distinct increase in the courts' grasp of the issues, but progress in resolving them successfully has been uneven and generally slow.

We have also seen substantial differences between the state courts in how objective, explicit, and principled their decisions have been. In this regard the courts have done much better in their treatment of general questions concerning the procedures they will generally follow in conducting their reviews (for example, the pool of cases to be considered) than they have in the application of their general procedures in specific cases.

Nevertheless, even on the basic procedural issues, some courts have been quite obscure about the general policies they apply in their reviews.[40] Especially in recent years, however, an increasing number of courts have clarified the issues, systematically reviewed the pattern of decisions in other states, and clearly explained the course of action they have chosen to follow. Good examples are recent decisions from Delaware and Maryland addressing the issue of the pool of cases to be considered in a proportionality review.[41] Nevertheless, even the courts that have clearly explained what they are doing have rarely explained why they have preferred one approach to another. Generally, the policy implications of the decisions are simply ignored. Moreover, as we noted earlier, not a single judicial opinion has, to our knowledge, squarely addressed the basic question of whether the court should apply a frequency or a precedent-seeking approach in conducting proportionality review.

As noted above, the performance of the courts in explaining and justifying their decisions in individual cases has been even less satisfactory. Opinions of some courts have completely obscured the review process that led to the decision. No hint is given of the selection criteria used, how they were applied, and what cases the court deemed to be comparable to the case under review. Such opinions are purely perfunctory and conclusory. A typical opinion of this genre limits its proportionality-review analysis to an assertion that the court had compared the case before it to all previous death sentences in the jurisdiction and concludes that the death sentence under review is not excessive or disproportionate.[42] Not surprisingly, the opaqueness of such undocumented opinions has produced criticism and disgruntled dissents.[43]

A slightly more principled class of opinions are those in which the case characteristics used to define similar cases are identified, but nothing further is specified beyond the legal conclusion that the death sentence is not excessive or disproportionate. This pattern, frequently found in early Georgia cases, is quite common elsewhere.[44]

Next, a growing number of opinions first define a broad category of a potentially relevant type, such as armed robbery. They then go on to identify and summarize the particular facts of the cases deemed most comparable to the review cases but offer no explanation as to why the specific cases chosen are similar to the case under review.[45]

Finally, there are opinions that push the analysis further by making specific factual comparisons between the review case and the life- and death-sentence cases called to the court's attention by the parties. The courts most often reach this level of analysis in cases involving claims of disproportionality between the sentences of one or more coperpetrators, one of whom received a death sentence while the other(s) did not. The opinions regularly make fine-grain factual comparisons to justify a conclusion that a coperpetrator is more or less culpable than the death-sentenced defendant before the court.[46] The problem, however, is that the opinions consistently fail to explain why, as a matter of policy, the factual distinction that the court considers sufficient to "distinguish" one or more life-sentence cases from the death-sentence case under review should or should not justify a death sentence. Sometimes the court will make the completely speculative assertion that the factual differences it has identified as important explain why juries or prosecutors treated the coperpetrators differently.[47] Normally, however, we are left with no more than the court's conclusion that the factual distinction specified by the court meaningfully distinguished the death case from the life-sentence cases offered to the court by the defendant. As a result, these decisions have a distinctly ad hoc and result-oriented quality.[48]

There are two principal sources of difficulty in cases involving claims of disproportionality between the sentences of coperpetrators. The first is the inability of the court to ever know what motivated the jury or a prosecutor in a given case; the second is the limitation imposed by the inevitably small sample of cases involved in comparison between two or three people. Without some external objective measure of culpability that would allow the court to compare the death-sentenced defendant under review and his coperpetrator with larger pools of defendants, the court has no choice but to rely on its own intuition as to whether factual differences between the cases should "distinguish" them as a matter of law.[49] This problem can be avoided, however, by expanding the inquiry to consider how defendants similar to the review case and each of the various coperpetrators are treated generally. If a high proportion of offenders similar to a life-sentenced coperpetrator generally receive a life sentence, and most defendants similar to the death-sentenced offender before the court receive death-sentences, the court will have a basis for believing that the factual differences between the defendant under review and his coperpertrators are generally important in the eyes of juries and prosecutors and, therefore, a "material" basis for distinguishing their cases. However, if defendants similar to a life-sentenced coperpetrator normally receive death sentences, factual differences between the coperpetrator and the review case would not be viewed as material; the life sentence imposed in such a coperpetrator's case would be properly viewed as itself aberrant and appropriately discounted as a reason for holding the death sentence under review to be excessive. In both of these situations, the reference to an external measure of defendant culpability, that is, how frequently death sentences are imposed in similar cases, avoids the highly subjective and ad hoc nature of so many of these cases. The main point is that no matter how appealing intracase comparisons may be, they should not distract the court from the central issue in the case, which is how offenders similar to the death-sentenced defendant before the court are normally sentenced.

We see the same problems of inconsistency and unpredictability when courts undertake case-by-case factual comparisons in cases involving claims of intercase disproportionality. Without reference to a common measure of culpability, it is impossible to justify in a principled manner why certain factual differences between cases are or are not "material." *Munn v. State*,[50] an Oklahoma decision, is illustrative on this point. The court defined the relevant pool of cases as those "in which an accused has killed a close family member without provocation and raised a reasonable doubt as to his insanity at the time of the crime."[51] On the basis of this classification, the court found the defendant before it to be "remarkably similar in regard to both the defendant and the crime" in a life-sentence case and, on that basis, declared the death sentence to be disproportionate within the meaning of the statute. In a special concurrence, Justice Brett questioned the narrow choice of the two case characteristics used to define the class of similar cases, since they ignore that the defendant had knocked down his parents' bedroom door, beat and stabbed his father forty times, eviscerated his abdominal organs and heart, and tried to stab a police officer while resisting arrest. Justice Brett argued that the court's comparative analysis would have looked quite different had all of these factors been used to identify similar cases.[52]

This case illustrates the point that without some external and predetermined measure of overall culpability, it is simply impossible to determine which characterization of any two cases is correct. An overall measure used for this purpose should be based on a classification of the cases that takes into account all factors that could conceivably be considered relevant, thereby avoiding debate over the materiality of any given facts. The court would then have compared the frequency with which death sentences were imposed among the near neighbors of both the case under review and the life case relied upon by the court for evidence of any material difference in rates at which they result in a death sentence.

The dangers of ad hoc, unprincipled decisions exist even in a system like Pennsylvania's, which appears to come closest to the model envisioned by the NCSC task force. For example, in one case the Pennsylvania court treated as similar all cases with the statutory aggravating circumstance that the defendant had been convicted earlier of a crime carrying a life or death sentence,[53] while in another case it treated as similar cases with that aggravating circumstance and one additional mitigating circumstance.[54] And in yet another example, the court's classification embraced cases that did not present any mitigating circumstances and in which the prosecution proved at least one, and in most cases two or more, aggravating circumstances. The court also considered relevant a subset of those cases in which there were "no mitigating circumstances and the same two aggravating circumstances (killing a person while in the perpetration of a felony and the defendant having a significant history of felony convictions involving the use or threat of violence to the person)."[55] Although there may well be some basis for the use of these different case classifications, in the absence of a rationale that can be applied consistently across cases, the appearance of an ad hoc, result-oriented jurisprudence is inevitable.

The appearance of unprincipled decision making is also enhanced by the failure of courts to document the results of their proportionality-review process. There is no justification for failing to describe briefly all of the cases (with outcome) it deems similar to the case under review.

WHY HAS PROPORTIONALITY REVIEW FAILED THUS FAR?

The general failure of state supreme courts to monitor their death-sentencing systems effectively is regrettable. This is especially so, we believe, because state appellate courts are, in fact, capable of providing the necessary oversight to eliminate instances of excessiveness or discrimination from their capital-sentencing systems.[56] Thus, it becomes particularly important to determine why the state supreme courts have generally failed to meet this challenge. There are several possible explanations; some are quite speculative, while others are suggested by court opinions.

First, some state supreme courts may have taken the view that the sort of demanding investigation required for an effective proportionality review is unnecessary. The United States Supreme Court has ruled that, as a matter of constitutional procedure, proportionality review is not necessary in death-sentence cases; and most state statutes mandating proportionality review are relatively vague concerning the reviewing courts' precise responsibilities. Now post–*McCleskey v. Kemp* defendants can no longer allege that their death sentences are unconstitutionally excessive or discriminatory in violation of the Eighth or Fourteenth Amendments.[57] But even before *McCleskey* defendants bore the burden of proof, and they were notably unsuccessful in persuading reviewing courts to conduct full-scale comparative reviews.[58]

Second, some state supreme courts may regard this sort of systematic review procedure as unnecessary because, based on intuition and anecdotal evidence, they believe their state's death-sentencing system is operating satisfactorily. Of course, the available empirical evidence strongly suggests that such intuitive judgments are wrong. Without systematically scrutinizing the operation of the entire system, however, no court can accurately assess the degree of consistency in sentencing results. Furthermore, value-laden considerations can strongly influence such perceptions. It is noteworthy that many defense attorneys believe the capital-sentencing process is as arbitrary and discriminatory today as in the pre-*Furman* era, while most prosecutors strongly argue the opposite view. The available data fully support neither position, thereby suggesting the danger of relying upon intuitive judgments when evaluating the operation of a complex social process.

A third possible explanation for the failure of state supreme courts to implement effective oversight procedures is that they do not feel competent to perform the functions that such a process requires. Normally, appellate courts decide cases on an individual basis, not by analyzing broad decision-making processes.[59] Some courts may be reluctant to undertake a task that is more familiar to statisticians and social scientists than to judges and lawyers. In particular, they may be deterred by what they believe to be the necessity of using computers and arcane statistical procedures and the responsibility that the typical state statutes place on its supreme court to develop the review system. In a typical discrimination case, by way of contrast, the burden is on the litigants to develop any technical analyses that are required.

Finally, some courts may be persuaded that the analytic methods currently available can never provide sufficiently reliable answers about the excessiveness or discriminatory character of any given death sentence for the purposes of judicial decision making. They may believe that the highly discretionary nature of the death-sentence selection process and the large number of tangible and intangible factors that may legitimately influence each step of the process make it impossible to collect all the necessary information required for a reliable analysis. This concern may be particularly great with respect to certain intangible but potentially influential factors such as the strength of the evidence of guilt, the defendant's appearance or demeanor, and the eloquence of the attorneys.[60]

Another argument in favor of this "impossibility" hypothesis is the difficulty of choosing other cases that are similar in terms of the relevant criteria to the death-sentence case being reviewed. Notwithstanding the presence of common factors, there are always differences between cases. Unless a court can confidently select pools of truly comparable cases, it cannot effectively monitor the degree of excessiveness or discrimination in the system.[61] Advocates of this view may acknowledge that social scientists have devised methods to overcome such problems, but only, they will argue, for academic or research purposes. They will insist that greater reliability than social science methods can provide is essential for deciding cases. They may also contend that such statistical techniques as multiple-regression analysis are simply incomprehensible to most litigants and judges and, therefore, have no place in the courts.[62] Our research has convinced us, however, that the conduct of a systematic proportionality review is entirely within the competence of the state supreme courts as presently constituted without reliance on sophisticated statistical or computer-based methodology.[63]

One final possible explanation for the reluctance of state supreme courts to undertake systematic proportionality review is the discomfort they might experience when assessing the relative deathworthiness of different capital defendants and deciding which of those defendants who received death sentences should be spared. To be sure, in some cases a systematic-frequency approach to proportionality review would provide clear answers. However, the findings reported in chapters 5 and 7 suggest that the question of excessiveness is often quite close. In such cases the court's decision would be subject to close scrutiny. Moreover, this process would involve the court in making life or death decisions on the basis of relatively nebulous factors.[64] It is at least possible, therefore, that, either consciously or unconsciously, state supreme courts are avoiding this potential discomfiture by employing a pro forma system of proportionality review, which substantially leaves the question of who should die to prosecutors and juries.

THE FUTURE OF PROPORTIONALITY REVIEW

In spite of the limited effectiveness thus far of proportionality review on the part of state supreme courts, we do not believe that the impossibility hypothesis advanced by Chief Justice Rehnquist and Professor Dix has been proven. The state courts have made important progress in identifying the issues that arise in the proportionality-review process. It should be recalled that the 1964 Civil Rights Act presented the federal judiciary with similar methodological and legal problems, and for the first ten or more years the quality of analysis in the federal courts in discrimination cases left much to be desired. In contrast, today we see a deep appreciation on the part of most federal judges of the legal and methodological issues involved in discrimination cases, which are very similar to the methodology issues presented by proportionality review. The current thinking in the state courts on the proportionality-review issue compares with what we saw in the federal courts on the discrimination issue a decade or so ago. Given the foundations now in place in the state courts, we believe that state supreme courts interested in doing so can master new problems of methodology and proof in the same way as the federal courts did,[65] particularly if they involve the parties in the development of the data and procedures needed to establish an effective system.

We recognize, however, that the incentives for improving the effectiveness of proportionality reviews have been substantially reduced by the Supreme Court's decision in *McCleskey v. Kemp*.[66] In fact, state courts motivated solely by the fear of federal judicial intervention can now be expected to reduce even further the vigor of their reviews or request their state legislatures to repeal the requirement altogether. Nevertheless, in terms of improving the effectiveness of proportionality review in the state courts, we consider the following four steps to be most important. The first is the adoption and principled application of a frequency approach to proportionality review. The record to date demonstrates the inability of precedent-seeking systems to limit death sentencing to the worst cases.

Second, regardless of the basic system of review that the court adopts, we consider it essential that the universe of cases examined in the review process be broad enough to embrace the effects of both prosecutorial and jury decisions. Our third recommendation is that, whatever system is used, the court should document and explain the results of its individual decisions.

Our fourth and perhaps most important recommendation also applies regardless of the basic approach used. It is that the courts should supplement their fact-specific matching methods with some overall measures of culpability that will allow the courts to classify and compare all of the death-eligible cases in their jurisdictions, regardless of their factual comparability. Indeed, we believe that until such measures can be undertaken, proportionality review procedures will be plagued with the inconsistency and ad hoc nature that has characterized most state systems to date.

NOTES

1. *See* ALA. CODE §13A-5-53(b)(3) (Supp. 1986); CONN. GEN. STAT. §53a-46b(b)(3) (1987); DEL. CODE ANN. tit. 11, §4209(g)(2) (Supp. 1986); GA. CODE ANN. §17-10-35(c)(3) (Supp. 1987); IDAHO CODE §19-2827(c)(3) (1987); KY. REV. STAT. ANN. §532.075(3)(c) (Michie Bobbs-Merrill Supp. 1987); LA. CODE CRIM. PROC.

ANN. art. §905.9.1(1)(c) (West 1987); MISS. CODE ANN. §99-19-105(3)(c) (Supp. 1985); MO. ANN. CODE art. 27 §414(e)(4) (Supp. 1985); MO. ANN. STAT. §565.035(3)(3) (1984); MONT. CODE ANN. §46-18-310(3) (1985); NEB. REV. STAT. §29-2521.03 (1984); NEV. REV. STAT. §177.055(2)(d) (repealed 1985); N.H. REV. STAT. ANN. §630:5(VII)(c); N.J. STAT. ANN. §2C:11-3e (West Supp. 1985); N.M. STAT. ANN. §31-20A-4(c)(4) (Supp. 1986); N.C. GEN. STAT. §15A-2000(d)(2) (Supp. 1985); OHIO REV. CODE ANN. §2929.05(A) (Anderson 1987); OKLA. STAT. ANN. tit. 21, §701.13(c)(3) (repealed 1985); PA. CONS. STAT. ANN. tit. 42, §9711(h)(3)(iii) (Purdon Supp. 1987); S.C. CODE ANN. §16-3-25(c)(3) (Supp. 1986); S.D. CODIFIED LAWS ANN. §23A-27A-12(3) (Supp. 1987); TENN. CODE ANN. §39-2-205(c)(4) (Supp. 1987); VA. CODE ANN. §17-110.1(c)(2) (Supp. 1987); WASH. REV. CODE §10.95.130(2)(b) (1985); WYO. STAT. §6-2-103(d)(iii) (Supp. 1987).

2. Woodson v. North Carolina, 428 U.S. 280, 304 (1976) (invalidating mandatory death sentencing); Lockett v. Ohio, 438 U.S. 586, 606-9 (1978) (all relevant mitigating evidence admissible).

3. NEV. REV. STAT. §177.055(2)(d) (repealed 1985) and OKLA. STAT. ANN. tit. 21, §701.13(c)(3) (repealed 1985). We expect this trend will strengthen when the implications of McCleskey v. Kemp are fully appreciated. *See infra* Chapter 10.

4. *See* Woodson v. North Carolina, 428 U.S. 280, 316 (1976) (Rehnquist, J.); Dix, *Appellate Review of the Decision To Impose Death*, 68 GEO. L.J. 97, 160–61 (1978) (hereinafter Dix); and *supra* chap. 7, text accompanying notes 3 and 4, for a discussion of the Dix and Rehnquist impossibility hypotheses.

5. 465 U.S. 37, 73 (1984) (Brennan, J., dissenting).

6. Henry v. State, 278 Ark. 478, 488-89, 647 S.W.2d 419, 425 (1983), *cert. denied*, 464 U.S. 835 (1983); Sumlin v. State, 273 Ark. 185, 190, 617 S.W.2d 372, 375 (1981); Neal v. State, 274 Ark. 217, 219, 623 S.W.2d 191, 192 (1981)(vacation based on excessiveness and ineffective counsel); Wilson v. State, 493 So. 2d 1019, 1023-24 (Fla. 1986); Ross v. State, 474 So. 2d 1170, 1174 (Fla. 1985); Caruthers v. State, 465 So. 2d 496, 499 (Fla. 1985); Herzog v. State, 439 So. 2d 1372, 1381 (Fla. 1983); Blair v. State, 406 So. 2d 1103, 1109 (Fla. 1981); McCaskill v. State, 344 So. 2d 1276, 1280 (Fla. 1977); Thompson v. State, 328 So. 2d 1, 5 (Fla. 1976); Halliwell v. State, 323 So. 2d 557, 561-62 (Fla. 1975); Tedder v. State, 322 So. 2d 908, 910 (Fla. 1975); Slater v. State, 316 So. 2d 539, 542-43 (Fla. 1975); Taylor v. State, 294 So. 2d 648, 652 (Fla. 1974); Hall v. State, 241 Ga. 252, 258-60, 244 S.E.2d 833, 838-39 (1978); Ward v. State, 239 Ga. 205, 208, 236 S.E.2d 365, 368 (1977); State v. Scroggins, 110 Idaho 380, 386-89, 716 P.2d 1152, 1158-61 (1985), *cert. denied*, 479 U.S. 989 (1986); State v. Windsor, 110 Idaho 410, 420-23, 716 P.2d 1182, 1192-95 (1985), *cert. denied*, 479 U.S. 964 (1986); People v. Gleckler, 82 Ill. 2d 145, 171, 411 N.E.2d 849, 856-61 (1980); Smith v. Commonwealth, 634 S.W.2d 411, 413-14 (Ky. 1982) (upholding trial court's refusal to allow prosecution to introduce evidence of aggravating circumstances at penalty stage where defendant's triggerman accomplice had received life imprisonment in previous trial and, therefore, imposition of death penalty on defendant would be disproportionate); State v. Sonnier, 380 So. 2d 1, 6-9 (La. 1979); Coleman v. State, 378 So. 2d 640, 649-50 (Miss. 1979); State v. McIlvoy, 629 S.W.2d 333, 341-42 (Mo. 1982); Munn v. State, 658 P.2d 482, 487-88 (Okla. Crim. App. 1983); Biondi v. State, 101 Nev. 252, 258-60, 699 P.2d 1062, 1066-67 (1985); Harvey v. State, 100 Nev. 340, 342-45, 682 P.2d 1384, 1385-87 (1984); State v. Rogers, 316 N.C. 203, 234-36, 341 S.E.2d 713, 731-33 (1986); State v. Young, 312 N.C. 669, 686-91, 325 S.E.2d 181, 192-95 (1985); State v. Hill, 311 N.C. 465, 475-80, 319 S.E.2d 163, 170-72 (1984); State v. Jackson,

309 N.C. 26, 45–47, 305 S.E.2d 703, 716-18 (1983); State v. Bondurant, 309 N.C. 674, 692-95, 309 S.E.2d 170, 181-83 (1983).

7. Van Duizend, *Comparative Proportionality Review in Death Sentence Cases: What? How? Why?* 8 STATE CT. J. 9 (Summer 1984) (hereinafter Van Duizend).

8. When the court is unable to find any other case that it considers comparable, some courts indulge a presumption that the death sentence under review is not excessive. *See, e.g.*, State v. Plath, 281 S.C. 1, 20, 313 S.E.2d 619, 630 (1984), *cert. denied*, 467 U.S. 1265 (1984); State v. Groseclose, 615 S.W.2d 142, 150 (Tenn. 1981), *cert. denied*, 454 U.S. 882 (1981). Others decide the excessiveness issue on the merits without reference to prior decisions. *See, e.g.*, Callahan v. State, 471 So. 2d 447, 457 (Ala. Crim. App. 1983), *rev'd*, 471 So. 2d 463 (Ala. 1985); State v. Buell, 22 Ohio St. 3d 124, 144, 489 N.E.2d 795, 813 (1986), *cert. denied*, 479 U.S. 871 (1986); State v. Singleton, 284 S.C. 388, 394, 326 S.E.2d 153, 156-57 (1985), *cert. denied*, 471 U.S. 1111 (1985); State v. Cone, 665 S.W.2d 87, 95 (Tenn. 1984), *cert. denied*, 467 U.S. 1210 (1984). *Cf.* Coleman v. State, 378 So. 2d 640, 650 (Miss. 1979) (no comparable cases, but death sentence held excessive because less aggravated than death cases with which it was compared). *See supra* chap. 7, note 50 and accompanying text, for further discussion of precedent-seeking and frequency proportionality-review systems.

9. Van Duizend, *supra* note 7, at 9.

10. *See* State v. Welcome, 458 So. 2d 1235, 1255-56 (La. 1983), *cert. denied*, 470 U.S. 1088 (1985); State v. Young, 312 N.C. 669, 687- 88, 325 S.E.2d 181, 192-93 (1985)(emphasizes that death-sentencing frequency is not dispositive of the proportionality review); Commonwealth v. Smith, 511 Pa. 343, 359, 513 A.2d 1371, 1379 (1986), *cert. denied*, 107 S.Ct. 1617 (1987); Commonwealth v. Whitney, 511 Pa. 232, 254, 512 A.2d 1152, 1161-62 (1986); Commonwealth v. Morales, 508 Pa. 51, 72-73, 494 A.2d 367, 378-79 (1985); Commonwealth v. Pirela, 510 Pa. 43, 60-61, 507 A.2d 23, 32 (1986); Poyner v. Commonwealth, 229 Va. 401, 435, 329 S.E.2d 815, 834-35 (1985), *cert. denied*, 474 U.S. 865 (1985) (court uses the language of a frequency approach; however, it does not document its conclusion).

11. In a recent dissenting opinion in State v. Jeffries, 105 Wash. 2d 378, 431-40, 717 P.2d 722, 742-46 (1986) (Utter, J., dissenting), *cert. denied* 479 U.S. 922 (1986), Justice Utter both presented the case for a frequency approach to proportionality review and demonstrated its application:

> The second step [of a proportionality review] would then be to compute the frequency of death sentences within the pool of similar cases. If the frequency is less than "generally," the death sentence should be reversed. Use of the word "generally" suggests that the "threshold frequency" at which a death sentence becomes appropriate is significantly greater than 50 percent. *See Webster's Third New International Dictionary* 944 (1971) (defining "general" as "applicable or pertinent to the majority of individuals involved" or "prevalent, usual, widespread").

Id. at 437, 717 P.2d at 744.

12. Although the courts do not characterize their proportionality analyses as "precedent-seeking," it is explicit in the opinions that the courts will hold that the imposition of the death penalty on a defendant is not excessive if documentation can be found for its imposition in other similar cases. *See* Henderson v. State, 279 Ark. 414, 422, 652 S.W.2d 26, 31, *cert. denied*, 464 U.S. 1012 (1983); Skaggs v. Commonwealth, 694 S.W.2d 672, 681 (Ky. 1985), *cert. denied*, 476 U.S. 1130 (1986); Gray v. State, 472 So. 2d 409, 423 (Miss. 1985); State v. Malone, 694 S.W.2d 723, 728 (Mo. 1985), *cert.*

denied, 476 U.S. 1165 (1986); State v. Mapes, 19 Ohio St. 3d 108, 118-19, 484 N.E.2d 140, 149 (1985), *cert. denied,* 476 U.S. 1178 (1986); State v. Singleton, 284 S.C. 388, 394, 326 S.E.2d 153, 157, *cert. denied,* 471 U.S. 1111 (1985); State v. Copeland, 278 S.C. 572, 595, 300 S.E.2d 63, 77 (1982), *cert. denied,* 460 U.S. 1103 (1983); State v. Smith, 695 S.W.2d 954, 960 (Tenn. 1985).

13. Numerous state courts do not indicate explicitly what type of analyses they apply. Although the opinions are basically consistent with a "precedent-seeking" approach, these courts purport to examine life cases as well as death cases and do not rule out a frequency approach. *See, e.g.,* Riley v. State, 496 A.2d 997, 1027 (Del. 1985), *cert. denied,* 478 U.S. 1022 (1986); State v. Byrne, 483 So. 2d 564, 577 (La. 1986); Tichnell v. State, 297 Md. 432, 471-72, 468 A.2d 1, 21-22 (1983), *cert. denied,* 479 U.S. 871 (1986); State v. Williams, 205 Neb. 56, 76-77, 287 N.W.2d 18, 29-30 (1979); State v. Garcia, 99 N.M. 771, 780-81, 664 P.2d 969, 978-79 (1983), *cert. denied,* 462 U.S. 1112 (1983).

14. Van Duizend, *supra* note 7, at 11. Whichever population of cases is used, an additional implicit requirement is that, whether a defendant's case was tried or pled, its evidence must have been sufficiently strong to support a finding beyond a reasonable doubt that the *mens rea* requirement for capital murder was satisfied and that one or more statutory aggravating circumstances (e.g., armed robbery) were present in the case. This requirement is easily satisfied when the universe of cases is limited to penalty-trial cases. When it embraces more than penalty-trial cases, the determination of whether such a case is death-eligible inherently involves a risk of error. The first such error (a false negative) results when the court erroneously *excludes* from the universe a case that, had it been prosecuted as a capital case, would have resulted in a capital murder conviction and a finding that one or more statutory aggravating circumstances were present in the case. The second type of error (a false positive) results when the court erroneously *includes* in the universe a case that, had it been prosecuted as a capital case, would not have resulted in a capital murder conviction and a finding that one or more statutory aggravating factors were present in the case. The legal question in specifying the universe is how much risk of what type of error can be tolerated in the system.

The empirical literature on sentencing and our experience in evaluating homicide cases support three relevant observations concerning this issue. The first is that the strength of the evidence concerning death eligibility varies considerably from case to case. In many cases, the evidence clearly was or was not sufficient to support a death-eligibility finding. There are also numerous cases where the record is mixed and, while it would support such a finding, that outcome would be far from certain. The second observation is that in evaluating these marginal cases, the heavier or stricter the burden of proof applied for inclusion into the universe, the lower will be the risk of false positives. But at the same time, an increase in the burden of proof increases the risk of false negative decisions. For example, an extremely high burden of proof for inclusion into the universe is likely to exclude from it cases that did not result in a capital conviction but whose evidence of death eligibility is stronger than that found in some cases that actually resulted in a death sentence. The third observation is that one can only estimate the likelihood that a case is death-eligible. As a result, there is no bright-line rule that will guide and permit the specification of a universe without any risk of an erroneous classification.

There are several possible evidentiary standards a court might use as a possible basis for including cases in the universe that did not result in a penalty trial. One is the rational basis test used by trial courts to determine whether a jury should be charged on a capital murder count (at both the guilt and penalty trial), i.e., would the evidence rationally support a unanimous finding beyond a reasonable doubt that the defendant is guilty of capital murder and that a statutory aggravating circumstance is present in the case? This standard will bring into the universe cases with evidentiary strength on death eligibility that is roughly equivalent to the weakest cases that resulted in a capital murder conviction and a unanimous finding on the presence of one or more statutory aggravating factors in the case. However, this test will also bring into the universe cases with evidentiary strength on death eligibility comparable to that found in cases that have gone to trial on capital murder and resulted in an acquittal or a finding of guilt on a lesser included offense. For this reason, a court may want to apply standards that impose higher burdens of proof for inclusion in the universe, thereby reducing the risk of false positives (but also increasing the risk of false negatives). Leading alternative standards are "clear and convincing," "substantial," or "conclusive" evidence of death eligibility.

15. See Tichnell v. State, 297 Md. 432, 478-80, 468 A.2d 1, 23-24 (1983), cert. denied, 466 U.S. 993 (1984) (Eldridge, J., concurring)(criticizing limitation of pool to penalty-trial cases because it excludes from the court's scrutiny the exercise of prosecutorial discretion); id. at 483, 468 A.2d at 26 (Cole, J., concurring) (same criticism); id. at 489-92, 468 A.2d at 29-31 (Davidson, J., dissenting) (same criticism); State v. Harper, 208 Neb. 568, 586, 304 N.W.2d 663, 673 (1981), cert. denied, 454 U.S. 882 (1981) (Krivasha, C.J., dissenting) (comparison pool should include all murder cases because one "cannot ignore the reality of [prosecutorial discretion] in attempting to determine whether the death penalty is imposed in a nonarbitrary and noncapricious manner in this state"); State v. Campbell, 103 Wash. 2d 1, 42, 691 P.2d 929, 953 (1984), cert. denied, 471 U.S. 1094 (1985) (Utter, J., dissenting) (criticizing reliance on penalty-trial cases because it fails to take into account the consequences of prosecutorial discretion).

16. The following courts consistently include only death cases in their comparison pools. The only exception is Alabama, which may look at a codefendant's life sentence in an intracase situation: Beck v. State, 396 So. 2d 645, 664 (Ala. 1980); Skaggs v. Commonwealth, 694 S.W.2d 672, 681 (Ky. 1985), cert. denied, 476 U.S. 1130 (1986); Gray v. State, 472 So. 2d 409, 423 (Miss. 1985), rev'd on other grounds, 107 S.Ct. 2045 (1987); State v. Mapes, 19 Ohio St. 3d 108, 118-19, 484 N.E.2d 140, 149 (1985), cert. denied, 476 U.S. 1178 (1986); State v. Koon, 285 S.C. 1, 4, 328 S.E.2d 625, 626 (1984), cert. denied, 471 U.S. 1036 (1985); State v. Smith, 695 S.W.2d 954, 960 (Tenn. 1985).

Other states have, on occasion, considered only death cases in their comparison pool; however, in most instances these states include both life and death cases. See State v. Correll, 148 Ariz. 468, 484-85, 715 P.2d 721, 737-38 (1986); Hayes v. State, 280 Ark. 509, 509-H, 660 S.W.2d 648, 654 (1983), cert. denied, 465 U.S. 1051 (1984); State v. Jones, 474 So. 2d 919, 938 (La. 1985), cert. denied, 476 U.S. 1178 (1986); State v. Smith, 705 P.2d 1087, 1108 (Mont. 1985), cert. denied, 474 U.S. 1073 (1986); Milligan v. State, 101 Nev. 627, 639, 708 P.2d 289, 296 (1985), cert. denied, 479 U.S. 870 (1986); State v. Gardner, 311 N.C. 489, 514-15, 319 S.E.2d 591, 607 (1984), cert. denied, 469 U.S. 1230 (1985). Additionally, the Washington Supreme Court has, on at least one occasion, appeared to have ignored the legislative mandate requiring the court to compare both life and death penalty-trial cases by comparing only cases where the death penalty was imposed. See State v. Jeffries, 105 Wash. 2d 398, 437-40, 717 P.2d 722, 745-46 (1986), cert. denied, 479 U.S. 922 (1986) (Utter, J., dissenting).

17. Idaho Supreme Court Justice Bistline has noted in several dissenting opinions that the absence of life cases from the comparison pool is not a result of judicial dis-agreement over policy, but, rather, is a result of the court's lack of information—the Idaho statute has no provision for gathering information in life cases. "Any respectable proportionality review has to include findings made in *all* cases where the sentencing court decides between life and death." State v. Gibson, 106 Idaho 54, 65, 675 P.2d 33, 44 (1983) (Bistline, J., dissenting), *cert. denied*, 468 U.S. 1220 (1984). Justice Robertson has expressed similar concern in a concurrence in Wiley v. State, 484 So. 2d 339, 361 (Miss. 1986), *cert. denied*, 479 U.S. 906 (1986): "Of greater concern is our refusal to include in proportionality review those capital murder cases which have resulted in affirmed life sentences." Similar criticism has been expressed by justices in Montana and Washington. *See* State v. Coleman, 185 Mont. 299, 381, 605 P.2d 1000, 1045 (1979) (Shea, J., dissenting), *cert. denied*, 446 U.S. 970 (1980) ("To use only cases imposing the death penalty as a comparison with a case under review, fails miserably in this objective [i.e., the rational and fair administration and enforcement of Montana's statutory scheme of capital punishment]"); State v. Jeffries, 105 Wash. 2d 398, 432, 717 P.2d 722, 742 (1986) (Utter, J., dissenting), *cert. denied*, 479 U.S. 922 (1986) ("As is clear from the statute and contrary to the majority, 'similar cases' includes aggravated first degree murder cases where the prosecutor did not seek the death penalty").

Legal commentators have also been critical of reviewing courts' failure to examine similar life-sentence cases. *See* Hubbard, Burry, & Widener, *A "Meaningful" Basis for the Death Penalty: The Practice, Constitutionality, and Justice of Capital Punishment in South Carolina*, 34 S.C.L. Rev. 391, 441-63 (1982) (hereinafter Hubbard, Burry, & Widener); Rodriguez, Perlin, & Apicella, *Proportionality Review in New Jersey: An Indispensable Safeguard in the Capital Sentencing Process*, 15 RUTGERS L.J. 399, 429 (1984); Van Duizend, *supra* note 7, at 11; Note, *Criminal Procedure: Comparative Proportionality Review of Death Sentences: Is It a Meaningful Safeguard in Okla-homa?* 38 OKLA. L. REV. 267, 275-78 (1985) (hereinafter *Criminal Procedure*). Skene, *Review of Capital Cases: Does the Florida Supreme Court Know What It's Doing*, 15 STETSON L. REV. 263, 296-97 (1986).

18. Coleman v. State, 378 So. 2d 640, 650 (Miss. 1979).

19. *See* Riley v. State, 496 A.2d 997, 1027 (Del. 1985), *cert. denied*, 478 U.S. 1022 (1986); Tichnell v. State, 297 Md. 432, 464, 468 A.2d 1, 17 (1983), *cert. denied*, 466 U.S. 993 (1984); State v. Foster, 700 S.W.2d 440, 445 n.5 (Mo. 1985), *cert. denied*, 476 U.S. 1178 (1986); Biondi v. State, 101 Nev. 252, 258, 699 P.2d 1062, 1066 (1985); State v. Williams, 308 N.C. 47, 79, 301 S.E.2d 335, 355, *cert. denied*, 464 U.S. 865 (1983); State v. Harris, 106 Wash. 2d 784, 797-99, 725 P.2d 975, 982-83 (1986), *cert. denied*, 480 U.S. 940 (1987) (however, nonpenalty-trial cases considered when no other penalty-trial cases available for review); State v. Jeffries, 105 Wash. 2d 398, 430, 717 P.2d 722, 740 (1986), *cert. denied*, 479 U.S. 922 (1986).

20. For example, in the Maryland watershed case Tichnell v. State, 297 Md. 432, 468 A.2d 1 (1983), *cert. denied*, 466 U.S. 993 (1984), which set forth the procedure of proportionality review, three justices criticized the majority's selection of capital cases that advanced to penalty trial as the relevant universe of potentially comparable cases. *Id.* at 477-80, 468 A.2d at 233-35 (Eldridge, J., concurring); *id.* at 482-83, 468 A.2d at 27 (Cole, J., concurring) (Justice Cole concedes that the majority will address similar cases that did not reach a penalty trial when presented by defendant; however, he clearly demonstrates his preference for placing this burden on the state's attorney); *id.* at 487-89, 468 A.2d at 29 (Davidson, J., dissenting) (Justice Davidson strongly criti-

cizes the majority's statutory construction of "similar cases" in light of the purposes of proportionality review).

21. *See, e.g.*, Henry v. State, 278 Ark. 478, 488, 647 S.W.2d 419, 425 (1983), *cert. denied*, 464 U.S. 835 (1983); State v. Williams, 205 Neb. 56, 76, 287 N.W.2d 18, 29 (1979), *cert. denied*, 449 U.S. 891 (1980); Brogie v. State, 695 P.2d 538, 547 (Okla. Crim. App. 1985); Commonwealth v. Pursell, 508 Pa. 212, 240-41, 495 A.2d 183, 197-98 (1985). An extension of the universe to include cases that did not advance to a penalty trial does create a risk of erroneously including in the universe cases that, had they been prosecuted as capital cases, would not have resulted in a capital murder conviction and a finding that one or more statutory aggravating factors were present in the case. *See supra* note 14. This concern provides no basis, however, for limiting the universe to death-sentence cases, since the only relevant penalty-trial cases would normally be those in which the fact finder found the defendant guilty of capital murder and that one or more statutory aggravating circumstances were present in the case.

22. *See, e.g.*, State v. Harding, 141 Ariz. 492, 501, 687 P.2d 1247, 1256 (1984); Gray v. State, 472 So. 2d 409, 423 (Miss. 1985), *rev'd on other grounds*, 107 S.Ct. 2045 (1987); State v. Smith, 705 P.2d 1087, 1108 (Mont. 1985), *cert. denied*, 474 U.S. 1073 (1986); State v. Bondurant, 309 N.C. 674, 692, 309 S.E.2d 170, 181-82 (1983).

23. It is the extremely aggravated cases with a real risk of a death sentence in which the defendants have a very substantial incentive to plead guilty as a way of avoiding the risk of the death sentence. Although no state court regularly considers capital-murder cases that result in a conviction for a noncapital crime, some opinions have referred to such cases on occasion. *See, e.g.*, State v. Aragon, 107 Idaho 358, 378-89, 690 P.2d 293, 313-14 (1984) (Bistline, J., dissenting from denial of petition for rehearing)(noting majority's inclusion of a case where defendant was charged and convicted of second-degree murder); Munn v. State, 658 P.2d 482, 487 (Okla. Crim. App. 1983) (citing numerous cases where the defendants were convicted for less than capital murder). The inclusion of such cases in the universe would be appropriate in guilty plea cases where there was sufficient evidence of death eligibility and the plea bargain was based on a prosecutorial judgment of death-worthiness. Even tried cases resulting in conviction for noncapital crimes may be appropriately included in the universe if there was sufficient evidence of death eligibility and the fact finder had no opportunity to convict the defendant of capital murder (because of an earlier prosecutorial charging decision) or there is clear evidence of jury nullification on the guilty verdict as a means of eliminating the risk of a death sentence.

24. *See, e.g.*, State v. Ford, 489 So. 2d 1250, 1264 (La. 1986), *vacated*, 479 U.S. 1077 (1987); State v. Brogdon, 457 So. 2d 616, 632 (La. 1984), *cert. denied*, 471 U.S. 1111 (1985); State v. Wingo, 457 So. 2d 1159, 1169-70 (La. 1984), *cert. denied*, 471 U.S. 1030 (1985). In Ohio, proportionality review is conducted by the court of appeals and the supreme court. At the court of appeals level, the review consists of only those cases within the court's jurisdiction. The policy stated in support of this limitation is to ensure an "extremely thorough and accurate" review with cases intimately familiar to the court. At the supreme court level of review, the court considers similar cases statewide. State v. Rogers, 17 Ohio St. 3d 174, 186, 478 N.E.2d 984, 996 (1985), *vacated*, 474 U.S. 1002 (1985).

25. This practice has drawn considerable criticism, however, and may explain why the court recently appears to be more inclined to look outside the parish for similar cases. *See* State v. Prejean, 379 So. 2d 240, 250-51 (La. 1979) (Dennis, J., dissenting from denial of rehearing), *cert. denied*, 449 U.S. 891 (1980); Note, *Capital Sentencing*

Under Supreme Court Rule 28, 42 LA. L. REV. 1100, 1117-19 (1982); *see, e.g.*, State v. Williams, 490 So. 2d 255, 264 (La. 1986), *cert. denied*, 107 S.Ct. 3277 (1987); State v. Loyd, 489 So. 2d 898, 906 (La. 1986); State v. Brogdon, 457 So. 2d 616, 632 (La. 1984), *cert. denied*, 471 U.S. 1111 (1985).

26. Wyoming appears to be the only state that routinely looked for "similar cases" in other jurisdictions—particularly death cases in Florida and Georgia. *See* Engberg v. State, 686 P.2d 541, 555-56 (Wyo. 1984), *cert. denied*, 469 U.S. 1077 (1984). However, the practice was employed by a few larger states during the period immediately following enactment of proportionality-review statutes when there was an insufficient backlog of cases under the post-*Furman* death-penalty statutes with which to compare.

27. *See, e.g.*, Tucker v. State, 245 Ga. 68, 74, 263 S.E.2d 109, 113 (1980), *cert. denied*, 449 U.S. 891 (1980) (citing in the appendix a case decided in 1970); State v. Windsor, 110 Idaho 410, 421-22n.2, 716 P.2d 1182, 1193-94n.2 (1985), *cert. denied*, 479 U.S. 964 (1986) (citing similar cases dating back to 1953); Skaggs v. Commonwealth, 694 S.W.2d 672, 681-82 (Ky. 1985), *cert. denied*, 476 U.S. 1130 (1986); State v. Smith, 705 P.2d 1087, 1109 (Mont. 1985), *cert. denied*, 474 U.S. 1073 (1986) (citing a 1947 death case); Munn v. State, 658 P.2d 482, 487 (Okla. Crim. App. 1983) (citing two pre-*Furman* life cases as support for finding a death sentence disproportionate); Osborn v. State, 672 P.2d 777, 801 (Wyo. 1983), *cert. denied*, 465 U.S. 1051 (1984).

28. *See, e.g.*, *Criminal Procedure, supra* note 17, at 276.

29. Van Duizend, *supra* note 7, at 11-12. To the extent that reliance on a previously vacated death sentence may bias a court's proportionality review, good practice calls for recognition of the risk and presentation of a justification for the use of the case.

30. *See, e.g.*, State v. Copeland, 278 S.C. 572, 592, 300 S.E.2d 63, 75, *cert. denied*, 460 U.S. 1103 (1983), *cert. denied*, 463 U.S. 1214 (1983); Gray v. State, 472 So. 2d 409, 423 (Miss. 1985), *rev'd on other grounds*, 107 S.Ct. 2045 (1987); *cf.* State v. Garcia, 99 N.M. 771, 780, 664 P.2d 969, 978 (1983) (affirmed life and death cases), *cert. denied*, 462 U.S. 1112 (1983).

31. *See, e.g.*, State v. Nash, 143 Ariz. 392, 407, 694 P.2d 222, 237, *cert. denied*, 471 U.S. 1143 (1985); Stanley v. State, 240 Ga. 341, 351-52, 241 S.E.2d 173, 180 (1977), *cert. denied*, 439 U.S. 882 (1978) (considering a death penalty vacated in a comparable kidnapping case); Skaggs v. Commonwealth, 694 S.W.2d 672, 681-82 (Ky. 1985), *cert. denied*, 476 U.S. 1130 (1986); State v. McDonald, 661 S.W.2d 497, 507 (Mo. 1983); State v. Reeves, 216 Neb. 206, 231-32, 344 N.W.2d 433, 449, *cert. denied*, 469 U.S. 1028 (1984) (although vacated/reversed cases are listed in the addendum, it is unclear to what extent they are used); Coleman v. State, 668 P.2d 1126, 1137 (Okla. Crim. App. 1983), *cert. denied*, 464 U.S. 1073 (1984).

32. *See, e.g.*, Stebbing v. State, 299 Md. 331, 374-75, 473 A.2d 903, 925 (1984), *cert. denied*, 469 U.S. 900 (1984); Commonwealth v. Travaglia, 502 Pa. 474, 504n.4, 467 A.2d 288, 303n.4 (1983), *cert. denied*, 467 U.S. 1256 (1984).

33. *See, e.g.*, State v. Correll, 148 Ariz. 468, 484, 715 P.2d 721, 737 (1986) (no cases similar on every factual point); Collins v. State, 261 Ark. 195, 223, 548 S.W.2d 106, 122 (1977), *cert. denied*, 434 U.S. 878 (1977) (no similar cases because this was the first case reviewed under the new statute); Flamer v. State, 490 A.2d 104, 144 (Del. 1983), *cert. denied*, 464 U.S. 865 (1983) (three cases involving multiple unprovoked murders of helpless elderly victims; one case involving a rape-murder of an elderly woman followed by invalid husband's death; two cases involving shopkeeper robbery–murder); State v. Stuart, 110 Idaho 163, 175-77, 715 P.2d 833, 845-47 (1985) (first murder-by-torture case); Tichnell v. State, 297 Md. 432, 469-71, 468 A.2d 1, 20-21 (1983),

cert. denied, 466 U.S. 933 (1984); State v. Smith, 705 P.2d 1087, 1108-10 (Mont. 1985), *cert. denied*, 474 U.S. 1073 (1986) (three murder-kidnapping cases); State v. Rault, 445 So. 2d 1203, 1220 (La. 1984), *cert. denied*, 469 U.S. 873 (1984) (the Louisiana court has a distinct problem with having too few cases in its comparison pool because it makes a parishwide rather than a statewide comparison—here there were no other cases of aggravated rape, kidnapping, and murder available for comparison in this particular parish); State v. Plath, 281 S.C. 1, 20, 313 S.E.2d 619, 630, *cert. denied*, 467 U.S. 1265 (1984) ("[l]acking precisely identical cases with which to compare these verdicts"); State v. Young, 312 N.C. 669, 686-88, 325 S.E.2d 181, 192-93 (1985) (three armed-robbery–murder cases that were more aggravated than the review cases, but resulted in life sentences).

34. Although computer-based data-management systems may be helpful in jurisdictions with very large numbers of cases, we believe the development of (a) effective measures of case culpability and (b) procedures for the conduct of systematic and comprehensive proportionality review, while difficult, is within the capacity of any court committed to the task. Two such measures are described *supra* chap. 4, note 21 and accompanying text (a qualitative *a priori* measure that weighs aggravating and mitigating circumstances), and *supra* chap. 4, note 29 and accompanying text (three-dimensional case-classification system), and illustrated *supra* chap. 5 at Table 12 and Figure 14.

35. *See, e.g.*, State v. Scroggins, 110 Idaho 380, 386-89, 716 P.2d 1152, 1158-61 (1985), *cert. denied*, 479 U.S. 989 (1986), and State v. Windsor, 110 Idaho 410, 421-22, 716 P.2d 1182, 1193-94 (1985), *cert. denied*, 479 U.S. 964 (1986) (using culpability measure when comparing intracase sentences); State v. Williams, 205 Neb. 56, 77, 287 N.W.2d 18, 29 (1979), *cert. denied*, 449 U.S. 891 (1980); State v. Gaskins, 284 S.C. 105, 130, 326 S.E.2d 132, 147 (1985), *cert. denied*, 471 U.S. 1120 (1985) ("The facts are not the same in any two cases and, accordingly, our review of the facts relate largely to *degree of culpability of the defendants and the viciousness of the killing*" [emphasis added]); State v. Carter, 714 S.W.2d 241, 251 (Tenn. 1986) (using an assessment of culpability to distinguish accomplice's life sentence); Watkins v. Commonwealth, 229 Va. 469, 494, 331 S.E.2d 422, 440 (1985), *cert. denied*, 475 U.S. 1099 (1986) (compared defendant's future dangerousness and vileness of the crime with previous defendants'); State v. Jeffries, 105 Wash. 2d 398, 430, 717 P.2d 722, 740 (1986), *cert. denied*, 479 U.S. 922 (1986).

Other states may be making comparisons based on overall measures of culpability but do not declare so explicitly. Such comparisons may be inferred from the fact that the "similar" cases used are not identified as factually similar; therefore, one might assume them to be of similar culpability. *See, e.g.*, Harper v. Commonwealth, 694 S.W.2d 665, 671 (Ky. 1985), *cert. denied*, 476 U.S. 1178 (1986); Gallego v. State, 101 Nev. 782, 793, 711 P.2d 856, 864 (1985), *cert. denied*, 479 U.S. 871 (1986).

36. Van Duizend, *supra* note 7, at 22.

37. *See, e.g.*, Skaggs v. Commonwealth, 694 S.W.2d 672, 682 (Ky. 1985), *cert. denied*, 476 U.S. 1130 (1986) (the public defender is not entitled to the data compiled for the court under KRS 532.075(6)). Some state supreme courts have argued that it is not their duty to provide the defendant with the information used in comparison because "the transcripts, briefs and opinions in those cases used for comparison purposes are public records; thus, the defendant in fact has access to the same information available to the Court." State v. Thompson, 278 S.C. 1, 6n.1, 292 S.E.2d 581, 584n.1 (1982), *cert. denied*, 456 U.S. 938 (1982). However, the Tennessee court appeared to give

defendants access to the trial-judge reports used for comparison purposes. State v. Coe, 655 S.W.2d 903, 913 (Tenn. 1983), *cert. denied*, 464 U.S. 1063 (1984).

38. *See* State v. Garcia, 99 N.M. 771, 780n.11, 664 P.2d 969, 978n.11 (1983), *cert. denied*, 462 U.S. 1112 (1983) ("It is the duty of the defendant's attorney to supply the Court with information of similar cases"); Tichnell v. State, 297 Md. 432, 466, 468 A.2d 1, 18 (1983), *cert. denied*, 466 U.S. 993 (1984) (defendant bears the burden of presenting similar noncapital cases).

39. Several states have addressed issues of discrimination but have rejected such claims. Moreover, the data available to the courts were clearly insufficient to analyze these claims. *See, e.g.*, Beck v. State, 396 So. 2d 645, 653 (Ala. 1981) ("[W]e cannot reach any conclusion whether racial discrimination infected the jury verdicts") *rev'd on other grounds*, 447 U.S. 625 (1980); State v. Carriger, 143 Ariz. 142, 159-60, 692 P.2d 991, 1008-9 (1984) (summarily rejected defendant's claim of race-of-victim discrimination in imposition of the death penalty), *cert. denied*, 471 U.S. 1111 (1985); Cooks v. State, 699 P.2d 653, 661 (Okla. Crim. App. 1985) (black principal defendant's argument that his death sentence was based on discrimination because white coperpetrator received life sentence rejected), *cert. denied*, 474 U.S. 935 (1985) .

40. *See, e.g.*, Callahan v. State, 471 So. 2d 447, 457 (Ala. Crim. App. 1983), *rev'd*, 471 So. 2d 463 (Ala. 1985); Henderson v. State, 279 Ark. 414, 422, 652 S.W.2d 26, 31 (1983), *cert. denied*, 464 U.S. 1012 (1983); State v. Buell, 22 Ohio St. 3d 124, 144, 489 N.E.2d 795, 813 (1986), *cert. denied*, 479 U.S. 871 (1986); State v. Singleton, 284 S.C. 388, 394, 326 S.E.2d 153, 157 (1985), *cert. denied*, 471 U.S. 1111 (1985); State v. Cone, 665 S.W.2d 87, 90 (Tenn. 1984), *cert. denied*, 467 U.S. 1210 (1984).

41. Flamer v. State, 490 A.2d 104, 138-45 (Del. 1983), *cert. denied*, 464 U.S. 865 (1983); Tichnell v. State, 297 Md. 432, 457-66, 468 A.2d 1, 13-18 (1983), *cert. denied*, 466 U.S. 993 (1984). *See also* State v. Williams, 205 Neb. 56, 74-77, 287 N.W.2d 18, 28-30 (1979), *cert. denied*, 449 U.S. 891 (1980); State v. Copeland, 278 S.C. 572, 586-97, 300 S.E.2d 63, 75-78 (1982), *cert. denied*, 460 U.S. 1103 (1983), *cert. denied*, 463 U.S. 1214 (1983).

42. *See supra* note 40. *See also* Brown v. State, 473 So. 2d 1260, 1271 (Fla. 1985), *cert. denied*, 474 U.S. 1038 (1985); People v. King, 109 Ill. 2d 514, 551, 488 N.E.2d 949, 967-68 (1986), *cert. denied*, 479 U.S. 872 (1986); People v. Kubat, 94 Ill. 2d 437, 502-4, 447 N.E. 2d 247, 277, *cert. denied*, 464 U.S. 865 (1983); State v. Brooks, 25 Ohio St. 3d 144, 156, 495 N.E.2d 407, 417 (1986); State v. Cooper, 718 S.W.2d 256, 260 (Tenn. 1986), *cert. denied*, 479 U.S. 1101 (1987).

43. *See, e.g.*, Wiley v. State, 484 So. 2d 339, 361 (Miss. 1986), *cert. denied*, 479 U.S. 906 (1986) (Robertson, J., concurring) ("In the end we merely list all of the death penalty cases we have decided since enactment of the revised statute post-*Gregg*. More normally we merely recite that the penalty is not 'disproportionate'"); State v. Cheadle, 101 N.M. 282, 290, 681 P.2d 708, 716 (1983), *cert. denied*, 466 U.S. 945 (1984) (Sosa, J., dissenting) ("[no] meaningful proportionality review as is evidenced by the cursory discussion in the majority opinion"). *See also* Hubbard, Burry, & Widener, *supra* note 17, at 463-65.

44. *See, e.g.*, Clisby v. State, 456 So. 2d 102, 104 (Ala. Crim. App. 1983); Skaggs v. Commonwealth, 694 S.W.2d 672, 682 (Ky. 1985), *cert. denied*, 476 U.S. 1130 (1986); Wilson v. State, 101 Nev. 452, 454, 705 P.2d 151, 153 (1985); State v. Rogers, 17 Ohio St. 3d 174, 187-88, 478 N.E.2d 984, 996-97 (1985), *vacated*, 474 U.S. 1002 (1985); Tuggle v. Commonwealth, 228 Va. 493, 517-18, 323 S.E.2d 539, 553-54 (1984), *vacated*, 471 U.S. 1096 (1985); State v. King, 694 S.W.2d 941, 947 (Tenn. 1985).

45. *See, e.g.,* State v. Correll, 148 Ariz. 468, 484-85, 715 P.2d 721, 737-38 (1986); State v. Welcome, 458 So. 2d 1235, 1255-58 (La. 1983), *cert. denied,* 470 U.S. 1088 (1985); State v. Preston, 673 S.W.2d 1, 11-12 (Mo. 1984), *cert. denied,* 469 U.S. 893 (1984); State v. Lawson, 310 N.C. 632, 648-52, 314 S.E.2d 493, 503-5 (1984), *cert. denied,* 471 U.S. 1120 (1985).

46. *See, e.g.,* Hendrickson v. State, 285 Ark. 462, 466-67, 688 S.W.2d 295, 298 (1985) (age and initiation of crime); Brown v. State, 473 So. 2d 1260, 1268 (Fla. 1985), *cert. denied,* 474 U.S. 1038 (1985) (degree of participation in crime); People v. Szabo, 94 Ill. 2d 327, 353, 447 N.E.2d 193, 205 (1983) (age and culpability); Trimble v. State, 300 Md. 387, 436, 478 A.2d 1143, 1168 (1984), *cert. denied,* 469 U.S. 1230 (1985) (culpability); State v. Gilmore, 681 S.W.2d 934, 946 (Mo. 1984) (degree of participation); State v. Mak, 105 Wash. 2d 692, 721-26, 718 P.2d 407, 426-28 (1986) (evidence of mental instability).

47. *See, e.g.,* State v. Scroggins, 110 Idaho 380, 387, 716 P.2d 1152, 1159 (1985) ("jury's verdict reflected that [defendant's] level of participation in the crime did not rise to the same level [as an accomplice who received death penalty]"); State v. Windsor, 110 Idaho 410, 421-22, 716 P.2d 1182, 1193-94 (1985) (degree of participation primary factor that justified disparity in both defendants' jury sentences), *cert. denied,* 479 U.S. 964 (1986).

48. Professor Dix's observation on proportionality review in Florida in the 1970s appears to have broad applicability: "Yet, because the court can easily distinguish earlier cases, these [proportionality review] comparisons have added little substance to the court's analysis." Dix, *supra* note 4, at 132-33.

49. *See supra* note 34 for discussion of measures of overall case culpability.

50. 658 P.2d 482 (Okla. Crim. App. 1983). *Accord* State v. Jones, 705 S.W.2d 19, 24-25 (Mo. 1986) (Blackmar, J., concurring in part and dissenting in part) (case under review factually distinguishable from majority's similar cases because it lacks element of torture), *cert. denied,* 477 U.S. 909 (1986); State v. Noland, 312 N.C. 1, 32-33, 320 S.E.2d 642, 661-62 (1984) (Exum, J., dissenting) (cases used by majority "easily distinguishable from the instant case" because defendant was suffering from mental or emotional disturbance), *cert. denied,* 469 U.S. 1230 (1985); State v. Hill, 311 N.C. 465, 482-83, 319 S.E.2d 163, 173-74 (1984) (Meyer, J., dissenting) (similar cases used by majority are "clearly distinguishable").

51. Munn v. State, 658 P.2d at 487.

52. *Id.* at 488-89 (Brett, J., specially concurring).

53. Commonwealth v. Morales, 508 Pa. 51, 73, 494 A.2d 367, 379 (1985), *cert. denied,* 469 U.S. 971 (1984).

54. Commonwealth v. Pirela, 510 Pa. 43, 60-61, 507 A.2d 23, 32 (1986).

55. Commonwealth v. Maxwell, 505 Pa. 152, 169, 477 A.2d 1309, 1318 (1984), *cert. denied,* 469 U.S. 971 (1984).

56. State courts are better situated to provide effective judicial oversight of their capital-sentencing process than are the federal courts. The latter must obey jurisdictional rules that drastically limit their oversight capacity in state criminal cases—e.g., 28 U.S.C. §32254(a)–(d)(1985). Federal courts also lack the staff and authority needed to collect and analyze the data required for an effective monitoring process, and they do not have the flexible statutory tools available to state supreme courts when they determine a sentence to be excessive or disproportionate.

57. *See infra* chap. 10, note 107 and accompanying text, for a discussion of the vitality of the constitutional concept of comparative excessiveness post-*McCleskey.*

58. Spinkellink v. Wainwright, 578 F.2d 582, 613-14 (5th Cir. 1978), *cert. denied,* 440 U.S. 976 (1979):

> In order to ascertain through federal habeas corpus proceedings if the death penalty had been discriminatorily imposed upon a petitioner whose murder victim was white, a district court would have to compare the facts and circumstances of the petitioner's case with the facts and circumstances of all other Florida death penalty cases involving black victims in order to determine if the first degree murderers in those cases were equally or more deserving to die. The petitioner thus requests the same type of case-by-case comparison by the federal judiciary that we have previously rejected in considering the petitioner's contention that Florida's death penalty is being imposed arbitrarily and capriciously. We need not repeat the myriad of difficult problems, legal and otherwise, generated by such federal court intrusion into the substantive decision making of the sentencing process which is reserved to the Florida state courts under Section 921.141.

Id. at 613.

59. Galanter, *Why the 'Haves' Come Out Ahead: Speculation on the Limits of Legal Change,* 9 L. & Soc. Rev. 95, 136-37 (1974) ("The architecture of courts severely limits the scale and scope of changes they can produce in the rules. Tradition and ideology limit the kinds of matters that come before them; not patterns of practice but individual instances, not 'problems' but cases framed by the parties and strained through requirements of standing, case or controversy, jurisdiction and so forth").

60. State v. Williams, 308 N.C. 47, 80, 301 S.E.2d 335, 355 (1983), *cert. denied,* 464 U.S. 865 (1983) ("The factors to be considered and their relevancy during proportionality review in a given capital case are not readily subject to complete enumeration and definition. Those factors will be as numerous and as varied as the cases coming before us on appeal").

61. Blake v. Zant, 513 F. Supp. 772, 825 (S.D. Ga. 1981) *rev'd in part* (Appendix) ("the Georgia law cannot be seen as a legislative failure, so much as still another reflection of the impossibility of the task. . . . The state judiciary can hardly be faulted for not following patterns which do not now exist and never have"); State v. Vereen, 312 N.C. 499, 519, 324 S.E.2d 250, 263 (1985) (although other cases "offer guidance" on the issue of disproportionality, "ultimately each case must rest on its own unique facts. An analysis which involves further inquiry into the endless combinations, variations, permutations, and nuances that an indepth review of every case in the pool would yield would be a fruitless endeavor"), *cert. denied,* 471 U.S. 1094 (1985); State v. Williams, 205 Neb. 56, 77, 287 N.W.2d 18, 29 (1979) ("It would be virtually impossible to find two murder cases which are the same in all respects"), *cert. denied,* 449 U.S. 891 (1980); Flamer v. State, 490 A.2d 104, 138, 143-44 (Del. 1983):

> The chief problem in proportionality review, and the one complained of by defendant, is selecting an array of similar cases with which to compare the death penalty imposed below. . . . Each of the 18 cases in our universe represents a horrible, senseless killing. To compare one against the other is a difficult task, almost like trying to compare the proverbial oranges and apples. In each there are different facts, different aggravating and mitigating circumstances, different prosecutors and defense counsel, and, above all, juries of 12 different persons who are cloaked with the discretion of reaching a unanimous verdict of death. . . . Therefore definitive comparison of cases is almost impossible and necessarily touches upon the realm of speculation.

Id., cert. denied, 464 U.S. 865 (1983).

62. State v. Williams, 308 N.C. 47, 80, 301 S.E.2d 335, 355-56 (1983):

We do not propose to attempt to employ mathematical or statistical models involving multiple regression analysis or other scientific techniques, currently in vogue among social scientists, which have been described as having "the seductive appeal of science and mathematics." . . . Even those with extensive training in data collection and statistical evaluation and analysis are unable to agree concerning the type of statistical methodology which should be employed if statistical or mathematical models are adopted for purposes of proportionality review.

Id., cert. denied, 464 U.S. 865 (1983). See also Thompson v. Aiken, 281 S.C. 239, 241-42, 315 S.E.2d 110, 111 (1984) :

In the final analysis, the allegation of statewide "patterns" raised by a specific capital defendant has no real bearing upon his individual guilt or innocence nor upon the correctness of any sentence imposed in his particular case. . . . Far less are we entitled to intrude upon the operations of executive officers when we have no more than general data complied [*sic*] for academic purposes.

63. *See supra* note 34.

64. Prosecutors and, to a lesser extent, juries appear to minimize this sort of discomfiture by imposing relatively few death sentences.

65. The Pennsylvania, Delaware, and Nebraska courts appear to have information on all death-eligible cases processed through their systems. While the Georgia Supreme Court considers only appealed cases, its data set is adequate to support an effective review system within that universe of cases. The New Jersey Supreme Court has not yet taken any proportionality-review decisions, but a recent decision discussing the issue suggests it may be amenable to the development of a comprehensive system of review with full involvement of the parties. *See* State v. Ramseur, 106 N.J. 123, 324-31, 524 A.2d 188, 291-94 (1987).

66. *See infra* chap. 10, note 110 and accompanying text.

CHAPTER TEN

McCleskey v. Kemp: Background, Record, and Adjudications

In this chapter we first describe the legal background against which the Mc-Cleskey case developed in the state and federal courts and the circumstances of our involvement in the case. We then describe the data from our Georgia studies that we presented in the McCleskey case, with special reference to the Charging and Sentencing Study (css). We also report some results that we developed for the McCleskey hearing but did not offer in evidence and some analyses of the css data that we conducted subsequent to the hearing. Finally, we describe in detail the rulings and analyses of the trial court, the Eleventh Circuit Court of Appeals, and the Supreme Court, with special reference to our Georgia studies and to issues of proof in discrimination cases. Chapter 11 critiques the rulings of the two appellate courts, while Appendix B presents a methodological critique of the district court's opinion.

THE BACKGROUND TO *McCLESKEY V. KEMP*

The Legal Context in Which *McCleskey* Arose

By the early 1980s, the decisions of the United States Supreme Court suggested three possible constitutional grounds for challenging the manner in which post-*Furman* capital-sentencing systems were being applied. The first possible "as applied" claim was that a death-sentencing system violated the cruel and unusual punishments provision of the Eighth Amendment because it routinely imposed comparatively excessive death sentences. The basis for this claim was language in *Furman v. Georgia* and the Court's decision in *Godfrey v. Georgia* (1980).[1] *Furman* characterized as arbitrary death sentences that could not be meaningfully distinguished from cases that generally received lesser sentences. *Godfrey* involved a death sentence imposed upon an estranged husband for the shotgun slaying of his wife and mother-in-law at a time in which he was distraught over a separation from his wife and child. The *Godfrey* majority vacated the death sentence on the ground that it had been imposed under circumstances that, on the basis of the Georgia Supreme Court's own prior decisions, did not establish the relevant, statutorily designated aggravating circumstance—vile and wanton slaying—upon which it was based. The majority opinion also quoted with approval the language of *Furman* requiring that a death-sentencing system must "in short, provide a 'meaningful basis for distinguishing the few cases in which [the penalty] is imposed from the many cases in which it is not.' "[2] Suggesting that most domestic homicides in Georgia did not result in a death sentence, the court stated that there was "no principled way to distinguish [Godfrey's] case, in which the death penalty was imposed, from the many cases in which it was not."[3]

There were two compelling reasons why a systemwide constitutional challenge on the theory of arbitrariness and comparative excessiveness did not appear promising. First, in spite of the outcome of *Godfrey*, the degree of support in the Supreme Court for any broader attack on comparative excessiveness was unclear. Indeed, of the original five supporters of the concept in *Furman v. Georgia*, only Justices Brennan, Marshall, and White remained on the Court. And no recent decision of the Supreme Court or any federal Court of Appeals had invalidated a death sentence on the ground of comparative excessiveness.[4]

The second problem with a challenge to a death-sentencing system on this theory of arbitrariness was the lack of an accepted standard for measuring excessiveness in an individual case and for challenging the constitutionality of an entire system on this basis. Both the *Furman* and *Godfrey* discussions of arbitrariness and excessiveness were based on quite general concepts, and there was no lower-court jurisprudence either defining the concept with particularity or identifying methods of proof that would be sufficient to support a successful claim.

The second possible basis for an as-applied challenge would focus on the lack of comparative-proportionality review in the supreme courts of those states whose statutes did not require such a review. The opinions of certain justices in *Gregg* implied that the Eighth Amendment might require an effective system of comparative-proportionality review, particularly in jurisdictions that gave sentencing juries extremely broad discretion.[5] Also, the *Godfrey* opinion had emphasized the importance of the appellate-review function in ensuring rational and consistent death sentencing.[6] On the basis of these decisions, a 1981 California federal habeas corpus case, *Pulley v. Harris*, challenged a death sentence on the grounds that the California statute did require a proportionality review in the case. Harris's claim was successful in the United States Court of Appeals but was ultimately rejected in the United States Supreme Court. By a 7–2 vote, *Pulley v. Harris* (1984) held that comparative proportionality was not constitutionally required, regardless of the degree of jury discretion involved.[7]

The third possible constitutional challenge suggested by the case law was a claim of racial discrimination. The Supreme Court's decisions in the 1960s and 1970s had previously applied the equal-protection clause of the Fourteenth Amendment to condemn state discrimination on racial grounds in such contexts as jury selection and public school administration. It seemed probable that these decisions would extend to discrimination in the application of a facially neutral death-sentencing statute if the required burden of proof could be met. Since *Washington v. Davis* (1976), it has been plain that in order to prevail under an equal-protection claim a claimant must establish purposeful or intentional discrimination.[8] It was unclear, however, whether an equal-protection claimant had to establish a "conscious" purpose or intent to discriminate, or whether evidence of a nonconscious but identifiable response to the racial characteristics of the cases would be sufficient. Finally, it was not clear whether proof of purposeful discrimination in the system as a whole would be a sufficient basis for granting a defendant relief if he were a member of a disadvantaged minority. For example, in Fourteenth Amendment jury-discrimination cases, a black defendant's conviction will be vacated if he can show purposeful discrimination against blacks in the selection of jury pools from which venires are drawn. Following this model, a black defendant's death sentence would be vacated if he can show classwide, purposeful race-of-defendant discrimination in his death-sentencing system. Alternatively, compelling evidence of classwide, purposeful discrimination might serve only to create a presumption of discrimination in individual cases, which the state could rebut with evidence of the particulars of the defendant's case. Whatever the uncertainties were on these issues, it was clearly perceived that evidence of classwide discrimination was relevant to a Fourteenth Amendment equal-protection claim.

The Supreme Court's decision in *Furman v. Georgia* also established the relevance of racial discrimination under the Eighth Amendment. Although the majority of the *Furman* justices considered the claims of racial discrimination to be unproven, their opinions clearly indicated that proof of purposeful discrimination would create a sufficient risk of arbitrariness and caprice to sustain a finding of arbitrariness under the Eighth Amendment's cruel and unusual punishments provision. The Court's post-*Furman* decisions, particularly *Zant v. Stephens*, strengthened this belief. In *Zant*, the Court stated that the defective statutory aggravating circumstance under attack in the case was not equivalent to attaching "the 'aggravating' label to factors that are constitutionally impermissible or totally irrelevant to the sentencing process, such as for example the race, religion, or political affiliation of the defendant."[9] This language clearly implied that race-of-defendant or race-of-victim discrimination, whether overt or covert, would be constitutionally impermissible.[10] What was unclear, however, was whether a discrimination-based Eighth Amendment claim required proof of purposeful discrimination in the same manner as the equal-protection clause. It was also unclear what the appropriate remedy would be for a defendant who successfully established an Eighth Amendment violation on the basis of racial discrimination.

In the post-*Furman* period the most detailed analysis of the proof that might be required of a claimant alleging arbitrariness and discrimination in the application of a death-sentencing system came in the 1982 Fifth Circuit case *Smith v. Balkcom*. Smith's allegation of race-of-victim discrimination was supported by a statewide statistical analysis that showed a race-of-victim disparity in death-sentencing rates among Georgia cases reported to the FBI. The court rejected the claim on several methodological grounds, the principal one being that the study controlled for only a single statutory aggravating circumstance—whether the case involved a serious contemporaneous offense. The court's criticisms of Smith's study suggested, however, the type of proof that might support a claim of arbitrariness and discrimination in capital sentencing.

> In some instances, circumstantial or statistical evidence of racially disproportionate impact may be so strong that the results permit no other inference but that they are the product of a racially discriminatory intent or purpose. . . . Smith's evidence, however, does not present such a case. The raw data selected for the statistical study bear no more than a highly attenuated relationship to capital cases actually presented for trial in the state. The leap from that data to the conclusion of discriminatory intent or purpose leaves untouched countless racially neutral variables. The statistics are not inconsistent with the proper application of the structured capital punishment law of the state found constitutional in *Gregg v. Georgia*. . . . Here, the proffered evidence would not have been of sufficient probative value to have required response and no hearing was required. . . .

> No data is offered as to whether or not charges or indictments grew out of reported incidents or as to whether charges were for murder under aggravating circumstances, murder in which no aggravating circumstances were alleged, voluntary manslaughter, involuntary manslaughter, or other offenses. The data are not refined to select incidents in which mitigating circumstances were advanced or found or those cases in which evidence of aggravating circumstances was sufficient to warrant submission of the death penalty vel non to a jury. No incidents resulting in not guilty verdicts were removed from the data. The unsupported assumption is that all such variables were equally distributed, racially, sexually, offender and victim, throughout the SHRs [Supplemental Homicide Reports to the FBI from the local police]. No conclusions of evidentiary value can be predicated upon such unsupported assumptions. [11]

The clear implication of the *Smith* opinion was that proof that met these requirements, as well as those of *Washington v. Davis*, would compel the court to consider classwide claims of discrimination under the Fourteenth and Eighth Amendments.

Our Involvement in *McCleskey*

In 1980, while we were completing the data-collection stage of the Procedural Reform Study (PRS), lawyers at the NAACP Legal Defense and Educational Fund, Inc. (LDF), requested us to undertake an empirical research study that might prove useful in their efforts to challenge the post-*Furman* application of the death penalty. We accepted their offer, but advised the LDF representatives that our results might prove to be of limited usefulness or even damaging to their cause. We agreed, however, that, if requested, we would testify concerning our findings in litigation on behalf of death-row inmates represented by the LDF. In exchange for this commitment, the LDF agreed to finance the study through a grant from the Edna McConnell Clark Foundation and to give us complete discretion as to the publication and dissemination of our findings.

In the summer and fall of 1980, we explored with the LDF's attorneys the focus and location of the contemplated study. It was agreed from the outset that the study should focus on racial discrimination. The most suitable state for the study was unclear, however, and we tentatively explored several possibilities. Georgia was finally selected because of its prominence as a death-sentencing jurisdiction, because a pilot study from the Procedural Reform Study gave us some idea of what a more extensive study might produce, and because of the high quality of the data on homicide cases that were available in that state.

In the winter of 1980 and the spring of 1981, we developed an expanded questionnaire for the new Charging and Sentencing Study (CSS), and we collected data over the summer and early fall of 1981. At the same time, we also began an analysis of the PRS data. By the spring of 1982 we had produced a set of preliminary findings from the PRS. In the summer and fall of 1982, the LDF cited these findings in several Georgia cases to support its request for a post-conviction hearing on the issue of arbitrariness and discrimination in the application of Georgia's post-*Furman* death-sentencing system. Only one of these requests was granted. On October 8, 1982, J. Owen Forrester, a federal district judge in Atlanta, ordered an evidentiary hearing on the issue. The petitioner in that case was Warren McCleskey.

McCleskey's Claims

McCleskey, a black man, had been convicted on October 12, 1978, in the Superior Court of Fulton County, Georgia, of the murder of police officer Frank Schlatt, who was white. The circumstances of McCleskey's crime, arrest, and trial were described by the United States Supreme Court as follows:

> The evidence at trial indicated that McCleskey and three accomplices planned and carried out the robbery. All four were armed. McCleskey entered the front

of the store while the other three entered the rear. McCleskey secured the front of the store by rounding up the customers and forcing them to lie face down on the floor. The other three rounded up the employees in the rear and tied them up with tape. The manager was forced at gunpoint to turn over the store receipts, his watch, and $6.00. During the course of the robbery, a police officer, answering a silent alarm, entered the store through the front door. As he was walking down the center aisle of the store, two shots were fired. Both struck the officer. One hit him in the face and killed him.

Several weeks later, McCleskey was arrested in connection with an unrelated offense. He confessed that he had participated in the furniture store robbery, but denied that he had shot the police officer. At trial, the State introduced evidence that at least one of the bullets that struck the officer was fired from a .38 caliber Rossi revolver. This description matched the description of the gun that McCleskey had carried during the robbery. The State also introduced the testimony of two witnesses who had heard McCleskey admit to the shooting.[12]

McCleskey's postconviction petition asserted a number of constitutional claims. Most relevant to the subject of this book was his assertion that his death sentence was unconstitutional because it had been imposed discriminatorily on the basis of his race and the race of his victim. In support of his request for a hearing on this issue, McCleskey's petition argued that the evidence he planned to present would support a finding that Georgia had applied its death-sentencing statute in a manner that violated the Fourteenth Amendment's equal-protection clause because it purposefully discriminated against defendants who were black and defendants whose victims were white. He also argued that such a discriminatory application of the death penalty constituted an arbitrary, capricious, and irrational application of the death sentence and violated the Eighth Amendment of the United States Constitution.

THE *McCLESKEY V. KEMP* RECORD

The hearing that Judge Forrester ordered in *McCleskey* took place over two weeks in August 1983. It began with several days of testimony describing the background of our empirical studies and the data-collection process we employed. Next, we presented our empirical findings and our interpretation of their meaning and validity.[13] The State then presented two expert witnesses who challenged the validity both of our data base and of our statistical procedures, and who explained how, in their opinion, these imperfections might have affected the validity of our empirical findings.[14] The State's experts also argued that the more aggravated nature of the white-victim cases explained the racial disparities in our findings; these experts did not, however, offer their own multivariate analyses of our data or of any other data that estimated a race-of-defendant or race-of-victim effect. The State's experts also pointed out that, even in the life-sentence cases included in our study, white-victim cases were generally more aggravated than black-victim cases. This, they argued, undercut McCleskey's claim of race-of-victim discrimination because if, as McCleskey asserted, such discrimination did occur, those white-victim cases that resulted in life sentences should be less aggravated than the pool of life-sentence cases involving black victims. In rebuttal to the State's arguments, McCleskey's lawyers offered additional testimony, including that of Richard Berk, a sociologist and expert on criminal justice.[15]

Findings from the Procedural Reform Study (PRS)

The findings of the Procedural Reform Study constitute only a small part of the statistical evidence presented in the *McCleskey* hearing. Because this book discusses the findings of the Procedural Reform Study so extensively, we will describe those findings that were presented in the *McCleskey* hearing only briefly.[16]

The first set of PRS findings addressed in the hearing were a series of multiple-regression analyses that estimated race-of-victim disparities in the rates at which defendants convicted of murder at trial were sentenced to death. We estimated the race-of-victim coefficients in these analyses after simultaneously adjusting variously for 5 to 150-plus nonracial aggravating and mitigating factors. As chapter 4 describes, we selected these factors on either *a priori* grounds or on the basis of both *a priori* considerations and the statistical significance of their relationship to the sentencing outcome. These analyses showed average race-of-victim disparities among defendants convicted of murder at trial ranging between 8 and 9 percentage points, all of which were statistically significant beyond the .05 level. We also presented the results of small-scale logistic-regression analyses that controlled for from 5 to 10 legitimate background factors such as the defendant's prior record or the number of victims. These results produced odds multipliers of 2.8 and 3.0, significant at the .01 level.[17] These results were quite comparable to the race-of-victim findings reported in chapter 6 of this book, which were produced after the *McCleskey* hearing.

The second set of PRS findings presented were race-of-victim disparities in prosecutorial and jury decision making, estimated with partial-regression coefficients. The largest prosecutorial linear model, which included simultaneous controls for more than 150 legitimate background variables, showed a statistically significant race-of-victim effect of 13 percentage points, while a smaller model, which limited background factors to 21 variables showing a statistically significant nonperverse relationship to the prosecutorial decision to seek a death sentence, produced a race-of-victim odds multiplier of 3.4, significant at the .0001 level.[18] The linear jury analyses, which controlled for all statutory aggravating factors and forty-three mitigating factors, showed race-of-victim disparities ranging from 16 (p = .05) to 23 (p = .04) percentage points.[19]

The results of the logistic-regression analyses of the prosecutorial and jury decisions that we presented showed mixed results. The prosecutorial results consisted of race-of-victim disparities estimated in four separate procedures that controlled for from five to twenty-one background variables; the estimated death-odds multipliers for the race-of-victim variables were from 2.8 to 3.4, all significant beyond the .01 level.[20] In contrast, comparable jury analyses produced only small death-odds multipliers (from 1.2 to 1.4), none of which was statistically significant beyond the .10 level.[21]

The PRS regression results on jury decision making presented in the McCleskey hearing provided weaker evidence of race-of-victim discrimination than the results presented in chapter 6, which were produced after the hearing. Although the race-of-victim disparities in both sets of findings have a sign consistent with the discrimination hypothesis, the magnitude and level of statistical significance of the disparities in the McCleskey PRS evidence is considerably lower.[22] We note, however, that the jury race-of-victim findings reported in chapter 6 were also mixed in terms of the observed level of statistical significance. On balance, we place the most confidence in the chapter 6 jury results estimated in cross-tabular analyses, which show a race-of-victim effect of approximately 14 percentage points (statistically significant at approximately the .10 level).[23]

Findings Presented from the Charging and Sentencing Study (CSS)

As noted above, our findings from the Procedural Reform Study constituted only a small part of the evidence that we presented in the McCleskey hearing. Our second investigation, the Charging and Sentencing Study, is the principal source of evidence in the McCleskey record.[24]

The Statewide Evidence from the Charging and Sentencing Study (CSS)

The findings from the Charging and Sentencing Study that we presented in the McCleskey case parallel to a striking degree the statewide results from the Procedural Reform Study reported earlier in this book. By and large, the results of the two studies differ only with respect to the race-of-defendant effects estimated within the white-victim cases.

The primary objective of the CSS discrimination analyses presented to the court was to estimate racial disparities in death-sentencing rates among defendants indicted for murder. Such disparities would reflect the combined effects of all decisions made from the point of indictment through the jury's sentencing decision.

To place in perspective the racial disparities estimated within this population of cases, we note that the death-sentencing rate for all defendants indicted for murder was 5 percent (128/2,484). This average rate is substantially lower than the 18 percent death-sentencing rate reported in the Procedural Reform Study for defendants convicted of murder at trial. The reason, of course, is that it is based on the very much larger pool of defendants indicted for murder, most of whom never reach trial because they plead guilty to murder or to a lesser offense.[25]

Table 50 presents the unadjusted race-of-victim and race-of-defendant effects in the CSS for all defendants indicted for murder.[26] Part I shows a 10-percentage-point difference in the rates at which white- and black-victim cases result in death sentences. And when characterized with a ratio measure, the death-sentencing rate for the white-victim cases is 8.3 times (.11/.0133) higher than the rate for the black-victim cases.[27]

Although the unadjusted −3 point race-of-defendant disparity in part II of Table 50 suggests that, overall, black defendants enjoy a slight advantage in the system, the breakdown of rates by the defendant-victim racial combinations shown in part III of the table suggests that, within the white-victim cases, black defendants may be treated more punitively than white defendants—that is, the death-sentencing rate is .21 (50/233) for the black defendants with white victims, versus .08 (58/748) for the white defendants with white victims.

Starting with these unadjusted racial disparities, we developed a series of multivariate analyses to estimate statewide race-of-defendant and race-of-victim effects after adjustment for a variety of legitimate nonracial background factors.

Statewide Adjusted Race-of-Victim Disparities: Overall Effects We commenced the analysis using cross-tabular techniques that controlled for variables our prior research indicated were important in terms of explaining which Georgia homicide defendants received a death sentence. Figure 31 presents the results of one such analysis offered in the *McCleskey* hearing.[28] It estimates, among defendants indicted for murder, race-of-victim effects after adjustment for the contemporaneous "felony circumstances" and "serious prior record" variables. The "All cases" row of figures indicates the death-sentencing rates among the four subgroups of cases produced with these two control variables. It shows sharply rising death-sentencing rates as the cases become more aggravated.

The next-to-bottom row of figures in Figure 31 measures the race-of-victim

Table 50. Unadjusted Race-of-Victim and Race-of-Defendant Disparities in Death-Sentencing Rates, among All Murder and Voluntary Manslaughter Cases (Post-*Furman* Georgia)[1]

	Rates and Disparities
I. Race-of-victim disparity	
White-victim cases (WV)	.11 (108/981)
Black-victim cases (BV)	.0133 (20/1,503)
Difference (WV−BV)	10 pts.
Ratio (WV/BV)	8.3
II. Race-of-defendant disparity	
Black-defendant cases (BD)	.04 (68/1,676)
White-defendant cases (WD)	.07 (60/808)
Difference (BD−WD)	−3 pts.
Ratio (BD/WD)	.57
III. Defendant/victim racial composition	
1. Black defendant/white victim (B/W)	.21 (50/233)
2. White defendant/white victim (W/W)	.08 (58/748)
3. Black defendant/black victim (B/B)	.01 (18/1443)
4. White defendant/black victim (W/B)	.03 (2/60)
All cases	.05 (128/2484)

1. The disparities are estimated for the universe of all cases that resulted in a murder or voluntary manslaughter conviction. When the analysis is limited to death-eligible cases, the race-of-victim disparity is 12 percentage points (.14 for white-victim cases versus .02 for black-victim cases), while the race-of-defendant disparity is −3 points (.07 for black defendants versus .10 for white defendants). The rates by defendant/victim racial combination in the death-eligible cases are B/W .23, W/W .11, B/B .02, and W/B .04. *See supra* chap. 4, note 38, on the use of all cases and those deemed death-eligible by our measures as a basis for estimating racial disparities.

disparities within each of the four subgroups of cases. It shows a distinct association between the aggravation level of cases and the magnitude of the race-of-victim effects. Among the less aggravated cases, in which the death-sentencing rates are quite low, the race-of-victim effects are also quite modest. But among the more aggravated cases, which show .16 and .27 death-sentencing rates, the race-of-victim disparities are 13 and 25 percentage points, respectively.

While cross-tabular analyses have the virtue of simplicity and clarity, they are dependent on large sample sizes to develop stable estimates. Even with a universe of over 2,400 cases, Figure 31 makes plain that the death-sentencing activity in the system is substantially confined to the 501 cases involving a

Figure 31. Race-of-Victim Disparities in Overall Death-Sentencing Rates, Controlling Simultaneously for Felony Circumstances and Prior Record (Charging and Sentencing Study)[1]

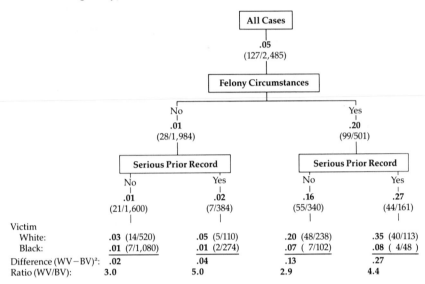

Victim				
White:	.03 (14/520)	.05 (5/110)	.20 (48/238)	.35 (40/113)
Black:	.01 (7/1,080)	.01 (2/274)	.07 (7/102)	.08 (4/48)
Difference (WV−BV)[2]:	.02	.04	.13	.27
Ratio (WV/BV):	3.0	5.0	2.9	4.4

1. Entries in this table are estimated death-sentencing rates for the indicated case categories. The rates are computed as numbers of death sentences divided by estimated numbers of cases in each category. The estimated numbers of cases are weighted counts of sampled cases. The totals of 2,485 and 127 (rather than 2,484 and 128) reflect roundoff error.
2. The average difference is .055, which is significant at the .0001 level (Mantel-Haenszel $Z = 5.39$).

contemporaneous felony. With this many cases, the limits of a fine-grained cross-tabular analysis are quickly reached. Thus, we relied primarily on multiple-regression analyses to produce the principal multivariate support for McCleskey's claims.

The centerpiece of McCleskey's race-of-victim evidence was the partial-regression coefficient for the race-of-victim variable estimated in a logistic-regression analysis after controlling for a core model of thirty-nine legitimate variables. We selected these thirty-nine variables because, from both a theoretical and statistical standpoint, they appeared to exercise the greatest influence in determining which defendants indicted for murder would actually receive a death sentence. The odds multiplier calculated from the race-of-victim coefficient in this analysis was 4.3, significant at the .005 level.[29] This figure is virtually identical to the race-of-victim disparity estimated for the Procedural Reform Study in a comparable analysis of defendants found guilty of murder at trial.[30]

The linear-regression coefficient estimated for the race-of-victim variable, after adjustment for the 39 core background variables, was .08, significant at the .001 level. We supplemented this analysis with a series of linear and logistic multiple-regression analyses, reported in Table 51, which controlled for varying numbers of background variables. The linear analyses (part I of Table 51) produced race-of-victim coefficients ranging from .06 to .07, all significant beyond the .05 level.[31] The largest of these analyses, which controlled simultaneously for more than 230 background variables, estimated a race-of-victim partial-regression coefficient of .06, significant at the .01 level.[32] These estimates are quite similar to the race-of-victim disparities reported in chapter 6 that we estimated with comparable analyses of cases from the PRS that resulted in murder-trial convictions.[33] The alternative logistic analyses

Table 51. Race-of-Victim and Race-of-Defendant Disparities in Death-Sentencing Rates for Defendants Indicted for Murder, As Estimated with Regression Coefficients, Controlling for Alternative Sets of Nonracial Background Characteristics (CSS)

Part I. Weighted-Least-Squares Regression Results		
Nonracial Variables in the Analysis	Coefficients and Level of Statistical Significance	
	Race of Victim	Race of Defendant[1]
a. 230+ aggravating, mitigating, evidentiary, and suspect factors[2]	.06 (.01)	.07 (.02)
b. 10 statutory aggravating circumstances and 126 factors derived from the entire file by a factor analysis	.07 (.01)	.06 (.01)
c. 43 nonracial variables with a statistically significant relationship ($p \leq .10$) to death-sentencing results[3]	.06 (.004)	.06 (.005)
d. 14 legitimate, nonarbitrary, and statistically significant ($p \leq .10$) factors screened with W.L.S. regression procedures[4]	.06 (.005)	.06 (.01)
e. 13 legitimate, nonarbitrary, and statistically significant ($p \leq .10$) factors screened with logistic-regression procedures[5]	.06 (.02)	.05 (.08)

(continued on next page)

Table 51. *(cont.)*

	Part II. Logistic Regression Results			
	Race of Victim		Race of Defendant	
Nonracial Variables in the Analysis	Coefficient	Death-Odds Multiplier	Coefficient	Death-Odds Multiplier
a. 14 legitimate, nonarbitrary, and statistically significant ($p \leq .10$) factors screened with W.L.S. procedures[6]	1.28 (.003)	3.6	.76 (.08)	2.1
b. 13 legitimate, nonarbitrary and statistically significant ($p \leq .10$) factors screened with logistic-regression procedures[7]	1.11 (.007)	3.0	−.15 (.68)	.86

1. *See infra* note 48 and accompanying text for a discussion of race-of-defendant effects.
2. Variables are listed in app. L, sched. 3.
3. Variables are listed in app. L, sched. 7.
4. Variables are listed in app. L, sched. 5. W.L.S. means weighted least squares.
5. Variables are listed in app. L, sched. 6.
6. Variables are listed in app. L, sched. 5.
7. Variables are listed in app. L, sched. 6.

(part II of Table 51), which had fewer variables, showed smaller, but still statistically significant, race-of-victim effects than those observed in the main 39-variable model.

One basis for assessing the influence of the victim's race in Georgia's capital-charging-and-sentencing systems is a comparison of the statistical impact of the race-of-victim variable with the comparable impact of variables for important legitimate case characteristics. Table 52 compares the relative statistical impact of the race-of-victim variable with the impact of the variables for legitimate case characteristics in the 39-variable model plus the race-of-defendant variable. Those data indicate that the race of the victim has an importance of the same order of magnitude as "multiple stabbing," "serious prior record," and "armed robbery involved," and its effect is larger than several variables of well-recognized importance, such as the victim having been a stranger.[34]

The second main set of findings from the Charging and Sentencing Study presented at the *McCleskey* hearing demonstrated that the race-of-victim effects that we observed occurred primarily in cases that were in the midrange in aggravation level, and that, within that range, the effects were much larger

Table 52. Logistic-Regression Coefficients, Estimated for Selected Aggravating and Mitigating Factors and the Race of Victim and Defendant in an Analysis of Death-Sentencing Outcomes, css[1]

Variable Label and Name	Death-Odds Multiplier	Adjusted Logistic Regression Coefficient (with level of statistical significance)
1. Defendant was not the triggerman (NOKILL)	.06	−2.75 (.0001)
2. Defendant admitted guilt and no defense asserted (DEFADMIT)	.28	−1.27 (.12)
3. Defendant had a history of drug or alcohol abuse (DRGHIS)	.36	−1.01 (.007)
4. Defendant was under 17 years of age (SMYOUTH)	.41	−.88 (.23)
5. Jealousy motive (JEALOUS)	.47	−.74 (.53)
6. Family, lover, liquor, or barroom quarrel (BLVICMOD)	.54	−.61 (.15)
7. Defendant was retired, student, juvenile, housewife (MITDEFN)	.54	−.61 (.64)
8. Hate motive (HATE)	.71	−.34 (.69)
9. Pecuniary gain motive for self/other (LDFB4)[2]	.80	−.22 (.70)
10. *Defendant was black* (BLACKD)	.94	−.06 (.88)
11. Number of prior defendant felony prison terms (PRISONX)	1.1	.08 (.67)
12. Defendant caused death risk in public place to 2 or more people (LDFB3)	1.1	.14 (.74)
13. One or more coperpetrators involved (COPERP)	1.3	.24 (.56)
14. Defendant was a female (FEMDEF)	1.3	.28 (.70)
15. One or more convictions for a violent personal crime, burglary, or arson (VPCARBR)	1.35	.30 (.53)
16. Nonproperty-related contemporaneous crime (NONPROPC)	1.4	.35 (.64)
17. Killing to avoid, stop arrest of self, other (LDFB10)	1.5	.41 (.32)
18. Victim was a police or corrections officer on duty (LDFB8)	1.7	.52 (.58)
19. Defendant primary mover in planning homicide or contemporaneous offense (DLEADER)	1.7	.55 (.33)
20. Rape/armed robbery/kidnapping plus silence witness, execution, or victim pleaded for life (LDFB7D)	1.8	.60 (.16)
21. Coperpetrator received a lesser sentence (CPLESSEN)	2.2	.78 (.09)
22. Multiple shots (MULSH)	2.2	.79 (.04)
23. Victim was drowned (DROWN)	2.6	.96 (.24)
24. Victim was a stranger (STRANGER)	2.8	1.03 (.01)
25. Victim bedridden/handicapped (VBED)	2.8	1.04 (.33)

(continued on next page)

Table 52. *(cont.)*

Variable Label and Name	Death-Odds Multiplier	Adjusted Logistic Regression Coefficient (with level of statistical significance)
26. Kidnapping involved (KIDNAP)	2.9	1.06 (.17)
27. Victim weak or frail (VWEAK)	3.1	1.13 (.19)
28. Defendant had a prior record for murder, armed robbery, rape, or kidnapping with bodily injury (LDFB1)	4.1	1.40 (.009)
29. Armed robbery involved (ARMROB)	4.2	1.43 (.02)
30. *One or more white victims* (WHVICRC)	4.3	1.45 (.003)
31. Multiple stabbing (MULTSTAB)	4.7	1.54 (.002)
32. Victim was 12 or younger (VICCHILD)	4.8	1.56 (.03)
33. Number of defendant prior murder convictions (MURPRIOR)	5.2	1.66 (.27)
34. Murder for hire (LDFB6)	5.9	1.77 (.08)
35. Defendant was a prisoner or escapee (LDFB9)	7.7	2.04 (.002)
36. Defendant killed two or more people (TWOVIC)	7.9	2.07 (.005)
37. Mental torture involved (MENTORT)	9.7	2.27 (.009)
38. Rape involved (RAPE)	12.8	2.55 (.001)
39. Defendant's motive was to collect insurance (INSMOT)	20.1	3.01 (.01)
40. Victim was tortured physically (TORTURE)	27.4	3.31 (.003)
41. Motive was to avenge role by judicial officer, D.A., lawyer (AVENGE)	28.9	3.36 (.25)
Constant		−6.15 (.0001)

1. The table reports the odds multiplier and coefficients for the race-of-defendant and the race-of-victim variables in the 39-variable core model. The outcome variable was DSENTALL, coded: 1 = Death Sentence, 0 = Other Sentence. The model with supporting statistics is also presented *supra* chap. 4, note 43, and *infra* app. L, schedule 4.

2. The negative sign of the coefficient for LDFB4 (pecuniary gain motive) is perverse. (*See supra* chap. 4, note 44 and accompanying text, for a description of perverse variables.) We attribute the sign of LDFB4 to its correlation with the variable for armed robbery (ARMROB).

than the 6 to 7 percentage point average race-of-victim effect estimated for all 2,484 cases in the universe. Figure 32 shows the midrange concentration of the race-of-victim effects in the css's black-victim cases.[35] Based on a multivariate linear model containing both linear and quadratic culpability effects and a race-by-culpability interaction, it shows 95 percent confidence limits for the probability of a death sentence in black-defendant cases with white victims and in black-defendant cases with black victims. The left (Y) axis indicates the probability of a death sentence for the cases distributed along the X axis, which indicates the level of aggravation measured with a culpability index estimated with the thirty-nine core variable multiple-regression model referred to above. Figure 32 shows that in the midrange of cases, where McCleskey's case is located, there was a concentration of race-of-victim disparities on the order of from 11 to 29 percentage points, the best estimate being 17. Specifically, the model estimated that in black-defendant cases with a level of aggravation comparable to McCleskey's case, defendants with white victims faced an estimated death-sentencing rate of between .34 and .43, while defendants with black victims faced estimated rates of between .14 and .23.

We also demonstrated the concentration of race-of-victim effects in the midrange of cases by comparing the actual death-sentencing rates for white- and black-victim cases after adjustment for case culpability. Table 53 presents a distribution of the 472 most aggravated cases in our study along a culpability scale derived from the results of a linear multiple-regression analysis designed to explain which defendants indicted for murder actually received a death sentence.[36] The average death-sentencing rate for these cases, which account

Figure 32. Black Defendant Model, Georgia Charging and Sentencing Study, 1973–1979[1]

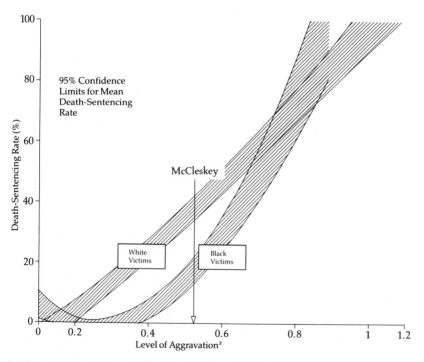

1. The curves represent 95% confidence limits on the average death-sentencing rate at increasing levels of aggravation (redrawn from computer output).
2. See *supra* chapter 4, note 43, for a description of this index.

Table 53. Race-of-Victim Disparities in Death-Sentencing Rates among Defendants Indicted for Murder, Controlling for the Predicted Likelihood of a Death Sentence and the Race of the Defendant (css)[1]

A	B	C	D	E	F	G	H	I	J
Predicted Chance of a Death Sentence, from 1 (low) to 8 (high)	Average Actual Sentencing Rate at Each Level	Death-Sentencing Rates for Black Defendants		Arithmetic Difference in Race-of-Victim Rates (Col.C − Col.D)	Ratio of Race-of-Victim Rates (Col.C/ Col.D)	Death-Sentencing Rates for White Defendants		Arithmetic Difference in Race-of-Victim Rates (Col.G − Col.H)	Ratio of Race-of-Victim Rates (Col.G/ Col.H)
		White-Victim Cases	Black-Victim Cases			White-Victim Cases	Black-Victim Cases		
1	.00 (0/33)	.00 (0/9)	.00 (0/19)	.00	0	.00 (0/5)	—	—	—
2	.00 (0/55)	.00 (0/8)	.00 (0/27)	.00	0	.00 (0/19)	.00 (0/1)	.00	Infinite
3	.08 (6/76)	.30 (3/10)	.11 (2/18)	.19	2.73	.03 (1/39)	.00 (0/9)	.03	0
4	.07 (4/57)	.23 (3/13)	.00 (0/15)	.23	Infinite	.03 (1/29)	—	—	—
5	.26 (15/58)	.35 (9/26)	.17 (2/12)	.18	2.06	.20 (4/20)	—	—	—
6	.17 (11/64)	.38 (3/8)	.05 (1/20)	.33	7.60	.16 (5/32)	.50 (2/4)	−.34	.32
7	.41 (29/71)	.64 (9/14)	.38 (5/13)	.26	1.68	.38 (15/39)	.00 (0/5)	.38	Infinite
8	.88 (51/58)	.91 (20/22)	.75 (6/8)	.16	1.21	.89 (25/28)	—	—	—

1. The overall race-of-victim disparity, estimated with a logistic-coefficient measure, was 1.31 (with a death-odds multiplier of 3.7), statistically significant at the .01 level (adjusted X^2 was 10.36). These results were produced with the procedure adopted from Cressie, *Playing Safe With Misweighted Means*, 77 J. AM. STAT. ASSN. 754 (1982). *See* Woodworth, *Analysis of a Y-Stratified Sample: The Georgia Charging and Sentencing Study*, in PROCEEDINGS OF THE SECOND WORKSHOP ON LAW AND JUSTICE STATISTICS: 1984, p. 18, Bureau of Justice Statistics, U.S. Dept. of Justice (E. Gelfand ed. 1985). The overall race-of-victim measure comparable to a least-squares regression coefficient is .06.

for 90 percent of the death sentences imposed, was .25 (116/472), but in the most aggravated subgroup of cases the rate rose to .88 (51/58). The race-of-victim disparities in the midrange (culpability levels 3 to 7) are in the 20- to 30-percentage-point range, a result strikingly similar to the effects estimated in a similar analysis in chapter 6 for the cases that resulted in a murder-trial conviction.[37]

We developed our third set of findings at the request of Judge Forrester. During the course of the hearing, he developed from our data collection instrument for the Charging and Sentencing Study a detailed model of the case characteristics that he believed would define the pool of cases that were the most aggravated and therefore the leading candidates for a death sentence. It turned out, however, that only 46 of the 2,484 cases in the universe of the Charging and Sentencing Study met his standards for inclusion in the category of most aggravated cases and only 33% (15/46) of these cases actually resulted in a death sentence. Moreover, among the white-victim cases in this sample, the death-sentencing rate was .38 (15/39), as contrasted to a rate of .0 (0/7) in the black-victim cases.[38]

Because of the small number of cases in Judge Forrester's sample (they accounted for only 12 percent [15/128] of the death-sentence cases), we relaxed some of the requirements of his model.[39] By doing so, we were able to identify a pool of 647 cases, which accounted for 76 percent (97/128) of the death sentences imposed.[40] The overall death-sentencing rate in this pool of cases was .15 (97/647), three times higher than the rate for all cases in the universe. Within this group, however, there was an 18-percentage-point race-of-victim disparity—a rate of .23 (84/369) for the white-victim cases versus a rate of .05 (13/278) for the black victim cases. We also conducted for these 647 cases a logistic regression analysis that controlled for the thirty-nine background variables in our core model mentioned above. The estimated race-of-victim effect yielded a statistically significant 4.0 odds multiplier.[41]

Our final analysis of race-of-victim effects among defendants indicted for murder paralleled the analysis of armed-robbery cases that we reported in chapter 6 of this book. We read narrative summaries of all of the cases from both the Charging and Sentencing Study and the Procedural Reform Study that were death-eligible under the contemporaneous-felony statutory aggravating circumstance (B2) and classified them into factually comparable subcategories. The data set consisted of 438 cases involving a murder committed contemporaneously with another murder, a rape, an armed robbery, a kidnapping, an aggravated battery, a burglary, or first-degree arson; it produced a death-sentencing rate of .30 (130/438). The results of our analysis, presented in Table 54, revealed strong race-of-victim effects, particularly among the midrange of cases in defendant culpability.[42]

Table 54. Race-of-Victim Disparities in Death-Sentencing Rates, Controlling for Type of B2 Statutory Offense (Murder, Rape, Armed Robbery, Kidnapping, Aggravated Battery, Burglary, First-Degree Arson) and Race of Defendant (CSS and PRS)

	A	B	C	D	E	F	G	H	I	J
	Percent of All B2 Cases	Average Death-Penalty Rate	Black Defendant/ White Victim	Black Defendant/ Black Victim	Arithmetic Difference (Col.C− Col.D)	Ratio (Col.C/ Col.D)	White Defendant/ White Victim	White Defendant/ Black Victim	Arithmetic Difference (Col.G− Col.H)	Ratio (Col.G/ Col.H)
All cases death-eligible under statutory aggravating factor B2[1]	100% (n = 438)	.30 (130/438)	.38 (60/160)	.14 (15/104)	.24**	2.71**	.33 (52/160)	.21 (3/14)	12	1.57
A. All armed robbery combined	63% (n = 275)	.26 (71/275)	.34 (42/123)	.05 (3/57)	.29**	6.80**	.27 (23/84)	.27 (3/11)	0	—
I. Defendant the triggerman										
a. With kidnap, arson, or burglary	7% (n = 30)	.70 (21/30)	.92 (11/12)	.00* (0/2)	.92*	Infinite	.60 (9/15)	1.00 (1/1)	−.40	.60
b. With more than one victim	2% (n = 8)	.63 (5/8)	.33 (1/3)	—	—	—	.80 (4/5)	—	—	—
c. With "other" contemporaneous offense	6% (n = 26)	.23 (6/26)	.36 (4/11)	.00 (0/7)	.36	Infinite	.14 (1/7)	1.00 (1/1)	−.86	.14
d. With no other contemporaneous offense:	34% (n = 150)	.23 (35/150)	.37 (25/68)	.06 (2/35)	.31**	6.17**	.18 (7/40)	.14 (1/7)	.04	1.29

1. Less aggravated armed robbery with no other offense	10% (n = 45)	.13 (6/45)	.25 (5/20)	.10 (1/10)	.15	2.50	.00 (0/11)	.00 (0/4)	0	—
2. Typical armed robbery with no other offense	14% (n = 62)	.18 (11/62)	.28 (7/25)	.00 (0/17)	.28	Infinite	.21 (4/19)	.00 (0/1)	.21	Infinite
3. More aggravated armed robbery with no other offense	10% (n = 43)	.42 (18/43)	.57 (13/23)	.13 (1/8)	.44	4.38	.30 (3/10)	.50 (1/2)	-.20	.60
II. Defendant not the triggerman	14% (n = 61)	.07 (4/61)	.03 (1/29)	.08 (1/13)	-.05	.38	.12 (2/17)	.00 (0/2)	.12	Infinite
B. Rape	12% (n = 52)	.50 (26/52)	.50 (8/16)	.44 (8/18)	.06	1.14	.59 (10/17)	.00 (0/1)	.59	Infinite
C. Kidnapping	8% (n = 33)	.42 (14/33)	.60 (3/5)	.29 (2/7)	.31	2.07	.45 (9/20)	.00 (0/1)	.45	Infinite
D. Burglary and/or arson	7% (n = 29)	.34 (10/29)	.63 (5/8)	.00 (0/8)	.63*	Infinite	.38 (5/13)	—	—	—
E. Another murder	7% (n = 31)	.29 (9/31)	.33 (2/6)	.29 (2/7)	.04	1.14	.28 (5/18)	—	—	—
F. Aggravated battery	4% (n = 18)	.00 (0/18)	.00 (0/2)	.00 (0/7)	0	—	.00 (0/8)	.00 (0/1)	0	—

1. These include all B2 death-eligible cases from both the Procedural Reform Study and the Charging and Sentencing Study.

** Significant at .01 level (chi-square ≥ 6.63)

* Significant at .05 level (chi-square ≥ 3.84)

The principal *McCleskey* statewide race-of-victim findings, from the Charging and Sentencing Study, are shown in Table 55.

Race-of-Victim Effects in Prosecutorial and Jury Decision Making   We also presented testimony on race-of-victim effects in the prosecutorial decisions to seek a death sentence following a murder conviction at trial and in the

Table 55. Summary of Charging and Sentencing Study Statewide Race-of-Victim Discrimination Findings Presented in *McCleskey v. Kemp*

Analytic Method and Background Variables Controlled for[1]	Death Sentences among Defendants Convicted of Murder or Voluntary Manslaughter, Statewide
1. Unadjusted disparity	10 pts.[a]
2. Adjustment for felony circumstances and prior record	From 2 to 27 pts., with average of 5.5 pts.[b]
3. Cross-tab controlling for a qualitative *a priori* measure (12 subgroups)	Average of 17 pts.[c]
4. Cross-tab controlling for a regression-based culpability index—most-aggravated 472 cases	3.7 o.m.[d]
5. Multiple-regression estimates for race-of-victim variables after adjustment for the following legitimate case characteristics and race of defendant:	
a. Main 39-variable culpability index	4.3 o.m.[e]
b. 13 to 136 variables (6 analyses)	6 to 7 pts.; 3.0 to 3.6 o.m.[f]
c. 230+ variables	6 pts[g]
d. 39-variable culpability index applied to 647 highly aggravated cases selected by model of Judge J. Owen Forrester	4.0 o.m.[h]

1. Arithmetic disparities are reported as points (e.g., 8 pts. means an 8-point difference in the average death-sentencing rate for white- and black-victim cases). The "odds multiplier" estimates in logistic-regression analyses are designated "o.m." All disparities are statistically significant beyond the .05 level, unless otherwise indicated. "T." stands for Table, "F." for Figure, and "n." for a footnote in this chapter.

a. T. 50.

b. F. 31 (the smaller disparities were not statistically significant beyond the .05 level; the 5.5-pt. average disparity was not in the *McCleskey* record).

c. T. 54 & n.42 (the overall disparity reported in n.42 was not in the *McCleskey* record).

d. T. 53.

e. T. 52.

f. T. 51 & n.30.

g. T. 51.

h. N.41 and accompanying text.

jury penalty-trial decisions. The second and third parts of Table 56 present the unadjusted race-of-victim effects for these two decision points.[43] The second part shows a strong (twenty-eight-point) unadjusted race-of-victim effect in the prosecutorial decisions and a lesser (fourteen-point) effect in the jury decisions. The results of the logistic multiple-regression analyses of prosecutorial decisions estimated odds multipliers on the order of 3.1, significant at the .001 level, and the linear results showed race-of-victim disparities ranging from approximately 15 to 25 percentage points.[44] Both these results were comparable to the results of similar analyses of data from the Procedural Reform Study reported in chapter 6.[45]

The results of multivariate analyses of racial discrimination in jury decisions were mixed. The linear analysis that controlled for all statistically significant background factors showed a weak race-of-victim effect that was not statistically significant, but a similar analysis using logistic procedures produced an odds multiplier of 3.4, significant at the .02 level.[46] These results

Table 56. Unadjusted Racial Disparities in Rates at Which Prosecutors Seek and Juries Impose Death Sentences (CSS)[1]

	Prosecutorial Decision to Seek a Death Sentence	Jury Penalty-Trial Decision
I. Race of defendant		
Black	.33 (125/374)	.54 (74/137)
White	.31 (103/333)	.57 (66/116)
Difference (B−W)	2 pts.	−3 pts.
Ratio (B/W)	1.06	.95
II. Race of victim		
White	.43 (186/437)	.58 (119/205)
Black	.15 (42/271)	.44 (21/48)
Difference (W−B)	28 pts.	14 pts.
Ratio (W/B)	2.9	1.3
III. Defendant/victim racial combination		
1. Black defendant/white victim	.70 (87/124)	.59 (55/93)
2. White defendant/white victim	.32 (99/312)	.57 (64/112)
3. Black defendant/black victim	.15 (38/250)	.43 (19/44)
4. White defendant/black victim	.19 (4/21)	.50 (2/4)

1. The prosecutorial analyses do not include multiple penalty trials, while the jury decisions do. The analysis includes cases that were not deemed death-eligible by our measures, *supra* chap. 4, note 38. When the analysis is so limited, the race-of-defendant disparity is 4 points (.39 for black-defendant cases v. .35 for white-defendant cases) and the race-of-victim disparity is 28 points (.47 for white-victim cases v. .19 for black-victim cases); the penalty-trial rates by defendant/victim racial combinations are B/W .70, W/W .37, B/B .19, and W/B .19. All cases in the jury analysis are death-eligible.

suggest, as did the findings of the PRS, that the principal posttrial source of race-of-victim discrimination is the prosecutorial decision to seek a death sentence.

The data presented in the *McCleskey* hearing further suggested that the largest race-of-victim effects in the pretrial stages of the process were in the prosecutorial decisions to allow defendants indicted for murder to plead to voluntary manslaughter. Such pleas were far more likely in cases with black victims.[47] The overall conclusion suggested by the data, therefore, was that the race-of-victim effects in death sentencing observed among defendants indicted for murder were attributable principally to prosecutorial decisions made both before and after trial.

Adjusted Race-of-Defendant Effects   It will be recalled that the unadjusted data shown in Table 50 (part II) revealed a -3 point race-of-defendant effect, suggesting that, overall, white defendants were at a slight disadvantage. However, when we focused the analysis on the white-victim cases, part III of Table 50 suggested that black defendants may be treated more punitively than white defendants. Indeed, the rate of .21 for the black-defendant/white-victim cases and the rate of .08 for the white-defendant/white-victim cases produces an unadjusted 13-percentage-point race-of-defendant disparity among the white-victim cases.

The findings from the multivariate analyses we presented in the *McCleskey* hearing were consistent with the unadjusted results. The results from the core thirty-nine variable logistic model estimated with all of the cases in the sample (see Table 52) shows no race-of-defendant effect.[48] Only when we limited the multivariate analyses to the most highly aggravated cases did we see a race-of-defendant effect that was particularly strong among the white-victim cases. For example, Table 57 presents a race-of-defendant analysis among the most aggravated 472 cases.[49] When all these cases are considered, there is a race-of-defendant effect equivalent to a 2.4 odds multiplier, which rises to 3.1 when the analysis is limited to the most aggravated white-victim cases (see columns C and D). Similarly, our race-of-defendant analysis of contemporaneous-felony (B2) cases presented in Table 58 (columns C, D, and B) shows a race-of-defendant effect that is more pronounced among the white-victim cases, although in neither case is the effect significant beyond the .10 level.[50]

The Impact of Appellate Review   We also testified in the *McCleskey* hearing about the impact of the Georgia Supreme Court's appellate-review process on the race-of-victim effects. For the purposes of this analysis, we treated all death-sentence cases that the Georgia Supreme Court reversed or vacated as

Table 57. Race-of-Defendant Disparities in Death-Sentencing Rates among the Most Aggravated Cases, Controlling for the Predicted Likelihood of a Death Sentence and the Race of the Victim (CSS)[1]

A	B	C	D	E	F	G	H	I	J
Predicted Chance of a Death Sentence, from 1 (low) to 8 (high)	Average Actual Sentencing Rate for Each Level	Death-Sentencing Rates for White-Victim Cases — Black Defendants	White Defendants	Arithmetic Difference in Race-of-Defendant Rates (Col.C − Col.D)	Ratio of Race-of-Defendant Rates (Col.C/ Col.D)	Death-Sentencing Rates for Black-Victim Cases — Black Defendants	White Defendants	Arithmetic Difference in Race-of-Defendant Rates (Col.G − Col.H)	Ratio of Race-of-Defendant Rates (Col.G/ Col.H)
1	.00 (0/33)	.00 (0/9)	.00 (0/5)	.00	–	.00 (0/19)	–	–	–
2	.00 (0/55)	.00 (0/8)	.00 (0/19)	.00	–	.00 (0/27)	.00 (0/1)	.00	–
3	.08 (6/76)	.30 (3/10)	.03 (1/39)	.27	10.00	.11 (2/18)	.00 (0/9)	.11	Infinite
4	.07 (4/57)	.23 (3/13)	.03 (1/29)	.20	7.67	.00 (0/15)	–	–	–
5	.26 (15/58)	.35 (9/26)	.20 (4/20)	.15	1.75	.17 (2/12)	–	–	–
6	.17 (11/64)	.38 (3/8)	.16 (5/32)	.22	2.38	.05 (1/20)	.50 (2/4)	−.45	.10
7	.41 (29/71)	.64 (9/14)	.38 (15/39)	.26	1.68	.38 (5/13)	.00 (0/5)	.38	Infinite
8	.88 (51/58)	.91 (20/22)	.89 (25/28)	.02	1.02	.75 (6/8)	–	–	–

1. The overall race-of-defendant disparity, estimated with a logistic-coefficient measure, was .87 (with a death-odds multiplier of 2.4), statistically significant at the .01 level (adjusted X^2 was 6.69). These results were produced with the procedure adopted from Cressie, *Playing Safe With Misweighted Means*, 77 J. Am. Stat. Assn. 754 (1982). *See* Woodworth, *Analysis of a Y-Stratified Sample: The Georgia Charging and Sentencing Study*, in Proceedings of the Second Workshop on Law and Justice Statistics: 1984, p. 18, Bureau of Justice Statistics, U.S. Dept. of Justice (E. Gelfand ed. 1985). The overall race-of-defendant measure comparable to a least-squares regression coefficient is .05. Among the white-victim cases alone, the race-of-victim disparity, estimated with a logistic-coefficient measure, was 1.13 (with a death-odds multiplier of 3.1), statistically significant at the .001 level (adjusted X^2 was 11.4). The overall race-of-defendant measure among white-victim cases comparable to the least-squares regression coefficient is .08.

Table 58. Race-of-Defendant Disparities in Death-Sentencing Rates, Controlling for Type of B2 Statutory Offense (Murder, Rape, Armed Robbery, Kidnapping, Aggravated Battery, Burglary, First-Degree Arson) and Race of Victim (CSS and PRS)

	A	B	C	D	E	F	G	H	I	J
	Percent of All B2 Cases	Average Death-Penalty Rate	Black Defendant/ White Victim	White Defendant/ White Victim	Arithmetic Difference (Col.C − Col.D)	Ratio (Col.C/ Col.D)	Black Defendant/ Black Victim	White Defendant/ Black Victim	Arithmetic Difference (Col.G − Col.H)	Ratio (Col.G/ Col.H)
All cases death-eligible under statutory aggravating factor B2[1]	100% (n = 438)	.30 (130/438)	.38 (60/160)	.33 (52/160)	.05	1.2	.14 (15/104)	.21 (3/14)	−.07	.67
A. All armed robbery combined	63% (n = 275)	.26 (71/275)	.34 (42/123)	.27 (23/84)	.07	1.3	.05 (3/57)	.27 (3/11)	−.22	.19
I. Defendant the killer										
a. With kidnap, arson, or burglary	7% (n = 30)	.70 (21/30)	.92 (11/12)	.60 (9/15)	.32	1.5	.00 (0/2)	1.0 (1/1)	−1.0	—
b. With more than one victim	2% (n = 8)	.63 (5/8)	.33 (1/3)	.80 (4/5)	−.47	.41	—	—	—	—
c. With "other" contemporaneous offense	6% (n = 26)	.23 (6/26)	.36 (4/11)	.14 (1/7)	.22	2.6	.00 (0/7)	1.0 (1/1)	−1.0	—

	.23 (35/150)	.37 (25/68)	.18 (7/40)	.19	2.1	.06 (2/35)	.14 (1/7)	−.08	.43
d. With no other contemporaneous offense 34% (n = 150)	.23 (35/150)	.37 (25/68)	.18 (7/40)	.19	2.1	.06 (2/35)	.14 (1/7)	−.08	.43
1. Less aggravated armed robbery with no other offense 10% (n = 45)	.13 (6/45)	.25 (5/20)	.00 (0/11)	.25	Infinite	.10 (1/10)	.00 (0/4)	.10	Infinite
2. Typical armed robbery with no other offense 14% (n = 62)	.18 (11/62)	.28 (7/25)	.21 (4/19)	.07	1.3	.00 (0/17)	.00 (0/1)	—	—
3. More aggravated armed robbery with no other offense 10% (n = 43)	.42 (18/43)	.57 (13/23)	.30 (3/10)	.27	1.9	.13 (1/8)	.50 (1/2)	−.37	.26
II. Defendant not the actual killer 14% (n = 61)	.07 (4/61)	.03 (1/29)	.12 (2/17)	−.09	.25	.08 (1/13)	.00 (0/2)	.08	Infinite
B. Rape 12% (n = 52)	.50 (26/52)	.50 (8/16)	.59 (10/17)	−.09	.85	.44 (8/18)	.00 (0/1)	.44	Infinite
C. Kidnapping 8% (n = 33)	.42 (14/33)	.60 (3/5)	.45 (9/20)	.15	1.3	.29 (2/7)	.00 (0/1)	.29	Infinite
D. Burglary and/or arson 7% (n = 29)	.34 (10/29)	.63 (5/8)	.38 (5/13)	.25	1.7	.00 (0/8)	—	0	—
E. Another murder 7% (n = 31)	.29 (9/31)	.33 (2/6)	.28 (5/18)	.05	1.2	.29 (2/7)	—	0	—
F. Aggravated battery 4% (n = 18)	.00 (0/18)	.00 (0/2)	.00 (0/8)	0	1.0	.00 (0/7)	.00 (0/1)	0	—

1. These include all B2 death-eligible cases from both the Procedural Reform Study and the Charging and Sentencing Study.

life-sentence cases. Using this convention, we estimated that the Georgia court's review process probably reduced the observed race-of-victim effects by about one-third.[51] In spite of this reduction, the overall race-of-victim effects among cases involving murder indictments persisted at a statistically significant level.[52]

Diagnostic and "Worst-Case" Analyses   Our final series of statewide analyses was designed to estimate the stability and validity of our substantive results. We first determined the extent to which the estimated race-of-victim disparities varied over time. The results of this analysis indicated that the estimated race-of-victim effects were quite stable between 1973 and 1979.[53]

Next, we sought to determine the probability that our estimated race-of-victim effects were an artifact of (1) the concentration of white-victim cases in judicial circuits with high death-sentencing rates;[54] (2) missing data for the race-of victim variable[55] or for the variable that indicated whether a murder case had advanced to a penalty trial;[56] (3) our coding protocol that treated legitimate case characteristics as not present when the files of the parole board provided no basis for inferring whether or not the characteristic was present in the case;[57] and (4) the failure of other technical assumptions underlying multiple-regression analyses. The results of all of these diagnostic and "worst case" analyses convinced us that our race-of-victim estimates were not statistical artifacts and reflected the influence of the race of the victim in Georgia's charging-and-sentencing system.[58]

The Fulton County Evidence of Racial Discrimination

Counsel for McCleskey also requested us to determine whether the statewide race-of-victim disparities we had observed in Georgia's capital-charging-and-sentencing system also occurred in Fulton County, the jurisdiction in which McCleskey's sentence was imposed. Specifically, the purpose of this investigation was to provide a basis for determining the likelihood that McCleskey's sentence had been influenced or determined by his race or the race of his victim. The analysis would also indicate whether the risk that we observed statewide that the race of the victim would play a decisive role in the death-sentencing process existed in Fulton County.

To examine whether McCleskey's race or the race of his victim influenced the decisions leading to his death sentence, we applied an approach modeled after those developed by the federal courts to evaluate claims of purposeful discrimination in a single decision brought under the equal-protection clause of the Fourteenth Amendment, the First Amendment, and Title VII. (Title VII is a provision of the 1964 Civil Rights Act that prohibits racial discrimination in employment.[59]) Proceedings brought under each of these laws may raise issues of whether the defendant treats the claimant adversely for such impermissible reasons as the claimant's sex, race, or exercise of a First Amendment right. In such cases, the issue is not whether the defendant harbored hostile feelings toward the claimant; rather, it is whether the objective evidence is sufficient to support an inference of purposeful discrimination.

In individual claims brought under both the First Amendment and the equal-protection clause of the Fourteenth Amendment, the Court does not apply the concept of a prima facie case, as it does in jury-discrimination cases. Instead, the Court examines the entire record to determine whether the claimant's evidence of discrimination remains persuasive despite whatever evidence the defendant may offer to show that the plaintiff was disadvantaged for legitimate, noninvidious reasons. Particularly relevant on such issues is comparative evidence that individuals with qualifications similar to the plaintiff's were treated differently than the plaintiff, or that there were procedural irregularities in the decision that adversely affected the plaintiff.[60]

In purposeful discrimination cases involving an individual claimant under Title VII, the Supreme Court has developed a more elaborate prima facie case methodology, but the logic of the analysis and the ultimate inferences of purposeful discrimination against an individual are the same as they are in First and Fourteenth Amendment cases. Under Title VII, the plaintiff employee must establish a prima facie case that disproves or discounts the most likely legitimate reasons for the act of alleged employment discrimination. The logic of the approach is that "when all legitimate reasons for rejecting an applicant have been eliminated as possible reasons for the employer's actions, it is more likely than not the employer, who we generally assume acts only with *some* reason, based his decision on an impermissible consideration such as race."[61] If a prima facie case is established, the employer can offer rebuttal evidence to establish that the adverse decision was the result of a legitimate factor, which the employee may then challenge as pretextual. In considering the pretext issue, the courts principally examine "comparative evidence," which indicates how other similarly situated employees were treated; procedural irregularities in the decision adversely affecting the plaintiff; and evidence that the defendant has discriminated against minorities or women as a class.[62]

The factual issue in *McCleskey* was quite comparable to those addressed in individual Title VII and equal-protection cases, since the state argued that there was a perfectly plausible explanation for McCleskey's death sentence— he was guilty of killing a police officer and of committing a contemporaneous armed robbery (both of which constitute statutory aggravating circumstances). Our task was to test whether these legitimate case characteristics could plausibly explain McCleskey's sentence. Our principal approach was to develop comparative evidence illustrating the treatment of Fulton County defendants whose cases were comparable to *McCleskey* in their overall aggravation levels but whose victims were black. We also presented evidence of classwide race-of-victim discrimination in Fulton County. All of these data were offered against a backdrop of testimony that, through the exercise of peremptory challenges and challenges for cause, McCleskey's prosecutor excluded all but one black juror from McCleskey's jury.[63]

The Comparative Evidence   In Warren McCleskey's case, there were two groups of comparable defendants. The first group consisted of the sixteen other Fulton County defendants who had been involved in the killing of a police officer; ten of the deceased officers in these cases were white and six were black. Although none of these other defendants received a death sentence, their disposition does not create a strong inference of purposeful discrimination because the majority of their cases were less aggravated than McCleskey's case. More relevant for purposes of comparison were the six cases involving triggerman defendants who, like McCleskey, were convicted of killing a police officer in the course of a contemporaneous felony. Four of these cases involved white victims and two involved black victims. One of the black-victim cases advanced to a penalty trial, and it resulted in a life sentence. The inference of jury discrimination from the disposition of this single black-victim case is not strong, however. Moreover, only one of the four white-victim cases, McCleskey's, even advanced to a penalty trial.[64]

Because of the small number of police-officer murders in Fulton County, we developed our second group of cases comparable to *McCleskey* using a culpability-index method. This approach allowed us to identify cases that were factually distinct yet appeared to be comparable to *McCleskey* in overall culpability. Specifically, we selected the twenty-seven cases with the highest culpability scores in Fulton County, plus five additional cases in which a penalty trial actually occurred. In these thirty-two cases, there were twenty-seven murder convictions and five voluntary manslaughter convictions. The twenty-seven murder-conviction cases included all ten of the Fulton County death sentences in our sample. Thus, the overall death-sentencing rate for this group of high-risk cases, with culpability levels comparable to *McCleskey*, was .31 (10/32). Among these "near neighbors" to *McCleskey*, seventeen of the cases involved a white victim and fifteen involved a black victim.

Table 59 presents an unadjusted race-of-victim analysis of these high-risk cases.[65] Part I of the table shows that defendants with white victims were three times more likely to receive a death sentence than those with black victims. Part II of Table 59 also presents a race-of-victim analysis of the thirty-two cases after further adjustment for the overall culpability of the offenders involved. An examination of the narrative summaries of the cases had suggested a three-tier classification system of relative aggravation.[66] The results shown in Table 59 indicate that further adjustment for the different aggravation levels

Table 59. Fulton County Unadjusted and Adjusted Race-of-Victim Disparities among Cases with the Highest Predicted Likelihood of Receiving a Death Sentence (css)[1]

A	B. Average Death-Sentencing Rate	C. White-Victim Cases	D. Black-Victim Cases	E. Arithmetic Difference (Col.C− Col.D)	F. Ratio (Col.C/ Col.D)
I. All cases	.31	.47	.13	.34	3.6
$n = 32$	(10/32)	(8/17)	(2/15)		
II. By aggravation level					
A. More aggravated	.57	.75	.33	.42	2.27
cases ($n = 14$)	(8/14)	(6/8)	(2/6)		
B. Typical cases	.25	.40	.00	.40	Infinite
($n = 8$)	(2/8)	(2/5)	(0/3)		
C. Less aggravated	.00	.00	.00	.00	Infinite
cases ($n = 10$)	(0/10)	(0/4)	(0/6)		

1. This sample also includes five penalty-trial cases that were not among the cases with the highest predicted likelihood of receiving a death sentence. The table includes *McCleskey*.

of the cases does not eliminate the race-of-victim disparities. It merely concentrates them in the "more aggravated" and "typical case" categories, for which the average death-sentencing rates were .57 and .25, respectively. The tabulation further indicates that in the "typical" case category, where *McCleskey's* case was found, there was a .0 (0/3) death-sentencing rate in the black-victim cases and a .40 (2/5) rate in the white-victim cases.

Table 59 indicates that, of the nine black-victim cases that equaled or surpassed McCleskey's case in overall culpability (rows IIA and IIB, column D), only two resulted in death sentences. We further examined the seven cases involving black victims in these culpability categories, all of which resulted in life sentences, for an indication of how McCleskey's case might have been treated had his victim been black. Summaries of those cases appear in Table 60.[67] They suggest a striking level of toleration for brutality and vileness in black-victim cases.[68]

Evidence of Classwide Disparate Treatment in Fulton County As noted above, we also conducted a countywide analysis for evidence of disparate treatment of black defendants or defendants whose victims were white. Table 61 indicates the disposition of cases at each stage in the Fulton County charging-and-sentencing system for the four groups of cases defined by the defendant/victim racial combination.[69] A comparison of columns C and D

Table 60. Thumbnail Sketches of Fulton County Black-Victim Cases Involving an Equal or Greater Level of Culpability than Warren McCleskey's Case with a Life Sentence Imposed (CSS)[1]

L16 (McCleskey)	Defendant, who had served a prison term for armed robbery, robbed a furniture store with three armed coperpetrators. Defendant entered the front door while the others entered the rear of the store. Employees and customers were forced to lie face down on the floor. The victim, a police officer responding to a silent alarm, was shot twice, including a fatal bullet to the face, by defendant.
**N64	Stabbing, rape, beating, and sodomy of victim. Rape of primary witness. Victim young female. Defendant followed victim home from work. May have known her.
**550	Victim was bound and shot several times. Primary witness also tied, blindfolded, beaten, kicked, shot several times, and left for dead in course of robbery.
**N63	Defendant shot a 17-year-old girl as he was trying to force her into his car. Victim, a stranger, shot twice in head. Earlier in day defendant had tried to force two other young women (separate occurrences) into his car. Defendant shot at each of them also, wounding one in the arm.
**855	Defendant gave victim, a stranger, a ride. Shot him, ran over victim twice with car.
*727	Defendant and two coperpetrators (third coperpetrator was in getaway car) entered grocery store. Once inside, all three pulled their guns. When the victim held the counter telephone out toward perpetrators, the defendant remarked that the victim was in contact with police. Coperpetrators left and as defendant left he shot victim in the chest.
*974	Defendant forced female cabdriver out of her cab; as she was backing away from defendant, he shot and killed her. Defendant then took $85 from victim's purse and fled in her cab, which he later abandoned.
*240	Defendant shot and killed employee of drive-in restaurant in course of armed robbery. Victim tried to grab defendant's gun.

1. All the cases listed received a life sentence for murder.
**More aggravated than McCleskey.
*With the same aggravation level as McCleskey.

provides even less evidence of race-of-defendant discrimination than do the statewide data, since, among the white-victim cases, the unadjusted figures indicate that black defendants are only slightly more at risk of receiving a death sentence than their white-defendant counterparts.

The evidence of race-of-victim discrimination, however, is perfectly consistent with the statewide pattern—black-victim cases are treated less punitively

Table 61. Fulton County, Disposition of Cases at Six Points in the Charging-and-Sentencing Process and Overall for All Cases, Controlling for the Defendant/Victim Racial Combination (css)

A	B	C	D	E	F
		Defendant/Victim Racial Combination			
	Average Rate	Black/White	White/White	Black/Black	White/Black
1. Indictment for murder	.92 (580/628)	1.00 (52/52)	.93 (108/116)	.91 (412/452)	1.00 (8/8)
2. Guilty plea to voluntary manslaughter after a murder indictment	.59 (340/580)	.38 (20/52)	.48 (52/108)	.63 (260/412)	1.00 (8/8)
3. Guilty plea to murder and no penalty trial	.21 (51/240)	.25 (8/32)	.34 (19/56)	.16 (24/152)	–
4. Murder conviction at guilt trial	.68 (128/188)	.83 (20/24)	.78 (29/37)	.62 (79/127)	–
5. Case advanced to a penalty trial after murder conviction at a guilt trial	.17 (19/110)	.29 (5/17)	.21 (6/29)	.13 (8/64)	–
6. Death sentence imposed at penalty trial	.53 (10/19)	.60 (3/5)	.83 (5/6)	.25 (2/8)	–
7. Combined effect of decisions after murder indictment resulting in a death sentence	.02 (10/581)	.06 (3/52)	.05 (5/108)	.005 (2/412)	.00 (0/8)

at each stage in the process. This is shown even more clearly in Table 62,[70] which focuses solely on the differential treatment of the black- and white-victim cases.

Because the death-sentencing rate is so low for the county as a whole, .02 (10/581), the absolute, percentage-point disparity in the death-sentencing rate for white- and black-victim cases indicted for murder is only 4.5 (see row 7). The ratio of those rates, however, is very large, 10 (.05/.005), and the race-of-victim effects at each stage in the process are consistent and substantial.

Table 63 presents the results of linear multiple-regression analyses conducted for the cases at each stage in the Fulton County criminal justice system.[71] Rows 2 and 4 indicate that the principal source of the race-of-victim disparity arises from plea bargaining before trial and the prosecutorial decision to seek a death sentence after a murder conviction is obtained at trial.

Table 62. Fulton County Race-of-Victim Disparities in the Disposition of Cases at Six Points in the Charging-and-Sentencing Process and Overall, for All Cases (CSS)

A	B	C	D	E	F
	Average Rate	Race of Victim		Arithmetic Difference (Col. C − Col. D)	Ratio (Col. C/Col. D)
		White	Black		
1. Indictment for murder	.92 (581/629)	.95 (161/169)	.91 (420/460)	.04	1.04
2. Guilty plea to voluntary manslaughter after a murder indictment	.59 (340/581)	.45 (72/161)	.64 (268/420)	−.19	.70
3. Guilty plea to murder and no penalty trial	.21 (51/241)	.30 (27/89)	.16 (24/152)	.14	1.88
4. Murder conviction at guilt trial	.68 (129/189)	.81 (50/62)	.62 (79/127)	.19	1.31
5. Case advanced to a penalty trial after murder conviction at a guilt trial	.17 (19/110)	.24 (11/46)	.13 (8/64)	.11	1.85
6. Death sentence imposed at penalty trial	.53 (10/19)	.73 (8/11)	.25 (2/8)	.48	2.92
7. Combined effect of decisions after murder indictment resulting in a death sentence	.02 (10/581)	.05 (8/161)	.005 (2/420)	.045	10

Also, row 4 shows a statistically significant race-of-defendant effect in the prosecutorial decision to seek a death penalty after the guilt trial. However, row 6 indicates neither a race-of-victim nor a race-of-defendant disparity after adjustment for important background factors.

McCleskey's attorneys also presented two items of nonquantitative evidence from Fulton County. The first was the deposition of Louis R. Slaton, who had been the Fulton County district attorney for eighteen years. He testified that there were no guidelines for assistant district attorneys regarding

Table 63. Race-of-Victim and Race-of-Defendant Disparities at Successive Steps in the Fulton County Charging-and-Sentencing Process (css)[1]

A	B	C
	Weighted-Least-Squares Regression Coefficients[2] (with Level of Statistical Significance in Parentheses)	
Stages in the Process	Race of Victim (1 = White; 0 = Black)	Race of Defendant (1 = Black; 0 = White)
1. Indictment (1 = Murder; 0 = Voluntary manslaughter)	−.03 (.60)	.04 (.44)
2. Guilty pleas		
A. Voluntary-manslaughter plea after a murder indictment (1 = Yes; 0 = No)	−.19 (.03)	−.06 (.52)
B. Plea to murder (1 = Yes; 0 = No)	−.29 (.0001)	−.16 (.01)
C. Prosecutor offer or agreement to a plea bargain (1 = Yes; 0 = No)	−.55 (.0001)	−.40 (.01)
3. Jury guilt-trial decision (1 = Murder; 0 = Voluntary manslaughter)	.01 (.76)	.01 (.77)
4. Case advanced to penalty trial after murder conviction at guilt trial (1 = Yes; 0 = No)	.20 (.01)	.19 (.02)
5. Penalty trial death-sentencing decision (1 = Death sentence; 0 = Life sentence)	—[3]	—[3]
6. Death sentence, given a murder indictment (1 = Death sentence; 0 = Other sentence)	−.01 (.83)	−.01 (.35)

1. The coefficients in columns B and C were estimated after controlling simultaneously for the nonracial background factors listed in schedule 3 of Appendix L that entered a stepwise weighted-least-squares regression analysis at the .10 level of statistical significance.
2. A positive regression coefficient in column B indicates that defendants with white victims had a higher probability of selection at the stage in the process to which it relates, while a negative coefficient reflects a lower probability of selection.
   A positive coefficient in column C indicates a higher probability of selection for black defendants and a negative coefficient indicates a reduced probability. *See supra* note 48 and accompanying text for a discussion of race-of-defendant effects estimated with linear regression procedures.
3. There were too few cases at this stage in the process to conduct a multiple-regression analysis.

either plea bargaining in death-eligible cases or when the prosecutors should seek a death sentence if a capital-murder conviction is obtained at trial. Mr. Slaton also indicated that neither he nor any of his deputies provided systematic oversight of the daily decisions of his office in death-eligible cases.

The second item of evidence offered by McCleskey was testimony that the jury that convicted him of murder and sentenced him to death included only one black juror.

THE COURT OPINIONS IN *McCLESKEY V. KEMP*

The Decision of the Federal District Court

In an extensive opinion, Judge Forrester rejected McCleskey's discrimination and arbitrariness claim on three grounds.[72] He found that our data base was not sufficiently trustworthy, that the statistical procedures used to analyze the data were flawed, and that even if McCleskey's data and statistical procedures were valid, the evidence was not sufficient to support a claim of purposeful discrimination under the Fourteenth Amendment or a claim of arbitrariness under the Eighth Amendment.

In support of his holding that the data were not "essentially trustworthy" and did "not in substantial degree mirror reality,"[73] Judge Forrester made six findings:

1. The design of the questionnaires was defective in that they did not comprehend all of the information available to the coders in the files of the parole board and Georgia Supreme Court.[74]
2. The data files in the parole board and the Georgia court were "very summary in many respects" and did not include all of the information available to the prosecutors and juries who processed the cases.[75]
3. The data set did not distinguish between information available only to prosecutors and that which was known by the sentencing juries.[76]
4. In numerous cases the data did not include the race of the victim or such procedural characteristics of the cases as whether a penalty trial occurred.[77]
5. There were numerous inconsistencies in the coding of the many variables common to both the Charging and Sentencing and Procedural Reform studies, suggesting that in these cases one or both of the codings was factually incorrect.[78]
6. The coding protocol erroneously treated a legitimate case characteristic as not present in a case when the coder coded the variable "unknown" because the file did not indicate whether or not the characteristic was present in the case.[79]

As for the statistical procedures used in the analysis of the data, Judge Forrester also identified a number of flaws. First, he held that multiple-regression analysis did not "compare identical cases" and was therefore inherently incapable of indicating whether similarly situated defendants were treated the same:

> [M]ultivariate analysis is ill-suited to provide the court with circumstantial evidence of the presence of discrimination, and it is incapable of providing the court with measures of qualitative difference in treatment which are necessary to a finding that a prima facie case has been established with statistical evidence. . . .[80] It is important to understand that the cases being compared in the regression analyses used here are not at all factually similar. . . . Their principal identity is that their aggravation index, the total of all positive regression coefficients minus all negative regression coefficients, is similar. . . . The whole study rests on the presumption that cases with similar aggravation indexes are similarly situated. R 1311. This presumption is not only rebuttable, it is rebutted, if by nothing else, then by common sense. . . . The same thought, it seems to the court, is apropos for the aggravation index. It allows a case with compelling aggravating circumstances, offset only by a series of insignificant mitigating circumstances, to be counted as equal to a case with the same level of aggravation and one substantial mitigating factor having the same numerical value as the series of trifling ones in the first case. The court understands that strength of the evidence measures generally are positive coefficients. To the extent that this is true, a strong evidentiary case with weak aggravating circumstances would be considered the same as a brutal murder with very weak evidence. Other examples abound, but the point is that there is no logical basis for the assumption that cases with similar aggravation indices are at all alike. Further, the aggravation index for any given case is a function of the variables that are included in the model. Any change in the variables included in the model will also change the aggravation index of most, if not all, cases.[81]

Judge Forrester further ruled that stepwise multiple regression was inherently flawed because of the atheoretical manner in which it identified variables as important, and as a result it *"cannot accord any weight to any evidence produced by the model created by stepwise regression."* [82]

Third, Judge Forrester held that plaintiff's burden was to show that race played a part in "either the decision of the prosecutor or the jury," and that regardless of its validity, statistical evidence of systemwide disparities was "incapable of saying whether or not any factor had a role in the decision to impose the death penalty in any particular case."[83] Judge Forrester also raised a number of quite technical objections concerning such matters as "multicollinearity" and "R^2" levels.[84]

Finally, Judge Forrester held that even if McCleskey's evidence were deemed sufficient to create a prima facie case, the State's evidence was sufficient to rebut it:

> A part of Baldus's hypothesis is that the system places a lower value on black life than on white life. If this is true, it would mean that the system would tolerate

higher levels of aggravation in black victim cases before the system imposes the death penalty.

The respondent postulates a test of this thesis. It is said that if Baldus's theory is correct, then one would necessarily find aggravation levels in black-victim cases where a life sentence was imposed to be higher than in white-victim cases. This seems to the court to be a plausible corollary to Baldus's proposition. To test this corollary, Katz [the state's primary expert], analyzing aggravating and mitigating factors one by one, demonstrated that in life sentence cases, to the extent that any aggravating circumstance is more prevalent in one group than the other, there are more aggravating features in the group of white-victim cases than in the group of black-victim cases. Conversely, there were more mitigating circumstances in which black-victim cases had a higher proportion of that circumstance than in white-victim cases. R 1510-15, 1540, Res. Exh. 43, 53, 54.

Because Katz used one method to demonstrate relative levels of aggravation and Baldus used another, his index method, the court cannot say that this experiment alone conclusively demonstrates that Baldus's theory is wrong. It is, however, direct rebuttal evidence of the theory, and as such, stands to contradict any prima facie case of system-wide discrimination based on race of the victim even if it can be said that the petitioner has indeed established a prima facie case. This court does not believe that he has.[85]

In spite of Judge Forrester's rejection of McCleskey's statistically based claims, he vacated McCleskey's murder conviction and thereby granted him relief from his death sentence. Judge Forrester held that, in violation of *Giglio v. United States*, the jury had not been properly informed that a key witness, Offie Evans, had been promised assistance by a detective in connection with federal criminal charges pending against him at the time in exchange for his testimony that McCleskey had admitted his guilt to him in a "jailhouse confession."[86]

In December 1987, eight months after the United States Supreme Court's decision in *McCleskey v. Kemp*, Judge Forrester granted McCleskey habeas corpus relief from his death sentence on a second habeas corpus petition which alleged that detectives had, in violation of McCleskey's constitutional rights, placed Offie Evans in the cell next to him for the sole purpose of obtaining incriminating evidence. McCleskey presented an affidavit of Offie Evans, not discovered until June 1987, which strongly suggested, but did not state, that he had been put in the cell next to McCleskey for that purpose. In addition, the jailer, Ulysses Worthy, testified that detectives had requested him to move the informant Evans into the cell next to McCleskey. Persuaded on the facts, Judge Forrester held that the detectives' conduct was unconstitutional and ordered a new trial on McCleskey's murder charge.[87]

The Decision of the Court of Appeals

Appeals were filed by both McCleskey and the State and argued before the entire membership of the Eleventh Circuit Court of Appeals (en banc) in June

1984. By a 7–5 vote, the court reversed the district court's decision granting a new trial on the *Giglio* theory and by a 9–3 vote affirmed the district court's findings that the petitioner had failed to prove his claim of arbitrariness and discrimination. In contrast to the district court, however, the majority of the court of appeals did not evaluate the validity of the petitioner's data base or the statistical procedures used to analyze it. Instead, the court expressly assumed both the "validity of the research" and that it proved what it claimed to prove. [88]

> We assume without deciding that the Baldus study is sufficient to show what it purports to reveal as to the application of the Georgia death penalty. Baldus concluded that his study showed that systematic and substantial disparities existed in the penalties imposed upon homicide defendants in Georgia based on race of the homicide victim, that the disparities existed at a less substantial rate in death sentencing based on race of defendants, and that the factors of race of the victim and defendant were at work in Fulton County.

The court proceeded, however, to hold that McCleskey's statistical evidence of discrimination "does not contain the level of disparity . . . so great as to inevitably lead to a conclusion that the disparity results from intent or motivation." [89]

The court offered several reasons for its dismissal of McCleskey's arbitrariness and discrimination claim. The first was that "statistics alone are insufficient to show that McCleskey's sentence was determined by the race of his victim, or even that the race of his victim contributed to the imposition of the penalty in his case." [90] The court appeared to believe, however, that the statistics presented a generally valid picture of Georgia's capital-sentencing process, which it characterized as "an essentially rational system, in which high aggravation cases were more likely to result in the death sentence than low aggravation cases. As one would expect in a rational system, factors such as torture and multiple victims greatly increase the likelihood of receiving the penalty." [91]

In spite of this implicit endorsement of the validity of McCleskey's statistical evidence, the majority of the appellate court nevertheless expressed strong skepticism that a statistical analysis could ever adequately demonstrate that a death-sentencing system operated in an unconstitutionally discriminatory or arbitrary fashion.

> From a legal perspective, petitioner would argue that since the [race-of-victim] difference is not explained by facts which the social scientist thinks satisfactory to explain the differences, there is a prima facie case that the difference was based on unconstitutional factors, and the burden would shift to the state to prove the difference in results from constitutional considerations. This approach ignores the realities. It not only ignores quantitative differences in cases: looks, age, personality, education, profession, job, clothes, demeanor, and remorse, just to

name a few, but it is incapable of measuring qualitative differences of such things as aggravating and mitigating factors. There are, in fact, no exact duplicates in capital crimes and capital defendants. The type of research submitted here tends to show which of the directed factors were effective, but it is of restricted use in showing what undirected factors control the exercise of unconstitutionally required discretion.[92]

In spite of its reservations about the relevance of classwide statistical analysis, the majority did examine McCleskey's evidence on that issue. It focused primarily on the average race-of-victim effects estimated in our large 230-plus linear-variable model (a 6-percentage-point disparity, which the court characterized as a "6%" effect)[93] and in our core 39-variable logistic model (a 4.3 race-of-victim odds multiplier) and held that these disparities were not of sufficient magnitude to establish intentional discrimination in the system.

> Taking the 6% bottom line revealed in the Baldus figures as true, this figure is not sufficient to overcome the presumption that the statute is operating in a constitutional manner. In any discretionary system, some imprecision must be tolerated, and the Baldus study is simply insufficient to support a ruling, in the context of a statute that is operating much as intended, that racial factors are playing a role in the outcome sufficient to render the system as a whole arbitrary and capricious.[94]

In considering the 4.3 odds multiplier calculated from the race-of-victim coefficient that we estimated with the core 39-variable logistic model, the court invoked recent Supreme Court decisions sustaining lower court decisions that had denied an evidentiary hearing on a claim of race-of-victim discrimination. The petitioners in those cases had relied on the study of Florida's death-sentencing system conducted by Samuel Gross and Robert Mauro:

> The bottom line figure in the Gross and Mauro study indicated a race-of-the-victim effect, quantified by a "death odds multiplier," of about 4.8 to 1. Using a similar methodology, Baldus obtained a death odds multiplier of 4.3 to 1 in Georgia.
>
> It is of course possible that the Supreme Court was rejecting the methodology of the Florida study, rather than its bottom line. It is true that the methodology of the Baldus study is superior. The posture of the Florida cases, however, persuades this Court that the Supreme Court was not relying on inadequacies in the methodology of the Florida study.
>
> Thus, assuming that the Supreme Court found the bottom line in the Gross and Mauro study insufficient to raise a constitutional claim, we would be compelled to reach the same result in analyzing the sufficiency of the comparable bottom line in the Baldus study on which McCleskey relies.[95]

As for the 20-percentage-point disparity operating in the midrange of cases, the court first questioned the validity of this finding:

The 20% figure in this case is not analogous to a figure reflecting the percentage disparity in a jury composition case. Such a figure represents the *actual* disparity between the number of minority persons on the jury venire and the number of such persons in the population. In contrast, the 20% disparity in this case does not purport to be an actual disparity. Rather, the figure reflects that the variables included in the study do not adequately explain the 20% disparity and that the statisticians can explain it only by assuming the racial effect. More importantly, Baldus did not testify that he found statistical significance in the 20% disparity figure for mid-range cases, and he did not adequately explain the rationale of his definition of the mid-range of cases. His testimony leaves this Court unpersuaded that there is a rationally classified, well-defined class of cases in which it can be demonstrated that a race-of-the-victim effect is operating with a magnitude approximating 20%.[96]

The court then went on to hold:

Assuming *arguendo*, however, that the 20% disparity is an accurate figure, it is apparent that such a disparity only in the mid-range cases, and not in the system as a whole, cannot provide the basis for a systemwide challenge. As previously discussed, the system as a whole is operating in a rational manner, and not in a manner that can fairly be labeled arbitrary or capricious. A valid system challenge cannot be made only against the mid-range of cases. Baldus did not purport to define the mid-range of cases; nor is such a definition possible. It is simply not satisfactory to say that the racial effect operates in "close cases" and therefore that the death penalty will be set aside in "close cases."[97]

The court of appeals also held that to establish a claim of arbitrary capital sentencing under the Eighth Amendment on the basis of racial discrimination, a defendant's evidence must be sufficiently strong to establish purposeful discrimination under the equal-protection clause. Since, in the court's opinion, McCleskey's evidence could not support such an inference, his Eighth Amendment claim also failed.[98]

The Decision of the United States Supreme Court

The Opinion of the Court

On April 22, 1987, the United States Supreme Court, by a 5–4 vote, affirmed the Eleventh Circuit's rejection of McCleskey's Fourteenth and Eighth Amendment claims of arbitrariness and racial discrimination.[99] Like the Court of Appeals, the majority assumed that "the study is valid statistically" without reviewing the methodological findings of the district court. Justice Powell did, however, characterize the trial court's opinion as having "considered the Baldus study with care," as having "found that the methodology of the . . . study was flawed in several respects," and for that reason as having concluded that it " 'fail[ed] to contribute anything of value' to McCleskey's claim."[100] Also, in an extensive footnote, the Court enumerated what it perceived to be the main methodological flaws identified by the trial court.[101]

On the merits, Justice Powell held first that, in a challenge to a capital-sentencing system based on the equal-protection clause, statistical evidence of classwide discrimination of the type offered by McCleskey was irrelevant and that McCleskey's other nonstatistical proof was clearly insufficient to support an inference that any of the decision makers in the case had acted with a discriminatory purpose.[102] Justice Powell made it plain that the normal methods for proving classwide purposeful discrimination claims under the Fourteenth Amendment, such as those employed in jury-discrimination cases, did not apply in the death-sentencing context.

Justice Powell's justification for rejecting the use of statistics to prove an equal-protection violation in the death-penalty context was primarily methodological. He acknowledged that statistical proof, including regression analysis, is appropriate to prove classwide, purposeful discrimination in cases involving employment or the selection of jury venires. In those types of cases, moreover, a claimant may establish a prima facie claim for relief by offering evidence of classwide discrimination:

> But the nature of the capital sentencing decision, and the relationship of the statistics to that decision, are fundamentally different from the corresponding elements in the venire-selection or Title VII cases. Most importantly, each particular decision to impose the death penalty is made by a petit jury selected from a properly constituted venire. Each jury is unique in its composition, and the Constitution requires that its decision rest on consideration of innumerable factors that vary according to the characteristics of the individual defendant and the facts of the particular capital offense. Thus, the application of an inference drawn from the general statistics to a specific decision in a trial and sentencing simply is not comparable to the application of an inference drawn from general statistics to a specific venire-selection or Title VII case. In those cases, the statistics relate to fewer entities, and fewer variables are relevant to the challenged decisions.[103]

Justice Powell pursued the latter points in two footnotes. In the first, he distinguished between employment and death-sentencing cases with respect to the number of relevant variables:

> While employment decisions may involve a number of relevant variables, these variables are to a great extent uniform for all employees because they must all have a reasonable relationship to the employee's qualifications to perform the particular job at issue. Identifiable qualifications for a single job provide a common standard by which to assess each employee. In contrast, a capital sentencing jury may consider *any* factor relevant to the defendant's background, character, and the offense. There is no common standard by which to evaluate all defendants who have or have not received the death penalty.[104]

In the second footnote, Justice Powell elaborated on his concern about inferring a policy from the decisions of a large number of seemingly autonomous decision makers:

> We refer here not to the number of entities involved in any particular decision, but to the number of entities whose decisions necessarily are reflected in a statistical display such as the Baldus study. The decisions of a jury commission or of an employer over time are fairly attributable to the commission or the employer. Therefore, an unexplained statistical discrepancy can be said to indicate a consistent policy of the decisionmaker. The Baldus study seeks to deduce a state "policy" by studying the combined effects of the decisions of hundreds of juries that are unique in their composition. It is incomparably more difficult to deduce a consistent policy by studying the decisions of these many unique entities. It is also questionable whether any consistent policy can be derived by studying the decisions of prosecutors. The District Attorney is elected by the voters in a particular county. See Ga. Const. Art. VI, §8, ¶1. Since decisions whether to prosecute and what to charge necessarily are individualized and involve infinite factual variations, coordination among DA offices across a State would be relatively meaningless. Thus, any inference from state-wide statistics to a prosecutorial "policy" is of doubtful relevance. [105]

Justice Powell also distinguished between employment cases and death-sentencing cases in terms of the capacity of the state to rebut a prima facie showing in a death-sentencing case:

> Another important difference between the cases in which we have accepted statistics as proof of discriminatory intent and this case is that, in the venire-selection and Title VII contexts, the decisionmaker has an opportunity to explain the statistical disparity. Here, the State has no practical opportunity to rebut the Baldus study. "[C]ontrolling considerations of . . . public policy" dictate that jurors "cannot be called . . . to testify to the motives and influences that led to their verdict." Similarly, the policy considerations behind a prosecutor's traditionally "wide discretion" suggest the impropriety of our requiring prosecutors to defend their decisions to seek death penalties, "often years after they were made." [106]

Justice Powell concluded his equal-protection analysis by distinguishing death-sentencing cases from jury-selection and employment cases on a broader and potentially more persuasive ground:

> Finally, McCleskey's statistical proffer must be viewed in the context of his challenge. McCleskey challenges decisions at the heart of the State's criminal justice system. "[O]ne of society's most basic tasks is that of protecting the lives of its citizens and one of the most basic ways in which it achieves the task is through criminal laws against murder." . . . Implementation of these laws necessarily requires discretionary judgments. Because discretion is essential to the criminal justice process, we would demand exceptionally clear proof before we would infer that the discretion has been abused. The unique nature of the deci-

sions at issue in this case also counsel against adopting such an inference from the disparities indicated by the Baldus study. Accordingly, we hold that the Baldus study is clearly insufficient to support an inference that any of the decisionmakers in McCleskey's case acted with discriminatory purpose.[107]

When addressing the Eighth Amendment issues in McCleskey, Justice Powell did not explicitly overrule *Furman*, nor did he appear to have intended to do so. Nevertheless, his discussion of the meaning of excessiveness and disproportionality under the Eighth Amendment repudiates much of what *Furman* has been understood to stand for over the past fifteen years. First, the opinion appears to reject the notion that comparative excessiveness is a matter of constitutional concern in death sentencing. At no point in the proceedings had McCleskey claimed that his death sentence was excessive in a comparative sense. His entire argument rested upon an assertion that the Georgia death-sentencing system operated in a racially discriminatory fashion and that his death sentence was a likely product of racial discrimination. Nevertheless, Justice Powell stated that McCleskey "argues that the sentence in his case is disproportionate to the sentences in other murder cases."[108] The opinion rejects this alleged claim, first by noting that McCleskey's case was found by the Georgia Supreme Court in a proportionality review to be "not disproportionate." The opinion then goes on to say that "McCleskey cannot prove a constitutional violation by demonstrating that other defendants who may be similarly situated did *not* receive the death penalty."[109] This point is further developed in a footnote that states, "The Constitution is not offended by inconsistency in results based on the objective circumstances of the crime."[110]

Justice Powell then turned to McCleskey's racial discrimination claim under the Eighth Amendment. Because the Supreme Court's prior decisions have vacated individual death sentences if they were ordered under circumstances that created a substantial risk that they were arbitrarily imposed, Justice Powell did not deny that McCleskey's proof would be highly probative if it, in fact, demonstrated such a risk with respect to his death sentence. Rather, the opinion sought to refute the principal inference suggested by McCleskey's statistical evidence—that the race of victim was an important influence in Georgia's capital-sentencing system. The first step in Justice Powell's refutation was a broad pronouncement on the capacity of a multivariate statistical analysis to support an inference that discrimination was an influence in a sentencing system:

> Our assumption that the Baldus study is statistically valid does not include the assumption that the study shows that racial considerations actually enter into any sentencing decisions in Georgia. Even a sophisticated multiple regression analysis such as the Baldus study can only demonstrate a *risk* that the factor of race entered into some capital sentencing decisions and a necessarily lesser risk that race entered into any particular sentencing decision.[111]

Turning to McCleskey's statistical evidence, Justice Powell next held that "[a]t most" it indicated "a discrepancy that appears to correlate" with race. However, because the case involved "the discretion that is fundamental to our criminal process," the Court would not "assume that what is unexplained is invidious." He concluded, therefore, that McCleskey's evidence "does not demonstrate a constitutionally significant risk of racial bias affecting the Georgia capital-sentencing process."[112]

Justice Powell also based his rejection of McCleskey's Eighth Amendment claim on a fear that a ruling for McCleskey would result in a flood of Eighth Amendment claims in both capital and noncapital cases and on both racial and nonracial grounds. Convictions and sentences might be threatened on the ground they were correlated illegitimately with the defendant's sex, the type of defense attorney, the identity of the judge, the defendant's facial character-istics, or the physical attractiveness of the defendant or the victim in a manner "that some statistical study indicates . . . may be influential in jury decisionmaking."[113] In support of this concern, Justice Powell presented a number of citations to empirical studies of discrimination and arbitrariness in judicial decision making.

Justice Powell's final reason for rejecting McCleskey's Eighth Amendment claim concerned the competence and authority of the Supreme Court to deal with the issue:

> McCleskey's arguments are best presented to the legislative bodies. It is not the responsibility—or indeed even the right—of this Court to determine the ap-propriate punishment for particular crimes. It is the legislatures, the elected representatives of the people, that are "constituted to respond to the will and consequently the moral values of the people." Legislatures also are better qual-ified to weigh and "evaluate the results of statistical studies in terms of their own local conditions and with a flexibility of approach that is not available to the courts."[114]

The Dissenting Opinions

Justices Brennan and Blackmun filed dissenting opinions in which Justices Marshall and Stevens joined to varying degrees. Justice Stevens also filed a dissent in which Justice Blackmun joined.

Justice Brennan's dissent asserted that both the statistical and the historical evidence proved that racial discrimination was a major characteristic of the Georgia death-sentencing system and, as a consequence, the system created an unacceptable risk that individual death sentences were arbitrary or capri-cious. Accordingly, in his opinion, the entire system violated the cruel and unusual punishments clause of the Eighth Amendment.[115] Justice Brennan also argued that the evidence supported a finding by a preponderance of the evidence that race had determined the outcome of McCleskey's case.

Justice Blackmun's dissent addressed McCleskey's equal-protection claims. He rejected as unpersuasive Justice Powell's rejection of the classwide model, which is routinely applied in jury- and employment-discrimination cases, in the death-sentencing context. Moreover, he found that McCleskey's evidence established a prima facie case of intentional discrimination under the equal protection clause that the state had failed to refute. Justice Blackmun also agreed with Justice Brennan that McCleskey's evidence established by a preponderance that race had been a factor in his own case. However, unlike Justice Brennan, Justice Blackmun did not believe the case called for the invalidation of Georgia's death-sentencing system—only a narrowing of death eligibility to the highly aggravated cases where there was no evidence of a race effect.[116]

Justice Stevens took a similar approach. He argued that the evidence established a "strong probability" that McCleskey was sentenced to death because of the race of his victim. In his view, this finding did not require the invalidation of Georgia's death-sentencing system. Rather, he urged that the case be remanded to determine whether, as he assumed, the studies were valid and whether McCleskey's case fell "within the range of cases that present an unacceptable risk that race played a decisive role in McCleskey's sentencing."[117]

NOTES

1. 446 U.S. 420 (1980).

2. Id. at 427.

3. Id. at 433.

4. Zant v. Stephens, 462 U.S. 862 (1983), provided further evidence that the Supreme Court's commitment to evenhanded death sentencing might be slipping. First, the Court reconceptualized the role of statutory aggravating circumstances under the Georgia statute in a manner that increased the risk of inconsistent death sentencing. The question in Zant was whether a defendant could be condemned to die based on a jury finding of three statutory aggravating circumstances, one of which was later found to have been constitutionally invalid. The defendant argued that the statutorily designated aggravating circumstances in the Georgia statute were intended not only to determine if the defendant was death-eligible, but also to guide the jury when it decided the actual sentence. In support of this argument the defendant cited various passages from Gregg that praised Georgia's statutory aggravating circumstances for guiding and channeling the jury's sentencing discretion in capital cases, thereby minimizing the risk of arbitrary or inconsistent sentences. See, e.g., Gregg v. Georgia, 428 U.S. 153, 192, 197–98 (1976). The defendant also noted that the trial judge's instructions in his particular case had suggested that the jury should consider the relevant statutory aggravating circumstances when deciding the defendant's fate. Zant v. Stephens, 462 U.S. at 865–66. The trial judge's instructions are quoted in full in Zant v. Stephens, 456 U.S. 410, 411n.1 (1982).

In contrast to the defendant's Gregg-based concept of the function of the statutory aggravating circumstances, the Georgia Supreme Court offered a substantially different construction. Responding to a certificate of inquiry from the United States Supreme Court, the Georgia court described its system for classifying capital defendants as a three-stage process with the following criteria governing each stage:

Stage One: Includes all defendants convicted of murder, that is, an unlawful killing with malice aforethought.

Stage Two: Includes those defendants convicted of murder who are death-eligible in that, beyond a reasonable doubt, a statutorily designated aggravating circumstance is present in their case.

Stage Three: Includes those death-eligible defendants who, based on all aggravating and mitigating factors in the case, actually receive a death sentence. See Zant v. Stephens, 462 U.S. at 870–72 (citing Zant v. Stephens, 250 Ga. 97, 99–100; 297 S.E.2d 1, 3–4 (1982)).

The significant difference between the defendant's *Gregg*- based model of the Georgia statute and that proposed in *Stephens* by the Georgia Supreme Court lies in the criteria determining inclusion in the third category. The defendant's *Gregg*-based model presumed that statutory aggravating criteria would play an influential role in guiding the jury's deliberations concerning what sentence to impose. Thus, the trial judge's instructions, which gave emphasis to a constitutionally defective criterion, might well have distorted the jury's decision.

On the other hand, the model suggested in *Stephens* by the Georgia Supreme Court downplayed the importance of the statutory aggravating circumstances with respect to the third-stage determination. According to the Georgia court, the statutory aggravating circumstances only served to determine whether the defendant was death-eligible. Once the jury made that determination, the statutory aggravating circumstances were of no further importance. When selecting those death-eligible defendants who would actually receive death sentences, according to the Georgia Supreme Court, the jury was entitled to consider any factors or circumstances that it deemed important; the legislative criteria were of no significance at this stage. Zant v. Stephens, 462 U.S. at 871–72 (quoting 250 Ga. at 99–100, 297 S.E.2d at 3). The Georgia court's description of the process appears to be an accurate portrayal of Georgia jury-charging practices before and after *Zant*.

In *Stephens*, the United States Supreme Court adopted the Georgia Supreme Court's construction of the statute as authoritative and ruled it was constitutional for two reasons. First, a majority of the justices rejected the defendant's argument that *Gregg* had attributed to the Georgia statutory aggravating circumstances the function of guiding the jury's sentencing discretion. *Id.* at 875. Second, the Court also rejected the contention that such guidance was constitutionally required. No such restriction on the jury's sentencing discretion was necessary, concluded the *Stephens* majority, because the Georgia statute requires a bifurcated sentencing procedure and "mandates meaningful appellate review of every death sentence," which would prevent the imposition of arbitrary or inconsistent death sentences. *Id.* at 875.

The second indication in *Stephens* of a possible retreat from the Court's earlier commitment to evenhanded death sentencing was Justice Stevens's suggestion that the two valid aggravating circumstances in the case "adequately differentiate this case in an objective, evenhanded and substantively rational way from the many Georgia murder cases in which the death penalty *may not be imposed*" (emphasis added). *Id.* at 879. The key shift was from the Court's earlier empirical test of whether a death-sentenced defendant's case could be distinguished from the many cases in which lesser sentences *are not imposed* to a nonempirical test of whether the death-sentenced defendant's case could be distinguished from cases in which death sentences are not authorized by law, regardless of the frequency with which death sentences are actually imposed in similar cases. In effect, the new test of excessiveness merely asks whether the death sentence imposed is authorized under the state law.

5. To be sure, the death-sentencing system approved in Jurek v. Texas, 428 U.S. 262 (1976), provided no provision for comparative-proportionality review. Yet in its decision approving the Texas system in *Jurek*, the United States Supreme Court characterized its system of appellate review as one capable of ensuring evenhanded death sentencing. *Id.* at 276. The expectation as to the importance of comparative-proportionality review was particularly strong with respect to jurisdictions that included a system of proportionality review as part of their post-*Furman* death-sentencing system.

6. 446 U.S. 420, 429 (1980).

7. 465 U.S. 37 (1984). Justice White's majority opinion did acknowledge that prior opinions (most recently in Zant v. Stephens) had emphasized the importance of proportionality review, but denied that such a review process was constitutionally required. *Id.* at 45–46. In *Gregg*, he explained, the Court had regarded comparative-sentence review as no more than "an additional safeguard against arbitrary or capricious sentencing." *Id.* at 45. Furthermore, in *Stephens*, it was "the jury's finding of aggravating circumstances, not the State Supreme Court's finding of proportionality" that made the death sentence rational. *Id.* at 50. In other words, suggested Justice White, so long as the jury had found at least one valid statutory aggravating circumstance to exist, that finding would adequately differentiate the defendant's death sentence from other life sentence cases "in an objective, evenhanded, and substantively rational way," thereby satisfying the relevant constitutional requirements. *Id.* at 50.n.12 (quoting Zant v. Stephens, 462 U.S. at 879).

There are at least two possible explanations for the Court's apparently revisionistic treatment of comparative-sentence review in *Harris*. One possibility is that, implicitly, the Court was endorsing the model of the Georgia death-sentencing system, which assumed that prosecutors and juries would regularly seek and impose the death penalty in death-eligible cases, thereby making comparative-sentence review constitutionally unnecessary. Justice White's majority opinion makes no reference to this presumption, but it does provide a logical explanation for the result.

The second possibility is that the Court had altered its earlier views of the constitutional importance of consistency in death sentencing. One can read *Harris* to suggest that sentencing juries may pick and choose among death-eligible defendants, exercising the sort of "untrammeled discretion" that *McGautha* endorsed and that *Furman* condemned, so long as at least one statutorily designated aggravating circumstance exists in the case of each defendant condemned to death. *Compare* McGautha v. California, 402 U.S. 183, 207–8 (1971), with Furman v. Georgia, 408 U.S. 238, 248 (1972) (Douglas, J., concurring). *See also* Zant v. Stephens, 462 U.S. at 906–12 (Marshall, J., dissenting). Although such a primitive model of a constitutionally satisfactory capital-sentencing procedure seems to run counter to the Court's opinions in *Gregg* and *Stephens*, it is, however, technically consistent with *Godfrey* and, of course, Pulley v. Harris itself. More to the point, such a minimally restrictive statutory procedure can avoid inconsistent, capricious sentencing results—which *Furman* specifically rejected—only if juries exercise their discretion when sentencing death-eligible defendants in a regular, consistent manner. In other words, whether or not the *Harris* majority intended to invoke the factual presumption that prosecutors and juries would regularly seek and impose death sentences in death-eligible cases, the accuracy of such a presumption was essential to the *Harris* ruling, if *Furman* was still good law. *Harris* also foreclosed constitutional claims that state courts that did conduct statutorily mandated proportionality reviews applied ineffective review procedures.

8. 426 U.S. 229 (1976).

9. 462 U.S. at 885.

10. More recently, in Turner v. Murray, a majority of the justices appeared to recognize the risk of discrimination in capital sentencing when they agreed that a defendant's Sixth Amendment right to an impartial jury in a capital case involving an interracial murder authorized him to voir dire prospective jury members concerning possible racial prejudice on their part. 476 U.S. 28 (1986). However, only a minority of the justices believed that the denial of this Sixth Amendment right to voir dire the jury invalidated the underlying conviction. Consequently, the Court vacated the death sentence, but declined to order a new trial. Justice White's opinion explained that the capital-sentencing proceeding merited this special protection because of the broad discretion jurors exercise under state law and the concomitant opportunity to discriminate on racial grounds. Although technically a Sixth Amendment case, therefore, *Turner* really applies only in the capital-sentencing context.

11. *Smith v. Balkcom*, 671 F.2d 858, 859–60 & n.33 (5th Cir. Unit B 1982) (citations omitted).

12. McCleskey v. Kemp, 107 S.Ct. 1756, 1762 (1987). The trial judge had also imposed two consecutive life sentences on McCleskey for his role in the armed robbery. McCleskey v. Zant, 580 F.Supp. 338, 344 (N.D.Ga. 1984).

13. McCleskey was represented by John C. Boger, NAACP Legal Defense and Educational Fund, Inc.; Tim Ford, Seattle; and Robert Stroup, Atlanta. Professor Baldus described the background of the study. Edward Gates then explained the data-collection efforts in which he participated in both the Procedural Reform and Charging and Sentencing Studies. Next Professor Baldus presented the substantive findings. Professor Woodworth then gave his opinion about the validity of the statistical procedures used, described the diagnostic and "worst-case" analyses he conducted, and presented his interpretation of our principal findings.

14. The state's experts were Dr. Joseph Katz, Assistant Professor, Department of Quantitative Methods, Georgia State University, and Dr. Roger Burford, Professor of Quantitative Business Analysis, Louisiana State University.

15. Richard Berk was then Professor of Sociology at the University of California at Santa Barbara and a member of the National Research Council sentencing panel. RESEARCH ON SENTENCING: THE SEARCH FOR REFORM (A. Blumstein, J. Cohen, S. Martin, & M. Tonry eds. 1983).

16. On the issue of race-of-defendant discrimination, in both the jury and prosecutorial statewide multiple-regression analyses from the PRS presented in the *McCleskey* hearing (whether conducted with linear or logistic-regression procedures), the coefficients estimated for the "black defendant" variable were generally negative, suggesting that black defendants had a lower chance of both advancing to a penalty trial and receiving a death sentence, although none of the estimates was statistically significant beyond the .10 level. *See infra* note tables 5, 6, & 7. These results were generally consistent with those reported in chap. 6 of this book.

17. The results were presented in DB 98, on which note table 4 is based. The exhibits presented in the *McCleskey* hearing were largely developed during the period March–June 1983. During that time and up until the hearing in August 1983 and

Note Table 4. Race-of-Victim Disparities in Death Sentencing: Among Defendants Convicted of Murder at Trial, Estimated with Ordinary Least-Squares and Logistic-Regression Coefficients, Controlling for Alternative Sets of Nonracial Background Factors and the Race of Defendant (Procedural Reform Study)

Nonracial Background Variables Controlled For	Ordinary-Least-Squares Regression Coefficient (with Level of Statistical Significance)	Death-Odds Multiplier	Logistic-Regression Coefficient (with Level of Statistical Significance)
1. Five legitimate factors[1]	.09 (.03)	2.8	1.03 (.002)
2. Nine legitimate factors[2]	.09 (.02)	2.8	1.02 (.005)
3. All statutory aggravating factors	.09 (.01)	3.0	1.1 (.01)
4. All statutory aggravating factors and 43 mitigating factors[3]	.09 (.02)	4.6	1.53 (.01)[a]
5. 150 + nonracial aggravating and mitigating factors and 4 suspect factors[4]	.09 (.01)	–	–[b]
6. 32 statistically significant variables from the file showing a statistically significant relationship ($p \leq .10$) with the death-sentencing result[5]	.08 (.02)	5.1	1.63 (.004)[a]

1. See app. L, sched. 10, for a list of these variables.
2. See app. L, sched. 11, for a list of these variables.
3. See app. L, sched. 14, for a list of the factors in the analysis.
4. See app. L, sched. 15, for a list of the full file of aggravating, mitigating, and suspect factors in the analysis. See also supra chap. 6, note 20 and accompanying text.
5. See app. L, sched. 16, for a list of these variables.
a. These logistic results were not presented in McCleskey.
b. The analysis involves too many variables for simultaneous adjustment in a logistic analysis.

beyond, we corrected any errors in the PRS and CSS data sets that we discovered in our cleaning of the data or that were brought to our attention by the State's experts in McCleskey. As a result, it is not possible to replicate exactly some of the exhibits that we submitted in McCleskey with the data in the archives at the University of Michigan (see supra chap. 4 note 15).

All references in the text to the record (R.) refer to the transcript of the evidentiary hearing held in the United States District Court for the Northern District of Georgia, August 8–22, 1983. "DB" and "GW" references indicate exhibits that were submitted by, respectively, Professors Baldus and Woodworth.

18. These results were presented through DB 95 & 96, on which note tables 5 & 6 are based.

19. The PRS jury results reported in column E of note table 5 were based on 19 variables screened with a linear stepwise procedure from the variables listed infra in app. L, sched. 15, minus the interaction terms. The procedure estimated a race-of-defendant coefficient of $-.03$ ($p = .61$).

20. These results were presented through DB 96, on which note table 6 is based. The background variables referred to in note 6 of note table 6 were nonperverse variables screened from the variables in app. L, sched. 15, minus the interaction terms with linear procedures. The logistic race-of-victim regression coefficient estimated in a

Note Table 5. Regression Coefficients (with the Level of Statistical Significance) for Racial Variables in Analyses of Prosecutorial Decisions to Seek and Jury Decisions to Impose Capital Punishment, Charging and Sentencing Study (CSS) and Procedural Reform Study (PRS)

A	B	C		D	E
		Controlling for			
		Full File of Statutory Aggravating Factors and Mitigating Factors[1]		All Factors in File[2]	
	All Statutory Aggravating Factors	All Factors Simultaneously	Factors with Statistical Significance at the .10 Level	Regardless of Statistical Significance	If Statistically Significant at the .10 Level
I. Prosecutor decision to seek a death sentence					
A. Race of victim					
1. CSS	.24[a] (.001)	.28[a] (.0001)	.28 (.0001)	.24 (.01)	.15 (.001)
2. PRS	.14 (.01)	.15 (.001)	.15 (.001)	.13 (.005)	.14 (.001)
B. Race of defendant					
1. CSS	.14[a] (.01)	.18[a] (.01)	.17 (.001)	.17 (.03)	.12 (.01)
2. PRS	.04 (.41)	.005 (.91)	−.001 (.98)	.00 (.99)	.01 (.73)
II. Jury sentencing decision					
A. Race of victim					
1. CSS	.11 (.19)	.26 (.01)	.13 (.08)	—[b]	.02 (.75)
2. PRS	.08 (.40)	.23 (.04)	.16 (.05)	—	.23 (.001)
B. Race of defendant					
1. CSS	−.02 (.76)	−.02 (.82)	.05 (.46)	—	−.00 (.91)
2. PRS	−.08 (.30)	−.06 (.46)	−.05 (.47)	—	−.03 (.61)

1. See app. L, sched. 1 (CSS) and sched. 14 (PRS), for a list of these variables.
2. See app. L, sched. 3 (CSS) and sched. 15 (PRS), for a list of these variables.
a. The computation of "safe" standard errors did not materially alter the level of statistical significance of the coefficients. See table 53, note 1.
b. Valid simultaneous adjustment for all factors in the files was not possible because of the limited number of penalty-trial decisions.

Note Table 6. Race-of-Victim and Race-of-Defendant Disparities in Prosecutorial Decision Making Estimated with Logistic-Regression Procedures, Controlling for Alternative Sets of Nonracial Background Variables

	Race of Victim		Race of Defendant	
A. Background Variables Controlled For	B. Death-Odds Multiplier	C. Regression Coefficient (w/level of statistical significance)[7]	D. Death-Odds Multiplier	E. Regression Coefficient (w/level of statistical significance)[7]
I. Charging and Sentencing Study				
A. Five legitimate factors[1]	4.8	1.56 (.0001)	2.0	.68 (.005)
B. Nine legitimate factors[2]	5.1	1.63 (.0001)	2.3	.82 (.02)
C. Ten statistically significant ($p<.10$) nonarbitrary factors[3]	3.3	1.21 (.02)	2.4	.86 (.10)
II. Procedural Reform Study				
A. Five legitimate factors[4]	2.8	1.03 (.002)	.73	−.32 (.23)
B. Nine legitimate factors[5]	2.8	1.02 (.005)	.81	−.21 (.47)
C. All statutory aggravating variables	3.2	1.15 (.0001)	1.1	.11 (.68)
D. 21 statistically significant nonarbitrary factors[6]	3.4	1.22 (.0001)	1.1	.12 (.71)

1. The five variables are (a) felony circumstances, (b) serious prior record, (c) family, lover, liquor, or barroom quarrel, (d) multiple victims, and (e) stranger-victim.
2. The nine variables are those listed in note 1 plus (a) defendant not the triggerman, (b) physical torture, (c) mental torture, and (d) rape or helpless victim or motive to silence a witness.
3. See app. L, sched. 8, for a list of these variables.
4. See app. L, sched. 10, for a list of these variables.
5. See app. L, sched. 11, for a list of these variables.
6. See app. L, sched. 12, for a list of these variables.
7. The race coefficients reported in this table were estimated with weighted logistic-regression analyses, while those reported in DB 96, which were in evidence in *McCleskey*, were estimated with unweighted procedures. The race-of-victim coefficients in DB 96 were, by row: IA (1.35); IB (1.5); IC (1.24), all significant beyond the .01 level. The race-of-defendant coefficients in DB 96 were, by row: IA (.82); IB (.94); IC (1.01), all significant at the .02 level.

model with 18 nonperverse legitimate background variables screened with logistic procedures was $b = 1.2$ ($p = .001$). *See supra* chap. 4, note 44 and accompanying text, and *infra* app. B, note 65, for a description of perverse variables.

Because the outcome variable in all of these analyses is binary (yes/no), we have greater confidence in estimates produced with logistic procedures than in estimates produced with linear procedures.

21. These results were presented through DB 97, on which note table 7 is based.

22. For example, *supra* chap. 6, note 37 and accompanying text, report an adjusted race-of-victim odds multiplier of 7 ($p = .001$) in a logistic regression.

23. *See, e.g.,* a 14-percentage-point disparity ($p = .12$) in an analysis with Barnett's three-dimensional culpability classification system (fig. 26); a 15-percentage-point disparity ($p = .055$) in a cross-tab with a regression-based culpability scale, *id.* at table 36; a 16-percentage-point disparity ($p = .10$) in cross-tab of armed-robbery–

Note Table 7. Race-of-Victim and Race-of-Defendant Disparities in Jury Decision Making Estimated with Logistic-Regression Procedures, Controlling for Alternative Sets of Nonracial Background Variables

	Race of Victim		Race of Defendant	
A. Background Variables Controlled For	B. Death-Odds Multiplier	C. Regression Coefficient (w/level of statistical significance)[7]	D. Death-Odds Multiplier	E. Regression Coefficient (w/level of statistical significance)[7]
I. Charging and Sentencing Study				
A. Five legitimate factors[1]	1.2	.18 (.63)	.76	−.28 (.34)
B. Nine legitimate factors[2]	1.4	.36 (.36)	.93	−.08 (.80)
C. Thirteen statistically significant nonarbitrary factors[3]	3.4	1.23 (.02)	1.3	.28 (.50)
II. Procedural Reform Study				
A. Five legitimate variables[4]	1.3	.24 (.57)	.67	−.41 (.21)
B. Nine legitimate variables[5]	1.4	.32 (.46)	.73	−.31 (.37)
C. All statutory aggravating factors	1.4	.36 (.43)	.67	−.41 (.27)
D. Eleven statistically significant nonarbitrary factors[6]	1.36	.31 (.57)	.57	−.57 (.21)

1. The five variables are (a) felony circumstances, (b) serious prior record, (c) family, lover, liquor, or barroom quarrel, (d) multiple victims, and (e) stranger-victim.
2. The nine variables are those listed in note 1 plus (a) defendant not the triggerman, (b) physical torture, (c) mental torture, and (d) rape or helpless victim or motive to silence a witness.
3. See app. L, sched. 9, for a list of these variables.
4. See app. L, sched. 10, for a list of these variables.
5. See app. L, sched. 11, for a list of these variables.
6. See app. L, sched. 13, for a list of these variables which were statistically significant at the .10 level in stepwise logistic analyses of all variables in the entire file.
7. The race coefficients reported in this table were estimated in weighted logistic-regression analyses, while those reported in DB 97, which were in evidence in *McCleskey*, were estimated with unweighted procedures. The race-of-victim coefficients in DB 97 were, by row: IA , .19 (p = .61); IB, .36 (p = .36); IC, 1.6 (p = .01). The race-of-defendant coefficients in DB 97 were, by row: IA, −.27 (p = .36); IB, −.65 (p = .88); IC, .43 (p = .01).

murder cases based on an *a priori* weighing measure, *id.* at table 35; *see also id.* at tables 36–39. We discuss our preference for disparities based on cross-tabular analyses (as opposed to regression coefficients) *infra* app. A, at p. 438. The regression analyses reported in chap. 6, which suggest stronger race-of-victim effects, are based on more variables (many interaction terms) than those presented in the McCleskey case.

24. The design and data in the Charging and Sentencing Study are described *supra* chap. 4, note 8 and accompanying text.

25. When the death-sentencing rates in the two studies are based on murder-trial convictions, the figures are virtually identical, .17 (128/762) for the Charging and Sentencing Study versus .18 (112/606) for the Procedural Reform Study.

26. Table 50 is based on exhibits DB 62 and DB 63.

27. The ratio measure used here is one of several commonly used "multiplier" methods for comparing two numbers. Other such measures would be the ratio of the death-sentencing rates in black- and white-victim cases, .12 (.0133/.11), and the ratio of the arithmetic difference between the two rates, .91 (.10/.11).

28. Fig. 31 is based on DB 76. The overall race-of-victim effect in fig. 31, calculated since the *McCleskey* hearing, is 6 percentage points, significant at the .0002 level (Mantel-Haenszel $Z = 6.1$).

29. The 39 legitimate variables in the core model are listed in app. L, sched. 4, and *supra* chap. 4, note 43. The results from the 39-variable model were introduced through exhibit GW 4 (table 1, line 9, "Midrange diagnostic model").

30. *See supra* chap. 6, note 19 and accompanying text (among cases resulting in a murder-trial conviction, a race-of-victim odds multiplier of 4.3, significant at the .001 level after adjustment for 23 nonracial background factors).

31. These results are based on exhibit DB 83. Table 51 has slight modifications reflecting corrections in the data set made since *McCleskey. See supra* note 17. Also, the logistic results reported in DB 83 were estimated with unweighted regression procedures, while the results in table 51 were estimated with weighted procedures. The race-of-victim estimates in Parts IIa and IIb of DB 83 were 1.0 ($p = .01$) and .85 ($p = .01$), respectively.

32. Table 51 at line I (a). *See infra* app. L, sched. 3, for a listing of the background variables used in this analysis; when the analysis was limited to B2 and B7 death-eligible cases, the race-of-victim linear coefficient estimated in each of the large 230-plus variable models was .10 ($p = .01$). Source: DB 85 (not reproduced here).

33. *See supra* chap. 6, note 20 and accompanying text.

34. A similar analysis based on the results of an unweighted stepwise logistic regression analysis was admitted as DB 82. It showed a 1.45 coefficient for the race-of-victim variable, significant at the .0003 level.

To estimate further the impact of the race of the victim in Georgia's capital-sentencing system, we compared the relevant characteristics of the defendants in the sample of the Charging and Sentencing Study who actually received death sentences with the death-row population that we estimated would have resulted from a hypothetical, color-blind charging-and-sentencing system that permitted fewer opportunities for the exercise of prosecutorial discretion. The trial court refused, however, to admit these estimates.

The hypothetical evenhanded death-row population was estimated as follows. First we selected the regression model that best identified the defendants that juries actually sentenced to death at penalty trials. We then applied the results of this analysis to all defendants convicted of murder (whether by plea or by verdict) and estimated which of them would have received death sentences if they had all faced penalty trials (whether or not they actually did). Thus, our hypothetical death row excluded the effects of all prosecutorial decisions to forgo a penalty trial following entry of a murder conviction. Our hypothetical system also secured evenhanded treatment at the penalty-trial stage by using the average death-sentencing rate that was actually observed among each group of similarly situated penalty-trial cases.

The results in note table 8 compare the racial characteristics of the defendants who were actually sentenced to death with our hypothetical death-row population. The distributions of cases in columns B and C indicate that we would see a substantial increase in the proportion of black-victim cases on the hypothetical death row and

Note Table 8. Distribution of Death-Sentence Cases by Racial Characteristics (CSS)

A	B. Hypothetical System without Prosecutorial Discretion after a Murder Conviction and with Even-handed Penalty Trials	C. Results of the Actual System (Proportion of Cases)	D. Changes in the Proportions: Hypothetical/ Actual (Col. B−Col. C)	E. Changes in the Proportions: Hypothetical/ Actual (Col. B/Col. C)
I. By defendant/victim racial combination				
A. Black defendant/ white victim	.24 (72/301)	.39 (50/128)	−.15	.62
B. White defendant/ white victim	.43 (128/301)	.45 (58/128)	−.02	.96
C. Black defendant/ black victim	.30 (90/301)	.14 (18/128)	+.16	2.14
D. White defendant/ black victim	.04 (11/301)	.02 (2/128)	+.02	2.0
II. By race of victim				
A. White	.66 (200/301)	.84 (108/128)	−.18	.79
B. Black	.34 (101/301)	.16 (20/128)	+.18	2.1
III. By race of defendant				
A. Black	.54 (162/301)	.53 (68/128)	+.01	1.02
B. White	.46 (139/301)	.47 (60/128)	−.01	.98

sharply reduce the proportion of black-defendant/white-victim cases. These adjustments change the overall proportion of black defendants on death row very little, however, since the higher death-sentencing rate in the black-victim cases is offset by the lower rate in the black-defendant/white-victim category.

We also estimated the size and racial characteristics of the death-row population we would expect if all defendants indicted for murder and later convicted of murder or voluntary manslaughter had been sentenced by an evenhanded penalty-trial jury. This analysis suggests that 49% of these defendants would run no risk of a death sentence, but 185 defendants would face a risk of over .90. The following tabulation indicates the distribution of this hypothetical death row among the four defendant/victim racial subgroups and compares it with the actual distribution from our sample:

	Proportion of Cases	
	Hypothetical System	Actual System
Black defendant/white victim	.19	.39
White defendant/white victim	.38	.45
Black defendant/black victim	.40	.14
White defendant/black victim	.03	.02

When estimating the effects of a hypothetical death row, we naturally found that its size depended on whether the "evenhanded" death-sentencing rate was based on the rate observed for white-victim cases, the rate in black-victim cases, or the average of these two rates. We found, however, that regardless of the rate we used, the distribution of cases in the hypothetical death row among the four defendant/victim racial categories remained the same.

Finally, we estimated how the racial characteristics of the death-row cases in our sample would differ under a system in which all defendants convicted of murder advanced to a penalty trial and evenhanded penalty-trial juries imposed an identical number of death sentences. To do this we adjusted the racial distribution of death-row cases in our sample to match the racial distribution of death-row cases we observed in the hypothetical death-row population shown in note table 8 (column B). The results shown in note table 9 indicate that the proportions of black and white defendants on death row would hardly change at all. What would change dramatically, however, is the identity of the black defendants on death row. If Georgia had employed our hypothetical evenhanded system, 19 black defendants whose victims were white would probably not be on death row. Instead, 20 other black defendants whose victims were black would probably have received death sentences. A similar, but much smaller, change would occur in the identity of the white defendants on death row; 3 white defendants whose victims were black would replace 4 white defendants whose victims were white.

See supra chap. 6, note 23 and accompanying text, for a similar hypothetical death-row analysis in the Procedural Reform Study.

35. Fig. 32 is based on GW 8. See supra chap. 4, note 43 and accompanying text, for a description of the aggravation index underlying fig. 32. It is a quadratic model that was fitted as part of a series of checks of the robustness of the race-of-victim effect. The model was also designed to determine if the "liberation hypothesis" effect, which is an intrinsic part of the logistic model, would also appear in an unconstrained model. Although this model predicts slightly better than a linear model, it does have some undesirable features. First, predicted probabilities for a few extreme cases at either end

Note Table 9. A Comparison of the Distribution of Death-Row Defendants by Defendant/Victim Racial Characteristics Actually Observed in Georgia and the Distribution Expected in an Evenhanded Charging and Sentencing System (css)

A	B. Defendants in Hypothetical System[1]	C. Actual Defendants	D. Difference (Col. B−Col. C)
I. By defendant/victim racial combination			
A. Black defendant/ white victim	31	50	−19
B. White defendant/ white victim	55	58	−3
C. Black defendant/ black victim	38	18	+20
D. White defendant/ black victim	5	2	+3
II. By race of victim			
A. White	85	108	−23
B. Black	44	20	+24
III. By race of defendant			
A. Black	69	68	+1
B. White	59	60	−1

1. Totals may exceed 128 cases because of rounding.

of the culpability index are "off scale"—either greater than one or less than zero. In practice, as shown in the figure, we interpret negative probabilities as zero and probabilities greater than one as unity. The perverse upward curl at the low end of the black-victim curve is an artifact of the use of a quadratic model; only a small number of cases are affected by it.

36. Table 53 is based on DB 90. The variables in the index underlying table 53 were the legitimate case characteristics listed *infra* app. L, sched. 5, plus CPLESSEN, which did not survive the .10 screen after corrections in the data set were made post-*McCleskey*. *See supra* note 17.

37. *See supra* chap. 6, note 17 and accompanying text and table 32.

38. The results of our analysis of Judge Forrester's model were submitted to the court by an affidavit dated September 15, 1983.

39. Judge Forrester's codes that had the greatest limiting effect on the sample size were those that excluded cases with certain mitigating factors and those with low scores for strength of evidence.

40. The 647-case count is a weighted number referring to cases in the universe; they are represented in the sample by 354 actual cases. *See supra* chap. 4, note 10 and accompanying text for a description of the CSS sampling plan.

41. The logistic-regression coefficient estimated in this model was 1.39, significant at .03 level.

42. Table 54 is based on DB 86. The overall race-of-victim effect among the cases in table 54, which we calculated subsequent to the *McCleskey* hearing, was 17 percentage points, significant at the .001 level (Mantel-Haenszel $Z = 3.4$). Among only the armed-robbery–murder cases, the race-of-victim effect was 13 percentage points, significant at the .02 level (Mantel-Haenszel $Z = 2.5$). A comparable analysis of the armed-robbery cases in the Procedural Reform Study, which are also included in table 54, produced a 25-point race-of-victim effect, significant at the .01 level. *Supra* chap. 6, note 15 and accompanying text and table 31.

43. Table 56 is based on DB 94.

44. *See supra* note 18 (note tables 5 & 6).

45. *See supra* chap. 6, table 44.

46. *Supra* note 18 (note table 5) and note 21 (note table 7); see *supra* chap. 6, table 44, for a summary of jury results from the Procedural Reform Study.

47. The evidence on race-of-victim disparities offered in *McCleskey* on pretrial prosecutorial decisions was unadjusted. The multivariate analyses of the separate pretrial stages developed for the hearing were not offered in evidence. They showed a statistically significant race-of-victim effect only in the prosecutorial decision to accept voluntary-manslaughter plea bargains. The analyses produced a least-squares regression coefficient of $-.15$ ($p = .001$) after adjustment for all background variables.

Since the *McCleskey* hearing, we have conducted extensive logistic analyses on each of the six stages in the Georgia charging-and-sentencing system, as well as a model of their combined effects. Each of these analyses screened hundreds of additional background variables beyond the original 230-plus background variables, as well as hundreds of interaction terms. The only models revealing a statistically significant race-of-victim effect were (a) the prosecutorial decision to accept a voluntary-manslaughter plea (.24 odds multiplier for white-victim cases, $p = .001$), (b) the prosecutorial decision to seek a death sentence after obtaining a guilt-trial conviction (3.2 odds multiplier for white-victim cases), and (c) the combined effects of all six decisions (i.e., indictment, plea to voluntary manslaughter, plea to murder, conviction for murder, advancement to a penalty trial after murder conviction, and jury sentencing decision) (5.1 odds multiplier for white-victim cases, $p = .02$).

48. The logistic results reported in table 51 are consistent with this finding. We discounted the least-squares race-of-defendant results in table 51 because logistic regression is a more valid measure for analyzing a dichotomous outcome variable like "life/death sentence." Also, when the white-victim cases were analyzed separately, no race-of-defendant effect was observed.

49. Table 57 is based on DB 90. Table 57 is based on the same index and scale as table 53. *See supra* note 36.

50. Table 58 is based on DB 87. Subsequent to the *McCleskey* hearing, we calculated an overall race-of-defendant effect in the cases in table 58. Among all of the cases with the contemporaneous-felony (B2) aggravating factor present, the race-of-defendant disparity was 7.1 percentage points, significant at the .20 level (Mantel-Haenszel $Z = 1.3$). Among the white-victim cases only, the disparity was 10 percentage points, significant at the .10 level (Mantel-Haenszel $Z = 1.75$).

51. *See* DB 102 (not reproduced here). The linear race-of-victim effect estimated, after adjustment for 230-plus background variables, dropped from 6 to 4 ($p = .05$) percentage points among all cases, and from 10 to 6 points ($p = .07$) in cases that were death-eligible under the contemporaneous-felony (B2) and wanton-and-vile (B7) aggravating circumstances. *See supra*, chap. 7, note 83 and accompanying text, for a discussion of the impact of appellate review in the Procedural Reform Study.

52. *See* DB 102 (not reproduced here).

53. *See* DB 103 (not reproduced here). The race-of-victim effects over time, after adjustment for 230-plus background factors, were 13 points, $p = .0001$ (1974–75); 3 points, $p = .23$ (1976–77); and 12 points, $p = .0001$ (1978–79).

54. As noted earlier, *supra* chap. 6, note 47 and accompanying text, we were concerned with the possibility that the race-of-victim disparities estimated in the CSS were simply the result of a disproportionate concentration of white-victim cases (especially those involving black defendants) in judicial circuits with high death-sentencing rates. After testing for this possibility, we discounted it as a threat to the validity of race-of-victim findings. *See infra* app. A, note 21 and accompanying text. This is not to suggest, however, that the racial disparities in the CSS are uniform throughout the state. As note table 10 illustrates, the race-of-defendant disparities, to the extent to which they exist, appear concentrated in rural areas. Moreover, the race-of-victim effects appear to be stronger there as well. Note table 11 indicates the extent to which these urban/rural differences exist after adjustment for background factors. Part I shows that the magnitude of the effects is about the same in rural and urban areas, although the disparity is not statistically significant in urban areas. A judicial circuit was coded "urban" in the CSS when more than 50% of the population was classified as urban in the 1970 census. The following circuits were so classified: Atlanta, Augusta, Brunswick, Clayton, Cobb, Dougherty, Eastern, Houston, Macon, Rome, Southern, Stone Mountain, and Western. The urban/rural race-of-victim disparities were more comparable in the PRS, which used a slightly different measure to define urban/rural distinctions. *Cf. supra* chap. 5, note 38 and accompanying text.

Part II of note table 11 estimates race-of-defendant and race-of-victim disparities with a logistic-regression model for urban and rural areas. It shows that the disparities are stronger in the rural areas for both race-of-victim and race-of-defendant effects, with the strongest race-of-defendant effects concentrated in the white-victim cases. Part II of the table embraces a weighted universe of 472 cases; there were only 285 cases

Note Table 10. Unadjusted Urban and Rural Death-Sentencing Rates and Racial Disparities among Defendants Indicted for Murder (DPMURIDT)

I. Death-sentencing rates, controlling for defendant/victim racial combination

	Black Defendant/ White Victim	White Defendant/ White Victim	Black Defendant/ Black Victim	White Defendant/ Black Victim
Urban ($n = 1,233$)	.13 (14/111)	.09 (27/307)	.01 (8/784)	.03 (1/31)
Rural ($n = 1,110$)	.30 (36/120)	.08 (31/403)	.02 (10/563)	.04 (1/24)

II. Race-of-Victim Disparities

	Race of Defendant			
	Urban Circuits		Rural Circuits	
	Black	White	Black	White
White victim	.13 (14/111)	.09 (27/307)	.30 (36/120)	.08 (31/403)
Black victim	.01 (8/784)	.03 (1/31)	.02 (10/563)	.04 (1/24)
a. Difference	12 pts.	6 pts.	28 pts.	4 pts.
b. Ratio	13:1	3:1	15:1	2:1
c. Overall measure[1]	.10 (.0004)		.25 (.0001)	

III. Race-of-Defendant Disparities

	Race of Victim			
	Urban Circuits		Rural Circuits	
	Black	White	Black	White
Black defendant	.01 (8/784)	.13 (14/111)	.02 (10/563)	.30 (36/120)
White defendant	.03 (1/31)	.09 (27/307)	.04 (1/24)	.08 (31/403)
a. Difference	−2 pts.	4 pts.	−2 pts.	22 pts.
b. Ratio	.33:1	1.4:1	.50:1	3.8:1
c. Overall measure[1]	.02 (.43)		.18 (.0001)	

1. The overall measures are the regression coefficients for the racial variable estimate, with no background controls for nonracial factors.

in the sample, which explains in part the low level of statistical significance of the estimated race effects. The urban/rural disparities in the PRS, by contrast, were estimated with a sample of 606 cases.

55. *See infra* app. A, note 36, and app. B, note 36 and accompanying text.

56. *See infra* app. B, note 41 and accompanying text.

57. *See infra* app. B, note 23 and accompanying text.

58. Judge Forrester's critique of these issues is presented *infra* note 73 and accompanying text.

59. 42 U.S.C. §§2000(e)–2000(e)(17).

60. Village of Arlington Heights v. Metropolitan Hous. Dev. Corp., 429 U.S. 252, 266–68 (1977) (denial of a rezoning request to construct racially integrated housing),

Note Table 11. Urban and Rural Racial Disparities in Death-Sentencing Rates, Controlling for 230 + Nonracial Background Variables in Multiple-Regression Analyses (CSS)

	Urban			Rural		
	Race-of-Victim Coefficient	Race-of-Defendant Coefficient		Race-of-Victim Coefficient	Race-of-Defendant Coefficient	
		All Cases	White-Victim Cases Only		All Cases	White-Victim Cases Only
I. Racial disparities after controlling simultaneously for 230 + nonracial background variables	.07 (.13)	.03 (.56)		.08 (.05)	.07 (.08)	
II. Racial disparity among the 472 cases with the highest predicted risk of receiving a death sentence, after controlling for 15 legitimate and statistically significant variables screened from 230 + nonracial background variables						
A. Arithmetic difference in average death-sentencing rates (in points)[1]	.07	.01	.04	.11	.07	.17
B. Death-odds multiplier	1.84	.76	1.17	2.7	2.48	5.36
C. Level of statistical significance of the disparities	.75	.86	.69	.11	.07	.01

1. As measured by the equivalent of a w.l.s. partial-regression coefficient for the race variables involved.

provides the best general guidelines for proving an equal-protection violation, while Mt. Healthy City Bd. of Educ. v. Doyle, 429 U.S. 274 (1977) (teacher fired in retaliation for protected speech), provides an overview of the elements required for a comparable First Amendment claim. Examples of the role of comparative evidence in constitutional cases are Lieberman v. Gant, 474 F. Supp. 848, 873 (D. Conn. 1979), aff'd, 630 F. 2d 60 (2d Cir. 1980) (denial of tenure challenged under both the First Amendment and Title VII, with similar methodology applied to each claim); Pinkington v. Bevilacqua, 439 F. Supp. 465, 471–72 (D. R.I. 1977), aff'd, 580 F. 2d 386 (1st Cir. 1979) (doctor claimed he was dismissed for criticizing public employer); Cherry v. Burnett, 444 F. Supp. 324, 330–31 (D. Md. 1977) (teacher allegedly fired for criticizing president of a public college).

61. Furnco Construction Corp. v. Waters, 438 U.S. 567, 577 (1978).

62. D. Baldus & J. Cole, STATISTICAL PROOF OF DISCRIMINATION, 18–22 (Cumulative Supplement 1987).

63. Normally, the development of comparative evidence first requires an identification of all employees who are comparable to the plaintiff in all relevant legitimate respects. The court then compares the treatment received by the plaintiff and that received by the nonprotected (i.e., men or nonminorities) employees within this category of comparable employees. For example, in the case of a female unskilled laborer claiming wage discrimination, the court might begin by examining the wages paid all unskilled laborers and then scrutinize the differences between the wages received by male laborers and the plaintiff. Of obvious relevance is evidence that employees in the nonprotected category who are no more qualified than the plaintiff receive more favorable treatment than the plaintiff. Such evidence obviously creates a strong presumption of purposeful discrimination and suggests that the reasons given by the employer were, in fact, pretextual.

64. The police-victim data were admitted in DB 116.

65. These data were admitted as exhibit DB 109. The index underlying table 53 was used to identify the initial group of high-risk cases in table 59. See supra note 36.

66. The more aggravated category included fourteen cases in which one or more of the following factors were present:

- torture, torment, or unnecessary pain to the victim
- murder for hire
- rape
- multiple victims
- helpless victim.

In the less aggravated category (C), there were ten cases in which none of the foregoing factors was present and one or more of the following mitigating factors were present:

- an established relationship between the defendant and the victim
- the defendant was not the triggerman
- the killing was accidental.

The remaining eight cases, which included none of these aggravating or mitigating factors, were deemed typical cases in the intermediate category (B), in which Warren McCleskey's case fell.

67. Admitted as exhibit DB 112.

68. The facts of the two Fulton County black-victim cases that did result in death sentences also support this proposition.

Case 1. The defendant, a twenty-three-year-old male with no prior convictions, was attending a church service. During the service, the defendant asked a woman near him about the location of the female victim's husband. She pointed him out, and the defendant began firing two .32-caliber handguns. He shot the seventy-year-old female victim, a nationally prominent civil rights figure, once in the chest and once in the head, killing her, and struck a sixty-six-year-old male victim in the chest, wounding him. The shots also wounded another female in the neck. Earlier that day, the defendant had been driven to the church twice, and he had asked at least one of the cab drivers whether the female victim would be at the service with her husband. (980)

Case 2. The defendant was a twenty-two-year-old male who had two prior convictions for felonies other than armed robbery or burglary. Victim's wife hired him to kill her husband for $1,500. He went to the youth detention center where the victim worked as a security guard, but he became reluctant to follow through with the act and left. After reconsidering, he returned to the guard station, forced the victim to lie on the floor, and shot him three times in the head. (898)

Both of these cases appear to be more aggravated than McCleskey's. In addition to involving an elderly, female, and politically prominent victim, the first was clearly premeditated and involved great risk to and the actual injury of other people. The second case, also clearly premeditated, involved an execution-style murder for hire. It can be argued, however, that the status of McCleskey's victim as a police officer and the terror of the customers and employees held on the floor under threat of death makes the cases comparable in overall aggravation level. The two summaries in the text were not offered in evidence in the *McCleskey* case.

69. Admitted as exhibit DB 106.

70. Admitted as exhibit DB 107.

71. Admitted as exhibit DB 114.

72. McCleskey v. Zant, 580 F. Supp. 338 (N.D. Ga. 1984).

73. *Id.* at 360.

74. *Id.* at 356.

75. *Id.* at 356, 361.

76. *Id.* at 356–57.

77. *Id.* at 358, 359–60.

78. *Id.* at 357.

79. *Id.* at 357–58.

80. *Id.* at 372.

81. *Id.* at 370–71 (emphasis in original).

82. *Id.* at 376 (emphasis in original).

83. *Id.* at 372.

84. Specifically, he found the multiple-regression analyses flawed by the presence of multicollinearity, which means that there is a statistical association between the race variable and other independent variables included in the multiple-regression analyses. *"The presence of multi-colinearity [sic] substantially diminishes the weight to be accorded to the circumstantial statistical evidence of racial disparity."* *Id.* at 364. (Emphasis in original.) He also found that because of their low R^2, "none of the models [used by petitioner's expert] . . . are sufficiently predictive to support an inference of discrimination." *Id.* at 361. Judge Forrester considered plausible the opinion of the State's expert that the race-of-victim effect estimated in the regression analyses "would become statistically insignificant with a model with a higher r^2 which better

accounted for all of the non-racial variables including interaction variables and composite variables which could be utilized." *Id.* at 362.

Judge Forrester also held that McCleskey's evidence was seriously undercut by the State's evidence that the white-victim cases were generally more aggravated than the black-victim cases. In this respect, the State's experts presented no results from multivariate analyses, either regression or cross-tabulation, that diminished the race-of-victim effects estimated in our analyses. The court was nevertheless persuaded that, because among cases with the same number of statutory aggravating circumstances white-victim cases tend to be more aggravated than black-victim cases with respect to the variables that are accounted for in the study,

> [I]n the white-victim cases there are unaccounted-for systematic aggravating features, and in the black-victim cases there are unaccounted-for systematic mitigating features. . . . Therefore, at least to the extent that there are unaccounted-for aggravating or mitigating circumstances, white-victim cases become a proxy for aggravated cases, and black-victim cases become a proxy, or composite variable, for mitigating factors.

Id. at 364.

Judge Forrester found two other technical flaws in the analysis—(a) the linear regressions inappropriately employed dichotomous (or dummy) independent variables, and (b) because frequently occurring factors that have no influence in the system may spuriously enter the equations, "the regression coefficients for the racial variables could have been artificially produced because of the high incidence of cases in which the victim was white." *Id.* at 370.

85. *Id.* at 372–73.

86. *Id.* at 380–84. Giglio v. United States, 405 U.S. 150 (1972), requires the disclosure to the jury of promises of leniency made to witnesses for the State who have been convicted of, charged with, or suspected of criminal activity. Particularly damaging evidence in McCleskey's guilt trial was the testimony of Offie Evans, an inmate of the Fulton County jail who occupied the cell next to McCleskey's. He testified that McCleskey had admitted to him that he was the triggerman. In McCleskey's trial, the State disclosed that at the time of Evans's testimony he had been charged with escaping from a federal halfway house, but it failed to disclose that the detectives investigating McCleskey's case had promised to "speak to federal authorities" on Evans's behalf. It was further revealed in McCleskey's habeas corpus proceedings that the federal charges against Evans were dropped after McCleskey's trial. Judge Forrester held that the failure to disclose the detectives' promise to Evans constituted a *Giglio* violation and that disclosure to the jury of this fact "would have affected the judgment of the jury" on the issue of whether McCleskey was the triggerman. *Id.* at 383.

87. McCleskey v. Kemp, No. C87-1517A (N.D. Ga. December 23, 1987). Judge Forrester's order left standing McCleskey's life sentences imposed for his participation in the armed robbery, which he admitted. The only issue in his murder case had been whether he was the triggerman, and Offie Evans's testimony on this issue was particularly damaging. The use of an informer in the manner found by Judge Forrester violates the rule of Massiah v. United States, 377 U.S. 201 (1964). Even in 1987, Judge Forrester's hostility toward the studies we presented on McCleskey's behalf persisted. In the opinion vacating McCleskey's murder conviction, he gratuitously remarked that the racial disparities we had estimated were the product of "arbitrarily structured little rinky-dink regressions that accounted for only a few variables. . . . They proved nothing other than the truth of the adage that anything may be proved by statistics." No. C87-1517A at 12.

88. McCleskey v. Kemp, 753 F. 2d, 877, 886 (11th Cir. 1985), *cert. granted in part*, 478 U.S. 1019 (1986).

89. *Id.* at 894–95.

90. *Id.* at 898.

91. *Id.* at 896.

92. *Id.* at 899.

93. *Id.* at 896.

94. *Id.* at 897.

95. *Id.* (citations omitted). The Gross and Mauro study is reported in S. Gross & R. Mauro, DEATH & DISCRIMINATION: RACIAL DISPARITIES IN CAPITAL SENTENCING (1989).

96. McKleskey v. Kemp, 753 F. 2d, at 898.

97. *Id.* at 898.

98. *Id.* at 891.

99. McCleskey v. Kemp, 107 S. Ct. 1756 (1987).

100. *Id.* at 1764.

101. *Id.* at 1764–65 & n.6. The first paragraph of the footnote listed three reasons why the trial court "noted that in many respects the data were incomplete" and had "concluded that McCleskey had failed to establish by a preponderance of the evidence that the data was trustworthy":

> In its view, the questionnaires used to obtain the data failed to capture the full degree of the aggravating or mitigating circumstances. *Id.*, at 356.
> The Court criticized the researcher's [*sic*] decisions regarding unknown variables. *Id.*, at 357–358.
> The researchers could not discover whether penalty trials were held in many of the cases, thus undercutting the value of the study's statistics as to prosecutorial decisions. *Id.*, at 359. In certain cases, the study lacked information on the race of the victim in cases involving multiple victims, on whether or not the prosecutor offered a plea bargain, and on credibility problems with witnesses. *Id.*, at 360.

The Supreme Court's footnote went on to list four "other problems with Baldus' methodology" that had been noted by the trial court:

> First, the researchers assumed that all of the information available from the questionnaires was available to the juries and prosecutors when the case was tried. The court found this assumption "questionable." *Id.*, at 361.
> Second, the court noted the instability of the various models. Even with the 230-variable model, consideration of 20 further variables caused a significant drop in the statistical significance of race. In the court's view, this undermined the persuasiveness of the model that showed the greatest racial disparity, the 39-variable model. *Id.*, at 362.
> Third, the court found that the high correlation between race and many of the nonracial variables diminished the weight to which the study was entitled. *Id.*, at 363–364.
> Finally, the District Court noted the inability of any of the models to predict the outcome of actual cases. As the court explained, statisticians use a measure called an "r^2" to measure what portion of the variance in the dependent variable (death sentencing rate, in this case) is accounted for by the independent variables of the model. A perfectly predictive model would have an r^2 value of 1.0. A model with no predictive power would have an r^2 of 0. The r^2 value of Baldus' most complex model, the 230-variable model, was between .46 and .48. Thus, as the court explained, "the 230-variable model does not predict the outcome in half of the cases." *Id.*, at 361.

The only other discussion in the Supreme Court majority's opinion of the methodology of our studies arose in connection with an examination of the relevance of the data from Fulton County:

Moreover, the statistics in Fulton County alone represent the disposition of far fewer cases than the state-wide statistics. Even assuming the statistical validity of the Baldus study as a whole, the weight to be given the results gleaned from this small sample is limited.

Id. at 1768 n.15.

102. *Id.* at 1767–69. Justice Powell's statement that in "rare cases" a "statistical pattern of discriminatory impact" was enough to establish an equal-protection violation may indicate that relief would be forthcoming in the death-penalty case if the racial disparities were dramatic enough, as, for example, they were in Yick Wo v. Hopkins, 118 U.S. 356 (1886). McCleskey v. Kemp, 107 S. Ct. at 1716n.12. Moreover, his comment that "absent a stronger proof, it is unnecessary to seek" a rebuttal from the prosecutor in McCleskey's case can also be construed to imply that extremely strong statistical proof may be enough to establish an equal-protection claim. *Id.* at 1769. However, we believe that Justice Powell's arguments based on the "nature of the capital sentencing system," which we describe below, and the subject matter of the two rare cases referred to (neither involved a death sentence) support the view that statistical evidence in death cases is irrelevant regardless of the strength of the inference it supports that a systemwide pattern of purposeful discrimination exists. Finally, even if statistics are still relevant, the level of proof implicitly required by the opinion is far beyond what we are likely to see in any United States death-sentencing jurisdiction.

103. *Id.* at 1767–68 (citations omitted).

104. *Id.* at 1768n.14 (citations omitted).

105. *Id.* at 1768n.15.

106. *Id.* at 1768 (citations omitted). Finally, on the matter of prosecutorial discretion, he distinguished a recent case that required a prosecutor to explain racial disparities in the exercise of peremptory voir dire challenges: "Requiring a prosecutor to rebut a study that analyzes the past conduct of scores of prosecutors is quite different from requiring a prosecutor to rebut a contemporaneous challenge to his own acts." *Id.* at n.17.

107. *Id.* at 1769.

108. *Id.* at 1774.

109. *Id.* (emphasis by the Court).

110. *Id.* at 1775n.28. The reason given was that the "outcome of a trial and a defendant's ultimate sentence" is influenced by many factors, such as the strength of the evidence in the case, the capability of the law-enforcement officers involved, and the wide variations in judgments of the various sentencing authorities. *Id.*

111. *Id.* at 1766n.7, 1775.

112. *Id.* at 1778. Another methodological basis for Justice Powell's Eighth Amendment ruling was his argument that, contrary to the suggestions of Justices Stevens and Blackmun, it would not be possible to limit death sentencing to the most aggravated cases as determined by the frequency with which prosecutors seek and juries impose death sentences. *Id.* at 1780n.45.

113. *Id.* at 1779–80.

114. *Id.* at 1781 (citations omitted).

115. *Id.* at 1786.

116. *Id.* at 1805.

117. *Id.* at 1806.

CHAPTER ELEVEN

McCleskey v. Kemp on Appeal:
A Methodological Critique

This chapter presents a critique of four methodological issues raised by the opinions of the Court of Appeals and the Supreme Court in *McCleskey v. Kemp*.[1] We first address the Supreme Court's rationale for holding that statistically based claims of classwide, purposeful racial discrimination are not cognizable under the equal-protection clause in death-sentencing proceedings. Second, we analyze the Court's further ruling that our statistics did not demonstrate the constitutionally requisite degree of "risk" of invidious discrimination that is necessary to establish an Eighth Amendment violation. Third, we address certain issues concerning the Supreme Court's and the Court of Appeals' interpretation of McCleskey's evidence of race-of-victim discrimination. Fourth, we consider the Supreme Court's judgment that a limitation of death sentencing to the worst cases—that routinely result in death sentences—is unworkable. We consider as well Justice Powell's fear that an Eighth Amendment ruling in favor of McCleskey would have resulted in a disruptive invasion of the criminal justice system by social scientists and statisticians.[2]

THE *MCCLESKEY* RATIONALE FOR PRECLUDING THE USE OF STATISTICAL EVIDENCE OF PURPOSEFUL DISCRIMINATION IN DEATH-SENTENCING CASES UNDER THE EQUAL-PROTECTION CLAUSE

Justice Powell held that McCleskey's equal-protection claim failed because he did not prove "that the decisionmakers in his case acted with discriminatory purpose." The failure of proof, he said, stemmed from the absence of "evidence specific to his own case that would support an inference that racial considerations played a part in his sentence."[3] Justice Powell implied that classwide statistical evidence alone was not relevant to the issue of discrimination in an individual defendant's case regardless of what it suggested about the policies of the state's prosecutors and jurors in general.[4] By so limiting capital punishment equal-protection claims, the Court in *McCleskey* created a nearly insuperable barrier to proof. In order to secure relief, it now appears that capital defendants must demonstrate the existence of purposeful discrimination based upon admissions by biased prosecutors or jurors or by circumstantial evidence of discriminatory intent affecting their individual cases, without reference to evidence of classwide discrimination against their racial group.

Justice Powell's opinion recognized that the Supreme Court has previously held that statistical evidence is relevant as proof of intent to discriminate—both in jury cases brought under the Fourteenth Amendment and in classwide purposeful discrimination cases brought under Title VII of the 1964 Civil Rights Act, which prohibits intentional employment discrimination.[5] He held, however, that to accept such a showing in capital cases "without regard to the facts of a particular case would extend [relief] to all capital cases in Georgia, at least where the victim was white and the defendant is black."[6] This alternative appeared particularly objectionable since the statistical evidence presented in McCleskey's case indicated that, in many highly aggravated black-defendant/white-victim cases, the race of the defendant and victim played no role at all.

Justice Powell's analysis of the probative value of statistical proof suggested, in short, that the Court confronted an "all or nothing" choice. Either it could accept statistical evidence as proof of an equal-protection violation "without regard to the facts of a particular case," or it could deny completely the relevance of statistical evidence of classwide discrimination and insist that McCleskey demonstrate strictly on the basis of case-specific evidence that his prosecutor or jury acted with a racial animus.[7]

In fact, however, the Court's choice of methods of proof was not as limited as Justice Powell suggested. The Court had itself developed a modified approach, which combined elements of both the statistical and the case-specific models in *International Brotherhood of Teamsters v. United States*, a Title VII classwide purposeful discrimination case.[8] This hybrid model relies initially on statistical proof to establish the existence of classwide, intentional discrimination but employs case-specific evidence of purposeful discrimination to fashion relief, thus retaining the advantages that statistical evidence can provide in discrimination cases.[9] At the same time, however, by conditioning relief on some further, case-specific showing of purposeful discrimination, it avoids the injustice that might result from uniformly granting relief to all affected parties without regard to their particular situation.

Justice Powell employs three arguments to justify his explicit rejection of the purely statistical model of proof and his implicit rejection of the hybrid model. First, he suggests that the imposition of an essentially unattainable burden of proof is necessary to maintain the legitimate discretion of prosecutors and jurors in the death-sentencing context. Indeed, his opinion even asserts that permitting the type of statistical proof of systemwide racial disparities in death sentencing that McCleskey offered would jeopardize the very heart of the state's criminal justice system. But he does not really develop the argument.[10]

Second, he rejects the strictly statistical model of proof on the ground that it would invalidate a significant number of death sentences without regard to whether they were a product of purposeful discrimination.[11] This is a reasonable basis for rejecting the exclusively statistical model, since, as noted earlier, it is plain that many death sentences are imposed in highly aggravated cases in which the race of victim or defendant clearly has no effect on the outcome.[12] This rationale does not, however, justify a rejection of the hybrid model, which contemplates a case-by-case inquiry into the specifics of each case as a basis for awarding relief.

Justice Powell's third and principal argument was based on methodological grounds that apply to both the purely statistical and hybrid models of proof. In essence, he held that the strength of the inference that could be drawn from evidence of classwide, purposeful discrimination was different in the death-sentencing context than it was in jury and employment cases: "[T]he nature of the capital sentencing decision, and the relationship of the statistics to that decision, are fundamentally different from the corresponding elements in the [jury] venire-selection or Title VII cases."[13]

Justice Powell offered three reasons for this judgment. First, there are more distinct and autonomous decision-making entities involved in a death-sentencing system, and they operate without any "coordination." Second, many more characteristics of each case may influence death-sentencing decisions. Third, there is "no common standard" by which a court can "evaluate all defendants who have or have not received the death penalty."[14] For these reasons, Justice Powell concluded that "the application of an inference drawn from the general statistics to a specific decision in a trial and sentencing simply is not comparable to the application of an inference drawn from general statistics to a specific venire-selection or Title VII case."[15]

To the extent that Justice Powell's conclusion rests upon his presumptions about the capacity of statistical methodology in the death-sentencing context, it is quite unpersuasive. First, the capacity of a multivariate statistical analysis to identify the factors that are influencing a discretionary decision-making system is not a function of the number of decision makers in the system. If decision makers apply similar selection criteria, a regression analysis will identify those criteria no matter how many people participate in the processing of each case and no matter how many different cases each participant handles. A multiple-regression analysis has the same power to identify commonly applied selection criteria in a system that requires a series of people to process each case and that limits each person's participation to only a single case as it has in a system that requires the same person to process each case in a single decision.

It is, of course, true that the probability of identifying the selection criteria being applied is reduced as the number of autonomous participants in a process increases, since the more autonomous actors there are in a system, the less likely it is that they will apply common selection criteria. Indeed, a characteristic that constitutes an aggravating factor in a case for some prosecutors and juries may mitigate it for others; the inconsistent statistical effects thereby produced within each subset of cases will be muffled and obscured in an analysis including all of the cases. For example, our Georgia data show that black offenders are treated more leniently than white offenders in urban districts, but more punitively in rural areas. However, when we analyze the data statewide those independent effects cancel each other out and the statistics show no statewide race-of-defendant effect. Similarly, within a single jurisdiction we have seen the effects of more favorable treatment of white defendants at early stages in the process offset by more favorable treatment for black defendants in the penalty-trial stage. The result is that an analysis of the combined effects of all of the stages in the system shows no race-of-defendant effect at all.

Within a system as large and decentralized as the Georgia capital-sentencing system, therefore, it is not surprising that relatively few factors emerge as statistically important. Moreover, because of the substantial risk that the effects of many factors will be potentially or wholly obscured in a statistical analysis, we can be confident that those that do emerge as important have a strong and consistent influence in the system. In fact, the factors that do emerge as important tend to be those that we would reasonably expect all participants in the system to recognize as significant—for example, the defendant's role in the homicide and the number of victims in the case.

Moreover, the presence or absence of "coordination" between decision makers in the system has nothing whatever to do with the capacity of a statistical analysis to identify the policies revealed by their decisions. Heretofore, the policy that decision makers believed they were applying has not been determinative or even particularly important. The ultimate concern was with the policy that in fact was applied, and that policy is precisely what a properly designed multivariate statistical analysis can reveal.[16]

We also found unpersuasive Justice Powell's argument about the number of variables that are relevant in the death-sentencing context and his concern about the absence of a "common standard" on which a court can determine whether the cases of two or more death-eligible defendants have similar levels of aggravation or blameworthiness. Justice Powell is correct in stating that there are common standards applied in employment cases. Examples would include economic worth, productivity, competence, and efficiency. Since these properties cannot be directly measured, proxies for them, which can be measured, are used to identify groups of cases that are similar and should be treated alike. Frequently used proxies in employment cases include such characteristics as years of prior experience, seniority, education, output, and supervisor evaluations. Variables for such case characteristics are then analyzed with cross-tabular and multiple-regression procedures to estimate sex and race disparities in treatment.

However, Justice Powell is unconvincing when he suggests that there exists "no common standard by which to evaluate" the treatment of death-eligible defendants. Indeed, his own characterization of the Georgia death-sentencing system belies his claim.

> The Baldus study in fact confirms that the Georgia system results in a reasonable level of proportionality among the class of murderers eligible for the death penalty. As Professor Baldus confirmed, the system sorts out cases where the sentence of death is highly likely and highly unlikely, leaving a mid-range of cases where the imposition of the death penalty in any particular case is less predictable.[17]

Implicit in this statement is the proposition that considerations of blameworthiness and overall moral culpability do explain the distribution of death sentences in the Georgia system. Those defendants who are most morally culpable and blameworthy are the most likely to receive a death sentence. More to the point, if, in fact, no common standard could be discerned in the operation of Georgia's capital-sentencing system, then that system would still offend the Supreme Court's ruling in *Furman*, which condemned death sentences imposed by Georgia because they "could not be meaningfully distinguished" from the many cases that resulted in lesser punishments.[18]

Justice Powell's third reason for imposing more exacting standards of proof in death-sentencing cases concerned the State's ability to respond to the claimant's statistical proof. In the death-sentencing context, stated Justice Powell, "the State has no practical opportunity to rebut" the evidence of classwide discrimination; this lack of opportunity stems both from " 'controlling considerations of . . . public policy,' " that prevent the testimony of jurors as witnesses, and from the impossibility of requiring prosecutors to defend decisions made years earlier.[19]

This reasoning lacks force for several reasons. First, as Justice Blackmun's dissent correctly points out, prosecutors are not barred from giving testimony in the same way as jurors are. Indeed, such testimony by prosecutors is particularly apt in cases involving claims of racial discrimination. Nor is the reliability of such testimony any more suspect than is the testimony of employers in Title VII cases, who routinely testify about decisions made years earlier.

Second, Justice Powell fundamentally misperceives the importance of verbal testimony in rebutting statistical evidence of classwide discrimination in jury-selection and Title VII cases. Although he suggests that such evidence is key, in fact it plays only a minor role. In jury cases, the self-serving testimony of jury commissioners that racial factors played no role in their decisions carries little weight. The persuasive rebuttal evidence in such cases is objective data, the adjustment for which eliminates the racial disparities.[20] Similarly, in employment cases alleging classwide intentional discrimination, defendants can rebut the plaintiff's case far more effectively by attacking the validity of the plaintiff's statistics or by introducing objective statistical evidence that explains away the disparities underlying the plaintiff's prima facie case than by offering the employer's self-serving denials of racial animus.[21]

Similarly, in the death-sentencing context, we would expect the testimony of prosecutors to be of minor importance in rebutting statistical evidence of excessiveness or discrimination. Far more effective would be the rebuttal evidence of the general type the State presented in *McCleskey*—attacks on the validity of the petitioner's statistics and quantitative efforts to explain away the observed racial disparities. Indeed, in *McCleskey* the State made no effort even to call as a witness the assistant district attorney who prosecuted the case.[22]

Similar considerations apply to the evidentiary disqualification of juror testimony. The state's inability to present such testimony would appear to be of little consequence, since, even if allowed, it would do little more in the great majority of cases than confirm which facts in the record were determinative for the jury. Furthermore, in most situations the party whom the juror-disqualification rule disadvantages is a prisoner seeking to establish juror misconduct or bias through juror testimony. Many prisoners are denied a decision on the merits of their claims for this reason. Thus, to deny prisoners the opportunity to assert statistically grounded claims of classwide discrimination in the capital-sentencing context because the juror-disqualification rule would disadvantage the State hardly seems to comport with parity of treatment.

THE *MCCLESKEY* RATIONALE FOR DISCOUNTING
STATISTICAL EVIDENCE OF DISCRIMINATION
AS SUPPORT FOR CLAIMS OF ARBITRARY
AND CAPRICIOUS SENTENCING UNDER
THE EIGHTH AMENDMENT

Justice Powell's holding in *McCleskey* rejecting evidence of classwide purposeful discrimination in death-sentencing cases as irrelevant to claims brought under the equal-protection clause of the Fourteenth Amendment did not dispose of McCleskey's Eighth Amendment arbitrariness claim. Indeed, the Court's prior decisions suggested that proof of a "significant risk" that a given death sentence was arbitrarily and capriciously imposed would be sufficient to establish an Eighth Amendment violation.[23] Thus, proof of a pattern and practice of purposeful racial discrimination in a death-sentencing system would appear to be extremely relevant under the Eighth Amendment. Indeed, it would appear to compel the reversal of any death sentences imposed by such a system. Nevertheless, Justice Powell rejected McCleskey's Eighth Amendment claim because he concluded that the statistical evidence that McCleskey offered, although relevant, failed to establish a "constitutionally significant risk" that racial bias affected Georgia's death-sentencing process.[24]

In reaching this conclusion, Justice Powell adopted a questionable distinction between evidence that was sufficient to "prove" the fact of racially discriminatory sentencing decisions and the type of statistical evidence presented in *McCleskey*. This latter sort of statistical evidence, suggested Justice Powell, could at best only establish a risk that such discrimination had occurred. Moreover, the risk of discrimination suggested by McCleskey's evidence was insufficient to establish a constitutional violation.

Justice Powell laid the groundwork for this analysis as follows:

> Even a sophisticated multiple regression analysis such as the Baldus study can only demonstrate a *risk* that the factor of race entered into some capital sentencing decisions and a necessarily lesser risk that race entered into any particular sentencing decision.[25]

Justice Powell's conclusion, that a multiple-regression analysis can only "demonstrate a *risk* that the factor of race entered into some capital sentencing decisions and a necessarily lesser risk that race entered into any particular sentencing decision," is unpersuasive on two levels. First, to the extent a regression analysis establishes "a risk" with respect to "some capital sentencing decisions," it will show exactly the same (not a lesser) risk with respect to "any particular sentencing decision." The Court's statement concerning a "necessarily lesser risk" is only correct if the factual proposition to be established is the existence of actual discrimination—not just the presence of a risk of discrimination—in a particular case. The reason is that a regression analysis can provide a firmer basis for concluding that racial factors determined the outcomes of "some" unspecified decisions than for concluding that discrimination occurred in a particular individual case.

The more basic issue raised by the foregoing quotation from Justice Powell's opinion, however, is whether statistics can ever "prove" the fact of purposeful discrimination in a legal sense or only the risk of its occurrence. In the context of a classwide claim of discrimination, therefore, the issue is whether statistical evidence can, in fact, prove that purposeful discrimination was the defendant's "standard operating procedure—the regular rather than the unusual practice."[26] In the context of an individual claim of discrimination, by contrast, the question is whether statistics can ever demonstrate that, in fact, the decision that adversely affected a specified claimant was based upon race or sex.

If, as we assume, Justice Powell intended to equate the concepts of "risk" and "probability," he may be partially correct, for it is true that the force of any causal inference based upon statistics depends upon an assessment of probabilities. For example, in a race-discrimination case involving wages, the ultimate factual inference of purposeful discrimination depends upon the magnitude of the likelihood that the disparity between the average wages of white and nonwhite employees is the product of some nonracial factor. The ultimate inference that discrimination is the actual cause of such a disparity necessarily rests upon a demonstration that neither chance nor other legitimate explanatory factors could produce the observed degree of disparity.

However, from this perspective, Justice Powell's observations simply underscore the truism that statistics are merely one more species of circumstantial evidence. In this regard, the courts do, indeed, treat statistical evidence in much the same way that they treat fingerprints, ballistic evidence, and similar forms of case-specific circumstantial proof in noncriminal cases. Such evidence is probative because, either standing alone or in combination, it decreases the perceived probability of the defendant's innocence. At some point, the accumulation of circumstantial evidence so reduces the plausibility of the claim that guilt is considered to be proved.

In a race-discrimination case, the probability or risk that a statistical correlation between race and the outcome variable of interest, such as wages paid, is attributable to purposeful discrimination depends upon three principal considerations. Each of these considerations affects in a different way the probability that the observed race disparity is the product of a legitimate noninvidious cause. The first two factors are the magnitude and statistical significance of the race disparity. For example, in Castaneda v. Partida, an equal-protection jury-selection case, the crucial first item of proof was a 40-percentage-point difference between the proportion of minorities in the community eligible for jury service (.79) and the proportion of minorities called for grand jury service (.39).[27] The second principal item of proof in Castaneda was a demonstration that the 40-point race disparity was highly significant statistically. This finding effectively eliminated the hypothesis that the low level of minority representation on grand juries was a coincidence or a product of chance.[28]

In such a case as Castaneda, in which the minority and majority group persons affected by a discretionary selection process are deemed to be equally qualified or their qualifications are considered to be irrelevant, the demonstration of a substantial statistically significant disparity is the only proof required. If, however, the selection process involves more numerous or more subjective criteria, there is a possibility that minority and majority group persons considered by the decision maker were not equally qualified. In such cases, the claimant must demonstrate that the disparity in treatment did not result from such nonracial factors as legitimate differences in qualifications.[29] The probative force of the statistical evidence in such a case depends upon its ability to eliminate alternate explanations besides purposeful discrimination for the observed disparity.

The type of statistical procedure normally employed for this purpose is known as a "multivariate statistical analysis." Its objective is to measure the observed disparity among cases with similar qualification levels. The most popular type of multivariate statistical analysis is multiple-regression analysis, a procedure that controls for the different qualification levels of the individuals involved through a process of algebraic adjustment.[30]

A recent Supreme Court decision involving the use of multiple-regression analysis is Bazemore v. Friday, a wage-discrimination case in which the plaintiff alleged a pattern or practice of discrimination in salaries paid to employees of the North Carolina Agricultural Extension Service.[31] Since the defendant had asserted that salary levels depended upon job performance and experience, the plaintiff adjusted the disparities between average salaries of white and black employees using a multiple-regression analysis that controlled for independent variables for education, job tenure, job title, and job performance. The results of this regression, which was conducted for several different years, showed that, after adjustment was made for the independent variables in the regression analysis, the average black employee earned from $300 to $400 less than the average white employee. These disparities were found to be statistically significant, and the Supreme Court held that the statistical evidence in the case would be sufficient to establish purposeful discrimination under Title VII.[32]

Against this background, Justice Powell's dismissal of McCleskey's statistical evidence as sufficient proof of only a risk of discrimination is disingenuous. As proof of classwide discrimination, the persistence of a statistically significant racial disparity of the magnitude estimated in McCleskey—after adjustment for all plausible background variables that would be expected to be an influence in the system—is commonly accepted as proof that race is an influence in a highly discretionary selection-process system and that race was the decisive factor in some decisions.[33] Moreover, it is possible with the McCleskey data to estimate how many fewer death sentences would have been imposed if all of the white-victim cases had been processed in the same manner as the black-victim cases, or how many more death sentences there would have been if the black-victim cases had been treated like the white-victim cases.[34] The same logic and methodology has been used not only to establish the now generally accepted fact that cigarette smoking causes cancer, but also to quantify the number of lung cancer deaths annually that are the product of cigarette smoking.[35]

One possible interpretation of Justice Powell's remarks is that a multiple-regression analysis can never prove purposeful discrimination, no matter how well it adjusts for relevant background factors or how stark and statistically significant the racial disparities it documents. Such a view seems questionable, however, for several reasons. First, it is contrary to the well-established doctrine that circumstantial evidence—of which multiple-regression analysis is, basically, a sophisticated, quantified variation—can be as probative as direct evidence of a given fact. Second, in its own rough and ready way, the Supreme Court in *Yick Wo v. Hopkins* employed the same analytic approach as does multiple-regression analysis to conclude that unconstitutional racial discrimination existed.[36] Certainly, we find it difficult to believe that Justice Powell would have voted to deny relief in *Yick Wo* in the face of the multiple-regression results that the circumstances of that case would have produced.

To be sure, the nature of the discriminatory action involved in *Yick Wo*—denial of governmental licenses to applicants of one particular ethnic background while granting them to all others—could be statistically documented by reference to fewer variables than those involved in the *McCleskey* case. But a flat, absolute refusal to acknowledge statistical findings in cases involving numerous possible explanatory variables, while accepting such findings (even on an intuitive, nonquantified basis) when such variables are few, cannot be supported either as a matter of statistical theory or as a matter of law. There is no logical or methodological reason why, with sufficient data and proper sample size, a properly constructed regression analysis is incapable of identifying causal connections in studies like those we did in Georgia.

Rather, we believe that the Court's refusal in *McCleskey* to accept the normal rules of statistical inference reflected a very different concern. Justice Powell's opinion strongly intimates that the potentially disruptive effects of a ruling in McCleskey's favor in Georgia and in other death-sentencing states significantly affected the Court's deliberations. We quoted above Justice Powell's concern that the use of statistical proof under the Fourteenth Amendment would threaten "all capital cases in Georgia." In his discussion of McCleskey's Eighth Amendment claim, he expanded on this theme:

> Where the discretion that is fundamental to our criminal process is involved, we decline to assume that what is unexplained is invidious. In light of the safeguards designed to minimize racial bias in the process, the fundamental value of jury trial in our criminal justice system, and the benefits that discretion pro-

vides to criminal defendants, we hold that the Baldus study does not demonstrate a constitutionally significant risk of racial bias affecting the Georgia capital-sentencing process.

Two additional concerns inform our decision in this case. First, McCleskey's claim, taken to its logical conclusion, throws into serious question the principles that underlie our entire criminal justice system. The Eighth Amendment is not limited in application to capital punishment, but applies to all penalties. . . . Thus, if we accepted McCleskey's claim that racial bias has impermissibly tainted the capital sentencing decision, we could soon be faced with similar claims as to other types of penalty. Moreover, the claim that his sentence rests on the irrelevant factor of race easily could be extended to apply to claims based on unexplained discrepancies that correlate to membership in other minority groups, and even gender. Similarly, since McCleskey's claim relates to the race of his victim, other claims could apply with equally logical force to statistical disparities that correlate with the race or sex of other actors in the criminal justice system, such as defense attorneys, or judges. Also, there is no logical reason that such a claim need be limited to racial or sexual bias. If arbitrary and capricious punishment is the touchstone under the Eighth Amendment, such a claim could—at least in theory—be based upon any arbitrary variable, such as the defendant's facial characteristics, or the physical attractiveness of the defendant or the victim, that some statistical study indicates may be influential in jury decisionmaking. As these examples illustrate, there is no limiting principle to the type of challenge brought by McCleskey. . . .

Second, McCleskey's arguments are best presented to the legislative bodies. It is not the responsibility—or indeed even the right—of this Court to determine the appropriate punishment for particular crimes. It is the legislatures, the elected representatives of the people, that are "constituted to respond to the will and consequently the moral values of the people."[37]

The clear implication of these remarks is that, for reasons unrelated to its probative force, the Court is simply unwilling to accept statistical proof of discrimination to support an Eighth Amendment claim in the death-penalty context. As indicated, McCleskey's evidence was strong. We find it to be significant that at no point does Justice Powell's opinion state exactly how or why the evidence failed to demonstrate "a constitutionally significant risk of racial bias."[38] Rather, Justice Powell's rejection of statistical evidence of discrimination in the death-sentencing context bespeaks an unwillingness to destabilize the capital-sentencing process in any fundamental respect, regardless of such evidence.[39]

In making this observation, we do not intend to suggest that the Court cares little about race-of-victim discrimination. Indeed, Justice Powell's opinion in *Booth v. Maryland* (decided two months after *McCleskey*) reflects the Court's continuing concerns.[40] *Booth* held that Maryland's use of detailed Victim Impact Statements (VIS) in penalty trials violated the Eighth Amendment.

The VIS in this case provided the jury with two types of information. First, it described the personal characteristics of the victims and the emotional impact of the crimes on the family. Second, it set forth the family members' opinions and characterizations of the crimes and the defendant. For the reasons stated below, we find that this information is irrelevant to a capital-sentencing decision, and that its admission creates a constitutionally unacceptable risk that the jury may impose the death penalty in an arbitrary and capricious manner.[41]

Moreover, Justice Powell explained his concern about the Victim Impact Statements' description of the personal characteristics of the decedent in the following footnote:

> We are troubled by the implication that defendants whose victims were assets to their community are more deserving of punishment than those whose victims are perceived to be less worthy. Of course, our system of justice does not tolerate such distinctions. Cf. *Furman v. Georgia.*[42]

This language clearly demonstrates a continuing commitment to a principled nondiscriminatory death-sentencing system, especially as it applies to the characteristics of the victim. Certainly, if the Court condemned jury consideration of the victim's character, it clearly would condemn the consideration of the victim's race by either prosecutors or jurors.

Of course, the *Booth* decision does raise an obvious question: How can one reconcile the Court's decision in *Booth*, which, on the basis of a completely undocumented risk, invalidated the use of Victim Impact Statements, with the Court's ruling two months earlier in *McCleskey* that empirical evidence was incapable of proving a "constitutionally significant risk of racial bias"? The likely explanation, we think, is that cases like *Booth*, which vacate death sentences on ad hoc grounds, will, at most, affect only a few defendants and lack any potential for producing a large-scale disruptive effect on state death-sentencing systems generally.

It may also be relevant that, in cases like *Booth*, the Court can comfortably assess the risk of arbitrariness and capriciousness in individual cases based solely on unproven hunches about the effects of certain rules and procedures, without recourse to empirical evidence about those effects. This preference for hunches or intuition may very well reflect an insecurity about the justices' own abilities properly to assess quantitative evidence of the type presented in *McCleskey*. The Court may very well fear that subsequent analyses will demonstrate that it incorrectly interpreted the empirical data on which its findings were based. Furthermore, one can understand why relatively untrained judges, confronted with massive quantities of data and conflicting expert opinions about the validity and probative force of statistically derived inferences, might have greater confidence in intuitively derived conclusions than in the pronouncements of statisticians. If the Court felt more confident about its ability to distinguish good from bad empirical studies, it might be more willing to accept such studies as a basis for its decisions. Certainly, without such confidence, one can understand a reluctance to rely upon an empirical study, no matter how well regarded by the "experts," as the basis for what is likely to be an unpopular and disruptive decision.[43]

Justice Powell's discussion of McCleskey's Eighth Amendment claim also referred to the difficulty of proving purposeful discrimination in an individual case. To be sure, as suggested above, the results of a regression analysis provide a weaker basis for inferring actual discrimination in an individual case than they do for inferring a general policy of purposeful discrimination. For example, the odds multiplier estimated for a variable in a logistic-regression analysis of a death-sentencing system, such as the number of victims, is an estimate of the average impact of the variable across all cases in the study. It does not necessarily represent the extent to which the odds that any given defendant will receive the death penalty are enhanced by the presence of the factor. As a result, the probability that race was a decisive factor in a given case cannot be inferred from the regression coefficient for race. Nevertheless, a close analysis of racial disparities among cases that closely resemble a given defendant's case in terms of the variables in the regression analysis does provide a basis for estimating the probability that race was a determinative factor in his case. For example, assume a court has indentified fifty cases of comparable blameworthiness, half involving black victims and half involving white victims. Assume further that the death-sentencing rate for the white-victim cases is .40 (10/25) and .12 (3/25) for the black-victim cases. If juries had sentenced defendants in the white-victim cases at the base rate of .12 observed for black-victim cases, the twenty-five white-victim cases would, on average, have produced only three death sentences, not ten. This suggests that the additional seven (10 − 3) death sentences in the white-victim cases resulted from racial discrimination. That finding does not, of course, tell which seven of the ten death sentences in the white-victim cases were racially infected. However, if the culpability level of all the death cases was substantially the same, one can conclude that there is a .70 (7/10) probability that the death sentence in any one of the white-victim cases is a product of race-based discrimination. The question then becomes whether this statistically demonstrable degree of risk is constitutionally significant.[44]

THE INTERPRETATION OF THE MAGNITUDE AND SUBSTANTIVE IMPACT OF THE RACE-OF-VICTIM EFFECTS ESTIMATED IN *MCCLESKEY V. KEMP*

Statistical Measures of the Overall Average Race-of-Victim Effect

In its discussion of the magnitude of the average race-of-victim effect in Georgia's capital-sentencing system, the Court of Appeals addressed almost exclusively what it styled a "6%" disparity. It presumably derived this figure from the .06 least-squares regression coefficient estimated for the race-of-victim variable in the 230-plus variable large-scale multiple-regression model in the CSS.[45] The court interpreted this "6%" average disparity to mean that "a white victim crime is 6% more likely to result in the [death] sentence than a comparable black victim crime."[46] This statement implies that the death-sentencing rate in white-victim cases would average 6 percent more than the rate for similar black-victim cases. Thus, for example, if the death-sentencing rate in a given class of black-victim cases were 10 percent, the white-victim rate would be 6 percent more, or 10.6 percent. But this interpretation of the .06 least-squares regression coefficient is incorrect and highly misleading. This race-of-victim regression coefficient indicates that the average death-sentencing rate in the system is 6 "percentage points" higher in white-victim cases than it is in similarly situated cases with black victims. Consequently, if the base rate for a given group of black-victim cases were 10 percent, the comparable rate for the white-victim cases would be 16 percent, a·60 percent increase. However, since the 6-percentage-point disparity is an *average* effect, it is more relevant to compare it to the average .01 death-sentence rate among all black-victim cases, which it exceeds by a factor of 6 (.06/.01), a 500 percent increase over the black victim rate.[47]

The Court of Appeals properly pointed out that the race-of-victim effect is concentrated in the midrange, where it is approximately 20 percentage points.[48] When the 20-point disparity in the midrange of cases is compared with the 14.2 percent average death-sentencing rate for black-victim cases in that range, the race-of-victim disparity exceeds the black-victim rate by a factor of 1.4 (.20/.144).[49] In other words, among this group of cases, the white-victim average death-sentence rate is at least 100 percent higher than the black-victim rate. And when the midrange race-of-victim disparity is compared with the 20 percent average death-sentencing rate among all cases in the midrange, the race-of-victim disparity is as large as the average death-sentence rate.[50] By any standard, these are strong substantive effects.[51]

We believe the logistic-regression coefficient, an alternative statistical measure of overall impact is somewhat less prone to misinterpretation than the least-squares regression coefficient and gives a clearer picture of the average impact of the race of the victim in the system. First, the estimates of impact produced with the logistic-regression coefficient avoid the ambiguous "percent higher" discussion found in the Court of Appeals' opinion. A simple calculation from the logistic-regression coefficient produces an "odds multiplier" that indicates the degree to which the average defendant's odds of receiving a death sentence are enhanced by having a white rather than a black victim after controlling statistically for all of the other independent variables in the analyses.[52] For example, the 4.3 odds multiplier calculated from the logistic-regression coefficient reported for the race-of-victim variable estimated in our core 39-variable model in the Charging and Sentencing Study indicates that the average defendant's odds of receiving a death sentence are enhanced by a factor of 4.3 when the victim is white after controlling for all of the legitimate case characteristics in the model.[53] Thus, if the odds of receiving the death sentence faced by defendants with black victims in a given category of cases are 1:2 (one death sentence in three cases, or a 33 percent probability), then the odds faced by defendants with white victims in this category of cases will be 4.3:2 or 2.15:1 (4.3 death sentences in 6.3 cases, or a 68 percent probability).

In spite of our preference for the use of odds multipliers as a measure of racial effects in a decision-making system, the opinions of the Supreme Court justices in *McCleskey* indicates that this measure is highly prone to another form of misinterpretation. The Supreme Court opinions generally avoid the problems of interpretation referred to in the Eleventh Circuit opinions. However, each justice who referred to the odds multiplier treated it as a multiplier of probabilities rather than odds. The difference between an odds multiplier and a probability multiplier is not trivial. A 4.3 probability multiplier increases a .20 probability to .86 (4.3 × .20). However, a 4.3 multiplier of the 1:4 odds (that are equal to a .20 probability) increases the odds to 4:4 (4 × .25), which is a probability of only .50. Since it appears that lawyers instinctively equate odds and probabilities, we believe it would be preferable to express the multiplier in terms of probabilities rather than odds.

Unfortunately, the logistic-regression procedure does not directly produce an average probability multiplier. However, a relatively straightforward procedure used in epidemiology can produce that measure.[54] Its application to the *McCleskey* case suggests an average race-of-victim probability multiplier of about 2 for the data from both the Procedural Reform Study and the Charging and Sentencing Study.[55]

THE FEASIBILITY OF THE "WORST-CASE-ONLY" SOLUTION AND THE INVASION OF THE SOCIAL SCIENTISTS

Our final thoughts about *McCleskey* concern two observations of Justice Powell, one an aside and the other central to the Court's imposition of an unattainable burden of proof for Eighth Amendment claims asserting racial discrimination.

The first observation concerns the feasibility of the worst-case-only proposal of Justices Stevens and Blackmun, according to which the death penalty would be limited to those categories of cases in which prosecutors consistently seek and juries consistently impose it without regard to the race of the victim or of the defendant.

> This proposed solution is unconvincing. First, "consistently" is a relative term, and narrowing the category of death-eligible defendants would simply shift the borderline between those defendants who received the death penalty and those who did not. A borderline area would continue to exist and vary in its boundaries. Moreover, because the discrepancy between borderline cases would be difficult to explain, the system would likely remain open to challenge on the basis that the lack of explanation rendered the sentencing decisions unconstitutionally arbitrary.
>
> Second, even assuming that a category with theoretically consistent results could be identified, it is difficult to imagine how Justice STEVENS' proposal would or could operate on a case-by-case basis. Whenever a victim is white and the defendant is a member of a different race, what steps would a prosecutor be required to take—in addition to weighing the customary prosecutorial considerations—before concluding in the particular case that he lawfully could prosecute? In the absence of a current, Baldus-type study focused particularly on the community in which the crime was committed, where would he find a standard? Would the prosecutor have to review the prior decisions of community prosecutors and determine the types of cases in which juries in his jurisdiction "consistently" had imposed the death penalty when the victim was white and the defendant was of a different race? And must he rely solely on statistics? Even if such a study were feasible, would it be unlawful for the prosecutor, in making his final decision in a particular case, to consider the evidence of guilt and the presence of aggravating and mitigating factors? However conscientiously a prosecutor might attempt to identify death-eligible defendants under the dissent's suggestion, it would be a wholly speculative task at best, likely to result in less rather than more fairness and consistency in the imposition of the death penalty.[56]

Justice Powell's assertion that no line can be drawn rationally between the worst cases, which routinely result in death sentences, and the remaining population of murder defendants can be viewed as rejecting the whole notion of proportionality review—since drawing that line is precisely what an appellate proportionality review, such as that which the Court approved in *Gregg v. Georgia*, purports to do. Furthermore, the success that some state supreme courts have already displayed in connection with the proportionality-review process, together with our own efforts to systematize techniques of drawing the line that Justice Powell eschews, persuades us that identifying the worst cases, while difficult, is not necessarily impossible. A ruling in *McCleskey* that limited death sentencing to only those cases in which death sentences are routinely sought and imposed would have imported a greater degree of rationality and consistency into state death-sentencing systems than any of the other procedural safeguards that the Supreme Court has heretofore endorsed.

To be sure, there would always be hard cases at the borderline of the worst-case category, but the level of arbitrariness involved in drawing that line would pale when compared to the arbitrariness of the current system.

Nor do the difficulties that Justice Powell feared prosecutors would encounter under a "worst-case-only" policy seem persuasive. He expressed concern that prosecutors would be unlikely to produce consistent results in their efforts to apply such a policy, even if they had good data on the operation of the system in their state. These concerns would be legitimate if the prosecutors were ultimately responsible for administering the system. The teaching of *Gregg*, however, is that the ultimate oversight of the system lies with the state appellate courts. It would be their function and responsibility to apply state-wide standards to identify the worst cases.[57] The prosecutor's responsibility in such a system is to apply his or her own judgment of blameworthiness, informed by the anticipated response of the sentencing juries. These decisions would then produce the universe of cases that the reviewing court would scrutinize in the course of articulating the "worst-case" standard. We cannot help but observe that, by declining to endorse such a system, the Supreme Court majority acted so as to preserve the ability of the state to impose death sentences in cases in which death sentences usually do not occur.

Justice Powell's second observation—which underscored the unsurmountable burden of proof imposed in Eighth Amendment cases involving claims of racial discrimination—was that he feared a ruling for McCleskey under the Eighth Amendment would open the entire criminal justice system to a disruptive invasion of social scientists and statisticians.[58] To be sure, a ruling favorable to McCleskey would have disrupted the death-sentencing systems of some states, at least for the short term; but Justice Powell's apprehension of a parade of social scientists disrupting the courts appears to be greatly exaggerated. In the first place, the only social science research relevant to judicial proceedings would be field research conducted in actual courts. Most of the social science studies cited by Justice Powell were not field studies but experiments that used students as mock jurors. Second, field research of the type Justice Powell fears is expensive, extremely time-consuming, and, because of its applied nature, generally not favored by funding sources. The relatively small amount of judicial field research done to date is suggestive of the few incentives that the system offers to produce it. Third, most of the field research conducted so far tends to undercut the farfetched claims that Justice Powell thinks social scientists would be inclined to support. That research does not suggest that the criminal justice system is systematically biased or invidious, or that it characteristically functions arbitrarily or irrationally. To be sure, there is substantial evidence of sentencing disparities among similarly situated offenders, but most of the available evidence does not suggest that these disparities are correlated with sex, physical appearance, or any of the other factors hypothesized by the Court. In fact, the literature suggests that, with respect to the issue of discrimination, further empirical inquiry may increase public confidence in the basic fairness of the system.

Finally, we find it distressing that a majority of the Supreme Court would choose to reject a claim based upon invidious racial discrimination because of the work load that a ruling in the claimant's favor might entail in later cases. Former Chief Justice Burger frequently urged Congress to conduct a "judicial impact study" before enacting new legislation. Justice Powell's avowed concerns in *McCleskey* have the same flavor but, given the constitutional character of the rights asserted, seem much less appropriate.

NOTES

1. The background record and rulings in the *McCleskey* case are described in detail in chap. 10.

2. We present our methodological critique of the district court's opinion in appendix B.

3. McCleskey v. Kemp, 107 S.Ct. 1756, 1766–67 (1987).

4. The opinion can also be read to grant the relevance of statistical disparities of a magnitude not likely to be seen in this country. *See supra,* chap. 10, note 101 and accompanying text.

5. *See* McCleskey v. Kemp, 107 S.Ct. at 1767. In alluding to Title VII cases, Justice Powell was referring to the use of statistics to prove classwide intentional or purposeful discrimination in what is known as a "disparate treatment case." International Bhd. of Teamsters v. United States, 431 U.S. 324, 336 (1977). His reference to Title VII was not to "disparate impact" cases, in which evidence of disproportionate impact is enough to establish liability and purpose and intent are irrelevant. *See id.* at 335–36n.15.

6. *Id.*

7. *See id.* The Fourteenth Amendment and Title VII cases in which courts rely primarily on case-specific evidence of discrimination normally involve a challenge to a single decision taken in relative isolation. The primary focus in such cases is on admissions, comparisons of the treatment the claimant received compared to the treatment received by a handful of similarly situated members of the nonprotected group, and any procedural irregularities in the decision-making process affecting the claimant and the relative plausibility of the reasons given for the action by the defendant. A good example of this approach, under the Fourteenth Amendment, is Village of Arlington Heights v. Metropolitan Housing Dev. Corp., 429 U.S. 252 (1977). This case involved a claim of purposeful racial discrimination in the village's denial of a request for a zoning change so that low-cost, racially integrated housing could be constructed. The focus of the court was almost exclusively on the plausibility of the explanations offered by the defendant to justify the denial of the rezoning request to exclude low-cost housing. *See also* United States v. City of Parma, Ohio, 494 F. Supp. 1049, 1096 (N.D. Ohio 1980); Resident Advisory Bd. v. Rizzo, 564 F.2d 126, 142 (3d Cir. 1977), *cert. denied,* 435 U.S. 908 (1978).

The approach that the federal courts have taken to evaluate claims of individual disparate treatment under Title VII is analogous to the *Arlington Heights* model, although the plaintiff's burden to establish liability is less onerous and it is substantially more difficult for the defendant employer to avoid a remedy once a degree of purposeful discrimination has been established. *See* Texas Dep't of Community Affairs v. Burdine, 450 U.S. 248, 252–54 (1981).

Arlington Heights also prescribed the proper remedy in such a case if a claimant has been able to establish that the defendant was "motivated in part by a racially discriminatory purpose"; such proof, said the Court, would shift to the defendant "the burden of establishing that the same decision would have resulted even had the impermissible purpose not been considered." Village of Arlington Heights v. Metropolitan Housing Dev. Corp., 429 U.S. at 270–71n.21. Thus, even if proof of a discriminatory motive is established, the issue in the remedial stages of the proceeding is whether it was a but-for cause of the decision at issue.

Courts have relied upon strictly statistical models of proof in cases brought under both the equal-protection clause and Title VII. Jury discrimination cases are the most prominent examples under the equal-protection clause. *See* Castaneda v. Partida, 430 U.S. 482, 493–94 (1977). Such cases first address whether the statistical showing of disparate treatment of the injured class will support a prima facie case of discrimination. If it does, the burden shifts to the defendant to rebut the showing with evidence establishing that the observed statistical disparity is the product of legitimate factors or chance. *Id.* The Court also applied a strictly statistical mode of proof in Yick Wo v. Hopkins, 118 U.S. 356 (1886), an equal-protection case in which local government officials approved all of the "eighty-odd" license applications from white applicants but none of more than 200 applications from Chinese applicants. A remedy followed without any further case-specific inquiry by the court. Courts have employed a similar model in Title VII employment cases when an individual approach is not feasible. *See, e.g.,* Stewart v. General Motors Corp., 542 F.2d 445, 452 (7th Cir. 1976), *cert. denied,* 433 U.S. 919 (1977), which states the following:

> [T]he utilization of an individualized method of calculation is impossible. Because General Motors had no objective standards by which to measure whether a given employee deserved a promotion, deciding in individual cases whether a particular person would have been promoted but for racial discrimination would lead the district court into a "quagmire of hypothetical judgments," . . . in which any supposed accuracy in result would be purely imaginary.

If liability is established in such cases and relief is a practical possibility, all affected class members are entitled to it without any further inquiry into the specifics of the individual cases. The common elements of the equal-protection and Title VII cases that use strictly statistical proof are compelling statistical evidence that purposeful discrimination is a standard operating procedure and the absence of a large number of legitimate criteria that would permit the defendant to distinguish between different individuals after a policy of classwide discrimination has been established.

8. In International Bhd. of Teamsters v. United States, 431 U.S. at 360–62, the Court stated the following:

> At the initial, "liability" stage of a pattern-or-practice suit the Government is not required to offer evidence that each person for whom it will ultimately seek relief was a victim of the employer's discriminatory policy. Its burden is to establish a prima facie case that such a policy existed. . . . If an employer fails to rebut the inference that arises from

the Government's prima facie case, a trial court may then conclude that a violation has occurred and determine the appropriate remedy. . . . When the Government seeks individual relief for the victims of the discriminatory practice, a district court must usually conduct additional proceedings after the liability phase of the trial to determine the scope of individual relief. . . . The Government need only show that an alleged individual discriminatee unsuccessfully applied for a job and therefore was a potential victim of the proved discrimination. . . . [T]he burden then rests on the employer to demonstrate that the individual applicant was denied an employment opportunity for lawful reasons. (Footnotes omitted.)

Under the first stage of the hybrid model, the statistical proof is highly relevant and liability is established primarily on its basis. However, in the remedy stage, the issue for each protected group member is whether her race or sex was a but-for cause of the decision under challenge. Stated differently, would the employer's decision have been any different had the claimant been a male or a majority group member? On this question, the defendant employer carries a heavy burden of demonstrating that the claimant's inadequate qualifications, and not her race or sex, produced the adverse decision.

9. In the employment context, evidence of classwide purposeful discrimination raises a question about the bona fides of each decision adversely affecting a minority person or a female.

10. *See* McCleskey v. Kemp, 107 S.Ct. at 1769.

11. *See id.* at 1767.

12. In Georgia, we estimate that from 30% to 40% of the death sentences fall into this highly aggravated category. *See supra* chap. 6, note 17 and accompanying text and table 32 (PRS); *supra* chap. 10, note 37 and table 53 (CSS).

13. McCleskey v. Kemp, 107 S.Ct. at 1767.

14. *Id.* at 1768n.14.

15. *Id.* at 1767–68. In addition, he stated that these same characteristics of the death-sentencing process impose institutional limits on the defendant's capacity to rebut statistical evidence of discrimination in a death-sentence case that do not exist in an employment- or jury-discrimination case. *See id.*

16. In his treatment of the "coordination" issue, Justice Powell discussed our separate analysis of data from Fulton County, since presumably within a single jurisdiction coordination between prosecutors would not be an issue. He gave these results only "limited" weight, however, because of the small sample involved. *See* 107 S.Ct. at 1768n.15. It is true that because the Fulton County sample included only ten death sentences, we could not conduct a reliable multivariate analysis of disparities in death-sentencing rates. However, the "coordination" issue primarily relates to prosecutorial decision making, and the Fulton County sample numbered 174 cases from a universe of 629 cases. This sample was of sufficient size to analyze several pretrial decisions, all of which showed a consistent pattern of race-of-victim discrimination. *See supra* chap. 10, tables 61, 62, & 63.

17. McCleskey v. Kemp, 107 S.Ct. at 1778n.36.

18. Justice Powell's finding of a "reasonable level of proportionality" in the Georgia death-sentencing system also implicitly recognizes the existence of measurable proxies for blameworthiness and moral culpability—that is, such case characteristics as the cruelty of the murder and the defendant's prior record. It is true that the number of relevant proxies bearing on the blameworthiness of candidates for the death penalty may sometimes be larger than the factors bearing on the productivity or economic

worth of a job candidate, but the number is not infinite, and to the extent they are known the methods of analysis in the two situations are identical.

19. *See* McCleskey v. Kemp, 107 S.Ct at 1768. In this respect Justice Powell's opinion is somewhat disingenuous. As Justice Blackmun points out, Justice Powell misstates the rationale of Imbler v. Pachtman and the extent to which it precludes judicial inquiry into a prosecutor's motivation outside of civil actions for damages. Justice Powell also suggested it is unfair to require a prosecutor to justify his or her decision to seek the death penalty in a particular case in the light of statistical evidence "that analyzes the past conduct of scores of prosecutors." *Id.* at 1768n.17. However, that is exactly what the Court requires employers to do when plaintiffs assert claims of classwide discrimination in Title VII employment cases.

20. We have found no recent Supreme Court case in which the testimony of a jury commissioner, or similar official, was deemed sufficient to rebut classwide racial disparities.

21. Moreover, even for such case characteristics, the objective evidence of the plaintiff's strengths and weaknesses (and how similarly situated employees were treated), rather than the employer's statements, provides the primary basis for the final resolution of whether sex or race determined the outcome. The employer's testimony explaining his or her decisions can be important in a classwide employment case at the remedy stage. In some cases, the employer can demonstrate that a particular member of the adversely affected class of minorities or women deserves no relief by showing that such a class member lacked the qualifications to be selected or promoted regardless of race or sex. However, even in this situation, objective evidence showing that no member of the favored class with equivalent or slightly superior qualifications received better treatment is more persuasive than the employer's own assertions.

22. There is one situation in which the prosecutor's testimony about why he or she chose to seek a death sentence might assume importance: the State might contend that some peculiar circumstance of the case, not included in the statistical analysis, justified a more punitive approach. The prosecutor's testimony concerning the nature of the circumstance and why it assumed importance would be of obvious relevance.

23. Zant v. Stephens, 462 U.S. 862 (1983).

24. *See* McCleskey v. Kemp, 107 S.Ct. at 1778.

25. *Id.* at 1766n.7 (emphasis in original).

26. This is the ultimate finding of fact required in a Title VII classwide, purposeful discrimination case. *See* International Bhd. of Teamsters v. United States, 431 U.S. at 336. A similar inference would be required to establish the fact of classwide purposeful discrimination under the Eighth Amendment.

27. *See* Castaneda v. Partida, 430 U.S. at 486–87.

28. *See id.* at 496–97n.17 (because of the level of statistical significance, "the hypothesis that the jury drawing was random would be suspect to a social scientist").

29. *See* Hazelwood School District v. United States, 433 U.S. 299, 308n.13 (1977) (adjustment for a qualification is required when it is not "one that many persons possess or can fairly readily acquire").

30. *See* Finkelstein, *The Judicial Reception of Multiple Regression Studies in Race and Sex Discrimination Cases*, 80 COLUM. L. REV. 736 (1980) (hereinafter Finkelstein); Fisher, *Multiple Regression in Legal Proceedings*, 80 COLUM. L. REV. 702 (1980).

31. Bazemore v. Friday, 478 U.S. 385, 398 (1986).

32. *Id.* at 401.

33. *See* Fisher, *Multiple Regression in Legal Proceedings*, 80 COLUM. L. REV. 702, 721–25 (1980); Finkelstein *supra* note 30; D. Baldus & J. Cole, STATISTICAL PROOF OF DISCRIMINATION 249–63 (1980).

34. *See supra* chap. 6, note 23 and accompanying text (PRS); *supra* chap. 10, note 34 and accompanying text (CSS).

35. *See* Gross, *Race and Death: The Judicial Evaluation of Evidence of Discrimination in Capital Sentencing*, 18 U.C. DAVIS L. REV. 1275, 1307–11 (1985). To be sure, the judgment about the relationship between cigarette smoking and cancer was based in part upon evidence from studies in which animals were exposed to high levels of cigarette "tar." In the *McCleskey* case, however, the history of racial discrimination in Georgia provides a comparable nonquantitative basis for believing that the race-of-victim effects observed in our study reflected a causal relationship and were not merely a statistical artifact.

36. *See* 118 U.S. 356, 359, 374 (1886) (Supervisors licensed "eighty odd" Caucasian-owned wooden laundries but refused to license over 200 similarly situated laundries owned by Chinese).

37. McCleskey v. Kemp, 107 S.Ct. at 1778–81 (footnotes omitted).

38. *See id.* at 1778.

39. A specification of why the evidence was insufficient would have invited a further attempt in a future case to cure the defects he might have specified in McCleskey's statistical proof.

40. *See* 482 U.S. 496 (1987).

41. *Id.* at 2533.

42. *Id.* at 2534n.8.

43. But why is the Court willing to rely routinely on quantitative evidence of discrimination in other areas of law such as employment, housing, and jury discrimination? Professor Joseph L. Hoffman of Indiana University Law School offers a plausible explanation:

> It seems to me that in some contexts, such as employment and housing, the Court's intuition tells it that discrimination is present and widespread. Moreover, the Court realizes that it would be impossible in many cases to "prove" that which the Court instinctively believes to be true, absent reliance on statistical inferences. The Court therefore adopts a statistics-based approach to establishing discrimination in employment and housing, not because it really "trusts" the approach in general, but because it is the only means available to accomplish an end that the Court sees as necessary and desirable.

Letter from Joseph L. Hoffman to David C. Baldus, September 8, 1987.

44. The validity of such an analysis, however, depends upon one's confidence that the white- and black-victim cases matched were, in fact, comparable in their blameworthiness.

Both Justices Brennan and Blackmun presented a similar type of analysis in their dissenting opinions in *McCleskey*. Justice Brennan wrote:

> The Baldus study indicates that, after taking into account some 230 nonracial factors that might legitimately influence a sentencer, the jury *more likely than not* would have spared McCleskey's life had his victim been black. The study distinguishes between those cases in which (1) the jury exercises virtually no discretion because the strength or weakness of aggravating factors usually suggests that only one outcome is appropriate; and (2) cases reflecting an "intermediate" level of aggravation, in which the jury has considerable

discretion in choosing a sentence. McCleskey's case falls into the intermediate range. In such cases, death is imposed in 34% of white-victim crimes and 14% of black-victim crimes, a difference of 139% in the rate of imposition of the death penalty. Supp. Exh. 54. In other words, just under 59%—almost 6 in 10—defendants comparable to McCleskey would not have received the death penalty if their victims had been black.

107 S.Ct. at 1784 (emphasis in original) (footnotes omitted).

In Justice Blackmun's view,

McCleskey also demonstrated that it was more likely than not that the fact that the victim he was charged with killing was white determined that he received a sentence of death— 20 out of every 34 defendants in McCleskey's midrange category would not have been sentenced to be executed if their victims had been black. S.E. 54.

107 S.Ct. at 1800.

Justices Brennan and Blackmun's analyses were hampered, however, by the fact that the record in *McCleskey* did not provide sufficiently fine-grained data on those cases that were closely comparable to *McCleskey* in their aggravation levels. As a consequence, the justices aggregated 320 cases that table 53 clearly indicates are distinguishable in their aggravation levels (as measured by the factors included in the regression model that underlies table 53). This puts into question the assumption that the white- and black-victim cases were of similar comparability. Following the *McCleskey* hearing, however, we located McCleskey's case in level 5 of table 53. Applying the same type of analysis to the 38 black-defendant cases at McCleskey's aggravation level (columns C and D), the probability that the race of the victim was a factor was .51. However, if the analysis also includes white-defendant cases at level 5 of table 53, the probability is only .40 (5.18/13). All the white-defendant cases involve a white victim at that level. *See generally*, Baldus, Pulaski, & Woodworth, *Arbitrariness and Discrimination in the Administration of the Death Penalty: A Challenge to State Supreme Courts*, 15 STETSON L. REV. 133, 204–7 (1986).

45. *See supra* chap. 10, note 32 and accompanying text.

46. McCleskey v. Kemp, 753 F.2d 877, 896 (11th Cir. 1985).

47. The 6-percentage-point disparity can also be usefully compared with the death-sentencing base rate for all cases indicted for murder of .05 (128/2,342).

48. The average 6-point disparity indicates that among the majority of cases in the system there is no or only a very slight race-of-victim effect. *See supra*, chap. 10, table 53.

49. Calculated from table 53, col. D, levels 3–7.

50. Calculated from table 53, col. B, levels 3–7.

51. To put the magnitude of this disparity in context, the Court has found in jury-discrimination cases the following disparities between the minority representation rate of the community and the minority representation of people called for jury service sufficiently substantial to justify relief: 40 percentage points (.79 v. .39) in Castaneda v. Partida, 430 U.S. at 486–87; 23 points (.60 v. .37) in Turner v. Fouche, 396 U.S. 346, 359 (1970); 18 points (.27 v. .09) in Whitus v. Georgia, 385 U.S. 545, 552 (1967); 19 points (.24 v. .05) in Sims v. Georgia, 389 U.S. 404, 407 (1967); and 15 points (.20 v. .05) in Jones v. Georgia, 389 U.S. 24, 25 (1967).

52. The odds-multiplier is the antilog (e^b) of the partial logistic-regression coefficient, b.

53. *See supra* chap. 4, note 43. The increase in the "average" defendant's odds among white-victim cases refers to white-victim cases with both black and white defendants.

54. *See* G. Friedman, PRIMER OF EPIDEMIOLOGY 178–79 (3d ed. 1987). Directly standardized, average death-sentencing rates for black- and white-victim cases can be computed by applying race-specific rates at each level of aggravation to a standard population—in this case the total number of cases (black-victim plus white-victim) at each level of aggravation. The ratio of these standardized rates is interpretable as an average-probability multiplier. However, unlike the case with the odds-ratio multiplier, the size of the probability multiplier will depend in part on the distribution of cases according to their culpability, as well as on the size of the disparity at each level of aggravation.

55. However, we believe that in contrast to the least-squares regression coefficient the logistic-regression coefficient is capable of giving a truer picture of the combined effects of the numerous decisions in Georgia's death-sentencing system (effects running from indictment to the penalty-trial sentencing decision). The property of an "arithmetic difference" measure, like the least-squares regression coefficient, is that when used to measure the combined effects of a multistage decision-making process like Georgia's capital-sentencing system, the overall disparity indicated will generally be smaller than the disparities observed at each point in the process that produce the observed overall disparity. The diminution in size is analogous to taking a fraction of a fraction, e.g., $\frac{1}{2} \times \frac{1}{2} = \frac{1}{4}$. To illustrate further, note *supra* chap. 10, note 18, note table 5, that the race-of-victim disparities estimated for the prosecutorial and jury decisions with a least-squares regression coefficient are quite large—.16 and .23 for the prosecutorial decision, and .22 and .23 for the jury decisions. Yet the combined effects of these two decisions show race-of-victim disparities in the range of 8 or 9 percentage points. *See supra* chap. 10, note 17, note table 4, col. B.

Interestingly, when one measures the combined effects of a series of decisions with a simple ratio or multiplier measure (e.g., white-victim rate/black-victim rate), the measure of their combined effects will be *larger* than the measure at a given stage in the process, provided the racial disparities run in the same direction. Its effect is analogous to compounding interest. For example, a 2-to-1 (white victim/black victim) ratio of selection rates at both the prosecutorial and jury levels will, in theory, result in a 4-to-1 (white victim/black victim) ratio when the combined effects of the two decision points are analyzed.

The odds multiplier estimated from the logistic-regression coefficient has neither of the effects just described. As a measure of the overall combined effects of multiple decision points in Georgia's capital-sentencing system, it does not substantially enhance or diminish the effects observed at the separate stages in the process. For this additional reason, we believe the logistic odds multiplier is the best single measure of the overall average race-of-victim effect in the system. And it can be supplemented by the measures based on arithmetic differences and ratios at different culpability levels in tabulations like those presented *supra* chap. 10, notes 53 & 54. *See also supra* chap. 6, note 36.

56. McCleskey v. Kemp, 107 S.Ct. at 1780n.45.

57. *See* Gregg v. Georgia, 428 U.S. 153, 198 (1976).

58. *See supra* text accompanying note 37.

CHAPTER TWELVE
Summary and Conclusions

This book has examined the extent to which three legal developments since 1972 have achieved their promise to end arbitrariness and discrimination in death sentencing in this country. Our two empirical studies in Georgia and the work of numerous scholars and reporters in other states indicate that the conditions that prompted *Furman v. Georgia* have improved somewhat in the last fifteen years. Nevertheless, the promise that two of these developments— post-*Furman* trial-court reforms and enhanced appellate oversight—would bring equal justice to the process remain substantially unfulfilled. The third development, embodied in several decisions of the Supreme Court in the 1970s, seemed to promise that the federal courts would require a minimal level of consistency in the state death-sentencing systems. However, the Supreme Court's apparent commitment to that promise weakened substantially in the early 1980s and is in serious question after the Court's 1987 decision in *Mc-Cleskey v. Kemp*.

In this chapter we summarize the methodology and findings of our two Georgia empirical studies that bear on these issues, as well as the findings from those studies that were presented on behalf of a death-sentenced defendant in *McCleksey v. Kemp*. We also summarize the evidence concerning arbitrariness, discrimination, and proportionality review outside Georgia. Finally, we discuss the implications of our principal findings.

SUMMARY OF METHODOLOGY[1]

The Research Design and Data

The Procedural Reform Study (PRS)

This book reports the results of two empirical studies of Georgia's capital charging-and-sentencing system during the 1970s. The first study, known as the Procedural Reform Study (PRS), which we commenced in 1980, was designed to evaluate the impact of the statutory reforms prompted by *Furman v. Georgia* (1972) on the levels of arbitrariness and discrimination in the final, sentencing stages of Georgia's capital-sentencing system. The pre-*Furman* sample (1970–72) consisted of 156 cases drawn from a universe of 294 cases that had resulted in a murder-trial conviction; 44 of these cases resulted in a death sentence. The post-*Furman* (1973–78) sample of 594 cases consisted of all Georgia cases that resulted in a murder-trial conviction between March 1973 and June 1978; 100 of these offenders received a death sentence. We obtained data on over 150 aggravating and mitigating case characteristics for each case from the records of the Georgia Supreme Court and the Georgia Board of Pardons and Paroles, and supplemented them with information from other public sources, defense counsel, and prosecutors.

These two data sets allowed us to analyze for both the pre- and post-*Furman* periods the combined effects of two decisions—the prosecutorial decision to seek a death sentence after a murder conviction was obtained at trial and the jury decision to impose a life or a death sentence when the prosecutor sought a death sentence. In addition, the post-*Furman* data set allowed us to analyze separately the prosecutorial decisions to seek a death sentence after obtaining a murder conviction at trial and the jury's penalty trial death-sentencing decisions.

The Charging and Sentencing Study (css)

The Charging and Sentencing Study (css) was undertaken on behalf of the NAACP Legal Defense and Educational Fund, Inc., in contemplation of possible litigation, which ultimately became *McCleskey v. Kemp*. The css embraces a universe of 2,484 defendants charged with homicide between 1973 and 1979 and subsequently convicted of murder or voluntary manslaughter. The data set is a stratified sample of 1,066 cases, 128 of which resulted in a death sentence.

The design of the css permitted us to track the movement of cases through five stages of Georgia's capital charging-and-sentencing system, from the point of indictment to the penalty-trial sentencing decision. [2] The design of the css also allowed us to examine the combined effects of these five stages.

The data for the css were obtained primarily from the Georgia Board of Pardons and Paroles, and supplemented with information from other public sources, defense lawyers, and prosecutors.

Measuring Arbitrariness, Excessiveness, and Discrimination

Under the Eighth Amendment of the United States Constitution, the concept of arbitrariness can refer to a death sentence imposed in an individual case or to the pattern of outcomes of a death-sentencing system in general without regard to the sentence imposed in any specific case. In its first, case-specific meaning, arbitrariness refers to the imposition of a death sentence in a case that cannot be distinguished in a "meaningful" or "principled" way from cases that generally result in a lesser sentence. Death sentences that are arbitrary in this sense are often referred to as "wanton," "capricious," "excessive," or "comparatively excessive." Our judgment of comparative excessiveness in an individual death-sentence case is based on the frequency with which death sentences are imposed in cases that are comparable to the death sentence under review in overall culpability or blameworthiness.

When used to characterize a death-sentencing system as a whole, arbitrariness has two possible meanings. One is that the system operates in a capricious or random fashion or that there is a substantial risk that death sentences are imposed in such a fashion. Our first measure of arbitrariness in this sense is the overall proportion of individual death sentences imposed that appear to be excessive in a comparative sense. Our second measure is the extent to which the death-sentenced cases as a group can be differentiated from the life-sentenced cases as a group in their overall culpability level. We determined this by estimating the degree of overlap of separate distributions of the death- and life-sentenced cases on a defendant culpability index. Our third measure is the extent to which legitimate case characteristics appear to explain the results of the system statistically and provide a basis for predicting which defendants receive death sentences.

Arbitrariness also embraces the concept of discrimination, and it may refer to the impact of discrimination on the system as a whole or in an individual case. From a systemwide perspective, discrimination refers to the extent to which (a) the death sentences imposed are the product of such legally irrelevant or impermissible factors as the race or socioeconomic status of the defendant or victim, or (b) there is a substantial risk that impermissible factors are influencing the system. Our first measure of discrimination in this sense is the magnitude and statistical significance of the disparities estimated for racial characteristics after adjustment is made for a variety of legitimate case characteristics, such as the number of victims and the defendant's prior record. The second measure of racial discrimination in the system is the proportion of all death sentences imposed that appear to be a product of race. In the case-specific sense, our concern is with the likelihood that a given death sentence is the product of discrimination.[3]

Analytic Methods

The measurement of arbitrariness, excessiveness, and discrimination requires the identification of cases that are similar in overall defendant blameworthiness or culpability. There are two basic approaches to this task— the *a priori* and the empirical. The *a priori* approach classifies cases as similar in overall culpability on the basis of criteria that, from a legal or moral perspective, one believes should govern the appropriate sentence. The empirical approach, by contrast, identifies similar cases on the basis of legitimate case characteristics, such as the number of aggravating circumstances or the defendant's role in the murder, that best explain the observed sentencing results statistically.

In the PRS, our core findings are based on two empirical methods for measuring overall defendant case culpability. The first employs indexes and scales developed with logistic multiple-regression analyses. These permit us to rank cases by defendant culpability and to identify subgroups of cases with similar levels of culpability. Within the subgroup of cases identified as similar according to these indexes and scales, we then estimate the levels of excessiveness and discrimination in the post-guilt-trial stages of Georgia's capital-sentencing process, before and after *Furman*.[4]

Our second empirical method for identifying cases of similar culpability in the PRS was a three-dimensional classification system developed by Professor Arnold Barnett. This system identified three dimensions of the cases (deliberateness of the killing, relationship of the defendant and victim, and the vileness of the murder) that allowed us to place them into eighteen subgroups of cases that were comparable in their overall culpability and blameworthiness. Within these subgroups of cases, we then conducted analyses of excessiveness and discrimination in the post-*Furman* period.

We also conducted alternative analyses to test the robustness of our core race-discrimination findings in the PRS. First, we constructed an *a priori* measure of case culpability that weighed aggravating and mitigating circumstances in an intuitive fashion. This was applied to the armed-robbery cases in both the pre- and post-*Furman* samples. Second, we conducted an ordinary-least-squares regression analysis that adjusted simultaneously for over 150 legitimate aggravating and mitigating circumstances.

The results of the Procedural Reform Study are reported in chapters 5, 6, and 7, which consider, respectively, the issues of comparative excessiveness, discrimination before and after *Furman*, and post-*Furman* comparative- proportionality review by the Georgia Supreme Court.[5]

In the CSS, our core measure of defendant culpability and blameworthiness was a 39-variable index estimated with a logistic multiple-regression procedure. This analysis was designed to identify the case characteristics that best explained which defendants from the entire universe of cases in the study received a death sentence. The variables in this model were selected on the basis of our general knowledge of the Georgia capital-sentencing system, the empirical literature on capital sentencing, and the empirical results from the PRS. We used this model to estimate race disparities produced by the combined effects of all decisions from indictment through penalty-trial sentencing.

We conducted a series of other analyses to test the robustness of the results produced with the 39-variable core model. First, we created culpability indexes and scales comparable to the ones described above for the PRS. Second, we estimated racial coefficients in a series of multiple-regression analyses controlling variously for from 5 to 136 variables selected in a variety of ways. We then conducted a large-scale linear multiple-regression analysis that controlled simultaneously for 230-plus variables. Third, we conducted an analysis of cases involving contemporaneous felonies sorted into subgroups according to the relative culpability of the offenders determined with an *a priori* measure.

Finally, we conducted a series of analyses which focused on Fulton County, where Warren McCleskey was sentenced, and the likely impact of racial factors in his case. The results of the Charging and Sentencing Study are reported in chapter 10, which describes the background, record, and adjudications in *McCleskey v. Kemp*.[6]

SUMMARY OF FINDINGS

The Frequency of Death Sentencing before and after *Furman*

The most striking feature of capital sentencing in the United States, both before and after *Furman*, is the infrequency with which death sentences are imposed. In both periods, the number of death sentences imposed annually was relatively stable and only a fraction of what the law authorized.[7]

In this respect, our findings conform to the perceptions of the Supreme Court justices who decided *Furman v. Georgia*. Although the five concurring justices each employed a different legal analysis, they were all concerned with the small number of death sentences imposed under pre-*Furman* law and with their inability to discern any principled distinction between the larger number of defendants who received life sentences or less and the relative handful who were condemned to die.[8] The finding that death sentences continue to be imposed infrequently in the post-*Furman* period is contrary to one of the court's major assumptions in *Gregg v. Georgia*—that, in death-eligible cases, prosecutors would regularly seek death sentences and that sentencing juries would regularly impose them.[9] However, in Georgia and elsewhere, a large proportion of death-eligible cases end with plea bargains involving a waiver of the death penalty or a reduction of charges to a noncapital crime. Moreover, in many jurisdictions, including Georgia, even after a jury has convicted the defendant of capital murder, prosecutors frequently choose to forgo a penalty trial, thereby waiving the death penalty. Finally, even when penalty trials do occur, the limited data indicate that juries generally impose death sentences in only about one-half of the cases.[10] Thus, in contrast to what the Supreme

Court anticipated, we find that prosecutorial discretion continues to dominate the system and that only a small portion of the death-eligible cases actually result in a death sentence.

Excessiveness and Discrimination

Pre-Furman Georgia

Infrequent death sentencing, however, does not necessarily mean excessive death sentencing. Justice Stewart's contrary suggestion in *Furman* notwithstanding, our results indicate that, at least in Georgia, the pre-*Furman* system was clearly not as random as a lottery. On the other hand, it was much more like a lottery than the highly selective system that Chief Justice Burger envisioned. We found no meaningful basis to distinguish a very large proportion of Georgia's pre-*Furman* death sentences, including that imposed on Furman himself, from the many other cases that resulted in life sentences. More significantly, only a fraction of these pre-*Furman* death sentences occurred in extremely aggravated cases in which Georgia juries regularly imposed death sentences.[11] The degree of excessiveness we observed in our pre-*Furman* sample of cases appears to have been partly attributable to geographic disparities in death-sentencing rates; the primary cause, as several justices suggested in *Furman*, appears to have been racial discrimination.

On this issue, our Georgia data from the pre-*Furman* era provide evidence of discrimination against both black defendants and defendants who killed white victims. By and large, race is a major case characteristic distinguishing cases that received a death sentence from the great bulk of life-sentenced cases. Black defendants and defendants with white victims received the worst treatment. On the average, the probability that a black defendant would receive a death sentence was 12 percentage points higher than the probability for white defendants after adjustment for case culpability. Moreover, defendants with white victims had a 12-percentage-point higher risk of receiving a death sentence than defendants with black victims.[12]

These racial effects occurred primarily in moderately aggravated, midrange cases in which the defendant's culpability was neither very high nor very low. Among these moderately aggravated cases, the racial disparities often exceeded 20 to 30 percentage points. This concentration of race effects in the midrange of cases is consistent with Kalven and Zeisel's liberation hypothesis, which posits that impermissible or inappropriate considerations have their most profound influence on juries in the midrange of cases in which legally relevant factors offset each other so that the decision might go either way.

We estimate that, after adjustment for case culpability, if black defendants in Georgia had been sentenced at the same rate as white defendants, 41 percent (18/44) fewer death sentences would have been imposed. We also estimate a 39 percent (17/44) decline in the total number of death sentences imposed if white-victim cases had been sentenced at the same rate as black-victim cases.[13]

Contrary to the suggestion of several justices in *Furman*, we found no compelling evidence, at least for its final two decision points, that Georgia's pre-*Furman* capital-sentencing system was influenced by the sex or socioeconomic status of the defendant or of the victim. We caution, however, that there is little variation in the socioeconomic status of our defendants, and our measures of defendant and victim economic status are far from perfect. Moreover, it is quite possible that these suspect characteristics influenced the earlier stages in the capital charging-and-sentencing process, for which we have no data.

*Post-*Furman *Georgia*

In terms of excessive death sentences, the results observed in the trial stages of Georgia's post-*Furman* system represent an improvement over the pre-*Furman* results. The degree of improvement, however, depends on which measure of defendant blameworthiness one uses to identify similar cases. Also, there is a possibility that record-keeping practices in the post-*Furman* period may have emphasized the importance of collecting case data on statutory aggravating circumstances, and may have thereby exaggerated somewhat the degree of consistency that we observe in the post-*Furman* period.[14] The most important change is a substantial reduction in the proportion of excessive death sentences, that is, those found among the least aggravated cases for which death sentences are quite infrequent. Also, a considerably higher proportion of death-sentence cases appear to be evenhanded, that is, they are imposed in categories of highly aggravated cases in which death sentences are common.

In spite of these improvements, the post-*Furman* system in Georgia is far from Chief Justice Burger's vision of a highly selective system that imposes death sentences only in the most extreme cases. There is still a significant amount of unpredictability in the Georgia system. Even when viewed in the most favorable light, only 50 percent to 60 percent of the death sentences in our study are presumptively evenhanded; and approximately one-quarter appear to be excessive.[15]

As in the pre-*Furman* era, geographic disparities in death-sentencing rates explain some of the excessiveness in Georgia's post-*Furman* system. A more important cause, however, appears to be the persistence of race-of-victim discrimination. Also, much of the variation in the distribution of excessive sentences is probably attributable to such factors as the luck of the draw in jury selection and the competence, experience, and diligence of the prosecutor, the defense counsel, and the judge presiding at the penalty trial, factors for which we have no data available.[16]

The post-*Furman* data on racial discrimination in Georgia present a mixed picture. Statewide, we found no evidence of race-of-defendant discrimination except among the more aggravated cases in the css. However, when we examined urban and rural areas separately, we found that rural prosecutors discriminated against black defendants, but the overall effect, taking into account the impact of jury decision making, was not statistically significant. More surprisingly, we found that in urban areas both prosecutors and juries appeared to discriminate against white defendants. Also, a comparison pre- and post-*Furman* of the reported aggravation levels of the white and black defendants whose victims were white suggested that altered record-keeping practices post-*Furman* may have suppressed somewhat evidence of discrimination against black defendants with white victims. Although this evidence is inconclusive, it does indicate that the actual post-*Furman* decline in race-of-defendant discrimination may not be as dramatic as the numbers at first suggest.[17]

The post-*Furman* evidence of race-of-victim discrimination that is summarized in Table 64 reveals a continuation of the pre-*Furman* pattern. After adjustment for case culpability among all cases in the PRS that resulted in a murder-trial conviction, the average defendant with a white victim faced a statistically significant 7- to 9-percentage-point higher risk of a death sentence than did a similarly situated defendant whose victim was black. This disparity persisted (a) in an analysis that adjusted for our main culpability index, consisting of three suspect variables and the 20 most important variables for legitimate case characteristics, (b) in an analysis employing a three-dimensional system for measuring case aggravation levels, and (c) in a large-scale linear multiple-regression analysis that simultaneously adjusted for over 150 legitimate background variables.[18] Also, a logistic-regression analysis estimated that defendants with white victims face average odds of receiving a death sentence that are 4.3 times larger than those faced by similarly situated defendants with black victims.[19]

In the css, we examined the combined effects of prosecutorial and jury decisions from indictment to the final sentencing decision; the results were comparable to those obtained in the PRS. A logistic-regression analysis suggested that the average odds of receiving a death sentence among all indicted cases were 4.3 times higher in cases with white victims. Linear-regression analysis controlling for from 13 to 230-plus variables showed an average 6- to 7-point higher death-sentencing rate in the white-victim cases. Table 64 summarizes the principal statewide race-of-victim findings produced by the PRS and the css.

These race-of-victim effects are much stronger, however, among the 30 to 40 percent of death-eligible cases that fall within the midrange of cases in relative culpability. Within this group there is, on average, a 20-percentage-point disparity in the death-sentencing rates between the white- and black-

Table 64. Summary of Statewide Race-of-Victim Disparities Reported in This Book[1]

I. Procedural Reform Study (PRS)[2]

A. Analytic Method and Background Variables Adjusted/Controlled for	B. Among Defendants Convicted of Murder at Trial	
	Pre-*Furman*	Post-*Furman*
1. Unadjusted disparities	8 pts.[a]	20 pts.[b]
2. Cross-tab controlling for main culpability index and scale	12 pts.[c]	7.4 pts.[d]
3. Cross-tab controlling for Barnett culpability index and scale	–	8 pts.[e]
4. Multiple-regression estimates after simultaneous adjustment for the following legitimate case characteristics and the race of defendant:		
a. Main culpability index	4.3 o.m.[f]	4.3 o.m.[g]
b. 150+ background factors	–	9 pts.[h]

II. Charging and Sentencing Study (CSS) Statewide[3]

A. Analytic Method and Background Variables Controlled for	B. Among Defendants Convicted of Murder or Voluntary Manslaughter
1. Unadjusted disparity	10 pts.[i]
2. Cross-tab controlling for a regression-based index—most aggravated 472 cases	3.7 o.m.[j]
3. Multiple-regression estimates after adjustment for the following legitimate case characteristics and the race of defendant:	
a. Main 39-variable culpability index	4.3 o.m.[k]
b. 13 to 136+ variables (6 analyses)	6 to 7 pts.[l]
c. 230+ variables	6 pts.[m]
d. Main 39-variable culpability index limited to 647 highly aggravated cases as determined by model of Judge J. Owen Forrester	4.0 o.m.[n]

1. Arithmetic disparities are reported as percentage-point differences (e.g., 8 pts. means an 8-percentage-point difference between the death-sentencing rates in the white- and black-victim cases); they are estimated in both crosstabular analyses and ordinary least-squares regression analyses (O.L.S.). The "odds multipliers" estimated in logistic-regression analyses are designated "o.m." *See supra* chap. 4, notes 54–55 and accompanying text, for an explanation of regression coefficients. All disparities are statistically significant beyond the .05 level. "T" and "F" in the footnotes refer to tables and figures in this book.

2. *See* chap. 6, tables 43 and 44, for a more detailed summary of the race-of-victim findings in the PRS.

victim cases. Like the pre-*Furman* results, the post-*Furman* findings are also consistent with Kalven and Zeisel's liberation hypothesis.[20]

The exercise of prosecutorial discretion is the principal source of the race-of-victim disparities observed in the system. Most important is the prosecutorial decision to seek a death sentence in cases that result in a murder-trial conviction. We observed another strong (but practically less important) race-of-victim effect in the prosecutorial decision to accept a voluntary-manslaughter plea in cases indicted for murder. The results of our analyses of jury penalty-trial decisions were mixed. Some estimates from the PRS showed a statistically significant race-of-victim effect, but the PRS results in which we have the most confidence, although fairly large, do not attain statistical significance at the .05 level,[21] nor do the jury race-of-victim results from the CSS.

The race of the victim appears to have determined the sentence imposed in up to one-third of the death-sentenced cases. We estimate that, if Georgia had processed all its post-*Furman* cases in the same manner as the black-victim cases, approximately 30 percent fewer death sentences would have resulted; and, if all defendants had received the same treatment as defendants in the white-victim cases, approximately 10 percent more defendants would have received a death sentence. In either of these situations, the increase in the proportion of defendants on death row whose victims were black would have risen slightly, as would the total proportion of black defendants on death row, since most black homicide victims die at the hand of a black defendant.[22]

Race-of-victim discrimination occurred in both urban and rural areas. Its effects were particularly strong in the decisions of urban and rural prosecutors and urban juries. Our findings regarding post-*Furman* Georgia are squarely at odds with two of the major factual presumptions underlying the Supreme Court's decision in *Gregg v. Georgia*. The Court's first presumption was that prosecutors would exercise their discretion solely on the basis of the strength of the evidence and the likelihood that the jury would impose a death sentence. The second presumption was that juries would exercise their discretion strictly on the basis of legitimate aggravating and mitigating circumstances. By contrast, we found there was a substantial degree of unpredictability in the deci-

---

Notes to Table 64 (*cont.*)

3. *See* chap. 10, table 55, for a summary of the race-of-victim findings from the CSS, and endnote tables 4 through 7 for the PRS findings presented in *McCleskey v. Kemp*.

a. T. 26.	f. App. J/model PREFURMA	h. Text at chap. 6,	m. T. 51.	
b. T. 30.	& text following	note 20.	n. Chap. 10, note 38 and	
c. T. 28.	chap. 6, note 7.	i. T. 50.	accompanying text.	
d. T. 32.	g. App. B/model OVERALLA	j. T. 53.		
e. F. 31.	and chap. 6, note 19	k. T. 52.		
	and accompanying text.	l. T. 51.		

sions of both prosecutors and juries in Georgia. Moreover, in addition to the race of the victim, other inappropriate factors, such as the socioeconomic status and residence of the defendant and the socioeconomic status of the victim, also influence sentencing results to varying degrees.[23]

The Impact of Georgia's Post-*Furman* Procedural Reforms

We found that the reduced frequency with which excessive death sentences occurred at the trial level in post-*Furman* Georgia was largely attributable to the new sentencing procedures that Georgia adopted in 1973 in response to the *Furman* decision.[24] We do not, however, perceive a connection between the post-*Furman* decline in race-of-defendant discrimination against black defendants and the 1973 reforms. Rather, we consider it more plausible that this development is a product of demographic and attitudinal changes and, most important, of the increased participation of black citizens on juries, and in political and civic affairs generally.[25]

Comparative-Proportionality Review in Georgia

The Georgia Supreme Court's process of proportionality review has not functioned as the United States Supreme Court contemplated in *Gregg v. Georgia*. For reasons that are not entirely clear, the Georgia court's procedures are biased in favor of findings that death sentences are not excessive or disproportionate. As a consequence, the Georgia Supreme Court has never vacated a death sentence because of the infrequency with which death sentences occur in other similar cases. The Georgia court does, however, reverse or vacate about one-third of the state's death sentences on other grounds, and these decisions reduce by approximately 40 percent the number of apparently excessive death sentences. We also estimate that the decisions of the Georgia court may have reduced the race-of-victim effects in the system by about 25 percent.[26]

Evidence Concerning Arbitrariness, Discrimination, and Proportionality Review outside Georgia

To a surprising degree, our findings concerning the frequency of excessive or discriminatory death sentences in Georgia before and after *Furman* parallel the findings in a number of other jurisdictions. The limited pre-*Furman* evidence from other states is generally consistent with our finding that most of Georgia's pre-*Furman* death-sentence cases could not be meaningfully distinguished from the larger group of cases in which there was no death sentence. The principal exception is our 1980 reanalysis of the capital system in California, which, in terms of comparative excessiveness, operated in the pre-*Furman* period in a manner comparable to Georgia's post-*Furman* system.[27] Our findings of strong race-of-victim and race-of-defendant discrimination in pre-*Furman* Georgia also parallel the results of other pre-*Furman* studies in the South, although many of these tended to be relatively small in scope and not well controlled. The results of studies from outside the South, which primarily addressed race-of-defendant discrimination, were generally mixed.[28]

For the post-*Furman* period, there is only limited evidence available concerning excessive death sentencing outside Georgia, and the results are also mixed.[29] The data from other states on racial discrimination, however, are considerably more extensive. They indicate no evidence of systematic discrimination against black defendants on the basis of their race. Indeed, the available statistics suggest that, nationwide, black defendants now receive on average slightly more lenient treatment than their white counterparts. The degree of leniency is only slight, however, and the statewide statistics may mask variations within states of the type we observed in Georgia.[30] There is persuasive evidence, however, that in many jurisdictions white-victim cases are treated more punitively than black-victim cases at various stages in the process. Furthermore, some studies that have examined the issue have also found, as we did in Georgia, that these race-of-victim effects occur primarily in cases falling within the midrange of cases in terms of relative culpability.[31]

The evidence on proportionality review indicates that other courts besides the Georgia Supreme Court have failed thus far to develop effective review systems. Several state courts have adopted the precedent-seeking approach and do not attempt to consider all similar cases or even a representative sample of similar cases.[32] Other courts limit their search for similar cases to cases that resulted in capital convictions, to cases in which there is an appeal, or to capital-murder cases that result in a penalty trial. Each of these limitations reduces the size of the pool of potentially similar cases, often substantially. Furthermore, this selective review of comparable cases insulates from appellate court oversight a significant number of cases in which prosecutorial decisions before and after trial eliminate the risk of a death sentence.[33]

Most state courts have failed to develop meaningful methods for selecting similar cases and principled standards for deciding whether or not a given death sentence is excessive. As a result, these courts have only a limited perception of their death-sentencing systems, and their review procedures are generally biased against finding that any individual death sentences are excessive or disproportionate.[34]

There are a number of possible explanations for the failure of the state courts to identify and to vacate the excessive and discriminatory death sentences that still frequently occur. Whatever the reasons, however, this failure is regrettable, especially because we believe state courts have the capacity to deal effectively with excessive or discriminatory death sentences.

McCleskey v. Kemp and the Supreme Court's Commitment to Comparative Justice

For all practical purposes, the decisions of the United States Supreme Court serve to define the minimal levels of evenhandedness that states must observe in death sentencing. In the 1970s the Court's decisions in *Furman* and *Gregg*, together with the principle articulated in other decisions that "death is different," created five important expectations related to equal justice in death sentencing:

1. An effective system of comparative proportionality review would be an important guarantee against arbitrariness and discrimination in death sentencing and might be required by the Eighth Amendment
2. Individual death sentences that are comparatively excessive violate the Eighth Amendment
3. Death-sentencing systems that consistently imposed excessive death sentences would probably violate the Eighth Amendment
4. Individual death sentences imposed on the basis of the defendant's or the victim's race would violate the equal-protection clause of the Fourteenth Amendment and the Eighth Amendment
5. Death-sentencing systems that routinely impose discriminatory death sentences would be unconstitutional in whole or in part under the Eighth Amendment.

The Supreme Court explicitly rejected the expectation that comparative-proportionality review was constitutionally required in *Pulley v. Harris* (1984). In an apparent retreat from several of its earlier pronouncements, the Court held in *Pulley* that the Eighth Amendment did not require state courts to conduct proportionality reviews, even in states with broad levels of jury discretion.

Several decisions in 1983 also suggested that the Court was becoming less committed to special safeguards to ensure reliability and, ultimately, consistency. However, *McCleskey v. Kemp* (1987), a 5–4 decision of the United States Supreme Court, threw into serious question the remaining equal-justice principles noted above.[35] *McCleskey* involved a claim that, between 1973 and 1979, Georgia had applied its capital-sentencing system in a racially discriminatory and unconstitutional manner. Part of the evidence before the Court in *McCleskey* consisted of selected findings of the Procedural Reform Study (PRS) reported in this book; the primary source of evidence before the court in *McCleskey*, however, was the second study reported in this book, the Charging and Sentencing Study (CSS). The central evidence in the CSS were the results of the 39-variable logistic multiple-regression analysis which indicated that the odds that the average defendant indicted for murder would receive a death sentence were enhanced by a factor of 4.3 if his victim was white. A second finding, derived from a linear multiple-regression model, indicated that after adjustment for 230-plus legitimate case characteristics, the average probability that a defendant indicted for murder would receive a death sentence was 6 percentage points higher if his victim was white.

The results of the CSS presented in *McCleskey* also indicated that the impact of the victim's race was substantially greater than average in the midaggravation range of cases, where McCleskey's case was located. In this category, the average defendant whose victim was white faced an approximately 20-percentage-point higher risk of receiving a death sentence than the average defendant whose victim was black.

The results of the CSS further indicated that, in highly aggravated white-victim cases, black defendants were at greater risk of receiving a death sentence than were similarly situated white defendants. Throughout the entire system, however, the CSS did not show a statistically significant race-of-defendant effect. Also before the *McCleskey* court was an analysis of the CSS cases from Fulton County. It showed race-of-victim effects at several stages in the process but no persistent race-of-defendant effects.

The trial court in *McCleskey* identified what it considered to be fatal flaws in the data and in the statistical methodology of the studies presented. The Court of Appeals did not scrutinize any of these methodological findings, however, assuming instead the validity of the research methodology. It held, nevertheless, that the evidence of race-of-victim discrimination was insufficient to establish a violation of the equal-protection clause or of the Eighth Amendment.

The Supreme Court also assumed the validity of the research methodology, with one major caveat: it did not accept the validity of our conclusion that the studies established that the race of the victim was a major influence in the system.

Although the parties to *McCleskey* presented no claims concerning comparative excessiveness, broad language in Justice Powell's opinion appears to be inconsistent with both the notion that comparatively excessive death sentences are impermissible and the proposition that death-sentencing systems that routinely impose excessive death sentences are constitutionally suspect. The holding of *McCleskey* also dramatically limited the reach of the equal-protection clause in death-sentencing cases by ruling that only case-specific evidence of purposeful discrimination in a claimant's case could establish an equal-protection violation, regardless of the strength of evidence that race influenced the system pervasively.

McCleskey also limited the usefulness of statistical evidence of classwide racial discrimination in the Eighth Amendment context, declaring that such evidence can only establish a *risk* of discrimination, not proof. The Court also held that the evidence of race-of-victim discrimination offered by *McCleskey* was insufficient to demonstrate a "constitutionally significant risk of racial bias affecting the Georgia capital-sentencing process."[36] Because the studies proffered in *McCleskey* and described in this book are among the most extensive and comprehensive sentencing studies reported to date, this particular finding bodes ill for any future efforts, at least in the near term. Thus, although the Court has not expressly overruled its earlier stated commitment to nondiscriminatory death sentencing, it has left future victims of such discrimination without an effective remedy.

A dissenting opinion by Justice Brennan argued that McCleskey had reliably established a constitutionally unacceptable risk that the death penalty was imposed in an arbitrary and capricious manner in violation of the cruel and unusual punishments provision of the Eighth Amendment. He also argued that McCleskey had shown by a preponderance of the evidence that racial factors determined the outcome of his penalty trial.

Also in dissent, Justice Blackmun rejected the idea that the ordinary equal-protection model of classwide disparate treatment did not apply in death-sentencing cases. He further argued that McCleskey's proof established a prima facie case of race-of-victim discrimination that had not been rebutted by the state. Moreover, he asserted that McCleskey had established by a preponderance of the evidence that race was a determinative factor in his case. However, unlike Justice Brennan, Justice Blackmun did not suggest the invalidation of Georgia's death-sentencing statute. Rather, he called for a narrowing of death-eligible cases under the Georgia statute, which would limit death sentencing to the most aggravated cases in which there was no evidence of racial discrimination.

Justice Stevens's brief dissent also found the risk of discrimination constitutionally intolerable, and like Justice Blackmun he would have limited relief to the invalidation of the death sentences imposed in cases that involved an unacceptable risk that race played a decisive role in sentencing.

IMPLICATIONS

A major finding of our Georgia study is that the promises of the two principal post-*Furman* procedural reforms—guided discretion at the trial-court level and enhanced oversight at the state-appellate level—remain unfulfilled. We retain great confidence in this finding, in part because of the consistent results we obtained when we tested and retested our findings using two independent data sets and many different statistical procedures. Also, the general consistency of our Georgia findings with the results of studies reported from other jurisdictions enhances our confidence about the validity of our Georgia results and convinces us that the problems with fairness and equal justice in Georgia's death-sentencing system are widespread.

We are less certain, however, about the implications of our findings. Certainly, we do not believe that our study answers every important question about equal justice in the administration of the death penalty, in Georgia or anywhere else. But we do believe that our findings help to illuminate certain features of the capital-sentencing process in the United States and what developments we can anticipate in the post-*McCleskey* era.

It seems to us that, when the United States Supreme Court decided in *Gregg v. Georgia* that Georgia's new sentencing procedures were capable of rendering evenhanded justice, it based that conclusion on three factual assumptions:

- that the statutory aggravating circumstances which state legislatures designate to identify those murder cases for which death is a permissible sanction would, in fact, serve to distinguish those defendants who received death sentences from the other convicted murderers who did not;
- that, in those cases in which the strength of the evidence and the aggravating circumstances warrant a death sentence, prosecutors would regularly seek and juries would regularly impose that penalty; and
- that systems of comparative-proportionality review of the type established in Georgia would be capable of identifying excessive or disproportionate death sentences when they occur, so that, despite the broad discretion that sentencing juries enjoy, an effective means of ensuring evenhanded death sentences would be available.

Our findings from Georgia, like the findings of researchers from other jurisdictions, indicate that none of these factual presumptions was correct. Nevertheless, we continue to believe that the promise of *Gregg v. Georgia* may not be impossible to achieve, and that the disinclination of state appellate courts, thus far, to provide rational and evenhanded sentencing in capital cases is attributable not to inherent inability, but an understandable reluctance of state supreme courts to confront and remedy the difficult problems of arbitrariness and discrimination in capital sentencing in their jurisdictions when the United States Supreme Court does not specifically require them to do so. The *McCleskey* decision will, of course, dramatically reduce any incentive for state courts to provide the oversight necessary to bring a minimal level of consistency to their systems. *McCleskey* is regrettable in this regard, for, if we have learned anything from our research, it is that fairness and consistency in capital sentencing is only possible with some effective system of posttrial oversight and review.

Statutory Aggravating Factors and Justice Harlan's "Impossibility" Hypothesis

In *McGautha v. California*, Justice Harlan contended that it was impossible to designate a statutory list of aggravating circumstances capable of guiding the exercise of the jury's discretion in any meaningful fashion.[37] Our findings do not fully support this first impossibility hypothesis. The statutory factors do effectively narrow the range of sentencing discretion that existed in the pre-*Furman* period. Moreover, at least in Georgia, the number of statutory aggravating factors present in a case is the single most powerful variable in explaining who is sentenced to death. On the other hand, it is also true that, except in this respect, the statutory aggravating factors do not appear to "guide" in any meaningful way either the exercise of prosecutorial descretion in deciding when to seek a death sentence or the exercise of jury sentencing discretion.

This appears to be so for two reasons. First, as Justice Harlan asserted, it may, indeed, be impossible to construct a verbal formula that would permit different juries to make reasonably consistent comparative judgments about the relative blameworthiness of different defendants, much less to decide in any consistent fashion which of those defendants should live and which of them should die.[38] Second, however, even if it is possible to devise such a formula, the current statutory guidelines clearly fail to do so. Indeed, they do not embrace among their sentencing criteria many of the case characteristics that our research reveals most strongly influence the decisions of prosecutors and juries.[39] The Supreme Court has held that the Eighth Amendment entitles juries to consider any mitigating circumstances that seem appropriate, but the law of Georgia, and of many other states, allows juries to consider nonstatutory aggravating factors as well.[40] As a consequence, the potential ability of the statutory aggravating circumstances to impose any degree of regularity upon sentencing decisions is substantially diminished. Indeed, our empirical results from Georgia indicate that the statutory aggravating circumstances account for only 43 percent of the explanatory power of our best statistical models of the process.[41]

Finally, the statutory guidelines and the typical jury instructions are also deficient in another respect: they make no reference to the goals of retribution or deterrence that the sentencing decision is supposed to implement. Such guidance would at a minimum ensure that different juries would approach the sentencing decision from a somewhat similar perspective when deciding how to evaluate the circumstances of particular cases. In short, it seems clear that, as currently drafted, Georgia's statutory aggravating circumstances are not capable of providing the guidance that *Gregg* anticipated, and this may explain why they exert such a modest influence on the actual sentencing results.[42]

The Infrequency of Death Sentences in Capital-Murder Cases

Another implication of our findings is that, in spite of the broad theoretical support for capital punishment reflected in public-opinion polls and in numerous death-sentencing statutes, in practice, support for the death penalty has been and continues to be quite limited. A variety of hypotheses have been offered to explain the infrequency of death sentencing in America, especially during the post-*Furman* period. Prominent among them are the high cost of capital trials and the close scrutiny by appellate courts, both state and federal, that makes it extremely difficult to carry out the death sentences once they are obtained. These explanations may be plausible for today, but they had much less weight during the pre-*Furman* period and even during the early years of the post-*Furman* era. Nevertheless, the overall rate of death sentencing in these earlier periods was quite comparable to more current results.

A more compelling hypothesis, we believe, is that the nation's historically low death-sentencing rates and even lower execution rates reflect society's efforts to resolve the profound value conflicts implicated in capital punishment. This country now appears to have a de facto national quota of 250 to 300 death sentences annually, which symbolizes its commitment to the value of life. At the same time, however, the widespread exercise of leniency by prosecutors and juries in the vast majority of death- eligible cases reflects the nation's unwillingness to take the lives of even our most culpable criminals on a wholesale basis.[43]

This explanation is consistent with the "perspective" theory of Franklin Zimring and Gordon Hawkins that "[t]hose who make and implement government policy . . . are much closer to the nexus between policy and practice, between 'the death penalty' as statute, and killing people as punishment. Thus, the difference between public attitudes and the government's or legislators' view may often be, in part, not so much a difference in opinion as a difference in perspective."[44] Also, Robert Weisberg has argued that the present approach to capital punishment in this country would represent a "logical if crude compromise between the extreme groups who want either no executions or as many as possible. . . . We might therefore imagine a socially stabilizing design for the death penalty which leads to just the right number of executions to keep the art form alive, but not so many as to cause excessive social cost." Weisberg, however, believes that state appellate and federal judges have constructed this "fiendishly clever" compromise, which he perceives primarily in terms of execution rates.[45] What our findings indicate is that low death-sentencing rates, which we have documented, are not the product of appellate decisions, either state or federal.[46] Rather, they are the result of thousands of pretrial and trial decisions of elected prosecutors and ordinary citizens. The low death-sentencing rates also suggest that prosecutors do not generally believe that high death-sentencing rates are necessary to maintain the deterrent effect of the death penalty.[47]

Proportionality Review and Chief Justice Rehnquist's Impossibility Hypothesis

Our findings about the Georgia Supreme Court, the results of our survey of proportionality-review practices in other states, and the results reported by other investigators provide significant support for a second impossibility hypothesis—that a system of comparative-sentence review is incapable of providing an effective safeguard against excessive or discriminatory death sentences. However, in spite of this discouraging performance to date, we are not fully persuaded that the task is impossible. We reject the idea that there is some inherent limit on the capacity of public officials, especially appellate courts, to monitor and police a death-sentencing system.

For one thing, in comparison to sentencing juries, each of which is different in its composition and considers only a single case, the body of judges who make up a reviewing court remain relatively stable; and, as they monitor capital cases passing through the system, they acquire useful experience in gauging the comparative culpability of different defendants. It was, for example, Justice White's more than ten years of experience reviewing homicide appeals on a daily basis before *Furman* that gave him the confidence to declare in *Furman* that he could not meaningfully distinguish the death cases he saw from the far more numerous murder cases that routinely resulted in lesser punishments.

Furthermore, we also believe that rational, workable methods for measuring the relative moral culpability and blameworthiness of different defendants are available. We make this assertion not only because of our own experience with respect to the data from Georgia and Colorado that we have analyzed both qualitatively and quantitatively, but also because some state supreme courts have succeeded in obtaining the data needed to conduct proportionality reviews effectively.

Highly technical statistical methods and computers, although helpful, are not necessary. It is within the capacity of any present-day appellate court to gather the necessary data and to classify all the cases within its pool of potentially similar cases. Having accomplished that task—which, although demanding, need not be repeated wholesale for each case review—the court is then in a position to conduct an effective form of proportionality review of all future death-sentence cases.[48]

Finally, an appellate court is in a position to determine the appropriateness of any individual death sentences in terms of the goals of the death-sentencing process. To be sure, a systematic and principled review process would involve many difficult moral and legal choices. But it would convert proportionality review into a meaningful safeguard instead of what it is now—largely a symbolic gesture.[49] Furthermore, the overview of its death-sentencing system that a state court would obtain from a comprehensive system of proportionality review would also enable the court to detect and eliminate the effects of any discrimination burdening the system.[50]

Why then the failure of most courts to put an effective review system in place? We believe the principal reasons are a lack of commitment to comparative justice in some courts, a belief that juries should make the life and death choices, an aversion to the task because of its emotional and technical difficulty, and the perceived political costs associated with vacating death sentences for reasons that may not enjoy much public support.

The United States Supreme Court's Fifteen-Year "Experiment" with Regularizing Capital Sentencing

One of the most interesting aspects of the data from the past fifteen years, we believe, is the framework it provides for assessing the Court's efforts from *Furman* to *McCleskey* to regularize state death-sentencing practices. Certainly, *Furman v. Georgia* represented the beginning of a high-minded effort to introduce an element of rationality and consistency into a process that, in *McGautha v. California*, decided only a year earlier, the Court had declared to be off limits. Moreover, those efforts did appear to achieve a partial success. Our findings indicate that the death sentences imposed in Georgia after its legislature responded to *Furman* appear to have been more rational and consistent than before, although as noted above we do not consider the decline of observed race-of-defendant discrimination in post-*Furman* Georgia to be a product of Georgia's 1973 capital-sentencing reforms.

Nevertheless, it is also true that the Supreme Court's "experiment" with capital sentencing fell well short of being a complete success. For example, one obstacle to eliminating excessive or discriminatory death sentences under the post-*Furman* statutes is the continuing reluctance of prosecutors and juries to favor the imposition of death sentences in all death-eligible cases. Not only is this reluctance contrary to the Supreme Court's apparent expectations when it decided *Gregg*, but there is no practical remedy for this inaction. No one involved in the criminal-justice process is going to argue that the Eighth Amendment requires the more frequent imposition of death sentences.[51] The fact remains, however, that when only a few of the many defendants convicted of capital murder actually receive death sentences the ability of the selection process to operate rationally and consistently in each case undergoes substantial strain.[52]

Of course, to the extent that the trial stages of the state capital-sentencing system do produce excessive or disproportionate death sentences, the Supreme Court's opinions, especially in *Gregg* and *Zant v. Stephens*, place great reliance on the state supreme court's process of proportionality review to provide the necessary safeguards. Many other states apparently agreed with the United States Supreme Court's assessment of the ability of proportionality review to ensure evenhanded death sentences. By legislation or court ruling, most of the states that presently employ capital punishment provide some sort of mandatory appellate review in death-sentence cases.[53]

However, neither in Georgia nor, apparently, anywhere else has proportionality review achieved its potential on a large scale. What is interesting about this failing is that, in contrast to its inability to compel prosecutors and juries to seek or to impose death sentences on a more regular basis, the United States Supreme Court has the power to effect a remedy. How state supreme courts conduct their review processes is subject to the United States Supreme Court's own scrutiny, and, as *Godfrey v. Georgia* illustrates, the high court is capable of granting relief when the state supreme court has failed to do its job.

Nevertheless, in *Pulley v. Harris* the United States Supreme Court refused to make some form of proportionality review a constitutional requirement in every death-sentence case. Similarly, the Court had the power to eliminate or substantially reduce the influence of race discrimination in death sentencing—through the direct intervention of the federal courts. More important, an occasional federal court intervention would give both prosecutors and state appellate courts an incentive to monitor their own systems more closely. *McCleskey*, however, terminated this feature of the Court's experiment.

One wonders, of course, why a majority of the Court gave up. It could be that the Supreme Court's perception of the level of excessiveness and racial discrimination in the current state death-sentencing systems is remarkably different from our findings and those of other investigators. This we doubt. It is more plausible, we believe, that some members of the Court either lack, or have lost interest in, the goals of consistency and fairness in capital sentencing, particularly if the attainment of those goals would require significant limitations on the exercise of discretion by prosecutors and, more important, by juries.[54]

It is also possible that some members of the Court endorse one or both of the impossibility hypotheses discussed above, that is, that the trial-level reforms will never work and that state supreme courts will never provide effective oversight. Some justices may also believe that, while the Court could improve the fairness of the system, doing so would require cumbersome, disruptive, and time- consuming procedures and would frustrate a perceived public demand for the resumption of routine executions. This latter hypothesis appears most plausible to us.

If this is, in fact, the case, it is unfortunate that the Supreme Court's opinion in *McCleskey v. Kemp* was not more straightforward. To be sure, Justice Powell did suggest that legislatures are better suited than the Court to resolve the problem of discriminatory death sentencing. Unfortunately, he also felt compelled to justify the majority's rulings on the equal-protection clause and the Eighth Amendment on the basis of unpersuasive methodological arguments about the function and limits of statistical proof. These arguments are troublesome, because lower courts may seize upon them to undercut the force of statistical argument in discrimination cases far removed from the domain of capital punishment.

The Goals of Capital Punishment

The emerging picture of the post-*Furman* capital-sentencing system in the United States raises obvious questions about that system's purpose. If Justice White was correct when he asserted that frequent death sentences in identifiable classes of cases are necessary to maintain a deterrent effect, then the system clearly is failing. Deterrence is, however, a difficult question.

It is quite possible that even a relatively few death sentences are sufficient to maximize the deterrent effect of capital punishment and that the marginal effect of imposing additional death sentences is slight. Indeed, the behavior of prosecutors and juries in post-*Furman* Georgia may reflect this view. Except for cases in which the motive for killing was to collect insurance proceeds, a defendant's having engaged in considerable premeditation appears to carry little weight with Georgia juries.[55] Prosecutors are somewhat more concerned with extensive premeditation,[56] but their willingness to forgo the death penalty in a vast number of capital-murder cases hardly suggests prosecutors believe securing additional death sentences would save additional lives.

With respect to the goal of retribution, the post-*Furman* results from Georgia are much clearer. The variables that best explain statistically the decisions of prosecutors and, especially, the decisions of juries all reflect retributive concerns (level of violence, the number of and vulnerability of victims, and the defendant's prior record). Our findings confirm the observation that, although legislators normally enact capital-sentencing statutes in order to create a deterrent, prosecutors and juries apply such statutes in individual cases from a retributive perspective.[57] Nevertheless, despite this concern with retribution, the low death-sentencing rates that exist nationwide and the number of presumptively excessive death sentences we found in Georgia suggest that the goal of retribution through the punishment of each defendant in accordance with his or her just deserts is satisfied in only a small number of cases. What is even more troublesome, from a retributive perspective, is that many of the nation's most egregious killers avoid the death penalty at various stages of the process. If, in fact, capital sentencing in the United States does not really advance in any meaningful way the goals of deterrence or retribution, its only remaining function must be symbolic.[58]

There is some evidence to support this hypothesis. Regardless of the small number of death sentences actually imposed, the strong political support in most states for the enactment of capital-sentencing statutes certainly expresses society's strong commitment to the sanctity of life and its outrage over the gratuitous infliction of extreme pain. Moreover, except for its corrosive effects on the legal process and the criminal-justice system, which are not widely perceived by the general public, maintaining the symbolic value of the system by imposing 250 to 300 death sentences each year appears to involve relatively little cost.

On the other hand, if the capital-sentencing system does serve a largely symbolic function, the moral and legal significance of our findings regarding excessiveness and discrimination become even more important. If the death penalty was the routine sanction for all aggravated murders, the comparative treatment of similarly situated defendants would be of little importance. But if society treats capital punishment as a scarce social resource to be imposed in only a few cases, then principles of comparative justice assume considerably greater weight.

In other words, the infrequent imposition of the death penalty, primarily for symbolic purposes, resembles the compulsory conscription of men for combat duty in wartime. Because only a fraction of those eligible for duty are selected, the evenhandedness of the selection process becomes a paramount consideration. For this same reason, if society is going to impose its most severe sanction upon a relatively small fraction of "eligible" defendants, not for reasons of retribution or deterrence, but as a moral gesture, surely that same social morality requires a selection process that reserves such symbolic executions for only the most culpable, blameworthy killers.

The Future of Equal Justice in Capital Sentencing

If we are correct that equal justice in death sentencing depends upon an effective system of oversight, the prospects for improvement in the post-McCleskey period appear to be slight. McCleskey has dramatically reduced the incentives for close oversight on the part of prosecutors and especially on the part of state supreme courts. Indeed, we expect that the process of proportionality review in many state supreme courts will continue as a mere formality or will be dropped altogether.

The *McCleskey* opinion did, to be sure, invite those concerned with the influence of race in death sentencing to seek relief from "the legislative bodies." Given the perceived public support for the death penalty and the lack of any compelling public concern about the fairness of the criminal process from the defendant's perspective, however, reform in the state legislatures seems unlikely.

The United States Congress, however, is a legislative body that has the power and may have the will to develop a system of oversight. Congress's authority to intervene in the criminal-justice system of the states flows from the enabling section of the Fourteenth Amendment, which gives it the "power to enforce, by appropriate legislation, the provisions" of the Fourteenth Amendment.[59] On several other occasions over the last twenty years, Congress has acted to protect minorities and disadvantaged people despite lukewarm public support or even overt opposition. Notable examples include civil-rights legislation concerning the vote, public accommodations, and housing.

To be sure, defendants convicted of murder beyond a reasonable doubt may not seem particularly deserving of similar protections, even if they receive death sentences that are attributable to their race or to the race of their victims. Certainly, the imposition of death sentences in such cases may not offend notions of disproportionality or "just deserts," since presumably any defendant whose only complaint is that his death sentence was racially discriminatory or otherwise comparatively excessive was convicted after a fair trial of a serious murder for which the legislature has authorized a death sentence. Nor do excessive or discriminatory death sentences cause injuries to particular minority groups comparable to those inflicted by housing or employment discrimination.[60] Nevertheless, trying to achieve consistency and rationality in capital sentencing is essential if we wish to maintain as a principle the dignity of the individual (including individuals convicted of capital crimes) and, equally important, to avoid the corrosive effect on society of judicially condoned racial discrimination. Society acknowledges and maintains the dignity of the individual by treating all persons with "equal concern and respect in the design and admininstration of the political institutions that govern them."[61] In the death-sentencing context, equal concern and respect requires a process that consistently evaluates each individual exclusively on the basis of those factors that genuinely relate to the legitimate penal objectives of capital punishment.

Racially discriminatory death sentences corrode the social order in at least two ways. First, they diminish respect for law and confidence in the administration of justice, particularly with respect to capital cases. Second, discriminatory death sentences demean the minority community and tacitly encourage racist behavior in other contexts. As Justice Brandeis said in 1928, in a different connection, "Our Government is the potent, the omnipresent teacher. For good or for ill, it teaches the whole people by its example. Crime is contagious. If the Government becomes a lawbreaker, it breeds contempt for law; it invites every man to become a law unto himself; it invites anarchy."[62] Regrettably, the corrosive effects of racially discriminatory death sentences can only be intensified when the highest court in the nation places its imprimatur on a death-sentencing system that demonstrably produces such results.

"The methods we employ in the enforcement of our criminal law have aptly been called the measures by which the quality of our civilization may be judged."[63] That quality has certainly declined since the days when, according to the Supreme Court, death sentences were valid only if meaningfully distinguishable from other cases that resulted in lesser sentences. Today, the law of the land is that objections based upon how others are treated are not cognizable because, if sustained, they would preclude the exercise of discretion. In the view of the *McCleskey* majority, at least, preserving discretion to impose death sentences in cases in which lesser sentences are usually imposed is more important than addressing the merits of the assertion that death sentences in such cases are comparatively unjust or discriminatory.

As we suggested earlier, the exercise by prosecutors and juries of their discretion to decide which capital defendants shall receive death sentences is an example of what Guido Calabresi and Phillip Bobbitt have described as "tragic choices"—those community or societal decisions to allocate or to withhold scarce resources that entail life-or-death consequences.[64] As a nation today, we convict between two and three thousand defendants each year of crimes for which capital punishment is an authorized sanction. Yet sentencing judges or juries only impose the death penalty in approximately 10 percent of those cases. The manner in which we select those who are condemned to die serves to define both those values that society espouses and those values that, operationally if not expressly, society rejects. As Calabresi and Bobbitt observed,

> We cannot know why the world suffers. But we can know how the world decides that suffering shall come to some persons and not to others. While the world permits sufferers to be chosen, something beyond their agony is earned, something even beyond the satisfaction of the world's needs and desires. For it is in the choosing that enduring societies preserve or destroy those values that suffering and necessity expose. In this way societies are defined, for it is by the values that are foregone no less than by those that are preserved at tremendous cost that we know a society's character.[65]

Over the last fifteen years the tension has increased in this country between the goal of preventing excessive or discriminatory death sentences and the demand for fewer restraints on capital sentencing and the resumption of routine executions. With the Supreme Court's significant withdrawal from the field, the future of equal justice in capital punishment now lies in the hands of state legislatures, the United States Congress, and state supreme courts acting under the authority of their state constitutions. Only time will tell whether these legislative and judicial bodies will reinstate our commitment as a nation to the principle of equal justice, without regard to race, even when dealing with those individuals whose conduct, quite rightfully, society most abhors.[66]

NOTES

1. *See supra* chap. 4 and app. A for a more detailed description of the methodology of the studies and the principal methodological issues they present.

2. Specifically, we were able to analyze separately the following decisions:

- prosecutorial and grand-jury indictment decisions;
- among cases indicted for murder, the prosecutorial decision to accept a plea bargain for voluntary manslaughter or murder;
- among cases that advanced to a guilt trial, the decision of the judge or jury to convict for murder or voluntary manslaughter;
- among cases that resulted in a murder conviction, the prosecutorial decision to advance the case to a penalty trial and seek a death penalty; and
- in penalty-trial cases, the jury death- sentencing decision.

The data-collection instrument in the CSS was an expanded version of the PRS instrument.

3. *See supra* chap. 2, note 48, and *supra* chap. 4, note 49 and accompanying text, for further discussion of the definition and measurement of the legal concepts involved.

4. Using these procedures, we developed indexes and scales for the following decision points in the PRS:

- pre-*Furman* death-sentencing decisions among defendants convicted of murder at trial;
- post-*Furman* death-sentencing decisions among defendants convicted of murder at trial;
- post-*Furman* decisions by prosecutors to seek a death sentence for defendants convicted of murder at trial; and
- post-*Furman* jury decisions to impose a death sentence in a penalty trial.

5. The race-of-victim results from the PRS are summarized fully in tables 43 & 44 of chap. 6 and briefly in table 64 of this chapter.

6. The statewide race-of-victim results from the CSS are summarized fully in tables 51 & 55 of chap. 10 and briefly in table 64 of this chapter. The Fulton County results are reported in tables 59–63 of chap. 10.

7. *See supra* chap. 8, table 48 and accompanying text.

8. *See supra* chap. 2, text accompanying note 38.

9. *See supra* chap. 3, text accompanying note 43.

10. *See supra* chap. 8, text accompanying notes 10–19.

11. *See supra* chap. 5, table 5 and accompanying text.

12. *See supra* chap. 6, tables 27 & 28 and accompanying text. The pre-*Furman* race-of-victim results are summarized *infra* table 64.

13. *See supra* chap. 6, note 10 and accompanying text.

14. *See supra* chap. 5, note 21 and accompanying text.

15. *See supra* chap. 5, table 10 and accompanying text.

16. *See supra* chap. 5, text accompanying note 46.

17. *See supra* chap. 6, note 56 and accompanying text.

18. *See supra* chap. 6, pages 186–87.

19. *See supra* chap. 6, table 43, for a summary of the post-*Furman* race-of-victim disparities.

20. *See supra* chap. 6, text accompanying notes 8 & 17.

21. *See supra* chap. 10, table 44 and accompanying text.

22. *See supra* chap. 6, note 22 and accompanying text.

23. *See supra* chap. 6, table 33 and accompanying text.

24. *See supra* chap. 5, text accompanying note 22.

25. *See supra* chap. 6, pages 183–84.

26. *See supra* chap. 7, table 46 and note 83 and accompanying text.

27. *See supra* chap. 8, text accompanying note 50.

28. *See supra* chap. 8, pages 251–53.

29. *See supra* chap. 8, pages 241–48.

30. The Georgia data revealed pockets of discrimination against black offenders (from rural prosecutors) and more punitive treatment of white defendants by urban prosecutors and juries—*see supra* chap. 6, table 42 and accompanying text (PRS); chap. 10, note 54 and note tables 10 & 11 (CSS).

31. *See, e.g., supra* chap. 8, text accompanying note 154.

32. *See supra* chap. 9, notes 8 & 16 and accompanying text.

33. *See supra* chap. 9, text accompanying note 19.

34. *See supra* chap. 9, text accompanying note 6.

35. The background record and rulings in the *McCleskey* decision are presented in chapter 10.

36. *See supra* chap. 10, note 112 and accompanying text.

37. *See supra* chap. 1, note 5, and chap. 2, note 18 and accompanying texts.

38. *See supra* chap. 2, text accompanying note 19.

39. Compare, for example, Georgia's statutory aggravating circumstances (*supra* chap. 3, note 18) with the factors that appear to be most influential in determining who is sentenced to death. *See supra* chap. 6, table 33 and accompanying text (PRS) & chap. 10, table 52 and accompanying text (CSS).

40. *See supra* chap. 10, note 4. However, not all state laws allow the juries to consider nonstatutory aggravating circumstances.

41. The R^2 of our best-fitting models based on legitimate case characteristics is .53, while the comparable R^2 for the model limited to statutory aggravating circumstances is .23.

42. We recognize, of course, that in Zant v. Stephens, 462 U.S. 862 (1983), *supra* chap. 10, note 4, the United States Supreme Court espoused a somewhat different role for statutory aggravating circumstances, one that did not contemplate the authoritative guidance of jury sentencing discretion, once the jury had found the defendant to be death-eligible. Nevertheless, Georgia courts do instruct sentencing juries concerning the particulars of the applicable statutory aggravating circumstances, and those juries do give specific attention to such instructions in the course of their deliberations. Consequently, it would be farfetched, indeed, to believe that those instructions have absolutely no influence on how juries decide to sentence death-eligible defendants.

43. The nation's response historically to capital punishment is comparable at sev-

eral levels to its response to other societal "tragic choices." *See* G. Calabresi & P. Bobbitt, TRAGIC CHOICES (1978); Hubbard, *"Reasonable Levels of Arbitrariness" in Death Sentencing Patterns: A Tragic Perspective on Capital Punishment*, 18 U.C. DAVIS L. REV. 1113 (1985).

44. F. Zimring & G. Hawkins, CAPITAL PUNISHMENT AND THE AMERICAN AGENCA 22 (1986) (hereinafter Zimring & Hawkins). The low post-*Furman* death-sentencing rates also support Hugo Bedau's hypothesis that the public-opinion polls strongly favoring of capital punishment probably reflect support for the legal threat flowing from "having the death penalty 'on the books' " rather than support for the execution of large numbers of convicted murderers. *American Attitudes Toward the Death Penalty*, in THE DEATH PENALTY IN AMERICA 68 (H. Bedau ed. 3d ed. 1980).

45. Weisberg, *Deregulating Death*, 1983 SUP. CT. REV. 305, 386–87 (hereinafter Weisberg).

46. The even lower execution rates of those sentenced to die, however, are in significant part the product of judicial decisions. *See* Greenberg, *Capital Punishment as a System*, 91 YALE L.J. 908, 919–22, 929–36 (1982).

47. If through deterrence each execution saves seven or eight innocent lives, as some proponents of capital punishment claim (Ehrlich, *The Deterrent Effect of Capital Punishment*, 65 AM. ECON. REV. 397, 414 [1975]), prosecutors are grossly derelict in their duties because they fail to seek death sentences in most of the death-eligible cases that they process. The low post-*Furman* death-sentencing rates strongly support Zimring and Hawkins's hypothesis that the Supreme Court in Gregg v. Georgia misinterpreted the post-*Furman* legislative backlash for public support for large-scale executions. Zimring and Hawkins also discuss the flow-control mechanism on the number of executions, the desire of actors in the process to "pass the buck," and the tendency of critics to blame the courts for the low level of executions. Zimring & Hawkins, *supra* note 44, at 95–105.

48. *See supra* chap. 9, text accompanying note 63.

49. Indeed, the workable premise of proportionality review is that it can "achieve a reasonable amount of harmony and consistency . . . so that at least in retrospect we can say we have acted in some sense" with the rationality we could have expected from a society seriously concerned with principles of comparative justice. *See* Weisberg, *supra* note 45, at 395.

50. If death sentencing is limited strictly to cases in which death sentences are the usual sentence, the risk of racial discrimination will be substantially reduced. *See supra* chap. 11, note 12 and accompanying text.

51. In his *Furman* dissent, Chief Justice Burger in fact attributed this complaint to Justices White and Stewart, but a reading of their respective concurring opinions indicates that their constitutional objections to standardless jury sentencing were somewhat more subtle than the chief justice suggested.

52. In fact, given the risk of excessiveness associated with low death-sentencing rates and the failure of its state supreme court to provide effective oversight, the proportion of evenhanded sentences imposed by Georgia's system is greater than one might expect to find. Besides Georgia, the only other state we have studied closely is Colorado. There, the death-sentencing rate is among the lowest in the nation, and that state's record for consistency in death sentencing is far less satisfactory than Georgia's. If adequate data are ever assembled, we would expect to find that the systems with the lowest death-sentencing rates also produce the highest proportion of excessive death sentences.

53. *See supra* chap. 9, note 1 and accompanying text.

54. *See* Special Project, *Capital Punishment in 1984: Abandoning the Pursuit of Fairness and Consistency,* 69 CORNELL L. REV. 1129 (1984).

55. Even though clearly relevant to the goal of deterrence, the duration of premeditation has no formal relevance under most death-sentencing statutes, including Georgia's.

56. The presence of substantial premeditation, which clearly brings the case into the deterrable category, has approximately the same statistical impact as the presence of a white victim.

57. *See* Rawls, *Punishment,* in PUNISHMENT: SELECTED READINGS 58, 59 (J. Feinberg & H. Gross eds. 1975).

58. *See* Zimring & Hawkins, *supra* note 44, at 10–15 for a perceptive analysis of the symbolic nature of capital punishment in this country:

> The experience of other Western countries illuminates an important aspect of death penalty legislation: its symbolic character. It also demonstrates the ritual or ceremonial function of the capital punishment statute, even if not invoked, and of the death sentence. The extensive ethnographic literature on ritual and symbolism focuses mainly on "primitive" societies, tending to overlook the collective ceremonials and focal rituals of large and complex modern societies. Our own twentieth-century institutions and practices, in which what Durkheim called the "collective consciousness" is expressed, have been largely ignored. But it seems likely that the symbolic significance of death penalty legislation, the ritual nature of the murder trial, and the incantatory power of the death sentence constitute a large part of the appeal for supporters of the death penalty.
>
> This may suggest an explanation for the curious ambivalence in contemporary societies that want to preserve death penalty legislation and murder trials yet appear to feel no need for executions. In a simple, homogeneous tribal society a human sacrifice performed with the intention of influencing or manipulating the course of human events is required. In larger, more complex societies the same psychological need is fulfilled, without an actual sacrifice, by the performance of the preliminary rituals. The latent social function is the same.

59. U.S. CONST. amend. XIV, §5.

60. Race-of-defendant discrimination against minority-group defendants disproportionately burdens members of the minority community. Also, race-of-victim discrimination that treats defendants with white victims more punitively than those whose victims are black denies the black community the same level of benefits from capital punishment enjoyed by the white community. For a "community-oriented" view of the consequences of race-of-victim discrimination that focuses on "the unfairness . . . [it] visits upon the black community by denying it equal treatment with respect to those who kill its members," *see* Kennedy, *McCleskey v. Kemp: Race, Capital Punishment and the Supreme Court,* 101 HARV. L. REV. 1388, 1391 (1988).

61. R. Dworkin, TAKING RIGHTS SERIOUSLY 180 (1977).

62. Olmstead v. United States, 277 U.S. 438, 485 (1928) (Brandeis, J., dissenting).

63. Coppedge v. United States, 369 U.S. 438, 449 (1962).

64. *See supra* note 43.

65. G. Calabresi & P. Bobbitt, TRAGIC CHOICES 17 (1978).

66. We can conceive of at least four congressional approaches to the problem, which vary in their potential for eliminating race discrimination in state capital-sentencing systems and in the level of federal intrusiveness in state capital-sentencing systems that they entail.

a. Further Study/Moratorium   One alternative would be major federal investigation of the scope and magnitude of the problem, similar to studies done in the 1960s on school segregation. *See* J. Coleman et al., EQUALITY OF EDUCATIONAL OPPORTUNITY (1966). A step in the this direction was a 1988 congressional requirement that the General Accounting Office

> conduct a study of the various procedures used by the several States for determining whether or not to impose the death penalty in particular cases, and shall report to the Congress on whether or not any or all of the various procedures create a significant risk that the race of a defendant, or the race of a victim against whom a crime was committed, influence the likelihood that defendants in those States will be sentenced to death. In conducting the study required by this paragraph, the General Accounting Office shall—
>
> (A) use ordinary methods of statistical analysis, including methods comparable to those rules admissible by the courts in race discrimination cases under title VII of the Civil Rights Act of 1964 [42 U.S.C.A. § 2000e et seq.]:
> (B) study only crimes occurring after January 1, 1976; and
> (C) determine what, if any, other factors, including any relation between any aggravating or mitigating factors and the race of the victim or the defendant, may account for any evidence that the race of the defendant, or the race of the victim, influences the likelihood that defendants will be sentenced to death.
>
> 1988 Anti-Drug Abuse Amendments to the Comprehensive Drug Abuse Prevention & Control Act; 21 U.S.C.A. § 484 (O) (2) (1989 Cumulative Annual Pocket Part)

A moratorium on executions pending the completion of a congressionally ordered study is another possibility.

However, the statistical and other evidence already available may be sufficient to justify more specific congressional intervention. The data presented and discussed in this book demonstrate, we believe, that, without some form of systematic oversight of state death-sentencing systems, many death sentences will be the product of race-of-victim discrimination.

b. Prohibition of Race Discrimination in State Death Sentencing   Another possibility would be to prohibit discrimination in state death-sentencing systems on the basis of the race and sex of the defendant and the race of the victim, in the same manner that federal law currently prohibits discrimination in employment, 42 U.S.C. §§2000e–2000e-17 (1982) ("Title VII"), and housing, 42 U.S.C. §§3601–3631 (1982) ("Title VIII"). Claims raised by individual death-row inmates would be subject to the burdens of proof generally applied under federal civil-rights statutes. Claimants could establish that their death sentences were discriminatorily imposed or that the statute was applied in a manner that was discriminatory in purpose and effect on the basis of the race or sex of the defendant or the race of the victim. If the burdens of proof in capital-sentencing cases were consistent with the standards applied in employment litigation, it would be possible for a defendant to base an individual claim of purposeful discrimination initially on statistical evidence of systemwide discrimination. When the state could not adequately explain such a discriminatory pattern of death sentencing, the burden of proof would shift to the state to prove that each death sentence was neither influenced by race or sex discrimination nor within the range of cases that present an unacceptable risk that race or sex influenced the claimant's death-sentencing decision. This approach is similar to the remedy suggested by Justice Stevens in *McCleskey*—"[I]t is necessary for the District Court to determine whether the particular facts of McCleskey's crime and his background place this case within the range of cases that present an unacceptable risk that race played a decisive role in McCleskey's sentencing." McCleskey v. Kemp, 107 S.Ct. 1756, 1806 (1987) (Stevens, J., dissenting). This burden-shifting function upon a showing of strong classwide disparities is analogous to the shift in the burden of proof that occurs in classwide disparate-treatment cases under the equal-protection clause in jury-discrimination cases and under Title VII in employment discrimination cases. International Bhd. of Teamsters v. United States, 431 U.S. 324, 360–62 (1977). *Supra* chap. 11, note 8.

A legislative approach modeled after Title VII is embodied in the proposed "Racial Justice Act," introduced in the House of Representatives by Congressman John Conyers in 1988 (H.R. 4442, 100th Cong., 2d sess. (1988)) and 1989 (H.R. 2466, 101st Cong., 1st sess. (1989)) and later in the Senate by Senator Edward Kennedy. The Senate version prohibits the execution by the federal government or any state of a death sentence "if that person's death sentence furthers a racially discriminatory pattern" based on the race of either the victim or the defendant. On October 17, 1989, the Senate Committee on the Judiciary adopted the Senate version of the Racial Justice Act as an amendment to the Federal Death Penalty Act of 1989 and reported the amended measure to the Senate without a recommendation. S. Rep. No. 101–170, 101st Congress, 1st sess. 5 (1989). The Senate bill further provides that racial disparities can be established with "ordinary methods of statistical proof" without the necessity of showing "discriminatory motive, intent, or purpose on the part of any individual or institution" (§2922(b)). A prima facie case of a "racially discriminatory pattern" may be established with statistical evidence that death sentences are "imposed or executed" with a "frequency that is [racially] disproportionate" (§2922(c)). To rebut a prima facie case, the government "must establish by clear and convincing evidence" that legitimate factors "persuasively explain" the observable racial disparities (§2922(2)).

Also, in October 1988, during the United States Senate debate leading to the enactment of a federal death penalty for certain drug-related murders, an amendment that would have applied the Racial Justice Act to the federal law was defeated by a 35–52 vote. 1988 U.S. Code Cong. & Admin. News, S 15755–56.

Following the Title VII and Title VIII models, it may be appropriate in legislation like the Racial Justice Act to empower the attorney general to bring actions claiming a pattern and practice of discrimination in a state capital-sentencing system. 42 U.S.C. §§20000e-6, 3613 (1982).

c. The Use of Federal Funding to Encourage Nondiscriminatory Death Sentencing
Another possible approach would be to use United States financial support for the state criminal justice systems as leverage to encourage the states to monitor their own systems to ensure that they are not racially discriminatory. In fiscal year 1986, for example, more than $70 million in federal funds were provided to support the criminal justice systems of the various states under the Justice Assistance Act of 1984. OMB, Budget of the U.S. Government, 1988, Appendix I- O25 (1987). States and local units of government receive discretionary grants for "technical assistance" and block grants to improve state criminal justice systems, "with special emphasis on violent crime and serious offenders." 42 U.S.C.A. §3761(a)(2), 3743(a) (West Supp. 1987). These funds are subject to suspension by the Office of Justice Programs through the attorney general in a specific program receiving funds if a "pattern or practice" of race or sex discrimination has been established in the program. 42 U.S.C.A. §3789d(c)(2)(A)(i), (C)(ii) (West Supp. 1987). Since it is unclear whether state death-sentencing systems are sufficiently supported by federal payments made under these programs to make this remedy applicable to most state death-sentencing systems, one alternative would be to extend the nondiscrimination requirement to include the operation of the state's

death-sentencing system regardless of the federal funds allocated to death sentencing. Also, the act could be amended to give death-row inmates a private right of action under the statute comparable to the private right of action under Title VI. *See* Regents of the University of California v. Bakke, 438 U.S. 265, 418–21 (1978) (Stevens, J., concurring in the judgment in part and dissenting in part).

d. Attorney General Oversight   Congress might also consider adopting a system of federal oversight similar to the one contained in section 5 of the 1965 Voting Rights Act. 42 U.S.C. §1973(c) (1982). That law requires "covered" local governments that seek to change their voting laws to demonstrate to the attorney general of the United States that the proposed changes are not discriminatory either in purpose or in effect.

Applied to capital sentencing, this model would simply require states whose death-sentencing systems reflect the symptoms of racial discrimination to satisfy the attorney general that, in fact, their death-sentencing statutes are operating in a manner that is nondiscriminatory in purpose and effect. Moreover, consistent with the Voting Rights Act model, the attorney general's certification that the system was or was not operating satisfactorily would be subject to federal judicial review under standards comparable to those generally applied in discrimination litigation under civil rights statutes.

The preliminary showing that would be required of a state to obtain the attorney general's certification might be a measure that considered the practical and statistical significance of both race-of-victim and race-of-defendant disparities in death-sentencing rates. The "⅘th" rule used by federal agencies in their oversight of employment practices is an example of such a measure. The "⅘th" rule triggers federal investigation of selection procedures when the selection rate for women or minorities is ⅘ (80 percent) of the selection rate for men or the majority group. *Uniform Guidelines on Employee Selection Procedures*, 29 C.F.R. §1607.4(D) (1986). The information needed to determine which cases are death-eligible under each state's laws, and which result in death sentences and executions under state laws, could be provided by the states to the Bureau of Justice Statistics of the Department of Justice, or added to the present Supplemental Homicide Reports provided to the FBI by local police.

APPENDIX A

Methodology Appendix

A major concern in any empirical study is the extent to which weaknesses in the research methods used may have biased the reported results. A major finding of our two empirical studies, the Procedural Reform Study (PRS) and the Charging and Sentencing Study (CSS), was that the sentences imposed during the first six years of Georgia's post-*Furman* capital-sentencing system were marked improvements over those imposed during the pre-*Furman* era in terms of excessiveness and race-of-defendant discrimination. We still found, however, that in the PRS approximately one-third of the post-*Furman* death sentences were presumptively excessive; we also found in both studies evidence of persistent race-of-victim discrimination among cases in the mid-aggravation range. How likely, therefore, is it that our research methodology may have artificially enhanced or suppressed the observed levels of arbitrariness or discrimination in either the pre- or post-*Furman* periods?

The validity of any research method is subject to challenge. The specific threats involved, however, depend on the method used. In both studies, this fact prompted us to employ a variety of measures, which allowed us to "triangulate" on the problems of excessiveness and discrimination.[1] Specifically, we used three principal measures to assess the relative culpability of each case, which in turn determined what cases should be considered "similar" in their blameworthiness:[2]

1. An *a priori* measure that weighed aggravating and mitigating circumstances on the basis of intuition and common sense (the "intuitive *a priori*" method)
2. An empirical measure that classified cases on three general dimensions according to the presence or absence of thirty-five specific case characteristics identified as relevant on the basis of intuition and common sense (the "intuitive empirical" method)
3. An empirical method that ranked cases by the presence of case characteristics identified with logistic and linear multiple-regression analyses as sharing a statistically significant association with sentencing results (the "regression-based-index" method).

An important basis for our confidence in the validity of our empirical findings is the generally consistent results produced with these three methods across both studies. This suggests that potential threats to validity unique to each study and to each of the three different methods probably did not distort the results they produced. This consistency tells us nothing, however, about the potential impact of threats to validity that were common to both studies and to all three measures.

In this appendix, we first discuss the threats to validity common to all three measures, with an emphasis on differences between the PRS and CSS. We then consider the threats to validity that were unique to one or both of the intuitively based measures or unique to the regression-based-index measure.

Several of the threats to the validity of our studies enumerated in this appendix were also raised by United States Federal District Judge J. Owen Forrester in his decision rejecting the discrimination claim of Warren McCleskey on methodological grounds. Because Appendix B of this book deals with those issues in detail, at several points in this appendix we refer the reader to its relevant portions.

THREATS TO VALIDITY COMMON TO ALL
   REPORTED RESULTS

Representativeness of the Samples

The PRS sample for the post-*Furman* period includes all cases in the universe of interest, that is, all Georgia cases that resulted in a murder-trial conviction or the imposition of a death sentence. Although we cannot generalize our results beyond 1978, other studies of later periods in Georgia show comparable race-of-victim effects.[3] However, because inclusion of a case in the study is conditioned on the presence of a jury-trial conviction, the results are potentially subject to sample-selection bias produced by earlier decisions for which the PRS has no data—pretrial prosecutorial charging and plea-bargaining decisions as well as the jury guilt-trial decisions. We discuss this problem below.

Because of both financial constraints and the unavailability of data in the Georgia Board of Pardons and Paroles before 1970, our PRS pre-*Furman* data set is smaller. It is also a nonrandom sample, since it includes during its time frame only a few death cases before 1970.[4] However, based on the death-sentencing rates in Georgia and nationally during the 1960s and 1970s, there is no reason to believe that the death-sentencing rates and the nature of the cases were substantially different for the 1970–72 period (for which we have both life- and death-sentence cases) and for the 1960s, a period for which our sample includes only a few life-sentence cases. Accordingly, we believe that our inclusion of the 1960s death-sentence cases did not bias the pre-*Furman* results. The pre-*Furman* sample is, however, also potentially subject to sample-selection bias in the same manner as the post-*Furman* PRS data.

The css sample is a stratified-probability sample that includes all death-sentence cases, all penalty-trial life-sentence cases of which we were aware during the study, and a sample of the remaining murder and voluntary-manslaughter cases. The sample, which is described in chapter 4, deviated from the strict probability model, however, with respect to the death-sentence cases. Twenty-eight of the 128 death-sentence cases were not on the Department of Corrections' list of prisoners from which our probability sample was drawn, even though they satisfied the requirements for inclusion in the study. We included those cases to ensure full coverage of death-sentence cases. The supplemental death-sentence cases were not on the Department of Corrections' list because the defendants were being held in local jails pending the completion of their appeals. Although we have no firm data on the question, we believe that defendants in death-sentence cases are more likely to be detained in local facilities longer than are other defendants who are less likely to appeal their convictions (a very large proportion of which are entered on guilty pleas), and when appeals are taken in those cases they are decided more rapidly than the average death-sentence case. However, to test for the possibility of bias from the inclusion of these death-sentence cases from outside the original sampling frame, we conducted a race-of-victim analysis with the supplemental cases excluded; the results were essentially the same.[5]

The css study is also potentially subject to sample-selection bias because, as is indicated in figure 1, chapter 4, it does not include information on death-eligible cases that did not result in a conviction for murder or voluntary manslaughter.

The Validity of the Data Bases

Both the PRS and the css involve the collection of data on hundreds of variables from a variety of data sources by a number of different coders. In an enterprise of this magnitude, a certain degree of coding and transcription error is inevitable. As we discuss more fully in Appendix B, however, we believe that the errors in our data base are random and would be quite unlikely to bias the central findings of the PRS and css concerning excessiveness and discrimination.[6]

The Potential for Bias from Omitted Variables

As noted in chapter 4, in order to identify excessive death sentences or a statistical disparity in the treatment of different racial subgroups, one must compare groups of cases that are similar in all the legally relevant features that might otherwise serve to distinguish one from another.[7] The possibility of overlooking such variables is the principal threat to the validity of this sort of analysis. Methodologists consider such an omission to be a form of model-specification error.

In the case of our Procedural Reform Study, one danger of overlooking relevant variables would be a distortion of our comparative-excessiveness analysis because we incorrectly estimated the relative culpability of the cases. If prosecutors and juries actually disposed of cases on the basis of some legitimate case characteristics of which we were unaware, our culpability ranking of the cases, whether done by intuition or by multiple-regression analysis, may be incorrect and may distort or bias our selection of groups of "similar" cases.

An omitted variable could also bias the results of our race-of-victim and race-of-defendant analyses in both the PRS and CSS if the variable omitted from the analysis influenced the decisions of prosecutors and juries and if certain values of that variable occurred more frequently in one racial subgroup than in the other. The omission of relevant variables could bias the race disparities estimated in the racial analysis upward or downward.

For example, suppose that we construct a system for arranging cases into five groups: "very mitigated," "somewhat mitigated," "neither aggravated nor mitigated," "somewhat aggravated," and "very aggravated." If all cases within any of these groups are similar in all legally relevant respects, then any racial disparities within those groups cannot be explained in any legally relevant way. For example, one might encounter a statistical analysis of jury death-sentencing decisions such as that shown in Table 65. In group 3, there are fifty cases (twenty-five with black victims and twenty-five with white victims) that resulted in a murder conviction after trial. Of these fifty cases, fourteen white-victim cases and eleven black-victim cases resulted in death sentences. In other words, juries imposed death sentences in 56 percent of the twenty-five white-victim penalty-trial cases and in 44 percent of the black-victim penalty-trial cases; this yields a 12-percentage-point disparity, suggesting a more punitive treatment of white-victim cases.

Now suppose that, in grouping cases, a legally relevant variable was overlooked—for example, the defendant's demeanor. If juries take into account whether defendants in a category such as group 3 have a negative or a positive demeanor (i.e., whether they seem remorseful or defiant and unrepentant), then the racial disparity shown in Table 65 may be distorted. For example, if negative defendant demeanor occurs relatively more frequently in white-victim cases than in black-victim cases, then in groups of cases that appear to be statistically indistinguishable the white-victim cases will actually be more aggravated on average than the data included in the study suggest. As a consequence, there would be an alternative explanation for some or all of the

Table 65. Death-Sentencing Rates for Five Groups of Hypothetical Cases that Resulted in a Capital-Murder Conviction

	A	B	C
	Jury Death-Sentencing Decisions[1]		Disparity (white victim– black victim rate)[2]
Matched Groups of Cases	White Victim	Black Victim	
Group 1. Very mitigated	1/12 (8%)	1/16 (6%)	2
Group 2. Somewhat mitigated	12/36 (33%)	6/24 (25%)	8
Group 3. Neither aggravated nor mitigated	14/25 (56%)	11/25 (44%)	12
Group 4. Somewhat aggravated	11/15 (73%)	13/19 (68%)	5
Group 5. Very aggravated	17/18 (94%)	24/26 (92%)	2

1. Expressed as the number of death sentences over the number of cases advanced to a penalty trial, and as the percentage resulting in a death sentence.
2. White-victim rate minus black-victim rate, expressed in percentage points.

black/white-victim disparities depicted in column C of Table 65, and the race-of-victim analysis would be biased by the omitted variable. To illustrate, Table 66 indicates how an omitted variable can create the appearance of racial bias in jury penalty-trial decisions for cases in group 3 of Table 65; we see that the 12-percentage-point race-of-victim disparity shown in Table 65 for this group, taken as a whole, vanishes when cases are further broken down according to the defendant's demeanor.

All nonexperimental, observational studies are vulnerable to this form of bias. For example, some commentators have criticized studies that link smoking with negative health effects because, they argue, the disparity between the

Table 66. Further Analysis of Racial Disparities in Group 3 Cases Shown in Table 65

	A	B	C
	Jury Death-Sentencing Decisions[1]		Disparity (white victim– black victim rate)
Matched Subgroups of Cases	White Victim	Black Victim	
Positive demeanor	2/5 (40%)	8/20 (40%)	0
Negative demeanor	12/20 (60%)	3/5 (60%)	0
Totals[2]	14/25 (56%)	11/25 (44%)	12

1. See supra table 65, note 1.
2. Same as group 3 in table 65.

medical histories of smokers and of comparable nonsmokers may, in fact, be due to some unobserved factor, perhaps genetic.[8]

However, the mere possibility of an "omitted variable bias" is not proof of bias. Three conditions must be present before a missing variable can bias a racial-discrimination analysis. First, one or more relevant factors must be omitted from the analysis. Second, alone or in combination with other variables, the omitted factor must be correlated with and actually influence outcomes of the process being studied. And third, within each group of matched cases, the omitted factor must be correlated with the racial variable at issue because it is distributed unequally between the racial subgroups involved (for example, between the white- and black-victim cases). Thus, in the omitted-demeanor hypothetical, missing-variable bias might very well occur if, for example, prosecutors and juries were influenced by negative defendant demeanor (the correlation with the outcome variable) and defendants with negative demeanor were substantially more common in white-victim cases (the correlation with the racial-status variable). In Appendix B we discuss the likelihood that the race-of-victim disparities estimated in the PRS and CSS are an artifact of omitted variables.[9]

Sample-Selection Bias

Missing-variable bias of the type described above can occur whether or not there are multiple selection steps involved in the process under investigation. However, when the individuals at risk at a particular decision point are themselves the product of a series of prior decisions in a winnowing-type system (like the American criminal justice system), the potential problem of omitted-variable bias can be exacerbated. In this study, our sample of PRS cases (murder-trial convictions) was the product of a series of decisions by police, prosecutors, judges, and juries commencing with the defendant's arrest.[10] The defendants in our data set had received repeated consideration at several points following arrest, at each of which the decision maker could have insulated the defendant from any further risk of a death sentence. The discretionary decisions that might have eliminated the defendant as a candidate for a death sentence are as follows:

1. A failure to charge with any crime, or a charge or indictment for a crime less than murder;
2. Reduction of the murder charge at the prosecutor's request to a lesser charge in exchange for a guilty plea;
3. Waiver by the prosecutor of the death penalty before trial in exchange for a guilty plea to the charge of murder; and
4. Acquittal, or conviction at trial of an offense less serious than capital murder.

The decisions made at each of these stages can alter the relative distribution of important omitted variables at the next stage in the process.

Thus sample-selection bias is a potential danger in studies of multistage selection processes like ours that estimate race effects through an analysis of cases that have been selected by an investigator for inclusion in the universe of a study on the basis of decisions of actors in the process that precede the decisions under investigation in the study. Sample-selection bias has the potential of distorting estimates of racial effects (or indeed any effects) because of biased selection of cases at earlier stages. There is a potential risk of sample-selection bias in the PRS because the sample of cases is limited to jury murder-trial convictions that were the result of prosecutorial pretrial decisions and the jury's guilt-trial decision. The risk is less in the CSS, since we have information on pretrial decisions in our sample. Nevertheless, we lack data on preindictment decisions and on postindictment decisions resulting in case dismissals or convictions for crimes less serious than voluntary manslaughter.

There are, however, four conditions that must exist before sample selection can introduce any additional bias.[11] The first is that there exist unmeasured characteristics of the cases, such as defendant demeanor, witness credibility, or the socioeconomic status of the defendant's attorney, which are not reflected in the models used to measure case culpability. The second and third conditions are that these unmeasured characteristics influence both the selection decisions of actors in the early stages of the process that are used to define the universe of cases being studied, and the substantive decisions that are the subject of the study. For example, in the PRS, a risk of sample-selection bias would exist if an unmeasured factor, such as defendant demeanor, were correlated with both the likelihood that a given defendant's case would result in a murder-trial conviction (the selection decision that brought the case into the study) and the likelihood that the defendant's case would be advanced to a penalty trial or result in a death sentence being imposed in a penalty trial. The fourth condition that must exist for sample selection to introduce additional bias is race-of-defendant or race-of-victim discrimination at the earlier selection stage or stages of the process, which define the universe of cases to be studied.

When these four conditions exist, there is a risk that the estimated racial disparities in the analysis of the data, produced by the earlier selection decisions, will be biased by the impact of the unmeasured factor on the previous selection decisions that produced the data being analyzed. The direction and degree of bias in the estimates produced from the sample depend upon the following three factors: the direction and magnitude of the correlations between the unmeasured factor(s) at the various decision points (in the PRS case, the pretrial and trial-selection decisions and the posttrial sentencing decisions); the direction and magnitude of racial discrimination at the earlier selection stage(s) of the process; and the rate at which the cases in the study were selected from similarly situated cases in the preselection pool of cases.[12] For example, assume in the PRS that defendants with white victims suffer discriminatory treatment at the earlier selection stages of the process and that an unmeasured factor such as prosecutorial aggressiveness is positively correlated with both the earlier selection decisions bringing the cases into the study and the post-guilt-trial sentencing decision being analyzed (that is, the more aggressive the prosecutor, the more likely the case will result in both a murder conviction and a death sentence after trial). Under these assumptions, the observed race-of-victim effects, suggesting that the defendants in the sample who killed white victims received more punitive treatment, will be biased downward. A recent discussion of a similar hypothetical concludes:

> Selection thus induces a correlation between race and prosecutor aggressiveness in the selected sample. When prosecutor aggressiveness is left unmeasured, some of its effect on more severe sentence outcomes will be picked up by the selected [black-victim cases], thus diminishing, or underestimating, the effect of any discrimination against [white-victim cases] in sentencing.[13]

Sample selection can also bias upward the racial effects observed in the sample in two different situations. The first arises when the direction of the bias at the selection stage is in the "unexpected" direction. For example, if, in the PRS example just described, the unmeasured variable of prosecutor aggressiveness was positively correlated with both the selection and sentencing decisions, but black-victim cases were treated more punitively at the selection stage, the race-of-victim effect at the sentencing stage would be biased upward rather than downward.

The second situation in which the race-of-victim effect will be biased upward occurs when the racial bias is in the expected direction at the selection stage and the unmeasured case characteristic is correlated with the selection and sentencing stages, but those correlations with the two stages are in opposite directions. For instance, in the PRS prosecutor-aggressiveness example, the race-of-victim effects in the sample could be biased upward if the unmeasured prosecutor-aggressiveness variable were positively correlated with the outcomes of the selection step (conviction of capital murder) but negatively correlated with imposition of a death sentence, or vice versa. It seems very unlikely that many, if any, variables exist that could produce reverse correlations in this manner. Accordingly, we consider it highly unlikely that the race-of-victim and race-of-defendant disparities we estimated for the sentencing stages of the PRS are statistical artifacts. More plausible, we believe, is the possibility that our estimated race-of-victim and race-of-defendant effects may have been biased downward by any sample-selection bias that may exist.

Quantitative Estimates of Selection Bias

Berk and Ray discuss two simple models of selection/decision processes embodying the relationships described above that can be applied to estimate the approximate size of a selection-bias artifact in logistic-regression models.[14] For this discussion, we use a somewhat more flexible form of the Gumbel type I bivariate-logistic model referred to in their paper.[15]

As noted above, three factors may combine to bias the race effects estimated with the cases in our sample:

1. The direction and magnitude of the effects of unmeasured variables (such as prosecutor aggressiveness) at the "selection" stage, which produced the sample of cases used in our studies, and at the "decision" stages, at which the defendants in our sample were sentenced to death or to life imprisonment; in the PRS, the "selection" stage embraces all of the decisions that culminated in a jury murder-trial conviction, while in the CSS the selection stage refers to the series of pre- and postindictment decisions that resulted in some outcome other than a conviction for murder or voluntary manslaughter (such a conviction being the predicate for inclusion in the CSS);

2. The direction and magnitude of the racial effects at the selection stages that brought the cases into the two studies; and

3. The odds, measured by a selection rate, that the cases in our studies had of being selected from similarly situated cases when they were in the preselection pool of cases.[16]

Of these three components, we are able to estimate in the PRS (on the basis of frequency cross-tabulations provided by Gross and Mauro) that the race-of-victim effect at the selection step, which brought the cases into our sample, is +.79, and the race-of-defendant effect is +.08, expressed as logistic-regression coefficients.[17] With these same data we estimate that the conviction rate[18] exceeds .54 for moderately aggravated cases (category 2 or higher on scale CSCALB).[19] The remaining component of selection bias (correlation between the unmeasured effects at the selection and decision stages) is unknown. However, if we assume the worst case (either $R = +1$ or $R = -1$), the formula in note 16 implies a selection bias in the range from $-.36$ to $+.13$ (in the logistic-regression coefficient) for race of the victim and a selection bias in the range of $-.04$ to $+.02$ for race of the defendant. A negative bias means that the estimate of the impact of the measured variables of interest understates the true disparity, while a positive bias implies that the estimate overstates the true disparity.[20] Since all the potential biases in either direction are small compared to our estimated race-of-victim effects, selection biases of the magnitude suggested by this analysis would not substantially alter our overall results. Moreover, the Gross and Mauro data indicate that there is race-of-victim discrimination in the selection stages in the expected direction. Thus, to the extent selection bias did influence our results, for the reasons stated above that influence would be to understate our race-of-victim estimates. In the case of the jury model, we have data for the selection step in which prosecutors advance murder-conviction cases to a penalty trial. As a result, we can more precisely estimate the magnitude of selection bias in our analysis of jury decisions by fitting the Gumbel type I bivariate-logistic model to both decision points. Using this method, we estimated selection biases of $-.24$ for race of victim and $+.07$ for race of defendant. This means the race-of-victim effect in the jury analysis would appear to be larger in the absence of selection bias, while the race-of-defendant effect would have been even smaller.

Also, in the Charging and Sentencing Study we were unable to detect any significant racial effects at the selection stage after comparing our data with Gross and Mauro's. Therefore, we believe that selection bias is unlikely to have distorted the racial effects which we estimated at later decision stages.

Threat from a Skewed Distribution of White- and Black-Victim Cases among Judicial Circuits

Another potential threat to the validity of our race-of-victim estimates is the possibility that they may have resulted simply from a disproportionate concentration of white-victim cases in judicial districts with high death-sentencing rates. For example, if white-victim cases occurred with a disproportionate frequency in judicial circuits with the highest death-sentencing rates, the death-sentencing rate for white-victim cases statewide might well exceed that for black-victim cases, even though the victim's race played no role in the sentencing decisions in any jurisdiction of the state. This would be an example of "Simpson's paradox."[21]

The possibility of this type of distortion concerned us because, as already noted, death-sentencing rates in different judicial circuits and geographic regions of Georgia vary considerably. To test the possibility that the race-of-victim effects observed in our PRS analysis reflected unusually high death-sentencing rates in the areas with a disproportionate number of white-victim cases, we estimated the race-of-victim effects after adjustment for the type "B" culpability index (estimated to measure racial disparities), the defendant's sex and socioeconomic status, the urban or rural character of the judicial circuit, the region of the state, and the identity of the judicial circuit.[22] In a similar analysis in the CSS, six circuits (Cobb, Northern, Eastern, Ocmulgee, Macon, and Toombs) emerged as having unusually high death-sentencing rates, and two (Fulton and Southern) had particularly low rates. The presence of background controls for these geographic variables (in an analysis with the control variables listed in Appendix L, schedule 10) did not, however, affect the magnitude or statistical significance of the race-of-victim disparities estimated statewide. If our estimated race-of-victim effects were an artifact of high death-sentencing rates in regions or circuits with a disproportionately high number of white-victim cases, adjustment for these geographic variables would eliminate or sharply reduce the observed race-of-victim effects. The results of these analyses indicated, however, that adjustment for the place of trial did not appreciably affect either the pre- or post-*Furman* results.[23] We are confident, therefore, that the racial disparities observed in the aggregate data did not result from a skewed distribution of white-victim cases among regions or circuits with high death-sentencing rates.

THREATS TO THE VALIDITY OF MEASURES BASED ON INTUITION AND COMMON SENSE

For two of our measures, one *a priori* (the weighing measure in the PRS) and one empirical (the Barnett classification system in the PRS), we relied to varying degrees on intuition and common sense when identifying important variables and weighing their relative significance as a means of estimating relative case culpability. The use of intuitive judgment permitted us to identify aggravating or mitigating circumstances that might dramatically affect the outcome in a particular case, but that occur so infrequently that they would be overlooked by a more systematic, statistical analysis.

Nevertheless, intuitive judgments are basically ad hoc. As a result, they pose a greater risk of inconsistency in the classification of cases and a real danger of overlooking important factors. The *a priori* weighing measure is particularly susceptible to these risks. By contrast, although Professor Barnett's classification system also employed intuition and common sense, its vulnerability to such risks is much smaller. Professor Barnett employed a classification system consisting of some thirty-five fairly objective factors.[24] In addition, he classified cases not on the basis of a single holistic judgment but on the basis of three separate judgments reflecting the three main characteristics of the case—a procedure that reduced the consequences of misclassifying a case on any one dimension. Finally, Professor Barnett tested the soundness of his measures with alternative coders and found it to be quite reliable.[25]

THREATS TO THE VALIDITY OF THE RESULTS PRODUCED WITH REGRESSION-BASED CULPABILITY-INDEX METHODS

There is considerable debate in the literature and in court opinions about the validity of multiple-regression analysis as a tool for evaluating complicated decision-making processes. Some of these objections apply to all regression analyses. Others, however, relate only to particular uses of regression. For example, if one uses regression procedure simply to rank the cases by relative culpability, one confronts substantially fewer potential threats to validity than if one employs partial-regression coefficients (for example, for the race-of-victim variable) as a measure of discrimination. For this reason, when the data permitted, we employed in the PRS the regression-based indexes simply as a vehicle for ranking cases; we used partial-regression coefficients as a supplemental, although important, measure of the impact of given variables. One should also note that the results of the race-of-victim and race-of-defendant analyses that we obtained using these alternative methods were quite comparable.[26] In the CSS, however, we relied more heavily on multiple-regression coefficients as a basis for estimating racial disparities.

There are two general threats to the validity of all regression results. The first is the circularity inherent in using factors identified as most predictive of the observed results as the basis for testing a system's consistency. The second is the tendency of multiple-regression analyses to generate a unique, overfitted solution with respect to a particular set of decisions, compounding the problem. The result is that matches based upon factors identified in a multiple-regression analysis utilizing all of the data generated by a system tend to exaggerate the degree of consistency within the system. For this reason we believe the measures of excessiveness produced by our regression- based index in the PRS underestimate the level of excessiveness in the Georgia death-sentencing system, both before and after *Furman*. We note, however, that the degree of underestimation does not appear to be large, since Professor Barnett's results, based upon a very different culpability measure, were quite similar.

To the extent to which we did rely on regression results, we generally preferred logistic to linear-regression procedures. However, we used least-squares regression methods in addition to logistic procedures for two reasons. First, for the purpose of developing a culpability index and scale for matching cases, as opposed to developing structural models of the charging-and-sentencing process, the index model produced by linear regression has the highest possible Pearson correlation with the outcome variable. Second, the index produced by linear regression is equivalent (apart from a change of origin and unit) to the index produced by linear-discriminant analysis, a widely accepted linear technique for analyzing a binary-outcome variable. Indeed, linear-discriminant analysis can be viewed as an alternative way of estimating the logistic model.[27] If case characteristics are approximately normally distributed, discriminant analysis produces a more accurate estimate of the culpability index; however, logistic regression is more robust than linear-discriminant analysis when case characteristics are not approximately normally distributed. Thus, OLS and logistic regression are reasonable ways to approach both the problem of modeling the effects of racial characteristics and the problem of sorting cases with respect to level of culpability. We are therefore reassured by the agreement using both linear and logistic methods. (See, e.g., Tables 43 and 44, which summarize the results from our race-of-victim analysis.)

We also conducted both regular and stepwise multiple regressions. The rationale for the use of stepwise regressions in this study is presented in Appendix B.[28] We also present there a discussion of the magnitude of the R^2 produced by our multiple-regression analyses.[29]

Another potential threat to the validity of our results concerns the basic characteristics of the logistic-regression model. A principal finding of our study of both pre- and post-*Furman* Georgia was that racial discrimination occurs primarily in the midaggravation range of cases. We made this observation when we measured the magnitude of the race effects with partial-regression coefficients and when we quantified the relative treatment of white-victim and black-victim cases in different culpability levels. However, there is at least a potential risk that the large race-of-victim effects on the midrange of cases may be an artifact of the basic characteristics of logistic-regression analyses. Specifically, the "sigmoid" curve of predicted probabilities generated with the logistic-regression model assumes that the impact of any given factor on the predicted probabilities will be largest in the midrange of cases.

This can be seen in Figure 33, which illustrates for the post-*Furman* PRS cases the relationship between the regression-based culpability score and the predicted sentencing outcomes produced by the logistic-regression analysis. The horizontal axis identifies the range of case culpability scores, while the vertical axis indicates the range of predicted death-sentencing probabilities. The plot of small dots locates each of the 594 post-*Furman* cases according to its culpability score and predicted likelihood of a death sentence. For example, the cases on the plot with an index score of 75 (point A) have a predicted death-sentencing probability of .76.

Figure 33 also illustrates the relationship between the predicted death-sentencing probabilities and actual death-sentencing rates. As noted earlier, we divided the post-*Furman* cases into six subgroups of cases with comparable culpability scores; the six heavy dots on Figure 33 indicate the actual death-sentencing rates for those subgroups. For example, dot A represents 34 cases with scores ranging from approximately 75 to 80 on the culpability index. The actual death-sentencing rate for those cases was .73. A comparison of the

Figure 33. Plot of Predicted and Actual Death-Sentencing Frequencies in Logistic Multiple-Regression Analysis (PRS)[1]

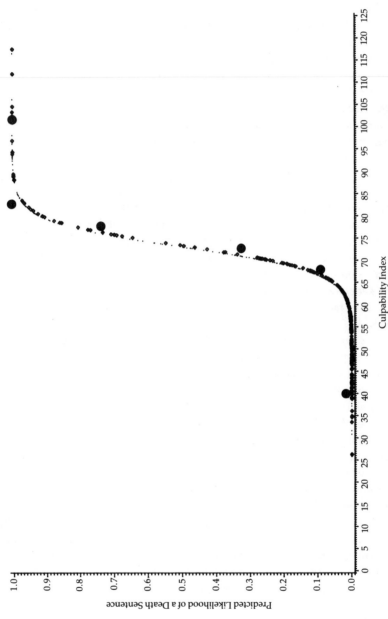

Predicted Likelihood of a Death Sentence

Culpability Index

1. The small plotted entries are the predicted death sentences. The large dots are the actual death-sentencing rates among similarly situated offenses.

predicted and actual rates shown in Figure 33 for the six subgroups of cases indicates that the predicted death-sentencing rates estimated by the logistic model match or "fit" the actual data quite well.

To test whether the race effects we observed in the midrange were an artifact of the logistic-regression model, we conducted diagnostic analyses with logistic models that permitted the pattern of predicted outcomes to deviate from this curve if that better explained the actual results. We also conducted similar analyses using linear multiple-regression models. In each analysis, the predicted outcomes gravitated toward the sigmoid curve underlying the logistic-regression procedure. We concluded, therefore, that for our data logistic-regression analysis best estimates the relationship between case culpability scores and death-sentencing outcomes, both actual and predicted, and that the concentration of race effects in the midrange of cases is not a statistical artifact of logistic regression.[30]

As noted above, our principal use of multiple-regression analysis in the PRS was to rank the cases by their relative culpability, as reflected by the decisions of prosecutors and jurors when seeking and imposing death sentences. The only additional threat to the validity of these rankings of any importance, besides those already mentioned, is multicollinearity. Multicollinearity exists when independent explanatory variables are correlated with both the outcome variable and each other. Severe multicollinearity could threaten the validity of the results by confounding the effects of race with those of other variables or by introducing a misranking of the cases, although there is no *a priori* basis for estimating how multicollinearity might bias either the excessiveness or the discrimination analysis.

To estimate the potential danger of multicollinearity to our results, we conducted multicollinearity diagnostics in the course of constructing our underlying logistic-regression models.[31] The results of these diagnostics indicate that multicollinearity poses no danger to our regression models. Appendix B presents further discussion of the multicollinearity issue.

To further validate our culpability rankings in the PRS, we read a 100–300-word narrative summary for each case and, based on intuition and common sense, determined if the rankings were correct. This process enabled us to consider intangible and subjective factors that were not reflected in the statistical models. As a result, we made a few minor adjustments to the case rankings, which did not change our substantive findings.[32]

To the extent that we employed partial-regression coefficients to estimate the race-of-victim and the race-of-defendant effects, there are other potential threats to validity. First is the problem of "misspecification," that is, the inclusion of inappropriate variables in the model or the exclusion from it of influential variables. None of the variables in our data set is inappropriate per se; each one might plausibly influence a capital-sentencing decision. We also conducted an extensive screening procedure to identify for inclusion in the model variables that shared a statistically significant relationship with the outcome variable. We conducted a similar analysis for large numbers of interaction terms that we constructed with the variables that shared statistically significant relationships with the outcome variables.[33]

Although all of the variables included in this screening process were plausibly related to the sentencing outcome, we found in both the PRS and CSS that for certain variables the multiple-regression analysis produced a regression coefficient, the sign of which was contrary to what we expected. For example, a mitigating variable might yield a positive regression coefficient, giving it an aggravating "weight." This suggested the possibility that including such variables in the model in the PRS was inappropriate. Alternatively, the sign of such a coefficient might reflect perversity or arbitrariness in the operation of the system. Our final post-*Furman* overall model in the PRS included two variables whose coefficients ran in an unexpected direction. On the basis of further analysis, we attributed one of these contrary coefficients to perversity in the system and the other to possible misspecification.[34]

MISSING DATA

Missing data is always a problem for empirical studies. It takes on statistical importance when data are missing from the file of one or more cases for a particular variable and the information represented by that variable was available to and known by the decision makers who processed the cases under study. For example, in a wage-discrimination case, if the measures of employee productivity in the study included education and experience, the absence of data in the case of one or more employees for either of these variables would create a missing-data problem so long as the employer-defendant was aware of the educational and experience levels of all employees. The standard practice in such cases is either to impute the missing data from other similar cases in which the data are present, or to delete from the analysis either the variable for which the data are incomplete or the cases in which the data are missing.

Because of the complexity of the death-sentencing process, our questionnaire sought information about a large number of legitimate, illegitimate, and suspect case characteristics as well as the procedural characteristics of the case. For any given defendant, the records we consulted might be silent about any number of the items covered by our questionnaire. In that regard, we treated cases in which the files contained no information about a legitimate characteristic differently from cases in which there was no information concerning illegitimate or suspect characteristics or procedural features of the case. If the missing information related to legitimate case characteristics, we coded the variable as unknown and treated the characteristic as not present in the case rather than as an instance of missing data. This protocol is explained in detail in Appendix B.[35]

Variables for illegitimate or suspect factors and for the procedural characteristics of the cases presented real missing-data problems.[36] That a case file does not include information concerning suspect or illegitimate factors does not mean that the officials who processed the case were ignorant of those factors. Because the characteristic involved is illegitimate or suspect, there is little incentive to include that information in any official record. Indeed, in some situations the incentive might be quite the opposite, even though the information is known by all concerned. Consequently, if the official records were silent, we had to make further efforts to learn the actual facts of each case with respect to suspect and illegitimate factors.

For the race of the defendant we were able to obtain information for all cases. We failed to obtain race-of-victim information in five cases in the PRS and in sixty-two cases in the CSS. These unknowns also presented a true missing data problem.

The files of the Department of Offender Rehabilitation, the Georgia Supreme Court, and the Georgia Board of Pardons and Paroles provided various indications of the defendant's socioeconomic status. There was, however, a substantial amount of missing information with respect to these variables. To deal with this problem, we created for each study a composite variable (LSTAT-DEF) that classified a defendant ("1") as being of low socioeconomic status based on the following criteria: Did he have appointed counsel? If that information was unknown, was he classified as being of low socioeconomic status in the Department of Offender Rehabilitation file? If that information was unknown, did he have an unskilled or blue-collar job? If that information was also unknown, did he have eight or fewer years of education?[37] After we classified the cases using this composite variable, there was only one case with a missing value for the defendant's socioeconomic status.

There was no missing information on the sex of the defendant; consequently, we could include this suspect variable in our analysis without difficulty. On the other hand, for the IQ of the defendant, the data provided by the Department of Offender Rehabilitation included substantial amounts of missing information that was correlated strongly with the sentencing outcome. As a result, we excluded the IQ variable from our study.

The files contained sufficient data concerning two additional suspect variables to include them in the analysis. One was the variable for high-status defendant (HISTD), for which information was missing in 3 percent of the cases (10 percent in death cases and 2 percent in others).[38] We coded this variable as absent when the information was missing because it seemed more likely that the status of the defendant would appear in the files if it was high. Besides, there were only an estimated sixty-four high-status defendants (3 percent) in our universe of cases. The second suspect variable was the defendant's out-of-state residence (DOUTSTAT). We were missing values for this variable in 2 percent of the cases (7 percent for death cases and 2 percent for others). We coded these defendants as in-state residents because 92 percent of the defendants with a known residence were from Georgia.

We also lacked information on whether a penalty trial occurred in a number of life-sentence murder cases. For every case appealed to the Georgia Supreme Court we were able to obtain this information; the problem concerned those cases in which there was no appeal. In these cases, we first sent questionnaires to prosecutors and defense attorneys, who were generally very cooperative; but we were still left with twenty-three cases in the PRS and twenty cases in the CSS for which the penalty-trial information was unknown. Our treatment of these missing-data issues is described in Appendix B.

MEASUREMENT ERROR

Another concern in a study of this type is whether the data we collected correctly reflected the status of the case characteristics that are included in the study. One question is whether the data in the files we consulted accorded with the perceptions of the prosecutors or juries who actually processed the cases. We coded about half of the cases from the files of the state supreme court, relying most heavily on the briefs because, as noted above, the prosecutors and defense counsel would have the greatest incentive to ensure accurate presentations of the aggravating and mitigating circumstances of each case.

We coded the other half of the cases from the files of the Georgia Board of Pardons and Paroles and the opinions of the Georgia Supreme Court in cases that were appealed.[39] The parole board investigators who prepared these files obtained the data from local court records, police reports, and conversations with police and prosecutors. Furthermore, they made their inquiries after the defendant had been sentenced. Thus, it is possible that the information presented in their reports might be biased in a way that supports the sentences imposed. To the extent such bias did exist, however, it would tend to minimize the observable race effects rather than to exaggerate them. It would also minimize the observed level of excessiveness in the system.

Another source of possible reporting bias might be a tendency by those who provided information to parole board investigators to describe the circumstances of the white-victim and black-defendant cases in an aggravated direction. This bias would cause such cases in our study to appear to be more aggravated than they actually were, thus reducing the observed race-of-victim and race-of-defendant effects.[40]

Another measurement-error question concerns the accuracy with which our coders recorded the data from the court and parole board records. We are reasonably confident that this is not a serious concern. First, our coders received extensive training. Second, to promote consistency in coding we prepared a detailed set of guidelines on the most frequent issues of interpretation. Third, coders periodically rechecked each other's work. Furthermore, to the extent coding errors did occur, we have no reason to think they were other than random and therefore would not bias our results. This is particularly true with respect to the race-of-victim analysis, because in most cases we learned the victim's race from sources other than court or parole board records.

NOTES

1. *See supra* chap. 4, note 19 and accompanying text.

2. These measures are described in detail *supra* chap. 4, at 49–52. For further discussion of methodological issues in capital-sentencing studies, see *Symposium, Statistical Studies of the Law and Justice System: Racial Discrimination in Capital Sentencing*, in PROCEEDINGS OF THE THIRD WORKSHOP ON LAW AND JUSTICE STATISTICS 1985, at 55–77, Bureau of Justice Statistics, U.S. Dept. of Justice (G. Woodworth ed. 1988).

3. *See supra* chap. 8, note 152 and accompanying text (a 7.2 race-of-victim odds multiplier estimated by Gross & Mauro after adjustment for five background factors for the period 1976–78).

4. The distribution of the life and death sentences in the pre-*Furman* sample is presented *supra* chap. 4, note 2, and chap. 5, and fig. 7.

5. When the twenty-eight supplemental cases were removed from the core thirty-nine-variable model (*see supra* chap. 4, note 43), the logistic coefficient for the race-of-victim variable declined from 1.45 ($p = .006$) to 1.19 ($p = .02$), while the coefficient for the race-of-defendant variable increased from .06 ($p = .87$) to .18 ($p = .68$).

6. *See infra* app. B, note 22 and accompanying text.

7. *See supra* chap. 4, at 46–50.

8. *See* Brown, *Statistics, Scientific Method, and Smoking* in STATISTICS: A GUIDE TO THE UNKNOWN 59 (J. Tanur et al. eds. 2d ed. 1978).

9. *Infra* app. B, at 460–61. This example illustrates the rather perverse behavior that must be postulated on the part of prosecutors to produce spurious race-of-victim effects.

10. The stages are described *infra* chap. 4, at 40–42 and fig. 1.

11. *See* 1 RESEARCH ON SENTENCING: THE SEARCH FOR REFORM 102–8 (A. Blumstein, J. Cohen, S. Martin, & M. Tonry eds. 1983) (hereinafter Blumstein et al.).

12. With respect to this third factor, all other things being equal, the lower the selection rate, the higher the potential for bias.

13. Blumstein et al., *supra* note 11, at 106.

14. *See* Berk & Ray, *Selection Biases in Sociological Data*, 11 SOC. SCI. REV. 352 (1982).

15. The Gumbel type I distribution of disturbances (effects of unmeasured variables) is a bivariate-logistic distribution,

$$F(u,v) = \frac{\exp(u+v)}{(1 - R + \exp(u) + \exp(v) + \exp(u+v))}.$$

Here, u and v represent the magnitude of the disturbances at the selection and decision stages, respectively, *exp* is the exponential function, and R is a parameter that determines the correlation between u and v. R lies between -1 and $+1$; a negative R implies negative correlation, and a positive R implies positive correlation. The actual correlation is a complex function of R; the most positive rank correlation is about .3 at R = 1 and the most negative is about $-.48$ at R $= -1$.

16. Selection bias is given by the following formula:

$$\text{Bias} = \log \frac{(1 - R + \text{odds of conviction for bv cases})}{(1 - R + \text{odds of conviction for wv cases})}$$

$$- \log \frac{(1 + \text{odds of conviction for bv cases})}{(1 + \text{odds of conviction for wv cases})}.$$

17. Estimated by weighted linear regression of empirical logits on predictors.

18. We excluded the least aggravated cases from this analysis because they contributed virtually nothing to the race-of-victim effects estimated in our sample. The "conviction rate" refers to the rate at which the cases in our sample were selected from similarly situated cases in the preselection stages of the process.

19. This is the scale used for estimating race effects in the overall model. It reflects the combined effect of both prosecutorial decisions to seek and jury decisions to impose death sentences. *See infra* app. J, part 1, for the model.

20. We also estimated separately the range of likely bias for the race-of-victim and race-of-defendant coefficients estimated in the prosecutorial and jury decisions in our sample. The results for the prosecutors' analysis also implied bias in the range of $-.36$ to $+.13$ for the race-of-victim and $-.04$ to $+.02$ for the race-of-defendant estimates. The results estimated for the jury analysis (which were obtained by using a slightly different procedure) are described in the next paragraph of the text.

21. A well-known study of graduate school admissions at the University of California at Berkeley provides an example of Simpson's paradox. The aggregated data in the Berkeley study indicated that men were accepted at a much higher rate than women, clearly suggesting sex discrimination. In fact, however, each department within the graduate school, which made the admission decisions, actually favored women over men. The aggregated data were misleading because women applied predominantly to the more competitive departments (e.g., English and History), for which overall admission rates were low, while the men applied predominantly to less competitive departments with high admission rates. *See* Bickel, Hammel, & O'Connel, *Sex Bias in Graduate Admission: Data from Berkeley*, in STATISTICS & PUBLIC POLICY 113–30 (W. Fairley & F. Mosteller eds. 1977).

22. *See supra* chap. 4, note 39 and accompanying text, for a description of the "type B" culpability indexes used in these analyses. The procedure involved a separate variable for each region and circuit.

23. The race-of-victim logistic coefficients estimated in the post-*Furman* analyses were: prosecutor, $b = 1.6$ ($p = .001$); jury, $b = 2.45$ ($p = .01$); and overall model, $b = 1.63$ ($p = .01$). For the pre-*Furman* analysis, the results were: $b = 2.1$ ($p = .001$)

for race of the victim and $b = 1.6$ ($p = .05$) for race of the defendant. In all of these runs, the geographic variables were forced in except for the circuits. Those variables were entered if they showed a statistically significant relationship (beyond the .05 level) with the dependent variable.

24. *See* Barnett, *Some Distribution Patterns for the Georgia Death Sentence*, 18 U.C. DAVIS L. REV. 1327, 1364–66 (1985). These factors are presented *infra* App. F.

25. *See id.* at 1370–71.

26. *E.g., cf.* the 8-percentage-point race-of-victim effect estimated after adjustment for the three Barnett dimensions (fig. 22) versus the 8.5-percentage-point disparity estimated after adjustment for the regression-based culpability index.

27. *See* Efron, *The Efficiency of Logistic Regression Compared to Normal Discriminant Analysis*, 70 J. OF THE AM. STAT. A. 892–98 (1975).

28. *See infra* app. B, note 60 and accompanying text.

29. *See supra* chap. 4, notes 52 & 53 and accompanying text, and *infra* app. B, note 55 and accompanying text, which discuss the magnitude and significance of the R^2 estimated with our linear models.

30. Letting C represent the culpability index with racial variables removed, we introduced C^2, CW, C^2W, CB, and C^2B into the logistic-regression model. Here B and W are dummy variables indicating a black defendant and/or a white victim, respectively. None of the additional terms (C^2, CW, C^2W, CB, or C^2B) was statistically significant at the 10% level. Thus, there is no evidence that culpability and racial effects are nonadditive on the log-odds scale. Consequently, it appears that the sigmoid logistic curve adequately describes the data.

A second test entailed fitting unweighted-least-squares regression involving C, C^2, C^3, B, W, CB, CW, C^2B, C^2W, C^3B, and C^3W. Here we used only 244 cases with culpability levels in the middle range so that the OLS model would not overshoot 0 or 1. We compared graphs of the resulting OLS curves and corresponding logistic curves to actual death-sentencing rates in graphs similar to fig. 33. The graphs for the OLS regression model mirrored the sigmoid character of logistic regression and followed the actual data within the limits of statistical error. It is significant that the OLS procedure selected this shape, since the model specification was flexible enough to allow a wide variety of curve shapes to be fit to the data.

The OLS curves for black- and white-victim cases exhibited the "liberation effect" feature of the logistic model; that is, the disparity in death rates between black- and white-victim case variables is small or nonexistent at each end of the culpability scale but large at intermediate culpability levels. Again, it is significant that the OLS procedure selected as the best model one that exhibited this characteristic. This OLS procedure considered a large set of candidate models, most of which did not exhibit this characteristic.

31. We generated multicollinearity diagnostics with the REG procedure of the SAS statistical software package. Logistic residuals, $(y-\hat{p})/\hat{p}\hat{q}$, were regressed against the independent variables; cases were weighted by $\hat{p}\hat{q}$. Here y is a binary outcome variable and $\hat{p}$ is the predicted probability that $y = 1$, given the values of the independent variables. Collinearity diagnostics produced by this program show the proportion of variance of each regression coefficient associated with each principal component of the variance-covariance matrix of the independent variables. Collinear sets of variables are identifiable by high proportions of variance associated with the same minor principal component. If a group of independent variables displayed high multicollinearity and involved a perverse sign, such as a positive regression coefficient for a mitigating factor,

we attributed the perverse sign to collinearity and removed from the model the least substantively meaningful variable in the collinear set. Neither the race-of-victim nor the race-of-defendant variable *ever* appeared in a collinear set; therefore, there is no ambiguity in their effects. Collinearity could not explain all perverse signs; these variables we left in the main models. *See* SAS USERS GUIDE: STATISTICS (1982); D. A. Belsley, E. Kuh, and R. E. Welsh, REGRESSION DIAGNOSTICS (1980).

32. But, one might ask, why use multiple-regression analysis at all if the investigator can modify the results by intuition and common sense? Why not simply rank the cases on this basis at the outset and avoid the cost and complexity associated with statistical analysis? In fact, if the total number of cases to be considered is sufficiently small, this can be an acceptable approach. The main advantages of regression analysis are its ability to process large numbers of cases and to identify explanatory variables that may be overlooked if one proceeds strictly on the bases of intuition and common sense.

33. The logistic model specifies the log odds of an adverse outcome at a decision point given the facts embodied in the independent variables. Outcomes of separate cases are assumed to be independent, given the facts. This assumption is probably not strictly true, since verdicts in prior similar cases may influence prosecutorial decisions in a subsequent case. However, this effect is likely to be weak. The principal specification problem is that of selecting what functions of the independent variables to include in the model. We addressed this difficulty using residual analysis.

Logistic residuals, *see supra* note 31, were correlated with variables not in the model and with interactions of variables in the model (see text above) to identify terms omitted from the model, which we then added. The log-linear form of the model was checked by offering nonlinear terms for inclusion in a stepwise logistic-regression analysis.

We also estimated racial effects in other ways that did not depend upon the specification of a regression equation. For example, we used cross-tabulations based on a regression-based index like table 32; case matching by expert raters, as in table 31; and the analysis produced with Arnold Barnett's three-dimensional classification system, as in fig. 22. All of these analyses revealed race-of-victim disparities among matched cases.

34. The overall model for the post-*Furman* period (OVERALLA) produced a large and statistically significant coefficient for the variable that the defendant had cooperated with the authorities, suggesting that such cooperation was an aggravating factor in the case. Even though the variable is included as an enumerated mitigating factor in many state death-sentencing statutes, cooperation frequently entails a confession and detailed description of the crime, including its gory details. This additional information in turn strengthens the state's case and will frequently enhance the perceived aggravation level of the case. It was for this reason that we considered this coefficient evidence, although understandable, of perversity in the system. The second variable with a perverse sign was one indicating when a crime involved both kidnapping and multiple shots. The presence of such a combination reduces the chances of a death sentence. We can conceive of no explanation for this result and therefore consider it likely evidence of misspecification. In the post-*Furman* jury model, we found two variables with unexpected signs; one we attribute to perversity, the other to misspecification. In the prosecutorial model, there was one variable with an unexpected sign (an interaction between the defendant's being a young adult and the case having no victim-mitigating circumstances), which we attribute to perversity in the system. In the pre-*Furman* model, all coefficients had signs in the expected direction.

35. *See infra* app. B, text accompanying note 23.

36. We consider the race of the victim and the race of the defendant to be illegitimate factors, while suspect factors include the sex, education, and socioeconomic status of the defendant. Current law suggests that these factors are either inappropriate to consider or, if they are considered, that the practice requires substantial justification.

37. At each step in this process, the LSTATDEF variable would be coded "1" for "yes" if the data justified the low-socioeconomic-status classification.

38. The defendant was classified as high-status if the record indicated he or she was a white-collar worker, proprietor/shop owner, professional, or executive. The post-*Furman* data set included twenty-five white collar workers, two proprietor/shop owners, two professionals, and no executives.

39. The opinions of the Georgia court were particularly rich in detail in the death-sentence cases. However, in the life-sentence cases, the appeal generally focused on errors in the guilt trial, and the description of the circumstances of the crime was often skimpy or omitted.

40. See *supra* chap. 6, at 161–62, for further discussion of this issue. For evidence of similar bias in the characterization of cases by prosecutors, see Radelet & Pierce, *Race and Prosecutorial Discretion in Homicide Cases*, 19 LAW & SOC'Y REV. 587 (1985).

APPENDIX B

McCleskey v. Kemp: A Methodological Critique of the District Court's Decision

This appendix is a critique of the district court's evaluation of the research findings we presented in *McCleskey v. Kemp*.

We first address the rulings and analysis of the district court concerning the validity of our research methodology. Judge Forrester's opinion identified as defective numerous features of our data bases and the statistical procedures that we employed. In many respects, we believe Judge Forrester either misread the record or simply misunderstood generally accepted standards of research methodology.[1] The Eleventh Circuit, by contrast, assumed the validity of our studies and did not review any of the district court's methodological rulings. It did not, however, accept the ultimate inferences concerning discrimination suggested by the studies. Moreover, the Eleventh Circuit's majority opinion made frequent, uncritical, and supportive references to Judge Forrester's methodological findings. Similarly, although the United States Supreme Court assumed the validity of our studies in the same manner as the Court of Appeals, Justice Powell's opinion stated that Judge Forrester considered our study "with care" and listed without comment the principal rulings of the district court faulting our research methodology.[2] The result is that Judge Forrester's rulings—which we believe to be erroneous—stand unchallenged and uncorrected. Indeed, other courts have relied upon some of those rulings.[3]

Because the empirical studies presented in *McCleskey* represent a major investment of our time and personal commitment, we cannot be regarded as objective either with respect to the validity of our research or with respect to Judge Forrester's rulings. We hope, however, that this appendix will clarify the methodological issues in the case and will facilitate an evaluation of the manner in which the courts treated our research by those who are more detached.

THE ACCURACY AND COMPLETENESS OF THE DATA BASE

Judge Forrester ruled that our data base was so substantially flawed that the petitioner had failed to establish by a preponderance of the evidence that it was "essentially trustworthy."[4] We believe that his analysis of our data base is deficient in three important regards. First, Judge Forrester ignored or minimized the strengths of the research-design and data-collection procedures used. Second, he identified what he considered to be numerous deficiencies in the study based on speculation or insufficient evidence, or in the face of unrefuted testimony directly to the contrary. Third, and most important, Judge Forrester failed to assess adequately whether and, if so, to what degree the deficiencies that he identified biased or in any way influenced the substantive results of the research.

It is also important to emphasize that McCleskey's case rests upon two distinct and independently conducted empirical studies. The first was the Procedural Reform Study (PRS), which we undertook as an empirical test of a theoretical model we developed as part of an interdisciplinary undertaking sponsored by the University of Iowa and supported by a National Institute of Justice grant. The second study, the Charging and Sentencing Study (CSS), was designed and conducted with litigation in mind. Consequently, we subjected the data-collection effort in the CSS to much more extensive and effective methods of quality control. Moreover, compared to the PRS, the CSS is more extensive in scope, and, as one might expect, McCleskey's claims rested more heavily on it than on the PRS. Judge Forrester failed to distinguish adequately between the different quality of the data-collection efforts in these two studies, thus creating the impression that the asserted deficiencies of either study are common to both.

Ignoring or Minimizing the Strengths of the Studies

In at least six different respects, we believe, Judge Forrester minimized the strength of the empirical studies that McCleskey offered. First, he understated the completeness of the information available to the coders. His opinion implied that the records of Georgia's Board of Pardons and Paroles were skimpy and incomplete. This is simply incorrect. To the contrary, the parole board's records reflect the results of an extensive investigation carried out by the parole board officials shortly after each homicide conviction occurred. The purpose of the investigations is to provide a complete picture of a case to be used as a basis for later parole or clemency decisions by the board. A representative of the Board of Pardons and Paroles testified that these investigations are especially thorough, and that the investigators routinely examine relevant court papers and all police records as well as interview prosecutors and police officers.[5]

Judge Forrester's characterization of the two- or three-page factual summary of each case found in the parole board files as "only" that long is surprising.[6] Two or three pages is far more than is needed to capture the essence of these cases. Few opinions of the Georgia Supreme Court devote two or three pages to a statement of the facts bearing on a defendant's culpability.[7]

Second, Judge Forrester's opinion simply ignored the scope of the research questionnaire and the richness of the resulting data sets, particularly for the CSS. No sentencing study to date had included as many variables as are found in the CSS. The judgment of Professor Richard Berk, who evaluated the quality and soundness of both studies in light of his prior comprehensive review of sentencing research for the National Academy of Sciences, is particularly relevant:

> [Baldus's studies] ha[ve] very high credibility, especially compared to the studies that [the National Academy of Sciences] reviewed. We reviewed hundreds of studies on sentencing . . . and there's no doubt that at this moment, this is far and away the most complete and thorough analysis of sentencing that's been done. I mean there's nothing even close.[8]

An examination of the variables listed in Appendix F gives the reader a sense both of the subtlety and variety of the variables included in that study and of the implausibility of the claim that important variables have been omitted from these data sets.[9]

Third, Judge Forrester minimized the extensive training and supervision that the coders received, particularly in the CSS. The CSS coders were law students who received training in Georgia under the personal supervision of Professor Baldus and the coding supervisor, Edward Gates, who himself had acquired extensive coding experience from his earlier work in Georgia on the PRS.[10] Thereafter, Gates maintained regular contact with Baldus by telephone and routinely supervised and spot-checked the work of the coders.[11]

Fourth, the trial court diminished the extensive efforts that were made, especially in the CSS, in developing coding protocols to promote consistency. The court incorrectly implied that the protocol embodied only two rules.[12] In fact, the CSS protocol ran to twenty-three pages and included more than one hundred rules.[13] The conventions to which Judge Forrester objected only came into play when a matter was not covered by one of the more specific rules.

Fifth, the court ignored evidence of the effort, particularly in the CSS, to ensure accurate entry of the data from the questionnaires into the computer. The estimate given by the professionals who entered the data was that there was an error rate of no more than one-sixth of 1 percent in the data-entry process.[14]

Finally, the court ignored the testimony concerning the extensive efforts that were made to "clean" the data after their entry into the computer, a process that included a cross-check (between the PRS and the CSS) of the coding for all of the variables for statutory aggravating circumstances.[15]

Exaggerating the Degree of Error in the Data Sets and the Extent
  to Which the Error Biased the Central Findings of the Studies

Coding Errors

The first major defect in the data base that Judge Forrester identified was a miscoding of the questionnaires. He based his findings in this regard primarily upon an analysis presented by the State's expert, who claimed that, among the more than 350 murder cases that appeared in the PRS and the CSS, there were a number of "mis-matches" resulting from the erroneous coding of the variables. However, this claim is unwarranted.[16]

First, evidence of a diverse coding for a particular variable in the two studies does not necessarily establish a coding or data-entry error. These studies used different data sources and, more important, different rules of interpretation. For example, in the PRS, on the basis of the available information, the coders exercised reasonable judgment as to what they believed had actually occurred in a case. For the CSS, the coders' task was simply to report the information available from the parole board's records.[17] In other words, the PRS coders exercised much more discretion than the CSS coders.[18] Moreover, the coding protocols used in the two studies were different.[19] Finally, although there were factual errors, a number of the claimed "mis-matches" involved judgments about which different observers could reasonably disagree.

In light of these claims of coder errors, Professor Baldus conducted two different investigations of alleged miscodings. He found that most of the inconsistencies were the product of different coding protocols or reasonable differences in the interpretation of the record.[20] On the basis of this study, Baldus testified that, at most, the error rate from coding and data entry for either study would be not more than one-half of 1 percent, and that the error rate for the PRS was higher than that for the CSS, the better-controlled study.[21]

What is most important, however, is that it is extremely unlikely that random errors of the sort that Judge Forrester identified would bias any of the central findings of the study. Although Judge Forrester accepted the State's assertions regarding alleged miscoding, he gave no consideration at all to Baldus's testimony on this point. Nevertheless, random coding or data-entry errors would not likely affect the validity of the substantive results, and the State did not refute or challenge this proposition in any respect during the *McCleskey* proceedings.[22]

Treatment of Variables Coded Unknown and of Missing Data

Variables for Legitimate Case Characteristics   According to Judge Forrester, the second major weakness in the data base was the CSS coding protocol applicable when the available records for a case did not indicate whether a legitimate case characteristic was present. In such a situation, the coders were instructed to code the variable "U" for "unknown."[23] For purposes of the statistical analysis, case characteristics coded "unknown" were treated as absent in the case and coded "0" (as contrasted to a coding of "1" when the records indicated that the factor was present). The presumption underlying this coding convention was that the parole board files reflected what information was known to the actors in the system.[24] We make this assertion because the briefs filed in the Georgia Supreme Court and the records of the Georgia Board of Pardons and Paroles, our principal data sources, generally included all the information concerning the legitimate case characteristics that were known to the prosecutors and juries. The reason is that those who prepare such documents recognize the importance of reporting fully and accurately all the relevant facts for later use.[25] We also read the opinions of the Georgia Supreme Court, which would often, especially in death-sentence cases, present a full description of the crime, the victim, and the defendant for each case that was appealed. Thus, when a file did not mention a legitimate case characteristic, the other information in the file would generally indicate that the unknown factor was not present in the case or, if it might have been present, that the prosecutor and jury were unaware of it. For example, if the case involved a convenience store holdup, the lack of any reference to a rape would support an inference that no rape took place, and the correct coding of such a case would be that no rape occurred.

In other situations, however, silence with respect to a legitimate case characteristic would not necessarily mean that it was absent. The variable "victim pled for his/her life" provides a good example. Sometimes the records include positive evidence of the variable; in many other cases there is clear evidence that no such pleading occurred. From time to time, however, when the defendant did not confess and no other witnesses were present, it is impossible to determine if the victim pled for his or her life. In this case, of course, the prosecutor and the jury would also have no way of knowing whether the variable was present.[26] We also presumed that, if the prosecutors and the juries were unaware of a particular fact concerning a case, it would not affect their decisions. Information, not ignorance, is the stimulus for a decision; without a stimulus, there can be no response.[27] For this reason, we do not consider such codings for legitimate case characteristics as "missing data" that were known to the decision makers but not known to the investigators.

However, Judge Forrester apparently misunderstood this statistical protocol and the meaning of an "unknown" coding. He stated that a coder would not have coded a variable as unknown "unless there was something in the file which made the coder believe that the factor could be present."[28] In other words, Judge Forrester construed an "unknown" coding to mean "unsure" or "uncertain." In fact, as we testified on several occasions, under the coding protocol for the css a variable would be coded "unknown" only when the record provided absolutely no information concerning a factor in the case and no basis existed for inferring either the presence or absence of the factor. [29]

This coding protocol for "unknowns" is the generally accepted procedure for sentencing studies based upon public records of the type involved in this case. [30] It is particularly appropriate when the people who prepared those records had every incentive to report all the relevant information about the case. As previously noted, parole board investigations in homicide cases usually included interviews of the prosecutors and the police. If either the investigating officers or the prosecuting attorneys considered a factor to be important, it seems highly unlikely the parole board investigator would omit it from his or her report. [31]

The State's experts made absolutely no effort to show that the "unknowns" were truly "missing data"—that is, variables that might have influenced the prosecutors or jurors, but for which our studies lacked the relevant information. Nor did the State's experts even attempt to show how any such "missing data" could have biased the results in any way. [32] In this connection, Richard Berk testified that, based upon the results of our statistical analyses, it was quite unlikely there would be a significant discrepancy between the information available to us from the files and what the prosecutor or, in the cases that went to trial, the jury actually knew about the case. He also stated that the impact of such errors, if any, would likely be slight. [33]

Finally, Professors Woodworth and Baldus performed a "worst case" analysis to test the potential impact of the "missing data" criticism. They reestimated the race effects after all of the variables originally coded "unknown" were recoded in the manner most supportive of the sentence imposed in the case; that is, they recoded "unknown" mitigators as present in life-sentence cases and as absent in death-sentence cases, and they recoded "unknown" aggravators as present in death-sentence cases and as absent in life-sentence cases. [34] As one might expect, these recoded adjustments reduced the observed race-of-victim effects somewhat, but they did not disappear or lose their statistical significance. [35]

Missing Data on Racial and Procedural Variables   Judge Forrester also identified four variables for which there were genuine "missing data." However, he overstated the magnitude of such omissions and ignored our demonstration that, at worst, the possible impact of such omissions on our results was trivial. [36] For example, Judge Forrester criticized the study because there were data missing concerning the race of certain victims. He stated that the studies lacked "any information on the race of the victim where there were multiple victims."[37] In fact, the record indicates that we did record the race of all victims in multiple-victim cases. Our problem was properly classifying a multiple-victim case as a white-victim or black-victim case when the victims were of both races. The coding protocol we adopted classified any case in which there was one or more white victims as a white-victim case.

It is also true that in .008 (5/593) of the cases in the PRS and in .06 (62/1,083) of the cases in the CSS[38] we could not determine the victim's race since, for these victims, no death certificates were available in the records of the Georgia Bureau of Vital Statistics. Because almost 90 percent of the cases in the study involved intraracial crimes, we presumed in these "missing data" cases that the victim and the defendant were of the same race. We also tried to estimate the potentially distortive effects of this presumption in two ways. First, we conducted a "listwise deletion" multiple-regression analysis—a reanalysis of the data after deleting the cases in which we did not know the race of the victim. We found that after this deletion the race-of-victim effects remained essentially unchanged.[39] We also conducted a "worst case" analysis with respect to these cases. We reanalyzed the data after recoding the missing race-of-victim variable in the manner most likely to offset our observed race-of-victim effects. Thus, if the defendant received a death sentence in such a case, we coded the victim's race black; if the defendant received a life sentence, we coded the victim's race white. Under this highly improbable set of assumptions, the race effect declined but remained substantial and statistically significant.[40]

Judge Forrester also criticized our data set because, in some cases, we were unable to determine whether there was a penalty trial. In part this criticism reflects a misreading of the record. Judge Forrester identified 62 murder cases in the CSS in which, he asserted, it was not known if there was a penalty trial. On this basis, he concluded that this information was missing in from "18 to 20%" of the relevant cases.[41] In fact, as we testified, in the sample of cases used for the CSS, whether a penalty trial occurred was known in all but 20 cases. For the universe of all cases in the CSS, this would generalize to 54 cases out of 762, or 7 percent rather than 18 to 20 percent.[42]

Based upon this misreading of the record, Judge Forrester further speculated that the missing penalty-trial data in the CSS "could have skewed the results."[43] However, whether there was a penalty trial is only relevant for analyses of the specific decision by the prosecutor whether to seek a death sentence after trial. It has no relevance to the principal objective of the CSS, which was to analyze those factors that influenced why certain defendants indicted for murder ultimately received death sentences.

Furthermore, the results of the PRS analyses of prosecutorial decision making were nearly identical to those results from the CSS. For the PRS, we lacked data for the penalty-trial variable in only 23, or 4 percent (23/594), of the cases. For these 23 cases we derived an imputed value for the penalty-trial variable using logistic multiple-regression analysis. We also reanalyzed the prosecutorial decision to seek a death sentence with the PRS data after deleting these 23 cases and obtained virtually identical results. [44]

THE VALIDITY OF THE STATISTICAL PROCEDURES

Judge Forrester faulted our substantive statistical analyses in a number of ways, ranging from a global assault on the validity of regression analysis to highly technical criticisms concerning such matters as the use of dichotomous independent variables in a linear-regression analysis.

The Central Findings

Perhaps the single most disturbing feature of Judge Forrester's evaluation of the CSS was his total rejection of our analyses based upon the 39-variable model, apparently because it included fewer variables than some of the alternative models we employed. Indeed, Judge Forrester's rejection of the 39-variable model reflected a profound misunderstanding of its features. First, he did not appear to realize that we considered the estimates it produced as our core model. On the basis of extensive analysis and study, we believed that it represented the best combination of variables that were conceptually important, statistically important in explaining who received death sentences, and sufficiently parsimonious to be understood. We developed the other alternative models (using between 5 and 230-plus variables that were selected with a variety of methods) to demonstrate the "robustness" of the race-of-victim effect found in the 39-variable model. [45] We presented the results produced with these alternative models because their use constitutes sound methodology in model building, not because their results are necessarily more reliable. [46]

The core 39-variable model in the CSS captured the essence of the charging-and-sentencing system. It is the result of our extensive efforts to reflect accurately the most relevant and important influences in the system. [47] However, with absolutely no support from the record, Judge Forrester concluded that any statistical model that did not include all 230 variables "may very possibly not present a whole picture." [48] On this basis, he simply dismissed the 39-variable model, together with the entire body of alternative regression results that we developed.

What Judge Forrester did not understand is that it would be unnecessary and undesirable to include all 230 variables in a meaningful statistical analysis, since many of these variables are redundant in the information they reflect. [49] It is far better to develop a more parsimonious model that captures the main characteristics of the system without overburdening the analysis with too many variables that convey essentially the same information.[50] Moreover, it is significant that the State's experts offered no other models as superior alternatives. In fact, the State offered no substantive analysis of any type employing racial variables to refute petitioner's claims. Indeed, the State's principal expert testified that during the seven months in which he had possession of our data he never attempted to conduct a single analysis designed to measure racial effects in Georgia's capital-sentencing system after adjusting for aggravating and mitigating factors.[51] The State's criticisms of our studies and Judge Forrester's opinion are based entirely on the speculation that the asserted deficiencies in the statistical procedures that we employed might be the actual source of the observed racial effects.[52]

The R^2 Problem

Although Judge Forrester stated that he regarded the 230-plus-variable model as superior to our 39-variable model, he ultimately rejected both as untrustworthy. His major reason concerned the R^2 statistic associated with each model. Essentially, Judge Forrester misinterpreted the R^2 multiple-regression statistic to be a measure of the trustworthiness of a statistical model.[53] The R^2 statistic describes only one thing—what percentage of the variation in the dependent variable (in this case, the death-sentencing result) is explained by all of the independent variables in the analysis. The R^2 statistic does not address the accuracy with which the effects of the independent variables (e.g., the race of the victim) are measured.[54] It simply indicates the extent to which the available data purport to explain changes in the dependent variable. The estimated R^2 for the midrange 39-variable model was .39. Judge Forrester found this statistic to be unacceptably low. However, the estimated R^2 for any analysis that employs a dichotomous (Yes/No) outcome or dependent variable, such as our 39-variable model, is always low compared to the R^2 in an equally predictive model with a continuously distributed outcome variable. Professor Woodworth used a "biserial R^2" to estimate that an equally predictive continuous-variable model would have a much higher R^2.[55]

Judge Forrester's opinion indicates also that he misunderstood the nature of the R^2 estimate in at least two respects. First, he incorrectly assumed that the R^2 estimate measures the validity of the model by indicating the proportion of cases correctly predicted as to sentencing outcome. An R^2 of .5 does not mean that only 50 percent of the cases are correctly predicted; as indicated above, it means only that the independent variables explain statistically 50 percent of the "variation" in the death-sentencing variable.[56] The State's experts never disputed either of these propositions. Indeed, the meaning of the R^2 statistic never became an issue at the hearing.

What the State's experts did suggest was that the race-of-victim effect estimated in our regression analyses would "become statistically insignificant with a model with a higher r^2 [sic] which better accounted for all of the nonracial variables including interaction variables and composite variables."[57] Judge Forrester found this suggestion to be persuasive, but, again, we believe he was mistaken.

This suggestion by the State's expert was speculation. He never identified any additional variables whose inclusion would have produced an increased R^2 or otherwise reduced the magnitude or statistical significance of the estimated race- of-victim effects. The sole basis for his opinion was the undisputed fact that the significance and magnitude of the unadjusted race-of-victim effect in our models declined after adjustment for the first dozen or so important background variables. This, of course, was no surprise. It would be astounding if adjustment for other variables did not modulate the unadjusted race effects. But the modulating effect of these intuitively obvious variables, such as the defendant's prior criminal record or the number of victims, certainly does not demonstrate that the inclusion of some hypothetical additional variables (which, in fact, were not included in our study) would have a further such effect. Indeed, the fact that the many other variables in our study exerted no modulating effect on the adjusted race effects would, given the logic of the State's experts, produce the opposite conclusion.

The failure of the State to demonstrate the validity of its R^2 hypothesis is particularly striking because we made the complete data files from both studies available to the State's experts. This gave them the opportunity to devise literally thousands of variables and interactions not included in our study and to show how they would further reduce the adjusted race effects estimated by our core models.[58] However, according to the testimony of these experts, they never even attempted to make this effort.[59]

The Stepwise-Regression Problem

Stepwise regression is a procedure involving the inclusion of additional variables in a multiple-regression model one at a time in the order of their respective statistical powers to explain the dependent variable. We employed this procedure in connection with our analyses of the *McCleskey* data, and Judge Forrester criticized us for doing so.[60] Again, we think he was mistaken. To be sure, a mechanical use of stepwise regression to determine which independent variables explain the dependent variable, without regard for prior knowledge, is inappropriate.[61] However, our testimony indicated we did not use stepwise regression in this mechanical fashion. We developed a pool of meaningful and plausible variables on the basis of the literature, the opinion of practitioners, and our earlier studies.[62] We then used stepwise regression, among other techniques,[63] as a screening device to determine whether any of these theoretically plausible variables were redundant.[64] As a result, none of the models contains variables that can be considered as implausible or inconsistent with prior knowledge.[65]

Furthermore, Judge Forrester's criticism of our actual use of stepwise regression was incorrect. Our core findings did not depend upon stepwise-regression analysis. Rather, we selected the variables we employed for our thirty-nine-variable core model in the CSS because, in our judgment, they constituted the most satisfactory model from both a theoretical and statistical perspective. We used the stepwise-regression analyses in the CSS to which Judge Forrester objected simply to test the robustness of this core model. In short, the strength of our race-of-victim findings rests not only on the single findings produced by our thirty-nine-variable core model but also on the consistency of results produced by other models that used other variables or different analytic techniques.[66]

The Omitted-Variables Problem

Judge Forrester's opinion faulted our statistical models for failing to include all of the information available to prosecutors or jurors that may have affected their decisions in the processing of capital defendants. The Court of Appeals also criticized the omission of data regarding such factors as "looks, age, personality, education, profession, job, clothes, demeanor, and remorse."[67] First, both studies did include variables for the defendant's age, education, profession, job, and remorse. Adjustment for these variables did not explain away the race-of-victim effect in either the PRS or the CSS. Moreover, we consider the variables for "looks, . . . education, profession, job, [and] clothes" to be suspect variables that are not relevant to the defendant's moral culpability and blameworthiness.[68] In addition, neither the Court of Appeals nor the district court actually evaluated the extent to which omitted variables of the sort described might have explained away the race-of-victim effects produced by our analyses.[69] For its part, the State presented little beyond speculation to suggest that any of the omitted variables would have affected the results of our studies.[70]

To be sure, a defendant's age, personality, and demeanor may properly influence how a prosecutor or jury choose to deal with a given offender. But this does not mean that the omission of variables for such characteristics from our analyses biased our findings. The omission of such a variable as the defendant's demeanor can only bias the estimated effect of the victim's race if two conditions exist. First, as noted earlier, the omitted variable must actually influence prosecutorial or jury decisions affecting the ultimate sentence. Second, the omitted variable also must be unequally distributed between white-

and black-victim cases—that is, it must be significantly correlated with the race-of-victim variable. In other words, the omission of a given variable could only bias the race-of-victim coefficients estimated in our studies if it were significantly correlated with both the race-of-victim variable and the outcome variable. We consider it quite unlikely that we omitted from our studies any significant variables that satisfy these two conditions. It is far more likely, we believe, that any omitted variables are randomly distributed with respect to the race of the victim. This is certainly true of the omitted variables (such as the defendant's demeanor, clothes, or attractiveness) to which the Court of Appeals referred. Although prosecutors or juries might be influenced by such variables in some cases, there is no reason to believe that, as a group, defendants characteristically differ in these respects depending upon the race of their victims.

The CSS includes a rich array of data concerning the defendant, the victim, the crime, and the strength of the evidence. The race-of-victim effects produced by that study persist after simultaneous adjustment for over 230 such variables.[71] Simultaneous adjustment for over 150 variables in the PRS also failed to eliminate the estimated race-of-victim effect.[72] Furthermore, since the *McCleskey* hearing we have constructed 1,078 additional variables and 406 interaction terms for the CSS, which we then tested for a statistically significant relationship with the death-sentencing outcome. If a variable or interaction term did display such a relationship, after adjustment for the variables in the overall model, we added it to the model. We found that these additions increased the estimated R^2 for our overall model but in no way diminished the magnitude of the race-of-victim effect.[73]

Consequently, we doubt that we have omitted many variables that would show a statistically significant relationship with the death-sentencing-outcome variable. Given the large number of statistically significant variables for which we have accounted and the large number of cases in our data set, unless the impact of an omitted unknown variable was statistically significant, no bias could result; its only effect would be to generate additional "noise." What seems even less likely, from an intuitive standpoint, is the possibility that such an omitted variable would also be positively correlated with the race-of-victim variable. On this basis alone, we regard the danger of omitted-variable bias to be quite small.

The Multicollinearity Problem

Multicollinearity exists when two or more independent variables in a multiple-regression analysis are correlated with each other. Judge Forrester rejected the results of our studies in part because he concluded that the "presence of multi-collinearity substantially diminishes the weight to be accorded to the circumstantial statistical evidence of racial disparity."[74] We believe this finding was erroneous on at least two grounds. First, Judge Forrester assumed the existence of severe multicollinearity despite reliable evidence to the contrary.[75] To be sure, the State's experts contended that severe multicollinearity existed, but their only evidence was a list of independent variables that were significantly correlated with the race of the victim or the race of the defendant. However, this is not persuasive evidence of severe multicollinearity, since in data sets of this size correlations as small as .10, which clearly do not constitute severe multicollinearity, may be statistically significant. Also, simple correlations are not a valid indication of multicollinearity because they do not indicate the degree of correlation between independent variables after adjustment for the other independent variables in the analysis.[76] Moreover, a well-established diagnostic measure of multicollinearity exists,[77] which, according to Berk's testimony, indicated the presence of only mild multicollinearity.[78]

Judge Forrester's second error with regard to multicollinearity was to "double count" its effects. Since the effect of multicollinearity on a regression coefficient is to reduce its statistical significance, it is inappropriate to discount even further the evidentiary weight attributable to the coefficient because of the presence of multicollinearity. Woodworth[79] and Berk[80] both made this point. Berk, for example, stated: "Multicollinearity, unless . . . so severe that your computer would probably balk in estimating the equations, . . . does not bias the regression coefficients. It just makes it more difficult to distinguish those regression coefficients from chance."[81] This principle is widely accepted in the statistical literature.[82]

To be more precise, the only effect of the presence of multicollinearity upon the regression coefficient estimated for the race-of-victim variable is to increase the magnitude of its standard deviation. Because the statistical significance of the coefficient estimated for a variable depends on the extent to which it exceeds the applicable standard deviation, multicollinearity can only reduce the statistical significance of the race-of-victim regression coefficient. There are no hidden additional effects of multicollinearity. If, despite any multicollinearity, the regression coefficient for race-of-victim exceeds its standard deviation by a factor of two, it is statistically significant beyond the .05 level, which gives one confidence that the race-of-victim disparity is not a chance result. In fact, the race-of-victim disparities in the PRS and the CSS regularly exceeded two standard deviations, thereby demonstrating their statistical significance well beyond the .05 level. No additional weight can be legitimately deducted from the coefficients for hidden effects of multicollinearity. The point, however, is that the effects of multicollinearity, if any, are fully captured in the measurement of the standard deviation. To discount the evidentiary weight, therefore, of a statistically significant coefficient for the victim's race, as Judge Forrester did, because of the possibility that multicollinearity is present is wholly inappropriate. It also strikes us as ironic that, on the one hand, Judge Forrester expressed concerns about the presence of multicollinearity (redundancy among explanatory variables) in our larger models while, on the other hand, he rejected our 39-variable model in favor of the highly redundant 230-plus-variable model.

The Spurious-Correlations Proposition

Another of Judge Forrester's criticisms of our research entailed what might be called the "spurious correlations proposition"—according to which, factors that occur frequently (but that do not influence death-sentencing decisions) may, nevertheless, spuriously bias the regression equations. To illustrate this proposition, Judge Forrester suggested that if an overwhelming majority of the defendants who received death sentences were right-handed, the regression equations might suggest the existence of discrimination against right-handed defendants even if right-handedness in no way influenced the sentencing results. On this basis, Judge Forrester concluded that "the regression coefficients for the racial variables could have been artificially produced because of the high incidence of cases in which the victim was white."[83] The flaw in Judge Forrester's analysis is that a frequently occurring factor will not emerge as a significant factor in a regression analysis unless it also occurs at different rates among life and death cases—that is, unless it is correlated with the outcome variable after adjustment for the other variables in the analysis. In other words, to return to Judge Forrester's right-handedness example, a regression analysis would not identify that trait as a factor influencing sentencing results, even if a large proportion of the defendants condemned to die were right-handed, unless right-handedness was much more common among defendants sentenced to death than among defendants who received lesser sentences.[84]

The State's "Rebuttal"

White-Victim Cases Are Generally More Aggravated than Black-Victim Cases

Judge Forrester's opinion noted with approval the demonstration by the State's chief expert witness, Dr. Joseph Katz, that among cases with the same number of statutory aggravating circumstances, white-victim cases tend to be more aggravated than black-victim cases.[85] Of course, no one disputed this point. Judge Forrester, however, erroneously concluded on this basis that "in the white-victim cases there are unaccounted-for systematic aggravating features, and in the black-victim cases there are unaccounted-for systematic mitigating features."[86]

This statement is subject to two interpretations, both exposing its flaws. The first is that Judge Forrester mistakenly assumed that our multiple-regression analyses did not account for the variables that Katz used to demonstrate the relatively more aggravated nature of white-victim cases. In fact, each of the variables used by Katz came from our data set, and we incorporated each of them simultaneously in our largest multivariate analyses. Consequently, Judge Forrester's statement that the aggravating or mitigating variables to which Katz referred were "unaccounted-for" is simply incorrect.

The second possible interpretation of Judge Forrester's conclusion is that, based upon Katz's demonstration that the white-victim cases are more aggravated in terms of the factors that are accounted for in the study, the judge mistakenly assumed that the white-victim cases are also characteristically more aggravated in terms of the factors that are not accounted for in the study. This interpretation, of course, is a restatement of the assertion already discussed, that the study omitted many important variables, which, if included in our analyses, would explain away the race-of-victim effect.

The Life-Sentence "Paradox": Black-Victim Cases Are Less Aggravated than White-Victim Cases

Another argument presented by the State concerned the observed aggravation levels in cases that resulted in life sentences.[87] Our data indicated that among life-sentence cases, those involving black victims were, on average, less aggravated than those involving white victims. The State argued that this evidence refuted the contention that Georgia treated defendants in white-victim cases more punitively than defendants whose victims were black. The theory was that if, as our statistical analyses suggested, white-victim cases resulted in more punitive treatment than similarly situated black-victim cases, one would observe a higher degree of aggravation in life-sentence cases involving black victims than in life-sentence cases involving white victims. Stated somewhat differently, the State's argument was that if cases of equivalent aggravation resulted in death penalties more frequently when the victim was white, the black-victim cases that resulted in life sentences would, as a group, tend to be more aggravated than those white-victim cases that did result in life sentences. The argument concludes that because our statistics clearly showed that the life-sentence cases involving black victims as a group were less aggravated than the white-victim life-sentenced cases, the data failed to support our hypothesis.

Judge Forrester apparently found this argument to be persuasive, possibly because he did not consider its logical corollary: that Georgia acted more punitively in black-victim capital cases. More important, however, Judge For-rester failed to recognize that the State's argument presupposed that the dis-tribution of cases in our studies in terms of aggravation levels was approxi-mately the same for both white- and black-victim cases. Otherwise, the State's argument would lack any real force, since if there were a substantial difference in the distribution of Georgia's white- and black-victim cases in their relative aggravation levels, it would be quite possible for Georgia to treat the white-victim cases more punitively than black-victim cases of equivalent aggravation levels and still produce a pool of relatively more aggravated white-victim cases that resulted in life sentences. In fact, when one examines the data, one finds that, as a group, the white-victim cases in our study are substantially more aggravated than the black-victim cases. Indeed, this was the very argument that the State itself made in an effort to explain away the racial effects that we observed. The magnitude of the differences in the aggravation levels for the two groups of cases is demonstrated in Table 67 from the Procedural Reform Study, which indicates (in column A) various culpability levels and (in col-umns B and C) the proportion of white-victim and black-victim cases with culpability scores below the level indicated in column A.

These data clearly indicate that, overall, the black-victim cases are much less aggravated than the white-victim cases. Indeed, the culpability index score of -5.50 for the white-victim case at the 50th percentile (col. B) is comparable to the culpability score for the black-victim case at the 70th percentile (col. C). One further measure of the difference in the relative culpability of the black- and white-victim cases is that in the Procedural Reform Study 87 percent of the

Table 67. Distribution of White- and Black-Victim Cases According to Case Culpability Scores (Procedural Reform Study)

A	B	C
Case Culpability Score (from least to highest)[1]	Proportion of Cases with Culpability Scores below the Level Indicated in Column A	
	White-Victim Cases	Black-Victim Cases
−10.49	.10	.15
−8.28	.25	.42
−5.50	.50	.70
−1.90	.75	.89
3.70	.95	.99
9.70	.95	1.00

1. The culpability index is based on model OVERALLC; see infra app. J.

white-victim cases were death-eligible, while only 70 percent of the black-victim cases were death-eligible. In the Charging and Sentencing Study, 76 percent of the white-victim cases were death-eligible, whereas the comparable figure for the black-victim cases was 58 percent.

This disparity in overall culpability levels effectively destroys the theoretical force of the State's argument concerning the life-sentence "paradox." This disparity in aggravation levels permitted Georgia to treat white-victim cases more punitively than black-victim cases of equivalent aggravation levels while still producing a pool of life-sentence white-victim cases that were more aggravated than the equivalent group of black-victim cases. The reason is that our study included so many more black-victim cases with low levels of aggravation that a comparison of all life-sentence cases is dominated by the generally low levels of aggravation in the black-victim cases.

NOTES

1. In this regard, Judge Forrester refused to admit into the record the detailed written reports prepared by the expert witnesses for both McCleskey and the State. He would only admit the statistical tabulations; all explanations of their origin and meaning were given orally.

2. In addition, the Supreme Court found that the results of our separate analysis of the data from Fulton County, where McCleskey was tried, should be given "limited" weight because of the "small sample" involved. *See* McCleskey v. Kemp, 107 S.Ct. 1768 n.15 (1987).

3. See, e.g., Griffin v. Board of Regents of Regency Univ., 795 F.2d 1281, 1291 (7th Cir. 1986) (R^2 analysis).

4. McCleskey v. Zant, 580 F. Supp. 338, 360 (N.D. Ga. 1984). Zant was the original defendant. Kemp became the new superintendent of McCleskey's detention facility and thus the new defendant while the case was on appeal.

5. *See* R. 1330–33. All "R" references are to the transcript of the evidentiary hearing held in the United States District Court for the Northern District of Georgia, August 8–22, 1983. "DB" and "GW" references are to exhibits offered, respectively, by Professors Baldus and Woodworth.

Contrary to the implication of Judge Forrester's opinion, even in the 75% of the parole board files that did not contain an actual copy of the police report, the investigator would have read that report and would have included its contents in his or her summary of the case. *See* R. 1331–32.

6. *McCleskey*, 580 F. Supp. at 357.

7. The data sources for the PRS, which was conducted earlier than the CSS, overlapped with those used in the CSS. One-half of the cases in the PRS were also coded from the files of the Georgia Board of Pardons and Paroles, the opinions of the Georgia Supreme Court, and the summaries and questionnaires prepared by Dennis York, a former special assistant to the Georgia Supreme Court on proportionality review. However, of the remaining three hundred cases in the PRS, one hundred death-sentence cases and one hundred life-sentence cases were coded in Iowa on the basis of elaborate narrative summaries prepared in Georgia from appellate opinions, the Dennis York

summaries and questionnaires, and the records of the Georgia Supreme Court. *See* R. 207–12. The remaining one hundred cases in the PRS were coded in Georgia directly from these supreme court documents. *See* R. 346. In their data collection from the supreme court's records, the coders relied principally on the published opinions and the briefs of the prosecutors and the defendants, but made frequent reference to the transcripts to obtain needed information that was not available in the briefs and opinions. *See* R. 538–42. The PRS also employed substantial data obtained from the Department of Offender Rehabilitation.

In addition to the extensive information available in the parole board's files, the coders had access to copies of the reported opinions of the Georgia Supreme Court in murder cases that resulted in an appeal. Particularly in death-sentence cases, these opinions contain rich descriptions of the circumstances of the offense as it was developed in the trial record. In addition, the Dennis York case summaries and questionnaires were prepared on the basis of his analysis of the entire record of the case. *See* R. 203–4. Finally, the CSS data files contained a broad array of information on the defendant's prior record provided by the Georgia Department of Pardons and Paroles.

8. R. 1766.

9. App. D presents a similar list of variables from the Procedural Reform Study. Judge Forrester also raised a question about the capacity of the questionnaires to carry the information available to the coders in the public records they used. He correctly noted that both the PRS questionnaire and the CSS questionnaire permitted only a limited number of responses with respect to a small number of questions. *See* McCleskey v. Zant, 580 F. Supp. at 356. This meant that, for those questions, there could be more items of information to enter than there were foils to hold them, thereby creating an "overflow" information problem. The problem can be illustrated by reference to variable 30 in the questionnaire for the Procedural Reform Study (at app. C). This variable for the special aggravating and mitigating features of the case provided only 6 foils, which meant that of the 33 special aggravating and mitigating features of the case listed for this variable only 6 could be entered. If the case involved more than 6 such characteristics, they could not be entered in the questionnaire as originally constructed and would represent overflow information. When we became aware of this problem, we added a potentially unlimited number of new foils to all the items in the questionnaires that might have an "overflow" information problem—that is, those for which there was a case in the study that had information in each original foil. Then, with narrative case summaries, we used these new foils to code any overflow information in the case with a potential problem. Upon analyzing these recoded cases, we found that the estimated race-of-victim effects actually increased slightly. *See* R. 1709–10. There was also an implication that the coding convention that treated equally (a) information in the parole board's files that "suggested" a factor was present in the case and (b) information positively stating it was present may have biased the results. Professor Baldus testified that he reran some of the analyses after taking these coding differences into account, and that the race-of-victim effects did not change. *See* R. 1677–78.

It was also suggested that the failure to include in the analysis all the information in the data base about each victim in multiple-victim cases would somehow bias the result. Baldus testified that he did a supplemental analysis that took account of available information on all of the victims in the multiple-victim cases. The result was a decrease in the linear race-of-victim coefficient of one-half of 1%. *See* R. 1678–79.

Judge Forrester faults the study for not including in the regression analyses the information embraced in the coding for "other" special aggravating features of the case, and suggests that this omission "might affect the outcome of the study." Baldus testified that the "other" category was included in addition to the many aggravating circumstances already coded in the study to enable him to see if any important factor, not anticipated at the time the questionnaire was designed, might appear after the questionnaires were coded. He further testified that he examined these answers and concluded that the omitted information was "unlikely to have any effect on the analysis, and it was for that reason that I did not break out that information and provide additional codes." R. 1709. He also testified that he did not believe that the addition of this information could plausibly explain away the race effects he and Professor Woodworth had estimated. See R. 1708–10. However, Judge Forrester's opinion never discussed these efforts—successful, in our judgment—to demonstrate that his concern with a potential "overflow" information problem was not well grounded.

10. The student coders were Lee Ann de Grazia, Matthew Estes, John Greeno, Orry Korb, and Martha Macgill. R. 308–10.

11. See R. 312–13, 345.

12. See McCleskey, 580 F. Supp. at 355.

13. DB 43.

14. R. 596–98.

15. See R. 606–16.

16. See R. 1716–20. First, Professor Baldus testified specifically that the mismatch count for one of the variables, "Two or More Victims in All," is erroneous because of an incompatibility between the two variables compared. He testified that the correct mismatch rate on that variable was 2%.

17. See R. 367–68, 371–73, 475–76.

18. See R. 406.

19. Cf. DB 34; DB 43.

20. In one investigation, he identified inconsistencies between the PRS and the CSS that existed with respect to the coding for the 10 statutory aggravating factors. This study identified several errors, which he corrected. R. 1719–24. In addition, he conducted an investigation of 17 of the variables that had been identified as having mismatches by the State's expert.

21. See R. 1719–20.

22. See id.

23. See R. 517–18, 520.

24. See R. 1684–86, 1690–91. Although we realize that this presumption was not always met, we consider it implausible that the error such discrepancies introduced into the data biased the central racial finding of the study.

25. The incentive of defense counsel and the attorney general to present all of the important aggravating and mitigating circumstances in their briefs to the Georgia Supreme Court is obvious. The records of the Georgia Board of Pardons and Paroles are the product of an extensive field investigation conducted by parole board officials shortly after a conviction is obtained. These field investigations include an examination of court records as well as conversations with police and either the district attorney or a representative of that office. The officials of the Board of Pardons and Paroles take great pride in the thoroughness of their investigations.

26. We believe that when decision makers are ignorant of the presence of potentially relevant factors, they disregard the factors on which they have no information and act on the basis of the positive information available to them.

27. This judgment is supported by all of the theoretical and empirical research of which we are aware on the subject of how people process information in decision making. Ignorance about a great many variables may lead one to seek more information or abstain from making a decision. But in all our cases dispositive decisions were made by a prosecutor or jury on the basis of the affirmative information at their disposal.

28. McCleskey v. Zant, 580 F. Supp. at 358.

29. *See* R. 517–18, 520–21. Judge Forrester's criticism of the practice of treating case characteristics coded as "unknown" as not being present in the case is based on the belief that the parole board records did not represent a reasonable proxy for what the actors in the process knew about the cases. This is apparent from Judge Forrester's statement describing a case in which a defendant had "told four other people about the murder." McCleskey v. Zant, 580 F. Supp. at 356. However, since the parole board files did not indicate whether the defendant had been "bragging about the murder or expressing remorse," the "bragging" and "remorse" variables were coded as unknown. Judge Forrester faults this coding because: "[a]s the witnesses to his statements were available to the prosecution and, presumably, to the jury, that information was knowable and probably known. It was not, however, captured in the study." *Id.* at 356–57.

Judge Forrester may have been correct with respect to what the jury and the prosecutor knew in this case. But the record does not show it. Nor does it indicate that in any other case the coding was inconsistent with what the prosecutor or jury knew about the case.

30. As Professor Berk (a member of the National Academy of Sciences Panel on Sentencing Research) testified, this is the generally accepted procedure for coding information that "was not available when a decision was made and was generally, . . . therefore, irrelevant to the decision maker's actions." R. 1763.

31. It is important to note the nature of the variables that have substantial numbers of "unknown" codes. The situation does not arise with respect to the basic facts of the cases (e.g., whether there was an armed robbery or a rape); the record nearly always permits an inference about whether these facts were present, even if they are not specifically mentioned in the record. However, as the range of variables embraced by a questionnaire expands, the possibility of inferring the presence or absence of a factor from a silent record declines. This is particularly so for variables related to the defendant's or the victim's state of mind, personal characteristics of the victim, certain conduct of the defendant before or during the crime that left no traces, relations between codefendants, and relations between the victim and defendant prior to the crime. These are the kinds of variables that have the highest proportion of unknown codes entered. In short, as the richness and detail of a data set expands, the number of variables with significant numbers of unknowns coded will inevitably grow.

Judge Forrester never explicitly considered the impact our coding protocol for unknown case characteristics was likely to have on the central findings of the study; and as noted above, the State was unable to show a single case where a mitigating or aggravating factor from the parole board's files coded "U" was in fact believed to have existed by a prosecutor or a jury. All statements in Judge Forrester's opinion to the effect that there were discrepancies between the parole board's files and the state of mind of the prosecutors are pure speculation.

32. There are true missing data for a variable when the information concerning it was known and acted upon by the relevant decision makers but was unknown to the researchers.

33. See R. 1790–91. Moreover, he testified that in two particulars the results of the studies indicated that it was quite unlikely that there was a real "missing data" problem of significant magnitude. First, he held that the estimates of the impact of the legitimate aggravating and mitigating circumstances in the system were plausible, which would probably not be so if there were large amounts of missing data in the case. See R. 1764–65. Second, he viewed the stability of the race-of-victim coefficients estimated across a variety of different analyses as also undercutting the likelihood that there was a large amount of genuine missing data in the studies. See R. 1765.

34. We also presented evidence, shown in note table 12, which puts the magnitude of the "unknown" problem in perspective. It indicates that the median case, in terms of the number of unknown variables coded, had 31 variables coded unknown (out of the full file of 230-plus variables); also, the 90th-percentile case (in the same terms) had 47 unknowns.

Note Table 12. Distribution of css Cases with One or More Unknown Codes by the Number of Variables Coded Unknown (css)

A	B	C	D	E
Number of Cases with Missing Information for the Number of Variables Indicated in Column B	Number of Variables with Missing Information per Case	Cumulative Frequency	Percent	Cumulative Percent
8	4	4	0.370	0.370
10	1	5	0.092	0.462
11	1	6	0.092	0.555
12	5	11	0.462	1.017
13	5	16	0.462	1.479
14	7	23	0.647	2.126
15	10	33	0.924	3.050
16	22	55	2.033	5.083
17	12	67	1.109	6.192
18	17	84	1.571	7.763
19	18	102	1.664	9.427
20	15	117	1.386	10.813
21	21	138	1.941	12.754
22	14	152	1.294	14.048
23	24	176	2.218	16.266
24	37	213	3.420	19.686
25	38	251	3.512	23.198
26	25	276	2.311	25.508
27	45	321	4.159	29.667
28	41	362	3.789	33.457
29	42	404	3.882	37.338
30	55	459	5.083	42.421
31	39	498	3.604	46.026
32	28	526	2.588	48.614
33	55	581	5.083	53.697
34	46	627	4.251	57.948
35	36	663	3.327	61.275

Note Table 12 (*cont.*)

A	B	C	D	E
Number of Cases with Missing Information for the Number of Variables Indicated in Column B	Number of Variables with Missing Information per Case	Cumulative Frequency	Percent	Cumulative Percent
36	49	712	4.529	65.804
37	37	749	3.420	69.224
38	32	781	2.957	72.181
39	34	815	3.142	75.323
40	26	841	2.403	77.726
41	29	870	2.680	80.407
42	24	894	2.218	82.625
43	16	910	1.479	84.104
44	23	933	2.126	86.229
45	20	953	1.848	88.078
46	15	968	1.386	89.464
47	12	980	1.109	90.573
48	14	994	1.294	91.867
49	7	1001	0.647	92.514
50	7	1008	0.647	93.161
51	6	1014	0.555	93.715
52	2	1016	0.185	93.900
53	5	1021	0.462	94.362
54	6	1027	0.555	94.917
55	3	1030	0.277	95.194
56	3	1033	0.277	95.471
57	2	1035	0.185	95.656
58	7	1042	0.647	96.303
59	4	1046	0.370	96.673
60	3	1049	0.277	96.950
61	2	1051	0.185	97.135
62	1	1052	0.092	97.227
63	2	1054	0.185	97.412
65	1	1055	0.092	97.505
66	2	1057	0.185	97.689
67	1	1058	0.092	97.782
71	1	1059	0.092	97.874
72	2	1061	0.185	98.059
79	1	1062	0.092	98.152
105	1	1063	0.092	98.244
124	1	1064	0.092	98.336
130	1	1065	0.092	98.429
134	1	1066	0.092	98.521
162	2	1068	0.185	98.706
165	1	1069	0.092	98.799
179	1	1070	0.092	98.891
181	2	1072	0.185	99.076
182	1	1073	0.092	99.168
184	1	1074	0.092	99.261

(continued on next page)

Note Table 12 (*cont.*)

A	B	C	D	E
Number of Cases with Missing Information for the Number of Variables Indicated in Column B	Number of Variables with Missing Information per Case	Cumulative Frequency	Percent	Cumulative Percent
187	1	1075	0.092	99.353
190	1	1076	0.092	99.445
191	1	1077	0.092	99.538
195	1	1078	0.092	99.630
198	1	1079	0.092	99.723
199	1	1080	0.092	99.815
202	1	1081	0.092	99.908
214	1	1082	0.092	100.000

35. *See* R. 1701–5; DB 122, 123; GW 4, table 1. Judge Forrester, however, rejected these analyses, including the one conducted for the core 39-variable model, because they did not include enough variables and, in the case of the 39-variable model, because it included too few variables with a large proportion of coded unknowns (a fact that would normally increase one's confidence in the model). *See* McCleskey v. Zant, 580 F. Supp. at 359. In addition, Judge Forrester overlooked the worst-case analysis Baldus conducted, which controlled simultaneously for all statutory aggravating factors and for more than 70 mitigating circumstances. It showed a linear race-of-victim coefficient of .04, significant at the .006 level. *See* DB 123; R. 1704.

36. Judge Forrester's statement that we were missing information in 40% of the cases about whether there was a plea bargain is correct, but the variable was included in no analysis. Also, Judge Forrester correctly states that our data were thin on whether there were credibility problems with the State's witnesses.

37. McCleskey v. Zant, 580 F. Supp at 360.

38. *See* R. 1706.

39. *See id.*

40. *See* R. 1706–7; DB 124.

41. *See* McCleskey v. Zant, 580 F. Supp. at 359–60.

42. *See* R. 1713–14.

43. McCleskey v. Zant, 580 F. Supp. at 359.

44. The race-of-victim logistic coefficient estimated in the model PROSCUTA (*see infra* app. J, part 2), after deleting the 23 cases in which there were missing data on the penalty-trial variables, was 1.74, significant at the .0001 level, which contrasts with a race-of-victim coefficient of 1.87, significant at the same level when the imputed data are included. Also, the coefficient for a race-of-victim interaction term declined to 1.6 ($p = .059$) from 1.71 ($p = .02$) in the model estimated with all the cases.

45. *See supra* chap. 10, note 31 and accompanying text.

46. As described by Richard Berk:

Perhaps the best way to proceed involves a clear distinction between two stages in model specification. In the first stage, one should pose several competing causal models and estimate all of them. Then, within the more recent traditions in causal modelings, one should select the model that fits the data best. Besides t-tests for individual coefficients, there are now a range of procedures that consider the model as a whole. In essence, one is comparing competing causal explanations based on how well they explain one's observed data. Once this exercise has been completed, a second stage may be undertaken in which the researcher fishes through the data in search of the big one that got away.

Berk, *Applications of the General Linear Model to Survey Data*, in HANDBOOK OF SURVEY RESEARCH 539 (P. Rossi, J. Wright, & A. Anderson eds. 1983); *see also* R. 812.

Exclusive reliance on the 230-variable model is particularly inappropriate. Not only is a model of such magnitude difficult to understand, it is overfitted, which means its coefficients may be overly sensitive to the particular 1000-plus case sample used in the analysis. Our sole purpose in employing such an unwieldy model was to test the persistence of the race-of-victim effect with a model that would be considered bizarre by normal social science standards. *See supra* chap. 10, table 55, for a summary of the results estimated with the alternative models.

47. *See* R. 808. Judge Forrester failed even to mention the logistic-regression results from this core analysis.

48. McCleskey v. Zant, 580 F. Supp. at 361.

49. *See* R. 808.

50. *See* R. 821.

51. *See* R. 1512.

52. One strong confirmation of the validity of the regression-based findings was Baldus's analysis in which cases were matched with a culpability index that we based solely on qualitative judgments, rather than on regression-based indexes (*see supra* chap. 10, table 54). The court failed to mention this analysis, which also showed substantial race-of-victim disparities.

53. *See* McCleskey v. Zant, 580 F. Supp. at 361.

54. *See* Fisher, *Multiple Regression in Legal Proceedings*, 80 COLUM. L. REV. 702, 719–20 (1980) (hereinafter Fisher); King, *How Not to Lie with Statistics: Avoiding Common Mistakes in Quantitative Political Science*, 30 AM. J. POL. SCI. 666, 675 (1986) (hereinafter King), states the following:

> R^2 is often called the "coefficient of determination." The result (or cause) of this unfortunate terminology is that the R^2 statistic is sometimes interpreted as a measure of the influence of X on y. Others consider it to be a measure of the fit between the statistical model and the true model. A high R^2 is considered to be proof that the correct model has been specified or that the theory being tested is correct. A higher R^2 in one model is taken to mean that that model is better. All these interpretations are wrong. R^2 is a measure of the spread of points around a regression line, and it is a poor measure of even that.

55. *See* R. 1289. J. Guilford & B. Fruchter, FUNDAMENTAL STATISTICS IN PSYCHOLOGY AND EDUCATION 311 (6th ed. 1978), gives the adjustment.

56. In a multiple-regression analysis, variation in the dependent variable (here the life- or death-sentencing outcome) is composed of two parts: a systematic part produced by the conceptually plausible influences in the system and potentially subject to a statistical explanation, and a random part, which cannot be explained statistically. Ideally, the researcher would always like to explain all of the variation of the systematic part and none of the random variation, which may be a product of how the sample was selected or reflect the influence of random shocks and influences in the decision-making process. Regrettably, however, one never knows what proportion of the total variation in the dependent variable is the systematic part of the dependent variable and

what proportion is the random part. Thus, in models of some decision-making systems, an R^2 of .10 might constitute all of the systematic part, while in another system an R^2 of .70 might represent all of it. Thus, there is no absolute standard for R^2; its only direct use is in comparing different models with the same dependent variable but different independent variables. In this context, it provides "a convenient goodness-of-fit statistic, providing a rough way to assess model specification and sensitivity." King, *supra* note 54 at 677. Indeed, as noted *supra* note 46, R^2 can be too high if the model is overfitted.

57. McCleskey v. Zant, 580 F. Supp. at 362.

58. Professor Woodworth testified (R. 1728–29) that our numerous analyses showed that after the initial big drop in the magnitude and statistical significance of the race-of-victim effect there was very little change in its significance. The State's R^2 hypothesis is simply further speculation, in disguise, that additional variables might be found to explain the race-of-victim effect. Judge Forrester further based his conclusions about the relationship between the magnitude of the R^2 statistic and the race-of-victim effect on the apparent decline in the magnitude and statistical significance of the race-of-victim effect when our large-scale linear model included 250 rather than 230 variables. *See* McCleskey v. Zant, 580 F. Supp. at 362. This comparison and the decline of the race of the victim in the 250-variable model was never mentioned by any of the experts in the *McCleskey* hearing. In fact, the decline in the size and significance of the race-of-victim effect was caused not by the addition of 20 more variables but by the adjustment for the effects of appellate review, a procedure in which we recoded the outcome variable so that any death sentence vacated on appeal was treated as a life-sentence case. The R^2 was virtually the same in the 230- and 250-variable models; the larger model was pruned to 230 variables because of the high multicollinearity between the 20 variables dropped and some of the remaining 230 variables. Unfortunately, the report of Judge Forrester's findings in Justice Powell's Supreme Court opinion leaves one with the false impression that it was the drop in the number of variables rather than the adjustment for the effect of appellate review that reduced the size and statistical significance of the estimated race-of-victim effect.

59. Since the *McCleskey* case, we have developed additional models that include substantial numbers of interaction terms and produce increased R^2 estimates. In each case, however, the models with the higher R^2 estimates produce a race-of-victim effect that is larger and more statistically significant than the models presented in the *McCleskey* case. For example, the race-of-victim odds multiplier in the logistic model analogous to the core thirty-nine-variable model rose from 4.3 to 5.1. These new variables were screened from hundreds of interaction terms. *See supra* chap. 11, note 47 and accompanying text. It is possible that the inclusion of these additional interaction terms may produce a degree of "over-fitting" in the models, which would be expected to enhance somewhat the statistical significance of all of the variables in the model. However, the over-fitting would not increase the *magnitude* of the estimated race-of-victim effect that in fact occurred. The key point, however, is that a higher R^2 in the models does not in any way reduce the magnitude or statistical significance of the estimated race-of-victim effects. The adjusted R^2 for the principal post-*Furman* model in the PRS was .50. *See supra* chap. 5, note 14.

60. *See* McCleskey v. Zant, 580 F. Supp. at 376. Indeed, at one point Judge Forrester rejected all regression models as an inappropriate basis for proving discrimination. The reason given was that, because such procedures did not "compare identical cases," they were inherently incapable of indicating whether similarly situated defendants were

treated the same. Judge Forrester's argument represents an attack on the use of any compensatory index that measures the similarity of cases on the basis of anything other than strict factual comparability. Such a standard is stricter than that used anywhere else in either the civil or criminal justice systems or in any field of science. For example, sentencing in noncapital cases normally involves an assessment of the defendant's moral culpability on the basis of a handful of variables, such as crime type, weapons used, violence involved, and prior record. Indeed, a requirement that cases may be examined only on the basis of strict factual comparability would, in many contexts, seriously limit the scope of legal analysis. This has been recognized in the capital-sentencing context by several state supreme courts in the conduct of their comparative-proportionality reviews. For example, the Georgia Supreme Court, in its analysis of "similar cases," regularly compares cases that are quite distinct factually but that the court believes are comparable in their overall culpability. *See supra* chap. 7, note 35 and accompanying text.

61. The source of the problem with stepwise regression is the manner in which the candidate variables are selected for inclusion in the final model. Most stepwise procedures select the first independent variable for inclusion in the model based on its univariate correlation with the dependent variable. The second independent variable is selected based on its partial correlation with the dependent variable, controlling for the first included variable, and so on through the entire list of candidate variables. There are two possible problems with this procedure. The first is that it "allows computer algorithms to replace logical decision processes in selecting variables for a regression analysis. . . . [S]ome a priori knowledge, or at least some logic, always exists to make selections better than an atheoretical computer algorithm." King, *supra* note 54, at 669n.6. The second problem is that stepwise regression procedures usually guarantee that some variables are omitted because the procedure will omit those variables that are (1) highly correlated with other already included variables and (2) possibly correlated with the dependent variable. The apparent problem is that this is also the definition of omitted-variable bias.

For the reasons stated in the text, we do not consider the atheoretical nature of the variable-selection process to be a serious problem in the context of this research. Nor, given the purposes to which our analysis was directed, do we consider the omitted-variable issue important. In contrast to the situation in most political science and econometric research, our primary objective was not to develop a structural model of a decision-making process in which it makes a great deal of difference which specific nonracial variables were included. Rather, our objective was to determine whether Georgia's death-sentencing system showed signs of being racially discriminatory and comparatively excessive after adjustment was made for every plausible and measurable case characteristic that could be influencing the system.

In our stepwise-regression analyses of racial discrimination, we sought first to develop regression models consisting of all of the nonracial variables that contributed to a possibly legitimate explanation of the death-sentencing outcomes, and then to add the racial variables to see if a race-of-victim or a race-of-defendant effect was apparent after adjustment for all of the other nonracial variables in the model that showed a relationship with the death-sentencing outcomes. Our approach was of the type used by epidemiologists seeking to "take into account several other known suspected causes [of a disease] in evaluating one potential cause." G. D. Friedman, PRIMER OF EPIDEMIOLOGY 194 (3d ed. 1987). For the purposes of this analysis, it was of no consequence which of three highly correlated variables (say, A, B, or C) was included in the model, since each had essentially the same relationship with the death-sentencing outcome and the race variables. So long as variables A, B, and C each carried the same information, the omission of variables A and B (whose information was redundant to variable C) would not bias the coefficients for the race variables so long as C was in the analysis.

We also used the results of stepwise-regression procedures to rank the cases according to an index that best explained who received a death sentence. Such rankings provided the basis for estimating excessiveness (through an analysis of death- sentencing frequencies among similar cases) and discrimination (through comparisons of death-sentencing rates for white- and black-victim cases with comparable index scores). Again, if variables A, B, and C all had the same relationship to the outcome variable, it made no difference to us from a conceptual standpoint whether A, B, or C was in the analysis, and the ranking of the cases through the final index would not materially differ whether one of variables A, B, or C was present and the other two were absent.

62. *See* R. 808.

63. *See* R. 821–22.

64. *See* R. 816, 822.

65. In some instances, the coefficient for a variable that entered a model had a "perverse" sign, in that it ran in the opposite direction of what prior knowledge predicted. (For example, the coefficient of a mitigating circumstance carried a positive sign, indicating that on average its presence aggravated rather than mitigated the offense.) In these cases, we removed the variables from the model if we determined that the perverse sign was a product of multicollinearity; otherwise, we left such variables in the model "type B" used to estimate racial discrimination but removed them from the "type C" list of variables used to measure excessiveness after adjustment for legitimate variables. *See supra* chap. 4, note 44 and accompanying text.

66. *See supra* chap. 10, table 55, for an overview of the race-of-victim findings from the css. Chapter 6 presents the results of race-of-victim analyses from the Procedural Reform Study not presented in *McCleskey* that do not depend on multiple-regression analysis and show results similar to those introduced in the *McCleskey* hearing. *See supra* chap. 6, table 43 (lines 2, 4).

67. McCleskey v. Kemp, 753 F.2d 877, 899 (11th Cir. 1985).

68. *See* chap. 6, note 25 and accompanying text for a discussion of suspect variables.

69. In a comparable Title VII case based on a claim of classwide purposeful discrimination, the defendant would have had exactly that burden, and it is a burden that cannot be satisfied with mere speculation:

> The burden is on the opposing party to clearly rebut statistical evidence; hypotheses or conjecture will not suffice. . . . When a plantiff submits accurate statistical data, and a defendant alleges that relevant variables are excluded, defendant may not rely on hypothesis to lessen the probative value of plaintiff's statistical proof. Rather, defendant in his rebuttal presentation, must either rework plaintiff's statistics incorporating the omitted factors, or present other proof undermining plaintiff's claims.

Segar v. Civiletti, 508 F. Supp. 690, 712 (D.C. Cir. 1981).

70. Under such circumstances, there is authority for applying a *"rebuttable* presumption of an equal distribution" of omitted variables in the absence of some basis for believing to the contrary. DeMedina v. Reinhardt, 686 F.2d 997, 1008–9 (D.C. Cir. 1982) (emphasis in original).

71. *See supra* chap. 10, table 55.

72. *See supra* chap. 6, table 43, row 5b, and note table 4, row 5 (DB 98). In the PRS there are no variables dealing explicitly with the strength of the evidence. However, the study has a built-in control for the strength of the evidence because all of the cases in the PRS universe of cases had evidence strong enough to result in a jury-trial conviction. We recognize this may not be a perfect control if, as some have suggested, the strength of evidence in murder cases is correlated with the race of the victim. This argument presumes that black-victim cases more frequently involve black witnesses who, for various reasons, may be less inclined to cooperate with law enforcement officials. To the extent either of these phenomena exists, we would see (as in fact we do) more missing data in black-victim cases than in white-victim cases. However, since these missing data are also presumably unknown to the prosecutors and jurors who process the cases, our ignorance of them introduces no bias to our results.

A related type of missing data may also be correlated with the race of the victim. It is possible that black-victim cases are treated more leniently than white-victim cases in the criminal justice system because the witnesses, who in black-victim cases are likely to be black, may be less credible as witnesses because of their lower socioeconomic status or prior records. To the extent this relationship between the race of the victim and witness credibility does exist, our lack of data on the latter would tend to bias upward our perception of case culpability in black-victim cases. This in turn would bias upward our race-of-victim estimates, since the weaker evidence in the black-victim cases would be expected to produce more lenient treatment than that observed in similarly situated cases. We note, however, that the propriety of a "witness credibility" variable is questioned to the extent that the reaction to black witnesses is racially motivated rather than a rational reaction to such things as witness articulateness and reputation.

73. *See supra* note 59.

74. McCleskey v. Zant, 580 F. Supp. at 364.

75. Multicollinearity is a somewhat subtle concept. According to R. Myers, CLASSICAL AND MODERN REGRESSION WITH APPLICATIONS 75 (1986) (hereinafter Myers): "The name *multicollinearity* has been used to such an extent that many potential users of statistical tools are aware that such a problem may exist before they really understand what it is" (emphasis in original). The precise meaning of the term is "*near* linear dependency among the [independent variables]." *Id.* at 76 (emphasis in original). As S. Swartz and R. E. Welsch state, "the [independent variables] are involved in exact or nearly exact linear relationships of their own." Swartz & Welsch, *Application of Bounded-Influence and Diagnostic Methods in Energy Modeling*, in MODEL RELIABILITY 162 (D. Belsley & E. Kuh eds. 1986) (hereinafter Swartz & Welsch).

76. Furthermore, there "are no definite guideline values on the [meaning of] the simple correlations," and they "do not always indicate the actual nature or the extent of multicollinearity." Myers, *supra* note 75, at 219. Richard Berk echoed this point in his testimony. *See* R. 1787–88.

77. The test is the "condition number," which Swartz and Welsch (*see supra* note 75, at 162) explain as follows:

> Numerical problems (multicollinearity) . . . will be reflected in enlarged standard errors [standard deviations] for the OLS estimates; beyond that, round-off error in the computer algorithms used to calculate the coefficients and standard errors adds a further degree of inaccuracy. . . . A flag for the existence of numerical instability is the condition number.

Berk testified that he had computed the condition number for the css data and found no serious multicollinearity problem: "The second thing I did was run some diagnostics on a larger regression model, particularly focusing on multicollinearity. There are within the sas statistical package state-of-the-art diagnostics that Belsley and his colleagues at m.i.t. have developed, . . . [a]nd I ran these diagnostics and somewhat to my surprise found rather little multicollinearity." R. 1756. The principal diagnostic provided by sas is the condition number referred to above by Belsley.

78. Aside from formal diagnostics, there are other earmarks of the presence of multicollinearity such as instability and/or wrong signs for regression coefficients. "One effect of multicollinearity . . . is the *instability* of the regression coefficients, i.e., coefficients that are very much dependent on the particular data set that generated them." Myers, *supra* note 75, at 79 (emphasis in original). It is therefore significant that throughout the analyses of two data bases and numerous sets of background variables the race-of-victim coefficient showed remarkable stability, remaining positive and statistically significant.

79. *See* R. 1281.

80. *See* R. 1758.

81. *See* R. 1782.

82. *See, e.g.,* Myers, *supra* note 75, at 79.

83. McCleskey v. Zant, 580 F. Supp. at 370.

84. Moreover, unless the right- or left-handedness of defendants was a factor known to prosecutors and juries and could plausibly and legitimately have influenced their decisions, it would not be properly included in the analysis. Finally, in the next paragraph of his opinion, Judge Forrester mistakenly stated that linear regression requires both continuous dependent and independent variables. *See* McCleskey v. Zant, 580 F. Supp. at 370. Neither assertion is correct. Woodworth discussed the use and interpretation of dichotomous (or dummy) independent variables. *See* October 17, 1983, testimony, p. 30. *See also* Fisher, *supra* note 54, at 722; J. Neter & W. Wasserman, Applied Linear Statistical Models chap. 9 (1974); *supra* app. A, note 27 and accompanying text.

85. *See* McCleskey v. Zant, 580 F. Supp. at 363 (in terms of variables that are accounted for in the study, such as torture or the number of victims).

86. *Id.* at 364.

87. *See id.* at 373.

APPENDIX C

Questionnaire/Codebook for the Procedural Reform Study

1. DEFENDANT DATA FROM DEPARTMENT OF OFFENDER REHABILITATION (DOR)

Variable Name	Variable Label
	A. General variables Blank, o = not reported, unless otherwise indicated
CASE	Case number
V3A	County in which sentence was imposed
	Current offenses #1 through #6
V4A	Current offense #1
V4B	Current offense #2
V4C	Current offense #3
V4D	Current offense #4
V4E	Current offense #5
V4F	Current offense #6
V6	Date sentence began (usually date arrested and confined)
V7	Date admitted to prison
	B. Physical characteristics
V11	Race and sex of the defendant

	Male	*Female*
White	1	6
Negro	2	7
Indian	3	8
Spanish-speaking	4	12
Other	5	13

Variable Name	Variable Label
V12	Birthdate
	C. Residency
V16	Residence of the defendant

Variable Name	Variable Label

D. Personal characteristics

1. Education

V29   Educational level of the defendant—years of schooling completed
    001–012. As indicated
    013. Any college
    014. Any graduate school

2. Employment record

V31   Occupational skill #1
V32   Occupational skill #2
V33   Employment status prior to apprehension
    1. Employed full-time
    2. Employed part-time
    3. Unemployed (recently) (6 mo. or less)
    4. Unemployed (long-time) (over 6 mo.)
    5. Never worked (nonstudent, capable)
    6. Student
    7. Incapable of working

V34   Defendant's socioeconomic status
    1. Welfare
    2. Occasionally employed
    3. Minimum standard of living ($3,000 or equivalent annual income)
    4. Middle class
    5. Other

V35   Defendant's marital status
    1. Single (never married)
    2. Married
    3. Separated
    4. Divorced (not remarried)
    5. Widowed
    6. Common-law marriage (established)

V36   Did the defendant have any children?
    1–9. (actual number)
    9. 9 or more

V37   Living arrangements prior to apprehension
    1. Living alone
    2. Living with spouse
    3. Illicit relationship

Variable Name	Variable Label

> 4. Living with one or more of same sex
> 5. No home
> 6. Inmate of institution
> 7. Living with another family member
> 8. Living with parents or pseudo-parents
> 10. Other

V38 Military record of the defendant

1.	Honorable	5.	Dishonorable
2.	General	6.	In service
3.	Undesirable	9.	Not applicable, no service
4.	Bad-conduct		

V41 Branch of service

1.	Air Force	5.	Coast Guard
2.	Army	6.	Other
3.	Navy	9.	No military service/not applicable
4.	Marines	0.	Not ascertained

V45 Number of prior arrests
V47 Prior conviction offense #1
V48 Prior conviction offense #2
V49 Prior conviction offense #3
V50 Prior conviction offense #4
V51 Prior conviction offense #5
V52 Prior conviction offense #6
V85A Was the defendant an escapee at time of the offense?
   1. No   2. Yes
V85B Was defendant a prisoner at the time of the offense?
   1. No   2. Yes
V88 Date of offense
V89 Date of arrest

2. CODEBOOK FOR DATA COLLECTED FROM THE RECORDS OF THE
   GEORGIA BOARD OF PARDONS AND PAROLES, SUPREME COURT,
   BUREAU OF VITAL STATISTICS, PROSECUTORS, AND DEFENSE
   ATTORNEYS

CASE Case number
W2 Date of offense   MM/DD/YY
W3 Defendant's plea to murder indictment
   Guilty = 1   Other = 3
   Not guilty = 2   Unknown = 0

Variable Name	Variable Label

W4 Date of trial on guilt   MM/DD/YY
   Not applicable = 000009 (e.g., guilty plea)
   Unknown = 0 or blank

W5 Sentence
   Life = 1   Other (specify) = 3
   Death = 2   Unknown = 0

W6 Status of principal defense counsel
   Retained = 1   Unknown = 0 or blank
   Appointed = 2

Variables W7, W8, and W9 coded only for post-*Furman* cases

W7 Did prosecution waive or fail to seek the death penalty?
   Yes = 1   No = 2   Unknown or pre-*Furman* = 0

W8 Did the judge otherwise take the penalty issue from the jurors or dismiss them before the penalty trial?
   Yes = 1   No = 2   Unknown or pre-*Furman* = 0

W9 Was there a penalty trial?
   Yes = 1   No = 2   Unknown or pre-*Furman* = 0

W10 Did the defendant appeal his/her conviction or sentence?
   Yes = 1   No = 2   Unknown = 0

W11 Outcome of the appeal:
   Death cases (if variable W5 = 2)
      Conviction and death sentence affirmed = 1
      Conviction sustained; death penalty reduced to life = 2
      Conviction reversed = 3
   Life cases (if variable W5 = 1)
      Conviction and life sentence affirmed = 4
      Conviction only reversed = 5
      Conviction affirmed; life sentence modified = 6
   Other (specify) _____ = 7
   Not applicable because no appeal = 9
   Unknown = 0 or blank

W12 Date of Supreme Court decision   MM/DD/YY
   Not applicable because no appeal = 9

W486 Outcome of the appeal (post-*Furman* death-sentence cases only)
   Conviction and death sentence affirmed = 1
   Conviction sustained but death penalty reduced to life = 2
   Conviction reversed and death sentence not passed on = 3
   Death sentence vacated by trial court = 4
   Not applicable because no appeal = 9
   Unknown = 0

W487 Georgia Supreme Court citation (post-*Furman* death-sentence cases only):
   Volume/page number in Georgia Reports
   Blank = Not applicable because no appeal

Variable
Name   Variable Label

Offender's criminal record before the event in which the murder occurred (enter
actual number; or 00 = none, −1 = unknown)

W14   Number of prior arrests
            Number of prior convictions
W15A1   Murder (1101)
W15B1   Armed robbery (1902)
W15C1   Rape (2001) and kidnapping (1311)
W15D1   Burglary (1601) and arson (1401)
W15E1   Other violent personal crimes
W15F1   Other nonviolent felonies and misdemeanors

W16   Prior incarceration in Georgia
            Yes = 1   No = 2   Unknown = 0

Characteristics of victim #1 (prepare supplemental sheets for additional victims)

W19   Sex
            Male = 1   Female = 2   Unknown = 0

W20   Race
            White = 1   Asian = 5
            Black = 2   Other = 6
            Native American = 3   Unknown = 0
            Spanish-speaking = 4

W21   Age (enter actual number of years, if known)
            Completely unknown = −1
            If phase of life cycle only is known:
            Aged adult (over 65) = 99   Teenager (13–19) = 96
            Middle-aged adult (35–65) = 98 Child (6–12) = 95
            Young adult (20–34) = 97   Preschool (under 6) = 94

Quest. 22   Relationship of victim to defendant (enter up to two foils)
                                            W22A _____   W22B _____
            01 = Husband, wife, or ex   13 = Employee or ex
            02 = Parent   14 = Employer or ex
            03 = Stepparent   15 = Coworker or ex
            04 = Child   16 = Friend or ex
            05 = Stepchild   17 = Homosexual relationship
            06 = Sibling   18 = Unrelated current or
            07 = In-law   prior confederate in crime
            08 = Other family member   19 = Other—known to victim
            10 = Neighbor   20 = Gang member
            11 = Other acquaintance   21 = Stranger
            12 = Boy- or girlfriend or ex
                 (intimate relationship)

Variable Name	Variable Label

22 = Parent-child relationship when it can't be determined whether foils 2, 3, 4, or 5 apply

23 = Business associate when it can't be determined whether foils 13, 14, or 15 apply

24 = Casual acquaintance when it can't be determined whether foil 10 or 11 applies

00 = Unknown

09 = Enter for end foil if only one applies

Quest. 23   Status of victim (enter up to two foils)   W23A ____   W23B ____

01 = On-duty police officer, corrections employee, or fireman

02 = Judicial officer (or former)/district attorney (or former)/lawyer

03 = White-collar worker

04 = Unskilled laborer

05 = Security guard (not sworn)

06 = Retired

07 = Housekeeper (for self or others)

08 = Student

10 = Juvenile (one not old enough to attend school)

11 = Unemployed or no occupation

12 = Drifter and nonresident

13 = Professional criminal

14 = Proprietor/shop owner

15 = Professional

16 = Executive

17 = Waitress, bartender, taxi driver, or similar service-person

18 = Blue-collar (all skilled laborers will be considered blue-collar; e.g., mechanics, factory workers, truck drivers, etc.)

19 = Store clerk

20 = Service-station attendant

21 = Military

22 = Apartment manager, hotel/motel manager

23 = Prostitute, pimp

24 = All other than above

25 = Farmer, fisherman

26 = Foil 8 or 10 applies, but it is not clear which

00 = Unknown

09 = Enter for second foil if only one applies

Quest. 24   Special aggravating and mitigating circumstances of victim (enter up to two foils)   W24A ____   W24B ____

01 = Bedridden/handicapped

02 = Mental defective

03 = Defenseless because of youth (1–13 years)

04 = Defenseless because of advanced age

05 = Defenseless because of physical condition or weakness (e.g., frail woman)

06 = Pregnant

07 = Supporting children

08 = Hostage

10 = Victim employed at time of crime

11 = Victim had a criminal record

12 = Other _____

13 = None

Variable Name	Variable Label

00 = Unknown	09 = Not applicable, and enter for second foil when only one applies

Characteristics of the offense(s)

Quest. 25   Where did the murder(s) occur? (enter up to three foils)

W25A _____   W25B _____   W25C _____

01 = Hotel, motel, or other commercial short-term residence	07 = Bar or cocktail lounge (and immediate environs)
02 = Victim's residence (initial entry without permission)	08 = Parking-lot area
	10 = Other place of business
	11 = Any vehicle
2A = Victim's residence (initial entry with permission, or outside)	12 = Street or sidewalk
	13 = Highway or freeway
	14 = County road in rural area
03 = Residence of offender	15 = Park or school grounds
3A = Residence of offender and victim	16 = Vacant field or woods
	17 = Jail/prison
04 = Other residence (initial entry without permission)	18 = Other _____
	19 = Other noncommercial public place
4A = Other residence (initial entry with permission, or outside)	00 = Unknown
	09 = Not applicable, and enter for second foil if only one applies
05 = Service station	
06 = Liquor store	

Quest. 26   Did the murder occur while the offender was engaged in the commission of another offense (whether or not the defendant was charged and convicted of the offense)? (enter up to four foils)   W26A _____

W26B _____   W26C _____   W26D _____

01 = Kidnapping
02 = Armed robbery
03 = Rape
04 = Aggravated battery
05 = Burglary or arson in the first degree
06 = Other violent personal crimes _____
07 = Theft
08 = Prostitution/commercial vice/narcotics
10 = Other nonviolent crime _____
11 = No contemporaneous offense
00 = Unknown
09 = Not applicable; enter for foils if fewer than four apply

Variable
Name   Variable Label

Quest. 27   Defendant's motive (enter up to four foils)   W27A ____
                                       W27B ____   W27C ____   W27D ____

            01 = Long-term hatred or revenge
            03 = Sex
            04 = Jealousy
            05 = Immediate rage (e.g., when conversation leads to argument and killing)
            06 = Killing for hire
            07 = To silence a witness to a crime
            08 = To facilitate obtaining money or other things of value for the defendant or another
            10 = To facilitate the commission of a non-property-related crime (e.g., kidnapping)
            11 = To collect insurance proceeds
            12 = Racial animosity
            13 = To escape custody from jail or prison
            14 = To facilitate the victim's suicide
            15 = To prevent arrest or recapture of the defendant or another
            16 = To avenge the role played by a present or former judicial officer, DA, or lawyer in the exercise of his/her duty
            17 = Other _____
            18 = Unclear whether 13 or 15 applies, but one of them does
            00 = Unknown
            09 = Not applicable (enter for extra foils if fewer than four apply)

Quest. 28   Special precipitating events (enter up to two foils)   W28A ____
                                                  W28B ____

            1 = Dispute between victim and defendant over money or property
            2 = Dispute because of influence of drugs or alcohol
            3 = Dispute between spouses or ex-spouses
            4 = Dispute between family members other than spouses or ex-spouses
            5 = Lovers' or ex-lovers' quarrel
            6 = Lovers' triangle
            7 = Assault on the defendant by the victim or by another
            8 = Other disputes and fights, where it is unknown who provoked the fights
            0 = Unknown
            9 = Not applicable (i.e., no precipating event), and enter for second foil if only one applies

Quest. 29   Method of killing/cause of death (enter up to four foils)
                     W29A ____   W29B ____   W29C ____   W29D ____
            01 = Gunshot wound

Variable Name	Variable Label

02 = Knife wound
03 = Bruises (beating from blunt object)
04 = Bruises (beating or stomping with such personal weapons as hands or feet)
05 = Fractures
06 = Crushing (e.g., with automobile)
07 = Hanging
08 = Strangulation with hands
10 = Strangulation with rope or garrote
11 = Choking
12 = Suffocation (e.g., in a refrigerator)
13 = Smothering (e.g., pillow, blanket)
14 = Drowning
15 = Burns (arson)
16 = Electrocution
17 = Explosion
18 = Deprivation/neglect
19 = Poisoning (including carbon monoxide)
20 = Drug or narcotic overdose
21 = Buried alive
22 = Flame or hot substance (nonarson)
23 = Victim thrown from high place
24 = Other _____
25 = Injuries from ax or similar sharp instrument
00 = Unknown
09 = Not applicable, and enter for extra foils if fewer than four apply

Quest. 30   Special aggravating and mitigating features of the offense (enter up to thirteen foils)   W30A ____   W30B ____   W30C ____
                  W30D ____   W30E ____   W30F ____   W30G ____
                  W30H ____   W30I ____   W30J ____   W30K ____
                                                 W30L ____   W30M ____

01 = Torture (methodical infliction of severe pain to punish victim, to extract information, or to satisfy sadistic urge)
02 = Other infliction of "unnecessary pain" (e.g., painful application or use of a weapon not necessary to swiftly kill the victim)
03 = Brutal stomping or beating (excessively painful or disfiguring abuse with hands or feet motivated by desire to cause pain)
04 = Lingering death of victim
06 = Violent struggle (participants injured and fight lasts for more than a few minutes)
07 = Bloody

Variable
Name   Variable Label

   08 = Victim bound and/or gagged
   10 = Luring, ambushing, lying in wait
   11 = Sniper
   12 = Execution-type murder (methodical, passionless killing of a subdued or defenseless victim)
   13 = Case involved contemporaneous felony, and the killing was unnecessary to complete the crime (e.g., storekeeper turned over money and offered no resistance)
   14 = Sexual perversion or abuse other than rape (sodomy, etc.)
   15 = Victim pleaded for life
   16 = Defendant expressed pleasure with the killing at the time of the crime
   17 = Mutilation (with knife or other)
   18 = Multiple shots to head
   19 = Multiple shots to body
   20 = Multiple stabbing
   21 = Slashed throat
   22 = Defendant on escape from jail or prison
   23 = Defendant actively resisted arrest
   24 = Defendant showed remorse for crime after capture
   25 = Defendant or coperpetrator disrobed victim
   26 = Victim was not clothed (in whole or in part) at the time of the killing
   27 = Defendant planned the killing for more than five minutes
   28 = Defendant planned a contemporaneous offense for more than five minutes
   29 = Defendant mutilated, dismembered, inflicted serious injury upon, or sexually assaulted the victim's body after death
   30 = Defendant attempted to dispose of or conceal the body after the murder
   31 = Defendant committed or is alleged to have committed additional crimes between the time of the murder and his/her arrest (whether or not charged)
   32 = Defendant gave him/herself up within twenty-four hours after the crime was committed
   33 = Other _____
   00 = Unknown
   09 = Enter for extra foils if fewer than thirteen apply
   34 = No special aggravating circumstances

Number of persons killed

W31   By defendant: enter actual number   Unknown = -1
      Count those actually killed by the offender, i.e., those killings for which defendant was the triggerman

Variable Name	Variable Label

W33   Number of victims killed by other coperpetrators: enter actual number
Unknown = -1 Not applicable, no coperpetrators = 99

Number of persons injured or endangered

Number of persons injured other than deceased victim(s)

W34   By defendant: enter actual number
Unknown = -1
Not applicable, victim only person involved in the incident = -2

W35   By coperpetrators: enter actual number
Unknown = -1
Not applicable, victim only person involved in incident or no coperpetrators = -2

W35A   If a gun was used, number of shots fired by defendant and coperpetrators: enter actual number or best estimate
Unknown = -1 Gun not used = -2

W36   How many more than one person was knowingly exposed to "Great Risk of Death" by the conduct of the defendant? Enter actual number or best estimate: Unknown = -1

W37   Was the "Great Risk of Death" referred to in question 36 centered in a public place?
Yes = 1   No = 2   Unknown = 0
No one other than victim exposed to "Great Risk of Death" by defendant = 9

W38   Status of defendant: Enter one foil

01 = On-duty police officer, corrections employee, or fireman	11 = Unemployed, sporadic, or no occupation
02 = White-collar worker (same definition as for victim, status of)	12 = Drifter
	13 = Professional criminal
	14 = Proprietor/shop owner
03 = Unskilled laborer	15 = Professional
04 = Security guard (not sworn officer)	16 = Executive
	17 = Waitress, bartender, taxi driver, or similar service-person
05 = Retired	
06 = Housekeeper, for self or others	18 = Blue-collar worker (all skilled laborers; see victim, status of)
07 = Student	
08 = Juvenile (one not old enough to attend school)	19 = Store clerk
	20 = Service-station attendant
10 = Babysitter of victim	21 = Military

Variable
Name   Variable Label

22 =	Apartment manager, hotel/motel manager	24 =	Farmer, fisherman
23 =	Prostitute, pimp	25 =	Other than above
		00 =	Unknown

Defendant's role in the victim's death and in any contemporaneous felony

W40   Number of coperpetrators: Enter actual number. Enter 00 if defendant acted alone. (If 00 is entered, enter 99 for questions 41 and 42.)

99 = Unknown how many coperpetrators, but there were coperpetrators

−1 = Unknown if there were any coperpetrators

Quest. 41   If there was a coperpetrator(s), did the defendant (enter up to two foils; for columns b and c):   W41A ____   W41B ____

A) Cause or direct another to commit murder? = 1

B) Participate directly and act as the prime mover:
   In the murder? = 02   In a contemporaneous felony? = 03

C) Participate directly as a coequal:
   In the murder? = 04   In a contemporaneous crime? = 05

D) Act as an underling or minor participant:
   In the murder? = 06   In a contemporaneous crime? = 07

E) Act as an agent or employee for another person:
   In the murder? = 08   In a contemporaneous crime? = 10

F) Not play a direct role (e.g., act as a lookout):
   In the murder? = 11   In a contemporaneous crime? = 12

G) Other = 13

H) Unknown = 00

I) Not applicable—no coperpetrators and no contemporaneous crime; also enter for second foil if only one applies = 09

Variables W41AA, W41AB, W41AC, and W41AD apply to type of liability trial and defense(s) invoked at that trial (enter up to four foils):   W41AA ____   W41AB ____   W41AC ____
                                                                                                          W41AD ____

Defendant's trial

1 = The liability trial was before a jury

2 = The liability trial was before a judge only

8 = The judge imposed sentence after the guilty plea

Defendant's defense at liability trial

3 = Alibi

4 = Accident

5 = Insanity or delusional compulsion

6 = Mistaken identity (someone else did it)

7 = Defendant claimed voluntary or involuntary manslaughter

Variable Name	Variable Label

9 = Enter for additional foils if fewer than four apply

0 = Unknown

Quest. 42   Mitigating circumstances

Relating to the offense from the defendant's perspective (enter up to eight foils)   W42A ____   W42B ____   W42C ____

W42D ____   W42E ____   W42F ____   W42G ____

W42H ____

The defendant:

01 = Acted under duress or the domination of another person

02 = Had used alcohol or drugs immediately before the crime

03–06 = The effect on the defendant at the time of the crime of the drugs or alcohol he/she consumed was:

     03 = Negligible   05 = Moderate

     04 = Slight   06 = Substantial

07 = Had a history of drug or alcohol abuse

08 = Was not the actual killer—only an accessory

10 = Had no intent to kill

11 = Had a questionable mental capacity to appreciate the wrongfulness of his conduct because of mental disease or defect

12 = Was emotionally disturbed at time of killing, as opposed to being under influence of drugs or alcohol

13 = Had a moral justification for killing (e.g., needed money for sick child; specify) _____

14 = Surrendered to authorities

15 = Cooperated with authorities (e.g., testified for prosecution)

16 = Coperpetrator(s) received life sentence(s), a lesser sentence, or no sentence

17–20 = Other extenuating circumstances relating to the defendant (specify and enter a foil 17, 18, 19, or 20 for each) _____

00 = Unknown

09 = Not applicable because no mitigating factors (enter for extra foils if fewer than eight apply)

Quest. 43   Relating to the victim (enter up to five foils)   W43A ____

W43B ____ W43C ____   W43D ____   W43E ____

01 = Aroused defendant's sexual desire

02 = Aroused defendant's rage just prior to killing

03 = Previous action to arouse defendant's hate

04 = Aroused defendant's fear for life (e.g., in a fight)

Variable
Name   Variable Label

05 = Provoked defendant with verbal abuse or attack

06 = Had abused (physically or verbally), assaulted, or injured a person that defendant cared about

07 = Provoked defendant by striking, attacking, or starting a fight

08 = Victim had used alcohol or drugs immediately prior to crime

10–13 = Effects on the victim of the alcohol or drugs used prior to the crime:

10 = Negligible   11 = Slight   12 = Moderate   13 = Substantial

14 = Victim showing or talking about large amounts of money

15 = History of bad blood between defendant and victim

16 = Victim consent

17 = Victim a fugitive at time of killing

18–20 = Other extenuating circumstances related to the victim (specify and enter numbers 18–20 for each) _____

21 = No apparent extenuating circumstances relating to the victim

22 = Had a criminal record

23 = Was a participant in the crime

00 = Unknown

09 = Enter for extra foils if fewer than five apply

W45	Number of supplemental victim forms completed for this questionnaire (regardless of actual number of victims). Enter actual number completed.

Coding for multiple victims

For 2d to 6th victim coding: See counterpart questions for first victim, e.g., WA20, see W20

WA19	2d victim—Sex
WA20	2d victim—Race
WA21	2d victim—Age
WA22	2d victim—Relation of vic. with def.
WA23A	2d victim—Status of victim
WA23B	2d victim—Status of victim
WA24A	2d victim—Spec. agg/mit. cir. of vic.
WA24B	2d victim—Spec. agg/mit. cir. of vic.
WB19	3d victim—Sex
WB20	3d victim—Race
WB21	3d victim—Age
WB22	3d victim—Relation of vic. to def.
WB23A	3d victim—Status of victim
WB23B	3d victim—Status of victim
WB24A	3d victim—Spec. agg/mit. cir. of vic.
WB24B	3d victim—Spec. agg/mit. cir. of vic.

Variable Name	Variable Label
WC19	4th victim—Sex
WC20	4th victim—Race
WC21	4th victim—Age
WC22	4th victim—Relation of vic. to def.
WC23A	4th victim—Status of victim
WC23B	4th victim—Status of victim
WC24A	4th victim—Spec. agg/mit. cir. of vic.
WC24B	4th victim—Spec. agg/mit. cir. of vic.
WD19	5th victim—Sex
WD20	5th victim—Race
WD21	5th victim—Age
WD22	5th victim—Relation of vic. to def.
WD23A	5th victim—Status of victim
WD23B	5th victim—Status of victim
WD24A	5th victim—Spec. agg/mit. cir. of vic.
WD24B	5th victim—Spec. agg/mit. cir. of vic.
WE19	6th victim—Sex
WE20	6th victim—Race
WE21	6th victim—Age
WE22	6th victim—Relation of vic. to def.
WE23A	6th victim—Status of victim
WE23B	6th victim—Status of victim
WE24A	6th victim—Spec. agg/mit. cir. of vic.
WE24B	6th victim—Spec. agg/mit. cir. of vic.

APPENDIX D

Variable Names and Labels and Frequency
Distribution of Case Characteristics Used in
Statistical Analyses Pre- and Post-*Furman:*
Procedural Reform Study

The number of cases in each data set is indicated below. The proportion of cases with the characteristic indicated follow each entry. The post-*Furman* data indicate separately the distributions among all cases and among the cases identified by our measures as death-eligible under Georgia's post-*Furman* statutory aggravating circumstances. Twelve post-*Furman* cases that received two death sentences are counted only once in both post-*Furman* counts. The 294 pre-*Furman* cases are estimates based on a sample, while the post-*Furman* counts include all cases in the universe. *See infra* chapter 4, note 2 and accompanying text, for a description of the pre-*Furman* sample.

		Post-*Furman*	
	Pre-*Furman* (*n* = 294)	Death-Eligible Cases (*n* = 471)	All Cases (*n* = 594)
I. THE DEFENDANT			
A. Age/Sex			
1. Defendant's age at time of crime (AGE)			
1–16	.02	.03	.03
17–20	.09	.21	.19
21–25	.26	.29	.26
26–35	.36	.27	.28
36–50	.21	.11	.14
over 50	.06	.08	.09
2. Defendant 50 + (OLDER)	.06	.08	.09
3. Female defendant (DFEM)	.04	.09	.10
4. Defendant aged 17 through 25 (YNGADLT)	.35	.50	.45
5. Defendant under 16 years of age (STMIT3)	.03	.07	.07
B. Physical/mental			

1. Defendant had a history
      of drug or alcohol abuse
      (DRGHIS)
	.32	.12	.13

| | | Post-*Furman* | |
	Pre-*Furman*	Death-Eligible	All Cases
2. Defendant lacked capacity to appreciate criminality of his conduct (STMIT1)	.10	.06	.07
C. Socioeconomic/geographic			
1. Defendant in military (MILDEFN)	.02	.04	.03
2. Defendant police/security guard (DPOLSEC)	.02	.01	.01
3. High-status defendant: white-collar, proprietor, professional, executive (HISTD)	.05	.05	.05
4. Low-status defendant (LSTATDEF)	.62	.67	.66
5. Defendant an out-of-country resident (DOUTCONT)	.45	.33	.30
6. Defendant an out-of-state resident (DOUTSTAT)	.16	.12	.10
D. Prior record			
1. Felony record			
a. Defendant had a felony record (FELREC)	.34	.35	.33
b. Defendant had a record for a serious violent felony (SERVFEL)	.11	.14	.14
2. Prior convictions			
a. The total number of defendant's prior convictions (CONVICTX)			
0	.27	.52	.53
1	.21	.14	.15
2	.11	.09	.08
3	.09	.06	.06
4	.08	.05	.05
5	.04	.04	.04
6	.03	.03	.03
7	.03	.02	.02
8	.05	.01	.01
9 or more	.05	.05	.05

	Pre-*Furman*	Post-*Furman*	
		Death-Eligible	All Cases
b. One or more prior convictions for murder, armed robbery, rape, kidnap (SVPCR)	.06	.08	.06
c. Number of prior convictions for murder, armed robbery, rape, kidnap (SVPCRX)			
0	.94	.92	.94
1	.05	.06	.05
2	.01	.01	.01
3 or more	.01	.01	.01
d. Number of prior convictions for murder, armed robbery, rape, kidnap, and other violent personal crimes as defined by Georgia Department of Corrections (VPCX)			
0	.77	.79	.79
1	.16	.13	.14
2	.03	.04	.04
3	.03	.02	.02
4	NC[1]	.01	.01
5 or more	.01	.01	.01
e. One or more prior convictions for violent personal crimes (VPERCR)	.20	.20	.20
f. Number of prior convictions: violent personal crimes (VPERCRX)			
0	.80	.80	.81
1	.14	.12	.13
2	.02	.03	.03
3 or more	.04	.05	.05
g. Number of prior felony convictions reported (PRIFEL)			
0	.67	.65	.67

1. NC means no cases.

	Pre-*Furman*	Post-*Furman*	
		Death-Eligible	All Cases
1	.21	.19	.19
2	.07	.05	.05
3	.02	.05	.04
4 or more	.04	.06	.06

h. Number of prior convictions for murder (W15A1)

	Pre-*Furman*	Death-Eligible	All Cases
0	.98	.99	.99
1	.02	.01	.01

i. Number of prior convictions for armed robbery (W15B1)

0	.97	.94	.95
1	.02	.05	.04
2	.01	.01	.01
3 or more	.01	.01	.01

j. Number of prior convictions for rape or kidnapping (W15C1)

0	.99	.99	.99
1	.02	.01	.01

k. Number of prior convictions for other violent personal crimes (W15D)

0	.93	.89	.89
1	.06	.07	.08
2 or more	.01	.03	.03

l. Number of prior convictions for arson or burglary (W15D1)

0	.79	.84	.86
1	.10	.09	.08
2 or more	.11	.07	.06

m. Number of prior convictions for felonies and misdemeanors other than h through l above (W15F1)

0	.34	.55	.55
1	.22	.14	.14
2	.11	.10	.10
3	.08	.04	.04

		Post-*Furman*	
	Pre-*Furman*	Death-Eligible	All Cases
4	.08	.03	.03
5	.04	.03	.03
6 or more	.13	.05	.06
n. Number of prior con- victions for serious crimes (SERCRIMX)			
0	.64	.70	.71
1	.19	.15	.16
2	.05	.05	.05
3	.04	.05	.04
4	.02	.02	.02
5 or more	.07	.03	.03
o. Defendant had a record of convictions for a felony or two or more violent misde- meanors (FEL–2VMD)	.37	.36	.34
p. Number of prior con- victions for violent personal crimes (W15E1)			
0	.84	.85	.84
1	.11	.10	.11
2	.01	.02	.03
3	.02	.02	.02
4 or more	.02	.01	.006
q. Number of serious felonies and violent personal crimes (SUMW15)			
0	.64	.70	.71
1	.19	.15	.16
2	.05	.05	.05
3	.04	.05	.04
4	.02	.02	.02
5	.05	.01	.01
6 or more	.01	.02	.01
3. No convictions			
a. No criminal convic- tions (NORECORD)	.25	.45	.45

| | Pre-*Furman* | Post-*Furman* | |
		Death-Eligible	All Cases
b. No conviction for a serious crime (NOSERCRI)	.61	.69	.70
c. No conviction for a serious violent felony (NOVPC)	.68	.73	.75
d. No felony convictions (NOFEL)	.67	.65	.67

II. THE VICTIM

A. Age/sex/physical

	Pre-*Furman*	Death-Eligible	All Cases
1. Victim was a female (FEMVIC)	.27	.27	.27
2. Victim was 65 years or more (OLDVIC)	.02	.10	.08
3. Victim defenseless/ youth (VICYNG)	.03	.04	.04
4. Victim pregnant, disabled, helpless (VICDEFS)	.12	.20	.17
5. Victim 12 or younger (YNGVIC)	.03	.04	.04
6. Victim nude (YNUDDIS)	.05	.11	.09

B. The number of victims

	Pre-*Furman*	Death-Eligible	All Cases
1. Either defendant or a coperpetrator individually killed two or more victims (TWOVIC)	.03	.08	.06
2. A total of two or more victims killed by defendant and coperpetrator(s) (TWOVICAL)	.06	.09	.07

C. Socioeconomic status

	Pre-*Furman*	Death-Eligible	All Cases
1. Victim low status (VICLSTAT)	.23	.14	.14
2. Victim a fugitive (VFUGIT)	NC	.01	.01

III. THE CRIME

A. Statutory aggravating circumstances

    1. Georgia post-*Furman* statutory aggravating circumstances

		Post-*Furman*	
	Pre-*Furman*	Death-Eligible	All Cases
a. B1—Prior record of murder/armed robbery, rape, kidnapping (PBQB1)	.07	.09	.07
b. B2—Contemporaneous murder, robbery, rape, kidnapping, burglary, arson (PBQB2)	.34	.55	.44
c. B3—Two or more people beyond victim at great risk of death (PBQB3)	.09	.20	.16
d. B4—Murder for money/value (PBQB4)	.33	.43	.34
e. B5—Victim a DA/judicial officer (PBQB5)	.03	NC	NC
f. B6—Murder for hire (PBQB6)	.01	.04	.03
g. B7—Murder wanton, vile, torture, depravation[2] (PBQB7)	.37	.63	.50
(1) Victim mutilated before or after death (PBQB7A)	.03	.10	.08
(2) Unnecessary multiple wounding (e.g., torture) (PBQB7B)	.30	.45	.36
(3) Kidnap or rape of a defenseless victim (PBQB7C)	NC	.03	.02
(4) To silence helpless, pleading witness (PBQB7D)	.01	.14	.11
(5) Sex perversion involved (PBQB7E)	.03	.14	.11

2. The wanton/vile factor was considered present in a case if one or more of factors PBQB7A through PBQB7F were present in the case. The coding of PBQB7A through PBQB7F is based on an analysis of the facts and the Georgia Supreme Court opinions for all cases in which that court reviewed a B7 finding in a post-*Furman* death-sentence case in this study.

	Pre-*Furman*	Post-*Furman*	
		Death-Eligible	All Cases
(6) Beat, strangle, drown, poison, torture (PBQB7F)	.11	.16	.12
h. B8—Victim police, corrections officer, fireman (PBQB8)	.07	.03	.03
i. B9—Defendant was prisoner or escapee (PBQB9)	.02	.04	.03
j. B10—Killing to avoid or stop arrest (PBQB10)	.26	.26	.20
2. Number of Georgia post-*Furman* death-eligible factors in case (PBQDELX)			
0	.28	.02[3]	.22
1	.28	.31	.24
2	.18	.27	.22
3	.15	.25	.20
4	.08	.13	.10
5	.03	.03	.02
6	.01	.004	.003
3. Number of Georgia post-*Furman* death-eligible factors with B7 elements expanded (DELB7EX)[4]			
0	.28	.02[5]	.22
1	.24	.28	.22
2	.16	.23	.19
3	.19	.22	.17
4	.08	.13	.10
5	.03	.08	.06
6 or more	.01	.06	.05
B. Contemporaneous offenses			
1. Armed robbery involved (ARMROB)	.21	.38	.31

3. These cases ($n = 7$) advanced to a penalty trial even though our measures classify them as not death-eligible. *See supra* chap. 4, note 38, for a discussion of this measurement problem.

4. This variable counts variables B1 through B6, B8 through B10, and the multiple subelements of B7 (PBQB7A through PBQB7F).

5. *See supra* note 3.

	Pre-*Furman*	Post-*Furman*	
		Death-Eligible	All Cases
2. Burglary or first-degree arson involved (BURGARS)	.06	.05	.04
3. Victim was kidnapped (KIDNAP)	.03	.11	.09
4. Case involved a hired killer (KILLHIRE)	.01	.02	.02
5. Rape involved (RAPE)	.03	.07	.05
6. Serious contemporaneous offense involved (SERCONOF)	.33	.51	.40
7. Kidnapping and multiple shots (KDNPAMSH)	.003	.03	.03
8. Neither kidnapping nor multiple shots (NKNPOMSH)	.94	.80	.84
C. Circumstances leading up to the crime			
1. Family or lover dispute (FAMLVDIS)	.23	.16	.19
2. Dispute influenced by drugs/alcohol (DRUGDIS)	.21	.14	.18
3. Killing occurred in escape from jail/prison (ESCAPE)	.01	.01	.01
D. Method of killing			
1. Killed by beating (BEAT)	.04	.13	.12
2. Bloody murder involved (BLOODY)	.09	.31	.29
3. Victim drowned (DROWN)	.003	.03	.03
4. Execution-style murder (EXECK)	.08	.05	.04
5. Killed by fractures (FRAC)	.003	.05	.04
6. Knife killing (KNIFE)	.09	.14	.14
7. Multiple shots (MULSH)	.04	.12	.10
8. Multiple stabs (MULSTAB)	.06	.10	.08
9. Victim killed with poison (POISON)	.01	.002	.002
10. Brutal stomping/beating (STOMP)	.07	.06	.04

	Pre-*Furman*	Post-*Furman*	
		Death-Eligible	All Cases
11. Killed by strangulation (STRANG)	.02	.05	.04
12. Killed by imprisonment/starvation (deprivation) (DEPRIVE)	.01	NC	.002
13. Victim's throat was slashed (SLASHTH)	NC	.03	.02
14. Torture involved (TORT)	.01	.05	.04
15. Victim was a hostage (HOST)	NC	.02	.01

E. Other aggravating factors related to the crime

	Pre-*Furman*	Death-Eligible	All Cases
1. Victim bound and/or gagged (VICBDGAG)	.03	.07	.05
2. Defendant lying in wait (AMBUSH)	.09	.12	.11
3. Mutilation involved (MUTIL)	.01	.10	.08
4. Sexual perversion involved (PERVR)	.01	.04	.03
5. Unnecessary pain involved (UNNEPAIN)	NC	.10	.08

F. Defendant's role in the crime

1. Motive for killing

	Pre-*Furman*	Death-Eligible	All Cases
a. Aggravated motive (AGGMOT)	.43	.58	.48
b. Hate/revenge motive (HATE)	.21	.18	.21
c. Insurance motive (INSMOT)	.01	.03	.03
d. Jealousy motive (JEALOS)	.10	.06	.07
e. Money motive (OBTMON)	.32	.41	.32
f. Motive to prevent arrest (PREESC)	.18	.12	.10
g. Race-hatred motive (RACE)	.03	.02	.01
h. Immediate-rage motive (RAGE)	.46	.26	.33
i. Sex motive (SEXMT)	.04	.11	.10

	Pre-*Furman*	Post-*Furman*	
		Death-Eligible	All Cases
j. Victim killed because a witness (SILWIT)	.06	.13	.11
k. Motive to facilitate a non-property-related crime (NONPCRM)	NC	.10	.08
l. An aggravated motive and one or more prior felonies (AGMOTAPF)	.22	.21	.17
2. Defendant's participation			
a. Defendant claimed a moral justification (DJUST)	.02	.02	.02
b. There were coperpetrators and defendant directly participated as coequal in the killing (DKILLER)	.13	.16	.14
c. Defendant was leader with coperpetrators in the murder or contemporaneous felony (DLEADMF)	.15	.25	.21
d. Defendant was an underling in the murder (DUNDERLG)	.07	.07	.07
e. Defendant injured one or more persons (INJURE)	.11	.09	.08
f. Defendant was not the triggerman (NOKILL)	.09	.19	.16
g. Defendant engaged in a nonviolent contemporaneous offense (NONVCOF)	.05	.13	.11
h. Defendant fired one shot (ONESHOT)	.34	.22	.27
i. Defendant fired five or more shots (SHOT5)	.13	.12	.11

	Pre-*Furman*	Post-*Furman*	
		Death-Eligible	All Cases
j. Defendant acted under the domination of another (STMIT2)	.02	.02	.02
k. Defendant under mental or emotional disturbance (STMIT5)	.07	.04	.04
l. Killing was not necessary (UNNEC)	.13	.17	.13
m. One or more coperpetrators involved (COPERP)	.36	.52	.45
n. Coperpetrator involved and defendant participated in contemporaneous offense (DIRROLCO)	.25	.34	.27
o. Five or more people at risk of death or serious bodily injury (RISK5)	.01	.05	.04
G. Miscellaneous case characteristics			
1. Defendant's emotions about killing			
a. Defendant showed remorse (DEFREM)	.01	.05	.05
b. Defendant expressed pleasure (DEFPLEA)	NC	.06	.05
c. Defendant expressed remorse or surrendered to authorities (1), did both (2), or did neither (0) (MITCIR1)			
0	.90	.90	.86
1	.09	.09	.12
2	.003	.01	.02
2. Defendant's condition at time of crime			
a. Defendant an escapee (DEFESC)	.02	.03	.02
b. Defendant heavily intoxicated (DDRG)	.18	.09	.11

	Pre-*Furman*	Post-*Furman*	
		Death-Eligible	All Cases
3. Defendant's actions before crime			
a. Defendant planned murder or contemporaneous offense more than five minutes (PREMED)	.60	.51	.46
b. Defendant planned contemporaneous offense more than five minutes (PREMEDF)	.36	.33	.28
c. Defendant planned killing more than five minutes (PREMEDK)	.33	.33	.30
4. Defendant's actions after crime			
a. Defendant actively resisted arrest (DEFRSARR)	.12	.16	.13
b. Defendant gave up within twenty-four hours (DFSUR24)	.09	.07	.10
c. Defendant surrendered to authorities (DSUR)	.10	.13	.17
d. Defendant cooperated with authorities (STMIT9)	.08	.04	.04
e. Defendant with a prior felony conviction resisted arrest (DEFRAAPF)	.06	.07	.06
f. Defendant committed an additional crime after the murder (ADCRIM)	.10	.12	.10
5. Victim's association with the defendant			
a. Bad blood (VBDBLD)	.10	.04	.03
b. Victim was a friend, relative, or intimate acquaintance (VICCLOSE)	.46	.41	.48

	Pre-*Furman*	Post-*Furman*	
		Death-Eligible	All Cases
c. Victim was a stranger (VICSTRAN)	.31	.36	.30
6. Actions by the victim affecting the defendant			
a. Victim aroused fear (DFEAR)	.25	.18	.20
b. Victim aroused hate (VACT)	.25	.20	.22
c. Victim verbally attacked defendant (VERATK)	.06	.03	.03
d. Victim aroused defendant's rage just prior to killing (VRAGE)	.42	.25	.32
e. Victim had attacked a third person defendant cared about (VINJD)	.01	.02	.02
f. Victim provoked defendant (VPROV)	.09	.05	.06
g. Victim offered no provocation (NOPROV)	.31	.57	.51
7. Barnett classification variables[6]			
a. Likelihood defendant was a deliberate killer (DELIBRAT)			
Low (0)	NC	.27	.26
High (2)	NC	.08	.06
Neither 0 nor 2 (1)	NC	.66	.68
b. Defendant-victim relationship (VICTIM) Intimate/friends			
(0)	NC	.58	.65
Strangers (1)	NC	.43	.36
c. Heinousness of the killing (VILE) Elements of self-			
defense (0)	NC	.10	.11

6. Data available only on post-*Furman* cases.

		Post-*Furman*	
	Pre-*Furman*	Death-Eligible	All Cases
A vile killing (2)	NC	.36	.29
Neither 0 nor 2 (1)	NC	.55	.60

IV. OTHER AGGRAVATING
AND MITIGATING FACTORS

A. Number of statutory aggravating circumstances—
from all jurisdictions
(ALSTAGCR)

	Pre-*Furman*	Death-Eligible	All Cases
0	.13	.002	.10
1	.24	.13	.19
2	.12	.18	.17
3	.14	.16	.13
4	.17	.15	.12
5 or more	.20	.38	.30

B. Nonstatutory aggravating
circumstances

1. Number of aggravating
factors (AGGCIRX)

	Pre-*Furman*	Death-Eligible	All Cases
0	.20	.07	.14
1	.26	.19	.22
2	.22	.23	.22
3	.16	.19	.16
4	.07	.10	.08
5 or more	.09	.22	.17

2. One or more aggravat-
ing methods of killing
(AGGMETKL)

	Pre-*Furman*	Death-Eligible	All Cases
	.06	.21	.19

3. Number of minor aggra-
vating circumstances
(MINAGCRX)

	Pre-*Furman*	Death-Eligible	All Cases
0	.32	.25	.31
1	.41	.32	.33
2	.16	.26	.23
3	.06	.10	.08
4 or more	.05	.07	.05

4. Number of major aggra-
vating circumstances
(MAJAGCRX)

	Pre-*Furman*	Death-Eligible	All Cases
0	.87	.65	.72
1	.10	.22	.18
2	.02	.07	.06
3 or more	.01	.06	.05

	Pre-*Furman*	Post-*Furman*	
		Death-Eligible	All Cases
5. One or more major aggravating circumstances (MAJAGCIR)	.13	.35	.28
6. One or more minor aggravating circumstances (MINAGGCR)	.68	.75	.69
7. No aggravating circumstances (NOAGGCIR)	.20	.07	.14
C. Mitigating circumstances			
1. One or more mitigating circumstances (MITCIR)	.85	.68	.73
2. The number of mitigating circumstances (MITCIRX)			
0	.15	.32	.27
1	.36	.36	.36
2	.39	.26	.29
3	.09	.06	.09
3. The number of mitigating circumstances concerning the defendant (MITCIR2)			
0	.42	.56	.51
1	.25	.32	.35
2	.24	.10	.12
3 or more	.09	.02	.03
4. The number of mitigating circumstances concerning the victim (MITCIR3)			
0	.26	.49	.43
1	.30	.24	.25
2	.29	.17	.19
3	.09	.08	.10
4 or more	.06	.02	.03
5. A mitigating defense present (MITDEF)	.42	.31	.38
6. A mitigating motive present (MITMOT)	.59	.41	.49
7. No victim mitigating circumstances (NOVMC)	.20	.40	.35

		Post-*Furman*	
	Pre-*Furman*	Death-Eligible	All Cases
8. No contemporaneous offense (NOCONTOF)	.48	.34	.44
9. Other mitigating circumstances (OTHMIT)	.19	.12	.12
10. A victim mitigating circumstance present (OTHVMIT)	.09	.05	.05
11. The number of victim aggravating circumstances (VITCIR)			
0	.50	.47	.54
1	.48	.48	.42
2	.02	.06	.05
D. Other			
1. Aggravated battery involved (AGGBAT)	.04	.07	.06
2. One or more precipitating events (PRECIPEV)	.59	.43	.50
3. Number of precipitating circumstances (PRECIPX)			
0	.41	.57	.50
1	.39	.33	.39
2	.20	.10	.11
V. DEFENDANT'S POSITION AT TRIAL			
A. Accident defense (ACCD)	.15	.08	.13
B. Victim assault (DEFENSE)	.06	.03	.03
C. No intent to kill (DNOINT)	.17	.08	.10
D. Insanity defense (INSANE)	.04	.09	.09
E. Manslaughter defense (MANSLAUG)	.27	.17	.21
F. Defendant believed actions were justified (STMIT8)	.02	.02	.02
VI. DEFENDANT AND VICTIM RACIAL CHARACTERISTICS			
A. Black defendant (BLACKD)	.62	.59	.60
B. One or more white victims (WHVICRC)	.61	.64	.59
C. Defendant/victim racial combinations (RACEVDRC)			
1. Black defendant/white victim	.26	.25	.21

| | | Post-*Furman* | |
	Pre-*Furman*	Death-Eligible	All Cases
2. White defendant/white victim	.35	.39	.38
3. Black defendant/black victim	.36	.33	.39
4. White defendant/black victim	.03	.03	.02

VII. GEOGRAPHIC AND PROCE-
DURAL CHARACTERISTICS

A. Five regions of the state (v3J)

	Pre-*Furman*	Death-Eligible	All Cases
1. North	.10	.10	.10
2. North Central	.32	.32	.31
3. Atlanta	.15	.15	.17
4. Southwest	.20	.21	.22
5. Southeast	.24	.21	.20
B. Trial in urban judicial circuit (URBN3D)	.46	.45	.45
C. Penalty trial sought by prosecutor against defendants convicted of murder at trial (x2481PRC)	NA[7]	.42	.33
D. Death sentences imposed among cases advanced to a penalty trial (x2481JRC)	NA[7]	.52	.52
E. Death sentences imposed among defendants convicted of murder at trial (x481C)	.15	.21	.17

7. NA—No information available for pre-*Furman* cases.

APPENDIX E

Questionnaire/Codebook for the Charging and Sentencing Study

Part I. Defendant data from Department of Offender Rehabilitation (DOR)

Variable name

DOC 33   Race
1 = White   2 = Black   3 = Native American
4 = Spanish-speaking   5 = Other

DOC 34   Sex
1 = Male   2 = Female

DOC 35   Birthdate   YY/MM/DD

DOC 41   Home county—code Georgia counties 1–159
999 = Out of state

DOC 42   State of birth

DOC 47   Socioeconomic class
0 = Not reported   3 = Minimum standard of living (be-
1 = Welfare   low official poverty levels)
2 = Occasionally employed   4 = Middle class
                                5 = Other or unknown

DOC 410   Marital status: this is marital status at time of entry to prison (#1).
Use status at time of conviction (#2) if (#1) is unknown, or status at
time of crime if #1 and #2 are unknown.
0 = Not reported   4 = Divorced (not remarried)
1 = Single (never married)   5 = Widowed
2 = Married   6 = Common-law marriage
3 = Separated

DOC 411   Number of children
Blank = Not reported   0 = None   1–8 = 1–8   9 = 9 or more

DOC 413   Educational level
00 = Not reported   17 = Master's degree
01– 12 = As indicated   18 = Doctor of philosophy (Ph.D.)
13 = One year of college   19 = Doctor of laws (LL.D.)
14 = Two years of college   20 = Doctor of medicine (M.D.)
15 = Three years of col-   99 = Had no school at all
       lege
16 = Four years of college
       (bachelor's degree)

DOC 414   Functional grade equivalent score (enter WRAT score): this is the average of the Wide-Range Achievement Test reading, math, and spelling

512

subtests. 000 = Not reported. The three-digit field has one implied decimal place; e.g., if the field contains "078," that inmate has the equivalent of 7.8 years of standard education. In general, WRAT scores are far below the self-reported grade levels.

DOC 433	Type military discharge		
	0 = Not reported	4 = Bad conduct	
	1 = Honorable	5 = Dishonorable	
	2 = General	6 = Was on active duty	
	3 = Undesirable	(not discharged)	

DOC 433 — Type military discharge
0 = Not reported 4 = Bad conduct
1 = Honorable 5 = Dishonorable
2 = General 6 = Was on active duty
3 = Undesirable (not discharged)

DOC 434 — Branch of military service
0 = Not reported 4 = Marines
1 = Air Force 5 = Coast Guard
2 = Army 6 = Other
3 = Navy 9 = No military service

DOC 54 — Number of sentences: this is the number of different sentences that the inmate is serving or is about to serve. Thus, if an inmate has three concurrent five-year sentences (and one three-year sentence to run consecutively to his five-year sentences), he will have "4" in this field.

DOC 61 — Most serious current offense
1101 = Murder
1102 = Voluntary manslaughter

DOC 612A — Prior arrests from FBI rap sheet (number)

DOC 612B — Prior convictions from FBI rap sheet (number)

DOC 612C — County of conviction

DOC 613 — Prior Georgia incarceration: based on rap sheet, code "Y" if yes, "N" if no, "U" if unknown, and blank if there was no rap sheet.

DOC 72 — Date sentence began

DOC 82 — Age at sentencing in years

D1125 — Arrest date: this is the date the inmate was arrested for the offense that resulted in the present incarceration. It is almost always the same as "date sentence began," except for revocations.

Part II. Codebook for data obtained from the Georgia Department of Pardons and Paroles and Records and Reports of the Georgia Supreme Court, Georgia Department of Vital Statistics, and Georgia prosecutors and defense attorneys*

Question
Number

1. Case number (CAS)

2. Sample code:
   1 = 25% sample   2 = 25% sample and all death   _____
                              on DOC list   (3)

*In Part II, question numbers appear on the left margin, while variable numbers or names are shown within parentheses; e.g., "Date of Arrest" is variable (4A).

3 = Death case not on DOC list   5 = 25% sample, death, life
    but before 12/31/79   penalty, and circuit supple-
4 = 25% sample, death and life   mentation
    penalty   6 = Other

3.   Date of offense   /_/_/
                                                               (4)

4.   Date of arrest   /_/_/
                                                             (4A)

5.   Date of sentence   /_/_/
                                                              (4B)

6.   County of conviction _____   _____   _____
                               Name   County Code #   (4C)

7.   Indictment #   _____
                                                                   (5)

8.   Procedure re: liability
    Part A
    Code: 1 = Jury trial   3 = No trial, guilty plea entered   _____
             2 = Bench trial   (6)
    Part B
    Code: 1 = First conviction   3 = Subsequent conviction   _____
             2 = Second conviction   (specify _____)   (7)

9.   Presiding judge's name _____
                                                                      (8)

9A. District attorney's name _____
                                                                    (9)

9B. Status of the defense counsel   _____
    1 = Retained   6 = Georgia Criminal-Justice   (10)
    2 = Appointed—private   Program
    3 = Public Defender   7 = Team Defense Project, Inc.
    4 = Legal Aid   8 = Appointed, but affiliation
    5 = Georgia ACLU   unknown

10.   Offender's present offenses
    (1) Crime code: 1 = Murder   8B = Aggravated battery
                    2 = Voluntary man-   (§1305) against one not a
                      slaughter   victim
                    3 = Involuntary man-   9 = Simple robbery
                      slaughter   10 = Aggravated assault
                    4 = Armed robbery   (§1302) against a victim
                    5 = Rape   10A = Aggravated assault
                    6 = Kidnapping   (§1302) against one not a
                    7 = Burglary   victim
                    8 = Arson in first degree   11 = Other personal violent
                  8A = Aggravated battery   felonies
                      (§1305) against a   12 = Other felonies
                      victim

13 = Personal violent   15 = Treason
     misdemeanors   16 = Aircraft hijacking
14 = Other misdemeanors

(3) *Final plea:* For guilty pleas, enter crime code (e.g., if plea is guilty to murder, enter 01; if multiple guilty pleas, enter plea to most serious offense). 20 = Not guilty. N = file does not indicate whether the defendant ever pleaded or was tried.

(4) *Jury/bench decisions:* For trials, enter appropriate crime code for guilty findings. 20 = Not guilty. N = Not applicable (no trial).

(5) *Number of counts convicted:* Enter actual number of counts the individual was convicted of for each crime. 8 = 8 or more. N = Not applicable, no conviction.

(6) *Term:* Fine = 97. Indicate amount in parens: e.g., 97 (500). Life = 98. Death = 99. Enter term of years the individual was sentenced to, with 96 = 96 or more years. For multiple counts of a single crime, enter the term that is the longest. If there is a range in years, enter the range (e.g., 15–20). N = Not applicable, no conviction. Use P suffix if sentence is probated.

	(1) Crime Code	(2) Number of Counts Indicted	(3) Final Plea	(4) Jury/Bench Decision	(5) Number of Counts Convicted	(6) Term
Crime #1	____ (11)	____ (12)	____ (13)	____ (14)	____ (15)	____ to ____ (16) (16A)
Crime #2	____ (17)	____ (18)	____ (19)	____ (20)	____ (21)	____ to ____ (22) (22A)
Crime #3	____ (23)	____ (24)	____ (25)	____ (26)	____ (27)	____ to ____ (28) (28A)
Crime #4	____ (29)	____ (30)	____ (31)	____ (32)	____ (33)	____ to ____ (34) (34A)
Number of Additional Felonies Totals		____ (35)			____ (36)	

11. Sentence: Total consecutive years sentenced to prison (actual number). For sentences consecutive to a life sentence, add number of consecutive years (beyond life) to 500 and enter.

          98 = Life   99 = Death
                                              ____ (37)

12. If the case resulted in a murder conviction, was there a penalty trial? (Omit 12 and 13 if no murder conviction.)
    1 = Yes (if answer is 1, go to question 14)
    2 = No (go to question 13)
                                            ____ (38)

13.   If there was no penalty trial, was it because: _____
    1 = The conviction was the result of a plea bargain under which the   (39)
        prosecution agreed not to seek the death penalty (go to question
        15)
    2 = Prosecution otherwise waived or refrained unilaterally from
        seeking the death penalty
    3 = Prosecution sought death penalty but the judge took the pen-
        alty issue away from the jurors and imposed life
    4 = Other _____

14.   Was a plea bargain *offered* or *agreed* to by the prosecution?   _____
    1 = Yes   (40)
    2 = No (go to question 14D if there was a penalty trial; if no penalty
        trial, go to question 15)

14A–C. If the prosecutor offered or agreed to a plea bargain,

14A.   To what crime was the defendant asked to plead guilty?   _____
    1 = Murder   2 = Voluntary manslaugher   3 = Other   (41)
    (specify _____)

14B.   Did the prosecutor agree to recommend a sentence to the court?   _____
    1 = Yes   2 = No   If yes, what sentence?   (42)
    1 = Life   2 = Term of years (specify _____)   _____
                                                                           (42A)

14C.   If the prosecutor offered the foregoing plea bargain, did the defen-   _____
    dant agree to it?
    1 = Yes   2 = No   (43)

14D.   (Omit if no penalty trial.) If there was a penalty trial, what aggra-
    vating circumstances were charged and found by the jury (or
    court)?
    1 = Charged and found   2 = Charged but not found

B1 = Prior record/serious		B6 = Murder for hire	_____ (43F)
assaultive conduct	_____ (43A)	B7 = Outrageous, vile	_____ (43G)
B2 = Contemporaneous		B8 = Peace officer, etc.	_____ (43H)
felony/aggravated			
battery, etc.	_____ (43B)	B9 = Defendant on	
B3 = Great risk of death	_____ (43C)	escape	_____ (43I)
B4 = Monetary gain	_____ (43D)	B10 = Avoid arrest	_____ (43J)
B5 = Judicial officer	_____ (43E)		

15.   Was there an appeal?   _____
    1 = Conviction and sentence affirmed   (44)
    2 = Conviction affirmed, sentence vacated or reduced
    3 = Conviction reversed and sentence vacated

4 = Appeal pending
5 = Yes, but outcome of appeal unknown
6 = No appeal

Characteristics of the defendant

16. Defendant's age at the time of the offense
_____
(46)

17. Defendant's living arrangements prior to apprehension
1 = Expressly stated in file
2 = Suggested by the file but not specifically indicated
Blank = Inconsistent with information in file
U = Unable to classify as 1, 2, or Blank

_____ Living alone
(47)

_____ Living w/ spouse and no
(48) children (including
common-law marriage)

_____ Living w/spouse and chil-
(49) dren

_____ Living w/paramour and no
(50) children

_____ Living w/paramour and chil-
(51) dren

_____ Living with one or more of
(52) same sex

_____ Living with parents or close
(53) family

_____ Living with another family
(54)

_____ Living with friends of both
(55) sexes

_____ Traveling on the road/hitch-
(56) hiking (temporary)

_____ No home
(57)

_____ Inmate of institution
(58)

_____ Other
(59)

18. Occupational skill of defendant (enter up to two foils)   _____   _____
Part I   (61)   (61A)

A Professional and managerial
01 = Professional (doctor, lawyer, other professional)
02 = Executive
03 = Judicial officer (or former),
district attorney (or former)
04 = Proprietor

B Law enforcement and military
05 = Policeman, fireman, or
corrections employee
06 = Military (enlisted)
07 = Military (officer)

C White-collar
08 = White-collar worker
09 = Apartment/hotel manager
10 = Store manager

D Blue-collar and unskilled
11 = Blue-collar (all skilled laborers will be considered
blue collar; e.g., mechanics, factory workers, truck
drivers)
12 = Farmer or fisher
13 = Unskilled laborer

E Outside of work force
14 = Juvenile (too young for
school)
15 = Student
16 = Retired
17 = Housekeeper

F Service workers
18 = Security guard (not sworn)
19 = Store clerk
20 = Service-station attendant
21 = Waitress, bartender, taxi driver, or similar service-person

G Unstable
22 = Drifter
23 = Professional criminal
24 = No occupation
25 = Prostitute or pimp

H Other
26 = Other _____
27 = Defendant has worked but precise skill is unknown (answer Part II)
U = Unknown whether defendant has ever worked at all (skip Part II and question 19)

Part II (To be answered if answer to Part I is 27, or if a specific skill is identified in Part I and the file also suggests a skill in a Part II general category.)
1 = Expressly stated in file
2 = Suggested by the file but not specifically indicated
Blank = Inconsistent with information in file
U = Unable to classify as 1, 2, or Blank

Group A _____
(62)

Group B _____
(63)

Group C _____
(64)

Group D _____
(65)

Group E _____
(66)

Group F _____
(67)

Group G _____
(68)

19.   Employment status of defendant prior to apprehension   _____
(69)

1 = Employed full-time
2 = Employed part-time
3 = Employed, but not sure if full- or part-time
4 = Seasonal laborer
5 = Unemployed six months or less
6 = Unemployed over six months
6A = Unemployed, but unsure how long

7 = Has never worked (nonstudent and capable)
8 = Incapable of working
9 = Student/juvenile/retired/housewife
10 = Unclear because in unstable category
U = Unknown

19A. Defendant's IQ (actual number)   _____
DNC = Offender doesn't comprehend or read or write enough to   (70)
be tested
L = Under 65 (exact number not given)

Offender's criminal record

20.   Number of prior felony arrests (actual number)   _____
00 = None   (71)

21. Reliability of this answer
    1 = File complete (exhaustive list)
    2 = File incomplete (list reliable)
    3 = File incomplete (list unreliable)
    U = Unable to make a judgment

    _____
    (72)

22. Number of prior misdemeanor arrests (actual number)
    00 = None

    _____
    (73)

23. Reliability of this answer
    1 = File complete (exhaustive list)
    2 = File incomplete (list reliable)
    3 = File incomplete (list unreliable)
    U = Unable to make a judgment

    _____
    (74)

24. Age of defendant at time of first felony arrest, including juvenile
    arrests
    N = Not applicable/no prior felony arrest

    _____
    (75)

25. Date of arrest for most recent violent crime (specify crime:_____
    _____)
    N = Not applicable/no prior violent-crime arrest

    _/_/_
    (76)

26. Date of arrest for most recent nonviolent crime, excluding traffic
    offenses not involving a homicidal crime or OMVI (specify crime:
    _____)
    N = Not applicable/no prior nonviolent-crime arrest

    _/_/_
    (77)

27. Date of most recent release from prison
    99 = Offender on escape at time of homicide
    N = Not applicable/no prior incarceration

    _/_/_
    (78)

28. Total number of years incarcerated in jail/prison (enter actual num-
    ber of years, months)
    N = Not applicable (never incarcerated)

    _____
    (79)

    If only approximate number of years incarcerated is known, enter:
    A = 1–2   E = 12–16
    B = 2–5   F = 16–20
    C = 5–8   G = 20–25
    D = 8–12   H = 26 or more

28A. Has offender ever been convicted of a crime in Georgia or else-
    where?
    1 = Yes (expressly stated in the file)
    2 = Yes (suggested by the file)
    3 = No (expressly stated in the file)
    4 = No (suggested by the file)

    _____
    (80)

    If the answer to 28A is 3 or 4 or blank (unknown), go to question 33 after
    answering question 29.

29. Did the homicide occur while the defendant was engaged in the
    commission of another offense (whether or not the defendant was
    charged with and convicted of the offense)?

1 = No contemporaneous offense
2 = Armed robbery
3 = Rape
4 = Kidnapping
5 = Burglary
6 = Arson in first degree
6A = Aggravated battery
against a victim
6B = Aggravated battery
against one not a victim
7 = Aggravated assault
against a victim
7A = Aggravated assault
against one not a victim
8 = Simple robbery
9 = Theft

10 = Commercial vice   _____
11 = Narcotics   (131)
12 = Motor-vehicle theft
(MVT)   _____
13 = Other personal violent   (132)
felonies (specify_____
_____)   _____
14 = Other felonies (specify   (133)
_____)
15 = Personal violent   _____
misdemeanors (specify___   (134)
_____)
16 = Other misdemeanors   _____
(specify_____   (134A)
_____)
17 = Aircraft hijacking

Number of prior convictions and sentences

29A. Crime code, Col. 1:

1 = Murder
2 = Voluntary manslaughter
3 = Involuntary manslaughter
4 = Armed robbery
5 = Rape
6 = Kidnapping
7 = Burglary
8 = Arson in first degree
9 = Simple robbery

10 = Aggravated assault
10A = Aggravated battery
11 = Other personal violent felonies
12 = Other felonies
13 = Personal violent misdemeanors
14 = Other misdemeanors, except
nonhomicidal and non-OMVI
traffic offenses

Code, Col. 2:
UC = Exact number unknown, but one or more

Code, Col. 3:
97 = Fine; indicate amount in parentheses: e.g., 97 (500)
98 = Life
99 = Death
UC = Exact sentence(s) unknown, but time was served following a conviction
N = No prison/jail sentence

Code, Col. 4:
99 = 99 or more
UC = Exact length unknown, but there were one or more probated sentences
N = No probated sentence

(1) Crime Code	(2) Enter Actual Number of Convictions	(3) Enter Combined Length of Prison/Jail Sentence (excluding concurrents)		(4) Enter Combined Length of Probated Sentences (excluding concurrents)
#1 ____ (81)	____ (82)	____ (83)	____ (83A)	____ (84)
#2 ____ (85)	____ (86)	____ (87)	____ (87A)	____ (88)
#3 ____ (89)	____ (90)	____ (91)	____ (91A)	____ (92)
#4 ____ (93)	____ (94)	____ (95)	____ (95A)	____ (96)
#5 ____ (97)	____ (98)	____ (99)	____ (99A)	____ (100)
#6 ____ (101)	____ (102)	____ (103)	____ (103A)	____ (104)

30. Prior incarceration following a conviction (jail or prison)   ____
     1 = Yes, in Georgia   3 = Yes, in and out of Georgia   (105)
     2 = Yes, outside Georgia   Blank = No

31. Number of times incarcerated (prison/jail) for a felony (enter actual
     number)   ____
     Blank = No felony convictions   (106)
     9 = Nine or more
     UC = Exact number unknown, but defendant has been incarcerated
          for a felony

32. Number of times incarcerated (prison/jail) for a misdemeanor, not
     concurrent to a felony sentence (enter actual number)   ____
     Blank = None   (107)
     9 = Nine or more
     UC = Exact number unknown, but defendant has been incarcerated
          for a misdemeanor

33. Stated number of times incarcerated in a youth detention center
     (enter actual number)   ____
     Blank = None   (108)
     9 = Nine or more
     UC = Exact number unknown, but defendant has been incarcerated
          in a youth detention center

Characteristics of victim 1

(Prepare supplemental sheets for additional victims. *)

---

*The supplemental sheets are omitted. They repeat for each victim questions 34–38, 40, 46, and 57.

34. Victim's name _____

        (If more than one victim, complete supplemental victim form.)

35. Victim's sex   _____

    1 = Male   2 = Female   (109)

36. Victim's race   _____

    1 = White   4 = Native American   (110)

    2 = Black   5 = Other _____

    3 = Spanish-speaking

37. Victim's age: enter actual number of years, if known   _____

    If only phase of life cycle is known, enter: (111)

    A = Aged adult (over 65)   D = Teenager (13–19)

    B = Middle-aged adult (35–65)   E = Child (6–12)

    C = Young adult (20–34)   F = Preschool (under 6)

38. Occupational skill of victim   _____

    Part I   (112)

A Professional and managerial

    01 = Professional (doctor, lawyer, other professional)

    02 = Executive

    03 = Judicial officer (or former), district attorney (or former)

    04 = Proprietor

B Law enforcement and military

    05 = Policeman, fireman, or corrections employee

    06 = Military (enlisted)

    07 = Military (officer)

C White-collar

    08 = White-collar worker

    09 = Apartment/hotel manager

    10 = Store manager

D Blue-collar and unskilled

    11 = Blue-collar (all skilled laborers will be considered blue collar; e.g., mechanics, factory workers, truck drivers)

    12 = Farmer or fisher

    13 = Unskilled laborer

E Outside of work force

    14 = Juvenile (too young for school)

    15 = Student

    16 = Retired

    17 = Housekeeper

F Service workers

    18 = Security guard (not sworn)

    19 = Store clerk

    20 = Service-station attendant

    21 = Waitress, bartender, taxi driver, or similar service-person

G Unstable

    22 = Drifter

    23 = Professional criminal

    24 = No occupation

    25 = Prostitute or pimp

H Other

    26 = Other _____

    27 = Victim has worked but precise skill is unknown (answer Part II)

    U = Unknown whether victim has ever worked at all. If code Part I with U, then skip Part II and question 39.

Part II   (To be answered if your answer to Part I is 27, or if a specific skill is identified in Part I and the file also suggests a skill in a Part II general category.)

1 = Expressly stated in file
2 = Suggested by the file but not specifically indicated
Blank = Inconsistent with information in file
U = Unable to classify as 1, 2, or Blank

Group A _____	Group E _____
(113)	(117)
Group B _____	Group F _____
(114)	(118)
Group C _____	Group G _____
(115)	(119)
Group D _____	
(116)	

39.   Employment status of victim

_____
(120)

1 = Employed full-time
2 = Employed part-time
3 = Employed, but not sure if full- or part-time
4 = Seasonal laborer
5 = Unemployed six months or less
6 = Unemployed over six months
6A = Unemployed, but unsure how long

7 = Has never worked (nonstudent and capable)
8 = Incapable of working
9 = Student/juvenile/retired/ housekeeper
10 = Unclear because in unstable category

40.   Victim's status in relationship to the defendant

Part I

_____
(121)

01 = Husband, wife, or ex
02 = Parent
03 = Child
04 = Sibling
05 = In-law
06 = Other family
07 = Paramour or ex (intimate relationship)
08 = Homosexual relationship
09 = Friend or ex
10 = Neighbor
11 = Other acquaintance
12 = Casual acquaintance (when it can't be determined whether 10 or 11 applies)

13 = Other: defendant known to victim
14 = Other: victim known to defendant
15 = Employer or ex
16 = Employee or ex
17 = Coworker or ex
18 = Business associate (when it can't be determined whether 15, 16, or 17 applies)
19 = Current or prior confederate or rival in crime
20 = Opposing gang member
21 = Stranger

22 = Specific relationship unknown but general relationship stated or suggested by file

U = Neither specific nor general relationship stated or suggested by the file; unknown

Part II   (If Part I is coded 22, complete Part II. Omit Part II if answer to Part I is 1 through 21 or U.)

1 = Expressly stated in file
2 = Suggested by the file but not specifically indicated
Blank = Inconsistent with information in file
U = Unable to classify as 1, 2, or Blank

_____ Family
(122)

_____ Friend or intimate
(123)

_____ Casual acquaintance
(124)

_____ Work associate
(125)

_____ Criminal associate or rival
(126)

_____ Stranger
(127)

Characteristics of the offense

41.   Where did the homicide occur (enter up to two foils)?   _____
                                                                                (128)
Part I
1 = Residence of victim
2 = Residence of victim's close friend or relative
3 = Residence of defendant
4 = Residence of defendant's close friend or relative
5 = Residence of coperpetrator
6 = Other residence
7 = Residence of victim and defendant
8 = Hotel, motel, or other short-term residence
9 = Victim's place of business or employment
10 = Defendant's place of business or employment
11 = Coperpetrator's place of business or employment
12 = Convenience or grocery store
13 = Liquor store
14 = Service station

15 = Bar or cocktail lounge (or immediate environs)   _____
                                                                                (129)
16 = Other place of business
17 = Cab/bus/other public vehicle
18 = Private vehicle of victim
19 = Private vehicle of third person other than victim
20 = Private vehicle of defendant
21 = Parking-lot area
22 = Highway or freeway
23 = Country road
24 = Street or sidewalk
25 = Park or school grounds
26 = Field or woods
27 = Other noncommercial public place
28 = Jail/prison/lawful custody of police or corrections officer
29 = Other _____

Part II   (Omit Part II if answer for Part I was 20–29.) If the answer
to question 41 is 1–19, the defendant's method of entry
was: _____

1 = Forcible entry without permission   (130)
2 = Other entry without permission
3 = Initial entry with permission
4 = Outside (invited)—applies only to foils 1–6 in Part I
5 = Outside (uninvited)—applies only to foils 1–6 in Part I

42.   [Omitted]

43.   Defendant's motive
1 = Expressly stated in file
2 = Suggested by the file but not specifically indicated
Blank = Inconsistent with information in file
U = Unable to classify as 1, 2, or Blank

_____ Long-term hatred
(135)

_____ Revenge
(136)

_____ Sex
(137)

_____ Jealousy
(138)

_____ Immediate rage
(139)

_____ To avenge the role played by
(140)   a present or former judicial
officer, DA, or lawyer in the
exercise of his/her duty

_____ To avenge the role played by
(141)   a present or former police
officer

_____ To facilitate obtaining
(142)   money or any other thing of
monetary value for the defendant or another

_____ Insurance proceeds
(142A)

_____ Racial animosity
(142B)

_____ To silence a witness to a
(143)   crime just committed by
defendant

_____ To silence a witness sought
(144)   out subsequent to the commission of an earlier crime

_____ Panic (e.g., defendant be-
(144A) came frightened when sur-
prised in the course of a burglary)

_____ Shoot-out
(145)

_____ To avoid/prevent/interfere
(146)   with lawful arrrest or lawful
custody of defendant or another

_____ To facilitate the victim's sui-
(147)   cide

_____ Gun fired during a struggle
(148)   for the gun

_____ Other _____
(149)   _____

44. Special precipitating events
1 = Expressly stated in file
2 = Suggested by the file but not specifically indicated
Blank = Inconsistent with information in file
U = Unable to classify as 1, 2, or Blank

_____ Dispute between victim and
(150)   defendant over money or
property
_____ Dispute while under influ-
(151)   ence of drugs or alcohol
_____ Dispute between spouses or
(152)   ex-spouses
_____ Dispute between family
(153)   members other than spouses
or ex-spouses

_____ Lovers' or ex-lovers' quarrel
(154)
_____ Lovers' triangle
(155)
_____ Other disputes and fights
(156)   where it is unknown who
provoked the fights

45. Method of killing—victim was: _____
1 = Shot with gun (specify   (158)
type _____
_____)   12 = Drowned
2 = Stabbed with sharp   13 = Burned (arson)
instrument (specify_____   14 = Burned by flame or hot   _____
_____)   substance (but not arson)   (159)
3 = Slashed or cut w/knife, ax, 15 = Electrocuted
or similar instrument   16 = Killed by an explosion   _____
(specify _____   17 = Crushed or struck by an   (160)
_____)   automobile
4 = Beaten with blunt object   18 = Given overdose of drugs/
5 = Beaten with fists or feet   narcotics
6 = Strangled with hands   19 = Poisoned (including
7 = Strangled with rope or   carbon monoxide)
garrote   20 = Neglected or deprived
8 = Hanged   21 = Thrown from high place
9 = Smothered (e.g., pillow,   22 = Traumatized by an assault
blanket)   that caused fatal heart
10 = Buried alive   attack/stroke
11 = Otherwise suffocated   23 = Starvation or imprison-
(e.g., in a refrigerator)   ment
24 = Other _____
_____

46. Special aggravating circumstances of victim
1 = Expressly stated in file
2 = Suggested by the file but not specifically indicated
Blank = Inconsistent with information in file
U = Unable to classify as 1, 2, or Blank

_____ Bed-ridden/handicapped
(161)

_____ Mental defect
(162)

_____ Defenseless because of
(163) youth
_____ Defenseless because of
(164) advanced age
_____ Pregnant
(165)
_____ Victim was asleep or had just
(166) awakened
_____ Defenseless because of gross
(166A) disparity in physical sizes,
e.g., defendant much larger
or two or more people
against one; code N for cases
where size is irrelevant given
mode of killing (e.g., gun)

_____ Defenseless because of
(167) physical condition or weakness, e.g., frail woman
_____ Peace officer, corrections
(168) employee, or fireman while
engaged in the performance
of his/her official duties
_____ Supporting children
(169)
_____ Victim offered no provoca-
(170) tion

47. Special aggravating features of the offense

    Part A   _____
                                                                                        (172)
    1 = Torture (methodical   8 = Slashed throat
        infliction of severe pain to   9 = Multiple stabbing (#__)   _____
        punish victim, to extract   9A = Other mode of *multiple*   (173)
        information, or to satisfy   lethal or painful attack
        sadistic urge; specify__   10 = Bloody   _____
        _____)   11 = Lingering death of victim   (174)
    2A = Mental torture (e.g.,   12 = Victim held hostage
         informing victim of   13 = Victim bound or gagged   _____
         impending death some-   14 = Victim forced to disrobe   (175)
         time before homicide)   or disrobed by perpetra-
    2B = Brutal clubbing or other   tor   _____
         unnecessarily painful   15 = Attempt to dispose of/   (175A)
         method of attack   conceal body
    2C = Brutal stomping or beat-   16 = Multiple victims   _____
         ing with hands or feet   17 = Bodily harm to one other   (175B)
     3 = Mutilation during the   than a victim
         homicide   18 = Sniper killing
     4 = Mutilation of body after   19 = Luring/ambushing/
         death   lying in wait
     5 = Shotgun homicide   20 = Victim killed in presence
     6 = Multiple gunshot   of family members or
         wounds (#__)   close friends
    6A = Single shot to head   21 = Other _____
     7 = Multiple gunshots to   22 = No special aggravating
         head (#__)   circumstances

Part B
1 = Expressly stated in file
2 = Suggested by the file but not specifically indicated
Blank = Inconsistent with information in file
U = Unable to classify as 1, 2, or Blank

_____ Homicide planned for more
(176) than five minutes

_____ Planned contemporaneous
(176A) offense for more than five
       minutes

_____ Execution-style homicide
(177) (homicide against subdued
       or passive victim)

_____ Case involved contempora-
(178) neous felony and homicide
       was unnecessary to com-
       plete the crime (e.g., store-
       keeper hands over money
       and offers no resistance)

_____ Victim beaten before killing
(178A)

_____ Victim pleaded for life
(179)

_____ Victim was not clothed (in
(180) whole or in part) at the time
       of the homicide

_____ Sexual perversion or abuse
(181) other than rape (sodomy,
       etc.)

Part C   (Special aggravating features of the offense specifically attributable to
            the defendant)
1 = Expressly stated in file
2 = Suggested by the file but not specifically indicated
Blank = Inconsistent with information in file
U = Unable to classify as 1, 2, or Blank

_____ Defendant showed no
(183) remorse for homicide

_____ Defendant expressed
(184) pleasure with the homicide

_____ Defendant committed or is
(185) alleged to have committed
       additional crimes between
       the time of the homicide and
       the time of his/her arrest
       (whether or not charged)

_____ Defendant left the scene of
(186) the crime

_____ Defendant otherwise
(187) actively resisted or avoided
       arrest

_____ Defendant was on escape
(188) from, or in lawful custody
       of, a peace officer or place of
       lawful confinement

_____ Defendant caused or
(189) directed another to commit
       murder or committed
       murder as an agent or
       employee of another

Coperpetrators

48. Were there coperpetrator(s) in the homicide or contemporaneous
     offense?
     1 = No, defendant acted alone (go to question 49)   _____
     2 = Yes   (191)
     U = Unknown (go to question 49)

48A. Actual number of coperpetrators   _____

     8 = eight or more   (192)

     UC = There were coperpetrators but actual number is unknown

48B. Defendant's role in the homicide and any contemporaneous offense vis-à-vis coperpetrators

     1 = Expressly stated in file

     2 = Suggested by the file but not specifically indicated

     Blank = Inconsistent with information in file

     U = Unable to classify as 1, 2, or Blank

     A. Acts of violence by the defendant

       _____ Defendant committed or participated in the act that caused the death of
       (193)   the victim (hereinafter, "the act")

       _____ Defendant did not commit the act but committed act(s) of violence
       (194)   against victim(s)

       _____ Defendant did not commit the act but committed act(s) of violence in the
       (195)   same incident against a person or persons other than the victim whose death is the basis of the defendant's prosecution

       _____ Defendant committed no acts of violence
       (196)

     B. Intention to use deadly force

       _____ Defendant intended to use deadly force
       (197)

       _____ Defendant was aware of an intention by coperpetrators to use deadly
       (198)   force

       _____ Defendant was not aware of an intention to use deadly force when it was
       (199)   inflicted by coperpetrators

     C. Defendant's role in planning

Homicide		Contemporaneous Offense*
_____ (200)	Defendant was prime mover in planning	_____ (208)
_____ (201)	Defendant was coequal in planning	_____ (209)
_____ (202)	Defendant was not planner but was aware of plan to commit	_____ (210)
_____ (203)	Defendant was not aware of plan to commit	_____ (211)
_____ (204)	There was no plan to commit	_____ (212)

*If there was a contemporaneous offense (i.e., if the foil for question 29 is other than 1), code right-hand margin; if no contemporaneous offense (i.e., question 29 is 1), omit items (208) through (215).

D. Defendant's presence

Homicide		Contemporaneous Offense
_____ (205)	Defendant was present at scene	_____ (213)
_____ (206)	Defendant was not present at scene but was present nearby in some related capacity	_____ (214)
_____ (207)	Defendant was neither present nor near the scene	_____ (215)

48C. Role of coperpetrators

(1)	(2) Acts of Violence against Victim	(3) Intention to Use Deadly Force	(4) Planning for		(5) Presence at	
			A Homicide	B Contemporaneous Offense**	A Scene of Homicide	B Contemporaneous Offense**
Coperpetrator Name: Code U if Name Unknown	Code A	Code B		Code C		Code D
#1 _____	_____ (216)	_____ (217)	_____ (218)	_____ (219)	_____ (220)	_____ (221)
#2 _____	_____ (222)	_____ (223)	_____ (224)	_____ (225)	_____ (226)	_____ (227)
#3 _____	_____ (228)	_____ (229)	_____ (230)	_____ (231)	_____ (232)	_____ (233)

List names of other coperpetrators _____

Code A

1 = Coperpetrator committed or participated in the act that caused the death of victim(s)

2 = Coperpetrator did not commit the act but committed act(s) of violence against victim(s)

3 = Coperpetrator did not commit the act but committed act(s) of violence against a person or persons other than the victim in the same incident

4 = Coperpetrator committed no acts of violence

U = Unknown

Code B

1 = Coperpetrator intended to use deadly force

2 = Coperpetrator had no intent to kill when coperpetrator committed the act that caused the death

3 = Coperpetrator was aware of an intention to use deadly force

4 = Coperpetrator was not aware of an intention to use deadly force when it was inflicted by defendant or another coperpetrator

U = Unknown

Code C

1 = Coperpetrator was prime mover in planning (A) the homicide or (B) a contemporaneous offense

2 = Coperpetrator was coequal in planning (A) the homicide or (B) a contemporaneous offense

3 = Coperpetrator was not planner but was aware of plan to commit (A) the homicide or (B) a contemporaneous offense

**If there was no contemporaneous offense, omit foils under 4B and 5B.

4 = Coperpetrator was not aware of plan to commit (A) the homicide or (B) a contemporaneous offense

5 = There was no plan to commit (A) the homicide or (B) a contemporaneous offense

U = Unknown

Code D

1 = Coperpetrator was present at scene of (A) the homicide or (B) a contemporaneous offense

2 = Coperpetrator was not present at scene but was present nearby in some capacity related to (A) the homicide or (B) a contemporaneous offense

3 = Coperpetrator was neither present nor near the scene of (A) the homicide or (B) a contemporaneous offense

U = Unknown

48D. Disposition of coperpetrators

Coperpetrator Name: Code U if Unknown (Use same number as in 48C)	Indictment Code A	Manner of Disposition Code B	Conviction Code C	Testimony Code D	Sentence Code E
#1 _____	___ (234)	___ (235)	___ (236)	___ (237)	___ (238)
#2 _____	___ (239)	___ (240)	___ (241)	___ (242)	___ (243)
#3 _____	___ (244)	___ (245)	___ (246)	___ (247)	___ (248)

Enter U if specific code for a known coperpetrator is unknown.

Code A: Indictment—indicate most serious crime

1 = Murder
2 = Voluntary manslaughter
3 = Involuntary manslaughter
4 = Armed robbery
5 = Rape
6 = Kidnapping
7 = Burglary
8 = Arson in first degree
9 = Simple robbery
9A = Aggravated battery
10 = Aggravated assault
11 = Other violent personal felonies
12 = Other felonies
13 = Violent personal misdemeanors
14 = Other misdemeanors
15 = No indictment, unknown if w/immunity
16 = No indictment, w/immunity
17 = No indictment, w/o immunity

Code B: Manner of disposition

1 = Jury trial as codefendant
2 = Jury trial: separate
3 = Bench trial as codefendant
4 = Bench trial: separate
5 = Plea w/o bargain
6 = Plea bargain including testifying for prosecution
7 = Plea but unknown if there was a bargain
8 = Plea bargain not including testimony
9 = Case dismissed, dead docketed, or nol-prossed

Code C: Conviction—enter most serious crime

1 = Murder
2 = Voluntary manslaughter
3 = Involuntary manslaughter
4 = Armed robbery

5 = Rape
6 = Kidnapping
7 = Burglary
8 = Arson in first degree
9 = Simple robbery
9A = Aggravated battery
10 = Aggravated assault
11 = Other violent personal felonies
12 = Other felonies
13 = Violent personal misdemeanors
14 = Other misdemeanors

15 = Acquittal
N = No indictment, case dismissed, dead docketed, or nol-prossed

Code D: Testimony—coperpetrator
1 = Testified on own behalf
2 = Testified as prosecution witness against defendant
3 = Did not testify
4 = Testified for defendant
N = No trial
U = Unknown

Code E: Sentence—Enter actual number of total consecutive years except, 97 = Fine (enter amount in parentheses)   98 = Life   99 = Death

For multiple counts, enter the term that is longest. If a range in years, enter the range (e.g., 15–20).
NC = No conviction

For sentences consecutive to a life sentence, add number of consecutive years beyond life to 500 and enter.

If sentence is probated, add P as suffix.

Number of persons killed

49.   Number of victims killed when defendant either was the trigger-man or physically participated in the killing (enter actual number)   _____
       0 = None   (249)
       U1 = Defendant's role unknown, plus 1 victim
       U2 = Defendant's role unknown, plus 2 or more victims

50.   Number of victims killed when the defendant was not the trigger-man and did not physically participate in the killing (enter actual number; omit if no coperpetrator)   _____
       0 = None   (250)
       U1 = Defendant's role unknown, plus 1 victim
       U2 = Defendant's role unknown, plus 2 or more victims

Number of persons injured

51.   Number of persons injured other than de-   by defendant _____
       ceased victims (enter actual number):   (251)
       0 = None, although other people were present
       N = Not applicable; victim only person involved   by coperpetrator _____
       UC = Some people injured, but exact number   (omit if no   (252)
              unknown   coperpetrator)
       U = Unknown

Number of shots fired

52. If no gun used, go to question 53. If a gun   by defendant _____
     was used, number of shots fired (enter actual   (253)
     number).
     00 = None   by coperpetrator _____
     UC = One or more shots   (omit if no   (254)
     If more precise estimation is possible: coperpetrator)
     A = 1–2   D = more than 7
     B = 3–4   E = more than one but
     C = 5–6   unclear how many

53. Did defendant create risk of death:
     a) to one or more people other than one victim? (If code = 2 or U, go
        to question 56.)   _____
        1 = Yes   2 = No   U = Unknown   (255)

     b) in a public place? (If code = 2 or U, go to question 56.)   _____
        1 = Yes   2 = No   U = Unknown   (256)
     c) with a gun or other device hazardous to lives of more than one
        person? (If code = 2 or U, go to question 56.)   _____
        1 = Yes   2 = No   U = Unknown   (257)
        If answer is yes, and if weapon other than gun was used, specify
        weapon_____

54. If answers to 53a, 53b, and 53c are all yes, how many people other
     than one victim were exposed to risk of death? Omit question 54 if
     an answer to 53a, 53b, or 53c is either 2 or U.   _____
                                                                      (258)

     1 = 1 person   6 = 6–10 people
     2 = 2 people   7 = 11–15 people
     3 = 3 people   8 = more than 15 people
     4 = 4 people   UC = more than 1 but exact number unknown
     5 = 5 people

55. [Omitted]

56. Defendant's behavior—*mitigating circumstances*
     1 = Expressly stated in file
     2 = Suggested by the file but not specifically indicated
     Blank = Inconsistent with information in file
     U = Unable to classify as 1, 2, or Blank
     The defendant:
     _____ Used alcohol or drugs im-   Blank = Not applicable, no
     (259)   mediately before the crime   alcohol or drugs
     _____ Was affected by this alcohol   U = Unknown effect but
     (260)   or drug consumption   D/A used
             1 = Substantially   _____ Had history of mental/
             2 = Moderately   (261) emotional illness
             3 = Slightly

_____ Had history of physical ill-
(262) ness

_____ Had history of egregious
(263) physical or economic deprivation

_____ Had impaired mental capac-
(264) ity to appreciate the wrongfulness of his/her conduct
because of mental disease or
defect

_____ Had impaired mental capac-
(265) ity to conform his/her conduct to the law

_____ Was under extreme mental
(266) or emotional disturbance
(specify_____
_____)

_____ Was physically injured by
(267) police in connection with
the homicide

_____ Had a moral justification
(268) for committing homicide
(e.g., needed money for sick
child; specify _____
_____)

_____ Was diagnosed mentally ill
(268A) after arrest (specify type
and time _____
_____)

_____ Did not kill victim deliber-
(269) ately, although he/she
caused death. Code N if
coperpetrator caused death.

If no coperpetrator, omit the next
three questions.

_____ Was not actual killer or par-
(270) ticipant in killing, only an
accomplice.

_____ His/her acts were not the
(271) sole cause of death. Code N
if foil 270 is 1 or 2.

_____ Coperpetrator(s) received
(272) life sentence(s) or a lesser or
no sentence before defen-
dant was sentenced

_____ Cooperated with authorities
(273) (e. g., testified for prosecution)

_____ Showed remorse
(274)

_____ Acted under duress or the
(275) domination of another person

_____ Surrendered within
(276) twenty-four hours of the
homicide (if later, code
277A)

_____ History of drug or alcohol
(276A) abuse

_____ Acted to aid victim after
(277) attack

_____ Surrendered more than
(277A) twenty-four hours after
homicide

_____ Other _____
(278) _____

57. Victim behavior
1 = Expressly stated in file
2 = Suggested by the file but not specifically indicated
Blank = Inconsistent with information in file
U = Unable to classify as 1, 2, or Blank
The victim:

_____ Had used drugs/alcohol
(279) immediately before homicide

_____ Was affected by this drug/
(280) alcohol consumption
1 = Substantially
2 = Moderately

3 = Slightly
Blank = Not applicable,
because no drug/
alcohol use
U = Unknown effect, but
D/A used

_____ Aroused the defendant's
(281)   fear for life

_____ Was armed with a deadly
(282)   weapon

_____ And defendant had history
(283)   of bad blood

_____ Accused defendant of mis-
(283A) conduct

_____ Physically ⎫
(284)   injured ⎪

_____ Physically ⎪ the defen-
(285)   assaulted ⎬ dant at the
                   time of the
_____ Verbally ⎪ homicide
(286)   threatened⎪

_____ Verbally ⎪
(287)   abused   ⎭

_____ Physically ⎫
(288)   injured   ⎪

_____ Physically ⎪ the defendant
(289)   assaulted ⎬ on an earlier
                     occasion
_____ Verbally   ⎪
(290)   threatened ⎪

_____ Verbally   ⎪
(291)   abused   ⎭

_____ Other provocation_____
(292)   _____

_____ Aroused defendant's sexual
(292A) desire

_____ Had a bad criminal reputa-
(292B) tion

_____ Showed or talked about
(293)   large amounts of money

_____ Was a participant in or con-
(294)   sented to his/her own death

_____ Was a fugitive at the time
(295)   of the homicide

_____ Had a criminal record
(296)

_____ Was a participant in the
(297)   contemporaneous crime
        (Omit if no contemporane-
        ous crime.)

_____ Physically ⎫
(298)   injured   ⎪

_____ Physically ⎪ a person the
(299)   assaulted ⎬ defendant
                     cared about
_____ Verbally   ⎪ at the time of
(300)   threatened ⎪ the homicide

_____ Verbally   ⎪
(301)   abused   ⎭

_____ Physically ⎫
(302)   injured   ⎪

_____ Physically ⎪ a person the
(303)   assaulted ⎬ defendant
                     cared about
_____ Verbally   ⎪ on an earlier
(304)   threatened ⎪ occasion

_____ Verbally   ⎪
(305)   abused   ⎭

_____ Other _____
(306)   _____

58.   Defendant's defense on liability
      1 = Expressly stated in file
      2 = Suggested by the file but not specifically indicated
      Blank = Inconsistent with information in file
      U = Unable to classify as 1, 2, or Blank

_____ Suicide by victim
(307)

_____ Accident
(308)

_____ Lack of intent to kill (e.g.,
(309)   mental illness, alcohol,
        drugs)

_____ Mistaken identity
(310)

_____ Voluntary manslaughter
(311)   (where murder is the
        charge): even if there was
        an intent to kill, the defen-
        dant acted solely as the re-
        sult of a sudden, violent,
        and irresistible passion re-
        sulting from serious provo-
        cation sufficient to excite
        such passion in a reasonable
        person

_____ Involuntary manslaughter
(312) (where murder or voluntary manslaughter is the
charge):
   a) defendant, in commis-
      sion of an unlawful act,
      caused the victim's death
      without any intention to
      do so by the commission
      of an unlawful act other
      than a felony
   b) defendant, in commis-
      sion of a lawful act in an
      unlawful manner, caused
      the victim's death with-
      out any intention to do
      so by the commission of
      a lawful act in an unlaw-
      ful manner likely to
      cause death or great
      bodily harm
_____ Coercion
(313)
_____ Defense of self or others
(314)

_____ Defense of home or
(315) dwelling
_____ Defense of property
(316)
_____ Justification: during course
(317) of arrest
_____ Justification: reasonable
(318) discipline of a minor by
      parent
_____ Coperpetrator caused the
(319) death
_____ Insanity
(320)
_____ Delusional compulsion
(321)
_____ Mistake of fact
(321A)
_____ Other _____
(321B) _____
_____ Unknown if a defense
(321C) plausible
_____ Admitted guilt and no de-
(321D) fense asserted

Strength of evidence

59. Police report indicates clear guilt.
    1 = Yes   2 = No   U = No police report filed

    _____
    (321E)

60. The file indicates that there was an identification witness with
    information on the items listed in question 60A.
    1 = Yes   2 = No

    _____
    (322)

    (If answer to question 60 is 2, go to question 62.)

60A. Witness accounts
    Identification: Enter actual number of witnesses under columns 1–2 and 5–6.
    Enter the type of I.D. in columns 3–4 and 7–8. (I.D. codes appear below.) The
    left-hand columns are for witnesses against the defendant. The right-hand col-
    umns are for witnesses against a coperpetrator, if there are coperpetrators. Omit
    columns 5–8 if no coperpetrators. For this question the "accused" is the defen-
    dant or coperpetrator. A witness should be included for only one observation
    regarding the defendant and one observation regarding the coperpetrator(s). If a
    witness saw several events, enter him/her only for the most incriminating event.
    The events are listed in decreasing order of incriminating potential (1 = most
    incriminating).

Defendant					Coperpetrator			
Police	Civil-ian	Type of I.D.			Police	Civil-ian	Type of I.D.	
(1)	(2)	(3)	(4)		(5)	(6)	(7)	(8)
(323)	(324)	(325)	(326)	1. Witness identified accused as person commiting the act that resulted in a homicide.	(343)	(344)	(345)	(346)
(327)	(328)	(329)	(330)	2. Witness identified accused as person with weapon at or near the scene of the homicide either immediately before or immediately after the act.	(347)	(348)	(349)	(350)
(331)	(332)	(333)	(334)	3. Witness identified accused as person at or near the scene of the homicide either immediately before or immediately after the act (but no weapon was noticed).	(351)	(352)	(353)	(354)
(335)	(336)	(337)	(338)	4. Witness identified accused as person with the victim close to the time of the homicide.	(355)	(356)	(357)	(358)
(339)	(340)	(341)	(342)	5. Witness identified accused as person at or near the scene close to the time of the homicide.	(359)	(360)	(361)	(362)

Defendant					Coperpetrator			
Police	Civil-ian	Type of I.D.			Police	Civil-ian	Type of I.D.	
(1)	(2)	(3)	(4)		(5)	(6)	(7)	(8)
(342A)	(342B)	(342C)	(342D)	6. Witness has knowledge of actions taken by the defendant in preparation for the crime(s).	(362A)	(362B)	(362C)	(362D)

Columns 3 and 7: Type of I.D.
1 = Witness observed the face of the accused.
2 = Witness identified the voice, gait, or general appearance of the accused.
3 = Witness identified the clothing of the accused.
U = Type of I.D. unknown.

Columns 4 and 8: Prior knowledge of the accused.
1 = Witness knew the accused prior to the offense.
2 = Witness did not know the accused prior to the offense.
3 = Unknown whether prior knowledge.

If there is more than one witness in a category (e.g., two witnesses saw the defendant kill), code "type of I.D." for the more incriminating witness, measured in terms of prior knowledge of accused, objectivity, and clarity of perception.

61. The file indicates that a witness (whether or not reported in question 60A) who identified the accused as a person at or near the scene of the homicide made an identification to the authorities before trial (omit if no witness). (If the answer to question 61 is 2, go to question 62; if blank, go to question 63.)

    1 = Yes   2 = No   (363)

61A. Method of identification to the authorities: (only one entry per witness—if multiple I.D.'s, enter the most incriminating)

Defendant			Coperpetrator	
Police	Civilian		Police	Civilian
			(Omit if no coperpetrator)	
(364)	(365)	1. Identified to police at scene of and immediately after the crime	(374)	(375)
(366)	(367)	2. From person line-up	(376)	(377)
(368)	(369)	3. From photo line-up	(378)	(379)
(370)	(371)	4. Show up—a one-on-one confrontation with accused *subsequent* to the crime (e.g., at crime scene, police station, etc.)	(380)	(381)

Defendant			Coperpetrator	
Police	Civilian		Police	Civilian
			(Omit if no coperpetrator)	

_____   _____   5. From single photo   _____   _____
(372)   (373)   (382)   (383)

_____   _____   6. Otherwise reported to police   _____   _____
(373A)   (373B)   (383A)   (383B)

62.   The file has information concerning (omit if no witness)   _____
(A) the primary witness's (PW) relationship to defendant/victim/   (384)
coperpetrator, or
(B) the PW's status, or
(C) corroborating witnesses, or
(D) the PW's credibility, or
(E) a written statement by PW
  1 = Yes   2 = No
(If the answer to question 62 is 2, go to question 63.)

62A.   Relationship of the primary witness to the defendant, coperpetrator(s), and the victim. The primary witness is the witness whose testimony would be most damaging in the case against the defendant or the coperpetrator(s).
  1 = Family   Primary witness to defendant   _____
  2 = Friend or intimate   (385)
  3 = Casual acquaintance   Primary witness to victim   _____
  4 = Work associate   (386)
  5 = Coperpetrator   Primary witness to coperpetrator   _____
  6 = Stranger   (Code N is witness was sole   (387)
  U = Unknown   coperpetrator; omit if there
                               was no coperpetrator)

62B.   Primary witness's status:
  1 = Civilian   2 = Police officer   3 = Unknown   _____
  Name, if known _____   (388)

62C.   Was the primary witness's statement corroborated by
another witness?   _____
  1 = Yes, by a police witness   4 = Yes, by a coperpetrator (a   (389)
  2 = Yes, by a civilian witness   second one if the primary
  3 = Yes, by a police and a   witness is a coperpetrator)
     civilian witness   5 = Yes, but witness's status is
  PC = Partial corroboration by one   unknown
       or more witnesses   6 = No
                                    U = Unknown

62D.   If the primary witness was a civilian, does the file indicate there was any problem with the witness's credibility?   _____
  1 = Yes   2 = No   U = Unknown   (390)
  (Specify if yes: _____)

62E. Is there a written copy of the primary witness's statement in the
Georgia parole-board files?

1 = Yes   2 = No   (391)

63. The file indicates a statement was made to the authorities by:

a) the defendant

1 = Yes   2 = No   (392)

(If answer to question 63 is 2, skip 63A Part I and questions 63B,
63C, and 63D; i.e., do 63A Part II if applicable and go to question
64.)

b) a coperpetrator (omit if no coperpetrator)

1 = Yes   2 = No   (393)

(If answer to question 63B is 2, skip 63A, Part II.)

63A. Statements to police by defendant or a coperpetrator connecting him/herself to
the crime (answer for as many as are appropriate).

01 = Oral, at scene, before custody

02 = Oral, at scene, after custody

03 = Oral, at scene, but not sure if before or after custody

11 = Oral, not at scene, within twenty-four hours of homicide, before custody

12 = Oral, not at scene, within twenty-four hours of homicide, after custody

13 = Oral, not at scene, within twenty-four hours of homicide, but not sure if
before or after custody

21 = Oral, not at scene, more than twenty-four hours after homicide, before
custody

22 = Oral, not at scene, more than twenty-four hours after homicide, after
custody

23 = Oral, not at scene, more than twenty-four hours after homicide, but not
sure if before or after custody

31 = Written or transcribed, within twenty-four hours of homicide

32 = Written or transcribed, more than twenty-four hours after homicide

33 = Written or transcribed, but unclear when

Part I Defendant Statement	A. Concerning the event	Part II Coperpetrator Statement*
(394)	Admitted deliberate homicide, no defense as- serted	(405)
(395)	Admitted deliberate homicide, with defense clearly asserted	(406)
(395A)	Admitted deliberate homicide, no clear defense asserted	(406A)
(396)	Admitted unintentional homicide	(407)
(397)	Admitted participation in homicide	(408)

*Leave blank if there were no coperpetrators.

_____ (398)	Admitted participation in contemporaneous of-fense	_____ (409)
_____ (399)	Made other inculpatory statement concerning homicide	_____ (410)
_____ (400)	Made other inculpatory remark concerning con-temporaneous offense	_____ (411)
_____ (401)	Admitted presence at scene but nothing more	_____ (412)
_____ (402)	Claimed ignorance	_____ (413)
_____ (403)	Claimed alibi	_____ (414)
_____ (404)	Other_____	_____ (415)

B. *Concerning motive*

_____ (416)	Described quarrel with victim	_____ (422)
_____ (417)	Claimed self-defense	_____ (423)
_____ (417A)	Claimed other provocation_____	_____ (424)
_____ (418)	Claimed accident	_____ (425)
_____ (419)	Admitted intentional use of force but no intent to kill	_____ (426)
_____ (420)	Claimed under heavy influence of alcohol/drugs	_____ (427)
_____ (420A)	Delusional compulsion	_____ (427A)
_____ (421)	Other_____	_____ (428)

63B. Did the defendant give conflicting statements to police?

1 = Yes—If so, on what issue(s)_____ _____ (428A)

_____

2 = Nothing in file to suggest such statements

63C. Were the defendant's statements consistent with a theory of self-defense?

1 = Yes _____ (429)

2 = No

N = File does not suggest the claim of self-defense was raised by defendant or that the claim is plausible

UC = Statements made but significance is unclear

63D. Were defendant's statements consistent with a theory of diminished responsibility (e.g., voluntary or involuntary manslaughter)?   _____

1 = Yes   (429A)

2 = No

N = File does not suggest the claim of diminished responsibility was raised by defendant or that the claim is plausible

U = Statements made but significance is unclear

63E. The file   _____

1 = Indicates defendant received a *Miranda* warning   (430)

2 = Indicates defendant did not receive a *Miranda* warning

3 = Does not indicate whether defendant received a *Miranda* warning

N = Defendant's statements were not incriminating

Coperpetrator statement (Omit 64–64B if no coperpetrator)

64. The file indicates that there was a coperpetrator who gave a statement to the authorities implicating defendant   _____   (431)

1 = yes   2 = no

(If the answer to 64 is 2, go to question 65.)

64A. Which coperpetrator was the witness in question 48C and in question 48D?   _____   (432)

64B. The coperpetrator implicated the defendant in (check more than one if more than one applies):

_____ the homicidal act   _____ planning the contempora-
(434)   (437)   neous offense

_____ planning the homicide   _____ unknown
(435)   (438)

_____ the contemporaneous of-
(436)   fense

65. The file indicates that there was a witness who heard an incriminating remark by the accused or a coperpetrator (do not include admission to the authorities here)   _____

1 = Yes   (446)

2 = No

(If the answer to question 65 is 2, go to question 66.)

65A and B. Incriminating remarks (enter only the most incriminating remark heard by a single witness)

1 = Admission of killing

2 = Concerning a killing

3 = An admission of the commission of a contemporaneous crime

4 = Concerning the contemporaneous crime

5 = Concerning weapons

6 = Other inculpatory remarks or behavior (specify _____ _____)

65A. Did witness hear remarks by accused that were in-   (Witness #1) _____
criminatory?   (447)
(N = only remark by coperpetrator; code only one
foil)   (Witness #2) _____
   (448)

65B. Did witness hear remarks by coperpetrator that were   (Witness #1) _____
incriminatory?   (449)
(N = only remark by accused; omit if no coperpetrator; code only one foil)   (Witness #2) _____
   (450)

66.   The file indicates there was scientific or real evidence other than the
murder weapon linking the defendant or a coperpetrator to the
event.   _____
1 = Yes   2 = No   (451)
(If answer to question 66 is 2, go to question 67.)

66A. The accused or a coperpetrator was linked to the scene of the crime by:

1 = Fingerprints at scene
2 = Footprints at scene
3 = Tiretracks at scene
4 = Personal belongings of defendant found at the scene
5 = Trace evidence at scene; e.g.,
   defendant's blood type, hair,
   etc.
   (specify_____)
5A = Trace evidence found on victim
6 = Trace evidence found on defendant or belongings of defendant; e.g., victim's blood type,
   spent gun shells, etc.
   (specify_____)

7 = Money or belongings of the victim or goods associated with the
   crime found in the defendant's
   possession and positively identified
8 = Money or belongings of the victim or goods allegedly associated
   with the crime found in the defendant's possession but not
   identified as such
9 = Other_____

Evidence against defendant
(N = Evidence links only coperpetrator—first foil only)

Evidence against coperpetrator
(N = Evidence links only defendant;
omit if no coperpetrator—first foil
only)

_____
(452)

_____
(455)

_____
(453)

_____
(456)

_____
(454)

_____
(457)

66B. If the answer to question 66A was 4, 6, 7, or 8, answer the following question;
otherwise go to question 67.

How was this property connected to the accused?

1 = Volunteered to police by defendant

2 = Volunteered to police by coperpetrator

3 = Found on defendant's person upon arrest

4 = Found on coperpetrator's person upon arrest

5 = Found in or traced to defendant's possession (in house, car, etc.) upon arrest

6 = Found in or traced to coperpetrator's possession (in house, car, etc.) upon arrest

7 = Found in or traced to defendant's possession during a search

8 = Found in or traced to coperpetrator's possession during a search   (458)

9 = Found in close proximity to defendant   (459)

10 = Found in close proximity to coperpetrator

11 = Defendant seen disposing of this property

12 = Coperpetrator seen disposing of this property

13 = Passed by defendant (e.g., forgery)

14 = Passed by coperpetrator (e.g., forgery)

15 = Witness saw defendant with property

16 = Witness saw coperpetrator with property

17 = Unknown

67. Does the file indicate the defendant or a coperpetrator sustained any injury at the scene of the crime that linked him/her to the homicide?

1 = Yes   2 = No   Defendant _____
                                                            (460)

                                               Coperpetrator _____
                                               (omit if no   (461)
                                               coperpetrator)

68. Does the file indicate defendant took out a life-insurance policy that linked him/her to the homicide?

1 = Yes   2 = No   _____
                                                             (462)

69. Did the homicide involve the use of a weapon (other than hands or feet)?

1 = Yes   2 = No   U = Unknown   _____
                                                             (463)

(If answer to question 69 is 2 or U, go to question 71.)

69A. Was the murder weapon found?   _____
1 = Yes   (464)

2 = No (if answer is 2, go to question 71)

U = Unknown (if answer is U, go to question 69C)

69B. If yes, how did police get the weapon?   _____
1 = Found at or near scene   (465)

2 = Found elsewhere

3 = Voluntarily surrendered to police by defendant

4 = Voluntarily surrendered to police by coperpetrator

5 = Voluntarily surrendered to police by other persons

6 = Accused led or directed the authorities to it

7 = Coperpetrator led or directed the authorities to it

8 = Confiscated during a search

9 = Other_____

U = Unknown

(Omit 69C if answer to 69B is 3 through 7.)

69C.   How was the weapon connected to defendant (D) or a coperpetrator (C)?

    1 = Weapon was not connected to D or C

    2 = Weapon was found on D's or C's person or in D's or C's possession

    3 = Weapon was found in close proximity to D or C

    3A = Saw D with weapon at scene of the crime

    4 = Witness positively saw D or C with weapon (on some other occasion than that of the homicide)

    5 = Witness saw D or C with weapon that looked like the homicide weapon (on some other occasion than that of the homicide)

    6 = D's or C's fingerprints were on weapon

    7 = D or C admitted ownership

    8 = D or C admitted possession

    9 = Paraphernalia such as holster or spent shells found on accused or coperpetrator

    10 = Other_____

    U = Unknown

Defendant   _____ _____   Coperpetrator _____ _____

    (466) (467)   (omit if no (468) (469)

        coperpetrators)

70.   Was there a ballistics report that   _____

    1 = Positively linked the fatal bullet(s) to the homicide weapon   (470)

    2 = Possibly linked the fatal bullet(s) to the homicide weapon

    3 = Failed to link fatal bullet(s) to the homicide weapon

    4 = Cleared the defendant's weapon

    5 = No ballistics report

    9 = Not applicable, no gun

    U = Gun used but unknown if report made

    N = Not contested that defendant's gun fired the shot

71.   Was there a report of medical evidence in the file that clarified the cause of death?

    1 = Yes, and it linked cause of death to accused's or coperpetrator's actions

    2 = Yes, but it did not link cause of death to accused's or coperpetrator's actions

    3 = No indication of medical evidence in file.

Defendant   _____   Coperpetrator _____

    (471)   (omit if no (472)

        coperpetrators)

72.   Nature of the arrest of accused and coperpetrator(s):

    1 = Voluntarily surrendered at scene shortly after the offense

    2 = Voluntarily surrendered within twenty-four hours of crime, but not at scene

    3 = Voluntarily surrendered but not within twenty-four hours of crime

4 = Apprehended at the scene shortly after the offense
5 = Apprehended within twenty-four hours of crime, but not at scene
6 = Apprehended, but not within twenty-four hours of the crime
7 = Coperpetrator not arrested
8 = Voluntarily submitted to arrest without admission of liability
9 = Other_____
U = Unknown

Defendant's arrest _____
                     (473)

Coperpetrator's arrest (omit if no coperpetrator—first foil only) (foil for each coperpetrator)

#1 _____	#2 _____	#3 _____	#4 _____
(474)	(475)	(476)	(477)

73. The file indicates that there was a witness with information on preparation or precipitating events: _____
    1 = Yes   2 = No (if so, go to question 74)   (477A)

73A. Preparation or precipitating events (enter number of witnesses; a witness may be entered for more than one piece of evidence)
Did witness:

Defendant			Coperpetrator*	
Police	Civilian		Police	Civilian
_____ (478)	_____ (479)	describe the accused as the aggressor in provoking a fight?	_____ (498)	_____ (499)
_____ (480)	_____ (481)	describe the victim as the aggressor in provoking a fight?	_____ (500)	_____ (501)
_____ (482)	_____ (483)	describe the accused as armed?	_____ (502)	_____ (503)
_____ (484)	_____ (485)	describe the victim as armed?	_____ (504)	_____ (505)
_____ (486)	_____ (487)	say that accused could have retreated from the scene but didn't?	_____ (506)	_____ (507)
_____ (488)	_____ (489)	describe the accused as being intoxicated or under influence of drugs?	_____ (508)	_____ (509)

*Leave blank if there were no coperpetrators.

Defendant			Coperpetrator*	
Police	Civilian		Police	Civilian
		describe the victim as being intoxicated or under influence of drugs?		
_____	_____		_____	_____
(490)	(491)		(510)	(511)
		describe hearing an argument between the accused and the victim?		
_____	_____		_____	_____
(492)	(493)		(512)	(513)
		testify to other events concerning possible claim of self-defense? (specify_____ _____)		
_____	_____		_____	_____
(494)	(495)		(514)	(515)
		testify to other events concerning a claim of diminished responsibility? (specify_____ _____)		
_____	_____		_____	_____
(496)	(497)		(516)	(517)

74. The file indicates that there was a witness with information on motive:

1 = Yes   2 = No (if so, omit question 74A)   _____ (518)

74A. Motive for crime (a witness may be entered for more than one piece of evidence)

Did witness:

Defendant			Coperpetrator*	
Police	Civilian		Police	Civilian
		ever hear the accused utter threats against the victim or a person the victim cared about?		
_____	_____		_____	_____
(519)	(520)		(529)	(530)
		ever hear the victim utter threats against the accused or a person the accused cared about?		
_____	_____		_____	_____
(521)	(522)		(531)	(532)
		deny that victim uttered threats against the accused?		
_____	_____		_____	_____
(523)	(524)		(533)	(534)

*Leave blank if there were no coperpetrators.

Defendant			Coperpetrator*	
Police	Civilian		Police	Civilian
		know of bad blood between accused and victim?		
_____	_____		_____	_____
(525)	(526)		(535)	(536)
		testify to any other motive on the part of the accused to kill the victim? (specify _____ _____)		
_____	_____		_____	_____
(527)	(528)		(537)	(538)

APPENDIX F

Frequency Distribution of Case Characteristics Used in the Charging and Sentencing Study

The proportions in this appendix are estimated for the universe of 2,484 murder and voluntary-manslaughter cases in the Charging and Sentencing Study from a stratified sample of 1,066 cases. *See supra* chapter 4, note 10, for a description of the sampling procedure used. Cases may not always add up to 2,484 because of rounding of weighted counts.

I. Defendant

    A. *Personal characteristics*

        1. Age

            a. Defendant's age at time of crime (DEFAGE):

Age	Proportion (Number)	Age	Proportion (Number)
13–17	.05 ($n=125$)	46–50	.05 ($n=130$)
18–25	.33 ($n=823$)	51–55	.05 ($n=119$)
26–30	.17 ($n=416$)	56–60	.02 ($n=49$)
31–35	.13 ($n=320$)	61–65	.02 ($n=45$)
36–40	.09 ($n=222$)	66–70	.007 ($n=18$)
41–45	.08 ($n=208$)	71–75	.004 ($n=9$)

            b. Defendant juvenile or student (DEFCHILD)   .02 ($n=42$)

            c. Defendant under 18 years of age (SMYOUTH)   .05 ($n=125$)

        2. Mental

            a. Impaired capacity (SMCAPIC)   .0004 ($n=1$)

            b. Defendant had impaired mental capacity (NOCONDUC)   .002 ($n=5$)

            c. Defendant had history of mental illness (MENTILL)   .10 ($n=254$)

        3. Physical

            a. Defendant had history of physical illness (PHYILL)   .06 ($n=158$)

            b. Defendant had history of physical or economic deprivation (DEPRIVED)   .008 ($n=20$)

            c. History of drug or alcohol abuse (DRGHIS)   .38 ($n=950$)

        4. Education or level of intelligence

            a. Defendant IQ over 100 (DBRIGHT)   .31 ($n=761$)

            b. Defendant had been to college or graduated (DCOLLEGE)   .04 ($n=96$)

    c. Defendant IQ 70 to 100 (DDULL)   .46 (n = 1,148)

    d. Defendant with six years or less education
       (DEFUNEDU)   .19 (n = 467)

    e. Defendant had third-grade education or less
       (WRATGGD)   .28 (n = 703)

    f. Defendant had high-school education
       (DHIGHSCH)   .23 (n = 581)

    g. Defendant IQ under 70 (DLOWIQ)   .23 (n = 574)

5. Economic

    a. Defendant blue-collar or unskilled (DBLUNSK) .78 (n = 1,948)

    b. Defendant not regular worker (DUNEMPLY) .20 (n = 500)

    c. High-status defendant (DHISTAT)   .03 (n = 65)

    d. Defendant retired, student, juvenile, housewife
       (MITDEFN)   .03 (n = 80)

    e. Court-appointed counsel (CTAPPATN)   .33 (n = 813)

    f. Low-status defendant (LSTATDEF)   .66 (n = 1,632)

6. Geographic

    a. Defendant from out of county (DOUTCO)   .28 (n = 684)

    b. Defendant from out of state (DOUTSTAT)   .08 (n = 194)

7. Sex of defendant

    a. Defendant a female (FEMDEF)   .13 (n = 324)

8. Other

    a. Defendant unsavory (BADDEF)   .03 (n = 76)

B. *Prior record*

1. Crimes committed

    a. Recent nonviolent crime by defendant (RECCRIM) .32 (n = 800)

2. Age

    a. Defendant sixteen or younger at first felony
       arrest (DAGEARST)   .14 (n = 349)

    b. Defendant's age at time of first felony arrest
       (DFSTCRIM):

Age	Proportion (Number)	Age	Proportion (Number)
none	.50 (n = 1,230)	36–40	.02 (n = 43)
8–17	.14 (n = 349)	41–45	.01 (n = 36)
18–25	.25 (n = 611)	46–55	.003 (n = 8)
26–30	.05 (n = 118)	56–91	.003 (n = 8)
31–35	.03 (n = 80)		

3. Detainers

    a. Defendant had one or more detainers (DETAIN) .04 (n = 108)

4. Arrests

    a. Defendant had one or more misdemeanor arrests
       (MISARST)   .70 (n = 1,738)

    b. Defendant had felony arrest (FELARST)   .49 $(n=1,217)$

    c. Defendant arrest for violent crime within two
        years of homicide (RECVCRIM)   .14 $(n=341)$

    d. Number of prior arrests (DARREST):

Number of Arrests	Proportion (Number)	Number of Arrests	Proportion (Number)
0	.35 $(n=863)$	11–15	.03 $(n=82)$
1–2	.29 $(n=728)$	16–20	.02 $(n=48)$
3–4	.15 $(n=375)$	21–30	.01 $(n=25)$
5–6	.07 $(n=186)$		
7–10	.07 $(n=172)$		

    e. Number of misdemeanor arrests (MISARSTX):   .67 $(n=723)$

Number of Arrests	Proportion (Number)	Number of Arrests	Proportion (Number)
0	.30 $(n=746)$	11–15	.05 $(n=113)$
1	.20 $(n=507)$	16–20	.02 $(n=39)$
2–3	.22 $(n=553)$	21–25	.006 $(n=14)$
4–5	.10 $(n=259)$	26–35	.004 $(n=11)$
6–10	.09 $(n=233)$	36–99	.004 $(n=9)$

    f. Number of felony arrests (FELARX):

Number of Arrests	Proportion (Number)	Number of Arrests	Proportion (Number)
0	.51 $(n=1,267)$	5–6	.04 $(n=106)$
1–2	.31 $(n=776)$	7–8	.02 $(n=55)$
3–4	.11 $(n=263)$	9–14	.007 $(n=17)$

5. Convictions

    a. Defendant had prior conviction, felony or
        misdemeanor (CONVICT)   .63 $(n=1,572)$

    b. One or more convictions: violent personal
        crime/burglary/arson (VPCARBR)   .32 $(n=794)$

    c. More than one violent-personal-crime
        conviction (besides homicide/armed robbery/
        rape/kidnapping) (OTHVPC)   .23 $(n=563)$

    d. Record of one or more misdemeanor convictions
        (MISDCONV)   .52 $(n=1,288)$

    e. Defendant had prior murder or manslaughter
        conviction (DPRIKILL)   .03 $(n=77)$

    f. Defendant had been convicted of a crime
        (RECORD)   .65 $(n=1,599)$

    g. Felony record/two or more violent
        misdemeanors (FEL 2VMD)   .35 $(n=879)$

    h. Defendant was convicted, felony or
        misdemeanor (DCONVICT)   .23 $(n=576)$

    i. Defendant had one or more prior murder
        convictions (MURPRIOR)   .01 $(n=20)$

j. Number of prior convictions for felonies,
misdemeanors (CONVICTX):

Number of Convictions	Proportion (Number)	Number of Convictions	Proportion (Number)
0	.37 ($n=912$)	11–15	.03 ($n=69$)
1–2	.26 ($n=656$)	16–20	.01 ($n=35$)
3–4	.15 ($n=378$)	21–30	.009 ($n=22$)
5–6	.09 ($n=234$)	above 30	.001 ($n=4$)
7–10	.07 ($n=176$)		

k. Number of convictions: violent personal crime,
burglary/arson in first degree (VPCARBRX):

Number of Convictions	Proportion (Number)	Number of Convictions	Proportion (Number)
0	.68 ($n=1,690$)	6–9	.01 ($n=26$)
1–2	.23 ($n=570$)	11–15	.003 ($n=7$)
3–5	.07 ($n=186$)	above 16	.002 ($n=5$)

l. Number of prior convictions for violent personal
crimes (RECVPLX):

Number of Convictions	Proportion (Number)	Number of Convictions	Proportion (Number)
0	.74 ($n=1,840$)	3–5	.04 ($n=106$)
1–2	.21 ($n=525$)	more than 5	.005 ($n=13$)

m. Number of violent-personal-crime convictions
beyond homicide, armed robbery/rape/
kidnapping (VIOLCVX):

Number of Convictions	Proportion (Number)	Number of Convictions	Proportion (Number)
0	.76 ($n=1,887$)	3–4	.03 ($n=82$)
1–2	.20 ($n=493$)	5 or more	.009 ($n=23$)

n. Number of violent-personal-crime convictions
(besides homicide/armed robbery/rape/kidnapping) (OTHVPCX):

Number of Convictions	Proportion (Number)	Number of Convictions	Proportion (Number)
0	.77 ($n=1,921$)	3–5	.03 ($n=79$)
1–2	.19 ($n=475$)	more than 5	.003 ($n=9$)

o. Number of convictions, felony and misdemeanor (DCONVICX):

Number of Convictions	Proportion (Number)	Number of Convictions	Proportion (Number)
0	.77 ($n=1,908$)	3–5	.03 ($n=82$)
1–2	.20 ($n=491$)	more than 5	.001 ($n=3$)

p. Number of prior felony convictions (PRIFELX):

Number of Convictions	Proportion (Number)	Number of Convictions	Proportion (Number)
0	.65 ($n=1,622$)	6–10	.02 ($n=51$)
1–2	.24 ($n=591$)	11–15	.003 ($n=8$)
3–5	.08 ($n=208$)	more than 15	.002 ($n=5$)

6. Prison
   a. Defendant released from prison within last year
      (DRECPRIS)   .06 ($n = 141$)
   b. Defendant has been incarcerated after conviction
      (PRISON)   .36 ($n = 888$)
   c. Number of times defendant in youth detention
      center (YTHDETX):

Number of Detentions	Proportion (Number)	Number of Detentions	Proportion (Number)
0	.93 ($n = 2,301$)	2	.01 ($n = 29$)
1	.06 ($n = 138$)	3	.006 ($n = 16$)

   d. Number of defendant felony prison terms
      (PRISONX):

Number of Terms	Proportion (Number)	Number of Terms	Proportion (Number)
0	.74 ($n = 1,838$)	3	.02 ($n = 49$)
1	.16 ($n = 406$)	4	.009 ($n = 23$)
2	.06 ($n = 151$)	5–6	.007 ($n = 17$)

   e. Months defendant previously incarcerated
      (MONTHJL):

Number of Months	Proportion (Number)	Number of Months	Proportion (Number)
0	.70 ($n = 1,744$)	49–60	.005 ($n = 13$)
1–12	.08 ($n = 198$)	61–84	.04 ($n = 96$)
13–24	.07 ($n = 173$)	85–120	.02 ($n = 50$)
25–36	.03 ($n = 70$)	121–216	.01 ($n = 33$)
37–48	.04 ($n = 109$)		

7. No prior record
   a. No prior arrests or convictions (NOARREST)   .21 ($n = 521$)
   b. No prior convictions (NOCONVIC)   .33 ($n = 822$)
   c. No serious prior convictions (NOSERCON)   .78 ($n = 1,940$)
   d. Defendant never incarcerated (NOPRISON)   .64 ($n = 1,592$)
   e. Defendant had no significant criminal history
      (SMNOSREC)   .78 ($n = 1,940$)

II. Coperpetrator

A. *Presence of coperpetrators*
   1. One or more coperpetrators involved (COPERP)   .21 ($n = 531$)
   2. Number of coperpetrators (COPERPX):

Number	Proportion (Number)	Number	Proportion (Number)*
0	.79 ($n = 1,953$)	4	.007 ($n = 19$)
1	.10 ($n = 254$)	6	.001 ($n = 3$)
2	.07 ($n = 166$)	8	.002 ($n = 4$)
3	.03 ($n = 86$)		

*Detail does not add up to 531 because of rounding.

B. *Role in crime*

 1. Coperpetrator caused the death (COPDIDIT)   .07 ($n = 164$)

 2. Coperpetrator injured one or more people
  (COPERHUT)   .003 ($n = 9$)

 3. Coperpetrator fired five or more shots (CPSHOOT5)   .007 ($n = 17$)

C. *Outcome*

 1. A coperpetrator received less than a death sentence
  prior to defendant's sentencing (CPLESSSN)   .03 ($n = 63$)

 2. A coperpetrator received a lesser sentence
  (CPLESSEN)   .08 ($n = 208$)

 3. A coperpetrator received a higher sentence
  (CPMORSEN)   .03 ($n = 65$)

III. Victim

A. *Characteristics*   *Proportion (Number)*

 1. Physical

  a. Victim mental defective (VDEFECT)   .002 ($n = 4$)

  b. Victim bed-ridden/handicapped (VBED)   .004 ($n = 9$)

  c. Defenseless victim because of youth (VDEFENLS)   .03 ($n = 68$)

  d. Victim pregnant, disabled, or helpless
   (VDEFNSLS)   .14 ($n = 339$)

  e. Victim defenseless because of advanced age
   (VDEFOLD)   .03 ($n = 86$)

  f. Victim used drugs or alcohol (VICDRUG)   .28 ($n = 694$)

  g. Victim pregnant (VPREG)   .009 ($n = 23$)

  h. Victim defenseless because of size difference,
   number of defendants (VSMALL)   .07 ($n = 179$)

  i. Victim weak or frail (VWEAK)   .02 ($n = 49$)

  j. Female victim (FEMVIC)   .31 ($n = 770$)

  k. Victim twelve or younger (YOUNGVIC)   .02 ($n = 58$)

  l. Victim's age (VICAGE):

Age	Proportion (Number)	Age	Proportion (Number)
0–1	.01 ($n = 25$)	46–50	.06 ($n = 161$)
2–10	.01 ($n = 30$)	51–55	.04 ($n = 105$)
11–15	.01 ($n = 32$)	56–60	.03 ($n = 65$)
16–20	.07 ($n = 166$)	61–65	.04 ($n = 107$)
21–25	.11 ($n = 262$)	66–70	.01 ($n = 32$)
26–30	.13 ($n = 335$)	71–75	.01 ($n = 35$)
31–35	.29 ($n = 712$)	76–80	.01 ($n = 29$)
36–40	.09 ($n = 230$)	81–85	.001 ($n = 2$)
41–45	.06 ($n = 154$)		

 2. Number of victims

  a. Defendant killed two or more people (TWOVIC)   .03 ($n = 63$)

  b. Two victims killed by defendant and/or
   coperpetrator (TWOVICAL)   .03 ($n = 75$)

3. Economic
    a. Victim blue-collar worker or unskilled (VBLUSKL)   .05 ($n=113$)
    b. Victim not regular worker (VUNEMPLO)   .006 ($n=14$)
    c. High-status victim (VHISTAT)   .05 ($n=129$)
    d. Victim supporting children (VSUPKID)   .18 ($n=451$)
4. General reputation
    a. Victim unsavory (BADVIC)   .03 ($n=69$)
    b. Victim had bad reputation (VBADREP)   .07 ($n=171$)
5. Criminal record
    a. Victim had a criminal record (VCRIMREC)   .03 ($n=86$)
    b. Victim had criminal record (VRECORD)   .03 ($n=86$)
    c. Victim was a fugitive (VFUGITIV)   NC*

IV. The crime

A. *Contemporaneous offense*
    1. Armed robbery involved (ARMROB)   .13 ($n=329$)
    2. Kidnapping involved (KIDNAP)   .04 ($n=100$)
    3. Rape involved (RAPE)   .02 ($n=58$)
    4. Non-property-related contemporaneous crime
       (NONPROPC)   .08 ($n=201$)
    5. Nonviolent contemporaneous crime (besides
       burglary/vice) (NOVIOLCR)   .04 ($n=90$)
B. *Circumstances leading up to crime*
    1. Family, lover, liquor, barroom quarrel (BLVICMOD)   .50 ($n=1,250$)
    2. Homicide arose from a dispute, fight (DISFIGHT)   .59 ($n=1,471$)
    3. Reasonable discipline of minor by parent (DISKID)   .002 ($n=4$)
    4. Dispute under influence of drugs, alcohol
       (DRUGDIS)   .25 ($n=624$)
    5. Dispute over money or property between victim,
       defendant (MONDIS)   .12 ($n=308$)
    6. Family dispute other than spouse, ex-spouse
       (FAMDIS)   .07 ($n=174$)
    7. Gun fired during struggle for gun (GUNSTRUG)   .03 ($n=70$)
    8. Defendant broke into victim's residence (RESBKIN)   .03 ($n=71$)
    9. Defendant panicked in course of burglary (PANIC)   .03 ($n=73$)
    10. Shoot-out (SHOOTOUT)   .02 ($n=49$)
    11. Dispute between spouses or ex-spouses (SPOUSESK)   .18 ($n=448$)
    12. Lovers' triangle (TRIANGLE)   .08 ($n=203$)
    13. Victim pleaded for life (VICPLEAD)   .06 ($n=150$)
C. *Method of killing*
    1. Brutal clubbing or stomping (BEAT)   .07 ($n=175$)
    2. Victim was drowned (DROWN)   .007 ($n=19$)

*NC means no cases.

3. Execution-style killing (EXECUT)   .10 ($n = 249$)
4. Victim killed with gun (GUN)   .72 ($n = 1,792$)
5. Multiple head shots (MULHDSHT)   .06 ($n = 137$)
6. Multiple gunshots (MULSH)   .25 ($n = 630$)
7. Multiple stabbing (MULSTAB)   .07 ($n = 167$)
8. Victim killed by neglect or deprivation (NEGLECT)   .0007 ($n = 2$)
9. Victim killed with poison (POISON)   .004 ($n = 10$)
10. Victim strangled (STRANGLE)   .02 ($n = 49$)
11. Slashed throat of victim (THROAT)   .02 ($n = 48$)

D. *Other aggravating factors related to the crime*
1. Bodily harm to other than victim (HARMOTH)   .08 ($n = 196$)
2. Victim bound or gagged (BDGAG)   .03 ($n = 78$)
3. Sex perversion other than rape (PERVER)   .01 ($n = 33$)
4. Victim forced to disrobe (NUDE)   .04 ($n = 91$)
5. Victim without clothes when killed (NOCLOTH)   .06 ($n = 151$)
6. Slow death (SLODIE)   .12 ($n = 298$)
7. Mutilation (MUTILATE)   .06 ($n = 140$)
8. Victim killed in presence of family/close friends (VFAMPRES)   .25 ($n = 618$)
9. Mental torture (MENTORT)   .01 ($n = 35$)
10. Victim tortured physically (TORTURE)   .01 ($n = 25$)
11. Ambush/lurking (AMBUSH)   .07 ($n = 172$)
12. Victim was a hostage (HOSTAGE)   .006 ($n = 15$)

E. *Defendant's role in the crime*
1. Motive for killing
   a. Motive to avenge role by judicial officer, district attorney, lawyer (AVENGE)   .001 ($n = 3$)
   b. Hate motive (HATE)   .11 ($n = 266$)
   c. Defendant motive to collect insurance (INSMOT)   .01 ($n = 29$)
   d. Rage motive (RAGE)   .60 ($n = 1,500$)
   e. Racial-hatred motive (RACEMOT)   .01 ($n = 33$)
   f. Revenge motive (REVENGE)   .14 ($n = 345$)
   g. Jealousy motive (JEALOUS)   .12 ($n = 294$)
   h. Defendant motive hate, revenge, jealousy, rage (MITMOTVE)   .66 ($n = 1,631$)
   i. Killing unnecessary to carry out contemporaneous offense (UNNECERY)   .06 ($n = 159$)
2. Defendant's participation
   a. Defendant aided victims (AIDVICT)   .05 ($n = 131$)
   b. Defendant committed or alleged to commit additional crime (ADDCRIME)   .07 ($n = 164$)
   c. Defendant injured one or more other people (DEFHURT)   .07 ($n = 182$)
   d. Defendant prime mover in planning homicide or contemporaneous offense (DLEADER)   .03 ($n = 67$)

    e. Defendant killed or participated in killing
       (DKILLER)   .14 $(n=339)$
    f. Defendant fired five or more shots (DSHOOT5) .06 $(n=147)$
    g. Defendant involved in felony at time of killing
       (FELMUR)   .20 $(n=500)$
    h. Defendant only an accomplice in killing
       (JOINTKIL)   .03 $(n=82)$
    i. Defendant did not kill but did violence to victim
       (DVIOLV)   .02 $(n=43)$
    j. Defendant not at scene (DABSENT)   .02 $(n=39)$
    k. Defendant unaware of plan to kill (DIGNORNT) NC
    l. Defendant unaware of intent to use force
       (DNOINT)   .003 $(n=7)$
    m. Coercion used on defendant (DCOERCED) .004 $(n=10)$
    n. Defendant not triggerman (NOKILL)   .06 $(n=161)$
    o. Defendant committed no violence (DNOVIOL) .04 $(n=110)$
    p. Defendant's only violence was against others
       (DVIOLOTH)   .004 $(n=11)$
    q. Defendant accomplice and minor participant
       (SMUNDRLG)   .06 $(n=140)$
    r. Defense of home, dwelling, or property
       (DPROPDEF)   .004 $(n=11)$
    s. Defendant acted under duress (SMDURESS) .002 $(n=4)$
    t. Defendant had moral justification for actions
       (SMDEFJUS)   .01 $(n=28)$
    u. Defendant under extreme mental or emotional
       disturbance (SMEMDIST)   .01 $(n=37)$
    v. Defendant was provoked (SMPROVOK) .48 $(n=1,194)$
    w. Lack of intent to kill (DNOINTNT)   .10 $(n=257)$

F. *Defendant's emotions about killing*
    1. Defendant showed no remorse for homicide
       (NOREMORE)   .06 $(n=140)$
    2. Defendant expressed pleasure with killing (DPLEAS) .02 $(n=40)$
    3. Defendant showed remorse (DEFREMOR) .05 $(n=131)$

G. *Treatment of defendant by police*
    1. Defendant physically injured by police (COPHURTD) .002 $(n=4)$

H. *Defendant's position at trial*
    1. Defendant admitted homicide—with no defense
       (DCONFESS)   .26 $(n=640)$
    2. Defendant admitted guilt and no defense
       asserted (DEFADMIT)   .06 $(n=150)$
    3. Mistake of fact claimed (DBADFACT)   .01 $(n=23)$
    4. Suicide by victim claimed (VSUICIDE)   .004 $(n=11)$
    5. Defendant claimed accident (ACCIDENT)   .14 $(n=339)$
    6. Defense of self or others (DSELFDEF)   .33 $(n=829)$

7. Defendant claimed involuntary manslaughter
   (INVOLMAN)   .02 $(n = 42)$
8. Defendant claimed voluntary manslaughter
   (VOLMANS)   .31 $(n = 775)$
9. Insanity or delusional compulsion (INSANDEF)   .02 $(n = 58)$

I. *Factors relevant to murder or voluntary-manslaughter liability*
   1. Malice/victim defenseless (VDEFENS)   .11 $(n = 271)$
   2. Malice/violence (VIOLENCE)   .56 $(n = 1,402)$
   3. Malice/no victim provocation (NOVPROV)   .09 $(n = 227)$
   4. Malice/deadly weapon without mitigation
      (DEADWEP)   .87 $(n = 2,172)$
   5. Malice/deliberation (DTHINK)   .32 $(n = 806)$
   6. Provocation or sudden passion (PROVPASS)   .13 $(n = 319)$
   7. Crime of anger (EMOTION)   .73 $(n = 1,812)$

J. *Defendant's condition at time of crime*
   1. Defendant used alcohol, drugs immediately prior to
      crime (DDRINK)   .38 $(n = 945)$
   2. Defendant substantially affected by alcohol,
      drugs (DEFINTOX)   .14 $(n = 340)$
   3. Defendant on escape (DEFESC)   .02 $(n = 43)$

K. *Defendant's actions before crime*
   1. Defendant lay in wait (DEFWAIT)   .07 $(n = 177)$
   2. Killing planned more than five minutes
      (PREMEDK)   .24 $(n = 592)$
   3. Contemporaneous offense planned more than five
      minutes (PLANCOF)   .16 $(n = 407)$

L. *Defendant's actions after crime*
   1. Defendant cooperated with authorities (SMDEFCO) .08 $(n = 198)$
   2. Defendant left the scene of crime (DEFLED)   .63 $(n = 1,573)$
   3. Defendant surrendered within twenty-four hours
      (DEFSUR)   .18 $(n = 437)$
   4. Defendant surrendered more than twenty-four
      hours after crime (DEFSURLT)   .02 $(n = 48)$
   5. Defendant tried to dispose of or conceal body
      (CONCELBD)   .08 $(n = 186)$
   6. Defendant resisted arrest (DRESIST)   .12 $(n = 299)$

M. *Victim's role in the crime*
   1. Victim was a coperpetrator (VCOPERP)   .002 $(n = 4)$
   2. Victim was witness (VWITNESS)   .06 $(n = 142)$
   3. Victim offered no provocation (NOVICPRO)   .13 $(n = 317)$

N. *Victim's association with the defendant*
   1. Victim and defendant had a history of bad blood
      (BDBLOOD)   .14 $(n = 348)$
   2. Victim a stranger (STRANGER)   .18 $(n = 449)$
   3. Victim family, friend, intimate (VICCLOSE)   .44 $(n = 1,103)$

O. *Actions by the victim affecting the defendant*
  1. Actions against the defendant
     a. Victim verbally abused defendant earlier
        (VABUSEAR)   .03 $(n=65)$
     b. Victim accused defendant of misconduct
        (VACCUSED)   .06 $(n=142)$
     c. Victim assaulted defendant (VASSAULD)   .14 $(n=335)$
     d. Victim assaulted defendant earlier (VASSDEAR) .06 $(n=155)$
     e. Victim verbally provoked defendant by
        accusation, abuse, threat (VICVERB)   .36 $(n=897)$
     f. Victim physically injured defendant earlier
        (VINJDEAR)   .02 $(n=56)$
     g. Victim aroused defendant fear (DEFFEAR)   .12 $(n=287)$
     h. Defendant fear/victim weapon (FEARVWEP)   .17 $(n=418)$
     i. Victim physically injured defendant (VINJURD) .02 $(n=46)$
     j. Victim threatened defendant earlier (VTHEAEAR) .03 $(n=76)$
     k. Victim verbally threatened defendant
        (VTHREATD)   .04 $(n=102)$
     l. Victim sexually aroused defendant (VSEXUP)   .006 $(n=16)$
     m. Victim showed, talked about much money
        (VSHOMON)   .01 $(n=30)$
  2. Actions against someone defendant cared for
     a. Victim verbally threatened person defendant
        cared for (VABSFEAR)   .002 $(n=5)$
     b. Victim verbally abused friend of defendant
        (VABUSEF)   .02 $(n=43)$
     c. Victim provoked defendant by abuse of person
        defendant cared for (VABUSFRD)   .06 $(n=139)$
     d. Victim assaulted person defendant cared about
        (VASSAULT)   .02 $(n=56)$
     e. Victim verbally threatened person defendant
        cared for (VASTFEAR)   .01 $(n=32)$
     f. Victim had earlier injured a person defendant
        cared for (VINJFEAR)   .006 $(n=16)$
     g. Victim injured person defendant cared about
        (VINJURF)   .007 $(n=18)$
     h. Victim threatened person defendant cared about
        (VTHREAT)   .006 $(n=15)$
     i. Victim verbally threatened person defendant
        cared for (VTRTFEAR)   .005 $(n=12)$
P. *Victim's condition at time of crime*
  1. Victim asleep or just awakened (VASLEEP)   .02 $(n=49)$
  2. Victim was armed (VICARMED)   .12 $(n=304)$
  3. Victim under substantial influence of
     drugs/alcohol (VICDRUNK)   .07 $(n=181)$
  4. Victim had deadly weapon (VICWEAPM)   .12 $(n=304)$

V. Other aggravating and mitigating factors

   A. *Statutory aggravating circumstances*
      1. Prior record of murder, armed robbery, rape, kidnapping/bodily injury, aggravated battery, burglary (LDFB1)   .04 ($n = 104$)
      2. Contemporaneous murder, armed robbery, rape, kidnapping/bodily injury, aggravated battery, burglary (LDFB2)   .20 ($n = 494$)
      3. Defendant caused death risk in public place to more than two people (LDFB3)   .15 ($n = 368$)
      4. Murder to get money/value for self/other (LDFB4)   .19 ($n = 464$)
      5. Victim was killed because of official duty (LDFB5)   NC
      6. Murder for hire (LDFB6)   .01 ($n = 35$)
      7. One or more B7 factors in case (LDFB7)   .51 ($n = 1,272$)
         7.1. Mutilation before or after death (LDFB7A)   .06 ($n = 140$)
         7.2. Unnecessary multiple wounding (LDFB7B)   .39 ($n = 976$)
         7.3. Rape/armed robbery/kidnapping/silence witness/exec/victim plead (LDFB7D)   .09 ($n = 227$)
         7.4. Torture/depravity (LDFB7E)   .10 ($n = 249$)
         7.5. Depravity/sex perversion (LDFB7F)   .07 ($n = 175$)
      8. Victim police/corrections/fireman on duty (LDFB8)   .01 ($n = 29$)
      9. Defendant prisoner or escapee (LDFB9)   .02 ($n = 44$)
     10. Kill to avoid, stop arrest of self, other (LDFB10)   .07 ($n = 165$)
     11. Number of Georgia statutory aggravating circumstances present (LDFBSUM):

Number of Circumstances	Proportion (Number)	Number of Circumstances	Proportion (Number)
0	.35 ($n = 864$)	4	.05 ($n = 115$)
1	.36 ($n = 882$)	5	.01 ($n = 30$)
2	.13 ($n = 324$)	6	.004 ($n = 10$)
3	.10 ($n = 259$)		

     12. Number of Georgia statutory aggravating factors, including a count of B7 factors (LDFB7EXP):

Number of Circumstances	Proportion (Number)	Number of Circumstances	Proportion (Number)
0	.35 ($n = 864$)	5	.04 ($n = 96$)
1	.32 ($n = 800$)	6	.02 ($n = 42$)
2	.13 ($n = 324$)	7	.01 ($n = 12$)
3	.08 ($n = 203$)	8	.002 ($n = 4$)
4	.06 ($n = 138$)	9	.001 ($n = 2$)

     13. Factor count with prior record (LDFSMRC2):

Number of Factors	Proportion (Number)	Number of Factors	Proportion (Number)
0	.25 ($n = 627$)	4	.06 ($n = 158$)
1	.34 ($n = 835$)	5	.03 ($n = 70$)
2	.18 ($n = 457$)	6	.01 ($n = 25$)
3	12 ($n = 306$)	7	.002 ($n = 6$)

B. *Nonstatutory aggravating factors*
1. No special aggravating circumstance (NOSPAGCR)   .14 (*n* = 355)
2. Number of minor aggravating factors in case (MINAGFCX):

Number of Factors	Proportion (Number)	Number of Factors	Proportion (Number)
0	.46 (*n* = 1,137)	4	.03 (*n* = 86)
1	.28 (*n* = 701)	5	.004 (*n* = 11)
2	.16 (*n* = 385)	6	.003 (*n* = 10)
3	.06 (*n* = 154)		

3. Number of major aggravating factors in case (MAJAGFCX):

Number of Factors	Proportion (Number)	Number of Factors	Proportion (Number)
0	.76 (*n* = 1,899)	3	.02 (*n* = 43)
1	.16 (*n* = 409)	4	.01 (*n* = 26)
2	.04 (*n* = 93)	5 or more	.004 (*n* = 13)

C. *Mitigating factors*
1. One or more mitigating factors involved (MITCIR)   .81 (*n* = 2,008)
2. No victim-related mitigating circumstances
   (NOVICMIT)   .32 (*n* = 789)
3. Number of mitigating factors involved (MITCIRX):

Number of Factors	Proportion (Number)	Number of Factors	Proportion (Number)
0	.19 (*n* = 476)	4	.11 (*n* = 279)
1	.26 (*n* = 628)	5	.05 (*n* = 128)
2	.21 (*n* = 519)	6	.01 (*n* = 27)
3	.17 (*n* = 417)	7	.005 (*n* = 10)

VI. Strength of evidence

A. *Identification*
1. Identification of the defendant not in doubt
   as killer (CLEARID)   .76 (*n* = 1,883)
2. Defendant seen in act by one who knew him
   (EYEWITID)   .25 (*n* = 622)
3. An ID witness of defendant or coperpetrator
   (IDWIT)   .78 (*n* = 1,940)
4. Two or more witness defendant commit crime,
   nearby (TWOWITD)   .47 (*n* = 1,160)
5. ID witness of defendant commit crime or near
   scene (IDWITDEF)   .75 (*n* = 1,871)
6. ID witness of coperpetrator commit crime or
   near scene (IDWITCOP)   .09 (*n* = 227)
7. ID witness of defendant with weapon near scene
   of crime (IDDEFGUN)   .12 (*n* = 300)
8. One or more witness re: preparation (PREPWITN)   .66 (*n* = 1,633)
9. There was a pretrial ID of defendant (PRETRID)   .69 (*n* = 1,725)
10. Witness heard incriminating remark by defendant

| | or coperpetrator (INCRREMK) | .29 $(n=723)$ |
| 11. | Mistaken identity (BADID) | .09 $(n=225)$ |

B. *Type of witness*
1. Primary witness police officer, civilian with no credibility problem (GOODWIT) .60 $(n=1,496)$
2. Police witnessed defendant commit crime, near scene (POLWIT) .02 $(n=41)$

C. *Statements or testimony*
1. Coperpetrator testified against defendant (COPERTES) .03 $(n=84)$
2. Coperpetrator statement implicated defendant in homicide (CPSTATEM) .08 $(n=187)$
3. Defendant statement supports voluntary manslaughter (DSTATVM) .29 $(n=719)$

D. *Other evidence*
1. Medical report links death to defendant action (INCMDRPT) .25 $(n=618)$
2. Police report indicated clear guilt (POLGUILT) .92 $(n=2,292)$
3. Science evidence other than weapon or medical (SCIEVID) .23 $(n=568)$
4. Murder weapon found, links defendant to homicide (WEAPON) .37 $(n=914)$
5. Number of major types of incriminating evidence against defendant (EVIDINDX):

Number of Types	Proportion (Number)	Number of Types	Proportion (Number)
0	.04 $(n=111)$	5	.17 $(n=418)$
1	.06 $(n=150)$	6	.07 $(n=174)$
2	.10 $(n=236)$	7	.02 $(n=47)$
3	.27 $(n=660)$	8	.007 $(n=17)$
4	.27 $(n=670)$		

6. Primary witness was corroborated (WITCOROB) .24 $(n=601)$
7. No witness, no pretrial identification, no coperpetrator statement (CIRCEVID) .01 $(n=27)$

VII. Racial characteristics

A. *Race of defendant and victim*
1. Defendant was black (BLACKD) .67 $(n=1,676)$
2. One or more white victims (WHVICRC) .40 $(n=980)$

B. *Defendant-victim racial combination* (RACEVCRC)
1. Black defendant/white victim .10 $(n=233)$
2. White defendant/white victim .30 $(n=748)$
3. Black defendant/black victim .58 $(n=1,443)$
4. White defendant/black victim .02 $(n=60)$

VIII. Outcome and geographic variables

    A. Death sentence imposed among all cases (DSENTALL)   .05 $(n = 128)$*

    B. Death sentence imposed among cases with a
        murder indictment (DPMURIDT)   .05 $(n = 128)$

    C. Death sentence imposed at penalty trial, including
        twelve cases with two penalty trials (DEATHSNT)   .56 $(n = 140)$

    D. Voluntary-manslaughter guilty plea and
        conviction among cases indicted for murder
        (MURVMPLE)   .42 $(n = 979)$

    E. Murder plea and conviction without penalty
        trial, among cases indicted for murder and not
        pleading guilty to voluntary manslaughter
        (MURPLEA)   .17 $(n = 237)$

    F. Jury-trial murder conviction (versus
        conviction for voluntary manslaughter) (JURCVMUR)   .68 $(n = 762)$

    G. Penalty trial if murder trial conviction (PSEENNGP)   .32 $(n = 228)$

    H. Five regions of Georgia (LDFX3J)
        1. North   .07 (176)
        2. North Central   .27 (681)
        3. Atlanta   .25 (629)
        4. Southwest   .23 (564)
        5. Southeast   .18 (434)

    I. Cases in urban judicial circuits with more than 50 percent
       urban population reported in 1970 census   .53 $(n = 1,321)$

*For items A through G, n equals the number of occurrences of the outcome indicated by the variable.

APPENDIX G

Listing of Post-*Furman* Georgia
Armed-Robbery–Murder Cases, in Order of
Culpability, As Determined with an *A Priori*
Measure that Weighs Aggravating and
Mitigating Circumstances[1]

POST-*FURMAN:* CATEGORY I (LEAST AGGRAVATED CATEGORY)

Case No.

618	rob (B2), defendant drove car, defendant claimed no responsibility in robbery and murder, 2 nonviolent priors
063	rob (B2), female defendant drove co-perps. to scene, no priors
037	rob (B2), female defendant waited in car during robbery and murder, split proceeds, 1 nonviolent prior [co-perp. #262] (wounded), V shot, police stopped car to search after robbery (B10), defendant no known priors
957	rob (B2), defendant driver, co-perp. hit V with gun and kicked him, elderly V, acquaintances, no priors
841	rob (B2), 1 prior armed robbery (B1), V shot, defendant 19-year-old, 2 priors (1 nonviolent)
983	rob (B2), V shot 5× by co-perp., defendant not at scene when robbery and murder occurred, 6 priors (2 nonviolent)
922	rob (B2), defendant stole car and waited outside, 3 co-perps. shot and robbed bus station attendant, no priors
385	same case as above, no priors[2]
434	rob (B2), 1 V, two injured (B3), defendant lookout, no priors
635	rob (B2), V and her invalid mother beaten to death (B7), defendant 16-year-old, defendant not trigger, V 55-year-old female neighbor, 7 priors (6 nonviolent)

1. The numbers in parentheses refer to the aggravating factors listed in the Georgia capital-sentencing statute. *See supra* chap. 3, note 18. Tables 12 and 31 include 7 cases (D13, D14, 641, 751, 753, 955, and 958) that resulted in the imposition of a second death sentence after the first death sentence was vacated by the Georgia Supreme Court. Because these cases are listed only once in this appendix, it includes 181 rather than 188 cases.
2. "Same case as above" means the defendant was a coperpetrator in the preceding case.

334   rob (B2), V struck with hammer, rocks, stick through skull (B7), defendant tried to run away and did not participate, defendant confessed and testified against co-perps., defendant 18-year-old, V 18-year-old friend, no priors

799   rob (B2), co-perps. beat V with gun butt and baseball bat, defendant paid to lure V to site, defendant 23-year-old female, no priors

798   same case as above, defendant role unknown [co-perp. C93, 801, 802, and 799]

C99   rob (B2), 11-year-old V shot, V's father injured, evidence that defendant neither shot nor threatened V, defendant 19-year-old, no priors

POST-*FURMAN:* CATEGORY II (LOW TO HIGH)

C88   rob (B2), victim killed, defendant not trigger, drinking, defendant 17-year-old, no priors

953   rob (B2), V shot in chest, defendant 15-year-old, V 19-year-old, lack of evidence, no priors

329   rob liquor store (B2), defendant not trigger, defendant age 16, V 16-year-old, no prior record

254   rob billfold (B2), 18-year-old defendant, friends, poss. alcohol, poss. self-defense (argument), poss. accidental shooting, 2 priors (1 nonviolent)

969   rob (B2), V shot, strangers, defendant mental problem (confined for 10 years in state hospital on manslaughter conviction), 4 priors

559   rob (B2), victim shot at defendant first, then defendant killed victim, confession, defendant cooperated with authorities, alcohol, defendant military, no priors

724   rob (B2), defendant and victim exchanged shots, victim killed, defendant injured, no priors

399   rob (B2), defendant shot V in head, dumped body in river, drugs and alcohol, friends, no priors

495   rob (B2), V lured out to aid wounded person, V kidnapped (B2), pled for life, defendant paranoid schizophrenic, 6 nonviolent priors

POST-*FURMAN:* CATEGORY III (LOW TO HIGH)

412   rob (B2), defendant killed V for his money bonus, friends, no priors

733   rob (B2), co-perps. shot V for refusing to give money, defendant not trigger, defendant 19-year-old, military, no priors

D16   rob (B2), V shot in head, defendant admits firing some shots but not trigger, defendant 19-year-old, no known priors

424   rob (B2), V stabbed, defendant claimed mistaken identity, 2 priors (1 nonviolent)

927	rob (B2), co-perp.'s gun accidentally fired, V female stranger, no priors
272	rob (B2), premeditation, poss. struggle, 8 priors (1 nonviolent)
D18	rob convenience store (B2), V (security guard) shot during struggle, 9 shots fired, 2 hits, 1 prior felony
648	rob (B2), V shot when walking toward defendant after refusing defendant's demand for money, 1 nonviolent prior
768	rob (B2), defendant drunk, V refused to sell wine to defendant, defendant later returned with gun, no priors, defendant 19-year-old, V 18-year-old
481	rob (B2), V stabbed, defendant 19 years old, defendant claimed influence of drugs, 1 nonviolent prior
502	rob (B2), V shot 2× by co-perp. after reaching for gun, defendant not trigger, defendant 19-year-old, no priors
565	rob gas station (B2), victim had gun and defendant shot victim in face, no priors
428	rob (B2), defendant shot liquor store employee, defendant 19 years old, defendant confessed, witness present, no priors
778	rob, $5 (B2), auto theft, defendant shot V, strangers, defendant 19-year-old, 5 nonviolent priors
275	rob (B2), V shot twice, poss. struggle, defendant turned self in, unknown priors, stranger
262	rob (B2), attempted rob, defendant shot V, store employee, 2 nonviolent priors
959	rob (B2), V and co-perp. struggled, V shot, defendant and co-perp. drugs and alcohol, strangers, 3 nonviolent priors
D17	rob (B2), defendant shot V, found standing over body, defendant confessed, defendant 18-year-old AWOL, V 62-year-old, no known record
981	rob store (B2), defendant and co-perp. shot 63-year-old V, possible personal motivation, V had injured defendant's brother in past, defendant 19-year-old, no priors
926	rob (B2), defendant beat and hit V over head with gun, V's dog shot, acquaintances, 8 priors (6 nonviolent)
D15	rob (B2), V's car blocked on road, co-perp. stuck gun in car window, gun went off, defendant 19-year-old, 2 priors (1 nonviolent)
D08	same case as above, 3 nonviolent priors
451	rob (B2), defendant shot V when attempting to flee, defendant 20-year-old, 1 prior
616	rob (B2), V college student shot while trying to aid 2 females, motive—defendant believed females robbed cousin, 7 priors (5 nonviolent)
725	rob store (B2), others refused to participate, defendant's car found at scene, 5 priors (2 nonviolent)
048	rob gas attendant (B2), V gave up money without a struggle, defendant took co-perp.'s gun and shot V, defendant 17-year-old, no priors

476   rob (B2), V's wife and friend injured (not grave risk), V robbed at friend's house and followed home at gunpoint to get more money, no priors

501   rob gas station (B2), premed., V shot by co-perp., no priors

407   rob (B2), V shot in head, V pled for life, defendant confessed, no priors, strangers, defendant 18-year-old

860   rob (B2), V beaten and stabbed, poss. motive—defendant believed V tried to rape defendant's girlfriend, poss. acquaintances, no priors

602   rob (B2), V shot once, no priors

517   rob liquor store (B2), V shot 2× with shotgun, motive—defendant recently fired by store, no priors

494   rob (B2), V shot 4× after argument, motive—defendant discussed loan problems with V (bank employee) at V's home, no priors

429   rob (B2), female V shot 4× after agreeing to give attempted robber (defendant) a ride home, defendant 19-year-old stranger, 1 nonviolent prior

584   rob (B2), V shot 3–4× in back of neck, defendant 18 years old, motive—defendant formerly worked for V (manager), 2 nonviolent priors

497   rob (B2), V shot in temple, no priors

D25   rob (B2), V shot in head by defendant, 1 nonviolent prior

745   rob (B2), 61-year-old V shot 2× in head, no priors

904   rob (B2), V beaten and shot, ambush, bloody, defendant female age unknown, no priors

POST-*FURMAN*: CATEGORY IV (LOW TO HIGH)

228   rob (B2), prior armed rob (B1), defendant panicked in rob and shot V, stranger, defendant trying to get money for heroin, 1 nonviolent prior

355   rob (B2), premed., 4 shots to head (B7), defendant 16-year-old, no priors

433   rob (B2), co-perp. cut V's throat, bloody (B7), defendant not trigger, stranger, no priors

411   rob, $200 (B2), defendant shot V in back (B7), premed., defendant turned self in, defendant exhibited remorse, friend, no priors

311   rob (B2), crime spree, V hand blown off, 6 priors (5 nonviolent)

373   rob (B2), defendant shot victim during rob without warning, premed. (defendant borrowed gun), 2 nonviolent priors

441   rob (B2), defendant waited in alley while co-perps. lured V there to rob (lying in wait), defendant not trigger, strangers, 1 nonviolent prior

440   same case as above, 2 priors (1 nonviolent)

755   rob (B2), V shot while calling police (B10), V shot in chest, defendant not trigger, strangers, defendant 19-year-old, 2 nonviolent priors

719   rob (B2), 1 prior armed robbery (B1), V beaten on head with gun, V's dog shot, 19 priors (18 nonviolent)

825   rob (B2), V shot 3×, ambush, premed., V neighbor, defendant 18-year-old, no priors

638   rob (B2), prior armed robbery (B1), V and defendant exchanged shots, eyewitness, 30 nonviolent priors

986   rob (B2), V shot in head and defendant slammed V's head on floor (B7), argue over coat, V female, 1 nonviolent prior

893   rob (B2), V shot in head (B7), V's wife gave defendant money, 5 priors (4 nonviolent)

427   rob (B2), 63-year-old V shot by co-perp. (B7), defendant and co-perp. hid in bushes awaiting V, motive—co-perp.'s brother shot by V a few years earlier, defendant 19-year-old, no priors

406   rob (B2), V 60-year-old (B7), defendant waited for V, defendant confessed, defendant 19-year-old, 4 priors (3 nonviolent)

D09   rob (B2), 69-year-old V (B7), defendant had stolen gun to commit rob, 1 prior

974   rob (B2), kidnap (B2), 1 shot in head, defendant confessed, V female cab driver, defendant 19-year-old, no priors

227   rob liquor store (B2), 1 prior armed robbery (B1), defendant shot V, a 16-year-old stockboy, 1 nonviolent prior

569   rob (B2), kidnapping (B2), 65-year-old V shot 3 times in head (B7), 17-year-old defendant, defendant not trigger, no priors

239   rob (B2), defendant stabbed V in back and choked V (B7), argument over money, defendant 18-year-old, no priors

737   rob (B2), co-perp. shot V in head (B7), wounded another, defendant not trigger, no priors

591   rob (B2), co-perp. shot V, defendant and co-perp. stomped V (B7), argument over woman, 2 nonviolent priors

384   rob bus station (B2), defendant shot V twice in head (B7), killed V so could not be identified, no priors

383   same case as above, 1 nonviolent prior, defendant confessed to everything but homicide

861   rob (B2), V pled for life (B7), V shot in head, defendant and co-perp. using drugs, defendant 19-year-old, defendant had tried to recruit V into aiding him in robbing gas station where V worked, no priors

D23   rob, $30 (B2), V tied up, beat with blunt object (B7), V gave statement prior to death, 3 priors

D22   same case as above, 2 nonviolent priors

824   rob (B2), hostage/kidnap own family (B2), V (friend) shot in leg when approaching defendant's home, defendant then shot V in head and fled town with family, 1 prior (manslaughter), defendant 18-year-old

401   rob (B2), mult. stabbing and bloody (B7), alcohol and drugs, defendant and police disagree on weapons used, no priors

038   rob (B2), stabbed 12× (B7), stole car, argument, poss. drugs and alcohol, V and defendant traveling together, defendant 39-year-old female, 4 priors (3 nonviolent)

614   rob (B2), 70-year-old V stabbed 13× with butcher knife (B7), several arguments in weeks before murder, V employer of defendant's girlfriend, no priors

563   rob (B2), V hit defendant, defendant stabbed V 16× (B7), defendant confessed, stranger, 1 nonviolent prior

810   rob (B2), vile (B7), defendant and co-perp. rob V's (neighbor) home, defendant beat V's mother, V shot with pellet gun and then defendant beat her to death, V 54-year-old female, unknown priors, defendant turned self in

881   rob (B2), defendant shot 62-year-old V 3× (B7), shot at others 3× as fled (B3), defendant thought V pushed silent alarm (B10), stranger, 5 priors (2 nonviolent)

D06   rob 2 hotels (B2), 2 Vs (B7), V #1 shot in head, V #2 37-year-old female, defendant had taken drugs and alcohol, defendant 19-year-old, strangers, 4 priors (3 nonviolent)

357   rob (B2), shot V 6× (B7), premed., poss. threat, poss. motive get even with two homosexuals, struggle for gun, defendant 20-year-old, 2 nonviolent priors

512   rob (B2), defendant stabs V 7× in back, chest, and face, beats with hammer (B7), V 22-year-old female stranger, 5 priors (2 nonviolent)

362   rob (B2), terrorize V's family (B7), V shot, poss. premeditation, 6 priors, past mental disorder

410   rob (B2), poss. grave risk (B3), V stranger, defendant stole gun, 4 priors (3 nonviolent)

790   rob (B2), defendant beat V with pipe wrench (B7), 6 priors (4 nonviolent)

955   rob (B2), prior armed robbery (B1), V 22-year-old female stranger, defendant beat V in head and shot in forehead, V found tied up with torn clothing

647   rob (B2), 1 prior murder (B1), 1 prior armed robbery (B1), 62-year-old stranger V shot, defendant not trigger, however intent to rob, 2 priors (1 nonviolent)

704   rob (B2), 1 prior armed robbery (B1), defendant shot V security guard (B8), wounded 2 others (B3), defendant took hostages, defendant mental disorder, 5 priors (3 nonviolent)

488   rob (B2), defendant shot V cab driver 2× in head (B7), 1 nonviolent prior

D24   rob (B2), V police (B8), police stopped car to search after robbery (B10), defendant took V's gun, killed V and other officer

L16   rob (B2), V police (B8), V shot in head, defendant found in possession of murder weapon, defendant caught during robbery

Do1   rob (B2), defendant kidnapped (B2) and shot 71-year-old V, defendant confessed and led police to body, stranger, defendant 17-year-old, no known priors

C94   rob gas station (B2), V taken to country and shot in eye (B7), V 19-year-old stranger, 1 prior

963   rob (B2), vile (B7), elderly victim, defendant struck V and ordered co-perp. to kill, co-perp slashed V's throat, unknown priors

459   rob (B2), elderly V, defendant beat and shot V with shotgun, V pled for life (B7), defendant also injured bystander, robbed another, and shot at another but narrowly missed (B3), 6 priors (5 nonviolent)

307   rob (B2), kidnap (B2), defendant shot V 3×, once in head (B7), V 27-year-old female stranger, taken to woods, attempt rape, shot, 1 prior

806   rob (B2), 19-year-old female V shot trying to escape, defendant raped and sexually assaulted 2 others present (B2), defendant 19-year-old, stranger, 6 priors (1 nonviolent)

Z18   rob, $20 (B2), 1 prior armed robbery (B1), defendant kidnapped (B2) and raped (B2), 23-year-old female V, defendant taunted V, V shot in neck causing slow death, strangers

D36   rob, $480 (B2), 2 prior armed robberies (B1), defendant raped (B2) 19-year-old female V, defendant shot her in right temple, V struggled, defendant disguised self as repairman to gain entry, 3 priors

672   defendant robbed (B2) and kidnapped (B2) 18-year-old female, V pled for life, defendant shot her in head and abdomen (B7), 3 priors (2 nonviolent)

814   rob, $2 and radio (B2), rape (B2), V 64-year-old female stranger, defendant 17-year-old, kicked V in chest, V died of cardiac arrest because of broken sternum (B7), poss. drugs and alcohol, no priors

855   rob (B2), shot V and ran over him twice with car, V hitchhiking, 6 priors (5 nonviolent)

880   rob (B2), premed., V tied up, V shot trying to aid other; other beaten, hit over head with gun and raped (B2), defendant went to apartment to buy drugs, V's friend beaten on neck before divulging location of money, unknown priors

202   rob (B2), stabbed 14×, V, a cab driver, drowned after being pushed in well (B7), defendant refused to pay taxi fare, 1 prior

Z20   rob (B2), defendant struck V, hitchhiker, with bottle, shot 3× in chest, once in scrotum (B7), defendant 19-year-old, poss. motive—to watch V die, no priors

630   rob (B2), defendant shot V 3× and kicked V 20 to 30 times (B7), threw body in river, stole car, V thought going on date with co-perp., defendant 20-year-old, V 20-year-old, 5 priors (4 nonviolent)

944   rob bank (B2), 2 hostages, co-perp.'s female hostage was killed, 5 priors (1 nonviolent)

557   rob (B2), kidnapping (B2), V shot 3× in head (B7), defendant not trigger, no prior record

523   rob (B2), kidnapped (B2), shot V 3× in head, defendant confessed, 63-year-old V wrote check and held until bank opened, V employed co-perp. as a maid, no priors

878   rob (B2), defendant slashed neck several times, pushed V off bridge, V paralyzed 73-year-old (B7), defendant previously took V on errands, 1 nonviolent prior

474   rob (B2), defendant held V while co-perp. cut V store clerk's throat to point of partial decapitation, poss. alcohol, no priors

279   rob (B2), 2 Vs (B7), Vs shot in head (B7), no priors, defendant and co-perp. were hitchhiking

760   2 robberies (B2), 1 prior armed robbery (B1), V 19-year-old gas-station attendant, shot, kidnap (B2), defendant 22-year-old female nontrigger, 2 nonviolent priors

D12   rob (B2), escape juvenile center (B9), V crippled, beaten (B7), stole car, defendant 17 years old, strangers, no known priors

862   rob (B2), V police shot in eye (B8), answering silent alarm, 4 priors (2 nonviolent)

312   rob (B2), kidnapped (B2), V shot in head, defendant took pictures of V for souvenirs (B7), strangers, 2 nonviolent priors

621   rob (B2), 70-year-old V, beat V with knife and hammer (B7), V's head swollen with hole in it, V died 3 mo. later, strangers, 6 priors (2 nonviolent)

074   rob (B2), 2 Vs, 3 shots (B7), premed., V #1 54-year-old female, V #2 16-year-old daughter of V #1, Vs knew co-perp., Vs bound with belts

576   rob (B2), 2 Vs, whom defendant and co-perps. beat, strangled with coat hanger, hands, and electrical cord (B7), V #1 75-year-old male, V #2, 73-year-old wife of V #1, forced to watch V #1 tortured before V #2 killed, motive—defendant and co-perps. trying to buy truck from V #1, unknown priors

579   same case as above, also unknown priors

323   rob (B2), defendant beat V to death with cement block (B7), another seriously injured, strangers, poss. premeditation, 2 priors

371   rob (B2), V police (B8), 8 people held hostage (B2), defendant not trigger, 1 prior

286   rob (B2), defendant shot a 62-year-old police V (B8), 8 hostages (B2), planned robbery, 7 priors (6 nonviolent)

285   same case as above, 4 priors (3 nonviolent)

958   rob (B2), V 61-year-old, defendant beat V's head, slashed face, hit in face with hammer, cut throat 2×, cut buttocks after death (B7), 4 nonviolent priors

991   rob (B2), kidnap (B2), defendant 17 years old, V 64 years old, V pled for life, defendant laughed at shooting, V shot 2× in head with shotgun (B7), motive—race, unknown priors

491   rob (B2), V shot in chest, another person shot in head, locked both in walk-in refrigerator (B7), stranger, 1 prior

964   rob (B2), escapee (B9), kidnap and auto theft (B2), 1 shot in head, weapon stolen from V's son, defendant and co-perp. caught during burglary, strangers, 13 priors (8 nonviolent)

570   rob (B2), 3 prior armed robberies (B1), 75-year-old V shot in head while waiting for wife (B7), stranger, 12 priors (8 nonviolent)

480   rob (B2), 2 Vs, V #1 74-year-old, V #2 72-year-old female (B7), tied Vs' hands and feet and choked them to find out where the money was (B7), strangled with coat hangers and cord, no priors

753   rob (B2), kidnap (B2), V police (B8), shot 5× in head, pt. blank (B7), 1 prior

507   rob (B2), 1 prior armed robbery (B1), V police chief (B8), defendant disarmed V and drove to swamp, let V flee and shot V 5× in head, defendant confessed, 4 priors (1 nonviolent)

751   rob (B2), escapee (B9), 18-year-old female V raped (B2), defendant not trigger, defendant 20-year-old, 2 priors

571   rob (B2), 3 elderly victims (B7), 2 others assaulted (B3), vile (B7), motive—search for drug money, 1 prior

333   rob (B2), defendant beat V with hammer, threw rocks at V's head, stuck stick through V's skull (B7), V lured to woods to buy drugs, no known priors

330   same as above, 3 nonviolent priors

066   rob (B2), 6 prior armed robberies (B1), defendant parolee (B9), V police (B8), V shot in eye after answering alarm, 6 priors (5 nonviolent)

743   rob (B2), 2 Vs, 63-year-old female Vs beaten, V #1 tied up and raped (B7), 1 victim forced to withdraw money from bank, both Vs died from beating with board and stomping (B7), strangers, defendant 20-year-old, no known priors

450   rob (B2), defendant demanded money from victim's family to disclose location of body (B2), stabbed 18× (B7), V pled for life, acquaintances, drugs and alcohol, V 17-year-old, defendant 18-year-old, 1 nonviolent prior

628   rob (B2), V bound, gagged, beaten, and shot 5×, then buried alive (B7), motive—prevent V from identifying, relationship unknown, defendant claims of drugs and insanity not substantiated, defendant confessed, no priors

627   same case as above, no priors

POST-*FURMAN:* CATEGORY V (MOST AGGRAVATED CATEGORY)

C82   rob (B2), defendant and co-perps. hired to rob, defendant designate trigger, however co-perp. shot V in head, 1 nonviolent prior

802	rob (B2), contract (B6), defendant lured V into store on sexual pretense, V beaten with baseball bat and butt of gun, motive—revenge, defendant confessed, 9 nonviolent priors
801	same case as above, defendant beaten and robbed V, no priors
C93	same case as above, defendant 36-year-old female, defendant hired other co-perps., 2 nonviolent priors
641	rob (B2), 56-year-old female V, slashed 2× almost disemboweling her (B7), rape (B2), neighbors, no priors
D10	rob (B2), contract (B6), shot V in head, no priors
C54	rob (B2), V tied to tree and shot (B7), defendant not trigger, defendant 15 years old, no priors
D21	rob, $1,000 (B2), V tied to tree, beat with butt of gun, stabbed 3× in neck (B7), defendant 19-year-old hitchhiker, V 58-year-old, unknown priors
550	rob (B2), V shot 2× in head, hands tied, blindfolded (B7), V 18-year-old neighbor, no priors
776	rob, $1,000 (B2), beat with blunt object, while still alive V was shot and set afire in his truck (B7), V playing cards with defendant, defendant and co-perp. motive to get V drunk and cheat him, V 66-year-old, 4 nonviolent priors
503	rob (B2), 70-to-80-year-old gas station attendant shot in back, V lying on ground, pled for life (B7), 1 prior
830	rob (B2), kidnap (B2), V (friend and gas station attendant) knocked unconscious, wrists tied, shot in head (B7), defendant not trigger, alcohol, 3 priors (2 nonviolent)
992	rob (B2), kidnap (B2), execution style, blindfolded, shot in face pt. blank with sawed-off shotgun (B7), 18-year-old defendant, V pled for life, strangers, unknown nonviolent priors
C77	rob (B2), 1 prior armed robbery (B1), kidnap (B2), 11-year-old V forced to lie down and shot in head, V's father injured, defendant 16-year-old, 1 nonviolent prior
C78	same case as above, 1 prior rape/kidnapping (B1), 15 priors (10 nonviolent)
395	rob, $4,200 (B2), V and family bound and gagged, V shot in back of head (B7), strangers, 4 priors (3 nonviolent)
D13	rob, $20 (B2), V forced to strip and sodomized, V pled for life (B7), V pushed into cab trunk and cab pushed into pond, V drowned in trunk, defendant 17-year-old soldier, strangers, no known priors
D14	same case as above, defendant 20-year-old, no priors
D03	rob (B2), bodies shot, ax, spear, and knife wounds (B7), 2 Vs (B7), former employer of defendant, no priors
266	rob (B2), 1 prior armed robbery (B1), family killed, daughter raped and mutilated (B2 and B7), 3 priors

265   rob (B2), escapee (B9), female V raped and sodomized (B2), 6 Vs (B7), kidnap (B2), female V's breast mutilated (B7), 2 priors

267   same case as above, 3 priors (2 nonviolent)

APPENDIX H

Classification Rules for Arnold Barnett's Three-Dimensional Measure of Case Culpability[1]

I. THE CERTAINTY THE DEFENDANT IS A DELIBERATE KILLER

Score the case either 0, 1, 2 on this dimension, applying the following criteria:

(i) The case is rated 0 if *any* of the following circumstances pertain:

    (1) The narrative indicates the evidence in the case seemed weak (e.g., "case based solely on circumstantial evidence").

    (2) The narrative mentions evidence that worked *against* the view that the defendant was guilty (e.g., tests for residue on the defendant's hand from firing a gun were negative).

    (3) It seems clear that the defendant neither ordered the killing nor was the triggerman. (Note that (3) *differs* from the weaker statement that it is uncertain whether the defendant was the triggerman.)

    (4) The killing has an "accidental" touch about it, because

        (a) a fairly long period (perhaps a week or more) elapsed between the incident and the victim's death, or

        (b) the death was caused by a shot fired somewhat randomly (e.g., through a door), or

        (c) the death was caused by a beating similar to previous beatings of the victim by the defendant.

    (5) There is reason to doubt that the defendant's actions *in themselves* would have caused the victim's death (e.g., (i) the defendant beat the victim, but it was a coperpetrator's stabbing that killed him, or (ii) the defendant's beating of the victim induced a heart seizure).

    (6) The defendant was one of several participants in a conspiracy to kill, but took no part in the actual killing.

    (7) The narrative mentions that the defendant was previously treated for mental problems (e.g., institutionalized). Neglect references to insanity if the defendant has no apparent medical history.

(ii) The case is rated 2 if any of the following elements were present:

    (1) The killing was a murder-for-hire, and the defendant was either the sole instigator or the executioner.

---

1. Barnett, *Some Distribution Patterns for the Georgia Death Sentence*, 18 U.C. Davis L. Rev. 1327, 1364–66 App. A (1985).

(2) The defendant plotted to kill the victim (e.g., a wife and her lover arrange to murder her husband). If, however, the defendant was one of several plotters, and clearly not the actual killer, assume (2) is not satisfied.

(3) The narrative mentions that the defendant was officially implicated in other killings.

(4) The narrative mentions that the defendant had tried previously to kill the victim.

(5) The defendant announced *in advance* to a third party an intention to kill the victim. (Neglect this condition in a lovers' triangle or lovers' quarrel case, or when the third party was a coperpetrator.)

(iii) If the killing warrants neither a 0 nor a 2, give the case a rating of 1. If the killing satisfies conditions for *both* 0 and 2, also rate it 1. Most "common" slayings, such as killings during armed robberies or during barroom fights, would warrant this intermediate classification. Indeed, a 2 reflects unusually clear evidence of premeditation, while a 0 reflects unusually large doubt that the defendant knowingly acted to cause the victim's demise.

II. THE STATUS OF THE VICTIM

On this dimension, the score is either 0 or 1. Give a score of 0 if:

(1) The victim was a relative of the defendant (even his or her child).

(2) The victim was a friend of the defendant. (Interpret the word "friend" loosely; if, for example, two people of similar age are riding together voluntarily in a car, consider them friends. However, the mere fact that two people know each other is not sufficient. Neighbors of vastly different ages, or the bank teller and the depositor, are not assumed friends barring other evidence of social ties.)

(3) The victim was an enemy of the defendant, though not the defendant's employer. (Interpret the word "enemy" loosely; if, for instance, the victim and defendant vied for the affections of the same woman, if the victim had harassed one of the defendant's loved ones, if there was a feud of some sort that turned violent, assume enmity existed. If, however, the victim could be viewed as the defendant's employer—whether as (say) his supervisor in a factory or the person who hired him to perform some chores—do not give a score of 0 under (3).)

(4) The victim, although a stranger to the defendant, acted in a highly provocative manner just prior to the killing (e.g., racial taunts).

(5) The victim was engaged in an illegal or often-disapproved activity at the time of the killing (e.g., a drug dealer, a prostitute or prostitute's customer, owner of a homosexual bathhouse, etc.).

If the case does not warrant the rating 0, give it the score 1. 1 is the appropriate rating for most stranger-to-stranger killings and those in which the defendant only knew the victim in the latter's official capacity (e.g., as employer, or attendant in a local gas station). If there are several victims, give the case a 0 if *any* of those slain qualify for it.

III. THE HEINOUSNESS OF THE MURDER

There are two aspects to this dimension: the question whether self-defense motivated the killing and how "gruesome" it was.

Self-defense is an element in the case under any of the following circumstances:

(1) the victim had *at hand* a deadly weapon at the time of the killing. (Merely having a gun in the store or house does not satisfy (1).)

(2) The victim was killed with his own weapon. (This is taken to imply (1) is satisfied even if the narrative does not explicitly say so.)

NOTE: If the victim was a police officer, do not invoke self-defense (1) or (2) unless the officer fired shots before the defendant did.

(3) The victim had threatened to kill the defendant or one of the defendant's loved ones.

(4) The victim had attacked the defendant at the time of the killing.

If none of the above conditions existed, self-defense was not a mitigating circumstance in the homicide.

NOTE: If the only evidence for self-defense is the defendant's uncorroborated claim, assume its absence even if any of (1)–(4) is alleged.

A homicide is classified as vile if one of the following circumstances is present:

(1) It was accompanied by rape or sexual abuse, either against the victim or someone in the company of the victim.

(2) There were at least two homicide victims.

(3) The deceased was a kidnapping victim at the time he was slain.

(4) Psychological torture preceded the killing (e.g., Russian roulette, a sustained period of terror).

(5) The victim was shot several times in the head at close range.

(6) The killing was execution style (i.e., victim forced to kneel or squat, then shot in head).

(7) The death was caused by strangulation or arson.

(8) The death was caused by a drowning in which physical force kept the victim below water.

(9) The killing involved ten (10) or more shots or stab wounds, except when the murder weapon was a penknife or other small cutting instrument.

(10) The physical details of the killing are unusually repulsive (e.g., the victim drowned in his own blood).

(11) The body was mutilated or otherwise grossly disfigured (except in an attempt to conceal the homicide).

(12) The killing was performed with a bizarre weapon (e.g., a hacksaw, a claw hammer, an icepick).

(13) The defendant apparently derived pleasure from the very act of killing. (This is distinct from his believing the victim deserved to die, and taking pleasure on that account.)

(14) The crime was specifically described in the narrative as extremely bloody.

Absent *all* these circumstances, the homicide is categorized as not vile. Despite the length of the list above, most "simple" shootings, stabbings, and beatings would not be classified as vile under these rules.

APPENDIX I

A Sample of Georgia Murder Cases,
As Classified with Arnold Barnett's
Classification System

A. Cases scoring a total of 0 on the three classification variables (0,0,0)

1. (0, 0, 0) The 2 coperpetrators drove to a shopping center with the male victim's girlfriend. During the drive coperpetrator #1 gave the girlfriend his gun. At the shopping center, the victim and the girlfriend argued and the girl took the gun out of her purse. At this point, the victim, the girlfriend, and her brother went to the victim's house. The two coperpetrators then met the defendant, and coperpetrator #1 told the defendant that the victim had his gun. The defendant, who had a pistol, and the 2 coperpetrators then went to the victim's house. The victim came to the door, unarmed, and said "Niggers, get out of my house." The defendant then shot the victim once in the thigh, at close range. The victim died 2 days later after going into shock and suffering cardiac arrest. (365)

2. (0,0,0) The 30-year-old male defendant called the male victim (defendant's uncle) and confirmed a rendezvous at a particular store at a specified time. The victim told his daughter that he knew the defendant had a gun, but stated that he himself had a knife. A witness stated that he saw the victim and the defendant in the parking lot, then he heard a shot and saw the victim crawl under a car, at which point he heard another shot and saw the defendant speed away. The defendant claimed self-defense. (555)

3. (0,0,0) The 32-year-old male defendant had been seeing the adult male victim's wife since they had separated 9 months earlier. The victim went to the defendant's home and demanded that his wife follow him to her mother's home. While the wife and the defendant were searching for her car keys, the victim approached the house yelling. The defendant told the victim to stay away from the house and the victim pulled a gun. There was a struggle for the gun, during which it discharged twice. The defendant took the gun and fired it one more time. The defendant claimed he fired the final shot into the ground. None of the 3 witnesses were sure which of the 3 shots hit the victim. (748)

B. Cases scoring a total of 1 on the three classification variables

1. (0,0,1) The 38-year-old female defendant and the male coperpetrator went to a friend's house for a party. The female victim and her husband were sitting next to the defendant when the victim's husband tried on the defendant's sunglasses. An argument erupted over the sunglasses, and the defendant

pulled a pistol out of her blouse and shot the victim in the arm. The coperpetrator grabbed the gun and shot 2 more times. The victim's husband tried to get the pistol, but the coperpetrator shot him in the foot. (050)

2. (0,0,1)   The male defendant and the 2 male coperpetrators were high school seniors. The male victim had previously assaulted the fiancée of one of the coperpetrators. The perpetrators arranged to lure the victim to the high school tennis courts. When they arrived at the tennis courts the 2 coperpetrators opened fire on the victim from the back of the defendant's station wagon. Both coperpetrators emptied their guns into the victim's car, and two shots hit the victim in the head and another in the shoulder. The defendant was driving the station wagon. The parties were arrested 2 months later on the basis of an anonymous tip. (519)

3. (0,0,1)   The 21-year-old male defendant and the adult male victim had an argument, and witnesses claim that the defendant tried to provoke the victim to fight. The victim walked away. Later, the defendant and the victim argued again and the defendant pulled a knife and stabbed the victim. The victim died 16 days later. The defendant claimed he was intoxicated and did not remember anything. (808)

4. (1,0,0)   The male defendant had been dating the female victim, who had a history of violence. The victim had previously assaulted the defendant with a knife. On the day of the offense, both the defendant and victim were armed with guns. There *may* have been an argument between the defendant and victim prior to the shooting. The defendant fired 4 shots, one hitting the victim in the temple and another hitting the victim's leg. (8)

C. Cases scoring a total of 2 on the three classification variables

1. (0,1,1)   The 26-year-old male defendant, the male coperpetrator, and a female companion (primary witness) went to a bar and were drinking when they saw the male victim and a male companion walk in. The defendant, coperpetrator, and female friend exchanged "funny looks" indicating they had a plan to rob the victim. The defendant, coperpetrator, and female friend went outside the bar to wait for the victim to come out. The coperpetrator beat the victim with a large cement block in the head and face causing multiple lacerations and exposing the inside skull. The defendant may have beaten the victim several times. The defendant also attacked the victim's friend with a knife, cutting him in the face and throat. The victim's friend was seriously injured, but did not die. The coperpetrator went through the pockets of the victim and his friend, taking some change and a wallet. The defendant dragged the bodies into some bushes and the 3 went to another bar to drink. (324)

2. (1,0,1)   The 50-year-old male defendant took his rifle and walked toward the male victim's house (defendant's neighbor). The defendant called out to the victim and the victim came outside. It is unclear as to whether an argument ensued, but soon after the victim came outside the defendant shot at him. In an effort to avoid the shots, the victim ran around the side of his house. The defendant followed and continued to shoot at the victim. The victim died of 5 gunshot wounds. The defendant admitted to the murder and stated that the

victim had been giving him a "bad time." Police investigators noted that both the defendant and the victim had been drinking. (643)

3. (1,0,1)   The 17-year-old male defendant and his girlfriend were having problems, and the girlfriend was dating the male victim. The defendant threatened to kill the victim if the girlfriend ever dated him again. The girlfriend went to a movie with the victim. The defendant was patrolling his girlfriend's home waiting for them to come home. When the victim left the girlfriend's home, the defendant began to follow him. The defendant got the victim to stop his car and then shot him twice in the chest. The defendant then called his girlfriend and stated, "You thought you could get away with it, didn't you?" The defendant left his .22 automatic rifle with a friend and then went home, where he was arrested. (656)

4. (1,0,1)   After consuming a pint of vodka, the male defendant was walking in his neighborhood when the victims began to follow him on bikes. The defendant walked into a wooded area and the victims followed. The defendant told them to stop bothering him, and, when they didn't, the defendant grabbed them. The defendant forced them to disrobe and then sodomized them before choking them to death. The defendant carried the nude bodies to a set of railroad tracks about 400 feet away. (553)

5. (0,1,1)   The male primary witness went into a liquor store and saw the 40-year-old male defendant behind the counter at the cash register and spoke to him. The defendant did not reply. The 34-year-old male coperpetrator then came up and forced the primary witness to the floor at gunpoint. The coperpetrator began to exchange fire with the 62-year-old male victim, a store employee. Both the victim and the defendant suffered wounds, the victim in the abdomen, the defendant in the chest and arm. The defendant and coperpetrator then left, and the primary witness called the police. The defendant claimed he knew nothing of the robbery until the coperpetrator forced him to participate. The primary witness stated that the defendant was not holding a gun, although the police found one on the counter near where the defendant had been standing. (647)

6. (0,0,2)   The 30-year-old male defendant, his brother (coperpetrator #1), and his father (coperpetrator #2) enticed the 66-year-old male victim into a poker game with the intention of getting him drunk and cheating him out of his money. The victim became too intoxicated to play cards. The defendant and coperpetrator #1 beat the victim with a blunt object until the victim was unconscious. They robbed the victim of over $1,000. Then, while the victim was still alive, they took him in his truck to a secluded area, where coperpetrator #1 shot him with a shotgun and set him and his truck on fire. (776)

D. Cases scoring a total of 3 on the three classification variables

1. (1,1,1)   The male victim was driving his wife and his small child in a car. The male defendant, his brother, and two females were driving behind the victim's vehicle. The victim, apparently, was not going fast enough for the defendant and his passengers, so they began hanging out the windows and yelling at the victim. Thinking that something was wrong, the victim stopped his car. As the

victim stepped out of his car, the defendant shot him several times and drove off. The victim's wife provided the police with a description of the defendant and the defendant's car. (D02)

2. (1,1,1)   The 20-year-old male defendant approached the male victim and a male friend from behind as they walked down the street. The defendant held a gun to the victim and demanded his money. The friend stated that the victim had no money. Then the friend and the defendant struggled for the gun. The defendant broke away, ran 10 feet, turned, and shot the friend in the leg. The victim then walked toward the defendant saying, "I'm not afraid of your gun." The defendant then shot the victim several times. The friend identified the defendant as the killer. (357)

3. (1,1,1)   The male victim, a marshal, went with other marshals to serve an eviction notice on a friend of the defendant. The friend started fighting with the marshals. At that point, the 25-year-old male defendant stuck a pistol out of the door and started firing. The defendant's bullets hit and killed the victim as he stepped out of the car and wounded another marshal in the abdomen. During the ensuing gun battle, the defendant's friend was hit and killed. The defendant surrendered after a SWAT team fired tear gas into the house. The defendant claimed someone else had fired the shots that killed the victim and had then escaped from the house. (796)

4. (1,0,2)   The 20-year-old male defendant and the male coperpetrator drove up beside the 19-year-old female victim's car and asked the victim and the female primary witness to smoke a joint. They all went to the high school parking lot and smoked marijuana. When the victim started her car to leave, the coperpetrator opened the door and pointed a gun at her. The defendant and the coperpetrator forced the girls into the defendant's car and bound and gagged them. They drove to a wooded area, where the defendant took the victim back into the woods and raped her. The coperpetrator tried to rape the primary witness, but failed. The perpetrators told the 2 girls, now nude, to stand off the side of the road. The defendant then turned his car around, got out, and stood next to the coperpetrator. There were two shots, one killing the victim and one injuring the primary witness. The primary witness did not see who shot. The perpetrators then left, burned and abandoned the car, and fled to Canada. (C67)

5. (1,0,2)   The male defendant and his wife (victim #1) had had marital problems for a long time, and victim #1 was living with her mother (victim #2). The defendant received a message from his mother-in-law that his wife wanted to speak with him. Victim #1 called and an argument ensued, at which point victim #1 said she was leaving the defendant for good. The defendant then picked up his shotgun and went over to the trailer in which the victims were living. The 2 victims and defendant's 11-year-old daughter were playing cards when the defendant shot both victims in the head. When the defendant's daughter ran to get help she ran into the defendant, who hit her on the head twice with the shotgun. The defendant then called the police and told them he had killed the victims and to come pick him up. The defendant went outside, placed the shotgun in a tree, and sat down to wait for the police. (Z15)

6. (0,1,2)   The male defendant was fired from a job with a waterproofing company and swore to get revenge. Victim #1 was the male general office manager of the company, and victim #2 was the female secretary. The defendant killed the victims with a large sword or machete, nearly decapitating victim #2. (250)

7. (1,0,2)   The male defendant and coperpetrator were hitchhiking, and the 2 victims picked them up. When the car broke down, the victims purchased another, and at this point the defendant saw how much money the victims were carrying. One day the victims were drinking and asked the defendant to drive. The defendant made a stop to allow the victims to relieve themselves in a ditch. As the victims came out of the ditch the defendant shot them both. The victims fell and the defendant ran over and shot each victim in the head. (279)

8. (1,0,2)   The male defendant was at the female victim's (his ex-wife) apartment when they got into an argument. The defendant threw an ashtray/vase at the victim. The defendant then taped the victim's mouth shut and stabbed her three times in the heart. At this point, the victim's mother returned with two female relatives. The defendant held them at gunpoint to prevent them from discovering the body, but they escaped. The defendant eluded arrest for about one week and then gave himself up. (578)

9. (0,1,2)   The male coperpetrator and the female primary witness, who lived with the 57-year-old male defendant, drove the defendant downtown. The defendant had been drinking and felt sick when he went into the 74-year-old male victim's barbershop. Later that night, the victim was found, badly beaten, in the barbershop. The barbershop appeared to have been the scene of a tremendous struggle and the victim's $300 was missing. The victim was comatose and died 3½ months later. The defendant claimed that the coperpetrator had hit him in the head with a hammer, and, when the defendant had recovered consciousness, he found the victim already beaten. (621)

10. (1,0,2)   The male defendant took the 10-year-old female victim into the woods and, according to the defendant, had sex with her by invitation. Afterward, the victim said she was going to tell on the defendant. The defendant stabbed her 4 times and then strangled her. The defendant claimed he did not remember the stabbing or strangling. (699)

11. (0,1,2)   The 20-year-old male defendant had escaped from prison. He and the male coperpetrator, a parolee whom the defendant had known in prison, planned to rob the store where the 18-year-old female victim worked. They robbed the store and abducted the victim in her car. While the coperpetrator was driving, the defendant told the victim to remove her clothes and then raped her. Then the defendant drove while the coperpetrator raped the victim. The victim's vagina was torn during these rapes. The coperpetrator then told the defendant to stop, and the coperpetrator and the victim got out of the car. The defendant then went to get gas, and, while he was gone, the coperpetrator shot the victim in the head, mutilating her beyond recognition. When the defendant returned they threw the body in some bushes and left the scene. Blood and pieces of flesh and bone were scattered at the scene. (751)

12. (0,1,2) The 2 male coperpetrators robbed a grocery store. The male victim, a police chief, heard a description of the getaway vehicle and apparently tried to stop the car. The coperpetrators kidnapped the victim, drove to an isolated spot in the country, and, when the victim ran from the car, the defendant shot him from long range, with a .38 caliber bullet, in the abdomen. The 2 coperpetrators then shot the victim at close range 4 times, in the right and left temple, between the eyes, and in the cheek. This occurred at a pond a short distance from the highway, where the victim's body was ultimately found. There was no explanation why the defendant was with the coperpetrators. He gave inconsistent statements to the police and finally admitted his presence at the murder scene. (753)

13. (1,0,2) The 29-year-old male defendant, the 2 male coperpetrators, and the male primary witness (coperpetrator #3, the defendant's father) were with the 60-year-old male victim and other family members when the victim became highly intoxicated. The perpetrators had planned to get the victim drunk and then to cheat him of money ($1,000) in a card game. The victim became too intoxicated to play cards, at which point the defendant and coperpetrator #1 beat the victim on the head with a wrench covered with a towel. The defendant and the 2 coperpetrators unsuccessfully attempted to get the victim's money. The defendant and coperpetrator #2, armed with a shotgun and a knife, respectively, then drove the victim to a secluded area, where the defendant poured gasoline on the victim while the victim begged him not to do so. The defendant shot the victim once with the shotgun. The victim and his truck were set afire. (777)

14. (1,0,2) The 22-year-old male defendant and his girlfriend (primary witness) met the male victim at a bar and had a few drinks. The victim invited the defendant and the primary witness to his apartment. The primary witness left the defendant and the victim in the living room and went to cook some steaks. When the primary witness returned to the living room, the lights were out. The defendant told her to leave them off. The primary witness turned the lights on and saw the defendant stab the victim twice. The primary witness then ran out and drove off with the defendant in the victim's car. The defendant took the victim's wallet, TV, and stereo. The victim suffered head lacerations caused by beating and four stab wounds, one a fatal chest wound. The defendant claimed that he had found the victim and the primary witness naked and that the victim had made sexual advances toward the primary witness. (860)

15. (1,0,2) The male defendant was a "good family man" who had been suffering marital problems. The defendant picked up the female victim, who was hitchhiking, after both his wife and girlfriend had refused to have sex with him. The defendant and victim drove around for a while and then went to a deserted house. The victim made a remark about the defendant's girlfriend, and the defendant took a knife out of the glove compartment and forced the victim to have sex with him. The victim then ran out and the defendant stabbed her 14 times in the face, chest, and abdomen. After the murder, the defendant turned himself in and confessed. (933)

16. (1,0,2) The male defendant, an escapee from prison, was living in the same rooming house as the male victim. The defendant, a coperpetrator, and the victim were drinking one night. After the victim went to bed, the defendant and coperpetrator went into his room and repeatedly stabbed him. Defendant made a statement that he had killed other people and had helped the coperpetrator kill the victim. (941)

E. Cases scoring a total of 4 on the three classification variables

1. (2,0,2) The male defendant and a coperpetrator went to the male victim's house and took him for a ride. The perpetrators and the victim were casual acquaintances. The perpetrators took the victim to a side road and shot him 3 times with a shotgun. The murder was very bloody. Immediately afterward, the defendant boasted that all they had to do now was to collect the money (murder for hire). (408)

2. (2,0,2) The male defendant and the female coperpetrator planned to kill the defendant's wife. On the morning of the murder the coperpetrator reconfirmed the plan. The coperpetrator entered the victim's home and shot the female victim five times with a .22 caliber pistol. Two shots to the head caused the victim's death. The defendant came home later that morning and called the police himself. The defendant denied having planned the murder. (498)

3. (2,0,2) The male defendant and the male coperpetrator were involved in a check-fraud scheme. They retained the male victim, manager of a local club, to act as a front. The defendant owed the victim money and had previously discussed getting rid of the victim. On the night of the offense, the three men left the bar to deliver some bootleg liquor. While the victim was driving, the defendant shot him several times in the head. The defendant claimed someone else committed the murder. (552)

4. (2,0,2) The victim, a female in her early thirties, had asked the 23-year-old male defendant for a divorce, and the defendant was afraid she would get possession of their mutual belongings. The defendant asked the coperpetrator to help him kill his wife in exchange for some insurance proceeds. The defendant invited the coperpetrator to his home and instructed the coperpetrator to hit the victim on the head with a wrench. At first the coperpetrator refused, but, when the defendant threatened him, he hit the victim. The victim ran from the room, but the defendant tackled her. With the help of the coperpetrator, the defendant held the victim down and strangled her until she was unconscious. The defendant then put the victim in the bathtub and drowned her. The perpetrators tried to conceal the crime by making it appear as if the victim had attempted suicide by driving her car into the river. (C66)

5. (2,0,2) The 23-year-old male coperpetrator asked the 26-year-old male defendant to help him kill his wife, the female victim in her early thirties. The coperpetrator offered to pay the defendant the life-insurance proceeds. The coperpetrator invited the defendant over to his house, and instructed him to hit the victim on the head with a crescent wrench. The defendant at first refused but complied when the coperpetrator threatened him. The defendant hit the victim, and, as she ran from the room, the coperpetrator tackled her. With the

help of the defendant, the coperpetrator held the victim down and strangled her until she was unconscious. They then put the victim in the bathtub and drowned her. The perpetrators tried to conceal the crime by making it appear as if the victim had attempted suicide by driving her car into the river. (574)

6. (2,0,2)   Prior to the day of the homicide the primary witness unsuccessfully attempted to recruit the 19-year-old male victim to rob the gas station where he was employed. On the day of the homicide, the defendant, the primary witness, and the coperpetrator were taking drugs (marijuana and barbiturates). In order to get more money the coperpetrator suggested they rob the gas station where the victim worked. The perpetrators decided that the defendant and the coperpetrator would "get rid of" the victim at a secluded area. They obtained a sawed-off shotgun, a knife, and a .30-.30 rifle. The perpetrators waited until the area was clear of police and then met the victim at his car. Once in the car, the defendant and coperpetrator robbed the victim of $150 at gun- and knifepoint. They drove to a wooded area and got out of the car. The victim dropped to his knees and pleaded for his life. The defendant took aim but could not shoot for about 5 minutes, during which time the coperpetrator encouraged him to shoot. The defendant shot the victim once in the head. The coperpetrator followed with another shot, either hitting or striking close to the victim's head. They fled in the victim's car. (861)

7. (1,1,2)   The 20-year-old male defendant and the 17-year-old male coperpetrator (both in the army) were drinking in an enlisted men's club. They ran out of money and decided to rob a cab driver. They called a cab, but changed their mind because the driver had a friend with him. The perpetrators then took a knife sharpener and a 14-inch butcher knife from the dining hall and called another cab. When the cab arrived, the 20-year-old male victim was driving. The perpetrators entered the cab and at an agreed signal they drew their weapons and forced the victim to the curb. The victim surrendered less than $20, so the defendant ordered the victim to take off his clothes, and the defendant searched each article for money and then threw them out the window. The defendant forced the victim to commit oral and anal sodomy. The perpetrators then bound the victim with the CB radio cord and put him naked in the trunk of the cab. They then picked up the primary witness and told him what they had done. The primary witness tried to talk them out of killing the victim. After they dropped the primary witness off, the perpetrators drove the cab to the woods, took the radio, and wiped the car clean of fingerprints. They opened the trunk and asked the victim if he was o.k. Then they closed the trunk and drove the car into a pond, leaping free before it went in. The victim died by drowning. (D14)

8. (1,1,2)   The male defendant and 3 coperpetrators planned to rob a convenience store where the male victim was working. When the victim squatted down by the store safe, the defendant struck him on the head with his gun and then leaned over and shot the victim in the temple. The defendant then fled the store with the money and joined the other coperpetrators. The defendant gave inconsistent statements but told another party that he killed the victim because he was "just another honky." (497)

9. (1,1,2) The 32-year-old male defendant and the coperpetrator went to a small barbershop where the 74-year-old male victim, the barber, was starting to close up shop. The coperpetrator and the defendant, who was wearing a disguise because the victim knew him, came into the shop. The defendant demanded the victim's money. The defendant then repeatedly beat the victim with a claw hammer, causing the victim's death after a violent struggle. The perpetrators stole $300 and the victim's watch. (991)

F. Cases scoring a total of 5 on the three classification variables

1. (2,1,2) The 31-year-old male defendant was hired by a criminal organization, consisting of coperpetrators #1, #2, and #3, to kill a deputy who was investigating cases against them concerning drugs and illegal liquor operations. The coperpetrators agreed to pay the defendant $3,000 for victim #1 (the male deputy) and an additional $500 if it was necessary to kill victim #2 (victim #1's wife). The defendant went to the home of the victims and shot them with a shotgun. (692)

2. (2,1,2) The 18-year-old female victim #1 and the male victim #2 were shotgunned to death in some woods. The male defendant flagged down a police car and reported finding the bodies while he was hunting. The police arrested the defendant more than a month later, after testing his shotgun. (573)

3. (2,1,2) The male defendant deeply hated his stepmother. On prior occasions he had gone to the mall to find someone to kill. On this trip he spotted the female victim at the mall. The defendant followed her and pulled a gun on her, forcing her to drive her car to the back of the lot. The victim, apparently, reminded the defendant of his stepmother. The victim pled for her life. The defendant covered the victim's head with her coat and then shot her twice. After the murder, the defendant bragged to his brother-in-law. (577)

4. (2,1,2) The 22-year-old male defendant, a student, was having money problems. The 22-year-old female primary witness (the coperpetrator) told the defendant she wanted her husband, the 28-year-old victim, killed because he had mistreated her. The defendant agreed to do the job for $1,500. The defendant took a friend's .22 pistol and went to find the victim at work as a security guard. The defendant recognized the victim from the primary witness's description but left without doing anything. After reconsidering, the defendant returned and forced the victim to lie on the floor, then shot him three times in the head. The defendant then fled. The defendant tried to collect his money from the primary witness for two months but was unable to do so. The primary witness then hired a person to kill the defendant; however, this person was an undercover police officer. After their arrests, both perpetrators made full written confessions. (898)

APPENDIX J

Logistic Multiple-Regression Models
Estimated for the Procedural Reform Study[1]

---

1. *See* chapter 4, note 38 and accompanying text, for a description of how the models in this appendix were estimated.

587

Part 1. Overall Models: These models identify the factors that explain which defendants convicted of murder at trial received a death sentence post-*Furman* (i.e., they reflect the combined influence of the prosecutorial decision to seek and the jury decision to impose a death sentence).

Variables	A. OVERALLA				B. OVERALLB			C. OVERALLC		
	Logistic Coefficient (Standard Error)	Odds Multiplier[2]	P Value	R Statistic	Logistic Coefficient (Standard Error)	Odds Multiplier	P Value	Logistic Coefficient (Standard Error)	Odds Multiplier	P Value
Black defendant (BLACKD)	-.57 (.50)	.56	.25	.00	—	—	—	—	—	—
White victim (WHVICRC)	2.66 (.65)	14.5	.0001	.16	—	—	—	—	—	—
One or more mitigating circumstances and a white victim (MCIRAWHV)	-1.65 (.54)	.19	.002	.11	—	—	—	—	—	—
Low-status defendant (LSTATDEF)	.85 (.48)	2.3	.08	.05	—	—	—	—	—	—
High-status defendant (HISTD)	1.88 (.95)	6.6	.05	.06	—	—	—	—	—	—
Female defendant (DFEM)	-.59 (1.03)	.56	.56	.00	—	—	—	—	—	—
Number of statutory aggravating circumstances, plus the number of B7 (vile-murder) circumstances in the case (DELB7EX)[3]	1.22 (.20)	3.4	.00001	.25	1.05 (.16)	2.9	.00001	1.22 (.20)	3.4	.0001

2. The odds multiplier is the antilog of the logistic partial-regression coefficient.
3. *See supra* appendix D, note 4, for a description of the variable.

Variable	b (SE)		p		b (SE)		p	b (SE)		p
Female victim (FEMVIC)	2.26 (.52)	9.5	.00001	.17	1.87 (.47)	6.5	.0001	2.26 (.52)	9.5	.00001
Defendant was underling in the murder (DUNDERLG)	−6.88 (1.51)	.001	.00001	.18	−4.95 (1.3)	.007	.0001	−6.88 (1.51)	.001	.00001
Victim stranger (VICSTRAN)	1.00 (.51)	2.7	.051	.06	1.34 (.47)	3.8	.005	1.00 (.51)	2.7	.051
Multiple stabs (MULSTAB)	1.71 (.71)	5.5	.01	.09	1.67 (.59)	5.3	.005	1.71 (.71)	5.5	.01
Defendant killed two or more people (TWOVIC)	1.66 (.65)	5.3	.01	.09	1.56 (.61)	4.8	.01	1.66 (.65)	5.3	.01
Victim hostage (HOST)	3.69 (2.03)	40	.07	.05	3.20 (1.45)	24.5	.027	3.69 (2.03)	40	.07
Defendant cooperated with authorities (STMIT9)	2.64 (.81)	14	.001	.12	2.24 (.75)	9.4	.003	—	—	—
Victim police- or fireperson (VICPFIR)	2.00 (.89)	7.4	.02	.07	.94 (.75)	2.6	.09	2.00 (.89)	7.4	.02
Victim twelve years or younger (YNGVIC)	2.3 (.97)	10	.02	.08	1.51 (.92)	4.5	.09	2.3 (.97)	10	.02
Defendant lay in wait (AMBUSH)	2.16 (.63)	8.6	.001	.13	1.78 (.55)	6.0	.001	2.16 (.63)	8.6	.001
Defendant in military (MILDEFN)	2.43 (.86)	11.4	.005	.10	1.86 (.80)	6.4	.02	2.43 (.86)	11.4	.005
Race-hatred motive (RACE)	4.68 (1.97)	108	.02	.08	4.12 (.54)	61.6	.008	4.68 (1.97)	108	.02
Victim low-status (VICLSTAT)	−2.63 (.80)	.07	.001	−.12	−2.49 (.78)	.08	.001	—	—	—
A bloody murder (BLOODY)	1.43 (.49)	4.18	.004	.10	1.05 (.42)	2.9	.01	1.43 (.49)	4.18	.004

Part 1. *(Continued)*

Variables	A. OVERALLA				B. OVERALLB			C. OVERALLC		
	Logistic Coefficient (Standard Error)	Odds Multiplier	P Value	R Statistic	Logistic Coefficient (Standard Error)	Odds Multiplier	P Value	Logistic Coefficient (Standard Error)	Odds Multiplier	P Value
Kidnap and multiple shots (KDNPAMSH)	-2.60 (1.03)	.07	.012	-.09	-1.22 (.94)	.30	.19	—	—	—
Neither kidnap nor multiple shots (NKNPOMSH)	-2.46 (.52)	.09	.00001	-.19	-2.14 (.45)	.12	.00001	-2.46 (.52)	.09	.00001
Aggravated motive and one or more prior felony convictions (AGMOTAPF)	1.69 (.58)	5.4	.004	.11	1.36 (.51)	3.9	.008	1.69 (.58)	5.4	.004
Number of convictions for violent personal crimes (other than murder, rape, armed robbery, kidnap) and number of statutory aggravating circumstances interaction (DLXXW15D)	0.36 (.19)	1.4	.07	.05	.25 (.18)	1.3	.17	.36 (.19)	1.4	.07
Defendant resisted arrest and one or more prior felony convictions (DEFRAAPF)	1.38 (.70)	4	.06	.05	1.22 (.65)	3.9	.06	1.38 (.70)	4	.06

Indexes OVERALLB and OVERALLC were used to create the following scales:

CSCALB	CSCALC
CSCALB = 6;	CSCALC = 6;
If OVERALLB LT 3.4557, then CSCALB = 5	If OVERALLC LT 2.2241, then CSCALC = 5
If OVERALLB LT 1.84301, then CSCALB = 4	If OVERALLC LT .5512, then CSCALC = 4
If OVERALLB LT .21251, then CSCALB = 3	If OVERALLC LT −1.0948, then CSCALC = 3
If OVERALLB LT −1.1983, then CSCALB = 2	If OVERALLC LT −2.8338, then CSCALC = 2
If OVERALLB LT −2.6786, then CSCALB = 1	If OVERALLC LT −4.4756, then CSCALC = 1

Part 2. Prosecutorial Models: These models identify the factors that explain which cases that resulted in a murder-trial conviction were advanced to a penalty trial by a prosecutorial decision, post-*Furman*.

Variables	A. PROSCUTA				B. PROSCUTB			C. PROSCUTC		
	Logistic Coefficient (Standard Error)	Odds Multiplier	P Value	R Statistic	Logistic Coefficient (Standard Error)	Odds Multiplier	P Value	Logistic Coefficient (Standard Error)	Odds Multiplier	P Value
Black defendant (BLACKD)	.15 (.39)	1.16	.6938	.00	—	—	—	—	—	—
White victim (WHVICRC)	1.87 (.40)	6.47	.00	.163	—	—	—	—	—	—
Low-status defendant (LSTATDEF)	.61 (.35)	1.84	.0787	.038	—	—	—	—	—	—
High-status defendant (HISTD)	.76 (.67)	2.14	.2556	.00	—	—	—	—	—	—
Female defendant (DFEM)	-1.33 (.65)	.26	.0417	-.053	—	—	—	—	—	—
One or more victims was white and a stranger (WHVXVSTR)	1.71 (.73)	5.55	.0193	.068	—	—	—	—	—	—
Brutal stomping/beating (STOMP)	2.48 (.67)	11.99	.0002	.126	1.93 (.62)	6.87	.0019	2.48 (.67)	11.99	.0002
Prior murder conviction (W15A1)	3.42 (1.37)	30.55	.0125	.075	3.14 (1.31)	23.00	.0164	3.42 (1.37)	30.55	.0125
Defendant killed two or more people (TWOVIC)	2.15 (.57)	8.56	.0002	.127	2.24 (.56)	9.41	.0001	2.15 (.57)	8.56	.0002

Variable	b (SE)	χ²	p	b (SE)	r	χ²	p	b (SE)	χ²	p
Victim a stranger (VICSTRAN)	.82 (.39)	2.28	.0357	1.37 (.35)	.057	3.93	.0001	.82 (.39)	2.28	.0357
Multiple stabs (MULSTAB)	1.44 (.52)	4.20	.0059	1.49 (.49)	.086	4.43	.0024	1.44 (.52)	4.20	.0059
Defendant actively resisted arrest (DEFRSAAR)	1.93 (.45)	6.90	.00	2.00 (.41)	.148	7.40	.00	1.93 (.45)	6.90	.00
Defendant's status sympathetic (MITDEFN)	−3.64 (1.07)	.03	.0006	−3.56 (1.05)	−.114	.03	.0007	−3.64 (1.07)	.03	.0006
Defendant engaged in a non-violent contemporaneous crime (NONVCOF)	1.82 (.47)	6.18	.0001	1.84 (.43)	.133	6.27	.00	1.82 (.47)	6.18	.0001
No victim mitigating circumstances (NOVMC)	1.00 (.32)	2.72	.0019	.97 (.30)	.101	2.65	.0011	1.00 (.32)	2.72	.0019
Defendant planned killing for more than 5 minutes (PREMEDK)	1.31 (.36)	3.71	.0003	1.10 (.33)	.120	3.01	.0009	1.31 (.36)	3.71	.0003
Murder for hire (PBQB6)	2.36 (.67)	10.62	.0004	2.15 (.65)	.119	8.55	.0010	2.36 (.67)	10.62	.0004
Defendant cooperated with authorities (STMTR9)	1.72 (.77)	5.57	.0253	1.62 (.77)	.063	5.07	.0361	—	—	—
Armed robbery involved (ARMROB)	1.07 (.41)	2.93	.0086	1.11 (.37)	.081	3.03	.0029	1.07 (.41)	2.93	.0086
Victim mutilated before/after death (PBQB7A)	1.18 (.61)	3.25	.0527	1.26 (.55)	.048	3.53	.0218	1.18 (.61)	3.25	.0527
Killing involved rape (PBQB7D)	1.18 (.53)	3.27	.0263	1.36 (.51)	.063	3.91	.0071	1.18 (.53)	3.27	.0263
Victim young (VICYNG)	1.61 (.73)	5.02	.0278	1.74 (.66)	.062	5.73	.0079	1.61 (.73)	5.02	.0278

Part 2. (Continued)

Variables	A. PROSCUTA				B. PROSCUTB			C. PROSCUTC		
	Logistic Coefficient (Standard Error)	Odds Multiplier	P Value	R Statistic	Logistic Coefficient (Standard Error)	Odds Multiplier	P Value	Logistic Coefficient (Standard Error)	Odds Multiplier	P Value
Number of prior convictions for less serious felonies and misdemeanors (W15F)	.76 (.24)	2.14	.0019	.101	.78 (.22)	2.18	.0004	.76 (.24)	2.14	.0019
Defendant was underling in killing (DUNDERLG)	−1.11 (.63)	.33	.0764	−.039	−.52 (.56)	.59	.3521	−1.11 (.63)	.33	.0764
Victim white-collar proprietor, professional, executive; number of defendant's convictions for other felonies and misdemeanors (VHSXW15F)	1.73 (.49)	5.66	.0005	.117	1.69 (.45)	5.40	.0002	—	—	—
Defendant not 17 to 25 years old and serious contemporaneous offense involved (NYADDSCO)	−1.84 (.44)	.16	.00	−.143	−1.70 (.41)	.18	.00	−1.84 (.44)	.16	.00
No multiple shots by major or aggravating circumstances interaction (NMSHTMAX)	.80 (.25)	2.23	.0016	.103	.66 (.21)	1.93	.0022	.80 (.25)	2.23	.0016

Victim not a stranger by number of prior convictions interaction (NVSTTCVX)	.13 (.04)	1.14	.0011	.108	.11 (.04)	1.12	.0035	.13 (.04)	1.14	.0011
Defendant aged 17 to 25 and no mitigating circumstances (YADXNOVM)	1.70 (.65)	5.50	.0090	.080	1.92 (.60)	6.80	.0014	1.70 (.65)	5.50	.0090

Indexes PROSCUTB and PROSCUTC were used to create the following scales:

PSCALB

If PROSCUTB LT −2.1325, then PSCALB = 1
If −2.1325 LE PROSCUTB LT −.9502, then PSCALB = 2
If −.9502 LE PROSCUTB LT .85668, then PSCALB = 3
If .85668 LE PROSCUTB LT 2.26365, then PSCALB = 4
If 2.26365 LE PROSCUTB LT 4.3758, then PSCALB = 5
If 4.3758 LE PROSCUTB, then PSCALB = 6

PSCALC

If PROSCUTC LT −4.0179, then PSCALC = 1
If −4.0179 LE PROSCUTC LT −2.4516, then PSCALC = 2
If −2.4516 LE PROSCUTC LT −.8871, then PSCALC = 3
If −.8871 LE PROSCUTC LT .66962, then PSCALC = 4
If .66962 LE PROSCUTC LT 2.22809, then PSCALC = 5
If 2.22809 LE PROSCUTC, then PSCALC = 6

Part 3, Jury Models: These models identify the factors that explain which defendants received a death sentence in a penalty trial, post-*Furman*.

Variables	A. JURYA				B. JURYB			C. JURYC		
	Logistic Coefficient (Standard Error)	Odds Multiplier	P Value	R Statistic	Logistic Coefficient (Standard Error)	Odds Multiplier	P Value	Logistic Coefficient (Standard Error)	Odds Multiplier	P Value
Black defendant (BLACKD)	-.53 (.61)	.59	.3857	.00	—	—	—	—	—	—
White victim (WHVICRC)	1.96 (.74)	7.09	.0082	.133	—	—	—	—	—	—
Low-status defendant (LSTATDEF)	.76 (.62)	2.14	.2188	.00	—	—	—	—	—	—
High-status defendant (HISTD)	.26 (1.29)	1.30	.8383	.00	—	—	—	—	—	—
White victim by number of statutory aggravating circumstances interactive (WVXDB7EX)	1.92 (.51)	6.79	.0002	.208	—	—	—	—	—	—
Female defendant (DFEM)	2.44 (1.80)	11.51	.1745	.00	—	—	—	—	—	—
Number of statutory aggravating circumstances, including the number of B7 (vile-murder) circumstances, in the case (DELB7EX)	1.12 (.24)	3.08	.00	.263	1.12 (.22)	3.08	.00	1.12 (.24)	3.08	.00

Female victim (FEMVIC)	2.97 (.73)	19.44	.0001	.225	1.73 (.55)	5.66	.0015	2.97 (.73)	19.44	.0001
Defendant cooperated with authorities (STMIT9)	2.81 (1.07)	16.58	.0089	.131	1.95 (.91)	7.07	.0327	— (—)	—	—
Defendant in military (MILDEFN)	2.08 (1.01)	8.00	.0403	.088	1.56 (.88)	4.74	.0778	2.08 (1.01)	8.00	.0403
Victim low-status (VICLSTAT)	−3.23 (1.01)	.04	.0014	−.17	−2.16 (.84)	.12	.0101	—	—	—
A bloody murder (BLOODY)	2.17 (.62)	8.73	.0004	.191	1.45 (.51)	4.25	.0042	2.17 (.62)	8.73	.0004
Kidnap and multiple shots (KDNPAMSH)	−4.84 (1.73)	.01	.0052	−.143	−3.41 (1.48)	.03	.0216	−4.84 (1.73)	.01	.0052
Defendant was accomplice to relatively minor act (STMIT6)	−9.24 (2.15)	.00	.00	−.24	−5.75 (1.42)	.00	.0001	−9.24 (2.15)	.00	.00
Multiple shots (MULSH)	2.21 (.86)	9.15	.01	.128	2.05 (.77)	7.77	.0082	2.21 (.86)	9.15	.01
Insurance motive (INSMOT)	3.65 (1.51)	38.36	.016	.116	2.76 (1.29)	15.89	.0323	3.65 (1.51)	38.36	.016
Victim kidnapped (KIDNAP)	3.57 (.97)	35.39	.0002	.201	2.86 (.81)	17.55	.0004	3.57 (.97)	35.39	.0002
Defendant had history of drug or alcohol abuse (DRGHIS)	−2.64 (.82)	.07	.0012	−.172	−1.68 (.70)	.19	.017	−2.64 (.82)	.07	.0012
One or more minor aggravating circumstances (MINAGGCR)	−2.43 (.97)	.09	.0128	−.121	−1.52 (.74)	.22	.0405	—	—	—

Part 3. (Continued)

Variables	A. JURYA				B. JURYB			C. JURYC		
	Logistic Coefficient (Standard Error)	Odds Multiplier	P Value	R Statistic	Logistic Coefficient (Standard Error)	Odds Multiplier	P Value	Logistic Coefficient (Standard Error)	Odds Multiplier	P Value
Prior conviction for murder/ armed robbery/ kidnap/ or other violent personal crime (VPCX)	1.14 (.50)	3.14	.0212	.108	.80 (.39)	2.22	.0391	1.14 (.50)	3.14	.0212

Indexes JURYB and JURYC were used to create the following scales:

JURYB

If JURYB LT −1.3094, then JSCALB = 1
If −1.3094 LE JURYB LT .2917, then JSCALB = 2
If .2917 LE JURYB LT 1.43452, then JSCALB = 3
If 1.43452 LE JURYB LT 2.77729, then JSCALB = 4
If 2.77729 LE JURYB LT 4.3296, then JSCALB = 5
If 4.3296 LE JURYB, then JSCALB = 6

JURYC

If JURYC LT −1.0308, then JSCALC = 1
If −1.0308 LE JURYC LT .8885, then JSCALC = 2
If .8885 LE JURYC LT 2.47058, then JSCALC = 3
If 2.47058 LE JURYC LT 4.24785, then JSCALC = 4
If 4.24785 LE JURYC LT 5.9593, then JSCALC = 5
If 5.9593 LE JURYC, then JSCALC = 6

Part 4. Pre-*Furman* Models: These models identify the factors that explain which defendants convicted of murder at trial received a death sentence pre-*Furman*. They reflect the combined effects of prosecutorial decisions to seek and jury decisions to impose death sentences.

Variables	A. PREFURMA				B. PREFURMB			C. PREFURMC		
	Logistic Coefficient (Standard Error)	Odds Multiplier	P Value	R Statistic	Logistic Coefficient (Standard Error)	Odds Multiplier	P Value	Logistic Coefficient (Standard Error)	Odds Multiplier	P Value
Black defendant (BLACKD)	2.49 (.80)	12.05	.002	.175	—	—	—	—	—	—
White victim (WHVICRC)	1.71 (.62)	5.55	.0054	.152	—	—	—	—	—	—
Low status–defendant (LSTATDEF)	.50 (.67)	1.65	.4544	.00	—	—	—	—	—	—
High-status defendant (HISTD)	−1.04 (1.77)	.35	.5566	.00	—	—	—	—	—	—
Female defendant (DFEM)	−4.79 23.37	.01	.8376	.00	—	—	—	—	—	—
One or more white victims and coperpetrators involved (WHVXCOPR)	2.13 (1.23)	8.38	.084	.063	—	—	—	—	—	—
Defendant committed additional crimes after killing (ADCRIM)	2.81 (.73)	16.58	.0001	.226	1.72 (.64)	5.58	.0071	2.81 (.73)	16.58	.0001
Defendant leader in murder or contemporaneous felony (DLEADMF)	2.84 (.96)	17.06	.0033	.164	2.55 (.97)	12.76	.0088	2.84 (.96)	17.06	.0033

Part 4. (Continued)

Variables	A. PREFURMA				B. PREFURMB			C. PREFURMC		
	Logistic Coefficient (Standard Error)	Odds Multiplier	P Value	R Statistic	Logistic Coefficient (Standard Error)	Odds Multiplier	P Value	Logistic Coefficient (Standard Error)	Odds Multiplier	P Value
Victim was sixty-five years or older (OLDVIC)	2.04 (.96)	7.72	.0331	.101	2.84 (1.19)	17.09	.0172	2.04 (.96)	7.72	.0331
Defendant killed two or more victims (TWOVIC)	5.77 (1.54)	320.0	.0002	.22	4.46 (1.61)	86.83	.0056	5.77 (1.54)	320.60	.0002
One or more coperpetrators involved (COPERP)	-2.12 (1.00)	.12	.0344	-.1	-1.73 (.91)	.18	.0577	-2.12 (1.00)	.12	.0344
Defendant actively resisted arrest (DEFRSAAR)	1.46 (.71)	4.33	.0401	.095	1.02 (.67)	2.78	.126	1.46 (.71)	4.33	.0401
Number of prior convictions for rape or kidnap (W15C1)	2.78 (1.14)	16.11	.0149	.126	2.87 (1.38)	17.58	.0377	2.78 (1.14)	16.11	.0149
Defendant engaged in nonviolent crime (NONVCOF)	1.89 (.88)	6.62	.0315	.103	1.65 (.97)	5.19	.0905	1.89 (.88)	6.62	.0315
Victim mitigating circumstances (OTHMIT)	-1.63 (.84)	.20	.0512	-.085	-2.08 (.97)	.12	.0323	-1.63 (.84)	.20	.0512
Defendant's age at time of crime (AGE)	-.58 (.25)	.56	.0201	-.117	-.78 (.24)	.46	.0013	-.58 (.25)	.56	.0201
Number of major aggravating circumstances (MAJAGCRX)	1.72 (.51)	5.6	.0007	.197	1.14 (.44)	3.12	.0102	1.72 (.51)	5.6	.0007

Indexes PREFURMB and PREFURMC were used to create the following scales:

PFSCALB	PFSCALC
If PREFURMB LT − 2.1511, then PFSCALB = 1	If PREFURMC LT − 5.7294 then PFSCALC = 1
If − 2.1511 LE PREFURMB LT 1.2160, then PFSCALB = 2	If − 5.7294 LE PREFURMC LT − 4.3717, then PFSCALC = 2
If 1.2160 LE PREFURMB LT .23261, then PFSCALB = 3	If − 4.3717 LE PREFURMC LT − 2.9925, then PFSCALC = 3
If .23261 LE PREFURMB LT .71560, then PFSCALB = 4	If − 2.9925 LE PREFURMC LT − 1.9879, then PFSCALC = 4
If .71560 LE PREFURMB LT 1.82528, then PFSCALB = 5	If − 1.9879 LE PREFURMC LT − .3348, then PFSCALC = 5
If 1.82528 LE PREFURMB, then PFSCALB = 6	If − .3348 LE PREFURMC, then PFSCALC = 6

APPENDIX K

A Sample of Georgia Murder Cases Ranked with a Multiple-Regression-Based Culpability Measure, from Least to Most Culpable

Culpability
Level
1 (least
culpable)

a. The defendant is a 19-year-old male with a prior conviction for a violent crime against a person and a conviction for a nonviolent crime. He and three coperpetrators noticed that the victim, a 27-year-old male, was carrying a lot of money. They followed him until they reached a secluded road, where they blocked the road with their car. A coperpetrator, carrying a shotgun, approached the victim while the victim was still in his car and demanded his money. When the victim started to back up his vehicle, the gun discharged, killing the victim. (D15)

b. The defendant is a 25-year-old male with a prior conviction for aggravated assault. The defendant and several friends, including the 24-year-old male victim, were playing pool and drinking at a club. The defendant got into an argument with a friend over $2 and the victim tried to break it up. The defendant and his cousin went to the cousin's house to get a pistol. Upon returning to the club, the scuffle broke out again. When the victim approached the defendant, the defendant fired twice, shooting the victim in the chest and stomach. The defendant also shot another male, who was going toward the victim, in the shoulder. (511)

c. The defendant is a 46-year-old male with no prior record. The defendant's family and the victims' family had feuded for years. There was an argument between the defendant and the two victims, a husband and wife. The defendant threatened the victims' family and the victims threatened to call the police. The defendant then shot both victims. The female victim was eight months pregnant. The defendant claims that he shot in the direction of the victims to distract them as he was trying to get away. The defendant claims that the same bullet struck both victims. (836)

d. The defendant is a female with two prior convictions for murder and involuntary manslaughter. The defendant and the victim, a female, began to argue over another woman; they had been drinking. The defendant grabbed a large butcher knife and stabbed the victim above the heart, killing her. The defendant tried to commit suicide by hanging herself in her cell. (034)

e. The defendant is a 22-year-old male with one prior conviction for a nonviolent crime. The defendant and a coperpetrator tried to purchase two life-insurance policies on the victim's life before committing the homicide. They offered an insurance agent money to help them. They also told another person that they were "coming into" some money. About two weeks before the homicide they finally obtained a policy on the victim's life. The defendant was the beneficiary of the policy. Subsequently, the victim, a male cousin of the defendant, was found dead with three bullets in his head. The defendant eventually admitted that the coperpetrator had killed the victim and that he helped the coperpetrator dump the body. (515)

f. The defendant, a female with no prior record, had been in love with the coperpetrator for some time. The defendant and coperpetrator planned the murder of the victim, the coperpetrator's wife. The coperpetrator gave the defendant a gun and she went to the victim's residence, where she shot the victim three times. The coperpetrator admitted the entire crime. The defendant led the police to the murder weapon. (052)

g. The defendant, a 28-year-old male with no prior record, was apparently in default on several outstanding loans from the bank where the victim, a 47-year-old male, worked. In order to discuss these matters, the defendant went to the victim's home, but the victim told the defendant to talk with him at the bank. The defendant left and later returned with a pistol. A fight occurred. The defendant struggled with the victim, hit him with the gun, and shot him four times. The defendant then robbed the victim and the bank where he worked. (494)

h. The victims, an elderly couple, had employed the defendant, a 32-year-old male with no prior convictions. The male victim was found dead in his home from a gunshot wound to the chest and from wounds to his shoulder and head caused by an ax and spear. The female victim had been stabbed in the back with a bread knife. There also were wounds to her left ear. There was approximately $3,500 worth of articles missing from the house. The defendant's girlfriend told the police that he had told her that he committed these homicides and numerous other homicides and thefts. (D03)

Culpability
Level
2

a. The defendant, a 21-year-old male with a prior conviction for a nonviolent crime, and three coperpetrators planned to rob the victim, a 41-year-old male. Two of the coperpetrators went to the victim's house, but the victim refused to go into a dark alley where the defendant and the other coperpetrator were hiding. The two coperpetrators then left, but later returned with a pistol. They had planned to hold the victim with the pistol, and then later kill him with a shotgun, but the victim struggled and one of the coperpetrators killed him with a shot to the chest. The defendant claimed he was at a party smoking marijuana when he heard the shots. The coperpetrators testified against him. (441)

b. The defendant, a 23-year-old male with three prior convictions for burglary, and two coperpetrators enticed the victim, an adult male, to a friend's house with the intent of getting him drunk and then "rolling" him for his money. They could not get the defendant drunk, so instead they stole his spark plugs and pretended they knew a mechanic who could fix the car. On the way to the mechanic, they beat the victim on the head with a blunt instrument, causing his death. The perpetrators then stole $30 from the body. (D23)

c. The defendant is a 28-year-old male prison escapee with five prior convictions, three of which are for nonviolent crimes. The coperpetrator waited in a car outside the victim's liquor store while the defendant, wearing a stocking mask and hat, went inside. The defendant told the victim, an adult male, not to move. The victim moved and the defendant shot him once through the eye. The defendant took $3,100 and fled. After his arrest, the defendant confessed to the shooting and led the police to the money pouch taken from the store. (893)

d. The 22-year-old male defendant, with no prior record, had been drinking and taking "street" drugs. He broke into the 78-year-old female victim's apartment and allegedly knocked her unconscious. He then assaulted, raped, and sodomized the victim. The cause of death was either suffocation or a heart attack. (D27)

e. The victim had been dating the defendant, a male with a prior conviction for a violent crime against a person. The victim had previously assaulted the defendant with a knife. On the day of the offense, both were armed with guns. It is unclear what happened prior to the shooting; there may have been a dispute between the parties. It is clear, however, that the defendant fired four shots, hitting the victim once in the temple and once in the leg. (008)

f. The defendant, a male with two prior convictions for burglary, and a coperpetrator heard the victim and the victim's friend talking about money while they were in a bar. The coperpetrator and the defendant went outside the bar and waited for the victims to come out. The defendant hit the victim over the head with a concrete block, killing him. The coperpetrator stabbed the victim's friend, but he did not die. The perpetrators then robbed the two and dragged their bodies behind some bushes. (323)

g. The defendant was a male with one prior conviction for burglary and two for nonviolent crimes. The victim was a peace officer who had earlier arrested the defendant. The officer was looking for the defendant in connection with an armed robbery. The victim pulled the defendant over, and both got out of their cars. The defendant shot the officer in the heart at close range. An accomplice testified against the defendant at trial. (580)

h. The defendant is an 18-year-old male, AWOL from the marines, with one prior conviction for a nonviolent crime. Two coperpetrators and the defendant demanded that the victim, a 62-year-old male, give them his money. It is not clear whether the victim resisted, but the defendant shot and killed the victim, and then he and the coperpetrators drove away. The police picked up the defendant and the coperpetrators. When their stories did not agree, the defendant confessed to the murder. (D17)

Culpability
Level
3

a. The defendant, a 36-year-old female with two prior convictions for nonviolent crimes, joined with four others in a plan to embarrass the victim, a 48-year-old male, by staging an armed robbery. The victim, an owner of a sporting-goods store, had allegedly made sexual advances toward the defendant. The plan was that one of the coperpetrators would lure the victim into the store by appearing to want to seduce him. While in the store, the other two coperpetrators planned to jump the victim, knock him unconscious, steal his money, and leave him half nude so that he would wake up embarrassed the next morning. However, as it happened, the victim suffered a serious beating and died three weeks later from head wounds. The defendant was not at the scene of the crime. She eventually made an admission to the police. (C93)

b. The defendant is an 18-year-old male with no prior convictions. He raped and shot to death a 25-year-old woman in the presence of her 4-year-old daughter. The defendant claimed the death was an accident; however, the victim was shot twice. (420)

c. The defendant, who had a prior history of assault, attacked a 62-year-old woman in a store and stabbed her four times in the chest. (426)

d. The defendant is a 19-year-old male who has one prior conviction for a nonviolent crime. He and two coperpetrators forced the victim, an adult male, to the victim's car at gunpoint. They drove to a secluded area, where they robbed the victim of about $1,000, shot him in the head, and stole his car. One of the coperpetrators claimed that the defendant shot the victim. However, the defendant claimed that they were discussing who would kill the victim when one of the coperpetrators shot at the victim. The victim then ran into the woods, and the defendant said that he shot at the victim several times. The defendant claimed that the coperpetrator fired the fatal shot. (D16)

e. The defendant, a 25-year-old male with one nonviolent prior conviction, and two coperpetrators took the victim to a secluded area. A coperpetrator struck the victim with a hammer. The defendant then struck the victim with a hammer and a rock, and drove a stick into his skull. They took the victim's money and left. (333)

f. The defendant had an alcohol problem and had allegedly previously assaulted the victim, his wife, with a pocket knife. The victim called the defendant on the telephone and said she was leaving him for good.

The defendant went over to his mother-in-law's house, where the victim was staying, and shot both his wife and mother-in-law in the head through the window of the home. He immediately turned himself in to the police. At the police station the defendant admitted that he had thought about committing the crime for eight years and that he would do it again. The defense argued he was not guilty by reason of insanity. (Z15)

g. The defendant is a 22-year-old male with fifteen prior convictions, eight of which are for nonviolent crimes. The victim, a 75-year-old male, was in a car in a parking lot when the defendant shot him in the head and stole $180 from him. The defendant was an escapee from prison at the time of the offense. He claims that someone else committed the crime. (570)

h. The defendant is a male, aged 22, with two convictions for nonviolent crimes, who was having financial problems. He agreed to kill the primary witness's husband, a 28-year-old male, for $1,500. At first he was reluctant to commit the act, but eventually he shot the victim in the head three times while the victim was lying on the floor. The primary witness never paid the defendant, and she hired a person to kill the defendant. This person was an undercover police officer who arrested both her and the defendant. Both perpetrators made full confessions. (898)

Culpability
Level
4

a. The defendant is a male, aged 45, with over 85 arrests, almost all for drunkenness. Both victims and the defendant had been drinking heavily at the time of the homicide. Victim #1, a 45-year-old female, may have been dating both the defendant and victim #2, a 32-year-old male, who was the defendant's brother. The victims were found dead from multiple stab wounds in victim #1's trailer. Witnesses had seen the defendant at the trailer earlier that day. The police found the defendant's fingerprints in victim #1's trailer and clothes with the victim's blood type in the defendant's house. (625)

b. The defendant is a male with an extensive prior history of violent crime. He escaped from custody in another county while awaiting the disposition of certain felony charges, including a homicide. The defendant and the coperpetrator encountered the victim, a 48-year-old male, while burglarizing the residence of the victim's son. The victim allegedly called the perpetrators "niggers." The defendant robbed and pistol-whipped the victim and then kidnapped him in the victim's vehicle. The perpetrators drove to a pasture, where the victim was shot in the head. They then robbed the victim of several hundred additional dollars. The defendant made a full admission upon capture and led the authorities to the victim's vehicle. (964)

c. The defendant, a male with no prior convictions, and other perpetrators entered the victim's home at night and demanded $5,000, which the victim said he did not have. The defendants decided to hold him captive until morning, when they would go to the bank to get the money. Meanwhile, the victim wrote the defendant a check for $300. In the morning, the defendant took the victim to a highway and shot him three times. The defendant claimed he had suffered Vietnam flashbacks and had heard voices telling him to shoot the "gook." (523)

d. The defendant, a male approximately 30 years old with three non-violent prior convictions, and two coperpetrators planned to rob the victim, an 18-year-old male. The perpetrators had consumed beer and marijuana prior to meeting the victim. They asked the defendant if he wanted to buy some marijuana. Thereafter, the victim and the perpetrators drove to a wooded area, where the defendant and a coperpetrator struck the victim in the head with a ball-peen hammer. The defendant then tried to cut the victim's throat. The victim pleaded with one of the coperpetrators for help. Subsequently, a coperpetrator struck the victim several times with a rock and then jabbed a stick into his skull. (330)

e. The 18-year-old male defendant robbed the store at which the victim was apparently employed. The defendant shot the 50-year-old male victim between the eyes. The victim had pleaded for his life. The defendant had no priors. (407)

f. The defendant is a 25-year-old male with one prior conviction for burglary and five for nonviolent crimes. He and the coperpetrators picked up the victim. The defendant then robbed the victim, shot him, and ran over him with a car. The perpetrators returned later to see if the victim was dead. (855)

g. The defendant, a male with no prior convictions, went to the victim's house to rob her. He stabbed her and slashed her in the throat, chest, abdomen, and vagina. There was evidence that he raped her before the killing. He also pulled out her intestines and laid them on her abdomen. The victim died from a loss of blood. The defense argued that the defendant was insane and that a coperpetrator had told him to kill the victim. (641)

h. The defendant is a 22-year-old male with no prior record. His sister and victim #1, a 30-year-old male, were getting a divorce. If victim #1 died before the divorce became final, she would receive the proceeds of a life-insurance policy. The defendant, a coperpetrator, victim #1, and victim #2 (a female) were in victim #1's car on the way to a party. On the way, the defendant shot victim #1 once in the head. The defendant shot victim #2 four times and told her to be silent as she cried for help. Just before the homicide, the defendant indicated to the coperpetrator that he was about to "do it." He had also told the coperpetrator sometime before that he was going to "ice somebody." (610)

Culpability Level 5

a. The defendant, a male aged 16 with no prior criminal record, and two coperpetrators pulled into his stepfather's Amoco station and stole the money in the register at gunpoint. Then they drove the stepfather and an 11-year-old boy to a deserted field, where the defendant told the two to lie down on the ground. Somebody shot and killed both victims, but it is unclear who did the shooting. There was some evidence that the defendant did it. Just before the killing, the boy told the defendant that he did not want to die. After his arrest, the defendant admitted to being the ringleader of the group and said that he wanted to be the biggest black gangster that ever lived. (C77)

b. The defendant, a male aged 19 with no prior criminal record, and the coperpetrator had been driving around, drinking, and talking about "rolling," or robbing, someone. The 28-year-old male victim was walking to his car when the defendant and a coperpetrator stopped and asked the victim if he needed a ride. The victim joined the perpetrators and they went to an isolated spot. The coperpetrator drove around in circles until the victim felt sick. The defendant then hit the victim on the head with an empty bottle, knocking him unconscious. The defendant then took the victim's wallet and watch, and shot the victim three times in the chest and once in the scrotum. The defendant admitted to the crime and said he killed the victim "to watch him die." (Z20)

c. The defendant and the coperpetrators robbed three foreign sailors while their ship was docked. The male victim died from wounds after being carried away in the defendant's car. It is not certain who actually killed the victim. The defendant heard the police wanted him and turned himself in. His alibi was that he attended a homecoming dance that night and later went home. The defendant is a male with no previous criminal record. (424)

d. The defendant, a 32-year-old male with one prior conviction for burglary, argued with the victim, a male, over some damage to the defendant's motorcycle. The victim apparently had damaged the motorcycle, but refused to pay for repairs. The defendant claimed that the victim pulled out a knife. The defendant then pulled out a pistol and shot the victim three times, killing him. The knife was found near the victim's body. (785)

e. The defendant is a male with three prior convictions for nonviolent crimes. He and two coperpetrators, who were relatives of the victim, obtained an insurance policy on the life of the victim. The defendant and one coperpetrator took the victim, a female, to a secluded area, where the defendant choked her and the coperpetrator stabbed her. The defendant claimed that the coperpetrators threatened him and his family if he did not commit the crime and denied that he was to receive any money. The defendant did admit his involvement in the crime, and the coperpetrators made statements implicating the defendant. (226)

f. The defendant, a 22-year-old male with five prior convictions, of which two were for nonviolent crimes, stabbed the victim, a female clerk, several times in the back, chest, and face and beat her in the course of a robbery. He had robbed and beaten another clerk the day before. The defendant gave conflicting statements to the police, confessing to the crime and then pleading insanity and denying his confession. (512)

g. The defendant, a male with no prior history of criminal charges, suffered from mental problems. He tried forcibly but unsuccessfully to have sex with his wife; his girlfriend also rejected him. Then he picked up the female victim, who was hitchhiking. They drove to a deserted house, where the victim made a remark about the defendant's girlfriend. The defendant took out a knife and forced the victim to have sex with him. Afterward, when she started to run, he stabbed her 14 times in the face, chest, and abdomen. The defendant then surrendered himself and confessed. (933)

h. The victim, a 17-year-old male, and the defendant, a male with one prior conviction for a nonviolent crime, went out together and had beer, marijuana, and barbiturates. They drove around in the country. At one point, the defendant demanded the car at knife point, and took the victim to the woods. The victim attempted to flee, but fell. The defendant then stabbed the victim 18 times while the victim was pleading for his life. Two weeks prior to the homicide the defendant had said that he needed to rob and kill someone. Two weeks after the homicide, the defendant called a radio station that had offered a reward for information about the location of the body. The defense claimed a lack of intent, possibly because the defendant was considered retarded. (450)

Culpability Level 6 (most culpable)

a. The defendant is a 20-year-old male who has no known record. Both victims were 63-year-old females, strangers to the defendant. The defendant and the coperpetrator came to garden in victim #1's yard. They grabbed her and forced her into the house, where they beat, tied, and raped her. They then took her to the bank and forced her to withdraw $600. When they returned, she tried to escape and attracted the attention of victim #2. After hitting victim #2 with a gun, the defendant and the coperpetrator drove both victims to a wooded area, where they beat them to death with a board and by stomping. (753)

b. The defendant, a 35-year-old male with a prior conviction for burglary and two convictions for nonviolent crimes, and three coperpetrators planned to burglarize a home. While the three coperpetrators were in the house, three male victims came home and the perpetrators shot them. Three more victims then arrived, two of whom were shot. The perpetrators took the remaining victim, the only female, to the woods, where she was raped and sodomized. They then shot her twice and mutilated her breasts. The defendant claimed to be in another state at the time of the killings, but a coperpetrator testified that the defendant killed one of the victims. (267)

APPENDIX L

McCleskey v. Kemp Variable Lists and Multiple-Regression Models

This appendix contains lists of variables that were included in a technical appendix submitted to the court in the *McCleskey* case. We also have included here the statistical models, including the racial variables, from which the variable lists were taken. The models were not submitted as evidence in *McCleskey*.

Most of the schedules include both logistic and least-squares multiple-regression models regardless of the method used to select the explanatory variables.*

Contents

*The statistical models in this appendix were estimated with the data sets archived at the Inter-University Consortium for Political and Social Research. *See supra* chap. 4, note 15. Because of data corrections and updates made immediately before, during, and after the *McCleskey* hearing in August 1983, the coefficients for some of the variables listed in this appendix are slightly different from those in the models used in the *McCleskey* hearing. These changes produced only trivial changes in the regression coefficients estimated for the race of defendant and victim on which McCleskey's legal claims were based.

†This model included variables in schedule 1 that showed a statistically significant relationship with the outcome variable DPMURIDT in a stepwise multiple-regression analysis.

7   Variables from the variable list in schedule 3 that show a statistically significant relationship ($p \le .10$) to the death-sentencing outcome in a linear stepwise-regression analysis of defendants indicted for murder, and the race of defendant and victim.

8   Nonperverse statistically significant ($p \le .10$) variables screened from the variable list in schedule 3 with logistic-regression analyses of prosecutorial decisions to seek a death penalty after a murder-trial conviction was obtained, and the race of defendant and victim.

9   Nonperverse statistically significant ($p \le .10$) variables screened from the variable list in schedule 3, using logistic-regression analyses of jury death-sentencing decisions, and the race of defendant and victim.

B. The Procedural Reform Study (PRS)

10   Five conceptually or statistically important variables and the race of defendant and victim.

11   Nine conceptually or statistically important variables and the race of defendant and victim.

12   Nonperverse statistically significant ($p \le .10$) variables screened from the list of variables in schedule 15 in a linear-regression analysis of prosecutorial decisions to seek a death sentence following a murder-trial conviction, and the race of defendant and victim.

13   Nonperverse statistically significant ($p \le .10$) variables screened from the variable list in schedule 15 in logistic regression analyses designed to explain which defendants received a death sentence at a penalty trial, and the race of defendant and victim.

14   All statutory aggravating circumstances, all mitigating circumstances in the file, and the race of defendant and victim.

15   The full file of 150 + factors plus the race of defendant and victim and a race-of-victim interaction term.

16   Variables from schedule 15 that show a statistically significant relationship ($p \le .10$) to the death-sentencing result among defendants convicted of murder at trial in a least-squares stepwise-regression analysis, and the race of defendant and victim. This model was estimated before the *McCleskey* hearing but the variable list was not included in the *McCleskey* Technical Appendix.

A. THE CHARGING AND SENTENCING STUDY (CSS)

Schedule 1—CSS

Outcome variable: Death sentence imposed in cases indicted for murder (DPMURIDT).
Explanatory variables: Statutory aggravating circumstances, all mitigating circumstances in the file, and the race of defendant and victim.

Model A. Weighted Logistic Regression

2342 Weighted observations
2214 DPMURIDT = 0
128 DPMURIDT = 1
Model chi-square[1] = 154.246 with 79 D.F.
R = .000[2]

Variable	Logistic Regression Coefficient	Safe[3]			Nominal[4]			Variable Label
		Standard Error	t[5]	p[6]	Standard Error	t[5]	p[6]	
CONST	−7.5004	1.3408	−5.59	0.000	1.131	−6.632	0.000	Constant
BLACKD	0.3437	0.4395	0.78	0.434	0.379	0.908	0.364	Def. was black
WHVICRC	2.3807	0.5071	4.69	0.000	0.458	5.201	0.000	One or more white victims (recode)
LDFB1	2.0661	0.5924	3.49	0.000	0.609	3.394	0.001	Prior rec. of mur., arm. rob., rape, kid.
LDFB2	1.6725	0.6360	2.63	0.009	0.481	3.476	0.001	Cont. mur., arm. rob., rape, kid./bod. inj., etc.
LDFB3	0.5315	0.5972	0.89	0.374	0.537	0.990	0.322	Def. caused death risk in pub. place to ≥2
LDFB4	0.4426	0.5604	0.79	0.430	0.441	1.004	0.316	Murder for money/value for self/other
LDFB6	2.4660	0.9411	2.62	0.009	0.816	3.021	0.003	Murder for hire
LDFB7	2.0617	0.5185	3.98	0.000	0.506	4.078	0.000	One or more B7 factors in case
LDFB8	0.6572	1.0762	0.61	0.541	0.845	0.778	0.437	Victim police/corrections/fire on duty
LDFB9	2.8300	1.0489	2.70	0.007	0.768	3.682	0.000	Def. prisoner or escapee

Variable							Description
LDFB10	1.0429	0.4303	2.42	0.015	0.349	2.991	0.003	Kill to avoid, stop arrest of self, other
BADID	0.9483	0.4558	2.08	0.037	0.398	2.380	0.017	Mistaken identity claimed
BDBLOOD	0.1004	1.0939	0.09	0.927	1.037	0.097	0.923	Vic. and def. had history of bad blood
BLVICMOD	−0.6767	0.9055	−0.75	0.455	0.811	−0.834	0.404	Family, lover, liquor, barroom quarrel
COPDIDIT	0.1816	0.5419	0.34	0.738	0.467	0.388	0.698	Coperpetrator caused the death
COPHURTD	3.2648	1.5925	2.05	0.040	2.516	1.298	0.194	Def. phys. injured by police
CPLESSEN	1.2565	0.4699	2.67	0.007	0.380	3.306	0.001	Coperp. received a lesser sentence
CPLESSSN	0.8092	0.6347	1.27	0.202	0.672	1.204	0.229	Coperp. w/life or less sent., earlier
DABSENT	−2.1949	1.7933	−1.22	0.221	1.275	−1.721	0.085	Def. not at scene
DBADFACT	2.3444	0.8031	2.92	0.004	1.066	2.199	0.028	Mistake of fact claimed
DCOERCED	1.4570	0.8980	1.62	0.105	0.917	1.589	0.112	Coercion used on def.
DDRINK	1.3112	0.4539	2.89	0.004	0.375	3.499	0.000	Def. used alcohol, drug immed. prior
DEFADMIT	−1.9327	0.6851	−2.82	0.005	0.686	−2.819	0.005	Def. admit guilt & no defense asserted
DEFAGE	−0.0266	0.0213	−1.25	0.212	0.018	−1.476	0.140	Def. age at time of crime
DEFCHILD	−0.8840	2.3102	−0.38	0.702	1.635	−0.541	0.589	Def. juvenile or student
DEPRIVED	1.6696	1.2178	1.37	0.170	1.573	1.061	0.289	Def. history of physical or econ. depriv.
DISKID	−5.8828	2.1565	−2.73	0.006	83.660	−0.070	0.944	Reasonable discipline of minor by parent
DNOINT	−6.3172	1.7608	−3.59	0.000	58.620	−0.108	0.914	Def. unaware of intent to use force
DNOINTNT	−0.6793	0.6211	−1.09	0.274	0.492	−1.381	0.167	Lack of intent to kill
DNOVIOL	−1.6871	1.1008	−1.53	0.125	0.981	−1.720	0.085	Def. committed no violence
DPROPDEF	−5.1610	1.6222	−3.18	0.001	50.830	−0.102	0.919	Defense of home, dwelling, or property
DRGHIS	−1.4722	0.5908	−2.49	0.013	0.477	−3.084	0.002	History of drug or alcohol abuse
DRUGDIS	−0.2415	1.2148	−0.20	0.842	1.045	−0.231	0.817	Dispute under influence of drugs, alcoh.
DSELFDEF	−2.4632	0.9145	−2.69	0.007	0.899	−2.739	0.006	Defense of self or others
DVIOLOTH	0.3682	1.2685	0.29	0.772	1.515	0.243	0.808	Def. only violence was against others
FAMDIS	1.0951	1.1436	0.96	0.338	1.183	0.926	0.355	Family dispute other than spouse, ex-spouse
GUNSTRUG	−0.0360	1.6902	−0.02	0.983	1.394	−0.026	0.979	Gun fired during struggle for gun
HATE	0.2114	1.1736	0.18	0.857	1.008	0.210	0.834	Hate motive
INSANDEF	2.6208	0.8659	3.03	0.002	0.602	4.353	0.000	Insanity or delusional compulsion
JEALOUS	−0.4958	0.8489	−0.58	0.559	1.662	−0.298	0.765	Jealousy motive
JOINTKIL	−0.9222	0.6014	−1.53	0.125	0.530	−1.740	0.082	Def. only an accomplice in killing

Schedule 1, Model A (*cont.*)

Variable	Logistic Regression Coefficient	Safe[3]			Nominal[4]			Variable Label
		Standard Error	t[5]	p[6]	Standard Error	t[5]	p[6]	
MITCIR	0.4103	0.6502	0.63	0.528	0.553	0.742	0.458	Mitigating factors involved
MITCIRX	−0.2856	0.2907	−0.98	0.326	0.260	−1.097	0.273	No. mitigating factors involved
MITDFFN	−0.3177	2.4716	−0.13	0.898	1.540	−0.206	0.837	Def. retired, student, juvenile, housekeeper
MITMOTVE	−2.9875	2.6098	−1.14	0.252	2.015	−1.483	0.138	Def. motive hate, revenge, jealousy, rage
MONDIS	−1.0203	0.8090	−1.26	0.207	0.694	−1.469	0.142	Dispute over mon. or prop. between vic., def.
NOCONDUC	−4.1940	2.9968	−1.40	0.162	1.594	−2.631	0.009	Def. had impaired mental capacity
NOSPAGCR	−6.2568	0.8460	−7.40	0.000	6.930	−0.903	0.367	No special agg. cir.
PANIC	1.9517	0.6910	2.82	0.005	0.679	2.873	0.004	Def. panic in course of burglary
PHYILL	0.6287	0.8468	0.74	0.458	0.830	0.757	0.449	Def. had history of physical illness
RAGE	3.3707	2.5991	1.30	0.195	1.996	1.689	0.091	Rage motive
REVENGE	0.3161	0.7252	0.44	0.663	0.727	0.434	0.664	Revenge motive
SHOOTOUT	0.0462	0.9099	0.05	0.960	0.911	0.051	0.960	Shootout
SMCAPIC	12.6660	2.5932	4.88	0.000	164.300	0.077	0.939	Impaired capacity
SMDEFCO	0.6529	0.5188	1.26	0.208	0.501	1.302	0.193	Def. coop with authorities
SMDEFJUS	1.3704	1.7341	0.79	0.429	1.392	0.984	0.325	Def. had moral just. for actions
SMDURESS	0.0666	1.1572	0.05	0.958	1.723	0.035	0.972	Def. acted under duress

Variable								Description
SMEMDIST	0.7209	1.2661	0.57	0.569	1.004	0.718	0.473	Def. under extreme ment. or emot. distress
SMNOSREC	0.0719	0.4326	0.17	0.868	0.368	0.195	0.845	Def. had no signif. criminal history
SMPROVOK	−3.1623	1.2870	−2.46	0.014	1.649	−1.918	0.055	Def. was provoked
SMUNDRLG	−1.2328	0.9715	−1.27	0.204	0.897	−1.375	0.169	Def. accomplice and minor participant
SMYOUTH	−0.8879	0.6743	−1.32	0.188	0.638	−1.393	0.164	Def. under 17 years of age
TRIANGLE	0.8006	1.2035	0.67	0.506	1.610	0.497	0.619	Lover's triangle
VABUSFRD	−1.4565	1.1217	−1.30	0.194	1.499	−0.972	0.331	Vic. prov def. by abuse person def. care for
VASSAULD	1.3202	1.5946	0.83	0.408	1.308	1.009	0.313	Vic. assaulted def.
VCOPERP	−7.3275	2.5049	−2.93	0.003	82.150	−0.089	0.929	Vic. was a coperp.
VDEFECT	−3.0332	2.2688	−1.34	0.181	164.400	−0.018	0.985	Vic. mental defective
VICVERB	2.7646	1.3206	2.09	0.036	1.596	1.732	0.083	Vic. verb provok def. by accus., abus., thrt
VINJDEAR	−7.6863	1.9275	−3.99	0.000	15.920	−0.483	0.629	Vic. physically injured def. earlier
VINJFEAR	−0.7954	1.5295	−0.52	0.603	37.450	−0.021	0.983	Vic. prior injur person def. care for
VINJURD	4.9501	1.4221	3.48	0.000	1.645	3.009	0.003	Vic. physically injured def.
VRECORD	1.2236	0.9166	1.33	0.182	0.754	1.623	0.105	Vic. had criminal record
VSEXUP	3.1808	1.0176	3.13	0.002	1.099	2.894	0.004	Vic. sexually aroused def.
VSHOMON	0.1781	1.0020	0.18	0.859	0.682	0.261	0.794	Vic. showed, talked about much money
VSUICIDE	6.4286	1.8159	3.54	0.000	1.552	4.142	0.000	Suicide by vic. claimed
VTHEAEAR	−4.3890	1.4687	−2.99	0.003	14.690	−0.299	0.765	Vic. threatened def. earlier
VTHREAT	−4.1813	2.0459	−2.04	0.041	36.960	−0.113	0.910	Vic. threatened person def. cared about
VTHREATD	2.9211	1.3782	2.12	0.034	1.277	2.287	0.022	Vic. verbally threatened def.
VTRTFEAR	2.4448	2.1279	1.15	0.251	36.530	0.067	0.947	Vic. verb threat person def. cared for

Model B: Weighted Least Squares

Source	DF	Sum of Squares	Mean Square	F Value	Prob>F
Model	79	38.82955732	0.49151338	5.593	0.0001
Error	935	82.17394818	0.08788658		
C Total	1014	121.00351			

Root MSE	0.2964567		R-Square	0.3209
Dep Mean	0.05466011		Adj R-Sq	0.2635

Variable	Safe[2]				Nominal[3]			Variable Label
	Regression Coefficient	Standard Error	t^4	p^5	Standard Error	t^4	p^5	
CONST	0.0689	0.0421	1.64	0.102	0.0415	1.658	0.097	Const
BLACKD	0.0965	0.0303	3.19	0.001	0.0226	4.264	0.000	Def. was black
WHVICRC	0.0705	0.0299	2.36	0.018	0.0228	3.096	0.002	One or more white victims (recode)
LDFB1	0.0711	0.0442	1.61	0.108	0.0346	2.055	0.040	Prior rec. of mur., arm. rob., rape, kid.
LDFB2	-0.0124	0.0302	-0.41	0.680	0.0247	-0.503	0.615	Cont. mur., arm. rob., rape, kid./bod. inj., etc.
LDFB3	0.0351	0.0141	2.49	0.013	0.0188	1.871	0.061	Def. caused death risk in pub. place to ≥2
LDFB4	0.0958	0.0372	2.58	0.010	0.0279	3.429	0.001	Murder for money/value for self/other
LDFB6	0.0343	0.0875	0.39	0.695	0.0602	0.570	0.569	Murder for hire
LDFB7	-0.0142	0.0103	-1.38	0.168	0.0146	-0.971	0.331	One or more B7 factors in case
LDFB8	0.1475	0.1118	1.32	0.187	0.0682	2.163	0.031	Vic. police/corrections/fire on duty
LDFB9	0.1830	0.0838	2.18	0.029	0.0493	3.710	0.000	Def. prisoner or escapee
LDFB10	0.0487	0.0524	0.93	0.353	0.0299	1.630	0.103	Kill to avoid, stop arrest of self, other
BADID	-0.0013	0.0255	-0.05	0.959	0.0227	-0.058	0.954	Mistaken identity claimed
BDBLOOD	-0.0075	0.0146	-0.51	0.610	0.0257	-0.290	0.772	Vic. and def. had history of bad blood
BLVICMOD	0.0211	0.0103	2.04	0.041	0.0183	1.147	0.251	Family, lover, liquor, barroom quarrel
COPDIDIT	0.2511	0.0478	5.25	0.000	0.0360	6.980	0.000	Coperp. caused the death

Variable								Description
COPHURTD	0.0501	0.2706	0.19	0.853	0.1551	0.323	0.747	Def. phys. injured by police
CPLESSEN	0.0401	0.0357	1.13	0.260	0.0250	1.604	0.109	Coperp. received a lesser sentence
CPLESSSN	-0.1033	0.0585	-1.76	0.078	0.0449	-2.301	0.021	Coperp. w/life or less, earlier
DABSENT	0.1131	0.0685	1.65	0.099	0.0619	1.826	0.068	Def. not at scene
DBADFACT	0.3088	0.0756	4.08	0.000	0.0637	4.848	0.000	Mistake of fact claimed
DCOERCED	0.0475	0.2817	0.17	0.866	0.0998	0.476	0.634	Coercion used on defendant
DDRINK	-0.0712	0.0170	-4.18	0.000	0.0178	-3.997	0.000	Def. used alcohol, drug immed. prior
DEFADMIT	0.0000	0.0272	0.00	0.999	0.0295	-0.001	0.999	Def. admit guilt & no defense asserted
DEFAGE	0.0174	0.0005	35.05	0.000	0.0006	27.092	0.000	Def. age at time of crime
DEFCHILD	0.0595	0.0655	0.91	0.364	0.0671	0.886	0.376	Def. juvenile or student
DEPRIVED	-0.1512	0.0590	-2.56	0.010	0.0741	-2.041	0.041	Def. history of physical or econ. depriv.
DISKID	-0.1238	0.1628	-0.76	0.447	0.1795	-0.690	0.490	Reasonable discipline of minor by parent
DNOINT	-0.0053	0.1874	-0.03	0.977	0.1268	-0.042	0.966	Def. unaware of intent to use force
DNOINTNT	-0.0807	0.0210	-3.83	0.000	0.0224	-3.603	0.000	Lack of intent to kill
DNOVIOL	-0.0286	0.0793	-0.36	0.718	0.0611	-0.468	0.640	Def. committed no violence
DPROPDEF	-0.0225	0.0406	-0.55	0.579	0.1060	-0.212	0.832	Defense of home, dwelling, or property
DRGHIS	-0.0261	0.0137	-1.91	0.056	0.0169	-1.547	0.122	History of drug or alcohol abuse
DRUGDIS	-0.0094	0.0161	-0.58	0.561	0.0238	-0.394	0.694	Dispute under influence of drugs, alcohol
DSELFDEF	-0.0955	0.0095	-10.00	0.000	0.0160	-5.964	0.000	Defense of self or others
DVIOLOTH	0.0126	0.1372	0.09	0.927	0.1088	0.115	0.908	Def. only violence was against others
FAMDIS	0.0107	0.0127	0.84	0.399	0.0272	0.394	0.694	Family dispute other than spouse, ex-spouse
GUNSTRUG	-0.0059	0.0234	-0.25	0.802	0.0384	-0.153	0.878	Gun fired during struggle for gun
HATE	0.2296	0.0162	14.14	0.000	0.0278	8.256	0.000	Hate motive
INSANDEF	-0.0171	0.0977	-0.17	0.861	0.0453	-0.376	0.707	Insanity or delusional compulsion
JEALOUS	-0.0693	0.0121	-5.73	0.000	0.0269	-2.573	0.010	Jealousy motive
JOINTKIL	-0.0208	0.0436	-0.48	0.633	0.0371	-0.562	0.574	Def. only an accomplice in killing
MITCIR	-0.0033	0.0233	-0.14	0.888	0.0225	-0.145	0.885	Mitigating factors involved
MITCIRX	-0.0340	0.0048	-7.04	0.000	0.0077	-4.442	0.000	No. mitigating factors involved
MITDFFN	-0.0102	0.0346	-0.29	0.769	0.0475	-0.214	0.831	Def. retired, student, juvenile, housekeeper
MITMOTVE	-0.0141	0.0203	-0.69	0.488	0.0360	-0.391	0.695	Def. motive hate, revenge, jealousy, rage
MONDIS	-0.3687	0.0114	-32.39	0.000	0.0201	-18.324	0.000	Dispute over mon. or prop. between vic. & def.

Schedule 1, Model B (*cont.*)

| Variable | Regression Coefficient | Safe² | | | Nominal³ | | | Variable Label |
		Standard Error	t⁴	p⁵	Standard Error	t⁴	p⁵	
NOCONDUC	−0.0056	1.2669	0.00	0.996	0.1448	−0.039	0.969	Def. had impaired mental capacity
NOSPAGCR	0.0727	0.0114	6.37	0.000	0.0204	3.565	0.000	No special agg. cir.
PANIC	0.0207	0.0510	0.41	0.685	0.0410	0.505	0.613	Def. panic in course of burglary
PHYILL	0.0224	0.0188	1.19	0.233	0.0270	0.829	0.407	Def. had history of physical illness
RAGE	0.0034	0.0166	0.20	0.838	0.0333	0.102	0.919	Rage motive
REVENGE	−0.0214	0.0131	−1.64	0.101	0.0206	−1.041	0.298	Revenge motive
SHOOTOUT	0.5159	0.0492	10.48	0.000	0.0501	10.305	0.000	Shootout
SMCAPIC	0.0010	0.2108	0.00	0.996	0.3123	0.003	0.997	Impaired capacity
SMDEFCO	0.0526	0.0242	2.17	0.030	0.0246	2.141	0.032	Def. coop. with authorities
SMDEFJUS	0.2040	0.0501	4.08	0.000	0.0608	3.355	0.001	Def. had moral just. for actions
SMDURESS	−0.0183	0.3612	−0.05	0.960	0.1629	−0.112	0.910	Def. acted under duress
SMEMDIST	−0.0040	0.0679	−0.06	0.953	0.0535	−0.075	0.940	Def. under extreme ment. or emot. distress
SMNOSREC	−0.0100	0.0174	−0.57	0.567	0.0173	−0.577	0.564	Def. had no signif. criminal history
SMPROVOK	−0.0717	0.0172	−4.18	0.000	0.0300	−2.390	0.017	Defendant was provoked
SMUNDRLG	−0.0395	0.0753	−0.53	0.599	0.0586	−0.675	0.500	Def. accomplice and minor participant
SMYOUTH	0.0075	0.0322	0.23	0.814	0.0331	0.228	0.820	Def. under 17 years of age
TRIANGLE	0.0035	0.0132	0.27	0.790	0.0297	0.119	0.905	Lover's triangle
VABUSFRD	0.0206	0.0231	0.89	0.372	0.0370	0.557	0.577	Vic. prov. def. by abuse person def. care for

VASSAULD	−0.1863	0.0123	−15.15	0.000	0.0248	−7.521	0.000	Vic. assaulted defendant
VCOPERP	−0.1708	3.7972	−0.04	0.964	0.1567	−1.090	0.276	Vic. was a coperp.
VDEFECT	0.0051	0.2830	0.02	0.986	0.3052	0.017	0.987	Vic. mental defective
VICVERB	−0.0050	0.0135	−0.37	0.713	0.0267	−0.186	0.853	Vic. verb provok. def. by accus., abus.
VINJEAR	−0.0161	0.0200	−0.81	0.420	0.0463	−0.348	0.728	Vic. physically injured def. earlier
VINJFEAR	0.0329	0.0480	0.69	0.493	0.0852	0.386	0.700	Vic. prior injur. person def. care for
VINJURD	−0.0069	0.0335	−0.21	0.836	0.0519	−0.134	0.894	Vic. physically injured def.
VRECORD	0.1361	0.0404	3.37	0.001	0.0376	3.620	0.000	Vic. had criminal record
VSEXUP	0.0088	0.1235	0.07	0.943	0.0773	0.114	0.909	Vic. sexually aroused defendant
VSHOMON	0.0965	0.0931	1.04	0.300	0.0585	1.650	0.099	Vic. showed, talked about much money
VSUICIDE	0.0282	0.1266	0.22	0.824	0.0943	0.299	0.765	Suicide by vic. claimed
VTHEAEAR	−0.0057	0.0177	−0.32	0.748	0.0417	−0.137	0.891	Vic. threatened def. earlier
VTHREAT	0.0239	0.0467	0.51	0.609	0.0963	0.248	0.804	Vic. threatened person def. cared about
VTHREATD	−0.0026	0.0203	−0.13	0.897	0.0384	−0.068	0.946	Vic. verbally threatened def.
VTRTFEAR	−0.0668	0.0316	−2.11	0.034	0.1015	−0.658	0.510	Vic. verb threat. person def. cared for

1. Model chi-square is −2 times the natural logarithm of the likelihood ratio.

2. R is the square root of R-square. For logistic regression, R-square is model chi-square minus twice the number of explanatory variables expressed as a proportion of total chi-square. Total chi-square is −2 times the natural logarithm of the likelihood of the intercept-only model. This definition of R is analogous to the C_p (a penalized R^2) in that it subtracts a penalty based on the number of predictor variables. Thus, an R value near zero indicates an overfitted model.

3. Safe inferential statistics are computed using methods described in Woodworth, Analysis of a Y-Stratified Sample: The Georgia Charging and Sentencing Study, in PROCEEDINGS OF THE SECOND WORKSHOP ON LAW AND JUSTICE STATISTICS, 1984, p. 18 (A. Gelfand ed. 1985).

4. Nominal inferential statistics are those reported by weighted logistic regression and weighted least-squares software.

5. The t statistic is the ratio of the parameter estimate to its standard error, safe or nominal.

6. The p value is the probability that a t-value this large or larger would occur by chance.

Schedule 3—CSS

Outcome variable: Death sentence imposed in cases indicted for murder (DPMURIDT).
Explanatory variables: The full file of 230+ variables and the race of defendant and victim.

Model A: Weighted Least Squares

Source	DF	Sum of Squares	Mean Square	F Value	Prob>F
Model	236	74.85726367	0.31719180	6.825	0.0001
Error	781	36.29892494	0.04647750		
C Total	1017	111.15619			

Root MSE 0.2155864   R-Square 0.6734
Dep Mean 0.1247541   Adj R-Sq 0.5748

Variable	DF	Parameter Estimate	Standard Error	Nominal[1] t for Ho: Parameter = 0	Prob.>t	Variable Label
INTERCEP	1	0.19270560	0.20701653	0.931	0.3522	Intercept
BLACKD	1	0.06635771	0.02707755	2.451	0.0145	Def. was black
WHVICRC	1	0.06464648	0.02658639	2.432	0.0153	One or more white victims (recode)
LDFB1	1	0.11579530	0.05847438	1.980	0.0480	Prior rec. of mur., arm. rob., rape, kid.
LDFB2	1	-0.01207822	0.06089701	-0.198	0.8428	Cont. mur., arm. rob., rape, kid., etc.
LDFB3	1	0.00730491	0.02650171	0.276	0.7829	Def. caused death risk in pub. place to ≥2
LDFB4	1	-0.00841213	0.04546880	-0.185	0.8533	Murder for money/value for self/other
LDFB6	1	0.03465062	0.07187000	0.482	0.6298	Murder for hire
LDFB8	1	-0.04205789	0.08180718	-0.514	0.6073	Vic. police/corrections/fire on duty
LDFB9	1	0.09656101	0.07918731	1.219	0.2231	Def. prisoner or escapee

Variable						Description
LDFB10	1	0.22275270	0.08099006	2.750	0.0061	Kill to avoid, stop arrest of self, other
LDFB7A	1	0.02225066	0.07165346	0.311	0.7562	Mutilation before or after death
LDFB7B	1	-0.04144860	0.04199425	-0.987	0.3239	Unnecessary multiple wounding
LDFB7D	1	0.08356927	0.04022732	2.077	0.0381	Rape/arm. rob./kid. + sil. wit./exec. or vic. pleaded
LDFB7E	1	-0.07856685	0.09159407	-0.858	0.3913	Torture/depravity
LDFB7F	1	0.04087783	0.13196239	0.310	0.7568	Depravity/sex perversion & vic. plead.
DEFWAIT	1	0.01651309	0.03236446	0.510	0.6100	Def. lay in wait
HOSTAGE	1	-0.11195218	0.10520910	-1.064	0.2876	Vic. was a hostage
NOVICPRO	1	-0.12903667	0.04965548	-2.599	0.0095	Vic. offered no provocation
POISON	1	0.02592878	0.14715665	0.176	0.8602	Vic. killed with poison
RACEMOT	1	0.08363829	0.06910831	1.210	0.2265	Racial hatred motive
VDEFNSLS	1	-0.11988029	0.08144355	-1.472	0.1414	Vic. pregnant, disabled, or helpless
VICCHILD	1	0.09205126	0.09806193	0.939	0.3482	Vic. was 12 or younger
VWITNESS	1	-0.15483066	0.08508266	-1.820	0.0692	Vic. was witness
SMDEFCO	1	-0.02279875	0.02944444	-0.774	0.4390	Def. coop. with authorities
SMDEFJUS	1	0.10137996	0.07142788	1.419	0.1562	Def. had moral just. for actions
SMDURESS	1	0.09032606	0.14909008	0.606	0.5448	Def. acted under duress
SMEMDIST	1	-0.00974303	0.06636650	-0.161	0.8718	Def. under extreme ment. or emot. distress
SMNOSREC	1	0.06402539	0.03865589	1.656	0.0981	Def. had no signif. criminal history
SMPROVOK	1	-0.03269300	0.03995718	-0.818	0.4135	Def. was provoked
SMUNDRLG	1	-0.02664779	0.08692196	-0.307	0.7593	Def. accomplice and minor participant
SMYOUTH	1	-0.02024314	0.04130593	-0.490	0.6242	Def. under 17 years of age
ACCIDENT	1	0.00533345	0.02581540	0.207	0.8364	Def. claimed accident
AIDVICT	1	-0.00548678	0.03770877	-0.146	0.8844	Def. aided victims
DEFREMOR	1	-0.02082733	0.03816410	-0.546	0.5854	Def. showed remorse
DEFSUR	1	0.00159314	0.02763843	0.058	0.9540	Def. surrendered w/in 24 hours
MULHDSHT	1	0.06040746	0.04407178	1.371	0.1709	Multiple head shots
OTHVPCX	1	-0.02896017	0.12176953	-0.238	0.8121	No. VPC conv. (besides hom./arm. rob./rape/kid.)
OTHVPC	1	-0.02449958	0.04283668	-0.572	0.5675	>1 VPC conv (besides hom./arm. rob./rape/kid.)
MURPRIOR	1	0.09575814	0.16972596	0.564	0.5728	No. of def. prior mur. convict.
MAJAGFCX	1	0.06362963	0.05398450	1.179	0.2389	No. of major agg. factors in case

Schedule 3, Model A (*cont.*)

Variable	DF	Parameter Estimate	Standard Error	Nominal[1] t for Ho: Parameter=0	Prob.>t	Variable Label
BADID	1	0.03410570	0.02786474	1.224	0.2213	Mistaken identity claimed
BDBLOOD	1	−0.01993938	0.03302877	−0.604	0.5462	Vic. and def. had history of bad blood
COPDIDIT	1	0.02160362	0.04271725	0.506	0.6132	Coperp. caused the death
COPHURTD	1	0.12955245	0.14002100	0.925	0.3551	Def. phys. injured by police
CPLESSEN	1	0.08359035	0.03408959	2.452	0.0144	Coperp. received a lesser sentence
CPLESSSN	1	0.03056500	0.04918561	0.621	0.5345	Coperp. w/life or less earlier
DABSENT	1	0.00664702	0.07862430	0.085	0.9326	Def. not at scene
DBADFACT	1	0.15569239	0.07096338	2.194	0.0285	Mistake of fact claimed
DCOERCED	1	0.27861443	0.09422828	2.957	0.0032	Coercion used on def.
DDRINK	1	−0.00252653	0.02340298	−0.108	0.9141	Def. used alcohol, drug immed. prior
DEFADMIT	1	−0.06564116	0.03671684	−1.788	0.0742	Def. admit. guilt & no defense asserted
DEFAGE	1	−0.00172868	0.00149674	−1.155	0.2485	Def. age at time of crime
DEFCHILD	1	0.00335856	0.07832991	0.043	0.9658	Def. juvenile or student
DEPRIVED	1	0.04314963	0.08387203	0.514	0.6071	Def. history of physical or econ. depriv.
DISKID	1	−0.02144875	0.26484188	−0.081	0.9355	Reasonable discipline of minor by parent
DNOINT	1	0.06904647	0.15655395	0.441	0.6593	Def. unaware of intent to use force
DNOINTNT	1	−0.01042785	0.02823214	−0.369	0.7120	Lack of intent to kill
DNOVIOL	1	0.04757397	0.11978725	0.397	0.6914	Def. committed no violence
DPROPDEF	1	−0.02537424	0.13760517	−0.184	0.8537	Defense of home, dwelling, or property
DRGHIS	1	−0.03208113	0.02428309	−1.321	0.1868	History of drug or alcohol abuse
DRUGDIS	1	0.00536482	0.03227718	0.166	0.8680	Dispute under influence of drugs, alcohol
DVIOLOTH	1	−0.05239485	0.15705857	−0.334	0.7388	Def. only violence was against others
FAMDIS	1	0.06055164	0.03659904	1.654	0.0984	Family dispute other than spouse, ex-spouse
GUNSTRUG	1	0.02927155	0.05434801	0.539	0.5903	Gun fired during struggle for gun

HATE	1	-0.03825159	0.03455557	-1.107	0.2687	Hate motive
INSANDEF	1	0.20463863	0.04981430	4.108	0.0001	Insanity or delusional compulsion
JEALOUS	1	-0.05181098	0.03436617	-1.508	0.1321	Jealousy motive
JOINTKIL	1	-0.07911921	0.04963662	-1.594	0.1113	Def. only an accomplice in killing
MITCIR	1	-0.03221876	0.02908912	-1.108	0.2684	Mitigating factors involved
MITCIRX	1	0.00842792	0.01288321	0.654	0.5132	No. mitigating factors involved
MITDFFN	1	-0.11074666	0.05485836	-2.019	0.0439	Def. retired, student, juvenile, housekeeper
MITMOTVE	1	-0.03371934	0.04678676	-0.721	0.4713	Def. motive hate, revenge, jealousy, rage
MONDIS	1	0.00204036	0.02702065	0.076	0.9398	Dispute over mon. or prop. between vic., def.
NOSPAGCR	1	0.03342399	0.02898320	1.153	0.2492	No special agg. cir.
PANIC	1	0.14417498	0.04661540	3.093	0.0021	Def. panic in course of burglary
PHYILL	1	0.01123067	0.03212513	0.350	0.7267	Def. had history of physical illness
RAGE	1	0.03104910	0.04524562	0.686	0.4928	Rage motive
REVENGE	1	-0.01373751	0.02758144	-0.498	0.6186	Revenge motive
SHOOTOUT	1	0.01249758	0.06509832	0.192	0.8478	Shootout
TRIANGLE	1	0.06544600	0.04026060	1.626	0.1044	Lover's triangle
DSELFDEF	1	-0.03201896	0.02325909	-1.377	0.1690	Defense of self or others
NOCONDUC	1	-0.05488019	0.20614900	-0.266	0.7901	Def. had impaired mental capacity
BLVICMOD	1	-0.02709064	0.02692052	-1.006	0.3146	Family, lover, liquor, barroom quarrel
VABUSEAR	1	-0.02046989	0.06543369	-0.313	0.7545	Vic. verbally abused def. earlier
VABUSEF	1	0.08337498	0.13225903	0.630	0.5286	Vic. verbal abuse friend of def.
VABUSFRD	1	0.00057524	0.12201212	0.005	0.9962	Vic. prov. def. by abuse. person def. care for
VACCUSED	1	-0.02594853	0.03760370	-0.690	0.4904	Vic. accused def. of misconduct
VASLEEP	1	0.13830136	0.07644290	1.809	0.0708	Vic. asleep or just awakened
VASSAULD	1	0.09567572	0.07063253	1.355	0.1760	Vic. assaulted def.
VASSAULT	1	-0.12578809	0.12187767	-1.032	0.3024	Vic. assaulted person def. cared about
VASSDEAR	1	0.00608072	0.04332375	0.140	0.8884	Vic. assaulted def. earlier
VASTFEAR	1	-0.04369621	0.11100809	-0.394	0.6940	Vic. verb. threat. person def. cared for
VBED	1	0.19461570	0.10497686	1.854	0.0641	Vic. bedridden/handicapped
VCOPERP	1	0.06713303	0.25392610	0.264	0.7916	Vic. was a coperp.
VDEFENLS	1	0.01157080	0.10247574	0.113	0.9101	Vic. defenseless due to youth

Schedule 3, Model A (*cont.*)

Variable	DF	Parameter Estimate	Standard Error	Nominal[1] t for Ho: Parameter = 0	Prob. >t	Variable Label
VDEFOLD	1	0.11575364	0.06572715	1.761	0.0786	Vic. defenseless due to advanced age
VICVERB	1	0.00428816	0.03540483	0.121	0.9936	Vic. verb. provok. def. by accus., abus.
VINJDEAR	1	0.01467182	0.06088190	0.241	0.8096	Vic. physically injured def. earlier
VINJFEAR	1	0.04920416	0.13771588	0.357	0.7210	Vic. prior injur. person def. care for
VINJURD	1	0.02313554	0.06402066	0.361	0.7179	Vic. physically injured def.
VINJURF	1	0.24029521	0.11698904	2.054	0.0403	Vic. injured person def. cared about
VPREG	1	0.21783920	0.10745807	2.027	0.0430	Vic. pregnant
VSMALL	1	0.11243043	0.05702527	1.972	0.0490	Vic. defnsls due to size diff., no. of def.
VSUICIDE	1	0.15587488	0.12848820	1.213	0.2254	Suicide by vic. claimed
VTHEAEAR	1	0.04947666	0.05885099	0.841	0.4008	Vic. threatened def. earlier
VTHREAT	1	-0.09687595	0.13800093	-0.702	0.4829	Vic. threatened person def. cared about
VTHREATD	1	0.05323704	0.04791356	1.111	0.2669	Vic. verbally threatened def.
VTRTFEAR	1	0.07806247	0.15632676	0.499	0.6177	Vic. verb. threat. person def. cared for
VWEAK	1	0.02962186	0.06170964	0.480	0.6313	Vic. weak or frail
STRANGER	1	0.02955185	0.02544706	1.161	0.2459	Vic. a stranger
FELMUR	1	-0.09953023	0.06624805	-1.502	0.1334	Def. involve in felony at time of killing
DISFIGHT	1	-0.02863956	0.03110081	-0.921	0.3574	Homicide arose from a dispute, fight
DEADWEP	1	0.02430502	0.04367736	0.556	0.5781	Malice/deadly weapon w/o mitigation
VDEFENS	1	-0.05266608	0.06601242	-0.876	0.3812	Malice/vic. defenseless
NOVPROV	1	0.06737556	0.05210048	1.293	0.1963	Malice/no vic. provocation
VIOLENCE	1	-0.03269385	0.02705943	-1.208	0.2273	Malice/violence
DTHINK	1	-0.07264396	0.03656007	-1.987	0.0473	Malice/deliberation
PROVPASS	1	-0.06330891	0.07267726	-0.871	0.3840	Provocation and sudden passion
FEARVWEP	1	0.01630237	0.06469249	0.252	0.8011	Def. fear/v. weapon

Variable		Coefficient	Std. Error	t	p	Description
SPOUSESK	1	0.02633554	0.03211559	0.820	0.4125	Dispute between spouses or ex-spouses
DSTATVM	1	0.03575725	0.02074490	1.724	0.0852	Def. statemnt support vol. manslaughter
DOUTSTAT	1	0.00865601	0.02939870	0.294	0.7685	Def. from out of state
FEMDEF	1	-0.00111976	0.02704050	-0.041	0.9670	Def. a female
COPERHUT	1	-0.06608021	0.10306779	-0.641	0.5216	Coperp. injure people beyond vic.
COPERTES	1	0.01713711	0.04433874	0.387	0.6992	Coperp. testified against def.
EYEWITID	1	-0.03484940	0.02306550	-1.511	0.1312	Def. seen in act by one who knew him
GOODWIT	1	0.04657899	0.01937953	2.404	0.0165	Prim. wit. pol. off., civil. w/no cred. prob.
IDDEFGUN	1	0.01534352	0.02632045	0.583	0.5601	ID wit. of def. w/weap. near scene of crime
IDWITCOP	1	-0.08724656	0.03524675	-2.475	0.0135	ID wit. of coperp. commit crime near scene
WITCOROB	1	-0.01690894	0.02084394	-0.811	0.4175	Primary wit. was corroborated
CLEARID	1	0.02871501	0.02716702	1.057	0.2908	Ident. of def. not in doubt as killer
LSTATDEF	1	-0.00383835	0.01730616	-0.222	0.8245	Low SES def.
COPERP	1	0.17438266	0.06469477	2.695	0.0072	One or more coperps. involved
COPERPX	1	-0.04604789	0.01595292	-2.886	0.0040	No. of coperps.
CPSHOOT5	1	0.04843561	0.10062081	0.481	0.6304	Coperp. fired 5 or more shots
CPMORSEN	1	-0.12947274	0.05397509	-2.399	0.0167	Def's coperp. received a higher sentence
DAGEARST	1	0.00810693	0.02751282	0.295	0.7683	Def. 16 or younger at 1st felony arrest
DARREST	1	-0.00174220	0.00297633	-0.585	0.5585	No. of prior arrests
DCONVICT	1	-0.04805977	0.03470445	-1.385	0.1665	Def. was convic., felony or misdem.
DCONVICX	1	0.00778475	0.01668679	0.467	0.6410	No. of convic., felony & misdemeanors
DEHURT	1	-0.01669712	0.04748895	-0.352	0.7252	Def. injured 1 or more other people
DEFLED	1	0.00402283	0.01947517	0.207	0.8364	Def. left the scene of crime
DETAIN	1	0.01951475	0.03964001	0.492	0.6226	Def. had 1 or more detainers
DFSTCRRC	1	0.00301272	0.00152240	1.979	0.0482	Def. age at first felony arrest (recode)
DKILLER	1	-0.09528188	0.06070705	-1.570	0.1169	Def. killed or participated in killing
DPRIKILL	1	0.01902355	0.14203192	0.134	0.8935	Def. had prior murder or mansltr convic.
DRECPRIS	1	-0.01280179	0.03536063	-0.362	0.7174	Def. released from prison w/in last year
DROWN	1	0.23267980	0.11678701	1.992	0.0467	Vic. was drowned
DSHOOT5	1	0.00070630	0.03238302	0.022	0.9826	Def. fired five or more shots
DVIOLV	1	-0.00381180	0.10313068	-0.037	0.9705	Def. not kill but did violence to vic.

Schedule 3, Model A *(cont.)*

Variable	DF	Parameter Estimate	Standard Error	Nominal[1]		Variable Label
				t for Ho: Parameter = 0	Prob. >t	
FELARST	1	0.05697584	0.0284695 7	2.001	0.0457	Def. had felony arrest
FELARX	1	-0.00556174	0.00808897	-0.688	0.4919	No. of def. felony arrests
FEMVIC	1	0.01330883	0.02239554	0.594	0.5525	Female vic.
GUN	1	0.03139088	0.03366973	0.932	0.3515	Vic. killed with gun
INSMOT	1	0.21032401	0.07789022	2.700	0.0071	Def. motive to collect insurance
KIDNAP	1	0.10335734	0.05914380	1.748	0.0809	Kidnapping involved
MENTORT	1	0.05575435	0.08244656	0.676	0.4991	Mental torture
MINAGFCX	1	0.02547123	0.01975548	1.289	0.1977	No. of minor agg. factors in case
MISARST	1	-0.02208985	0.02874131	-0.769	0.4424	Def. had one or more misdem. arrests
MISARSTX	1	-0.00062500	0.00200562	-0.312	0.7554	No. of misdemeanor arrests
MISDCONV	1	0.01777334	0.03157652	0.563	0.5737	Record of 1 or more misdemeanor convict.
MULSH	1	0.09594573	0.04066324	2.360	0.0185	Multiple gunshots
MULSTAB	1	0.11152060	0.05007905	2.227	0.0262	Multiple stabbing
NOCLOTH	1	0.02124360	0.04271614	0.497	0.6191	Vic. without clothes when killed
NONPROPC	1	0.07934841	0.05810087	1.366	0.1724	Nonproperty-related contemp. crime
NOREMORE	1	-0.01365219	0.04128902	-0.331	0.7410	Def. showed no remorse for homocide
NOVICMIT	1	-0.01865888	0.03038444	-0.614	0.5393	No. vic.-related mitigating cir.
NOVIOLCR	1	-0.08238330	0.03934051	-2.094	0.0366	Nonviol. cont. crime (besides burg./vice)
PLANCOF	1	-0.04013059	0.04294329	-0.935	0.3503	Contemp. offense planned more than 5 min.
PRIFELX	1	0.00922323	0.00955548	0.961	0.3367	Number of prior felony convictions
RAPE	1	0.02739283	0.06930233	0.395	0.6928	Rape involved
RECCRIM	1	-0.01639030	0.01962409	-0.835	0.4039	Recent nonviolent crime by def.
RECVCRIM	1	-0.02336028	0.02622038	-0.891	0.3732	Def. arrest. for viol. crime w/2 yrs homicide
RECVPCX	1	-0.03139166	0.02690929	-1.167	0.2437	No. prior convict. for viol. pers. crimes

SLODIE	1	0.05483626	0.02548924	2.151	0.0318	Slow death
STRANGLE	1	0.09059848	0.08762962	1.034	0.3015	Vic. strangled
TORTURE	1	0.15671138	0.08772941	1.786	0.0744	Vic. tortured physically
TWOVIC	1	0.06561742	0.06057214	1.083	0.2790	Def. killed two or more people
VIOLCVX	1	0.08141118	0.12153706	0.670	0.5032	No. of VPC conv. beyond hom./arm. rob./rape/kid.
YTHDETX	1	-0.00819695	0.02112258	-0.388	0.6981	No. times def. in yth detention center
VPCARBR	1	0.07997686	0.04639819	1.724	0.0852	One or more convictions: VPC/burg./arson
VPCARBRX	1	-0.00350406	0.01111259	-0.315	0.7526	No. convictions: VPC, burg/arson 1st deg.
CONVICTX	1	-0.00095479	0.00329375	-0.290	0.7720	No. of prior convic. for felonies, mis.
CONVICT	1	-0.13398098	0.05501612	-2.435	0.0151	Def. had prior convict, felony or mis.
DEFSURLI	1	0.03242639	0.05722619	0.567	0.5711	Def. surrend. more than 24 hr aft. crime
EMOTION	1	0.00522127	0.03977404	0.131	0.8956	Crime of anger
INVOLMAN	1	0.00946687	0.07176699	0.132	0.8951	Def. claimed invol. mans.
MENTILL	1	-0.01894994	0.02653571	-0.714	0.4754	Def. had history of mental illness
NOARREST	1	0.00655492	0.03548295	0.185	0.8535	No prior arrest or convictions
NOCONVIC	1	-0.21962448	0.05126052	-4.284	0.0001	No prior convictions
NOKILL	1	-0.11758763	0.08861368	-1.327	0.1849	Def. not triggerman
NOPRISON	1	-0.18213103	0.18040695	-1.010	0.3130	Def. never incarcerated
VICARMED	1	-0.05446832	0.05562666	-0.979	0.3278	Vic. was armed
VICCLOSE	1	-0.02507228	0.02328142	-1.077	0.2818	Vic. family friend, intimate
VOLMANS	1	0.00056410	0.02044429	0.028	0.9780	Def. claimed vol. mans.
DEFFEAR	1	-0.05702361	0.05446475	-1.047	0.2954	Vic. aroused def. fear
DEFINTOX	1	0.03821559	0.02794114	1.368	0.1718	Def. substant. affected by alcohol, drugs
DNOPLCOF	1	0.46105137	0.25730137	1.792	0.0735	No plan or def. ignt. of plan for cont. off.
DNOTINCO	1	-0.07885947	0.09284832	-0.849	0.3960	Def. not involved in contempt off.
ADDCRIME	1	-0.04670040	0.03714908	-1.257	0.2091	Def. commit or alleg. commit add. crime
BDGAG	1	-0.06359765	0.05296222	-1.201	0.2302	Vic. bound or gagged
CONCELBD	1	-0.01241826	0.03140286	-0.395	0.6926	Def. tried to dispose of or conceal body
DLEADER	1	0.05773082	0.04617247	1.250	0.2116	Def. prime mover plan homicide, contemp. off.
DPLEAS	1	0.14934706	0.08242322	1.812	0.0704	Def. expressed pleasure with the killing
DRESIST	1	-0.02001390	0.02537885	-0.789	0.4306	Def. resisted arrest

Schedule 3, Model A (*cont.*)

Variable	DF	Parameter Estimate	Standard Error	Nominal[1]		Variable Label
				t for Ho: Parameter = 0	Prob. >t	
HARMOTH	1	0.04830633	0.04686289	1.031	0.3030	Bodily harm to other than vic.
NUDE	1	0.18151464	0.06573710	2.761	0.0059	Vic. forced to disrobe
PERVER	1	−0.10039222	0.13075397	−0.768	0.4428	Sex perversion other than rape
PREMEDK	1	0.05080550	0.04147608	1.225	0.2210	Killing planned more than 5 minutes
PRISON	1	−0.17806037	0.18045132	−0.987	0.3241	Def. has been incarcer. after a convict.
PRISONX	1	0.03116893	0.01755911	1.775	0.0763	No. of def. felony prison terms
RESBKIN	1	−0.07507655	0.04855211	−1.546	0.1224	Def. broke into victim's residence
THROAT	1	−0.06260016	0.07831864	−0.799	0.4244	Slashed throat of vic.
UNNECERY	1	−0.04878269	0.04719573	−1.034	0.3016	Kill unnec. to carry out contemp. offense
VFAMPRES	1	0.04052795	0.02105321	1.925	0.0546	Vic. killed in pres. of fam./close friends
VICPLEAD	1	−0.04355732	0.14392931	−0.303	0.7623	Vic. pleaded for life
MONTHJL	1	−0.00029954	0.00036881	−0.812	0.4169	Months def. prior incarcerated
EXECUT	1	0.01574343	0.06378343	0.247	0.8051	Execution-style killing
RECORD	1	−0.11193428	0.06068478	−1.845	0.0655	Def. had been convicted of a crime
CIRCEVID	1	−0.01231026	0.08586228	−0.143	0.8860	No wit., no pretrial ID, no coperp. statement

CPSTATEM	1	0.04242059	0.03749764	1.131	0.2583	Coperp. statement implicate def. in homicide
DCONFESS	1	0.03915920	0.02154947	1.817	0.0696	Def. admitted homicide—with no defense
IDWITDEF	1	-0.01144650	0.04636104	-0.247	0.8051	ID wit. def. commit crime or near scene
INCMDRPT	1	0.08319024	0.01894505	4.391	0.0001	Med. report link death to def. actions
INCRREMK	1	0.00687834	0.01834654	0.375	0.7078	Wit. heard incrim. remark by def. or coperp.
POLGUILT	1	-0.04692738	0.03138287	-1.495	0.1352	Police report indicated clear guilt
POLWIT	1	0.01240804	0.05838154	0.213	0.8317	Police wit. def. commit crime, near scene
PREPWITN	1	-0.01556372	0.02101977	-0.740	0.4593	One or more wit. re. preparation
PRETRID	1	0.00741897	0.02239329	0.331	0.7405	There was a pretrial ID of def.
SCIEVID	1	0.06867405	0.02131105	3.222	0.0013	Science evid. other than weapon or medical
WEAPON	1	0.00974531	0.01698746	0.574	0.5664	Murder weapon found, link def. to homicide
IDWIT	1	-0.01168843	0.04719675	-0.248	0.8045	An ID witness of def. or coperp.
TWOWITD	1	0.03357250	0.02215769	1.515	0.1301	2 or more wit. def. commit crime, nearby
ARMROB	1	0.15497249	0.05346351	2.899	0.0039	Armed robbery involved
AVENGE	1	0.27964435	0.16989524	1.646	0.1002	Motive to avenge role by jud. off., DA, lawyer
BEAT	1	0.17741891	0.10610086	1.107	0.2688	Brutal clubbing or stomping

1. Nominal inferential statistics (standard error, t, and probability) were computed by a weighted least-squares program. Safe inferential statistics could not be computed because of the large number of independent variables.

Schedule 4—CSS

Outcome variable: Death sentence imposed among all cases (DSENTALL).
Independent variables: The 39-variable core model and the race of defendant and victim.

Model A: Weighted Logistic Regression

2484 Weighted observations
2356 DSENTALL = 0
128 DSENTALL = 1
Model chi-square¹ = 570.332 with 41 D.F.
R = .696²

Variable	Safe³				Nominal⁴			Variable Label
	Logistic Regression Coefficient	Standard Error	t^5	p^6	Standard Error	t^5	p^6	
CONST	−6.1497	0.6055	−10.16	0.000	0.5785	−10.630	0.000	Intercept
BLACKD	−0.0638	0.4104	−0.16	0.876	0.3428	−0.186	0.852	Def. was black
WHVICRC	1.4473	0.4801	3.01	0.003	0.4047	3.576	0.000	One or more white victims (recode)
ARMROB	1.4355	0.5938	2.42	0.016	0.5299	2.709	0.007	Armed robbery involved
AVENGE	3.3650	2.9462	1.14	0.253	1.7550	1.917	0.055	Motive to avenge role by jud. off., DA, lawyer
BLVICMOD	−0.6128	0.4264	−1.44	0.151	0.4226	−1.450	0.147	Family, lover, liquor, barroom quarrel
COPERP	0.2424	0.4116	0.59	0.556	0.3893	0.623	0.534	One or more coperpetrators involved
CPLESSEN	0.7851	0.4626	1.70	0.090	0.4032	1.947	0.052	Coperp. received a lesser sentence
DEFADMIT	−1.2747	0.8285	−1.54	0.124	0.6794	−1.876	0.061	Def. admit guilt and no defense asserted
DLEADER	0.5503	0.5625	0.98	0.328	0.4648	1.184	0.236	Def. prime mover in plan. homicide or contemp off.
DRGHIS	−1.0111	0.3778	−2.68	0.007	0.3404	−2.970	0.003	History of drug or alcohol abuse
DROWN	0.9625	0.8253	1.17	0.244	0.7837	1.228	0.219	Vic. was drowned
FEMDEF	0.2812	0.7323	0.38	0.701	0.6552	0.429	0.668	Def. a female

Variable								Description
HATE	−0.3426	0.8733	−0.39	0.695	0.7130	−0.480	0.631	Hate motive
INSMOT	3.0106	1.1911	2.53	0.011	0.8701	3.460	0.001	Def. motive to collect insurance
JEALOUS	−0.7452	1.1912	−0.63	0.532	0.6309	−0.689	0.491	Jealousy motive
KIDNAP	1.0601	0.7661	1.38	0.166	1.0810	1.680	0.093	Kidnapping involved
LDFB1	1.3985	0.5352	2.61	0.009	0.5037	2.776	0.005	Prior rec. of mur., arm. rob., rape, kid.
LDFB3	0.1400	0.4214	0.33	0.740	0.4353	0.322	0.748	Def. caused death risk in pub. place to ≥2
LDFB4	−0.2249	0.5794	−0.39	0.698	0.5259	−0.428	0.669	Murder for money/value for self/other
LDFB6	1.7724	1.0292	1.72	0.085	0.8122	2.182	0.029	Murder for hire
LDFB8	0.5163	0.9339	0.55	0.580	0.7684	0.672	0.502	Vic. police/corrections/fire on duty
LDFB9	2.0401	0.6653	3.07	0.002	0.6046	3.374	0.001	Def. prisoner or escapee
LDFB10	0.4118	0.4165	0.99	0.323	0.3544	1.162	0.245	Kill to avoid, stop arrest of self, other
LDFB7D	0.5981	0.4272	1.40	0.162	0.4016	1.489	0.136	Rape/arm. rob./kid. + sil. wit./exec./vic. pleaded
MENTORT	2.2735	0.8765	2.59	0.009	0.7099	3.203	0.001	Mental torture
MITDFFN	−0.6119	1.3249	−0.46	0.644	1.0940	−0.559	0.576	Def. retired, student, juvenile, housekeeper
MULSH	0.7885	0.3813	2.07	0.039	0.3325	2.371	0.018	Multiple gunshots
MULSTAB	1.5408	0.5007	3.08	0.002	0.4268	3.610	0.000	Multiple stabbing
MURPRIOR	1.6628	1.5202	1.09	0.274	1.2210	1.362	0.173	Num. of prior mur. convict def.
NOKILL	−2.7504	0.7716	−3.56	0.000	0.6269	−4.387	0.000	Def. not triggerman
NONPROPC	0.3505	0.7600	0.46	0.645	0.6166	0.568	0.570	Nonproperty-related contemp. crime
PRISONX	0.0814	0.1917	0.42	0.671	0.1522	0.535	0.593	No. of def. felony prison terms
RAPE	2.5475	0.7782	3.27	0.001	0.6909	3.687	0.000	Rape involved
SMYOUTH	−0.8758	0.7242	−1.21	0.226	0.6575	−1.332	0.183	Def. under 17 years of age
STRANGER	1.0345	0.4250	2.43	0.015	0.3307	3.128	0.002	Vic. a stranger
TORTURE	3.3126	1.1171	2.97	0.003	0.8638	3.835	0.000	Vic. tortured physically
TWOVIC	2.0693	0.7288	2.84	0.005	0.5377	3.848	0.000	Def. killed two or more people
VBED	1.0369	1.0580	0.98	0.327	0.9527	1.088	0.276	Vic. bedridden/handicapped
VICCHILD	1.5558	0.7334	2.12	0.034	0.6733	2.311	0.021	Vic. was 12 or younger
VPCARBR	0.3022	0.4792	0.63	0.528	0.3776	0.800	0.424	One or more convictions: VPC/burg./arson
VWEAK	1.1261	0.8645	1.30	0.193	0.7329	1.536	0.124	Vic. weak or frail

Model B: Weighted Least Squares

Source	DF	Sum of Squares	Mean Square	F Value	Prob>F
Model	41	45.92065864	1.12001666	15.194	0.0001
Error	1024	75.48337256	0.07371423		
C Total	1065	121.40403			

Root MSE	0.2715036	R-Square	0.3782
Dep Mean	0.05153101	Adj R-Sq	0.3534

Variable	Regression Coefficient	Safe[3] Standard Error	t^5	p^6	Nominal[4] Standard Error	t^5	p^6	Variable Label
CONST	0.0458	0.0248	1.85	0.065	0.0230	1.989	0.047	Intercept
BLACKD	0.0754	0.0244	3.09	0.002	0.0196	3.848	0.000	Def. was black
WHVICRC	0.0824	0.0244	3.38	0.001	0.0198	4.169	0.000	One or more white victims (recode)
ARMROB	0.4255	0.0490	8.69	0.000	0.0345	12.330	0.000	Armed robbery involved
AVENGE	−0.0009	0.4559	0.00	0.998	0.1688	−0.005	0.996	Motive to avenge role by jud. off., DA, lawyer
BLVICMOD	−0.0038	0.0084	−0.46	0.648	0.0127	−0.302	0.763	Family, lover, liquor, barroom quarrel
COPERP	0.0194	0.0241	0.80	0.421	0.0216	0.899	0.369	One or more coperpetrators involved
CPLESSEN	−0.0745	0.0350	−2.13	0.033	0.0255	−2.924	0.003	Coperp. received a lesser sentence
DEFADMIT	0.0734	0.0212	3.47	0.001	0.0240	3.053	0.002	Def. admit guilt and no defense asserted
DLEADER	−0.0211	0.0681	−0.31	0.757	0.0378	−0.556	0.578	Def. prime mover plan. homicide or contemp off.
DRGHIS	0.1362	0.0095	14.28	0.000	0.0120	11.385	0.000	History of drug or alcohol abuse
DROWN	0.0014	0.1395	0.01	0.992	0.0683	0.021	0.983	Vic. was drowned
FEMDEF	−0.0123	0.0096	−1.29	0.197	0.0169	−0.729	0.466	Def. a female
HATE	0.2291	0.0119	19.32	0.000	0.0185	12.399	0.000	Hate motive
INSMOT	−0.0071	0.1036	−0.07	0.946	0.0642	−0.110	0.912	Def. motive to collect insurance
JEALOUS	0.1789	0.0085	20.96	0.000	0.0177	10.126	0.000	Jealousy motive
KIDNAP	0.0761	0.0697	1.09	0.275	0.0421	1.810	0.070	Kidnapping involved
LDFB1	−0.0075	0.0449	−0.17	0.866	0.0328	−0.230	0.818	Prior rec. of mur., arm. rob., rape, kid.

Variable							Description
LDFB3	-0.0343	0.0119	-2.87	0.004	0.0161	-2.130	0.033	Def. caused death risk in pub. place to ≥2
LDFB4	0.0854	0.0405	2.11	0.035	0.0316	2.702	0.007	Murder for money/value for self/other
LDFB6	0.0302	0.0846	0.36	0.721	0.0559	0.540	0.589	Murder for hire
LDFB8	0.1062	0.0849	1.25	0.211	0.0588	1.806	0.071	Vic. police/corrections/fire on duty
LDFB9	0.0916	0.0716	1.28	0.201	0.0449	2.041	0.041	Def. prisoner or escapee
LDFB10	0.0657	0.0477	1.34	0.181	0.0287	2.216	0.027	Kill to avoid, stop arrest of self, other
LDFB7D	0.1631	0.0442	3.69	0.000	0.0294	5.556	0.000	Rape/arm. rob./kid. + sil. wit./exec./vic. pleaded
MENTORT	-0.0126	0.0832	-0.15	0.880	0.0497	-0.253	0.801	Mental torture
MITDFFN	0.0217	0.0224	0.97	0.333	0.0328	0.661	0.509	Def. retired, student, juvenile, housekeeper
MULSH	0.0734	0.0107	6.89	0.000	0.0132	5.550	0.000	Multiple gunshots
MULSTAB	0.0377	0.0251	1.50	0.133	0.0226	1.666	0.096	Multiple stabbing
MURPRIOR	-0.1252	0.0800	-1.57	0.117	0.0694	-1.805	0.071	Num. of prior mur. convict. def.
NOKILL	0.0094	0.0317	0.30	0.768	0.0269	0.348	0.728	Def. not triggerman
NONPROPC	0.0041	0.0419	0.10	0.921	0.0343	0.121	0.904	Nonproperty-related contemp. crime
PRISONX	0.1649	0.0079	20.92	0.000	0.0077	21.417	0.000	No. of def. felony prison terms
RAPE	-0.0405	0.0790	-0.51	0.608	0.0458	-0.883	0.377	Rape involved
SMYOUTH	0.0398	0.0286	1.39	0.165	0.0274	1.452	0.147	Def. under 17 years of age
STRANGER	0.3036	0.0221	13.76	0.000	0.0178	17.045	0.000	Vic. a stranger
TORTURE	0.1254	0.0977	1.28	0.199	0.0588	2.131	0.033	Vic. tortured physically
TWOVIC	0.1326	0.0570	2.32	0.020	0.0361	3.675	0.000	Def. killed two or more people
VBED	0.0559	0.1879	0.30	0.766	0.0946	0.591	0.555	Vic. bedridden/handicapped
VICCHILD	0.0054	0.0492	0.11	0.912	0.0405	0.134	0.894	Vic. was 12 or younger
VPCARBR	0.0564	0.0117	4.83	0.000	0.0144	3.912	0.000	One or more convictions: VPC/burg./arson
VWEAK	-0.0572	0.0495	-1.16	0.248	0.0416	-1.376	0.169	Vic. weak or frail

1. See supra schedule 1, note 1.
2. See supra schedule 1, note 2.
3. See supra schedule 1, note 3. When the variable for victim blue-collar or unskilled worker (VBLUSKL) is added to the logistic analysis, the partial regression coefficient for it is −1.29 (p = .18) and the coefficient for the race of victim is 1.40 (p = .001).
4. See supra schedule 1, note 4.
5. See supra schedule 1, note 5.
6. See supra schedule 1, note 6.

Schedule 5—CSS

Outcome variable: Death sentence imposed in cases indicted for murder (DPMURIDT).
Explanatory variables: Nonperverse statistically significant ($p \leq .10$) variables screened from the variable list in schedule 3 with linear-regression methods designed to explain which defendants indicted for murder received a death sentence, and the race of defendant and victim.

Model A: Weighted Logistic Regression

2342 Weighted observations
2214 DPMURIDT = 0
128 DPMURIDT = 1

Model chi-square[1] = 586.872 with 16 D.F.
R = .748[2]

Variable	Logistic Regression Coefficient	Safe[3]			Nominal[4]			Variable Label
		Standard Error	t[5]	p[6]	Standard Error	t[5]	p[6]	
CONST	-9.3017	0.8624	-10.79	0.000	0.6927	-13.428	0.000	
BLACKD	0.7585	0.4352	1.74	0.081	0.3428	2.213	0.027	Def. was black
WHVICRC	1.2770	0.4345	2.94	0.003	0.3803	3.358	0.001	One or more white victims (recode)
NOCONDUC	-5.5108	2.4282	-2.27	0.023	1.3310	-4.140	0.000	Def. had impaired mental capacity
NOKILL	-1.8542	0.5382	-3.45	0.001	0.5563	-3.333	0.001	Def. not triggerman
RACEMOT	1.4882	0.7628	1.95	0.051	0.8091	1.839	0.066	Racial hatred motive
AVENGE	1.8418	0.9403	1.96	0.050	1.3920	1.323	0.186	Motive to avenge role by jud. off., DA, lawyer
INSMOT	2.7977	0.6789	4.12	0.000	0.6327	4.422	0.000	Def. motive to collect insurance
KIDNAP	1.6536	0.4439	3.72	0.000	0.3756	4.403	0.000	Kidnapping involved
TORTURE	1.5253	0.7690	1.98	0.047	0.7776	1.962	0.050	Vic. tortured physically
DPLEAS	2.1471	0.7701	2.79	0.005	0.6873	3.124	0.002	Def. expressed pleasure with the killing
LDFB7EXP	0.7652	0.1269	6.03	0.000	0.1212	6.314	0.000	No. of statutory agg. fact. & B7 fact.
MAJAGFCX	0.2061	0.1864	1.11	0.269	0.1537	1.341	0.180	No. of major agg. factors in case
MINAGFCX	0.2393	0.1463	1.64	0.102	0.1366	1.752	0.080	No. of minor agg. factors in case
INSANDEF	2.0134	0.5859	3.44	0.001	0.4397	4.579	0.000	Insanity or delusional compulsion
DEFADMIT	-2.5557	0.8835	-2.89	0.004	0.6545	-3.905	0.000	Def. admit guilt and no defense asserted
EVIDINDX	0.4676	0.1117	4.19	0.000	0.0910	5.139	0.000	No. of major types of incrim. evid. v. def.

Model B: Weighted Least Squares

Source	DF	Sum of Squares	Mean Square	F Value	Prob>F
Model	16	48.16213147	3.01013322	41.242	0.0001
Error	988	72.8413740	0.07298735		
C Total	1014	121.00351			

Root MSE	0.2701617	R-Square	0.3980
Dep Mean	0.05466011	Adj R-Sq	0.3884

Variable	Regression Coefficient	Safe[3]			Nominal[4]			Variable Label
		Standard Error	t[5]	p[5]	Standard Error	t[5]	p[6]	
CONST	-0.1448	0.0281	-5.16	0.000	0.0228	-6.364	0.000	
BLACKD	0.0628	0.0246	2.55	0.011	0.0189	3.318	0.001	Def. was black
WHVICRC	0.0648	0.0233	2.78	0.005	0.0191	3.386	0.001	One or more white victims (recode)
NOCONDUC	-0.3914	1.2560	-0.31	0.755	0.1280	-3.059	0.002	Def. had impaired mental capacity
NOKILL	-0.1070	0.0232	-4.61	0.000	0.0236	-4.525	0.000	Def. not triggerman
RACEMOT	0.1167	0.0657	1.78	0.076	0.0489	2.384	0.017	Racial hatred motive
AVENGE	0.4124	0.3528	1.17	0.242	0.1572	2.623	0.009	Motive to avenge role by jud. off., DA, lawyer
INSMOT	0.1647	0.0822	2.00	0.045	0.0519	3.171	0.002	Def. motive to collect insurance
KIDNAP	0.1960	0.0636	3.08	0.002	0.0310	6.320	0.000	Kidnapping involved
TORTURE	0.1638	0.1049	1.56	0.118	0.0603	2.717	0.007	Vic. tortured physically
DPLEAS	0.2351	0.0716	3.28	0.001	0.0457	5.139	0.000	Def. expressed pleasure with the killing
LDFB7EXP	0.0287	0.0064	4.48	0.000	0.0057	5.071	0.000	Cnt. of statutory agg. fact. & B7 fact.
MAJAGFCX	0.0387	0.0131	2.96	0.003	0.0098	3.945	0.000	No. of major agg. factors in case
MINAGFCX	0.0173	0.0073	2.36	0.018	0.0069	2.491	0.013	No. of minor agg. factors in case
INSANDEF	0.1534	0.0925	1.66	0.097	0.0383	4.006	0.000	Insanity or delusional compulsion
DEFADMIT	0.0957	0.0251	-3.81	0.000	0.0249	-3.841	0.000	Def. admit guilt and no defense asserted
EVIDINDX	0.0135	0.0038	3.59	0.000	0.0038	3.586	0.000	No. of major types of incrim. evid. v. def.

1. See supra schedule 1, note 1.
2. See supra schedule 1, note 2.
3. See supra schedule 1, note 3.
4. See supra schedule 1, note 4.
5. See supra schedule 1, note 5.
6. See supra schedule 1, note 6.

Schedule 6—CSS

Outcome variable: Death sentence imposed in cases indicted for murder (DPMURIDT).

Explanatory variables: Nonperverse statistically significant ($p \leq .10$) variables screened from the variable list in schedule 3 with logistic-regression methods designed to explain which defendants indicted for murder received a death sentence, and the race of defendant and victim.

Model A: Weighted Logistic Regression

2342 Weighted observations

2214 DPMURIDT = 0

128 DPMURIDT = 1

Model chi-square[1] = 491.218 with 15 D.F.

R = .682[2]

Variable	Logistic Regression Coefficient	Safe[3]			Nominal[4]			Variable Label
		Standard Error	t[5]	p[6]	Standard Error	t[5]	p[6]	
CONST	−6.2697	0.5621	−11.15	0.000	0.5067	−12.374	0.000	
BLACKD	−0.1483	0.3582	−0.41	0.679	0.2929	−0.506	0.613	Def. was black
WHVICRC	1.1091	0.4087	2.71	0.007	0.3317	3.344	0.001	One or more white victims (recode)
DSHOOT5	1.0679	0.4298	2.48	0.013	0.3926	2.720	0.007	Def. fired five or more shots
MITMOTV	−0.8213	0.4153	−1.98	0.048	0.3362	−2.443	0.015	Def. motive hate, revenge, jealousy, rage
VRECORD	1.3162	0.7393	1.78	0.075	0.5837	2.255	0.024	Vic. had criminal record
DRGHIS	−0.6011	0.3378	−1.78	0.075	0.2830	−2.124	0.034	History of drug or alcohol abuse
DCOERCE	1.6544	0.8997	1.84	0.066	0.7826	2.114	0.035	Coercion used on def.
VICCHIL	1.9000	0.6236	3.05	0.002	0.5040	3.770	0.000	Vic. was 12 or younger
PRISONX	0.3671	0.1260	2.91	0.004	0.1111	3.305	0.001	No. of def. felony prison terms
EXECUT	0.7135	0.3197	2.23	0.026	0.2651	2.692	0.007	Execution-style killing
RACEMOT	2.4833	0.6263	3.97	0.000	0.6722	3.694	0.000	Racial hatred motive
NUDE	1.6102	0.4352	3.70	0.000	0.3257	4.944	0.000	Vic. forced to disrobe
LDFB7EX	0.7508	0.1068	7.03	0.000	0.0859	8.740	0.000	No. of statutory agg. fact. & B7 fact.
INSMOT	1.4539	0.6941	2.09	0.036	0.5420	2.682	0.007	Def. motive to collect insurance
PANIC	1.5118	0.5611	2.69	0.007	0.4701	3.216	0.001	Def. panic in course of burglary

Model B: Weighted Least Squares

Source	DF	Sum of Squares	Mean Square	F Value	Prob>F
Model	15	35.42781942	2.36185463	27.572	0.0001
Error	999	85.57568608	0.08566135		
C Total	1014	121.00351			

Root MSE 0.2926796 R-Square 0.2928
Dep Mean 0.05466011 Adj R-Sq 0.2822

Variable	Regression Coefficient	Safe[3]			Nominal[4]			Variable Label
		Standard Error	t[5]	p[6]	Standard Error	t[5]	p[6]	
CONST	-0.0875	0.0303	-2.89	0.004	0.0260	-3.364	0.001	
BLACKD	0.0466	0.0267	1.75	0.081	0.0205	2.272	0.023	Def. was black
WHVICRC	0.0644	0.0268	2.40	0.017	0.0206	3.127	0.002	One or more white victims (recode)
DSHOOT5	0.0210	0.0256	0.82	0.412	0.0256	0.822	0.411	Def. fired five or more shots
MITMOTV	-0.0011	0.0128	-0.08	0.934	0.0150	-0.070	0.944	Def. motive hate, revenge, jealousy, rage
VRECORD	0.0224	0.0324	0.69	0.490	0.0351	0.637	0.524	Vic. had criminal record
DRGHIS	-0.0198	0.0106	-1.87	0.061	0.0129	-1.543	0.123	History of drug or alcohol abuse
DCOERCE	0.3486	0.2514	1.39	0.166	0.0952	3.662	0.000	Coercion used on def.
VICCHIL	0.1203	0.0504	2.39	0.017	0.0394	3.050	0.002	Vic. was 12 or younger
PRISONX	0.0200	0.0085	2.37	0.018	0.0075	2.658	0.008	No. of def. felony prison terms
EXECUT	0.0764	0.0318	2.40	0.016	0.0219	3.494	0.000	Execution-style killing
RACEMOT	0.1544	0.0757	2.04	0.041	0.0527	2.930	0.003	Racial hatred motive
NUDE	0.2060	0.0737	2.80	0.005	0.0337	6.112	0.000	Vic. forced to disrobe
LDFB7EX	0.0393	0.0069	5.70	0.000	0.0051	7.745	0.000	No. of statutory agg. fact. & B7 fact.
INSMOT	0.1136	0.0975	1.17	0.244	0.0560	2.027	0.043	Def. motive to collect insurance
PANIC	0.0626	0.0581	1.08	0.282	0.0378	1.658	0.097	Def. panic in course of burglary

1. See *supra* schedule 1, note 1.   3. See *supra* schedule 1, note 3.   5. See *supra* schedule 1, note 5.
2. See *supra* schedule 1, note 2.   4. See *supra* schedule 1, note 4.   6. See *supra* schedule 1, note 6.

Schedule 7—CSS

Outcome variable: Death sentence imposed in cases indicted for murder (DPMURIDT).

Explanatory variables: Variables from the variable list in schedule 3 that show a statistically significant relationship ($p \leq .10$) to the death-sentencing outcome in a linear stepwise-regression analysis of defendants indicted for murder, and the race of defendant and victim.

Model A: Weighted Logistic Regression

2342 Weighted observations
2214 DPMURIDT = 0
128 DPMURIDT = 1
Model chi-square[1] = 733.668 with 46 D.F.
R = .805[2]

Variable	Logistic Regression Coefficient	Safe[3] Standard Error	t[5]	p[6]	Nominal[4] Standard Error	t[5]	p[6]	Variable Label
CONST	-8.3680	1.8385	-4.55	0.000	1.401	-5.973	0.000	
BLACKD	1.4283	0.5316	2.69	0.007	0.508	2.814	0.005	Def. was black
WHVICRC	2.0762	0.5369	3.87	0.000	0.521	3.987	0.000	One or more white victims (recode)
LDFB1	2.2213	0.8518	2.61	0.009	0.666	3.333	0.001	Prior rec. of mur., arm. rob., rape, kid.
LDFB10	3.8262	0.9388	4.08	0.000	1.118	3.422	0.001	Kill to avoid, stop arrest of self, other
LDFB7D	0.9904	0.6237	1.59	0.112	0.498	1.987	0.047	Rape/arm. rob/kid. + sil. wit./exec/vic. pleaded
RACEMOT	0.6121	0.8876	0.69	0.490	0.903	0.678	0.498	Racial hatred motive
VDEFNSLS	-0.4854	0.6945	-0.70	0.485	0.551	-0.881	0.378	Vic. pregnant, disabled, or helpless
VWITNESS	-2.9171	1.0448	-2.79	0.005	1.179	-2.474	0.013	Vic. was witness
NOCONVIC	-3.0442	1.3550	-2.25	0.025	0.862	-3.531	0.000	No prior convictions
NOKILL	-0.9415	0.6898	-1.36	0.172	0.842	-1.118	0.263	Def. not triggerman
DNOPLCOF	10.3530	1.7875	5.79	0.000	164.300	0.063	0.950	No plan or def. ignt. of plan for cont. off.
BDGAG	-3.7423	0.8710	-4.30	0.000	0.861	-4.346	0.000	Vic. bound or gagged

Variable								Description
DLEADER	0.4376	0.7973	0.55	0.583	0.678	0.645	0.519	Def. prime mover plan homicide, contemp. off.
DPLEAS	0.9974	1.3563	0.74	0.462	0.924	1.079	0.280	Def. expressed pleasure with the killing
HARMOTH	-1.0362	0.8949	-1.16	0.247	0.742	-1.396	0.163	Bodily harm to other than vic.
NUDE	2.3625	0.6995	3.38	0.001	0.675	3.499	0.000	Vic. forced to disrobe
CPSTATEM	1.4947	0.7447	2.01	0.045	0.557	2.683	0.007	Coperp. statemnt implicat def. in homicide
DCONFESS	1.8130	0.5465	3.32	0.001	0.477	3.797	0.000	Def. admitted homicide—with no defense
INCMDRPT	2.0645	0.5431	3.80	0.000	0.456	4.531	0.000	Med. report link death to def. actions
POLGUILT	-1.3005	0.7586	-1.71	0.086	0.685	-1.899	0.058	Police report indicated clear guilt
SCIEVID	2.1442	0.4972	4.31	0.000	0.420	5.105	0.000	Science evid. other than weapon or medical
AVENGE	3.6308	1.1217	3.24	0.001	2.655	1.368	0.171	Motive to avenge role by jud. off., DA, lawyer
CPMORSEN	-9.0831	1.2388	-7.33	0.000	15.660	-0.580	0.562	Def.'s coperp. received a higher sentence
DROWN	2.0261	1.4767	1.37	0.170	1.243	1.630	0.103	Vic. was drowned
INSMOT	2.1901	1.1895	1.84	0.066	1.094	2.002	0.045	Def. motive to collect insurance
KIDNAP	2.2867	0.7180	3.18	0.001	0.609	3.754	0.000	Kidnapping involved
MULSTAB	0.1204	0.6736	0.18	0.858	0.625	0.193	0.847	Multiple stabbing
NOVICMIT	0.3767	0.4624	0.81	0.415	0.405	0.929	0.353	No victim-related mitigating circum.
RECCRIM	-1.2044	0.4907	-2.45	0.014	0.444	-2.712	0.007	Recent nonviolent crime by def.
SLODIE	0.8161	0.6333	1.29	0.198	0.567	1.440	0.150	Slow death
TORTURE	3.8654	0.9228	4.19	0.000	1.122	3.445	0.001	Vic. tortured physically
VPCARBRX	0.2581	0.1220	2.12	0.034	0.142	1.822	0.069	No. convictions: VPC, burg./arson 1st deg.
CONVICT	-3.6375	1.3877	-2.62	0.009	0.916	-3.972	0.000	Def. had prior convict., felony or misdmr.
MAJAGFCX	0.8695	0.1989	4.37	0.000	0.196	4.425	0.000	No. of major agg. factors in case
BADID	1.6034	0.6214	2.58	0.010	0.579	2.768	0.006	Mistaken identity claimed
DCOERCED	4.4624	1.4017	3.18	0.001	1.384	3.224	0.001	Coercion used on def.
DEFADMIT	-1.9741	1.2850	-1.54	0.124	0.978	-2.019	0.044	Def. admit guilt and no defense asserted
INSANDEF	2.6972	0.6341	4.25	0.000	0.657	4.102	0.000	Insanity or delusional compulsion
MITDFFN	-1.6974	1.1071	-1.53	0.125	1.199	-1.416	0.157	Def. retired, student, juvenile, housekeeper
PANIC	3.3675	0.7988	4.22	0.000	0.741	4.543	0.000	Def. panic in course of burglary
NOCONDUC	-0.9306	2.5241	-0.37	0.712	1.625	-0.573	0.567	Def. had impaired mental capacity
VBED	2.4889	1.2167	2.05	0.041	1.183	2.104	0.035	Vic. bedridden/handicapped
DEADWEP	1.3839	0.6640	2.08	0.037	0.612	2.259	0.024	Malice/deadly weapon w/o mitigation
GOODWIT	1.7861	0.5530	3.23	0.001	0.492	3.630	0.000	Prim. wit. pol off., civil. w/no cred. prob.
IDWITCOP	-1.2759	0.7849	-1.63	0.104	0.591	-2.160	0.031	ID wit. of coperp. commit crime near scene

Model B: Weighted Least Squares

Source	DF	Sum of Squares	Mean Square	F Value	Prob>F
Model	45	61.54825774	1.36773906	22.291	0.0001
Error	969	59.45524776	0.06135732		
C Total	1014	121.00351			

Root MSE	0.2477041	R-Square 0.5086
Dep Mean	0.05466011	Adj R-Sq 0.4858

Variable	Regression Coefficient	Safe[3] Standard Error	Safe[3] t[5]	Safe[3] p[6]	Nominal[4] Standard Error	Nominal[4] t[5]	Nominal[4] p[6]	Variable Label
CONST	-0.0360	0.0434	-0.83	0.407	0.0389	-0.924	0.356	
BLACKD	0.0636	0.0228	2.79	0.005	0.0178	3.578	0.000	Def. was black
WHVICRC	0.0652	0.0224	2.91	0.004	0.0176	3.700	0.000	One or more white victims (recode)
LDFB1	0.0575	0.0368	1.56	0.118	0.0271	2.120	0.034	Prior rec. of mur., arm. rob., rape, kid.
LDFB10	0.2360	0.0876	2.70	0.007	0.0567	4.163	0.000	Kill to avoid, stop arrest of self, other
LDFB7D	0.0936	0.0352	2.66	0.008	0.0236	3.969	0.000	Rape/arm. rob./kid. + sil. wit./exec/vic. pleaded
RACEMOT	0.0845	0.0651	1.30	0.194	0.0457	1.848	0.065	Racial hatred motive
VDEFNSLS	-0.0413	0.0213	-1.94	0.053	0.0182	-2.268	0.023	Vic. pregnant, disabled, or helpless
VWITNESS	-0.1641	0.0950	-1.73	0.084	0.0614	-2.673	0.008	Vic. was witness
NOCONVIC	-0.0971	0.0304	-3.19	0.001	0.0264	-3.677	0.000	No prior convictions
NOKILL	-0.0510	0.0251	-2.03	0.042	0.0249	-2.049	0.041	Def. not triggerman
DNOPLCOF	0.6638	0.1311	5.06	0.000	0.2569	2.584	0.010	No plan or def. ignt. of plan for cont. off.
BDGAG	-0.1427	0.0706	-2.02	0.043	0.0355	-4.017	0.000	Vic. bound or gagged
DLEADER	0.0698	0.0564	1.24	0.215	0.0339	2.060	0.039	Def. prime mover plan homicide, contemp. off.
DPLEAS	0.1879	0.0728	2.58	0.010	0.0426	4.416	0.000	Def. expressed pleasure with the killing
HARMOTH	0.0323	0.0184	1.75	0.079	0.0192	1.679	0.093	Bodily harm to other than vic.
NUDE	0.1478	0.0615	2.40	0.016	0.0316	4.671	0.000	Vic. forced to disrobe
CPSTATEM	0.0480	0.0317	1.52	0.130	0.0230	2.088	0.037	Coperp. statemnt implicat. def. in homicide

							Description
DCONFESS	0.0333	0.0120	2.77	0.006	0.0124	2.690	0.007	Def. admitted homicide—with no defense
INCMDRPT	0.0519	0.0136	3.82	0.000	0.0129	4.032	0.000	Med. report link death to def. actions
POLGUILT	-0.0526	0.0202	-2.60	0.009	0.0202	-2.602	0.009	Police report indicated clear guilt
SCIEVID	0.0670	0.0162	4.15	0.000	0.0139	4.834	0.000	Science evid. other than weapon or medical
AVENGE	0.3698	0.2784	1.33	0.184	0.1490	2.482	0.013	Motive to avenge role by jud. off., DA, lawyer
CPMORSEN	-0.0805	0.0345	-2.33	0.020	0.0372	-2.162	0.031	Def.'s coperp. received a higher sentence
DROWN	0.2172	0.0982	2.21	0.027	0.0600	3.621	0.000	Vic. was drowned
INSMOT	0.1396	0.0730	1.91	0.056	0.0503	2.775	0.006	Def. motive to collect insurance
KIDNAP	0.1483	0.0570	2.60	0.009	0.0308	4.823	0.000	Kidnapping involved
MULSTAB	0.0513	0.0231	2.22	0.027	0.0213	2.409	0.016	Multiple stabbing
NOVICMIT	0.0165	0.0112	1.47	0.142	0.0117	1.406	0.160	No victim-related mitigating circum.
RECCRIM	-0.0230	0.0110	-2.09	0.036	0.0119	-1.925	0.054	Recent nonviolent crime by def.
SLODIE	0.0285	0.0147	1.94	0.053	0.0163	1.753	0.080	Slow death
TORTURE	0.2076	0.0936	2.22	0.027	0.0577	3.597	0.000	Vic. tortured physically
VPCARBRX	0.0083	0.0031	2.64	0.008	0.0037	2.241	0.025	No. convictions: VPC, burg./arson 1st deg.
CONVICT	-0.1094	0.0308	-3.55	0.000	0.0265	-4.128	0.000	Def. had prior convict., felony or misdmr.
MAJAGFCX	0.0532	0.0132	4.05	0.000	0.0090	5.940	0.000	No. of major agg. factors in case
BADID	0.0339	0.0184	1.84	0.066	0.0182	1.859	0.063	Mistaken identity claimed
DCOERCED	0.2588	0.2299	1.13	0.260	0.0844	3.066	0.002	Coercion used on def.
DEFADMIT	-0.0740	0.0234	-3.17	0.002	0.0236	-3.136	0.002	Def. admit guilt and no defense asserted
INSANDEF	0.1479	0.0806	1.83	0.067	0.0364	4.070	0.000	Insanity or delusional compulsion
MITDFEN	-0.0571	0.0256	-2.23	0.026	0.0297	-1.920	0.055	Def. retired, student, juvenile, housekeeper
PANIC	0.1025	0.0459	2.23	0.026	0.0328	3.122	0.002	Def. panic in course of burglary
NOCONDUC	-0.3849	1.2672	-0.30	0.761	0.1246	-3.088	0.002	Def. had impaired mental capacity
VBED	0.1668	0.2461	0.68	0.498	0.0867	1.925	0.054	Vic. bedridden/handicapped
DEADWEP	0.0621	0.0184	3.37	0.001	0.0186	3.334	0.001	Malice/deadly weapon w/o mitigation
GOODWIT	0.0299	0.0097	3.09	0.002	0.0110	2.730	0.006	Prim. wit. pol. off., civil. w/no cred. prob.
IDWTCOP	-0.0822	0.0275	-2.99	0.003	0.0219	-3.756	0.000	ID wit. of coperp. commit crime near scene

1. See *supra* schedule 1, note 1.
2. See *supra* schedule 1, note 2.
3. See *supra* schedule 1, note 3.
4. See *supra* schedule 1, note 4.
5. See *supra* schedule 1, note 5.
6. See *supra* schedule 1, note 6.

Schedule 8—CSS

Outcome variable: Prosecutorial decision to seek a death sentence after a murder-trial conviction was obtained (PSEEKNGP).
Explanatory variables: Nonperverse statistically significant ($p \leq .10$) variables screened from the variable list in schedule 3 with logistic-regression analyses of prosecutorial decisions to seek a death penalty after a murder-trial conviction was obtained, and the race of defendant and victim.

Model A: Weighted Logistic Regression

708 Weighted observations
480 PSEEKNGP = 0
228 PSEEKNGP = 1
Model chi-square[1] = 398.038 with 12 D.F.
R = .648[2]

Variable	Logistic Regression Coefficient	Safe[3]			Nominal[4]			Variable Label
		Standard Error	t[5]	p[6]	Standard Error	t[5]	p[6]	
CONST	-5.4597	0.9166	-5.96	0.000	0.5447	-10.023	0.000	Intercept
BLACKD	0.8648	0.5211	1.66	0.097	0.3039	2.846	0.004	Def. was black
WHVICRC	1.2083	0.5132	2.35	0.019	0.3222	3.750	0.000	One or more white victims (recode)
DBADFACT	1.4308	0.9985	1.43	0.152	0.7440	1.923	0.054	Mistake of fact claimed
DISFIGHT	-0.9443	0.3585	-2.63	0.008	0.2830	-3.337	0.001	Homicide arose from a dispute, fight
EVIDINDX	0.4208	0.1178	3.57	0.000	0.0856	4.916	0.000	No. of major types of incrim. evod. v. def.
IDWITCOP	-0.7564	0.4546	-1.66	0.096	0.3452	-2.191	0.028	ID wit. of coperp. commit crime near scene
JOINTKIL	-1.5704	0.6262	-2.51	0.012	0.4648	-3.379	0.001	Def. only an accomplice in killing
LDFBSUM	0.8915	0.1686	5.29	0.000	0.1227	7.266	0.000	No. of Ga. stat. agg. circumstances present
MAJAGFCX	0.5640	0.1431	3.94	0.000	0.1221	4.619	0.000	No. of major agg. factors in case
SMUNDRLG	-1.3308	0.5490	-2.42	0.015	0.3978	-3.345	0.001	Def. accomplice and minor participant
STRANGER	0.6510	0.4052	1.61	0.108	0.2748	2.369	0.018	Vic. a stranger
VBLUSKL	-2.4202	1.0326	-2.34	0.019	0.7440	-3.253	0.001	Vic. blue-collar worker or unskilled

Model B: Weighted Least Squares

Source	DF	Sum of Squares	Mean Square	F Value	Prob>F
Model	12	72.54613971	6.0455164	30.149	0.0001
Error	409	82.01420249	0.20052372		
C Total	421	154.56034			

Root MSE	0.4477988	R-Square	0.4694
Dep Mean	0.3221038	Adj R-Sq	0.4538

Variable	Safe[3]				Nominal[4]			Variable Label
	Regression Coefficient	Standard Error	t^5	p^6	Standard Error	t^5	p^6	
CONST	0.1152	0.0887	1.30	0.194	0.0701	1.644	0.100	Intercept
BLACKD	0.1724	0.0621	2.77	0.006	0.0461	3.738	0.000	Def. was black
WHVICRC	0.2288	0.0638	3.59	0.000	0.0486	4.704	0.000	One or more white victims (recode)
DBADFACT	−0.1072	0.2280	−0.47	0.638	0.1343	−0.798	0.425	Mistake of fact claimed
DISFGHT	0.0471	0.0439	1.07	0.283	0.0415	1.135	0.256	Homicide arose from a dispute, fight
EVIDINDX	−0.0703	0.0125	−5.60	0.000	0.0118	−5.975	0.000	No. of major types of incrim. evid. v. def.
IDWITCOP	−0.1923	0.0613	−3.14	0.002	0.0511	−3.762	0.000	ID wit. of coperp. commit crime near scene
JOINTKIL	0.1156	0.0941	1.23	0.219	0.0737	1.570	0.117	Def. only an accomplice in killing
LDFBSUM	0.0794	0.0193	4.12	0.000	0.0171	4.647	0.000	No. of Ga. stat. agg. circumstances present
MAJAGFCX	−0.1957	0.0161	−12.19	0.000	0.0171	−11.474	0.000	No. of major agg. factors in case
SMUNDRLG	0.1256	0.0724	1.74	0.083	0.0597	2.102	0.036	Def. accomplice and minor participant
STRANGER	−0.2299	0.0579	−3.97	0.000	0.0435	−5.282	0.000	Vic. a stranger
VBLUSKL	−0.2453	0.0871	−2.82	0.005	0.0766	−3.201	0.001	Vic. blue-collar worker or unskilled

1. See *supra* schedule 1, note 1.
2. See *supra* schedule 1, note 2.
3. See *supra* schedule 1, note 3.
4. See *supra* schedule 1, note 4.
5. See *supra* schedule 1, note 5.
6. See *supra* schedule 1, note 6.

Schedule 9—CSS

Outcome variable: Death sentence imposed at penalty trial (DEATHSNT).
Explanatory variables: Nonperverse statistically significant (p .10) variables screened from the variable list in schedule 3, using logistic-regression analyses of jury death-sentencing decisions, and the race of defendant and victim.

Model A: Weighted Logistic Regression

253 Weighted observations
113 DEATHSNT = 0
140 DEATHSNT = 1

Model chi-square^1 = 157.356 with 15 D.F.
R = .605^2

Variable	Logistic Regression Coefficient	Safe³			Nominal⁴			Variable Label
		Standard Error	t⁵	p⁶	Standard Error	t⁵	p⁶	
CONST	−4.7796	0.9089	−5.26	0.000	0.9742	−4.906	0.000	
BLACKD	0.2854	0.4265	0.67	0.503	0.4344	0.657	0.511	Def. was black
WHVICRC	1.2269	0.5369	2.29	0.022	0.5379	2.281	0.023	One or more white victims (recode)
NOKILL	−1.9513	0.4939	−3.95	0.000	0.6385	−3.056	0.002	Def. not triggerman
LDFB2	0.9916	0.5300	1.87	0.061	0.4718	2.102	0.036	Cont. mur., armrob., rape, kid.bod. inj., etc.
LDFB1	1.4530	0.7910	1.84	0.066	0.6887	2.110	0.035	Prior rec. of mur., armrob., rape, kid. wbod. inj
NOCLOTH	1.9798	0.4767	4.15	0.000	0.6016	3.291	0.001	Vic without clothes when killed
MULSH	1.1595	0.4299	2.70	0.007	0.4265	2.719	0.007	Multiple gunshots
DCOERCED	2.8497	1.9002	1.50	0.134	1.4320	1.990	0.047	Coercion used on def.
DRGHIS	−1.7491	0.5020	−3.48	0.000	0.4573	−3.825	0.000	History of drug or alcohol abuse
MITMOTVE	−1.3888	0.5602	−2.48	0.013	0.5295	−2.623	0.009	Def. motive hate, revenge, jealousy, rage
INSMOT	2.8532	1.5641	1.82	0.068	1.1330	2.518	0.012	Def. motive to collect insurance
MAJAGFCX	0.8486	0.1950	4.35	0.000	0.1771	4.792	0.000	No. of major agg. factors in case
INSANDEF	3.4602	0.9105	3.80	0.000	0.7705	4.491	0.000	Insanity or delusional compulsion
PANIC	2.0905	0.7442	2.81	0.005	0.7824	2.672	0.008	Def. panic in course of burglary
EVIDINDX	0.3794	0.1146	3.31	0.001	0.1213	3.128	0.002	No. of major types of incrim. evid. v. def.

Model B: Weighted Least Squares

Source	DF	Sum of Squares	Mean Square	F Value	ProbF
Model	15	28.64252277	1.90950152	13.298	0.0001
Error	236	33.88712150	0.14358950		
C Total	251	62.52964427			

Root MSE 0.378932   R-Square 0.4581
Dep Mean 0.5533597   Adj R-Sq 0.4236

Variable	Regression Coefficient	Safe[3]			Nominal[4]			Variable Label
		Standard Error	t^5	p^6	Standard Error	t^5	p^6	
CONST	−0.1082	0.1076	−1.00	0.315	0.1109	−0.975	0.330	Def. was black
BLACKD	0.0168	0.0586	0.29	0.775	0.0561	0.299	0.765	One or more white victims (recode)
WHVICRC	0.1144	0.0791	1.45	0.148	0.0702	1.629	0.103	Def. not triggerman
NOKILL	−0.2520	0.0706	−3.57	0.000	0.0777	−3.244	0.001	Cont. Mur., armrob., rape, kid.bod. inj., etc.
LDFB2	0.1683	0.0627	2.68	0.007	0.0589	2.858	0.004	Prior rec. of mur., armrob., rape, kid. wbod. inj.
LDFB1	0.1514	0.0847	1.79	0.074	0.0767	1.974	0.048	Vic without clothes when killed
NOCLOTH	0.2325	0.0592	3.93	0.000	0.0664	3.500	0.000	Multiple gunshots
MULSH	0.1571	0.0612	2.57	0.010	0.0573	2.740	0.006	Coercion used on def.
DCOERCED	0.2849	0.2082	1.37	0.171	0.1500	1.900	0.057	History of drug or alcohol abuse
DRGHIS	−0.2149	0.0585	−3.67	0.000	0.0553	−3.885	0.000	Def. motive hate, revenge, jealousy, rage
MITMOTVE	−0.1454	0.0685	−2.12	0.034	0.0642	−2.266	0.023	Def. motive to collect insurance
INSMOT	0.3711	0.1876	1.98	0.048	0.1362	2.724	0.006	No. of major agg. factors in case
MAJAGFCX	0.1034	0.0188	5.52	0.000	0.0184	5.636	0.000	Insanity or delusional compulsion
INSANDEF	0.3846	0.0896	4.29	0.000	0.0817	4.707	0.000	Def. panic in course of burglary
PANIC	0.2540	0.1236	2.06	0.040	0.1077	2.358	0.018	No. of major types of incrim. evid. v. def.
EVIDINDX	0.0503	0.0162	3.11	0.002	0.0156	3.233	0.001	

1. See *supra* schedule 1, note 1.
2. See *supra* schedule 1, note 2.
3. See *supra* schedule 1, note 3.
4. See *supra* schedule 1, note 4.
5. See *supra* schedule 1, note 5.
6. See *supra* schedule 1, note 6.

B. THE PROCEDURAL REFORM STUDY (PRS)

Schedule 10—PRS

Outcome variable: Death sentence imposed in cases indicted for murder at trial (x481c).
Explanatory variables: Five conceptually or statistically important variables and the race of defendant and victim.

Model A: Logistic Regression

606 Observations
494 x481c = 0
112 x481c = 1
Model chi-square[1] = 166.922 with 7 D.F.
R = .513[2]

Variable	Logistic Regression Coefficient	Safe[3]			Nominal[4]			Variable Label
		Standard Error	t[5]	p[6]	Standard Error	t[5]	p[6]	
CONST	−3.7476	0.4969	−7.54	0.000	0.4568	−8.204	0.000	
BLACKD	−0.3224	0.2695	−1.20	0.232	0.2771	−1.163	0.245	Black defendant
WHVICRC	1.0275	0.3389	3.03	0.002	0.3373	3.046	0.002	One or more white victims (recode)
BLVICMOD	−0.5922	0.3865	−1.53	0.125	0.3861	−1.534	0.125	Family, lover, liquor, barroom quarrel
VICSTRAN	0.5703	0.2779	2.05	0.040	0.2739	2.082	0.037	Victim was a stranger
SERCONOF	2.0749	0.3488	5.95	0.000	0.3256	6.373	0.000	A serious cont. offense involved
VPCX	0.3171	0.1696	1.87	0.061	0.1315	2.411	0.016	No. of prior conv. mur.arm. rob. rapekid. & other vpc
TWOVIC	2.1292	0.4132	5.15	0.000	0.4167	5.110	0.000	Two or more victims by def. or by coperp.

Model B: Ordinary Least Squares

Source	DF	Sum of Squares	Mean Square	F Value	Prob>F
Model	7	23.2287948	3.3183964	29.152	0.0001
Error	598	68.07153255	0.11383199		
C Total	605	91.3003003			

Root MSE	0.33739	R-Square	0.2544
Dep Mean	0.1848185	Adj R-Sq	0.2457

Variable	Regression Coefficient	Safe[3]			Nominal[4]			Variable Label
		Standard Error	t[5]	p[6]	Standard Error	t[5]	p[6]	
CONST	-0.0095	0.0470	-0.20	0.840	0.0439	-0.216	0.829	
BLACKD	-0.0147	0.0428	-0.34	0.732	0.0363	-0.405	0.686	Black defendant
WHVICRC	0.0902	0.0409	2.21	0.027	0.0376	2.401	0.016	One or more white victims (recode)
BLVICMOD	-0.0338	0.0262	-1.29	0.197	0.0325	-1.041	0.298	Family, lover, liquor, barroom quarrel
VICSTRAN	0.0898	0.0433	2.07	0.038	0.0356	2.522	0.012	Victim was a stranger
SERCONOF	0.2378	0.0385	6.17	0.000	0.0335	7.092	0.000	A serious cont. offense involved
VPCX	0.0439	0.0254	1.73	0.084	0.0172	2.555	0.011	No. of prior conv. mur./arm. rob./rape/kid. & other vpc
TWOVIC	0.3235	0.0736	4.39	0.000	0.0558	5.803	0.000	Two or more victims by def. or by coperp.

1. *See supra* schedule 1, note 1.
2. *See supra* schedule 1, note 2.
3. *See supra* schedule 1, note 3. Although this analysis is unweighted, we have included the safe computations to keep the table format the same.
4. *See supra* schedule 1, note 4.
5. *See supra* schedule 1, note 5.
6. *See supra* schedule 1, note 6.

Schedule 11—PRS

Outcome variable: Death sentence imposed in cases convicted of murder (x481c).
Explanatory variables: Nine conceptually or statistically important variables and the race of defendant and victim.

Model A: Logistic Regression

606 Observations
494 x481c = 0
112 x481c = 1
Model chi-square[1] = 204.070 with 11 D.F.
R = .560[2]

Variable	Logistic Regression Coefficient	Safe[3] Standard Error	t[5]	p[6]	Nominal[4] Standard Error	t[5]	p[6]	Variable Label
CONST	-3.8195	0.5086	-7.51	0.000	0.4794	-7.967	0.000	
BLACKD	-0.2128	0.2936	-0.72	0.469	0.3000	-0.709	0.478	Black defendant
WHVICRC	1.0182	0.3587	2.84	0.005	0.3558	2.862	0.004	One or more white victims (recode)
BLVICMOD	-0.6414	0.3596	-1.78	0.074	0.3924	-1.6535	0.102	Family, lover, liquor, barroom quarrel
VICSTRAN	0.7023	0.3096	2.27	0.023	0.2961	2.372	0.018	Victim was a stranger
SERCONOF	1.7281	0.3726	4.64	0.000	0.3485	4.959	0.000	A serious cont. offense involved
VPCX	0.3875	0.1520	2.55	0.011	0.1324	2.927	0.003	No. of prior conv. mur./arm. rob./rape/kid. & other vpc
TORT	1.3024	0.7683	1.70	0.090	0.6273	2.076	0.038	Torture involved
UNNEPAIN	0.6167	0.4908	1.26	0.209	0.4391	1.404	0.160	Unnecessary pain involved
NOKILL	-1.0876	0.4031	-2.70	0.007	0.3716	-2.927	0.003	Def. not the triggerman
PBQB7D	1.2367	0.3491	3.54	0.000	0.3403	3.634	0.000	Rape etc./sil wit. or vic. helpless. ex., plead.
TWOVIC	2.0517	0.4712	4.35	0.000	0.4438	4.623	0.000	Two or more victims by def. or by coperp.

Model B: Ordinary Least Squares

Source	DF	Sum of Squares	Mean Square	F Value	Prob>F
Model	11	30.24260751	2.74932796	27.747	0.0001
Error	594	61.05772252	0.10279078		
C Total	605	91.30033003			

Root MSE 0.32061 R-Square 0.3312
Dep Mean 0.1848185 Adj R-Sq 0.3189

Variable	Safe[3]				Nominal[4]			Variable Label
	Regression Coefficient	Standard Error	t[5]	p[6]	Standard Error	t[5]	p[6]	
CONST	-0.0035	0.0445	-0.08	0.936	0.0424	-0.084	0.933	
BLACKD	-0.0014	0.0409	-0.03	0.973	0.0347	-0.039	0.969	Black defendant
WHVICRC	0.0919	0.0392	2.34	0.019	0.0358	2.563	0.010	One or more white victims (recode)
BLVICMOD	-0.0448	0.0250	-1.79	0.074	0.0311	-1.441	0.150	Family, lover, liquor, barrom quarrel
VICSTRAN	0.0877	0.0416	2.11	0.035	0.0340	2.578	0.010	Victim was a stranger
SERCONOF	0.1694	0.0423	4.00	0.000	0.0348	4.875	0.000	A serious cont. offense involved
VPCX	0.0477	0.0227	2.10	0.036	0.0163	2.922	0.003	No. of prior conv. mur./arm. rob./rape/kid. & other vpc
TORT	0.1711	0.1111	1.54	0.124	0.0744	2.299	0.022	Torture involved
UNNEPAIN	0.0952	0.0657	1.45	0.147	0.0500	1.902	0.057	Unnecessary pain involved
NOKILL	-0.1377	0.0433	-3.18	0.001	0.0374	-3.683	0.000	Def. not the triggerman
PBQB7D	0.2508	0.0676	3.71	0.000	0.0467	5.373	0.000	Rape etc./sil wit. or vic. helpless. ex., plead.
TWOVIC	0.2560	0.0771	3.32	0.001	0.0540	4.741	0.000	Two or more victims by def. or by coperp.

1. See *supra* schedule 1, note 1.
2. See *supra* schedule 1, note 2.
3. See *supra* schedule 1, note 3. Although this analysis is unweighted, we have included the safe computations to keep the table format the same.
4. See *supra* schedule 1, note 4.
5. See *supra* schedule 1, note 5.
6. See *supra* schedule 1, note 6.

Schedule 12—PRS

Outcome variable: Prosecutorial decision to seek a death sentence following a murder-trial conviction (X2481PRCPSEEKNGP).

Explanatory variables: Nonperverse statistically significant (p.10) variables screened from the list of variables in schedule 15 in a linear-regression analysis of prosecutorial decisions to seek a death sentence following a murder-trial conviction, and the race of defendant and victim.

Model A: Logistic Regression

594 Observations
400 X2481PRC = 0
194 X2481PRC = 1
Model chi-square = 387.746 with 23 D.F.[1]
R = .675[2]

Variable	Logistic Regression Coefficient	Safe[3]			Nominal[4]			Variable Label
		Standard Error	t[5]	p[6]	Standard Error	t[5]	p[6]	
CONST	-4.7607	0.5122	-9.29	0.000	0.4926	-9.664	0.000	
BLACKD	0.1220	0.3301	0.37	0.712	0.3478	0.351	0.726	Black defendant
WHVICRC	1.2178	0.3473	3.51	0.000	0.3547	3.433	0.001	One or more white victims (recode)
SILWIT	0.7343	0.4110	1.79	0.074	0.4830	1.520	0.128	Victim killed because a witness

								Description
STOMP	1.8445	0.6726	2.74	0.006	0.6177	2.986	0.003	Brutal stompingbeating
TWOVIC	1.3296	0.4798	2.77	0.006	0.5346	2.487	0.013	Two or more victims by def. or by coperp.
NOKILL	-1.1712	0.4482	-2.61	0.009	0.4357	-2.688	0.007	Def. not the triggerman
VICSTRAN	1.1359	0.3061	3.71	0.000	0.3384	3.357	0.001	Victim was a stranger
MULSH	0.8488	0.5489	1.55	0.122	0.4750	1.787	0.074	Multiple shots
MULSTAB	1.4405	0.4745	3.04	0.002	0.4778	3.015	0.003	Multiple stabs
MAJAGCRX	0.6766	0.1961	3.45	0.001	0.2069	3.270	0.001	No. of major aggravating circumstances
DEFRSARR	1.6337	0.4062	4.02	0.000	0.4109	3.976	0.000	Def. actively resisted arrest
SERCONOF	1.7235	0.3283	5.25	0.000	0.3389	5.086	0.000	A serious cont. offense involved
MITDEFN	-3.1717	0.7322	-4.33	0.000	0.9882	-3.210	0.001	Def. status sympathetic
NONVCOF	1.4558	0.4186	3.48	0.001	0.4262	3.416	0.001	Def. engaged in a nonviolent crime
NOVMC	1.0621	0.2880	3.69	0.000	0.2955	3.594	0.000	No. of victim mitigating circumstances
PREMEDK	1.0274	0.3151	3.26	0.001	0.3252	3.159	0.002	Def. planned killing5 minutes
VICHST	0.4903	0.3602	1.36	0.173	0.3657	1.341	0.180	Victim wht. col., proprietor, prof., exec.
CONVICTX	0.0823	0.0381	2.16	0.031	0.3012	0.273	0.785	No. of defendant's prior convictions
PBQB6	2.4405	0.7706	3.17	0.002	0.6871	3.552	0.000	Murder for hire
PBQB7A	0.8989	0.4845	1.86	0.064	0.5400	1.665	0.096	Victim mutilated beforeafter death
VICYNG	1.2993	0.6828	1.90	0.057	0.6276	2.070	0.038	Victim defenselessyouth
ESCAPE	2.4991	1.0337	2.42	0.016	1.2950	1.930	0.054	Kill occurred in escape from jailprison
W40	-0.3134	0.1191	-2.63	0.009	0.1371	-2.286	0.022	No. of coperpetrators

Model B: Ordinary Least Squares

Source	DF	Sum of Squares	Mean Square	F Value	Prob>F
Model	23	68.45733268	2.97640577	27.283	0.0001
Error	570	62.18239796	0.10909193		
C Total	593	130.63973			

Root MSE	0.3302907	R-Square	0.5240
Dep Mean	0.3265993	Adj R-Sq	0.5048

Variable	Regression Coefficient	Safe[3]			Nominal[4]			Variable Label
		Standard Error	t^5	p^6	Standard Error	t^5	p^6	
CONST	-0.1125	0.0422	-2.67	0.008	0.0418	-2.694	0.007	
BLACKD	0.0369	0.0400	0.92	0.357	0.0371	0.993	0.321	Black defendant
WHVICRC	0.1390	0.0427	3.26	0.001	0.0384	3.623	0.000	One or more white victims (recode)
SILWIT	0.1048	0.0547	1.91	0.056	0.0516	2.030	0.042	Victim killed because a witness
STOMP	0.2009	0.0877	2.29	0.022	0.0691	2.910	0.004	Brutal stomping/beating
TWOVIC	0.1168	0.0690	1.69	0.091	0.0595	1.963	0.050	Two or more victims by def. or by coperp.
NOKILL	-0.1399	0.0494	-2.83	0.005	0.0445	-3.145	0.002	Def. not the triggerman

VICSTRAN	0.1336	0.0412	3.24	0.001	0.0369	3.617	0.000	Victim was a stranger
MULSH	0.1081	0.0588	1.84	0.066	0.0492	2.195	0.028	Multiple shots
MULSTAB	0.1808	0.0579	3.12	0.002	0.0529	3.421	0.001	Multiple stabs
MAJAGCRX	0.0681	0.0179	3.79	0.000	0.0176	3.868	0.000	No. of major aggravating circumstances
DEFRSARR	0.2130	0.0464	4.59	0.000	0.0427	4.983	0.000	Def. actively resisted arrest
SERCONOF	0.2297	0.0439	5.24	0.000	0.0371	6.193	0.000	A serious cont. offense involved
MITDEFN	-0.2039	0.0628	-3.25	0.001	0.0703	-2.902	0.004	Def. status sympathetic
NONVCOF	0.1743	0.0527	3.31	0.001	0.0467	3.733	0.000	Def. engaged in a nonviolent crime
NOVMC	0.1364	0.0377	3.62	0.000	0.0331	4.122	0.000	No. of victim mitigating circumstances
PREMEDK	0.1163	0.0338	3.44	0.001	0.0326	3.563	0.000	Def. planned killing >5 minutes
VICHST	0.0727	0.0474	1.53	0.125	0.0412	1.765	0.078	Victim wht. col., proprietor, prof., exec.
CONVICTX	0.0070	0.0032	2.18	0.029	0.0027	2.598	0.009	No. of defendant's prior convictions
PBQB6	0.3364	0.1130	2.98	0.003	0.0817	4.118	0.000	Murder for hire
PBQB7A	0.1248	0.0669	1.87	0.062	0.0599	2.082	0.037	Victim mutilated before/after death
VICYNG	0.1741	0.0916	1.90	0.057	0.0724	2.404	0.016	Victim defenseless/youth
ESCAPE	0.3496	0.1657	2.11	0.035	0.1424	2.455	0.014	Kill occurred in escape from jail/prison
W40	-0.0400	0.0152	-2.64	0.008	0.0145	-2.757	0.006	No. of coperpetrators

1. *See supra* schedule 1, note 1.
2. *See supra* schedule 1, note 2.
3. *See supra* schedule 1, note 3. Although this analysis is unweighted, we have included the safe computations to keep the table format the same.
4. *See supra* schedule 1, note 4.
5. *See supra* schedule 1, note 5.
6. *See supra* schedule 1, note 6.

Schedule 13—PRS

Outcome variable: Death sentence imposed at penalty trial (x2481JRC/JURYDSNT).
Explanatory variables: Nonperverse statistically significant ($p \leq .10$) variables screened from the variable list in schedule 15 in logistic regression analyses designed to explain which defendants received a death sentence at a penalty trial, and the race of defendant and victim.

Model A: Logistic Regression

206 Observations
94 X2481JRC = 0
112 X2481JRC = 1

Model chi-square[1] = 125.524 with 13 D.F.
R = .592[2]

Variable	Logistic Regression Coefficient	Safe[3]			Nominal[4]			Variable Label
		Standard Error	t[5]	p[6]	Standard Error	t[5]	p[6]	
CONST	−3.6785	0.7886	−4.66	0.000	0.7920	−4.645	0.000	
BLACKD	−0.5708	0.4590	−1.24	0.214	0.4881	−1.170	0.242	Black defendant
WHVICRC	0.3141	0.5501	0.57	0.568	0.5389	0.583	0.560	One or more white victims (recode)
W15D	1.1551	0.3075	3.76	0.000	0.4694	2.461	0.014	No. of prior conv. other viol. per. cr.
PBQB3	2.0000	0.5440	3.68	0.000	0.6168	3.243	0.001	Def. created risk/death/public place
PBQB4	2.1247	0.6038	3.52	0.000	0.5406	3.930	0.000	Murder for money/value
FEMVIC	1.8418	0.5654	3.26	0.001	0.5860	3.143	0.002	Victim was a female
KIDNAP	1.8035	0.6850	2.63	0.008	0.6233	2.893	0.004	Victim was kidnapped
RAPE	1.8500	1.0737	1.72	0.085	0.8624	2.145	0.032	Rape involved
MAJAGCRX	0.7998	0.2682	2.98	0.003	0.2293	3.488	0.000	No. of major aggravating circum.
VICPFIR	2.2664	0.7965	2.85	0.004	0.9007	2.516	0.012	Victim was police or fire
MULSTAB	1.0892	0.6166	1.77	0.077	0.6405	1.701	0.089	Multiple stabs
MULSH	1.8308	0.7192	2.55	0.011	0.6180	2.962	0.003	Multiple shots
STMIT6	−3.7727	1.9110	−1.97	0.048	1.2900	−2.925	0.003	Def. an accomplice role was rel. min.

Model B: Ordinary Least Squares

Source	DF	Sum of Squares	Mean Square	F Value	Prob>F
Model	13	21.86190381	1.68168491	11.041	0.0001
Error	192	29.24489231	0.15231715		
C Total	205	51.10679612			

Root MSE 0.3902783   R-Square 0.4278
Dep Mean 0.5436893   Adj R-Sq 0.3890

Variable	Safe[3]				Nominal[4]			Variable Label
	Regression Coefficient	Standard Error	t^5	p^6	Standard Error	t^5	p^6	
CONST	0.0176	0.1032	0.17	0.865	0.0966	0.182	0.856	
BLACKD	−0.0329	0.0686	−0.48	0.632	0.0651	−0.505	0.614	Black defendant
WHVICRC	0.0555	0.0920	0.60	0.547	0.0799	0.694	0.488	One or more white victims (recode)
W15D	0.1286	0.0312	4.12	0.000	0.0420	3.060	0.002	No. of prior conv. other viol. per. cr.
PBQB3	0.2178	0.0814	2.68	0.007	0.0783	2.783	0.005	Def. created risk/death/public place
PBQB4	0.2454	0.0650	3.78	0.000	0.0623	3.939	0.000	Murder for money/value
FEMVIC	0.2539	0.0795	3.19	0.001	0.0753	3.371	0.001	Victim was a female
KIDNAP	0.2479	0.0737	3.37	0.001	0.0718	3.455	0.001	Victim was kidnapped
RAPE	0.1431	0.1179	1.21	0.225	0.1032	1.387	0.166	Rape involved
MAJAGCRX	0.0788	0.0242	3.26	0.001	0.0229	3.447	0.001	No. of major aggravating circum.
VICPFIR	0.1912	0.1185	1.61	0.106	0.1134	1.686	0.092	Victim was police or fire
MULSTAB	0.1736	0.0939	1.85	0.065	0.0087	1.958	0.050	Multiple stabs
MULSH	0.1821	0.0884	2.06	0.039	0.0769	2.369	0.018	Multiple shots
STMIT6	−0.4269	0.1260	−3.39	0.001	0.1155	−3.695	0.000	Def. an accomplice role was rel. min.

1. *See supra* schedule 1, note 1.
2. *See supra* schedule 1, note 2.
3. *See supra* schedule 1, note 3. Although this analysis is unweighted, we have included the safe computations to keep the table format the same.
4. *See supra* schedule 1, note 4.
5. *See supra* schedule 1, note 5.
6. *See supra* schedule 1, note 6.

Schedule 14—PRS

Outcome variable: Death sentence imposed in cases convicted of murder at trial (x481c).
Explanatory variables: All statutory aggravating circumstances,[1] all mitigating circumstances in the file, and the race of defendant and
victim.

Model A: Logistic Regression

606 Observations
494 x481c = 0
112 x481c = 1

Model chi-square = 251.24 with 53 D.F.[2]
R = 0.620[3]

Variable	Beta	Std. Error	Chi-Square	P	R	Variable Label
INTERCEPT	-4.59671503	1.16230829	15.64	0.0001		
BLACKD	-1.17405303	0.44245419	7.04	0.0080	-0.093	Black defendant
WHVICRC	1.52715539	0.52654828	8.41	0.0037	0.105	One or more white victims (recode)
ACCD	-0.79705064	0.92077888	0.75	0.3867	0.000	Accident defense
DDRG	-0.85758549	1.47422935	0.34	0.5608	0.000	Def. heavily intoxicated
DEFENSE	2.15792163	1.79995287	1.44	0.2306	0.000	Vic. assault
DEFREM	1.32651909	0.83592635	2.52	0.1125	0.030	Def. showed remorse
DFEAR	-1.25053671	1.28579621	0.95	0.3308	0.000	Vic. arouse fear
DFSUR24	1.10873949	1.25197711	0.78	0.3758	0.000	Def. gave up within 24 hrs.
DJUST	1.53658292	1.82816570	0.71	0.4006	0.000	Def. with moral justification
DNOINT	-1.46118611	1.52698368	0.92	0.3386	0.000	No intent to kill
DRGHIS	-1.42382530	1.32951331	1.15	0.2842	0.000	Def. had history of drug or alco. abuse
DRUGDIS	-0.13800909	0.73441674	0.04	0.8509	0.000	Dispute influenced by drg/alcohol
DSUR	-1.36663325	1.36698355	1.00	0.3174	0.000	Def. surrendered to authorities
DUNDERLG	-2.79412067	1.10202715	6.43	0.0112	-0.087	Def. was underling in murder
FAMLVDIS	0.65834770	1.43514120	0.21	0.6464	0.000	Family or lover dispute
JEALOS	-0.64733391	1.84398846	0.12	0.7256	0.000	Jealousy motive
MANSLAUG	-3.17939811	0.93734034	11.51	0.0007	-0.128	Manslaughter defense
MINOR	1.70560911	0.70406152	5.87	0.0154	0.082	Def. 16 or younger

Variable	Description					
MITCIR	One or more mit. circumstances	-1.07571486	0.62463186	2.97	0.0850	-0.041
MITCIR2	Mit. cir. concern def. (count)	0.85338199	1.12157065	0.58	0.4467	0.000
MITCIR3	Mit. cir. concern vic. (count)	-1.57984428	0.77966611	4.11	0.0427	-0.060
MITDEF	Mitigating defense	2.88947268	0.70472094	16.81	0.0000	0.160
MITDEFN	Def. status sympathetic	-5.43491378	1.56457748	12.07	0.0005	-0.132
MITMOT	A mitigating motive	0.19528428	0.59869944	0.11	0.7443	0.000
NOCONTOF	No contemp. offense	0.02651960	0.70256736	0.00	0.9699	0.000
NOCONVIC	No prior convictions	-1.74358146	1.62435664	1.15	0.2831	0.000
NOFEL	No felony convictions	-0.81415606	0.56204331	2.10	0.1475	-0.013
NOKILL	Def. not the triggerman	-0.91055448	0.57197866	2.53	0.1114	-0.030
NORECORD	No criminal convictions	0.89134527	1.57884966	0.32	0.5724	0.000
NOSERCRI	No conviction for a serious crime	0.65750213	0.56557927	1.35	0.2450	0.000
NOVPC	No conviction for a serious viol felony	-1.53350009	0.76787952	3.99	0.0458	-0.059
OTHMIT	Other mit. cir.	-0.15861389	1.52848633	0.01	0.9174	0.000
OTHVMIT	Vic. mitigating circumstances	0.82681253	1.25576146	0.43	0.5103	0.000
STMIT1	Def. lack cap. to app. criminal. of cond.	-1.07543133	0.77047051	1.95	0.1628	0.000
STMIT10	Def. was provoked	3.41791745	1.04122831	10.78	0.0010	0.123
STMIT2	Def. acted under domin. of another	-0.73009441	1.31678057	0.31	0.5793	0.000
STMIT5	Def. under mental or emot. disturb.	0.46863909	1.16645778	0.16	0.6879	0.000
STMIT9	Def. cooperated with authorities	1.25788805	0.77404747	2.64	0.1041	0.033
VACT	Vic. aroused hate	-1.56854107	1.20797839	1.69	0.1941	0.000
VBDBLD	Bad blood	0.39429512	1.81808167	0.05	0.8283	0.000
VERATK	Vic. verbal attack	0.76306642	1.77999648	0.18	0.6681	0.000
VICCLOSE	Vic. friend, rel., int. acquaintance	0.08623270	0.49813337	0.03	0.8626	0.000
VPROV	Vic. provoked def.	2.58557952	1.42507142	3.29	0.0696	0.047
VRAGE	Vic. aroused def. rage just pri. to kill	-1.56775122	1.23131373	1.62	0.2029	0.000
MINROLCO	Coperp. invol. & def. minor role cont. off.	-1.29656465	1.62163254	0.64	0.4240	0.000
PBQB2	Cont. mur., rob., rape, kid., burg., arson	2.58742466	0.69058874	14.04	0.0002	0.144
PBQB3	Def. created risk/death/public place	1.96639598	0.54184713	13.12	0.0003	0.138
PBQB4	Murder for money/value	0.98525889	0.44467857	4.91	0.0267	0.071
PBQB6	Murder for hire	2.50617871	0.89344201	7.87	0.0050	0.101
PBQB7	Murder wanton, vile, tort., depra.	2.60005863	0.47264102	30.26	0.0000	0.221
PBQB8	Vic. police, corrections, fireman	1.21145566	1.01123221	1.44	0.2309	0.000
PBQB9	Def. prisoner/escapee	3.91182266	1.04958374	13.89	0.0002	0.143
PBQB10	Kill to avoid or stop arrest	0.54611488	0.41563959	1.73	0.1889	0.000

Model B: Ordinary Least Squares

Source	DF	Sum of Squares	Mean Square	F Value	Prob>F
Model	54	37.85210580	0.70096492	7.226	0.0001
Error	551	53.44822423	0.09700222		
C Total	605	91.30033003			

Root MSE 0.3114518   R-Square 0.4146
Dep Mean 0.1848185   Adj R-Sq 0.3572

Variable	DF	Parameter Estimate	Standard Error	t for Ho: Parameter = 0	Prob. >t	Variable Label
INTERCEP	1	0.12106246	0.08338541	1.452	0.1471	Intercept
BLACKD	1	-0.02332903	0.03630166	-0.643	0.5207	Black defendant
WHVICRC	1	0.08665562	0.03743560	2.315	0.0210	One or more white victims (recode)
ACCD	1	-0.07627942	0.05382831	-1.417	0.1570	Accident defense
DDRG	1	-0.04295685	0.10156957	-0.423	0.6725	Def. heavily intoxicated
DEFENSE	1	0.009894681	0.10243012	0.097	0.9231	Vic. assault
DEFREM	1	0.003559939	0.06188871	0.058	0.9542	Def. showed remorse
DFEAR	1	-0.008660624	0.06036553	-0.143	0.8860	Vic. arouse fear
DFSUR24	1	0.009031677	0.06554192	0.138	0.8904	Def. gave up within 24 hrs.
DJUST	1	0.05560421	0.13489373	0.412	0.6803	Def. with moral justification
DNOINT	1	-0.11134538	0.09946068	-1.119	0.2634	No intent to kill
DRGHIS	1	-0.11595691	0.09445679	-1.228	0.2201	Def. had history of drug or alco. abuse
DRUGDIS	1	-0.01653070	0.04715356	-0.351	0.7260	Dispute influenced by drg/alcohol
DSUR	1	-0.01652396	0.10140863	-0.163	0.8706	Def. surrendered to authorities
DUNDERLG	1	-0.13577432	0.06848266	-1.983	0.0479	Def. was underling in murder
FAMLVDIS	1	0.02594646	0.05131173	0.506	0.6133	Family or lover dispute
JEALOS	1	-0.04608835	0.06610840	-0.697	0.4860	Jealousy motive
MANSLAUG	1	-0.17440552	0.05055824	-3.450	0.0006	Manslaughter defense
MINOR	1	0.10983836	0.05654239	1.943	0.0526	Def. 16 or younger
MITCIR	1	-0.13570024	0.04629786	-2.931	0.0035	One or more mit. circumstances
MITCIR2	1	0.07698068	0.08618742	0.893	0.3722	Mit. cir. concern def. (count)
MITCIR3	1	-0.06156802	0.04805525	-1.281	0.2007	Mit. cir. concern vic. (count)
MITDEF	1	0.20460471	0.04845034	4.225	0.0001	Mitigating defense

Variable	df	Coefficient	Std. Error	t	p	Description
MITDEFN	1	-0.19529136	0.07397701	-2.640	0.0085	Def. status sympathetic
MITMOT	1	-0.006980202	0.04480495	-0.156	0.8763	A mitigating motive
NOCONTOF	1	0.02511874	0.04025124	0.624	0.5329	No contemp. offense
NOCONVIC	1	-0.09703561	0.12586368	-0.771	0.4411	No prior convictions
NOFEL	1	-0.04230841	0.04573955	-0.925	0.3554	No felony convictions
NOKILL	1	-0.08817610	0.04919347	-1.792	0.0736	Def. not the triggerman
NORECORD	1	0.02313835	0.12716158	0.182	0.8557	No criminal convictions
NOSERCRI	1	0.04633355	0.0441002	1.050	0.2940	No conviction for a serious crime
NOVPC	1	-0.11052394	0.05785630	-1.910	0.0566	No conviction for a serious viol. felony
OTHMIT	1	-0.02521823	0.11127520	-0.227	0.8208	Other mit. cir.
OTHVMIT	1	-0.01602826	0.07870727	-0.204	0.8387	Vic. mitigating circumstances
STMIT1	1	-0.05237698	0.05804822	-0.902	0.3673	Def. lack cap. to app. criminal. of cond.
STMIT10	1	0.1192819	0.05630224	2.130	0.0336	Def. was provoked
STMIT2	1	0.07463797	0.1056684	0.707	0.4799	Def. acted under domin. of another
STMIT5	1	0.04369881	0.06941494	0.630	0.5293	Def. under mental or emot. disturb.
STMIT9	1	0.17350421	0.07045798	2.463	0.0141	Def. cooperated with authorities
VACT	1	0.002743636	0.05969865	0.046	0.9634	Vic. aroused hate
VBDBLD	1	0.000258919	0.08801019	0.003	0.9977	Bad blood
VERATK	1	-0.03529982	0.08978628	0.393	0.6944	Vic. verbal attack
VICCLOSE	1	-0.02969499	0.03370533	-0.881	0.3787	Vic. friend, rel., int. acquaintance
VINJD	1	-0.006517842	0.11852293	-0.055	0.9562	Vic. attack 3rd person
VPROV	1	0.07119133	0.08253370	0.863	0.3887	Vic. provoked def.
VRAGE	1	0.0125839	0.06470493	0.194	0.8464	Vic. aroused def. rage just pri. to kill
MINROLCO	1	-0.09697166	0.12086549	-0.802	0.4227	Coperp. invol. & def. minor role cont. off.
PBQB2	1	0.15394461	0.04370670	3.522	0.0005	Cont. mur., rob., rape, kid., burg., arson
PBQB3	1	0.09088537	0.03796659	2.394	0.0170	Def. created risk/death/public place
PBQB4	1	0.11655943	0.03984284	2.925	0.0036	Murder for money/value
PBQB6	1	0.10050139	0.08201604	1.225	0.2210	Murder for hire
PBQB7	1	0.16981869	0.02866943	5.923	0.0001	Murder wanton, vile, tort., depra.
PBQB8	1	0.06474403	0.08677295	0.746	0.4559	Vic. police, corrections, fireman
PBQB9	1	0.27997668	0.07974706	3.511	0.0005	Def. prisoner/escapee
PBQB10	1	0.06270914	0.03616231	1.734	0.0835	Kill to avoid or stop arrest

1. Statutory aggravating circumstance B1 (PBQB1) was deleted because of high collinearity with other variables in the model. Aggravating circumstance B5 (PBQB5) was omitted because it was not present in any case. The file contains 51 mitigating factors, but 8 were deleted for multicollinearity. Variable NOCONVIC was omitted from the logistic regression because of computing errors.

2. See supra schedule 1, note 1.

3. See supra schedule 1, note 2.

Schedule 15—PRS

Outcome variable: Death sentence imposed in cases convicted of murder at trial (x481c).
Explanatory variables: The full file of 150+ factors, plus the race of defendant and victim and a race-of-victim interaction term.[1]

Model A: Ordinary Least Squares

Source	DF	Sum of Squares	Mean Square	F Value	Prob>F
Model	165	64.33285133	0.38989607	6.362	0.0001
Error	440	26.96747870	0.06128972		
C Total	605	91.30033003			

Root MSE	0.2475676	R-Square	0.7046
Dep Mean	0.1848185	Adj R-Sq	0.5939

Variable	DF	Parameter Estimate	Standard Error	t for Ho: Parameter=0	Prob. >t	Variable Label
INTERCEP	1	-0.10732691	0.22985752	-0.467	0.6408	Intercept
BLACKD	1	0.03320042	0.03434556	0.967	0.3342	Black defendant
WHVICRC	1	0.19322469	0.05713595	3.382	0.0008	One or more white victims (recode)
AGGMOT	1	0.11689898	0.06445599	1.814	0.0704	Aggravated motive
ALSTAGCR	1	0.02405587	0.06717015	0.358	0.7204	No. of stat. agg. cir. (all jurisdictions)
AMBUSH	1	0.07241559	0.08608563	0.841	0.4007	Def. lying in wait
ARMROB	1	0.16594833	0.07503990	2.211	0.0275	Armed robbery involved
BEAT	1	-0.01809214	0.08822787	-0.205	0.8376	Killed by beating
BLOODY	1	-0.22990701	0.11040359	-2.082	0.0379	Bloody murder involved
BURGARS	1	0.23186119	0.08337334	2.781	0.0057	Burglary or first-degree arson inv.
CONVICTX	1	0.18503231	0.05568711	3.323	0.0010	No. of defendant's prior convictions

Variable		Coefficient	Std. error	t	p	Description
COPERP	1	-0.01967447	0.06291377	-0.313	0.7546	Coperpetrators involved
DDRG	1	-0.02937341	0.10475307	-0.280	0.7793	Def. heavily intoxicated
DEFENSE	1	-0.00637462	0.07959548	-0.080	0.9362	Vic. assault
DEFESC	1	-0.29070150	0.21121893	-1.376	0.1694	Def. on escape
DEFPLEA	1	-0.08187118	0.11180063	-0.732	0.4644	Def. expressed pleasure
DEFREM	1	0.06206379	0.06668073	1.023	0.3070	Def. showed remorse
DEFRSARR	1	0.13634569	0.10976844	1.242	0.2149	Def. actively resisted arrest
DELB7EX	1	-0.05003298	0.09597496	-0.521	0.6024	No. of Ga. death-elig. fac. B7 exp.
DEPRIVE	1	-0.10747483	0.35006553	-0.307	0.7590	Kill by imprison/starve (deprivation)
DFEAR	1	0.00715948	0.05971267	0.120	0.9046	Vic. arouse fear
DFSUR24	1	0.01715890	0.06767284	0.254	0.8000	Def. gave up within 24 hrs.
DJUST	1	0.06753339	0.12839548	0.526	0.5992	Def. with moral justification
DKILLER	1	0.07240391	0.05702507	1.270	0.2049	Def. directly participated in killing
DLEADMF	1	0.03648770	0.05691184	0.641	0.5218	Def. leader murder/con. fel.
DNOINT	1	-0.03387967	0.10076193	-0.336	0.7369	No intent to kill
DPOLSEC	1	0.00424351	0.17196149	0.025	0.9803	Def. police/sec.
DRGHIS	1	-0.03031700	0.10236553	-0.296	0.7672	Def. had history of drug or alco. abuse
DROWN	1	0.07063148	0.12878311	0.548	0.5837	Vic. drowned
DRUGDIS	1	0.02627435	0.05075637	0.518	0.6050	Dispute influenced by drg/alcohol
DSUR	1	0.02081387	0.10520844	0.198	0.8433	Def. surrendered to authorities
DUNDERLG	1	-0.05112984	0.07602388	-0.673	0.5016	Def. was underling in murder
ESCAPE	1	-0.23810375	0.14070533	-1.692	0.0913	Kill occurred in escape from jail/prison
EXECK	1	0.13905089	0.12640091	1.100	0.2719	Execution-style murder
FAMLVDIS	1	-0.02933304	0.04581314	-0.640	0.5223	Family or lover dispute
FEMVIC	1	0.09209684	0.03578714	2.573	0.0104	Vic. was a female
FRAC	1	-0.15716309	0.07933344	-1.981	0.0482	Killed by fractures
HATE	1	0.02142468	0.05071826	0.422	0.6729	Hate/revenge motive
HOST	1	0.31791027	0.12468440	2.550	0.0111	Vic. a hostage
INJURE	1	0.05144563	0.04907054	1.048	0.2950	Def. injured 1 + person
INSANE	1	-0.00657421	0.07236481	-0.091	0.9277	Insanity defense

Schedule 15, Model A (*cont.*)

Variable	DF	Parameter Estimate	Standard Error	t for H0: Parameter = 0	Prob. >t	Variable Label
INSMOT	1	0.25126121	0.21265622	1.182	0.2380	Insurance motive
JEALOS	1	0.05976721	0.05650170	1.058	0.2907	Jealousy motive
KIDNAP	1	−0.18233325	0.10200310	−1.788	0.0745	Vic. was kidnapped
KILLHIRE	1	−0.17045486	0.14651189	−1.163	0.2453	Case involved hired killer
KNIFE	1	−0.01244992	0.05421525	−0.230	0.8185	Knife killing
MAJAGCIR	1	−0.00095972	0.06084729	−0.016	0.9874	One or more major agg. cir.
MAJAGCRX	1	0.12711625	0.09248893	1.374	0.1700	No. of major aggravating circumstances
MANSLAUG	1	−0.07258660	0.05817382	−1.248	0.2128	Manslaughter defense
MILDEFN	1	0.18056011	0.07162075	2.521	0.0121	Def. in military
MINAGCRX	1	0.32074734	0.10762572	2.980	0.0030	No. of minor agg. circumstances
MINAGGCR	1	−0.08786108	0.05015216	−1.752	0.0805	One or more minor agg. circumstances
MINOR	1	0.17209850	0.05666096	3.037	0.0025	Def. 16 or younger
RACE	1	0.04213364	0.14142557	0.298	0.7659	Race-hatred motive
RAGE	1	0.08937537	0.05579999	1.602	0.1099	Immediate rage motive
RAPE	1	0.15974932	0.09478642	1.685	0.0926	Rape involved
RISK5	1	−0.05274276	0.06462426	−0.816	0.4149	Five or more people at risk
RPUBPLC	1	−0.06190716	0.21649022	−0.286	0.7750	Def. created great risk in pub. place
SERCONOF	1	0.01653332	0.12923653	0.128	0.8983	A serious cont. offense involved
SERCRIMX	1	−0.18966378	0.05718778	−3.317	0.0010	No. of ser. prior crimes
SERVFEL	1	−0.08330649	0.11035004	−0.755	0.4507	Def. record serious violent felony
SEXMT	1	−0.14880714	0.06623974	−2.246	0.0252	Sex motive
SHOT5	1	−0.00576638	0.04425348	−0.130	0.8964	Def. fired 5 or more shots
SILWIT	1	−0.01187277	0.08279572	−0.143	0.8860	Vic. killed because a witness
SLASHTH	1	−0.05097319	0.13184846	−0.387	0.6992	Victim's throat was slashed
STMIT1	1	−0.07819135	0.05175106	−1.511	0.1315	Def. lack cap. to app. criminality of cond.

STMIT2	1	-0.0644428	0.09898297	-0.671	0.5024	Def. acted under domin. of another
STMIT5	1	-0.03761173	0.06295579	-0.597	0.5505	Def. under mental or emot. disturb.
STMIT9	1	0.10431585	0.06340627	1.645	0.1006	Def. cooperated with authorities
ACCD	1	-0.10918796	0.06060971	-1.801	0.0723	Accident defense
ADCRIM	1	-0.29779634	0.11289228	-2.638	0.0086	Def. comm. add. crime after killing
AGE	1	0.05046501	0.02023281	2.494	0.0130	Def. age at time of crime
AGGBATT	1	-0.09845070	0.06690701	-1.471	0.1419	Aggravated battery involved
AGGCIRX	1	-0.00022361	0.02473207	-0.009	0.9928	No. of aggravating factors
FEL_2VMD	1	0.01864740	0.14543241	0.128	0.8980	Record/fel. or 2 + viol. misd.
AGGMETKL	1	0.08025621	0.09232897	0.869	0.3852	One or more agg. method of killing
MITCIR	1	0.10838497	0.06589427	1.645	0.1007	One or more mit. circumstances
MITCIRX	1	-0.06710575	0.04360772	-1.539	0.1246	No. of mit. cir.
MITCIR2	1	0.03101820	0.09114312	0.340	0.7338	Mit. cir. concern def. (count)
MITCIR3	1	-0.01629829	0.04882035	-0.334	0.7387	Mit. cir. concern vic. (count)
MITDEF	1	0.11796612	0.06676145	1.767	0.0779	Mitigating defense
MITMOT	1	-0.08222348	0.06301262	-1.305	0.1926	A mitigating motive
MULSH	1	-0.11077607	0.10195046	-1.087	0.2778	Multiple shots
MULSTAB	1	0.14339384	0.07583418	1.891	0.0593	Multiple stabs
MUTIL	1	0.09321234	0.12499243	0.746	0.4562	Mutilation involved
NOAGGCIR	1	-0.06016132	0.04735746	-1.270	0.2046	No aggravating circumstances
NOCONTOF	1	0.05578625	0.04165350	1.339	0.1812	No contemp. offense
NOCONVIC	1	-0.02597148	0.12691940	-0.205	0.8380	No prior convictions
NOFEL	1	-0.02570138	0.15338516	-0.168	0.8670	No felony convictions
NOKILL	1	-0.07420293	0.04710239	-1.575	0.1159	Def. not the triggerman
NONPCRM	1	0.12559132	0.06054926	2.074	0.0386	Motive to facl. nonprop.-related crime
NONVCOF	1	0.07808913	0.04673550	1.671	0.0955	Def. engaged in nonviolent contemp. off.
NORECORD	1	0.04844864	0.12940902	0.374	0.7083	No criminal convictions
NOSERCRI	1	0.06637212	0.09773015	0.679	0.4974	No conviction for a serious crime
NOVMC	1	0.03061927	0.04379779	0.699	0.4849	No vic. mitigating circumstances
NOVPC	1	0.06682309	0.09907187	0.614	0.5396	No conviction for a serious viol. felony

Schedule 15, Model A (cont.)

Variable	DF	Parameter Estimate	Standard Error	t for Ho: Parameter = 0	Prob. >t	Variable Label
NOPROV	1	−0.14775593	0.09005574	−1.641	0.1016	Vic. offered no provocation
OBTMON	1	0.02577936	0.21505976	0.120	0.9046	Money motive
OLDER	1	−0.08158252	0.05604468	−1.456	0.1462	Def. 50+
OLDVIC	1	−0.17447147	0.06124125	−2.849	0.0046	Vic. was 65 years or more
ONESHOT	1	0.01484361	0.03234756	0.459	0.6465	Def. fired one shot
OTHMIT	1	0.01119781	0.11444842	0.098	0.9221	Other mit. cir.
OTHVMIT	1	0.03338898	0.07342635	0.455	0.6495	Vic. mitigating circumstances
PBQB10	1	−0.24709362	0.23692068	−1.043	0.2975	Kill to avoid or stop arrest
PBQB2	1	−0.12082570	0.24750467	−0.488	0.6257	Cont. mur., rob., rape, kid., burg., arson
PBQB4	1	−0.23806586	0.30302954	−0.786	0.4325	Murder for money/value
PBQB6	1	−0.08370289	0.24338400	−0.344	0.7311	Murder for hire
PBQB7	1	−0.31190962	0.23758334	−1.313	0.1899	Murder wanton, vile, tort., depra.
PBQB7B	1	0.14755821	0.11638361	1.268	0.2055	Unnessary multiple wounding (tort.)
PBQB7D	1	0.17959158	0.12568700	1.429	0.1537	Rape, etc./sil. w. or vic./helpless. ex., plead.
PBQB7E	1	0.07555123	0.14324565	0.527	0.5982	Sex perversion involved
PBQB7F	1	0.14268485	0.13581846	1.051	0.2940	Vic. beat, strang., drown, poison, torture
PBQB8	1	−0.13209910	0.23444829	−0.563	0.5734	Vic. police, corrections, fireman
PBQB9	1	0.02377194	0.26523930	0.090	0.9286	Def. prisoner/escapee
PBQDELX	1	0.15422674	0.23811848	0.648	0.5175	No. of Georgia death-elig. factors in case
PERVR	1	−0.17548172	0.09764147	−1.797	0.0730	Sexual perversion involved
POISON	1	−0.20670421	0.30851987	−0.670	0.5032	Vic. killed with poison
PRECIPEV	1	−0.00244402	0.05922509	−0.041	0.9671	One or more precip. evts.
PRECIPX	1	0.00721485	0.04671055	0.154	0.8773	Number of precip. cir.
PREESC	1	0.11250040	0.10625714	1.059	0.2903	Prevent arrest motive
PREMED	1	0.08808241	0.06424729	1.371	0.1711	Def. plan murder or cont. off. >5 min.

PREMEDF	1	-0.40163518	0.11592193	-3.465	0.0006	Def. planned cont. off. >5 minutes
PREMEDK	1	-0.37601482	0.12390027	-3.035	0.0025	Def. planned killing>5 minutes
PRIFEL	1	0.02237292	0.008128991	2.752	0.0062	No. of prior felony convictions reported
STOMP	1	-0.33064252	0.16775913	-1.971	0.0494	Brutal stomping/beating
STRANG	1	-0.09825812	0.12289482	-0.800	0.4244	Killed by strangulation
SVPCR	1	-0.13320195	0.23562557	-0.565	0.5721	1+ prior conv.: murder, arm. rob., rape, kidnap
SVPCRX	1	0.20753524	0.16999996	1.221	0.2228	No. of prior conv.: murder, arm. rob., rape, kidnap
TORT	1	-0.04152011	0.11259134	-0.369	0.7125	Torture involved
TWOVIC	1	0.14969602	0.14841051	1.009	0.3137	Two or more vic. by def. or by coperp.
TWOVICAL	1	0.01832125	0.13862386	0.132	0.8949	Two or more vic. total by def. and coperp.
UNNEC	1	-0.37137176	0.11166837	-3.326	0.0010	Killing was not necessary
UNNEPAIN	1	-0.16330073	0.11322298	-1.442	0.1499	Unnecessary pain involved
DIRROLCO	1	-0.08665378	0.04840941	-1.790	0.0741	Coperp. invol. & def. partic. in cont. off.
VACT	1	-0.01294147	0.06567447	-0.197	0.8439	Vic. aroused hate
VBDBLD	1	-0.04359501	0.08509073	-0.512	0.6087	Bad blood
VERATK	1	-0.05918646	0.08437712	-0.701	0.4834	Vic. verbal attack
VFUGIT	1	-0.10840197	0.1458418	-0.740	0.4600	Vic. a fugitive
VICBDGAG	1	-0.24808028	0.13525952	-1.834	0.0673	Vic. bound and/or gagged
VICCLOSE	1	-0.01606519	0.03404084	-0.472	0.6372	Vic. friend, rel., int. acquaintance
VICSTRAN	1	0.07686636	0.04045072	1.900	0.0581	Vic. was a stranger
VICYNG	1	-0.02904288	0.22133541	-0.131	0.8957	Vic. defenseless/youth
VINJD	1	0.00999014	0.11012700	0.091	0.9278	Vic. attack 3rd person
VITCIR	1	-0.01109722	0.02990834	-0.371	0.7108	No. of vic. agg. cir.
VPCX	1	0.00575766	0.05216276	0.110	0.9122	Prior conv. mur./arm. rob./rape/kid./& oth. VPC
VPERCR	1	0.04760031	0.0874119	0.549	0.5834	1+ prior convics.: violent person crimes
VPERCRX	1	-0.00833849	0.05138888	-0.162	0.8712	No. of prior convics.: violent person crimes
VPROV	1	-0.01390989	0.07768287	-0.179	0.8580	Vic. provoked def.
VRAGE	1	-0.07398683	0.06755171	-1.095	0.2740	Vic. aroused def. rage just pri. to kill
W15A1	1	0.11008702	0.19141978	0.575	0.5655	No. of prior conv. mur.
W15B1	1	-0.16562556	0.14493278	-1.143	0.2538	No. of prior conv. arm. rob.

Schedule 15, Model A (cont.)

Variable	DF	Parameter Estimate	Standard Error	t for Ho: Parameter = 0	Prob. >t	Variable Label
W15D	1	0.07722703	0.04701167	1.643	0.1012	No. of prior conv. other viol. per. cr.
W15F	1	−0.0067992	0.01584113	−0.425	0.6712	No. of convictions: other felonies, misdem.
W15F1	1	−0.1885069	0.05539166	−3.405	0.0007	No. of pri. conv. for oth. fel. & mid. (DOC & PBQ)
YNGADLT	1	0.06597016	0.04034779	1.635	0.1028	Def. aged 17 thru 25
YNGVIC	1	0.1367043	0.21726820	0.629	0.5295	Vic. 12 or younger
YNUDDIS	1	−0.2847049	0.12655956	−2.279	0.0231	Vic. nude
HISTD	1	−0.0478895	0.05900555	−0.811	0.4177	High-status def.: wh-coll., propr., prof., exec.
LSTATDEF	1	0.0191783	0.02609758	0.533	0.5941	Low SES def.
DFEM	1	0.02958932	0.04319305	0.685	0.4937	Female def.
VICLSTAT	1	−0.06425784	0.03617356	−1.776	0.0764	Vic. low stat.
NKNPOMSH	1	−0.32056749	0.10248459	−3.128	0.0019	No KIDNAP or MULSH
AGMOTAPF	1	0.11760086	0.05529469	2.127	0.0340	AGGMOT and PRIFEL
DLXXW15D	1	0.03670512	0.01363056	2.693	0.0074	DELB7EX − 2.1631 × W15D − .54932
DEFRAAPF	1	0.09823240	0.07516209	1.307	0.1919	DEFRSARR and PRIFEL
MCIRAWHV	1	−0.14200481	0.05966779	−2.380	0.0177	MITCIR and WHVICRC

1. Some factors were deleted because of multicollinearity or because the factor was not present in any case. The variable list submitted in the *McCleskey* case did not include any interaction terms.

2. For one case in which the socioeconomic status of the defendant was not known, we set the variable LSTATDEF to equal its average value.

3. Nominal inferential statistics (standard error, t, and probability) are computed by a least-squares program. Safe inferential statistics could not be computed because of the large number of independent variables.

Schedule 16—PRS

Outcome variable: Death sentence imposed in cases convicted of murder at trial (x481c).
Explanatory variables: Variables from schedule 15 that show a statistically significant relationship ($p \le .10$) to the death-sentencing result among defendants convicted of murder at trial in a least-squares stepwise-regression analysis, and the race of defendant and victim.[1] This model was estimated before the McCleskey hearing but the variable list was not included in the McCleskey Technical Appendix.

Model A: Logistic Regression

606 Observations
494 x481c = 0
112 x481c = 1
Model chi-square[1] = 401.332 with 34 D.F.
R = .758[2]

Variable	Logistic Regression Coefficient	Safe[3]			Nominal[4]			Variable Label
		Standard Error	t[5]	p[6]	Standard Error	t[5]	p[6]	
CONST	−7.8441	0.8789	−8.92	0.000	1.0990	−7.137	0.000	
BLACKD	0.0650	0.4584	0.14	0.887	0.5251	0.124	0.901	Black defendant
WHVICRC	1.6277	0.5660	2.88	0.004	0.6385	2.549	0.001	One or more white victims (recode)
AGGCIRX	0.5470	0.1753	3.12	0.002	0.1729	3.164	0.002	No. of aggravating factors
ARMROB	0.7077	0.6549	1.08	0.280	0.6335	1.117	0.264	Armed robbery involved
BURGARS	2.0751	1.1175	1.86	0.063	0.9461	2.193	0.028	Burglary or first-degree arson inv.
DELB7EX	0.7273	0.2247	3.24	0.001	0.2532	2.872	0.004	No. of Ga. death-elig. fac. B7 exp.
DROWN	1.4189	1.4173	1.00	0.317	1.2030	1.179	0.238	Vic. drowned
DUNDERLG	−4.9222	3.2713	−1.50	0.132	1.8450	−2.668	0.008	Def. was underling in murder

Schedule 16, Model A (*cont.*)

Variable	Logistic Regression Coefficient	Safe[3]			Nominal[4]			Variable Label
		Standard Error	t[5]	p[6]	Standard Error	t[5]	p[6]	
EXECK	0.7666	1.0123	0.76	0.449	1.4280	0.537	0.591	Execution-style murder
FEMVIC	1.2226	0.5962	2.05	0.040	0.5949	2.055	0.040	Vic. was a female
HOST	2.6821	1.0514	2.55	0.011	1.3970	1.920	0.055	Vic. a hostage
INSANE	0.8734	0.5726	1.53	0.127	0.7336	1.190	0.234	Insanity defense
INSMOT	2.7116	0.9559	2.84	0.005	0.9440	2.872	0.004	Insurance motive
KIDNAP	0.5661	0.6033	0.94	0.348	0.6705	0.844	0.399	Vic. was kidnapped
MINAGGCR	-0.5120	0.6132	-0.83	0.404	0.6971	-0.734	0.463	One or more minor agg. circumstances
MULSH	2.0921	0.7263	2.88	0.004	0.6884	3.039	0.002	Multiple shots
MULSTAB	2.1518	0.5850	3.68	0.000	0.7840	2.745	0.006	Multiple stabs
NOKILL	-0.3636	0.6153	-0.59	0.555	0.6601	-0.551	0.582	Def. not the triggerman
OLDVIC	-1.8791	1.1510	-1.63	0.103	0.8767	-2.143	0.032	Vic. was 65 years or more
PBQB7	-1.2830	0.7311	-1.75	0.079	0.6776	-1.893	0.058	Murder wanton, vile, tort., depra.
PBQB7D	0.3717	0.9631	0.39	0.700	0.8359	0.445	0.657	Rape, etc./sil. w. or vic./helpless. ex., plead.
PRIFEL	0.2960	0.1692	1.75	0.080	0.1748	1.693	0.090	No. of prior felony convictions reported
RACE	3.6457	0.8612	4.23	0.000	3.3140	1.100	0.271	Race-hatred motive
RAPE	1.4390	1.1768	1.22	0.221	0.9057	1.589	0.112	Rape involved
STMIT9	2.7195	0.7792	3.49	0.000	0.8689	3.130	0.002	Def. cooperated with authorities
TWOVIC	1.7451	0.6756	2.58	0.010	0.6242	2.796	0.005	Two or more victims by def. or by coperp.
UNNEC	-1.3242	0.6497	-2.04	0.042	0.6063	-2.184	0.029	Killing was not necessary
VICBDGAG	-1.3967	0.7728	-1.81	0.071	1.1250	-1.242	0.214	Vic. bound and/or gagged
VICSTRAN	1.9281	0.6033	3.20	0.001	0.5338	3.612	0.000	Vic. was a stranger
VITCIR	-0.6638	0.4634	-1.43	0.152	0.4677	-1.419	0.156	No. of vic. agg. cir.
W15D	0.9520	0.2895	3.29	0.001	0.3433	2.773	0.006	No. of prior conv. other viol. per. cr.
W15F1	-0.2366	0.1552	-1.52	0.127	0.1458	-1.623	0.105	No. of pri. conv. for oth. fel. & mid.
YNGVIC	1.7975	0.8105	2.22	0.027	1.0920	1.646	0.100	Vic. 12 or younger
VICLSTAT	-1.1097	0.6817	-1.63	0.104	0.7086	-1.566	0.117	Vic. low stat.

Model B: Ordinary Least Squares

Source	DF	Sum of Squares	Mean Square	F Value	Prob>F
Model	34	54.8084612	1.6120143 0	25.224	0.0001
Error	571	36.4918391	0.06390866		
C Total	605	91.3003003			

Root MSE 0.2528016   R-Square 0.6003
Dep Mean 0.1848185   Adj R-Sq 0.5765

Variable	Regression Coefficient	Safe[3]			Nominal[4]			Variable Label
		Standard Error	t^5	p^6	Standard Error	t^5	p^6	
CONST	-0.1083	0.0354	-3.06	0.002	0.0361	-2.996	0.003	
BLACKD	0.0206	0.0329	0.63	0.531	0.0287	0.719	0.472	Black defendant
WHVICRC	0.0763	0.0322	2.37	0.018	0.0296	2.574	0.010	One or more white victims (recode)
AGGCIRX	0.0429	0.0100	4.29	0.000	0.0085	5.054	0.000	No. of aggravating factors
ARMROB	0.0924	0.0455	2.03	0.042	0.0373	2.479	0.013	Armed robbery involved
BURGARS	0.1673	0.1036	1.61	0.106	0.0612	2.736	0.006	Burglary or first-degree arson inv.
DELB7EX	0.0339	0.0158	2.14	0.032	0.0137	2.480	0.013	No. of Ga. death-elig. fac. B7 exp.
DROWN	0.1413	0.0898	1.57	0.116	0.0655	2.156	0.031	Vic. drowned
DUNDERLG	-0.1749	0.0599	-2.92	0.004	0.0526	-3.325	0.001	Def. was underling in murder
EXECK	0.1964	0.0845	2.32	0.020	0.0714	2.752	0.006	Execution-style murder
FEMVIC	0.0636	0.0277	2.30	0.022	0.0280	2.273	0.023	Vic. was a female
HOST	0.3489	0.1477	2.36	0.018	0.0954	3.656	0.000	Vic. a hostage
INSANE	0.0890	0.0423	2.10	0.035	0.0392	2.270	0.023	Insanity defense
INSMOT	0.2350	0.1208	1.94	0.052	0.0714	3.292	0.001	Insurance motive
KIDNAP	0.1794	0.0612	2.93	0.003	0.0436	4.119	0.000	Vic. was kidnapped

Schedule 16, Model B (cont.)

Variable	Logistic Regression Coefficient	Safe[3]			Nominal[4]			Variable Label
		Standard Error	t[5]	p[6]	Standard Error	t[5]	p[6]	
MINAGGCR	−0.0583	0.0260	−2.24	0.025	0.0285	−2.047	0.041	One or more minor agg. circumstances
MULSH	0.1580	0.0576	2.74	0.006	0.0396	3.995	0.000	Multiple shots
MULSTAB	0.1816	0.0503	3.61	0.000	0.0434	4.181	0.000	Multiple stabs
NOKILL	−0.0600	0.0402	−1.49	0.136	0.0367	−1.636	0.102	Def. not the triggerman
OLDVIC	−0.0969	0.0645	−1.50	0.133	0.0471	−2.060	0.039	Vic. was 65 years or more
PBQB7	−0.1067	0.0311	−3.43	0.001	0.0301	−3.541	0.000	Murder wanton, vile, tort., depra.
PBQB7D	0.0912	0.0732	1.25	0.213	0.0501	1.819	0.069	Rape, etc./sil. w. or vic./helpless. ex., plead.
PRIFEL	0.0193	0.0044	4.33	0.000	0.0056	3.458	0.001	No. of prior felony convictions reported
RACE	0.2168	0.0960	2.26	0.024	0.1002	2.163	0.031	Race-hatred motive
RAPE	0.1456	0.0824	1.77	0.077	0.0551	2.644	0.008	Rape involved
STMIT9	0.1658	0.0874	1.90	0.058	0.0561	2.955	0.003	Def. cooperated with authorities
TWOVIC	0.1839	0.0738	2.49	0.013	0.0466	3.942	0.000	Two or more victims by def. or by coperp.
UNNEC	−0.1473	0.0469	−3.14	0.002	0.0368	−4.002	0.000	Killing was not necessary
VICBDGAG	−0.1629	0.0755	−2.16	0.031	0.0604	−2.696	0.007	Vic. bound and/or gagged
VICSTRAN	0.1269	0.0378	3.35	0.001	0.0292	4.345	0.000	Vic. was a stranger
VITCIR	−0.0529	0.0252	−2.10	0.035	0.0221	−2.395	0.017	No. of vic. agg. cir.
W15D	0.0715	0.0246	2.91	0.004	0.0202	3.536	0.000	No. of prior conv. other viol. per. cr.
W15F1	−0.0069	0.0027	−2.59	0.009	0.0023	−3.012	0.003	No. of pri. conv. for oth. fel. & mid.
YNGVIC	0.1149	0.0638	1.80	0.072	0.0596	1.930	0.054	Vic. 12 or younger
VICLSTAT	−0.0489	0.0313	−1.56	0.118	0.0317	−1.540	0.124	Vic. low stat.

1. *See supra* schedule 1, note 1.
2. *See supra* schedule 1, note 2.
3. *See supra* schedule 1, note 3. Although this analysis is unweighted, we have included the safe computations to keep the table format the same.
4. *See supra* schedule 1, note 4.
5. *See supra* schedule 1, note 5.
6. *See supra* schedule 1, note 6.

GENERAL INDEX

INDEX OF CASES

SELECTED SOURCES

American Trial Lawyers Foundation, *The Penalty of Death: Final Report* (1980), Roscoe Pound Conference, 6n.4

Amsterdam, "Race and the Death Penalty,"7 *Crim. Jus. Ethics* 2 (Winter/Spring 1988)

Amsterdam, "The Supreme Court and Capital Punishment," 14 *Human Rights* 14 (A.B.A. Sec. on Individual Rights & Responsibilities) (Winter 1987), 137n.39

Arkin, "Discrimination and Arbitrariness in Capital Punishment: An Analysis of Post-*Furman* Murder Cases in Dade County, Florida, 1973–1976," 33 *Stan. L. Rev.* 75 (1980), 241–42, 256, 270n.53, 275n.136

Baldus, D., & Cole, J., *Statistical Proof of Discrimination* (1980), 70n.31, 191n.18, 365n.62, 391n.33

Baldus, Pulaski, & Woodworth, "Arbitrariness and Discrimination in the Administration of the Death Penalty: A Challenge to State Supreme Courts," 15 *Stetson L. Rev.* 133 (1986), 22, 34n.6, 34n.14, 68n.17, 267n.11

Baldus, Pulaski, & Woodworth, "Comparative Review of Death Sentences: An Empirical Study of the Georgia Experience," 74 *J. Crim. L. & Criminology* 661 (1983), 21n.51, 34n.15, 36n.25, 135n.22, 222n.37, 222n.44

Baldus, Pulaski, Woodworth, & Kyle, "Identifying Comparatively Excessive Sentences of Death: A Quantitative Approach," 33 *Stan. L. Rev.* 1 (1980), 34n.14, 37n.25, 78n.55, 133n.7, 241, 252, 267n.6, 270n.50, 270n.51, 274n.105

Baldus, Woodworth, & Pulaski, "Arbitrariness and Discrimination in Colorado's post-*Furman* Capital Charging and Sentencing Process: A Preliminary Report" (1986; unpublished manuscript), 233–35, 243–44, 262, 268n.20, 270n.64, 277n.171

Baldus, Woodworth, & Pulaski, "Monitoring and Evaluating Contemporary Death Sentencing Systems: Lessons from Georgia," 18 *U.C. Davis L. Rev.* 1375 (1985), 70n.29

Barnes, D., & Conley, J., *Statistical Evidence in Litigation* (1986), 70n.31

Barnett, "Some Distribution Patterns for the Georgia Death Sentence," 18 *U.C. Davis L. Rev.* 1327 (1985), 51–52, 70n.29, 94–95, 116–17, 134n.13, 152–53, 161, 189n.16, 447n.24, 448n.33

Baumeister & Parley, "Reducing the Biasing Effect of Perpetrator Attractiveness in Jury Simulation," 8 *Personality & Soc. Psychology Bull.* 286 (1982), 188–89n.8

Bedau, "Capital Punishment in Oregon, 1903–64," 45 *Or. L. Rev.* 1 (1965), 274n.113

Bedau, H., *Death is Different: Studies in the Morality, Law, and Politics of Capital Punishment* (1987)

Note: When applicable, sources are followed by page number and, where cited, note number ("n").

Bedau, "Death Sentences in New Jersey, 1907–1960," 19 *Rutgers L. Rev.* 1 (1964) (Appendix II: "Abstract of Analysis of Jury Sentencing in Capital Cases: New Jersey: 1937–1961," by E. Wolf), 251–52, 267n.6, 274n.99, 274n.112

Bedau, "Felony Murder and the Mandatory Death Penalty: A Study in Discretionary Justice," 10 *Suffolk U. L. Rev.* 493 (1976), 241, 252, 270n.49, 274n.107

Bedau, H., ed., "American Attitudes Toward the Death Penalty," in *The Death Penalty in America* (3d ed. 1980), 421n.44

Bedau, H., ed., *The Death Penalty in America* (3d ed. 1982), 6n.4, 16n.2, 16n.3, 34n.5

Belsley, D. A., Kuh, E., & Welsh, R. E., *Regression Diagnostics* (1980), 448n.31

Bentele, "The Death Penalty in Georgia: Still Arbitrary," 62 *Wash. U. L. Q.* 573 (1985), 37n.25, 126–27, 138n.43, 206, 219n.6, 223n.48, 223n.49, 224n.62, 246, 271n.78

Berk, "Applications of the General Linear Model to Survey Data," in *Handbook of Survey Research* 539 (P. Rossi, J. Wright, & A. Anderson eds. 1983), 473n.46

Berk & Lowery, "Factors Affecting Death Penalty Decisions in Mississippi" (June 1985; unpublished manuscript), 258–60, 268n.19, 268n.27, 276n.155, 277n.162

Berk & Ray, "Selection Biases in Sociological Data," 11 *Soc. Sci. Rev.* 352 (1982), 445n.14

Berns, "Defending the Death Penalty," 26 *Crime & Delinquency* 503 (1980), 6n.4

Bickel, Hammel, & O'Connel, "Sex Bias in Graduate Admission: Data from Berkeley," in *Statistics & Public Policy* 113 (W. Fairley & F. Mosteller eds. 1977), 446n.21

Bienen, Weiner, Denno, Allison, & Mills, "The Reimposition of Capital Punishment in New Jersey: The Role of Prosecutorial Discretion," 41 *Rutgers L. Rev.* 27 (1988), 68n.11, 244, 261–62, 265, 268n.18, 268n.28, 271n.66, 271n.68, 277n.167

Black, C., *Capital Punishment: The Inevitability of Caprice and Mistake* (2d ed. 1981), 6n.4

Blumstein, A., Cohen, J., Martin, S., & Tonry, M., eds., 1 *Research on Sentencing: The Search for Reform* (1983), 68n.11, 72n.40, 278n.180, 353n.15, 445n.11

Bowers, W., *Legal Homicide* (2d ed. 1984), 16n.2, 16n.10, 16n.12, 205–6, 219n.6, 223n.46, 224n.62, 249, 274n.87, 274n.91

Bowers, "The Pervasiveness of Arbitrariness and Discrimination Under Post-*Furman* Capital Statutes," 74 *J. Crim. L. and Criminology* 1067 (1983), 37n.25, 245–46, 256, 271n.75, 271n.77, 271n.79, 275n.138

Bowers & Pierce, "Arbitrariness and Discrimination under Post-*Furman* Capital Statutes," 26 *Crime & Deling.* 563 (1980), 245, 255, 271n.71, 275n.124

Brearley, "The Negro and Homicide," 9 *Soc. Forces* 247 (1930), 249, 273n.84

Brown, "Statistics, Scientific Method, and Smoking," in *Statistics: A Guide to the Unknown* 59 (J. Tanur, F. Mosteller, W. Kruskal, R. Link, R. Pieters, G. Rising, & E. Lehman eds. 2d ed. 1978), 445n.8

Bruck, "On Death Row in Pretoria Central," 197 *The New Republic,* July 13 & 20, 1987, 273n.83

Bunker, J., Forrest, W., Jr., Mosteller, F., & Vandam, L., *The National Halothane Study* (1969), 70n.32

Calabresi, G., & Bobbitt, P., *Tragic Choices* (1978), 418, 421n.43, 422n.65

Coleman, J., et al., *Equality of Educational Opportunity* (1966), 423n.66

Coleman, K., ed., *A History of Georgia* (1977), 137n.38

Converse, P., *American Social Attitudes Data Sourcebook, 1947–1978* (1980), 136n.30

DeParle, "A Matter of Life or Death," *Times Picayune* (New Orleans), Apr. 7, 1985, 269n.36

Dix, "Appellate Review of the Decision to Impose Death," 68 *Geo. L. J.* 97 (1979), 34n.14, 37n.25, 198–99, 219n.4, 219n.6, 222n.40, 267n.3, 280, 292, 294n.4, 303n.48

Dixon, W. J., ed., *BMDP Statistical Software 1981* (1981), 70n.34

Dorin, "Two Different Worlds: Racial Discrimination in the Imposition of Capital Punishment in Rape Cases," 72 *J. Crim. L. & Criminology* 1667 (1981), 16n.15

Dworkin, R., *Taking Rights Seriously* (1977), 422n.61

Efron, "The Efficiency of Logistic Regression Compared to Normal Discriminant Analysis," 70 *J. of the Am. Stat. A.* 892 (1975), 447n.27

Ehrhardt & Levinson, "Florida's Response to *Furman*: An Exercise in Futility," 64 *J. Crim. L. & Criminology* 10 (1973), 23

Ehrlich, "The Deterrent Effect of Capital Punishment," 65 *Am. Econ. Rev.* 397 (1975), 421n.47

Ekland-Olson, "Structured Discretion, Racial Bias, and the Death Penalty: The First Decade after *Furman* in Texas," 69 *Soc. Science Q.* 853 (1988)

Exum, "The Death Penalty in North Carolina," 8 *Campbell L. Rev.* 1 (1985)

Finkelstein, "The Judicial Reception of Multiple Regression Studies in Race and Sex Discrimination Cases," 80 *Colum. L. Rev.* 737 (1980), 70n.31, 390n.30, 391n.33

Fisher, "Multiple Regression in Legal Proceedings," 80 *Colum. L. Rev.* 702 (1980), 70n.31, 390n.30, 391n.33, 473n.54, 478n.84

Fisher & Kadane, "Empirically Based Sentencing Guidelines and Ethical Considerations," in 2 *Research on Sentencing: The Search for Reform* (A. Blumstein, J. Cohen, S. Martin, & M. Tonry eds. 1983), 45, 69n.18

Foley, "Florida After the *Furman* Decision: The Effect of Extralegal Factors on the Processing of Capital Offense Cases," 5 *Behavioral Sciences & the Law* 457 (1987)

Foley & Powell, "The Discretion of Prosecutors, Judges, and Juries in Capital Cases," 7 *Crim. Just. Rev.* 16 (1982), 256, 275n.134

Fox, "Death Verdict More Frequent in South Jersey," *Sunday Record* (Bergen, N.J.), February 15, 1987, 268n.18, 271n.70

Friedman, G. D., *Primer of Epidemiology* (3d ed. 1987), 393n.54, 475n.61

Galanter, "Why the 'Haves' Come Out Ahead: Speculation on the Limits of Legal Change," 9 *Law & Soc. Rev.* 95 (1974), 304n.59

Gallup, G., *The Gallup Poll: Public Opinion 1983* (1984), 137n.30

Gallup, G., *The Gallup Poll: Public Opinion 1985* (1986), 196n.61

Garfinkel, "Research Notes on Inter- and Intra-racial Homicides," 27 *Soc. Forces* 369 (1949), 250, 274n.90

General Accounting Office, *Death Penalty Sentencing: Research Indicates Pattern of Racial Disparities*, GAO/GGD-90-57 (Feb. 1990)

Gillers, "Deciding Who Dies," 129 *U. Pa. L. Rev.* 1 (1980), 15n.1, 33n.4

Goldberg, "The Death Penalty and the Supreme Court," 15 *Ariz. L. Rev.* 355 (1974), 17n.29

Gottfredson, M., & Gottfredson, D., *Decision Making in Criminal Justice: Toward the Rational Exercise of Discretion* (2d ed. 1988), 189n.8

Greenberg, "Capital Punishment as a System," 91 *Yale L. J.* 908 (1982), 15n.1, 33n.1, 267n.3, 421n.46

Greenfeld & Hinners, "Capital Punishment 1984," in U.S. Dept. of Just., Bureau of Just. Statistics Bull. 1 (1985), 254, 275n.122, 275n.123

Gross, "Race and Death: The Judicial Evaluation of Evidence of Discrimination in Capital Sentencing," 18 *U.C. Davis L. Rev.* 1275 (1985), 391n.35

Gross, S., & Mauro, R., *Death & Discrimination: Racial Disparities in Capital Sentencing* (1989), 71n.34, 271n.76, 368n.95

Gross & Mauro, "Patterns of Death: An Analysis of Racial Disparities in Capital Sentencing and Homicide Victimization," 37 *Stan. L. Rev.* 27 (1984), 15n.1, 19n.48, 38n.52, 78n.55, 196n.62, 258, 271n.76, 276n.150, 276n.152, 276n.154, 445n.3

Guilford, J., & Fruchter, B., *Fundamental Statistics in Psychology and Education* (6th ed. 1978), 473n.55

Haller, "Capital Punishment Statutes After *Furman*," 35 *Ohio State* L. J. 651 (1974), 16n.6

Hancock, "The Perils of Calibrating the Death Penalty Through Special Definitions of Murder," 53 *Tul. L. Rev.* 828 (1979), 34n.16

Henderson & Taylor, "Racist Justice: Discrimination Even in Death," Dallas *Times Herald*, Nov. 17, 1985, at A-17, col. 4, 264–65, 267n.13, 268n.23, 269n.34, 269n.37, 278n.177

Hood, R., *The Death Penalty: A World-Wide Perspective* (1989)

Hubbard, "'Reasonable Levels of Arbitrariness' in Death Sentencing Patterns: A Tragic Perspective on Capital Punishment," 18 *U.C. Davis L. Rev* 1113 (1985), 421n.43

Hubbard, Burry, & Widener, "A 'Meaningful' Basis for the Death Penalty: The Practice, Constitutionality, and Justice of Capital Punishment in South Carolina," 34 *S.C. L. Rev.* 391 (1982), 298n.17, 302n.43

E. Johnson, "Selective Factors in Capital Punishment," 36 *Soc. Forces* 165 (1957), 252, 274n.111

G. Johnson, "The Negro and Crime," 217 *Annals* 93 (1941), 249, 274n.88

L. Johnson, "The Executioner's Bias," 37 *National Rev.*, Nov. 15, 1985, 194n.45

O. Johnson, "Is the Punishment of Rape Equally Administered to Negroes and Whites in the State of Louisiana?" in *Civil Rights Congress, We Charge Genocide* 216 (W. Patterson ed. 1970), 252, 274n.111

S. Johnson, "Black Innocence and the White Jury," 83 *Mich. L. Rev.* 1611 (1985), 279n.181

Kalven, H., & Zeisel, H., *The American Jury* (1966; 2d ed. 1971), 137n.35, 188n.8, 239–40, 269n.40

Kennedy, "*McCleskey v. Kemp*: Race, Capital Punishment and the Supreme Court," 101 *Harv. L. Rev.* 1388 (1988), 422n.60

King, "How Not to Lie with Statistics: Avoiding Common Mistakes in Quantitative Political Science," 30 *Am. J. Pol. Sci.* 666 (1986), 473n.54

Kleck, "Life Support for Ailing Hypotheses: Modes of Summarizing the Evidence for Racial Discrimination in Sentencing," 9 *Law & Hum. Beh.* 271 (1985), 278n.179, 278n.180

Kleck, "Racial Discrimination in Criminal Sentencing: A Critical Evaluation of the Evidence with Additional Evidence on the Death Penalty," 46 *Am. Soc. Rev.* 783 (1981), 249, 253–54, 275n.115, 275n.116, 275n.120, 278n.179, 278n.180

Klemm, M. F., "The Determinants of Capital Sentencing in Louisiana, 1979–84," dissertation, University of New Orleans (1986), 262, 268n.15, 277n.170

Knowlton, "Problems of Jury Discretion in Capital Cases," 101 *U. Pa. L. Rev.* 1099 (1953), 16n.9

Kopeny, "Capital Punishment—Who Should Choose," 12 *W. St. U. L. Rev.* 383 (1985), 267n.7, 267n.10, 268n.25, 268n.29, 271n.76

Ledewitz, "The New Role of Statutory Aggravating Circumstances in American Death Penalty Law," 22 *Duquesne L. Rev.* 317 (1984), 34n.5

Liebman, "Appellate Review of Death Sentences: A Critique of Proportionality Review," 18 *U.C. Davis L. Rev.* 1433 (1985), 36n.25, 219n.6, 222n.40, 222n.43, 224n.61

Mellow & Robson, "Judge over Jury: Florida's Practice of Imposing Death over Life in Capital Cases," 13 *Fla. State U. L. Rev.* 31 (1985), 23

Meltsner, M., *Cruel and Unusual: The Supreme Court and Capital Punishment* (1973), 16n.13

Morris, P., "Sentence Reversals and Subsequent Disposition of Georgia Death Cases: 1973–86" (mimeo 1986), 228n.85

Mosteller, "Assessing Unknown Numbers: Order of Magnitude Estimation," in *Statistics and Public Policy* 163 (W. Fairley & F. Mosteller ed. 1977), 69n.19

Murphy, "Application of the Death Penalty in Cook County," 73 *Ill. B. J.* 90 (1984), 257, 267n.12, 268n.24, 268n.29, 269n.38, 276n.147

Myers, R., *Classical and Modern Regression with Applications* (1986), 477n.75, 477n.76, 478n.78, 478n.82

Nakell, B., & Hardy, K., *The Arbitrariness of the Death Penalty* (1987), 68n.11, 242, 260–61, 265, 268n.17, 268n.26, 270n.57, 277n.163

Neter, J., & Wasserman, W., *Applied Linear Statistical Models* (1974), 478n.84

Nisbett & Bellows, "Verbal Reports About Causal Inferences on Social Judgments: Private Access Versus Public Theories," 35 *J. Personality & Soc. Psychology* 613 (1977), 79n.59

Nisbett & Wilson, "Telling More Than We Can Know: Verbal Reports on Mental Processes," 84 *Psychological Rev.* 231 (1977), 79n.59

Note, "Capital Sentencing Under Supreme Court Rule 28," 42 *La. L. Rev.* 1100 (1982), 299–300n.25

Note, "Criminal Procedure: Comparative Proportionality Review of Death Sentences: Is It a Meaningful Safeguard in Oklahoma?" 38 *Okla. L. Rev.* 267 (1985), 298n.17, 300n.28

Note, "Discretion and the Constitutionality of the New Death-Sentencing Statutes," 87 *Harv. L. Rev.* 1690 (1974), 33n.2

Note, "Distinguishing Among Murders When Assessing the Proportionality of the Death Penalty," 85 *Col. L. Rev.* 1786 (1985), 19n.49

Note, "*Furman* to *Gregg*: The Judicial and Legislative History," 22 *How. L. J.* 53 (1979), 33n.2

Note, "The Two-Trial System in Capital Cases," 39 *N.Y.U. L. Rev.* 50 (1964), 16n.9

Note, "Washington's Comparative Proportionality Review: Toward Effective Appellate Review of Death Penalty Cases Under the Washington State Constitution," 64 *Wash. L. Rev.* 111 (1989)

Olmesdahl, "Predicting the Death Sentence," 6 *SACC/SASK* 201 (1982), 272–73n.83, 278n.178

Partington, "The Incidence of the Death Penalty for Rape in Virginia," 22 *Wash. & Lee L. Rev.* 43 (1965), 250, 274n.92

Paternoster, "Prosecutorial Discretion in Requesting the Death Penalty: A Case of Victim-Based Racial Discrimination," 18 *L. & Soc. Rev.* 437 (1984), 257, 268n.29, 276n.144, 276n.145

Paternoster, "Race of Victim and Location of Crime: The Decision to Seek the Death Penalty in South Carolina," 74 *J. Crim. L. & Criminology* 754 (1983), 257, 276n.144

Radelet, "Racial Characteristics and the Imposition of the Death Penalty," 46 *Am. Soc. Rev.* 918 (1981), 255, 275n.129

Radelet, "Rejecting the Jury: The Imposition of the Death Penalty in Florida," 18 *U.C. Davis L. Rev* 1409 (1985), 267n.15, 269n.33

Radelet & Mellow, "Executing Those Who Kill Blacks: An Unusual Case Study," 37 *Mercer L. Rev.* 911 (1986), 195n.60

Radelet & Pierce, "Race and Prosecutorial Discretion in Homicide Cases," 19 *Law & Soc'y Rev.* 587 (1985), 194n.56, 275n.130, 449n.40

Radelet & Vandiver, "Race and Capital Punishment: An Overview of the Issues," 25 *Crime & Soc. Jus.* 94 (1986), 278n.177

Rawls, "Punishment," in *Punishment: Selected Readings* 58 (J. Feinberg & H. Gross, eds. 1975), 422n.57

Riedel, "Discrimination in the Imposition of the Death Penalty: A Comparison of the Characteristics of Offenders Sentenced Pre-*Furman* and Post-*Furman*," 49 *Temp. L. Q.* 261 (1976), 254, 275n.118

Rodriguez, Perlin, & Apicella, "Proportionality Review in New Jersey: An Indispensable Safeguard in the Capital Sentencing Process," 15 *Rutgers L. J.* 399 (1984), 298n.17

Saks, M., *Small Group Decision Making and Complex Information Tasks* (Federal Judicial Center 1981), 137n.35

Sarat & Vidmar, "Public Opinion, the Death Penalty, and the Eighth Amendment: Testing the Marshall Hypothesis," 1976 *Wis. L. Rev.* 171, 18n.31

Schwartz, "The Supreme Court and Capital Punishment: A Quest for a Balance Between Legal and Societal Morality," 1 *L. & Policy Q.* 285 (1979), 38n.51

Sellin, T., *The Penalty of Death* (1980), 249, 274n.86

Shapiro, "First-Degree Murder Statutes and Capital Sentencing Procedures: An Analysis and Comparison of Statutory Systems for the Imposition of the Death Penalty in Georgia, Florida, Texas, and Louisiana," 24 *Loy. L. Rev.* 709 (1978), 16n.5

Skene, "Review of Capital Cases: Does the Florida Supreme Court Know What It's Doing," 15 *Stetson L. Rev.* 263 (1986), 298n.17

Smith, "Patterns of Discrimination in Assessments of the Death Penalty: The Case of Louisiana," 15 *J. of Crim. Jus.* 279 (1987)

Special Issue, "A Study of the California Penalty Trial in First-Degree-Murder Cases," 21 *Stan. L. Rev.* 1297 (1969), 68n.12, 251, 270n.50, 274n.103

Special Project, "Capital Punishment in 1984: Abandoning the Pursuit of Fairness and Consistency," 69 *Cornell L. Rev.* 1129 (1984), 16n.1, 422n.54

Swartz & Welsch, "Application of Bounded-Influence and Diagnostic Methods in Energy Modeling," in *Model Reliability* (D. Belsley & E. Kuh eds. 1986), 477n.75, 477n.77

Tabak, "The Death of Fairness: The Arbitrary and Capricious Imposition of the Death Penalty in the 1980's," 14 *N.Y.U. Rev. L. & Soc. Change* 797 (1986), 137n.39, 139n.46, 246–47, 271n.80

Thomas, R. H., & Hutcheson, J. D., Jr., *Georgia Residents' Attitudes Toward the Death Penalty, the Disposition of Juvenile Offenders and Related Issues* (December 1986), 196n.61

Timms & McGonigle, "Blacks Rejected From Juries in Capital Cases," Dallas *Morning News*, Dec. 21, 1986, 263, 277n.172

Timms & McGonigle, "Race Bias Pervades Jury Selection," Dallas *Morning News*, March 9, 1986, 264, 277n.176

"Uniform Guidelines on Employee Selection Procedures," 29 C.F.R. §1607.4D (1986), 425n.66

van den Haag, "The Collapse of the Case Against Capital Punishment," 30 *National Rev.* 395 (March 1978), 6n.4

van den Haag, "In Defense of the Death Penalty: A Legal—Practical—Moral—Analysis," 14 *Crim. L. Bull.* 15 (1978), 6n.4

Van Duizend, "Comparative Proportionality Review in Death Sentence Cases: What? How? Why?" 8 *State Ct. J.* 9 (Summer 1984), 281, 285–86, 295n.7, 295n.9, 296n.14, 298n.17, 300n.29, 301n.36

von Hirsh, A., *Past or Future Crimes* (1985), 20n.50

Waseleski, "Grim Equality," Pittsburgh *Post-Gazette*, Nov. 28, 1985, 269n.35

Weisberg, "Deregulating Death," 1983 *Sup. Ct. Rev.* 305, 34n.7, 135n.24, 267n.4, 411, 421n.45, 421n.49

White, "Disproportionality and the Death Penalty: Death as a Punishment for Rape," 38 *U. Pitt. L. Rev.* 145 (1977), 37n.27

White, W., *The Death Penalty in the Eighties: An Examination of the Modern System of Capital Punishment* (1987)

Wilbanks, W., *The Myth of a Racist Criminal Justice System* (1987), 278n.179, 278n.180

Wolfgang & Riedel, "Race, Judicial Discretion, and the Death Penalty," 407 *Annals* 119 (1973), 16n.4, 68n.12, 250, 267n.8, 274n.94

Wolfgang & Riedel, "Rape, Race, and the Death Penalty in Georgia," 45 *Am. J. Orthopsychiatry* 658 (1975), 251, 274n.97

Wolfgang, Kelly, & Nolde, "Comparison of the Executed and the Commuted among Admissions to Death Row," 53 *J. Crim. L., Criminology & Police Sci.* 301 (1962), 253, 275n.114

Woodworth, "Analysis of a Y-Stratified Sample: The Georgia Charging and Sentencing Study," in *Proceedings of the Second Workshop on Law and Justice Statistics: 1984*, 18, Bureau of Justice Statistics, U.S. Dept. of Justice (E. Gelfand ed. 1985), 322n.1, 329n.1

Woodworth, G., ed., "Symposium, Statistical Studies of the Law and Justice System: Racial Discrimination in Capital Sentencing," in *Proceedings of the Third Workshop on Law and Justice Statistics 1985*, 55, Bureau of Justice Statistics, U.S. Dept. of Justice (1988), 445n.2

Zeisel, "Race Bias in the Administration of the Death Penalty: The Florida Experience," 95 *Harv. L. Rev.* 456 (1981), 196n.62, 255, 275n.131

Zimring, Eigen, & O'Malley, "Punishing Homicide in Philadelphia: Perspectives on the Death Penalty," 43 *U. Chi. L. Rev.* 227 (1976), 240, 252, 270n.47, 274n.109

Zimring, F., & Hawkins, G., *Capital Punishment and the American Agenda* (1986), 33n.2, 37n.27, 411, 421n.47, 422n.58